through your apparent attitudes and your actions. For communication encompasses all human behavior that results in an exchange of meaning. How well you manage depends upon how well you communicate in this broad sense. These ten commandments are designed to help you improve your skills as a manager by improving your skills of communication—with superiors, subordinates, and associates.

6. Take the opportunity, when it arises, to convey something of help or value to the receiver.

Consideration of the other person's interests and needs—the habit of trying to look at things from his point of view—will frequently point up opportunities to convey something of immediate benefit or long-range value to him. People on the job are most responsive to the manager whose messages take their own interests into account.

7. Follow up your communication.

Our best efforts at communication may be wasted, and we may never know whether we have succeeded in expressing our true meaning and intent, if we do not follow up to see how well we have put our message across. This you can do by asking questions, by encouraging the receiver to express his reactions, by follow-up contacts, by subsequent review of performance. Make certain that every important communication has a "feedback" so that complete understanding and appropriate action result.

8. Communicate for tomorrow as well as today.

While communications may be aimed primarily at meeting the demands of an immediate situation, they must be planned with the past in mind if they are to maintain consistency in the receiver's view; but, most important of all, they must be consistent with long-range interests and goals. For example, it is not easy to communicate frankly on such matters as poor performance or the shortcomings of a loyal subordinate—but postponing disagreeable communications makes them more difficult in the long run and is actually unfair to your subordinates and your company.

9. Be sure your actions support your communications.

In the final analysis, the most persuasive kind of communication is not what you say but what you do. When a man's action or attitudes contradict his words, we tend to discount what he has said. For every manager this means that good supervisory practice—such as clear assignment of responsibility and authority, fair rewards for effort, and sound policy enforcement—serve to communicate more than all the gifts of oratory.

10. Last, but by no means least: Seek not only to be understood but to understand—be a good listener.

When we start talking, we often cease to listen—in that larger sense of being attuned to the other person's unspoken reactions and attitudes. Even more serious is the fact that we are all guilty, at times, of inattentiveness when others are attempting to communicate to us. Listening is one of the most important, most difficult—and most neglected—skills in communication. It demands that we concentrate not only on the explicit meanings another person is expressing, but on the implicit meanings, unspoken words, and undertones that may be far more significant. Thus we must learn to listen with the inner ear if we are to know the inner man.

Effective Communication In Business

with Management Emphasis

by

Robert R. Aurner, Ph.D.

Vice President,
Management Consultant Division,
Scott, Incorporated

and

Formerly: Dean of the College of
Commerce of the United States Army
American University, Biarritz, France;
and Professor of Business Adminis-
tration in the University of Wisconsin

 Fourth Edition

Published by the

SOUTH-WESTERN PUBLISHING COMPANY

CINCINNATI 27 CHICAGO 5 SAN FRANCISCO 3 DALLAS 2 NEW ROCHELLE, N.Y.

E49

LIBRARY OF CONGRESS
CATALOG CARD NUMBER: 58-7338

H360
Printed in the United States of America

Preface

Communication in Tomorrow's World. Yesterday's World of the Future is here today. Today's World of the Future will be here tomorrow. And Tomorrow's World of the Future is just over the horizon. Little wonder why, in this jet age, we must learn how to live in Tomorrow's World. Yet, we have just begun to learn the art of How to Live in the World of the Future.

Like all other activities in the World of Tomorrow, communication has taken on a significant new character. Undergoing a subtle evolution that reflects sharp increases in population, ever-increasing gross national product, wide enlargement of personal services, and acceleration of every form of research, communication is emerging as a new *management giant.* Top management has within just a few years "discovered" communication as one of its most powerful resources for operating success. Management men of all three major levels—top management, middle management, and operating management—have accepted the swiftly emerging truth that written communication is an indispensable resource for supporting the industrial process by transmitting executive actions. Accordingly, communication in unprecedented degree has taken on multiplied importance, and has grown in size, in scope, in stature, and in overriding significance.

The New Title Reflects the New Emphasis. The new title EFFECTIVE COMMUNICATION IN BUSINESS—WITH MANAGEMENT EMPHASIS appropriately reflects the dominant theme of the new edition: communication by and for management. The management concept is established on the front end-sheet and the opening page of Chapter 1 and is expanded, chapter by chapter, through the remainder of the book.

The new Fourth Edition reflects the amazing growth, the automation trends, and the sharp change in character of communication. The author has described and illustrated the wide and enthusiastic acceptance of communication as the great new power tool of management. In one chapter after another it has been the aim to present, describe, and illustrate the many different and fascinating roles of communication in carrying out the different kinds of management responsibilities.

The New Emphasis on Effective Human Relations. An essential part of the management emphasis in communications is the mastery of the art of getting along with other people; the demonstration of the ability to work harmoniously with others; the development of effective human relations. Chapters 1, 6, 7, and 8, among others, discuss and illustrate this valuable art in new detail and give concrete, sharply defined examples and suggestions on how to enjoy effective human relations as an essential part of communications-management success.

The New Organization. The Table of Contents of the new Fourth Edition reflects a number of significant changes and improvements in organization. There are now ten major parts in the book, each part presenting an important organic division of the communications field. Parts I to VIII in the new organization cover the major functional divisions. Part IX is a new *Refresher Division of Communication Skills,* containing five reorganized sections. Part X is a *Reference Division,* containing a new Section 1 on Letter Layout, and six valuable additional reference sections for student and office guidance.

Chapter 1, entitled *The New Management Target: Communications Power,* is, in large part, entirely new in concept, in plan, and in material. It discusses in detail for the first time the two great new developments of the past ten years in the communications field: "Communications Power for the World of the Future" and "Communications Power for Effective Human Relations." The new Part II, Chapters 3-7 inclusive, carefully reorganized with new materials and illustrations, develops this theme of Effective Human Relations in greater detail under the general heading of Positive Planning.

Chapter 2, *The First Target of Management: Creating a Good First Impression,* combines the basic elements of Chapters 2, 3, and 4 of the Third Edition. The new chapter is devoted to a discussion of the "look" of the message and how to make it attractive. Much of the detailed material on the mechanics of letter layout variations has been transferred to Section 1 of the Reference Division. This transfer of material makes possible an earlier introduction of principles, problems, and procedures of writing business messages—the real objective of the communications course.

Chapter 8, *How to Dictate a Business Letter,* is in most respects an entirely new chapter, greatly enlarged and completely reorganized on the basis of much fresh material, new illustrations, new examples, and concrete procedures drawn directly from modern executive action. Formerly Chapter 23 in the Third Edition, the "how to dictate" chapter has been moved up to become Chapter 8 in the Fourth Edition to provide students with an *early* introduction to the idea of TALK-writing. Many students of communication will, soon after graduation, find themselves in positions requiring the immediate dictation of business messages in many and varied forms. The evidence is overwhelming that they should be introduced to the idea of dictation early, and that recurring experience should be provided —from Chapter 8 on—in dictating "with speed." The author hopes that all instructors will encourage students to seize many opportunities during the course to practice the enormously important art of effective dictation.

Chapters 13-16 inclusive, comprising Part VI, *Effective Sales Messages*, have been sharply reorganized with the former five chapters streamlined to four in what is believed to be a highly desirable change. Part VI now opens with a discussion of business promotion to acquaint the reader quickly with an over-all concept of the activity. That, in turn, is followed by a discussion of techniques of product analysis and sales potential. With this kind of background, the student is ready for truly effective sales work.

The New End-of-Chapter Problems. For each chapter entirely new problems and case situations have been prepared, each one drawn carefully from successful management practice. A quick review will reveal the realistic, interesting, and usable character of these materials. Each problem and case situation has been planned to stimulate the sense of realistic, immediate, worth-while progressive achievement. To this end, many illustrative examples, based on the most up-to-the-minute executive action, light up and motivate the successful application of the discussion material.

The New Incentive Motivations. In the Fourth Edition incentive motivations have been provided continuously from chapter to chapter. Each chapter subject has been freshly organized and developed to invite swift and easy reading and to stimulate the sense of realistic, progressive achievement. Fresh examples and case illustrations have been drawn directly from the author's consulting experience and from the files of successful executives to dramatize, and to make vivid and dynamic, the high-lighted topics. Swift-moving episodes, concrete examples, and up-to-the-minute illustrations have been used to drive home, through dramatic-story technique, salient points in the discussion.

The New Workbook. For use with EFFECTIVE COMMUNICATION IN BUSINESS—WITH MANAGEMENT EMPHASIS an optional workbook has been prepared. The workbook situations, like the end-of-chapter materials, are planned to stimulate the reasoning powers of the student, and to apply, in tested realistic ways, the main text's major principles.

Other New Features. Those who consult the Fourth Edition will also note (1) the new front end-sheet, *Ten Commandments of Good*

Communication, that will serve as a continuous reference guide for students and executives alike; (2) the fresh, new physical appearance; (3) the new pictorial illustrations, cartoons, special panels, and other artwork to add "eye interest" from page to page; (4) the new and sharply different chapter headings; (5) the new "within the text" display headings of a fresh panel-type format; (6) the fresh paragraph headings to intrigue the reader's eye and attention ("How Do You Rate on These Real-Life Challenges?" and "Executive Action—How to Take It."); and (7) the complete rewriting of many topics, the careful chiseling of words in direct writing style, and the painstaking streamlining of material.

Communication Management, the Final New Key. Whether an executive creates a one-sentence directive, a one-page memorandum, a two-hundred page report, or any one of a thousand other written executive actions in between, the principles that apply are relatively uniform. They apply to every written executive action that he takes. The Fourth Edition presents this important new orientation through a carefully motivated discussion of the role of the written word, the persuasive word, the informative word, placed in the hands of top management men, executive decision-makers at all levels, and potential executives, all of whom must be expert communicators to carry out their executive functions and management responsibilities.

The key, over all, is this: Management at every level has discovered the indispensable ingredient of successful executive action— dynamic communication through the communication "power line."

The author will be deeply gratified if EFFECTIVE COMMUNICATION IN BUSINESS—WITH MANAGEMENT EMPHASIS contributes in some degree toward the success of American management in Tomorrow's World.

ROBERT R. AURNER

Development of the Problems

Of the greatest importance in bringing this new work to completion has been the contribution of those outstandingly able individuals who have prepared case and problem material for the several chapters. The author wishes to express his deepest thanks and most sincere acknowledgment to the following for their special services in case and problem preparation:

Dr. Ray W. Arensman, Evansville College; Dr. John E. Binnion, University of Denver; Dr. Jean C. Halterman, Indiana University; Dr. William C. Himstreet, University of Southern California; Professor Lyda E. McHenry, Wayne State University; Professor Mary C. Robertson, North Texas State College; Dr. William G. Savage, Wayne State University.

These colleagues, through their valuable and constructive contributions, have effectively extended the teaching radius of the problems and cases for classroom discussion and assignment.

Acknowledgments

The author takes great pleasure in expressing the fullest measure of appreciation to the many whose thoughtful suggestions and able contributions to this book have been so significantly helpful.

To those top management executives who have contributed many valuable ideas and items relating to management responsibilities, executive techniques, business procedures, competitive strategies, and the amazing newer developments of commerce and industry; to those professional associates who, in connection with the author's management consulting work, have so generously shared some of their most valuable case materials for use in the Fourth Edition; to the maturing students of former academic years, many of them now experienced management executives in their own right, and all of whom have expressed such deep and lasting interest in the author's development of this edition—to all of these groups go most earnest and unstinted thanks.

Deepest appreciation is due, likewise, to the many teachers of long classroom experience who, after generous mention that they have enjoyed using the First, Second, and Third Editions, have offered helpful criticisms and constructive suggestions toward the improvement of the new Fourth Edition. If, as is hoped, the new edition becomes an even more effective teaching instrument than its predecessors, a generous portion of this effectiveness will flow from the rigorous testing of much of its materials by both skilled classroom leaders and expert professional management men.

The author hopes that the flowing together of the deep insights and the top skills of these advisory groups has been reflected in the pages of the new EFFECTIVE COMMUNICATION IN BUSINESS—WITH MANAGEMENT EMPHASIS and that the volume will be found even more acceptable than its widely used predecessor editions. Certain it is that every management man in the country will attest to the crucial importance of the subject and to the enormously growing demand for the services of its trained exponents. The field is there. The opportunity is brilliant. If this volume helps in its swift development, the author will be deeply gratified.

Especially pleasant is the opportunity to express most grateful thanks to Mrs. Kathryn D. Aurner for valuable and sustained assistance in bringing the work to completion.

For permission to use certain materials, special appreciation is also expressed to the following sources:

Addressograph-Multigraph Corporation; American Airlines; American Automatic Typewriter Co.; American Business Writing Association; American Management Association, Inc.; Dr. Ray W. Arensman, Evansville College; *Banking*, Journal of the American Bankers Association; Ray Baxandall, Baxandall Company; Buckley, Dement & Company; *Chicago Times Syndicate;* Crocker-McElwain Company; Dictaphone Corporation; Encyclopaedia Britannica; *Fortune* Magazine; Fox River Paper Corporation (Communications Improvement Division); General Electric Company; Grey Advertising Agency, Inc.; James R. Hare; Harper & Brothers; The Harvard Alumni Bulletin.

Home Savings and Loan Association; Ketchum, MacLeod & Grove, Inc.; Kimball Associates; Professor Thomas A. Kirby, Louisiana State University; Marshall Field & Company; *Life* Magazine; J. F. McFadden, President, American Credit Indemnity Company; G. & C. Merriam Company; Merrill Lynch, Pierce, Fenner & Smith; *Milwaukee Journal; Monsanto Magazine;* National Broadcasting Company, Inc.; The National Cash Register Company; New Departure, Division General Motors Corporation; New York Life Insurance Company; *New York Times;* The Pacific Telephone and Telegraph Company; Phoenix Mutual Life Insurance Company; Pitney-Bowes, Inc.; R. L. Polk & Co.; *Printers' Ink; Publishers Syndicate, Inc.;* The *Reader's Digest;* Remington Rand, Division of Sperry Rand Corporation; The Royal Bank of Canada.

Saturday Evening Post; Harry H. Scott, President, Scott, Inc.; Professor Hyla M. Snider, Connecticut College; Standard Federal Savings and Loan Association; Standard Oil Company of California; The Reverend William L. Stidger; Dr. James E. Silverthorn, Oklahoma State University; Professor James M. Thompson, Eastern Illinois State Teachers College; *Time* Magazine; Union Carbide Corporation; United States Post Office Department; *The Wall Street Journal;* Wenger-Michael, Inc.; Olga B. Werner, Joseph T. Ryerson & Sons, Inc.; Westinghouse Electric Corporation; Whiting-Plover Paper Company.

Other credits appear in later pages.

The standing hope of the author of this book is that its usefulness may be brought to ever-higher levels. To this end, constructive suggestions from those who are using this volume will be warmly welcomed.

ROBERT R. AURNER

Table of Contents

Page

PART I   The Management Concept

Chapter I

The New Management Target:
Communications Power

| Communications Power for the World of the Future |

Executive Action in a New Kind of World. You and I are paying a visit to the executive area of a great business enterprise. By invitation we look through the open doorway of a handsomely appointed office. The diffused lighting glows from luminescent walls, with pushbutton controls for any color-shading and any level of intensity. The solar air-conditioning system gathers its year-around level-temperature energy from the rays of the sun.

Seated at his electronic desk, a top management executive closely watches a closed-circuit full-color television three-dimensional wall screen showing a succession of key activities in all branches and divisions of his company throughout the world.

Turning from the television screen, the executive swiftly picks up the electronic recording microphone and dictates a series of business messages into a whisper-silent direct-dictation typewriter that instantaneously reproduces his words in perfect form the moment after he has spoken the final syllable.

Preparing Today for the World of Tomorrow. Full-color, flat wall-screen, three-dimensional television—direct-dictation typewriters that *directly* reproduce the human voice in flawless letters of perfect form—these developments are already in the laboratory on their way to reality.

Other developments equally astonishing are already here: "Ultra-fax"—a system of high-speed communications, capable of transmitting and receiving written or printed documents at the rate of a million words a minute; and "Electrofax"—a high-speed electronic-photographic printing process for reproducing any type of visual information by electronic means directly upon any solid surface, as a basis for multiplying important business communications instantly for transmission in exact facsimile copy to key executives.

1

—New Departure, Division General Motors Corporation

Automation and the Written Word: The Coming Direct-Dictation Typewriter

"TOMORROW: You dictate! The machine types and hustles your letters to the mail. Electronics does it all. Think of dashing through your correspondence with this imaginary scribe! It converts your voice into electronic impulses which type, micro-record, fold, insert, seal, address and stamp letters almost as fast as you can dictate!"

Gearing Your Career to the Challenges Ahead. It is not merely interesting and entertaining to hear something of the miracles now emerging from the research laboratories. Far more than that, it is both important and essential to your career that you acquaint yourself with some of these startling developments in order that you may have a useful working background for the pages that lie ahead.

Accordingly, let us look a little further at some of the things coming up over the distant horizon. And we had better take a really long look at this World of the Future and the demands it will make upon us in terms of communication training and skill, because it is in this World of the Future that you and I and all of us will spend the rest of our lives.

In the featured column at the right, *Time* magazine glimpses the coming age of electronics, the age that is ushering in a second Industrial Revolution. The electronic direct-dictation typewriter; the TV set that hangs like a picture, flat against the wall; the radio only as big as a golf ball; the telephone, now a movielike screen projecting both the caller's image and his voice—the impact of technical progress on *these four great channels of written and spoken communication* is gigantic in its challenge to you to bring your own communication training and skill up to the required level in the New Age in which you are going to live.

More of the Background Story. Go back to the year you (or most of you, now reading this book) were born: In about that year there was still no television industry. No one knew how to split the atom. There was no jet aircraft, guided missile, man-launched satellite, or electronic digital computer. And the medical profession had never heard of antibiotics. Yet that time was scarcely two decades ago.

THE NEW AGE

The house was like none ever built before. Its roof was a honeycomb of tiny solar cells that used the sun's rays to heat the house, furnish all the electric power. Doors and windows opened in response to hand signals; they closed automatically when it rained.

The TV set hung like a picture, flat against the wall—so did the heating and air-conditioning panels. The radio was only as big as a golf ball. The telephone was a movie-like screen, which projected both the caller's image and voice. In the kitchen the range broiled thick steaks in barely two minutes. Dishes and clothes were cleaned without soap or water.

The house had no electrical outlets; invisible radio beams ran all appliances. At night, the walls and ceilings glowed softly with glass-encased "light sandwiches," which changed color at the twirl of a dial. And throughout the house, tiny, unblinking bulbs of a strange reddish hue sterilized the air and removed all bacteria.

• • •

Such a house, fully described in fiction and partly pictured in advertisements, is today a reality in the laboratories that are moving deeply into the coming age of electronics—the age that is ushering in a second Industrial Revolution.

—*Time*, Vol. LXIX, Number 17, pp. 84-90.

Today we are in a different kind of world typified by UNIVAC II (one of the great electronic digital computers, popularly known as giant brains)—an ultra-modern new-world instrument that makes possible *an entirely new kind of communication based upon a combination of coded words, symbols, and figures*. The high point for special note is this: the automatic programing system feeds *coded English words* into the computer's "memory," which then puts the

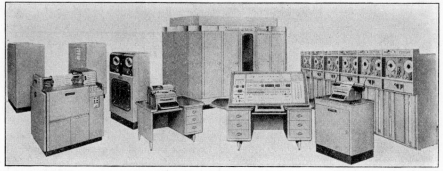

—*Sperry Rand Corporation*

UNIVAC II: An Entirely New Kind of Communication for the
World of Tomorrow

computer to work automatically. At the end of the program, UNIVAC II presents its own "business report" for the use of the executive who needs it in solving management problems. From these report data, the executive can then communicate information and directions for the entire business to his subordinates.

Speaking to The Economic Club of Chicago on "Looking Ahead in Communications," the president of the American Telephone and Telegraph Company put it this way:

"Research is opening up startling new prospects for communications. New ways of *transmitting* information are being developed, and also new all-electronic methods for *interconnecting*. . . . The goal is a communication system that will carry every conceivable kind of information over any distance, long or short—words . . . pictures, raw data . . . your business reports, and your best girl's smile."

Higher Skills Are a "Must" for the Future. It is comforting, of course, to know that "electronic captains" in a mysterious array of little black boxes can fly supersonic planes, guide enormous missiles through thousands of miles of space, run machines and whole factories, and easily solve scientific and mathematical problems that were impossible to tackle only a decade ago (automation).

But one moment, please! What impact is all this going to have upon *you*? *You will have to develop much higher skill than you would have needed only ten short years ago.* To fill your future job successfully, you will have to know more about more things than did your older colleagues of only ten short years ago. You will gain this specialized knowledge *through association with and input of the written word.* And you will demonstrate your skill in your future job much of the time through *trained output of the written word*—in all forms of office communication.

4

Effective Communication Is a Management Problem

Management executives call upon the art of communication almost every hour of every business day. Sometimes, in fact, management men may spend entire business days, one after another, solving intricate and immensely important communication problems at the top management level.

For example, here is the controller-treasurer of a corporation doing a business volume of $125,000,000 a year. He is faced with a typical communication-management problem. It is his responsibility to dictate a business message that is to go to a government agency and that will explain in precise technical detail the exact earnings status of certain dollar amounts presented in the company annual report. *If he is able to dictate the message with expert accuracy, bringing out the exact facts of a complicated situation,* he will save the company $375,000. This huge sum may equal the net profit on millions of dollars of sales, representing the efforts of scores of sales representatives over many months. *The crucial outcome of his final message draft represents a classic application of the written word for the purpose of solving a top management problem.*

Back to the Executive on Page One. Now we are ready to go back to the "executive on page one" and pick up his story. You will recall that he had just finished dictating a series of messages to his world-wide industrial empire. What happens now? Those dictated messages will shortly go forth as written communications carrying administrative directives that may affect the procedures and activities of a half million employees, including all the management levels throughout the vast enterprise.

The executive who issues these directives is a top management man. He *depends upon the power of the written word*—the force and clarity of effective communication—to carry out his management responsibilities.

All Levels of Management Depend on Group Action Through Communication. Among the several levels of management there are three general groupings, commonly known as top management, middle management, and operating management. Each group manages at different levels of responsibility and authority through the able use of communication.

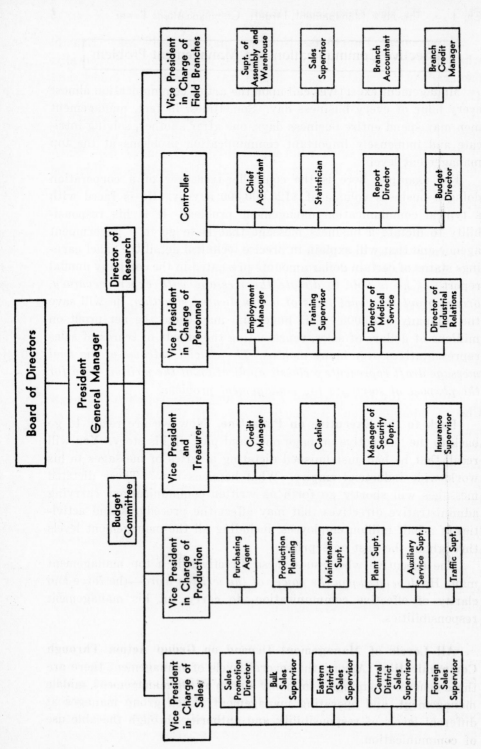

Typical Organization Chart of a Manufacturing Concern

Management Functions. Now we may properly ask: Exactly what does management do in carrying out its functions? Specifically, management (1) controls, (2) directs, (3) conducts, (4) guides, and (5) administers the affairs of business enterprise.

A management function is an activity or procedure necessary to develop an organization and lead it toward the successful attainment of its goals. It is a subdivision of the total management job. When the size or the nature of the group organization justifies it, then the management function is best performed by a specialist—an expert trained in a specialized field such as:

- Accounting
- Distribution and Sales
- Engineering and Design
- Finance
- Industrial Relations
- Inspection and Quality Control
- Legal Counsel

- Manufacturing
- Market Research
- Organization
- Personnel
- Production Planning
- Public and Human Relations
- Purchasing
- Training

Knitting the Groups—and Their Functions—Together Through Clear Communication. As you will see, each of these functions of management requires an elaborate communication system to knit the several group activities together into a smoothly working whole. We might also put it this way: When two or more persons decide to pool their efforts in a common cause, somebody has to define the target and plan the program. The larger and the more complex the organization, the more numerous are the types of management leadership required, the greater the number of specialized functions that must be performed, and inevitably the *greater the need for expert intercommunication in every form of the written word.* Management, therefore, seeks out those who are *articulate* because "language is the picture and counterpart of thought" flowing smoothly into action.

Communication in business is really the human subject of how we all live together and earn our way in life—"our *interdependence,* the relationships of small enterprises to large enterprises, and again, their *interdependence,* one on the other now and in all our tomorrows," as Henry J. Taylor puts it. "For surely there is a lesson that we should learn in our country—*we are never working alone.*"

For example, the Radio Corporation of America buys materials, components, products, and services from more than ten thousand independent suppliers. The majority of them are comparatively small businesses located throughout the United States. In a recent year RCA's purchases from these sources amounted to $593,479,000. At the next level down, these ten thousand independent suppliers, by *their* employment of thousands of workers, stimulate business in their own communities, support the national economy, and distribute locally the benefits of this national network of stabilized business interdependence. And out of all this interdependent network flow millions upon millions of communications necessary to the conduct of the business interchange: messages containing informative words, explanatory words, and perhaps persuasive words, all with one overriding management target: CLEAR UNDERSTANDING AND CLEAN-CUT ACTION THROUGH THE COMMUNICATION POWER LINE. Indeed, the one absolutely indispensable ingredient for efficient executive action is *clear communication*.

As later pages of the book will disclose, we shall be privileged to watch management apply the written word to the solving of business problems. We shall watch management develop a continuous program to strengthen the power and multiply the effectiveness of the entire communication process. Management's purpose? To assure swift efficiency in the solution of its daily problems.

Now we can see how executive action and communication efficiency are interlinked. We can see how the executives at every level, men of skill and inquiring minds, use intra-company, inter-company, and general communications—the power of the written word—to develop a favorable human relations climate for understanding and achievement, for progress and success, both inside and outside their own enterprise.

Communication Power for Effective Human Relations

Effective Communication As a Human Relations Instrument. Effective communication is a challenging art. But, more than that, it is also a powerful human relations instrument that you will call upon every day of your life. This instrument you will use for multiple purposes. What are some of them? Here are some examples that reflect typical human relations activities.

You use effective communication to:

1. Inquire, reply, announce, inform, invite, appoint, direct, acknowledge, make purchase orders, and pay for them.

2. Ask favors, grant favors, decline favors, express appreciation, congratulate, praise, introduce, and recommend.

3. Present an analysis of yourself and your abilities and skills, compile job opportunities, apply for jobs.

4. Prepare product descriptions and market reports.

5. Through the written word, sell, adjust, settle trouble, extend credit, collect money.

6. Develop written reports through which top management gets the information needed to make command decisions, and then to take final executive action.

Communication in Business Is Basically a Program in Effective Human Relations. More than ever before, management now understands that every policy decision, every operating move, has a human relations aspect that must be considered. Industry and business today regard human relations as a management function along with research, engineering, distribution, manufacturing, and personnel. As for individuals themselves, the matter is even more important. Any way you look at it, human relations are the daily concern of every person in all walks of life.

Do you have broad interests? Today there is a growing emphasis on what personnel experts call the *flexible* man—one whose talents, interests, and abilities reach out beyond a restricted, highly specialized area. This emphasis is a sharp change from a few years ago, when the narrow specialist was the fair-haired favorite.

Reason for the change is ably expressed by an executive of a major chemical company: "A purely technical background will enable a man to solve immediate technical problems, but it may leave him unprepared to cope with today's highly involved human problems of management."

Now look back again for a moment at Items 1 to 6 given above, listing various written-communication activities. You will note that each item involves human relations, the contacts and relationships of one human being with another, or of one group of human beings with another group.

Each item in these lists of communication actions *tests your ability to get along with others.* Do you *really* like people? You had better begin to do so—because human relations have taken on new value and new importance in all business thinking. Knowing how to get along with others is a vital necessity for everyone in the world of tomorrow.

Big Companies Recognize the Trend, Train Their People. One of America's largest life insurance companies, alert to the need for continuous improvement in communication standards, has expressed in a letter the new approach of modern management:

> In order to improve the general character and tone of our correspondence with policyholders, agents, and general public, we have the authorization to add to our consulting staff an expert on business communication to help us improve this powerful channel of public and human relations and to guide us on correspondence policy and procedure. We fully recognize our need for consultation and counsel on our problems.

How to Get Along Successfully with Others: The Art of Human Relations. Getting along with other people is sometimes not easy. Getting along with other people at a distance, when they are out of sight and must be reached through the written word, is often genuinely difficult. Certainly the art of getting along is one that calls for study and practice, one that challenges the best effort, as seasoned executives well know. Yet, astonishing though it may seem, vast numbers of mature persons seem

—Dale McFeatters and Publishers Syndicate, Inc.

to be wholly ignorant of how to get along successfully with other people, either nearby or at a distance. But there is a constructive answer to this deficiency. Here it is:

Knowing how to handle the English language is really knowing how to get along successfully with others. Can you see why this is true? It is true because in adjusting to other people, either nearby or at a distance, you make most of your adjustments through using oral or written words. You talk with others in order to indicate your interest or your curiosity, your agreement or your opposition.

> The liberally educated man is articulate. . . . He has a respect for clarity and directness of expression. . . . He is at home in the world of quantity, number, and measurement. He thinks rationally, objectively, and knows the difference between fact and opinion. When the occasion demands, however, his thought is imaginative and creative. . . . His mind is flexible and adaptable, curious and independent. . . . He can use the written word with judgment and discrimination.

—*The Harvard Alumni Bulletin*

On the other hand, if the other people—the people to whose ideas, and thoughts, and prejudices you must adjust, and with whom you must successfully get along—if these other people are at a distance, then most of the time you use that long-tested and highly successful alternative for talking: YOU WRITE. YOU USE THE WRITTEN WORD TO COMMUNICATE AS FORCEFULLY AND AS SKILLFULLY AS YOU KNOW HOW.

How Much Does Management Depend on Communications?

A famous investment advisory service, commenting recently on an executive action of the president of the Dow Chemical Company, writes, "He has created a special department whose aim is for *better communication*, first with employees and stockholders, then with the communities in which Dow operates, and finally with the public itself." Obviously, the top management of Dow Chemical Company is sensitive to the force of effective communication.

How much, in fact, does management, along with our whole industrial society, depend on communications to carry out its management duties? As part of the answer, we know that more and more powerful channels are available each year to carry business messages to the American people: 55 million newspapers are put into consumers' hands each day; 184 million single copies of magazines (measured monthly, biweekly, and weekly by the Audit Bureau of Circulations) enter American homes; 121 million radio sets, and 40 million homes with one or more television sets, are supplemented by car cards in 80,000 vehicles in 400 markets, and 345,000 outdoor posters in 12,000 markets. And of course, just "around the corner of time" and just over the horizon but coming up fast are three-dimensional color-television and telephonovision.

But more important than all of these together, for *direct, private, personal, individual* communication are FIFTY BILLION PIECES OF MAIL! We shall hear more about this in a moment.

Production Lines Depend upon Communication Lines. "No physical activity of production or distribution goes on in our modern age without a piece of paper moving along to guide it." So comments a former president of General Motors Corporation who later became U. S. Secretary of Defense. Charles E. Wilson, in making this comment, said that he learned very early in his career, and continued to learn through a long succession of executive posts in the General Motors organization, how utterly and completely production lines depend upon effective communication lines. *"That piece of paper, carrying the necessary written words* (or facts, or data) must be moving alongside at every moment to guide everything that we do."

"Operation Everywhere" Through the Written Word. Consider, for example, these illustrative sentences from a business report of The Charles Pfizer Company:

> Operation Everywhere . . . Today, Pfizer products are manufactured in 14 countries and are distributed in nearly 100 other countries throughout the world. Month after month over the past five years, production and packaging operations have been expanded in Europe, the Far East, and North and South America. Plants have been erected in France, England, and Japan. New production facilities have been blueprinted or are under construction in Argentina, Italy, Mexico, and Turkey.

> Through an international labyrinth of shipping regulations, import licenses, currency exchange restrictions, and customs laws, Pfizer has traced smooth-flowing lines of distribution, with matching smooth-flowing lines of written communication, that penetrate to the outermost edges of the world map.

Automation Helps to Speed the "Pieces of Paper" Carrying the Coded Written Word. Let us consider one more concrete case: The Standard Oil Company of California issues an all-plastic featherweight credit card. On the front of the carrying case transmitting the card is this "science-fiction" sentence which, however, happens to be true: "This card will print your credit information so clearly that electronic machines will read your charge slips." Thus does automation—a word mentioned briefly at an earlier point in this chapter—begin to emerge as a future important channel for the written word.

Is Top Management Happy with Present Levels of Communication Skill? The Answer: No

Top management is almost universal in its call for better communication skill, and for better control of the written and spoken word, on the part of its new employees.

Of any given thousand graduating seniors of a collegiate institution only a disappointingly small number can intelligently handle even the simpler business situations involving business communication. The majority of college graduates show gross deficiencies when they come face to face for the first time with modern communication problems. Except for those who have been trained in a course like the one you are now taking, college graduates do not know how to handle themselves in business communication and are needlessly hamstrung by that lack. This statement is supported by the overwhelming testimony of scores of experts, both in and out of business, as well as scores of personnel and top management executives.

Management Wants Better Training, Higher Skill in Communication. Scores of top management and personnel men are constantly searching for college graduates competently trained in business communication at the college level. It is significant to learn of the almost universal disappointment of these men in finding that the majority of college graduates had been allowed by the authorities to slide through without a hint of training in the subject so vital to business—communication control—intelligent competence in written business expression. Nor were these executives at all hesitant in expressing their amazement that this kind of educational deficiency should be allowed to go on and on.

The story is told by Russell Kirk, in *Fortune* magazine, of a dinner party attended by an investment broker who happened to sit next to a professor of education.

"Do you think," said the investment broker to the professor, "that young people are better educated now than they were in 1900?"

The professor did indeed think so: much better educated; integrated with the group; adjusted to the environment.

"I had wondered about it," the investment broker observed, "because when I bring young men into my office, I GENERALLY FIND THAT THEY CANNOT WRITE DECENT LETTERS. . . ."

Good Writers Are Scarce: Make Yourself One. "Bill Pensyl, our creative director, and Harry Bender, our copy chief, never cease moaning over the scarcity of good writers," runs the comment of a management executive of Ketchum, MacLeod & Grove, Inc., writing in *Dividends*, a company publication. "And," he continues, "every other creative organization in the country is having the same trouble. *There has never been a time in the past 16 or 18 years when companies have been able to get all the good writers they want. . . . The great aim is to get enough people to use the right words in the right sequences. . . . There will be a premium on the people who know the greatest number of the right words in the right situation.*" Memorize that last sentence: ". . . the people who know (1) the greatest number of (2) the right words in (3) the right situation."

From these statements you can draw one simple and undeniable conclusion: train yourself as an effective communicator in business, and management will make you welcome when you apply for your job!

IF YOU ARE THINKING OF BUSINESS,
HERE IS WHAT A BUSINESSMAN HAS SAID . . .

I know of no subject that deserves more extensive exploration than the relationship between effective communication and the executive career. . . .

Ideas are valueless if they cannot be conveyed. The executive must know how to convey ideas succinctly, for the slightest obscurity in his directives will result in confusion. . . . He must know the power . . . of language.

**From a Statement of the
President, Steuben Glass,
Incorporated**

> ## Communication Power in Action

Examples of Communication Power

The World's Power Line. Mail is one of the world's greatest business channels. Most universal of all, available to every man, it is the one medium that everyone can command. Instrument of personal power, it is yours to put to use for future success. The world's mail is a line of communication for carrying vital information from (a) where it is, to (b) where it is needed, through (c) the written word.

The book you are now reading keynotes these three steps from first page to last. Literally millions of business transactions call for transmitting, through the written word, great quantities of information from where it is—the data file, the investigation, the survey, the report, the executive's head—to where it is needed in other business offices, on the desks of other management executives, and in all similar places where the information will be valuable.

Imagine, if you can, the sudden vanishing of the daily newspaper, the telegraph, the cable, the telephone, and the United States postal service. Then you will have a sweeping demonstration of how completely business enterprise depends upon swift communication channels.

"The One Who Knows How to Say It." In modern business the top man is he who marshals the facts, puts them in the right order, and knows how to say what must be said. This man, knowing how to think straight and how to put his thoughts into words, can almost name his own price in the business world. He can write well. He can talk well. With his ability to express himself, he has the confidence to go anywhere and can effectively meet his daily problems. Using his skill *like a switchboard* in an electronic telephone exchange, *he connects his mind with the mind of his correspondent*, and he keeps the connection open and clear as long as the two minds wish to continue their communication.

How Do You Rate on These Real-Life Challenges? Can you write a letter that—in competition with other determined applicants —will win you an interview for a job you want? Can you organize a business report that will please the "boss"? Can you stand confidently before a group of your associates and command attention by forceful expression of ideas and precision of word-choice—the same clear expression and word-precision you will have to use when you start to dictate letters in your future job?

The purpose of this book is to help you answer "Yes" to these practical questions and to many others like them.

A Bank Executive "Lays It on the Line." Dr. Benjamin M. Anderson, Jr., an executive of the Chase Manhattan Bank of New York, has this to say: "The ability to write a good communication, courteous in tone, with a right adaptation of words to ideas, with a sure sense of the human relations effect of the message upon its reader, conveying precisely the information it means to convey, wasting no words, . . . this ability is a great business asset, as is the ability to write clean-cut and clear reports and memorandums. The ability to speak well in the business conference, and in dictating forceful letters is likewise a first-rate business asset. Mastery of the English language and of the art of writing—*from the standpoint of practical business*—comes close to being the one thing of highest importance."

What Other Management Men Say. "Your students will find their writing ability the best possible lever for obtaining positions in the business world when they graduate," says R. E. Smallwood, executive of a business magazine. Thousands of companies need trained business writers. Particularly note this, however: the ordinary English course won't do the job. Top management men want college graduates who have completed the course in business communication."

Supplementing this statement with even greater emphasis, the former chairman of the board of a famous mail-order firm testifies that hundreds of millions of dollars is the sum wasted every year in lost customers through clumsy, negative, and poorly prepared communications. "More today," he says, "than at any previous time, the world needs people who can write themselves into persuasive and positive English."

Fortune May Ride the Mails. Why does one letter get a job, an order, a check, or a forgiving smile from a ruffled customer? Why does another lose business and turn customers angrily away? Why do some letters hit the bull's-eye while others hit the wastebasket?

To find the secrets, Westinghouse, Armco, Fox River Paper, National Cash Register, Marshall Field and Company, Standard Oil, Cellucotton Products Division of Kimberly-Clark Corporation, and many other famous organizations set up special training methods and retain expert consultants in communication.

Says the National Cash Register Company, "The men and the concerns that use letters and follow them up promptly are reaping the rich rewards. Letters are one of the most powerful forces in business today."

Pulling Power: Some Examples of the Powerful Force. The strength with which it draws replies is called the *pulling power* of a message. Different messages ask for wholly different actions. For example, one seeks inquiries. Another seeks orders on approval. Still another seeks orders paid in full. A fourth invites you to check a return post card or to fill out a questionnaire. Whatever the request may be, the test is: How did it pull? How strong was it in getting replies? How much business did it produce?

One Message Helps Win Millions in Business (Case I). Read the invitation in the opening paragraphs of the tested letter reproduced on page 19. Hidden in that tested message is the practical magic that produced millions of dollars of new business:

```
As you will see from the enclosed card, we are reserving
for your use a memorandum pad, "Things to Do Today," hand-
fashioned of genuine leather - black morocco grain with
renewable filler.  Embossed with your name in gold, it will
be forwarded promptly on the receipt of the card completed.
```

Here are picture-facts, concrete details that can be seen and felt and appreciated. They tell about something that you may want: a memorandum pad, hand-fashioned of genuine leather, black morocco grain, renewable filler, embossed with your name in gold.

This multi-million-dollar example is a canvassing letter. It aims to stimulate interest and draw inquiries. It develops prospective buyers who are further informed through other steps in a planned program. The pulling power of this message is a matter of record. With virtually the same copy, this letter has been in successful use for more than 30 years and has been instrumental in selling millions of dollars of life insurance. This spectacular record is only one of many similar examples.

Can You Move 50 Carloads Through the Written Word? (Case II). "We have developed a powerful system for drawing inquiries," says the vice president of a leading rubber company. "One letter we recently sent to a hundred companies brought inquiries for 50 carloads of material. Totaling $120,000 in volume, these inquiries were turned into orders. It was the power of the written word that did it."

What Was the Mystery Power in the $22,000 Message? (Case III). Sometimes messages of extraordinary power almost baffle analysis. The power is there. But like an elusive mystery it seems to lie hidden. Later on in this book we are going to take a famous letter apart to discover the reasons for its mystery power. Here is an opening clue:

<u>$22,267.64 from a single letter!</u>

The General Manager was amazed. He hadn't the remotest idea that <u>he</u> could write a letter that would bring in more than $20,000 worth of business. But there were the returns to prove it--order after order from his circular-letter campaign to win back 1,305 old customers.

Was this $22,267.64 letter pure luck?

Not exactly! For when the General Manager heard of our unusual publication on business communication, containing the actual working methods of Dr. J. C. Harvey, the well-known specialist, he was among the first to send for a copy. A few weeks later he wrote us: "I must say that I never knew there were so many fine points in business letters as I found in Dr. Harvey's <u>Effective Business Writing Techniques</u>. Below are the detailed results of my circular-letter campaign to win back 1,305 old customers. I most certainly owe the unusually good results to your publication."

Seizing your attention is a gripping, concrete opening fact. The following paragraphs inflame the curiosity and put you in the middle of a drama. Later on in this book you will get the rest of the story.*

---

* Everything in this example is documented and factual except the names, which have been changed.

PHOENIX MUTUAL
LIFE INSURANCE CO.   HARTFORD, CONN.
ORGANIZED 1851

October 17, 19

Mr. Charles A. Cochrane
2210 Gaston Avenue
Dallas 4, Texas

Dear Mr. Cochrane:

As you will see from the enclosed card, we are reserving
for your use a memorandum pad, "Things to do Today," hand-
fashioned of genuine leather - black morocco grain with
renewable filler. Embossed with your name in gold, it will
be forwarded promptly on the receipt of the card completed.

Frankly, we are taking this means of calling to your attention
a newly announced "Series Ninety," an effective combination
of savings, investment, and protection.

There are unique features in this plan of special interest
to those who want to provide for dependents and at the same
time guarantee financial security for later years.

Seventy-one out of every hundred of our clients select the
"Ninety Series," feeling that there is no other plan which
provides more securely for possible developments in the
future.

When you return the card with your date of birth, we will
gladly supply the details as they would apply to you
personally.

Very truly yours,

G. W. Cheney

G. W. Cheney:NS   Second Vice President

"Pulling Power" in Action

This letter has been in successful use for more than 30 years. With only minor changes
in copy, it has been instrumental in selling millions of dollars of life insurance. This
spectacular record is only one of many in the annals of letter power.

Communication Volume

The United States Post Office Department Is a Big Business.
How many pieces of mail do you think the U. S. Post Office Department
handles in one fiscal year? How would you answer that question, just on an offhand guess? Would you say a billion? Maybe
two billions? Five billions? Ten billions, perhaps? On all those
guesses you are wrong. You may have a little trouble believing the
correct figure because it is a staggering FIFTY-SIX BILLIONS. If you
will take pains to inquire, Uncle Sam will tell you that this astro-
nomical figure is correct.

Here are the figures for a typical fiscal year showing the number of pieces of mail handled by the United States Post Office Department, as reported through the courtesy of the office of the United
States Postmaster General. You will notice that the total number
of pieces of *first-class mail alone*—the class in which personal and
business letters fall—reaches the stratospheric figure of more than
thirty billions. From every point of view the Post Office Department
is BIG BUSINESS indeed.

CLASS OF MAIL	PIECES
FIRST CLASS: letters and other written and sealed matter	30,077,567,376
SECOND CLASS: news-papers, magazines, and other periodicals bearing notice of second-class entry	6,914,504,058
THIRD CLASS: circulars and other miscellaneous printed matter	14,676,073,050
FOURTH CLASS: parcel post: merchandise, books, printed matter, other mailable matter not in first or second class	1,173,248,992
OTHER CLASSES	3,599,822,795
GRAND TOTAL	56,441,216,271

Communication Volume in the United States: Via Mail

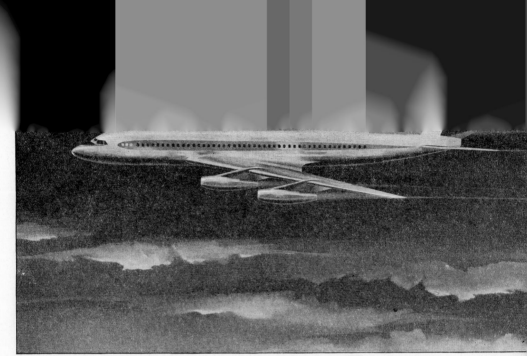

—Convair, a Division of General Dynamics Corporation

Get Ready for the World of Tomorrow . . . Today!

In jet airliners like these, traveling at speeds up to 2,000 miles an hour, your future world will travel, and the world's airmail will flash around the globe. Business communication, too, must be swift and dynamic in the World of Tomorrow.

Airmail Volume Also Skyrockets to Ever Higher Levels. Air travel telescopes the miles, and users of the mails are finding air speed more desirable with each passing year. "Of all inventions," wrote Lord Macaulay, the English historian, "the alphabet and printing press alone excepted, those inventions which abridge distance have done most for civilization." The mail-carrying airliners of America now cut national and international distances to a fraction of what they once were by carrying increasing billions of pound-miles of airmail. A "pound-mile" means one pound of mail flown one mile.

Again through the courtesy of the Post Office Department, here is the figure of pound-miles of airmail flown in one recent year:

TOTAL NUMBER OF POUND-MILES OF AIRMAIL FLOWN IN ONE YEAR: 120,438,064,000.

Because business transactions carried on over distances, great or small, must as a rule be put into writing, they require use of the mails in these colossal figures, both on the ground and in the air.*

* Three fourths of all the world's mail is now written in the English language. H. L. Mencken, *The American Language* (New York: Alfred A. Knopf), pp. 590-591. Also interesting is the fact that the English language is used in printing more than half the world's newspapers, and it is the language of three fifths of the world's radio stations.

Post Office Department

ASSISTANT POSTMASTER GENERAL
BUREAU OF TRANSPORTATION
AIR MAIL SERVICE
WASHINGTON 25, D. C.

July 19--

To Help You Get the Most
From Air Postal Services...

Here's an instructive folder that will show you how Air Parcel Post
and Air Mail can benefit your business. And, as explained below,
we'll be glad to send you a complimentary copy of a 12-page booklet
which describes the advantages of Air Postal Services even more
completely.

We think you'll agree that the first thought in regard to Air Parcel
Post or Air Mail is its speed - and rightly so. It's common knowledge that Air Parcel Post takes only one-fourth as long as surface
Parcel Post, and Air Mail reaches its destination overnight - arrives
anywhere in the world within 60 hours.

But have you ever thought of the other advantages of these Air Postal
Services? For example, consider the economy of Air Parcel Post. It
flies with Air Mail on the same planes, gets the same preferred handling - is delivered to off-airline points at no extra charge. Yet,
rates are extremely low.

Then look at the prestige and profit angles. Air Parcel Post has
action-value that is reflected in greater prestige for your firm -
businessmen recognize and appreciate your desire to furnish prompt,
efficient service.

Air Mail, too, has the advantages of economy, prestige and profit.
And besides all this, there is the dependability of Air Postal Service - backed by the U. S. Post Office Department and the Scheduled
Airlines of the U. S. Naturally, you'll get best results from Air
Postal Service by installing clear-cut Air Parcel Post and Air Mail
policies of your own. How to do that most successfully is explained
briefly in the enclosed folder - more fully in the booklet.

We'll be glad to send you a copy of the Air Postal Service Booklet
- without cost or obligation. Just fill in and return the enclosed
reply card. No postage is necessary - and I'll be glad to see that
your copy is sent promptly.

Sincerely yours,

Robert S. Burgess

Robert S. Burgess
Deputy Assistant Postmaster General
Air Mail Service

RSB/DR
Encs.

The United States Government Uses Powerful Letters

An effective message setting forth the many advantages of airmail.

Communication Costs

American Business Spends Millions Each Day—On Its Letters! How much do letters cost American business *every day*? If you were asked to make an offhand guess, what would your answer be? Two million dollars? Five millions? Ten millions, perhaps? These guesses are impressive. Possibly they sound too big. But the fact is, they fall far short of the actual mark. The correct figure is even more astonishing. *Business spends over thirty million dollars a day on letters.* And this it does every day of the calendar year.

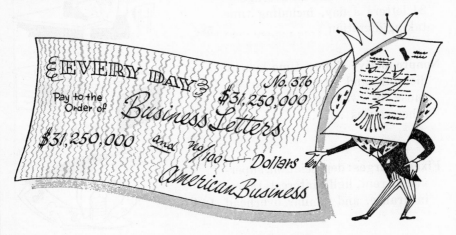

"What," You May Ask, "Does This Have to Do With Me?" Thirty million dollars a day is a fair-sized king's ransom. And how the cost of business letters in every 24-hour period could be so high is at first hard to understand. Your natural reaction may be to ask, "What does all this have to do with me?" Of course it has a great deal to do with you because it is a part of *your* future management problem and that of thousands of others like you: how to cut costs. Perhaps you ask, "Where do these colossal costs come from? I always thought letters cost just a few cents apiece." "Just a few cents apiece" is a common, nationwide misconception.

An Average Business Letter Costs . . . Much More Than You Think! The average personally dictated business letter costs about a dollar and a half. A short letter dictated by a lower-salaried executive may cost slightly less. A long letter dictated by a higher-salaried executive may cost a great deal more. Letters costing two or three dollars apiece are today not at all unusual.

$1.50 IS THE COST OF THE AVERAGE-LENGTH DICTATED BUSINESS LETTER. THIS LETTER-COST CHART SHOWS WHY.

Dictator's Time: based on an average salary of $168 a week; a 40-hour week; and an average of eight minutes for each letter written .... 56¢

Stenographic Cost: based on an average salary of $70 a week; a 40-hour week; and an average of 24 letters a day, including time taking dictation .... 58¢

Nonproductive Time: time lost by dictator and stenographer because of waiting, illness, and other causes .... 4.62¢

Fixed Charges: depreciation, supervision, rent, light, interest, taxes, insurance, and similar overhead 18.48¢

Materials: letterheads, envelopes, carbon papers, typewriter ribbons, pencils, and other supplies 6.75¢

Filing Costs: clerical time, costs of filing supplies .... 1.67¢

Mailing Costs: postage, gathering, sealing, stamping, and delivering to the post office .... 4.48¢

Total Cost . . . $1.50

If a secretary transcribes 24 letters a day and the cost is $1.50 apiece, the total production cost for the letters transcribed by that one secretary is $36 a day. In 10 working days $360 worth of time and energy, materials, overhead, and all the other factors on the cost chart, have been consumed.

How to Save One and One-Eighth Billion Dollars: Make Business Letters 10% More Effective. About one fourth of the thirty billion pieces of annual first-class mail gets costly personal attention, according to reasonable estimate. If 7,500,000,000 of our letters cost $1.50 each, our annual bill is $11,250,000,000. The U. S. Postal Service spends another billion and a half each year to *carry* the mail.

Now sharpen a pencil for some brief arithmetic: If dictated letters can be made just 10 per cent better, figure how many tens of millions of dollars can be thriftily recaptured each year.*

The 10% Improvement Parade

A 10% improvement may be only the beginning. You may **energize** your mail with so much new power that your better results will more than repay your full cost per message.

For example, if you dictate 24 letters a day, each costing $1.50, your daily letter cost is $36. Improve these letters 10% and that improvement will equal a saving of $3.60 each day, $18 each week, $72 each month (4 weeks), and $900 each year (50 weeks) for your company.

* Every year the United States Government writes a billion (1,000,000,000) letters to carry on its work. The Government spends $4,000,000,000 a year on paper work; $40,000,000 a year to store records; $180,000,000 for office space for paper work; $36,000,000 on office machines (automation); with no less than 750,000 federal employees engaged exclusively in paper work. Each year the Government adds 9,000,000,000 documents to its store of records. See *Findings of the Second Hoover Commission*, Washington, D. C., for these and other significant facts and figures.

$\boxed{\textbf{Summary}}$

The new management target is greater communication power to be used in a new kind of world for more effective human relations. You are wisely preparing today for the world of tomorrow because you recognize that higher skills will be a "must" for the future. You have discovered that effective communication is basically a management problem, and that all levels of management, whether at the top, at the middle, or at the operating level, must depend upon communication for effective group action.

In coming chapters your search will be for clear understanding and clean-cut action through the communication power line. Your aim throughout the book will be to put communication power into action for better human relations, and to generate higher skill and ability in getting along with others.

Having seen how much top management depends on efficient communications, having learned new facts concerning the huge volume and costs of communication, you are now ready to study new examples of communication power, to find out how the experts produce their powerful messages, and to see if you can do it yourself.

Your aim is basic and simple: to learn how to solve management problems through the written word. To this end you will strive to master the central principles and the important power elements set forth, in systematic order, in coming chapters.

Communication Problems

● 1. You are the newly appointed Program Chairman for a businessmen's group in your community. In addition to planning, with your committee, the first fall meeting of the year, one of your first duties as Chairman is to write to all members inviting them to the meeting. You are to write the message on October 1 for the meeting to be held October 20. Since the letter is to be duplicated, you should omit the inside address and use a salutation that is appropriate for all members.

Data to Be Used: This first meeting is to be a dinner meeting on Wednesday, October 20, at 6:30 p.m. The meeting is to be held in the Crystal Room of the Park-Vue Hotel. Members are to be notified that they may invite guests. The price of the dinner will be $3.75, including tax and tip. A social hour, with refreshments, in the Hunt Room will precede the dinner. The dinner speaker will be Dr. Harold B. Bolen, President of the American Business Writing Association and Chairman of the Department of Business Communication at State University. Dr. Bolen has chosen as his topic: "Plain Talk Makes for Readable Writing." A discussion period will follow Dr. Bolen's presentation.

Directions: Arrange the data into a letter to be sent to the members of this businessmen's group. Strive in your writing for brevity, clarity, and logical arrangement of ideas. Choose words that will add a fraternal tone to the message.

Date your message October 1. Assume that it will be accompanied by a reservation card. This card is to be returned to you by October 15. (Use the illustration on page 44 of this book as a model of effective layout.)

● **2.** One of the objectives of this course in effective communication is to develop the ability to detect errors and weaknesses in business messages and to correct them. The following problem will acquaint you with some of the kinds of situations you will face.

Directions: Assume that a new office assistant composed and typed the following letter and presented it to you for evaluation and suggestions. Analyze the letter carefully and list the changes you would ask him to make before you would be willing to sign it.

Sept. 15, 19--

Dear Mr. Taylor,

I am sorry that I have to inform you that we do not have in stock at the present time any Time Master alarm clocks furthermore we do not know when we will have any in stock.

For your information we do have Bel Aire electric alarms. In fact, we are overstocked with them and can certainly supply you with this particular model if you so wish.

I hope that the Bel Aire model will be okey to ship to you.

At your service, we are.

Sincerely,

● **3.** Mr. Edward M. Simms, Communications Supervisor of Electronic Enterprises, Inc., has received a letter offering to send a complimentary copy of a booklet entitled "Writing Out Loud." The booklet contains 36 pages of up-to-date and refreshingly presented pointers on dictating effective business messages. Mr. Simms believes this booklet will be useful to him and his staff in improving their dictating techniques. Assume that you are an assistant to Mr. Simms, who has asked you to write for a copy of the booklet.

Directions: Set up a heading in which you use your home or a nearby city as the address for Electronic Enterprises, Inc. Your request is to be sent to: Mr. Lloyd M. Powell, President, Dictaphone Corporation, 420 Lexington Avenue, New York 17, New York. As a guide for arrangement and punctuation, use the letter illustrated on page 44. Since you are making the request for Mr. Simms, you will sign the letter.

Suggested Plan: Mention the source of your information about the booklet. Make the request. Indicate that Mr. Powell's courtesy in sending this publication will be appreciated.

● 4. *Effective Communication Is a Management Problem!* You read this as one of the section headings in Chapter 1. Any business, large or small, has to communicate and can therefore profit from the use of good communication techniques. If the cost of the average dictated business communication is $1.50, and if you can reduce the cost 10 per cent by study and practice, then every management executive should require his employees to work toward improvement.

Directions: As a three-day class project study the Cost Analysis shown on page 24 and report on ways and means of reducing the expense of writing for business. Work on an individual basis at first. Later, at the direction of your instructor, you may work as a member of a group.

How to Begin. (1) Collect ten business messages and analyze them for possible improvement. (2) Talk to several businessmen or businesswomen who write or dictate as a part of their regular duties. Ask them for opinions or for suggestions based on their experience. (3) Time an executive on his dictation and a secretary on her transcription. Does the time from your experiment substantially "match" the time given in the book illustration? (4) Do some outside reading to find possible ways of cutting down on normal communication costs.

Make Your Report. After you have completed these four steps, then (under the direction of your instructor) join forces as a group-team. Pool your findings. Hold a "brain-storming" session. Compile your own individual list of positive suggestions for the improvement of business communication and for cost reduction. Present these suggestions to the class, complete with illustrations, in a short but carefully prepared one- or two-page report.

● 5. Study the examples you collected in Problem 4. How did they involve human relations as outlined on pages 8 and 9 of this chapter? Were the messages effective? Make a list of the words that appealed to you. List the words that created a negative impression.

Suggestions for the Problem: In order to have class uniformity, follow the general classifications given on page 9. It will be obvious that the different purposes for which communications are written will affect the selection of words. The messages will also have to attack the human relations problem from different approaches. Fit your examples into the six different classifications given, and select your human relations words on the basis of that classification.

● 6. From library sources such as the *Statistical Abstract of the United States* or United States Post Office publications, secure comparative figures on the mail volume for several years. Is the volume of mail up or down? Is there a difference in the trend between the various classes of mail—that is, is one class of mail increasing in volume while another class of mail is declining? What influence should these figures have on management policies?

Suggestions: Try to secure at least ten figures—either year-by-year or by five-year periods.

● **7.** The purpose of this problem is to give you an opportunity to share with your instructor your thoughts about the significant factors in your life that may affect your progress in this course and that may have an influence on your success in your business or professional career.

A. Prepare a typewritten or neatly handwritten data sheet in which you outline your previous training, your present activities, and your plans for the future. An annotated outline is given below as a guide for headings to be used and subjects of interest that you might cover.

PERSONAL DATA SHEET

MAJOR FIELD OF STUDY:

Indicate your major field of specialization and how you plan to use this training when you receive your diploma.

MINOR FIELD OF STUDY:

Indicate your minor field of specialization and how you plan to use this training when you receive your diploma.

EXPECTED DATE OF GRADUATION:

Indicate month and year.

RELATED COURSES PREVIOUSLY TAKEN:

List courses in English, psychology, and business that you believe will be helpful to you in this course in effective communication.

RELATED ACTIVITIES:

List such activities as writing for the school paper, dramatics, debating, or offices in organizations that require writing business messages, reports, and announcements.

WORK EXPERIENCE:

List summer, part-time, and military experience—especially if this experience included correspondence or report writing, or special opportunities for learning to understand people.

PRESENT EMPLOYMENT (IF ANY):

Give the name of the company or organization, nature of duties and responsibilities, and number of hours you are working.

OTHER COURSES BEING TAKEN THIS SEMESTER OR TERM:

PERSONAL RESPONSIBILITIES:

List all personal responsibilities that may affect or limit your activities—marital, parental, or others.

SPECIFIC PERSONAL PROBLEMS IN WRITING:

Indicate such problems as difficulty in organization of materials, lack of ability to express yourself clearly, and weaknesses in grammar, spelling, and punctuation that you hope to master in this class.

B. Consider your own qualifications and your reasons for taking this course. Write a one-page letter to your instructor in which you state your primary objective in taking this course, indicate what courses and experiences you have had that you think will be most helpful in completing this course successfully, and describe your plans for using what you learn to help you in your business or professional career. Select from the personal data sheet you have just prepared the highlights to be included. Mention in the letter that you are enclosing a personal data sheet that gives more detailed information about you and your future plans.

Directions: Use your own address for the heading of the letter. Use your instructor's full name with the complete address of your college or university as the inside address. (Consult a current catalog of your college for this information.) An appropriate salutation is "Dear" followed by the instructor's title and surname.

Although this message is necessarily about yourself, avoid the too frequent use of *I* at the beginning of sentences and paragraphs, especially of consecutive ones. Starting some of the sentences with an introductory phrase or clause will help avoid this possible suggestion of egotism.

"Sincerely yours," and "Sincerely," are appropriate closings for this type of writing. Sign your name carefully so that it is completely legible. Help the reader to recognize it easily.

> NOTE: Use the illustration on page 44 of this book as a model for the layout. You will use your own address instead of the letterhead as the heading, however.

From time to time throughout this course you will be called upon to analyze business messages according to various writing criteria. For that reason, you not only should keep the ten messages collected for Problem 4 of this chapter, but you should also add to your collection throughout the course.

PART I

Chapter 2
The First Target of Management: Creating a Good First Impression

| Make the Look of Your Message Command Respect |

Do You Make Snap Judgments? Most People Do. A top management executive, discussing the subject of business success and how to win it, has some salty and unvarnished words about first impressions.

"People look at you," he writes. "They judge you, and they trademark you. They put you in a pigeonhole saying, 'That is where you belong.' They do that just by looking at you!"

When a reader opens and unfolds a written message, he does exactly the same thing. He makes a snap judgment.

To draw quick conclusions, to make snap judgments on the first impression of a person, an object, a situation, or a letter, is a natural human habit that you must expect.

You have watched a speaker stride to the platform to open a meeting. Before he utters a word, you start sizing him up. You make a snap judgment about him. Perhaps you like him at first sight.

The Interesting Example of Mr. Bell. Take the case of Mr. Bell. He's a lucky man. In the first place, he's a good management executive who has had one promotion after another because he deserves them. He stands high in his company. People seem to like him at first sight.

You may hear his associates making comments like these: "Why not send Bell over to the meeting? They'll listen to him." "Let Bell write that campaign. *He can talk on paper.*" "Have Bell handle that letter." "Ask Bell to draft our next report . . . he can take a complicated situation and write it so that it seems simple and easy." "Yes, Bell's your man . . . *he knows how to say it so that anybody can understand it.*"

31

—Lichty, *Chicago Times Syndicate*

"That letter is rather urgent, Miss Truffle —better use two fingers!"

But you may as well know the truth at the outset: there are very few people like Bell. A few, like him, are born with the "gift." But they are very rare. Most others have reached their success through steady personal effort and careful study. And they all find out, sooner or later, that their *articulateness*—that is, their ability *to put words meaningfully on paper, to express themselves clearly*—is taking them farther along the road to success than any of their other personal assets. Now—what is the first step, the very first step, along that road?

Management Requirement Number 1: A High Standard of Excellent Form. Management man Bell, and all his fellow executives, lay down one standard "Number 1" requirement to be observed throughout the company: EVERY LETTER THAT LEAVES THE COMPANY MUST REACH A HIGH STANDARD OF EXCELLENT FORM. Their standing instruction to the secretarial staff is this: "Make the LOOK of Our Letters COMMAND Respect!" Why these instructions? Because these skilled management people have learned by experience that the first great step to success is handsome form and appearance—*an excellent first impression*.

"Lady, you're it!"

Visualize the Picture

The First Impression May Be the Final Impression! What does your message look like? What kind of a first impression does it make? It had better be good because the first impression it makes may easily be the final impression it leaves. The form of the message is the first thing the reader sees. Make it measure up to Management Rule Number 1: Make it COMMAND respect.

Your message is always doubly forceful if it looks right on the sheet of paper. If it looks wrong because of slovenly handwriting, or careless typing, then you have ruined the effect, no matter how vivid your ideas, no matter how thoughtful your plan, no matter how careful your word choice.

So frame your letter like a picture. Make it attract the eye. Get it off to a flying start.

Let's Look In on a Brief Drama. A management executive sits at his desk. The time? Nine o'clock in the morning. Lying before him is the incoming mail. Preferring to open his own messages, he draws a slender metal paper knife through the flap of the first envelope, takes out the letter, unfolds it with a snap, and there before his eye is a striking picture!

"Handsome," is the unspoken thought. "Important! Better give this message special attention." The knife slits the second envelope. "My word! . . . What a damaging contrast! Can't Carter's, Inc.

He's Giving Your Letter a Second Look

Perhaps he is a management executive who is considering you for a job. He's giving your letter a second look . . . and that's worth money to you. Why? Because when you become part of a business organization, that one letter (if average) will cost you more than $1.50.

find a secretary who can spell? . . . Slovenly strikeovers . . . Do
you suppose their management is slipping? . . . That reminds me,
I'd better check up on our own letters . . . I don't want anything like
this happening, believe me! Next!"

The paper knife slits on. The fragmentary thoughts continue to
flow. The unspoken thoughts reflect the fleeting first impressions
that may make or break the message success. Every morning—all
over America—this drama repeats itself, tearing down or building
up the company reputation.

Do You, Like Others, Read Between the Lines? You have often
heard people speak of "reading between the lines." How would a
letter look if the unrecorded thoughts between the lines were actually
written there?

Dear Mr. Bell:

On the basis of the cost figures with which
  There is something about this letter that I

you supplied us, we have arrived at the annual
  like. . . . Wonder what it is. . . . I have a

cost of operating your plant under your present
  feeling that this is an established, dependable

system. We have prepared a chart showing how
  company that knows its business. . . . Odd,

much you will now be able to save by installing
  because I never heard of it before last week

the Kendall System, and how much the plant
  when I gave it those figures. . . . Now I know

output can be increased. May our representa-
  what I like about it. . . . handsome layout,

tive call with some additional facts?
  good bond paper, beautiful letter form, fine content.

                    Very sincerely yours,
  Excellent! Certainly, I'll see the representative.

                    KENDALL SYSTEMS, INC.

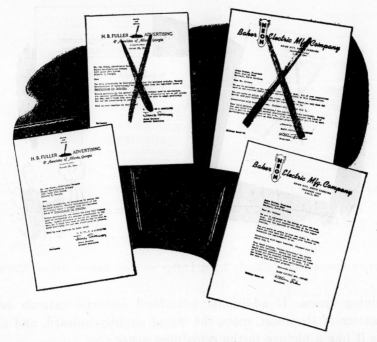

Use the "Picture Frame" for Every Kind, Size, and Shape of Letterhead

The "Picture-Frame" Guide. *Make your letter assume the same proportions as those of the sheet upon which it is placed. Keep the side and bottom margins equal in width, so that the letter, under its letterhead, looks like a picture in a handsome frame.* This is the "picture-frame" guide. No matter how short or how long the letter is, no matter what the shape of the sheet may be, apply this guide. If you are writing on a half sheet, a three-quarter sheet, a full sheet measuring 8½ by 11 inches—or a sheet of stationery with other dimensions—make your letter look like a picture on the page.

If you carefully observe the picture-frame guide, you will win these four desirable results:

1. The form will be attractive.
2. It will be high in attention value.
3. It will guide the message smoothly into the mind.
4. It will make the message stand out in importance.

Even if the page is of unusual shape or design, the picture-frame guide still applies. If, for instance, the letterhead material extends down the left margin (committee names, branch office addresses, and like data), move the layout slightly to the right and frame it in the

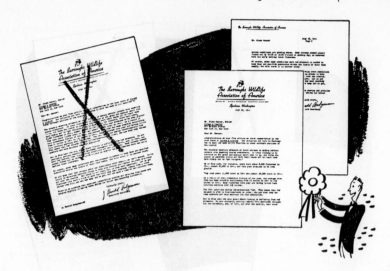

"Picture Frame" an Unusually Long Letter on Two Pages—Never Crowd!

remaining space. If additional letterhead material extends across the bottom of the sheet, move the layout slightly upward, and again frame it like a picture in the remaining space.

You may doubt that the message will go on one sheet. In that case leave more white space in the margins—the "frame of your picture" —and use a second sheet. *Never crowd.* Crowding ruins visual form. Use the same side margins on the second sheet as on the first.

Can You Visualize? Visualize in your mind's eye how to frame a letter. Train your eyes for symmetry. Make the message a picture in its frame.

Look at the First National Bank letter on page 37 and the National Broadcasting Company letter on page 38. Note how crispness of form generates respect. Form, the first thing you see, flashes a picture upon the brain. If you train yourself to observe excellent standards, your message will always be:

1. Attractive to the eye
2. High in attention value
3. Strong in visual contrast
4. Well-shaped
5. Well-centered
6. Interesting to look at
7. Easy to read

You can expect these seven important results as soon as you begin to apply the picture-frame guide to the layout of your messages.

THE FIRST NATIONAL BANK

ESTABLISHED 1854

MADISON 1, WISCONSIN

June 1, 19--

A SPECIAL LETTER TO OUR DEPOSITORS:

Through the years, the First National Bank has taken much pride in using the most up-to-date methods and equipment available for servicing its Checking Accounts.

Now, something new has been introduced to banking . . . equipment for the electronic-mechanical sorting and posting of checks and deposits . . . and our bank has recently made arrangements to acquire this equipment which will permit greater speed and accuracy in keeping Checking Account Records. This new procedure represents a major change from the past conventional bookkeeping methods, but it is the unanimous opinion of leading bankers of the nation that this is the answer to the problem of processing the ever-increasing volume of check activity.

These machines require the use of an individual "sorting-code number" on all checks and deposit tickets for each separate Checking Account. This number will be printed on each check at a place near the signature line on the check. When making deposits, the number is to be written in the space provided on the deposit ticket.

If you are already using checks with your name imprinted on them, the code number will be printed near the signature line on all subsequent reorders. If you are not presently using checks with your name imprinted on them, we will write you again regarding the imprinting of checks, including your assigned code number.

We sincerely believe that this system will greatly increase efficiency as we will have a positive identification of your account, your checks, and your deposits by both signature and number.

With your cooperation in this important undertaking, we are sure the results will be mutually beneficial.

Sincerely yours,

T. R. Hefty, President

TRH:dmk

COMMERCIAL ··· SAVINGS ··· TRUST

A Long Letter Well Framed

An interesting message discusses management communication and financial control by code number. This is an example of "Automation" in banking—a development similar to others discussed in Chapter 1.

NATIONAL BROADCASTING COMPANY, INC.

A SERVICE OF RADIO CORPORATION OF AMERICA

RCA Building, Radio City. New York 20, N.Y.

CIRCLE 7-8300

February 18, 19--

Dr. Thomas R. Clinton
P. O. Box 3434
Chicago 17, Illinois

Dear Dr. Clinton:

Your interest in Mr. Guthrie Janssen's portion
of "Weekends" on February 6 is deeply appreciated.

The surveys mentioned by Mr. Janssen were conducted by the United States Chamber of Commerce,
Washington 6, D. C. Further information is available
through their Education Department. We are sorry
that because of copyright restrictions, scripts are
not available for distribution.

It will be a pleasure to forward your gracious
comments directly to Mr. Janssen for notation.

Sincerely yours,

K S Cole

K. S. Cole, Manager
Department of Information

ld

A Short Letter Well Framed

A brief message, in a pleasant tone, gives information that has been requested. Note
how carefully the message opens and closes on the keynote of courtesy.

Make the "Comparison" Check

Select 10 typewritten letters. Lay them out on a desk for observation. Some will draw your favorable attention; others you will disregard. Next, sort out the ones that strike your eye. Compare them with one another. As you examine the sheets, do you find yourself forming impressions from the looks of the printed letterheads? the placement and spacing of the message? the appearance of the typing? the feel of the paper?

Use Top-Quality Materials

Selected Stationery. White, unruled, high-quality bond paper of firm texture and surface, of standard size 8½ by 11 inches, is most popular. For short notes the half sheet of 8½ by 5½ inches is used, but it cannot always be filed well with larger sheets. Other sizes appear, but in smaller volume. Tinted paper with matching envelopes is used to an increasing extent.

Second-sheet stationery should equal the first sheet in quality, color, weight, and size. Carbon copies for office files are typed on "copy" stationery, thin but firm in texture to assure a clear carbon impression.

Letterheads in Modern Design. Handsome letterheads can be created by the use of simple lines and angles and blocks of type. An attractive letterhead adds to the power of the message and to the

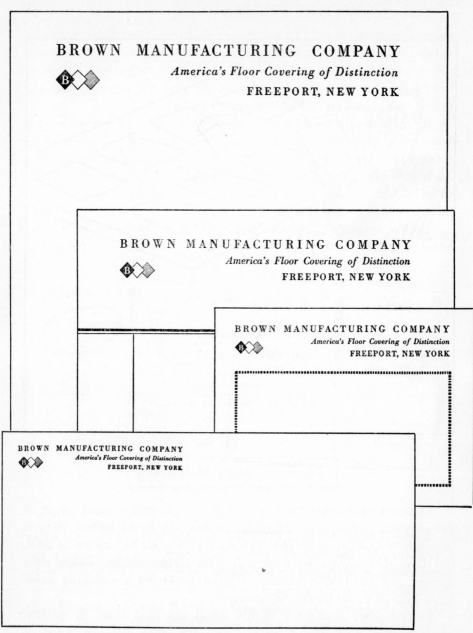

—*Crocker-McElwain Company*

Unified Stationery Is Modern Practice

reputation of the firm. Note the handsome modern qualities of the letterheads appearing on pages 40, 44, 340, 343, 427, 431, and other pages of this book.

Your letterheads may be printed, lithographed, engraved, or embossed. Expensive designs, impressive trademarks, and elaborate colors sometimes appear on the theory that letterhead space is of high value for sales purposes. For such work "heavy" letterheads may prove suitable. But in general communication a "shouting" letterhead draws your attention from the message, where it belongs, and may defeat the object for which the letter was sent.

Letterhead information normally fills a depth of not more than two and a half inches. In this space you will find the name of the concern, the mail address, and sometimes the nature of the business. Such information as the telephone number, the address of the chief office of the company, the location of branch offices, and the cable address is sometimes supplied.

Note carefully the twelve items listed in the letterhead rating chart on page 42. Each question should have a "yes" answer.

❶ **The Paper:**

Is it fine bond — bright, crisp, and strong? Does it crackle with quality?

❷ **The Printing:**

Does it show pleasing design and fine craftsmanship?

❸ **The Typing:**

Does your letter emerge like a picture in a frame — skilled, expert, in beautiful letter layout?

❹ **YOUR WORDS:**

YOU . . . What YOU say . . . How YOU say it . . . Do you say it well — or otherwise?

These Four Simple Tests Lead to Success

Every Letter Is an INDIVIDUAL Message. Although letters travel through the mails by the billion, each one represents a personal message addressed to a definite destination. Each firm stakes its reputation for the moment on the impression that a single message will make on the person getting it. If that one message succeeds, the firm succeeds. If that one message fails, the firm fails as far as the one reader is concerned.

Remember: *Each letter is a personal message read by an individual.* The sum total of the impressions made upon your individual readers by these personal messages, from the first glance at the physical form to the final appraisal of the message, makes up a large part of your success.

Letterhead Rating Chart

For _____

Type of Business _____

How well does our letterhead tell <u>who</u> we are?

    1. Is the name legible and clear at a glance?............................ _____

How well does our letterhead tell <u>where</u> we are?

    2. Has it full address for convenience of out-of-town visitors?......... _____

    3. Has it telephone number to save out-of-town customers time and trouble?.. _____

How well does our letterhead tell <u>what</u> we are?

    4. Is our business simply and accurately described?...................... _____

    5. If an illustration is used, is it legible, attractive and does it help tell our story?.. _____

    6. Is the type-face or lettering of good design?.......................... _____

    7. Are the various elements (name, business, address, etc.) well-arranged, or are they cluttered up?........................... _____

    8. Do the various elements follow in logical order, to tell their story at a glance?... _____

    9. Is the printing sharp, clean and attractive?.......................... _____

    10. If colors are used, are they pure, of proper strength, appropriate?... _____

    11. Is the paper of substantial thickness, good crisp feel and proper permanence? .... _____

    12. Is the heading equal to competitors' headings, or up to the standard of the industry? .... ════════

                                Total Points

      Divide by number of rating points used

                                 RATING   _____

It is impossible to give a just rating without full knowledge of the letterhead user's business. But this chart puts letterhead rating on, at least, a semi-scientific basis, in which utility is considered first and design is subordinate to it. The most beautiful letterhead, deficient in the information it should convey, is not a good letterhead in the business world.

—Whiting-Plover Paper Company

Letterhead Rating Chart

These questions may be used as a check-chart for appraising the value of a letterhead.

Layout

Effective Layout. Layout, a term from the field of art that applies well to letter form, refers to the arrangement of the several parts of a finished letter. Layout has three purposes: (1) to make the letter handsome in appearance; (2) to draw attention to the important parts of the letter; and (3) to present the message clearly.

Ask yourself these questions in planning your letter layout: How can I make it most attractive? How can I design it to secure the highest attention? How can I build it so that the message will be understood most easily?

Standard Structure. The business letter has seven main parts: (1) heading, (2) address, (3) salutation, (4) body, (5) complimentary close, (6) signature, and (7) signature identification and stenographic reference.*

The letter on page 44 shows the arrangement and the relative position of each of these parts.

Letter Styles. Letters may be arranged in several different styles, of which the *modified block* is the most popular.

In the modified block style typed on letterhead paper, the date line is ordinarily centered under the letterhead or typed to end at the right margin. When letterhead paper is not used, the heading is ordinarily typed to end at the right margin. The paragraphs may be typed in the complete block style, each line flush with the left margin, or the first line of each paragraph may be indented five to ten spaces. The closing lines are blocked (a) beginning about five spaces to the left of the center of the letter, or (b) beginning at the center of the letter, or (c) beginning at a point so that the longest line will end flush with the right margin.

The modified block style of letter with mixed punctuation is illustrated on page 44. Note that mixed punctuation requires a colon after the salutation and a comma after the complimentary close. No other end-of-line punctuation is used in the opening and closing lines. Other letter and punctuation styles are illustrated on pages 596 and 598 in the Reference Division.

* In some letters certain special guide lines, such as the *attention line*, the *subject line*, and the *reference line*, may appear. These guide lines are discussed and illustrated on pages 603 and 604 in the Reference Division of this book.

APEX TYPEWRITER COMPANY

520 Boylston Street • Boston 3, Massachusetts

MAin 1-2437

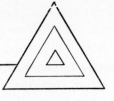

October 12, 19--

Mr. Kent J. Evans, President
Fisher Textile Corporation
2140 Cobblestone Avenue
Boston 13, Massachusetts

Dear Mr. Evans:

Few things are more personal than the letters you
write. They express your thoughts, your ideas,
your ideals. They are <u>you</u>--on paper. But are
the letters that bear <u>your</u> signature giving <u>you</u>
fair representation?

Study this letter for a moment and decide for yourself. Note, first of all, how it is centered upon
the page. Observe that the margins are balanced
and clearly defined; that the paragraphs are well
proportioned.

Note also that every type character is clean-cut,
uniform in impression and evenly spaced. The capitals, which in so many letters show a tendency to
jump above the line, are in perfect alignment.

Compare this letter with <u>your</u> letters. Or, better
still, permit us to deliver a new Apex Electric
Typewriter to your office where your own secretary
can use it and show you how much better your own
letters will look.

Sincerely yours,

John Sinnott

John Sinnott
Branch Manager

JS:lc

Correct Letter Layout of a Modified Block Letter

In arranging the parts of the letter, guide yourself by the picture-frame rule: Make your letter assume the same proportions as those of the sheet upon which you put it.

1. **Heading.** The heading shows where the letter comes from and when it was written. As the name and address of the business are printed on a letterhead, the typed heading includes only the date. On letterhead paper the date is typed on the second line space (a double space) below the city and state line.

   When the letter is prepared on plain paper, both the exact address of the writer and the date must be typed or written. The first line of the heading begins slightly to the right of the horizontal center of the sheet and, for a letter of medium length, is typed about an inch and a half below the top.

2. **Address.** The address contains the name of the person (if used) to whom the letter is to be sent and his official title (if he has one), the name of the business, the street address, the city name and postal zone number (if a zone number is used), and the state name. Each line of the address is typed even with the left margin. The number of line spaces between the date line and the address is determined by the length of the letter.

3. **Salutation.** The salutation is the complimentary greeting with which a letter begins (Examples: *Dear Mr. Evans:* or *My dear Evans:*). The salutation is typed even with the left margin on the second line space (a double space) below the last line of the address.

4. **Body.** The body of the letter is the material between the salutation at the beginning and the complimentary close at the end. The body begins two line spaces (a double space) below the salutation. The body of a single-spaced letter requires double spacing between paragraphs. Single spacing is standard usage for practically all business letters, no matter what their length.

5. **Complimentary Close.** The complimentary close is typed two line spaces (a double space) below the last line of the body. The longest of the closing lines should not extend noticeably beyond the right margin.

6. **Signature.** The signature may consist only of the name of the writer with his name typed, for clear identification, directly below his written signature, on the fourth line below the complimentary close. This typed signature is begun even with the beginning of the complimentary close.* The official title (when used) is typed on the line immediately below the typed name, or it may be typed on the line with the name separated by a comma.

7. **Signature Identification and Stenographic Reference.** The signature identification and stenographic reference are devices to indicate who has dictated the letter and who has transcribed it. These items should be typed flush with the left margin on a line even with, or two line spaces below, the typed signature.**

---

* A number of firms still follow the practice of typing the company name in all capital letters a double space below the complimentary close. *This practice is unnecessary if the company name appears in the letterhead.*
** Variations in spacing and positioning the letter parts for letters typed in the basic styles are given on pages 597-613 in the Reference Division of this book.

Single-spaced, blocked, four-line address. Note the method of emphasizing the city and the state. ▶

Double-spaced, indented, three-line address. This form is used with the indented letter when the address is typed in three lines. ▶

CALLAWAY ADVERTISING AGENCY
1050 Pike Boulevard
Colorado Springs, Colorado

```
                    Mr. John E. Binnion
                    Manager, The Frontier Hotel
                    315 Corral Street
                    ESTES PARK, COLORADO
```

Palette Artist Supplies
502 Eggleston Avenue • Detroit 12, Michigan

```
          Century Sports Car Company

            13958 Gratiot Boulevard

                Flint 4, Michigan
```

Attention Mr. Jean Vedier

<hr>

Envelopes for Business Letters

Addressing the Envelope. Although the envelope address should be essentially the same as the address in the letter, a few exceptions should be noted. Three-line addresses for envelopes are often double-spaced for more legibility and hence more accuracy in the handling of mail. When four or more lines are to be used, however, the envelope address should be single-spaced. To improve appearance, use at least three lines for an envelope address. If no street address is given, type the names of the city and the state on separate lines. The city and zone number should be separated from the state name by a comma when typed on the same line. Do not use the word *City* in the place of the correct name of the city.

The top line of the address should not rise above the middle of the envelope and should be centered from left to right. With the exception of the points noted above, the envelope address duplicates the address in the letter in form (block or indented) and in punctuation (close or open). The form should present the maximum in attractiveness and clearness, in accuracy and symmetry.

The envelopes illustrated above show two popular styles of addresses.*

* Procedures for folding letterheads to fit various sizes of envelopes are illustrated on page 614 in the Reference Division of this book.

46

Different-Sized Envelopes. The smaller envelope is generally used for sending a one-page letter or a one-page letter with a small enclosure that is folded not more than twice, such as a circular or a card. The larger envelope is often used when a letter contains more than one page or when accompanying enclosures might make a smaller envelope seem too bulky. In some offices the larger size envelope is used for all letters because of its superior attention value. When a quantity of material is to be sent with a letter, or if material is to be sent unfolded, it is sometimes necessary to use large envelopes of heavy stock. Commonly used sizes are 6½ by 9½ inches, 9 by 12 inches, and 10 by 13 inches.

Checking the Letter Address with the Envelope Address. As the letter is folded, its address should be checked with the address on the envelope to be sure they correspond, and to avoid the danger that the letter may become separated from its matching envelope.

Postal Cards

Postal Cards: Their Advantages. For routine or brief and impersonal correspondence, postal cards enjoy these advantages: (1) Their postal-carrying charge is less than that of the first-class letter; (2) they obviate all costs of stationery, envelopes, folding, sealing, and stamping; (3) they call for the simplest arrangement, making for ease in writing the message and for speed in its preparation.

Layout for Postal Cards. Because the space is so limited, it is well to use a typewriter with the smaller elite type in order to get the message on the card without sacrificing appearance. Pica type permits ten strokes to an inch of line space; elite type permits twelve strokes. Hence, elite type allows 20 per cent more material in the same amount of space, or 20 per cent more margin for the same amount of material. For the details of standard postal card layout, see the illustration on page 48.

After the heading has been typed on the message side of the card, the typist next types the salutation, omitting what would be the address of a letter. (The address on the stamped side of the card is enough.) As the heading supplies the address of the sender, no return address is used on the stamped side of the card. One can still further lessen the work by having the address of the sender printed on the message side of the card.

111 Alvarado Street
Monterey, California
January 11, 19

Dear Mr. Grant:

Please accept our invitation to attend the convention of the Allied Chambers of Commerce of
Monterey County at Hotel San Carlos, Monterey,
California, January 21, 22, and 23. The sessions will take up problems of interest to every
merchant on the Peninsula and in Monterey County.
Plan to attend. Mark your calendar now.

                        Sincerely,

                        RRGreene

RRGreene:KD   Convention Chairman

A Standard Postal Card Layout

From: G. W. Franklin, 1727 Park Avenue, New York 17, N. Y.

                        September 13, 19

Dear Mr. March

As you requested in your letter of September 11,
we have made a reservation for you at the Hotel
Georgian for the week of September 16.

We are very glad to be able to be of assistance to
you. When you arrive in New York, we shall appreciate your calling us if there is anything that
we can do to make your stay a pleasant one.

                        Sincerely yours

                        G. W. Franklin

**Arrangement of the Straight-Line Return Address in a Standard
Postal Card Layout**

To save space, the return address (normally a part of the heading) may be arranged in straight-line style, with the name of the individual or firm, the street, the city and zone number, and the state written on one line across the top of the card. See the illustration of this arrangement, page 48.

Penwritten signatures add force to any message. If the number of cards is not too great, it is better to sign all cards. But on routine acknowledgments and mass announcements sent to large numbers of firms and individuals, penwritten signatures are seldom used. For sales promotion purposes, use of postal cards is rapidly increasing.

Decision to use the postal card depends upon common sense, sound judgment, and good taste. If the card will bring the desired results without sacrificing prestige, use the card. Otherwise, use the letter.

Summary

Day in and day out, people are making snap judgments, perhaps about *you*. Of course snap judgments are not always right. But whether they are right or wrong, people will go right ahead making them for the rest of your life.

Because you will be under this kind of constant scrutiny, and because every piece of your work will be under it too, every experienced management executive would advise you to *make the first impression count*. Make it a good one! This chapter has told you how you can do it.

Communication Problems

● 1. Rate the ten (or more) examples collected for Problem 4 in Chapter 1 according to the factors presented in the Letterhead Rating Chart printed on page 42. After each example has been individually rated, your instructor will appoint one member to summarize the ratings for the entire group.

Suggested Procedure: (a) Be more than merely critical. Rate your examples accurately. Then be prepared to show the other members of the group some of your suggested improvements, together with the reasons for the change.

(b) Discuss the summary that was compiled from the individual rating sheets. Is there a visible pattern—that is, do certain industrial, business, or professional groups tend to have certain group characteristics? Is there an indication of a trend from "traditional" to "modern" designs? Is there an increasing use of color or tint in printing or in stationery? And so forth.

● 2. The examples you collected for Problem 4 in Chapter 1 are to be used as a basis for this problem. Choose an example that has an unattractive letterhead design. Redesign the letterhead so that it will be more attractive and better meet the standards given in the Letterhead Rating Chart on page 42.

Suggestions for the Assignment: Many firms can best be represented by the use of appropriate color (a shop selling western wear, for example, would have better appeal if brown or tan colors were used, rather than aqua or red). Printing type styles may fit one kind of business but be quite inappropriate for another.

Design a letterhead to replace the one you believe is in need of improvement. Make it simple, modern, and in good taste. The layout for a firm using the NOMA simplified style would probably not be quite the same as for the firm using the modified block or indented style.

● 3. On the letterhead you designed for Problem 2, retype the message that appeared on the original letterhead.

Suggested Procedure: (a) Study the various styles of letter layout that are described and illustrated on pages 596-598 in the Reference Division of this book.

(b) Choose a style that you believe will be effective on the letterhead you have designed.

(c) Type the message in the style of your choice, correcting only the glaring errors in the original.

● 4. Make yourself familiar with certain expressions that apply to letterheads, envelopes, and paper. Look up the following terms and bring illustrations to your next meeting. Be prepared to explain and define.

watermark	window envelope	offset printing
bond paper	engraved stationery	16-pound paper
Monarch-size paper	embossed stationery	kraft paper
letter-size paper	legal-size paper	rag content

● 5. Business houses today are using more and more postal cards to simplify and expedite their mounting volume of correspondence. If the use of a postal card will bring the desired results without sacrifice of prestige and the reader's good will, the advantages of using the card will probably far outweigh any of the common objections usually associated with the use of postal cards.

Directions: Using your name and address and the current date, set up the message at the top of page 51 on two separate postal cards. Use the two styles for postal card layout illustrated on page 48. Address these cards to one of the members in your class.

I am pleased to send you two free copies of WRITING BETTER BUSINESS REPORTS.

These booklets are sent with the compliments of my company. Should you wish additional copies, please write to me.

I know that you will find these booklets of value in improving the quality of report writing in your company.

● **6.** The following message, confirming a hotel reservation, was sent on the letterhead of the Stapleton Hotels, Inc., to a group of attorneys.

Directions: Analyze the weak points of this message, and rewrite it using the modified block style with mixed punctuation. In correcting letter-arrangement errors, refer to the letter on page 44; for errors in punctuation and English usage, refer to pages 527-595 in the Reference Division of this book.

November 23, 19--

Messrs Gray, Grayson, & Brayson
Boston, Mass.
30 Duke Place

Dear Sirs,

As you requested in your letter of November 20th, we have made reservations for you gentlemen at our hotel for the week of 2 December.

We are glad to be able to be of special assistance to you and to help you in whatever way we can to make your stay at our hotel a most pleasant one.

When you arrive in New York, we shall appreciate your checking in at the Reservation Desk before 6 o'clock, P.M.

Enclosed with this letter is your reservation card. Present this at the time of your arrival to the clerk on duty.

Sincerely

STAPLETON HOTELS, INC.

Mrs. Wilma Harrison,
Reservation Manager

WH/jc

The National Cash Register Company

Dayton 9, Ohio

TO OUR LETTER WRITERS:

Next to the personal call, letter writing may be
considered the most powerful and influential medium
in business.

By this medium contact is made with merchants and
opportunity is afforded for the creation and promotion of good will.

Through this medium members of the selling force
are influenced by the letters sent to them. If
the letters are helpful, results are reflected in
increased sales.

To be helpful, brevity should be practiced, but
not at the expense of completeness and clarity.
Good letters are as short as their subjects will
permit--not curt.

Courtesy, an influence for success in business,
should be displayed in every letter. If you have
to make an unpleasant demand, make it firmly but
kindly. You can be definite and firm without
being discourteous.

To assist in writing effective letters, embodying
these suggestions, and to assist correspondents,
stenographers, and transcribers to have a better
understanding of each other's requirements, this
manual was prepared.

It includes but a small part of the material that
has been written on this subject, but it is hoped
the contents will be useful and act as a stimulus
to the seeking of additional information for the
betterment of the Company's correspondence.

                    THE NATIONAL CASH REGISTER COMPANY

"Next to the Personal Call . . . the Most Powerful and Influential Medium in Business"

A well-known company addresses a general message to its executive staff as an introduction to an excellent company correspondence-manual. Note the emphasis laid upon
the qualities of Completeness, Courtesy, Clearness, and Brevity.

PART II Positive Planning for Effective Human Relations

Chapter 3

The Positive C-Qualities: Completeness; Courtesy; Consideration

The World of Tomorrow Will Ask You Ten Top Questions. The time is not far off when you will face at least ten top questions from the World of Tomorrow. Here they are:

1. Can you say what you mean and say it well?
2. Can you make yourself unmistakably understood?
3. Do you know the path to personal power?
4. Do you know what makes a leader a leader?
5. What does management look for when it hires you?
6. If *you* did the hiring, what qualities would *you* want?
7. Would you like to be a top management executive?
8. How would you help to make your company articulate?
9. How would you help to make every one of your staff members an expert communicator?
10. How and why would your management program help to maintain effective human relations?

There are sound answers to all these questions, but the road leading to these answers is not necessarily simple and easy to travel; nor, on the other hand, is it necessarily frustrating and difficult. As is always the case, everything depends on you. With the help of the coming pages, you can make the road whatever you want it to be. And in those pages, together with the pages of succeeding chapters, we shall begin to unfold some of the answers to the ten top questions that the World of Tomorrow will surely ask you.

Can You Reach Other People's Minds? Those who have made themselves experts in handling the written word develop high skill in reaching other people's minds. In so doing, they keep a million secretaries busy 250 working days a year transcribing billions of costly messages designed to reach other people's minds. These messages complete, or help to complete, management transactions involving billions of dollars of cash and credit in payment for materials and labor and other services.

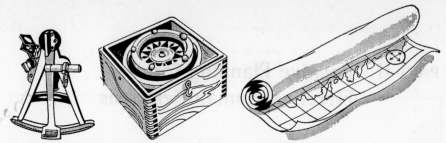

The Sextant ... To Tell Where You Are   **The Compass ... To Tell Where You're Going**   **The Map ... To Tell You How to Get There**

If you know where you are, where you're going, and how to get there, you are thinking clearly and you have a good plan. If you can think clearly and plan well, you have a good job waiting for you. Management will welcome you on the staff.

Your First Goal: Learn How to Put Straight Thinking on Paper. "How can you tell what road to take unless you know where you are going?" Those are the English words reflecting the classic question that Alexandar Dumas, the son, first asked in French a good many years ago. But suppose we now reframe the question: "How can you ever hope to 'write straight' unless you learn to think straight?" The answer is: you can't. Good writing is simply straight thinking put on paper—in such expert form that *the reader's mind easily lifts it off the page.*

How, then, does the efficient management man plan his messages so that they command the vital seven C-Qualities: completeness, courtesy, consideration, clearness, conciseness, concreteness, and correctness? The following pages will tell the story.

Planning the Message. Expert management men recommend the following steps in planning a business message:

1. Visualize your reader. Picture him. How does he look? How does he act?
2. Get all the facts, figures, examples, and illustrations you will need to make a planned and complete reply.
3. Organize this material into thought units, each of which is clear in its relation to the others. Determine what data are needed, how the data should be arranged, and what elements should come first.
4. Double-check the material to see that it is complete and that its arrangement is right.

Give *all* the information asked for, to the extent that you have it. For instance, if you are answering a request, jot down notes on the several points of the reply you plan to make. Pencil these in the margin in the order of their importance to make sure you will cover them all. But do not start to write until the object at which you aim is as clear as a flare and as sharp as a spike.

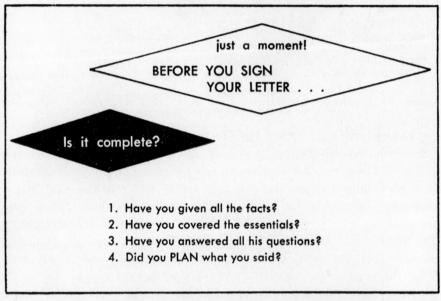

Connect Your Mind with the Minds of Others—Through the "Switchboard" of the Written Word. To assure completeness, say enough, but *just enough*. The knack is to know when just enough has been said. For example, brief sales letters often fail. A short letter may not get enough ideas into the mind of the reader to bring him to the point of action.

The test is this: Will your inclusion of the material make it easier to understand? Will it help the message on its errand? Will it help you to reach your aim? No letter is too long if a reading proves every word necessary.

> The chief art in writing is to know:
> 1. How much to put in
> 2. What to leave out
> 3. When to quit

A Classic of Completeness. You will find on page 56 of this book the famed original text of Lincoln's Gettysburg Address, thought by many competent judges to be the greatest utterance ever made by any President of the United States. As you study it, note how complete, yet how clear it is. This is not to say that all the words are simple. Not all of them are. But it would be hard to find a document into which is packed greater meaning and significance in the astounding conciseness of two hundred sixty-eight words.

FOUR SCORE AND SEVEN YEARS
AGO OUR FATHERS BROUGHT FORTH
ON THIS CONTINENT A NEW NATION
CONCEIVED IN LIBERTY AND DEDICA-
TED TO THE PROPOSITION THAT ALL
MEN ARE CREATED EQUAL

NOW WE ARE ENGAGED IN A GREAT
CIVIL WAR TESTING WHETHER THAT
NATION OR ANY NATION SO CON-
CEIVED AND SO DEDICATED CAN LONG
ENDURE · WE ARE MET ON A GREAT
BATTLEFIELD OF THAT WAR · WE HAVE
COME TO DEDICATE A PORTION OF
THAT FIELD AS A FINAL RESTING
PLACE FOR THOSE WHO HERE GAVE
THEIR LIVES THAT THAT NATION
MIGHT LIVE · IT IS ALTOGETHER FIT-
TING AND PROPER THAT WE SHOULD
DO THIS · BUT IN A LARGER SENSE
WE CAN NOT DEDICATE - WE CAN NOT
CONSECRATE - WE CAN NOT HALLOW -
THIS GROUND · THE BRAVE MEN LIV-
ING AND DEAD WHO STRUGGLED HERE
HAVE CONSECRATED IT FAR ABOVE
OUR POOR POWER TO ADD OR DETRACT·
THE WORLD WILL LITTLE NOTE NOR
LONG REMEMBER WHAT WE SAY HERE
BUT IT CAN NEVER FORGET WHAT THEY
DID HERE · IT IS FOR US THE LIVING
RATHER TO BE DEDICATED HERE TO
THE UNFINISHED WORK WHICH THEY
WHO FOUGHT HERE HAVE THUS FAR
SO NOBLY ADVANCED · IT IS RATHER FOR
US TO BE HERE DEDICATED TO THE
GREAT TASK REMAINING BEFORE US-
THAT FROM THESE HONORED DEAD
WE TAKE INCREASED DEVOTION TO
THAT CAUSE FOR WHICH THEY GAVE THE
LAST FULL MEASURE OF DEVOTION -
THAT WE HERE HIGHLY RESOLVE THAT
THESE DEAD SHALL NOT HAVE DIED IN
VAIN - THAT THIS NATION UNDER GOD
SHALL HAVE A NEW BIRTH OF FREEDOM-
AND THAT GOVERNMENT OF THE PEOPLE
BY THE PEOPLE FOR THE PEOPLE SHALL
NOT PERISH FROM THE EARTH ·

Lincoln's Gettysburg Address

Punctuation is often omitted on plaques of this kind.

Incompleteness Multiplies Costs. One message well planned and complete will accomplish everything that otherwise might require three. An appalling number of needless messages are exchanged because the first ones were dictated by persons who had no grasp of the problem. Out of the first answer that fails because of a faulty plan, a string of others must issue to clear up the matter. The correspondent, for example, may answer only half your question because he reads too hurriedly. Or, in his desire to be brief, he may fail to cover the situation. In either case you must write a second time, and he must answer a second time.

One investigator, examining two thousand messages, found that five out of six had neither objective nor plan. Such planlessness penalizes everyone because it complicates management, thieves profits, and raises costs.

Oversight Multiplies Costs. Mail-order houses and the mail-order divisions of department stores know how often customers forget to mention the number of yards, or the color, or the size, or the dimensions, or the catalog number, or some other similar important detail necessary to the filling of an order. Forgetting essential facts like these is so commonplace that stores can predict how many mail orders out of every hundred will be so incomplete as to require further correspondence. Private citizens are probably much more guilty of carelessness than is business. People forget the most obvious things.

Actions themselves may also be incomplete. Enclosures are carelessly omitted. The correspondent has to write for them. An inquiry or an agreement may be neglected for several days. Along comes a reminder—a second needless message. The delay has cost everyone money. Had the action in each instance been completed—had the enclosure been made, the inquiry answered promptly, or the agreement fulfilled—had a well-made plan been followed, needless waste could have been avoided.

Management Calls for Completeness. From a management bulletin of one of the country's biggest firms, here is a vigorous caution:

> Replies that are incomplete, indefinite, or obscure irritate and confuse the inquirer, delay progress, create distrust, and increase the volume of correspondence. Haste and inattention lead to unnecessary messages. Too often we fail to concentrate on the question asked. Too often we fail to reread the questions asked and the answers we have given to assure ourselves that the latter will not be misunderstood, and that every part of our reply is complete.

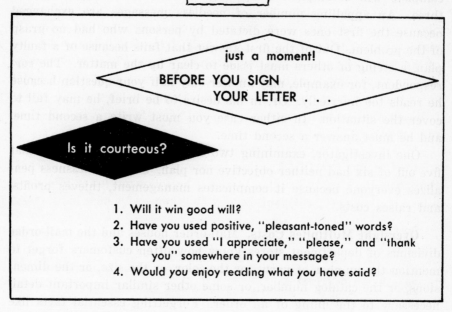

Courtesy

just a moment!
**BEFORE YOU SIGN
YOUR LETTER . . .**

Is it courteous?

1. Will it win good will?
2. Have you used positive, "pleasant-toned" words?
3. Have you used "I appreciate," "please," and "thank you" somewhere in your message?
4. Would *you* enjoy reading what *you* have said?

One Golden Key to Success. *"Life is not so short but there is always time for courtesy,"* writes Emerson. And another philosopher, an executive of very keen mind, puts it in these words:

> I do not know of a more certain key to success than courtesy. It will carry you further in this world and cost you less than any other single quality you could possess. If I could talk in twenty languages, I would preach courtesy in all of them!

Of course, courtesy is far more than the generous use of the words *Please* and *Thank you.* You must not only *write* these words but you must also *feel* them toward your reader. Courtesy is an attitude of mind, expressed in its most genuine form by (1) the manner you assume toward others, (2) the generous attitude you take toward others, and (3) the language and tone in which you express yourself.

Words Like These Make Small Firms Big

How to Generate Good Will. You owe courtesy to others as a matter of decent politeness. But if you want to look at it from the dollars-and-cents standpoint, courtesy is also good business policy. Showing courtesy is one of the many instances in which doing the right thing is doing the profitable thing. "Good will is the decision of the customer to return to the place where he has been well served," says an important legal decision. The value of the good will in which some businesses are held runs into the millions. This public esteem is based upon a good product plus public satisfaction with the courtesy shown.

Cooling the World's Friction Points. Courtesy is the "lubricant" that cools the world's friction points. The following letter introduces a book on business friendship, the whole theme of which is courtesy:

```
Does Every Communication Leaving
Your Desk Build Good Will?

    The present trend of legislation is to make everything
in business equal except friendship. You should, therefore,
see to the developing of this most valuable of all assets.
You must build a close feeling between your organization
and your customers. Your customers must have the desire to
return to your house over and over again when the need for
your commodity arises.

    You can get real aid in this important problem--the
building of good will--from J. K. Park's book, Courtesy in
Business.

    Mr. Park discusses the value of friendship and the part
it plays in getting and holding more business. He shows in
detail how good will may be acquired and held, how friend-
ship may be built by the written word. He gives plans for
developing better communication and shows how you can put
more good-will building power into your words.

    "Mr. Park shows the business world," writes one re-
viewer, "how to leave an ever-widening trail of good will
after the job is completed."

    If, like most of us, you are guilty of spending large
sums for general public contact, but nothing to see that
each message typed on your letterhead is courteously and
carefully written, see this book.
```

Courtesy, with a Large "C," Wins Friends. No business ever grows without the good will of the public, won through fair dealings and courtesy. Three employees of Montgomery Ward and Company gave the following answers to the question: What are our responsibilities as communicators?

"To convey to the customer the facts in an honest, concise, tactful way and to instill good will and friendliness are our responsibilities,"

wrote the first. "This can be best accomplished by a thorough knowledge of the company's policies, the catalog, and the inquiry we are
answering."

"We have the responsibility, first of all, of satisfying the customer," concluded the second. "A good correspondent should be able
to put himself in the customer's place. What he writes should be
the kind of message he would like to receive—friendly, courteous,
and sympathetic. All questions should be answered accurately and
fully, and the message should be honestly written."

"Our messages," said the third, "represent this company, and they
should show our friendliness. The customer's good will depends on
what we say."

Courtesy-Power Is Yours for the Asking. You will tap undreamed
of resources if you learn to recognize and apply the power of courtesy. Some of the blue-ribbon corporations of the country did so
long ago.

In each of its hundreds of district offices the Metropolitan Life
Insurance Company displays the following instructions:

> Every patron of the Company must receive courteous atten-
> tion, unstinted service, and helpful counsel. Our policyholders
> own the Company. Their good will must be cherished and sus-
> tained by the exertion of every reasonable effort to comply
> with their wishes.

A major hotel corporation uses every imaginable device to insure
that each guest shall receive courteous treatment. Says one of their
management bulletins:

A doorman can sling the door
in such a way as to make the incoming guest expect to find a rusty
pen stuck in a potato when he gets
to the desk, or he can so swing the
door as to make him feel that this
is HIS HOTEL.

Millions of cash-register receipts go into the hands of buyers each day with *Thank you, call again* printed upon them.

People of the United States willingly pay millions upon millions just to add the word *please* to their telegrams. The money is well spent. Returns are three of the most valuable assets a business can have—respect, friendship, and good will.

Customers, Too, Can Be Courteous. Interesting is The Case of the Dull Razor Blades. A customer writes:

> I know you can't make magic blades, and I know it's human to make a mistake--I just got a package of five of those mistakes--each one duller than the one before. Of course I didn't get the shaving mileage you intended I should.
>
> Enclosed is the guilty package so you can find out what went wrong--and I wish you luck.

You'll agree that this customer has cushioned his complaint with courtesy. Now—can you do as well as he? "But the sale is only fifty cents!" someone exclaims. True, but experience proves that no expression of complaint or customer dissatisfaction is ever too trivial for courtesy. So play it safe—ALWAYS BE COURTEOUS. In doing so, you will be following the ABC rule—a rule that has made many a company great.

LIFE IS *NOT SO SHORT* BUT THERE IS ALWAYS TIME FOR COURTESY

MARSHALL FIELD & COMPANY

STATE, WASHINGTON, RANDOLPH & WABASH

CHICAGO

February 6, 19—

Mrs. Alice Canter
6248 Beechmont Avenue
Cincinnati 30, Ohio

Dear Mrs. Canter:

If there's one place in the world where every member of your family can have a completely rounded and highly enjoyable vacation--it's Chicago!

There's everything here! Restaurants of all nationalities, gala dining and dancing, Ravinia's symphony concerts, bathing beaches, boat regattas, one of the largest aquariums in the world, outstanding zoos and museums--a whole world of enter-tainment in one great city. And this year the celebration of Chicago's Charter Jubilee will make your visit brimful of excitement.

Marshall Field & Company is eager to help you get the most out of every minute of your time in Chicago, whether it is a full-length vacation, a gay weekend, or just a day between trains. Think of our store as your own personal tour headquarters.

You'll find our Personal Service Bureau ready to give you detailed hotel information, to make your hotel reservations, to assist in solving your transportation problems, to help plan your sightseeing and your day and evening entertainment.

As soon as you arrive in Chicago, we hope you will come in, present the enclosed card, and let us help you. If there is anything we can do for you now, let us hear from you by mail.

Sincerely yours,

George Carson

George Carson
Credit Manager

jac
Enclosure

STANDARD STATIONS, INC.

225 BUSH STREET   SAN FRANCISCO 20 · CALIFORNIA

August 5, 19—

TO ALL EMPLOYEES:

For many years Standard Stations, Inc. has tried to deserve a reputation for service and courtesy throughout the West. At it is our responsibility to carry forward this reputation. As we do, it is helpful from time to time to think about this part of our business, for we shall succeed as a company only if we serve those who come to us to meet their needs.

Customers are the lifeblood of our Company. In many cases they look to the quality of our service as much as to the quality of our products in deciding whether to do business with us. In these days of very severe competition, we owe it to ourselves to see that no customer is lost because of a shortcoming on our part.

When you greet a customer courteously and promptly at the pump block, service his car carefully and correctly in the lubrication unit or provide him with any of the other services which we offer at Standard Stations, Inc., you are contributing to the growth and prosperity of our Company, as well as to your own personal progress and security.

As a Standard Stations employee you meet thousands of people from all walks of life, each of whom forms his judgment of our Company from the treatment which he receives in his dealings with you. Courtesy, reliability and integrity should be your guide in dealing with these people just as they are in your own personal life.

A recent study by a national magazine showed that Standard Oil Company of California is considered one of the ten most courteous companies in the nation. This should be a source of satisfaction to us all, and I extend to each of you my thanks for your part in building this fine reputation. I hope that each of us will be alert in all of our dealings on behalf of the Company to help build an even finer reputation in the future.

Sincerely,

E. O. Thompson

President Thompson of Standard Stations, Inc. Hammers
Home . . . *Courtesy*

The YOU-Attitude Breathes from Every Paragraph of This
Highly Successful Message

Consideration: The YOU-Attitude

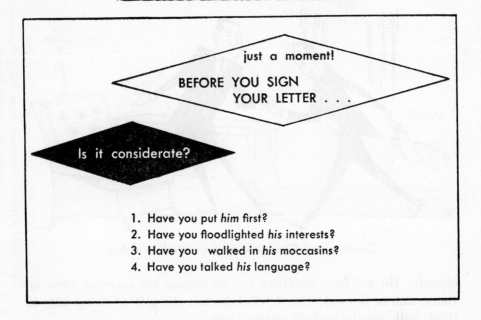

just a moment!
**BEFORE YOU SIGN
YOUR LETTER . . .**

Is it considerate?

1. Have you put *him* first?
2. Have you floodlighted *his* interests?
3. Have you   walked in *his* moccasins?
4. Have you talked *his* language?

The YOU-Attitude Is Now Famous. Many years ago people were mystified by a new discovery of writing technique known as "the YOU-attitude." Now, everyone who writes recognizes its force. The YOU-attitude is the ability to release yourself from self- centered attention to your own affairs, and to see, instead, through your reader's eyes, to get into your reader's shoes, and to assume your reader's point of view.

Imagine a business big enough to be called America, Incorporated, with an executive vice president of the stature such a position would demand. You are to have a conference with this executive tomorrow morning, and you can face it without nervousness. Here is why:

Most executives of his stature have a gift. That gift is the rare quality of concentrating on YOU. When you first enter the door of his office, our executive friend will glance up from his work, give you a friendly smile, an equally friendly hand, and motion you to a comfortable chair. From that moment on through to the end of the discussion, he will give you his undivided attention. He will listen carefully to you, to your statements, to your questions. He will consider them thoughtfully, give you replies that are intelligent and to the point of your interests. Through long experience he has learned to "other"

Courtesy and Consideration Can Work Wonders

himself. He will not interrupt you to impose his point of view on yours, unless you ask him to. For he has the gift of being able to think with you instead of against you.

Can You "OTHER" Yourself? Understand your reader's needs. Find out his characteristics and traits. Study him as a Wall Street investment counselor, a Delaware coastal fisherman, a western Pennsylvania coal miner, a harvest hand in the western wheat fields, a Vermont maple-syrup packer, a California rancher, a Detroit automobile executive, a New England hardware dealer, a middle western housewife—and a hundred more. Learn how to "other" yourself.

"If you want to put a thought through, you've got to get off self-center," says Harvey Campbell, an executive of the Detroit Board of Commerce. "When you want to win an argument, you'll be mighty wise to say, 'I can see it from your point of view.' In my messages I make it a rule to get the word *you* in the first sentence."

A Former President: A YOU-Attitude Expert. Even a former President of the United States practiced the knack of "getting in tune" with others. He studied other people. When a scientist or a lawyer or a banker was expected at the White House, the President informed himself as to his guest's business, profession, or hobby, found out in advance what his *visitor's* chief interests were, and centered the conversation on those interests. Often he astonished his guest with his detailed knowledge. He made the gathering of such information a regular technique. He went out of his way to learn what his caller was interested in. He took special pains to talk his caller's language. As a result, this President became a master of the strategy of successful associations. His thoughtfulness converted some of his worst enemies, won him a warm place in the hearts of many who dealt with him, and brought him new friends.

Emphasize THEIR Interests, Not Yours. Whether you meet your associates across a desk or across a thousand miles, think of *other* people's work, interests, and hobbies, *other* people's ambitions, hopes, and aims. Every writer must climb out of his own little world and learn to visit the worlds of others. Here is the secret of getting along with others and winning their cooperation. Being interested in what the other fellow is doing and thinking is a part of the preparation of the communicator who must make his words on paper carry sincere and friendly warmth.

Put Yourself in Your Reader's Shoes. When you talk about your reader, you are discussing the most interesting thing in the world— to him. Make his interests, his wishes, his preferences, his hopes as nearly as possible yours. See, if you can, what he sees, through his eyes. Assume his viewpoint. Talk about your business in his terms. Back up your appeal with the motive power of his self-centered attention. Take up your position beside him, look back at yourself, and ask, "What would I like to have myself say if I were over here with my reader instead of in my own office?" Put yourself in his shoes. Or, as the Indian saying goes, "Put your feet in his moccasins." When you "walk in his moccasins," you win his willing and cordial fellowship.

Step into His Moccasins!

What Kind of Person Is Your Reader? Study Him. Your reader, involved with his own personal and business problems, receives every message in the light of his own personal advantage. "What is there in this," he asks, "of advantage to *me*?" Accordingly, using the following channels, get all the vital information about him that you can.

(1) Correspondence Files. The study of a file of correspondence, or a careful "between-the-lines" examination of a single letter, will often yield valuable information on the type and character of the correspondent. Look for clues and build up a character-study from the growing record of your file in order to individualize each person.

(2) Information Cards. Information cards record useful facts about the character type and business needs of individuals. Additional personal information from field salesmen is also recorded to supplement the facts on the card.

(3) First-Hand Knowledge. To make immediate personal acquaintance with the men to whom they write, some correspondents for large firms travel for a month each year. Meeting and talking with their readers, they get live knowledge and face-to-face impressions.

(4) Study of the Business. The correspondent should study the reader's business, its nature, its environment, its social pattern, and its geographical location. The reactions of a Cape Cod, Massachusetts, fisherman will differ from those of a haberdasher in Marion, Ohio; the credit manager of a sporting goods chain in Chicago; or a drugstore proprietor in Missoula, Montana.

The YOU-WE Test. Suppose the following expressions were addressed to you? Which would command your attention and your consideration?

"YOU"	"WE"
You may have noticed	We wish to announce
Your experience may have shown	It is our opinion
Have you perhaps wondered	We are firmly of the belief
You will often find	We think that

The persons who dictated the opening expressions in the left column learned, somewhere, the priceless secret of thinking their dictation from the other fellow's side of the desk. But those who dictated the expressions in the right column were so wrapped up in their *own* point of view that they built a high wall around themselves.

When he begins to write, the average person thinks naturally of his own world—*our* company, *our* policy, *our* factory. Only with practice does he get over the barrier into *your* desires, *your* wants, and *your* interests.

Can You Pass the YOU-WE Test?

Welcome your customer by putting him in the center of your dictation. **Don't barricade yourself behind a wall of "We" and "Our Company."**

Put Double Power into What You Say. If you think ahead, you can put double power into what you say.

> **Power 1 :** Make What You Say Valuable to Your Reader
>
> **Power 2 :** Put Your Reader in the Center of What You Say

Suppose we set up some striking contrasts, showing on the left the double-powered writing that good dictators enjoy, and showing on the right the kind of mill-run jargon of which business still has too much.

THE RIGHT WAY: "YOU"	THE WRONG WAY: "WE"
Your inquiry of August 2 for Booklet No. 5 is greatly appreciated. It will be reprinted within 60 days, and you will be sent a copy the day it comes from the press.	In reply to inquiry of August 2, this is to say that Booklet No. 5 is out of print. It will not be reprinted for sixty days. We regret therefore that we cannot send a copy.
* * *	* * *
Thank you for your May 3 remittance of $11.29. It is a pleasure to credit it promptly to your personal account.	Acknowledging recent remittance of $11.29, we wish to state that it has been duly credited to the proper account.

If you can think of the advantages the reader wants at the same time you are thinking of what you want, you will fill your message with the attractive YOU-tone that generates good will. Each of the two pieces of dictation at the left on page 67 keeps the reader's interests foremost and thinks in terms of his advantage.

You'll Have to Be More than a "YOU-Sprinkler." Your first step in getting the right attitude is to substitute the word *you* for the word *we*. But this step is only a mechanical one and does not in itself make the attitude. It simply tends to make you think first of your reader's interest. You can perfect the YOU-attitude without once using the pronoun *you*. Writers who sprinkle *you's* all over the page are wrong if they believe that, by that act alone, they have developed the YOU-attitude; for the thought may still be intensely selfish.

The YOU-attitude comes from the heart out. It can never be faked. It is not simply one multiplied pronoun but something deeper and bigger—*the spirit back of the expression*. To have it, you must feel it; you must believe in it; you must live it.

Walk WITH Your Reader: Don't Talk AT Him. What happens when writers get over on the reader's side of the fence and begin to show him that his interests are theirs?

"If you are sincere," writes a successful management executive whose writing scores high, "and can show your reader you have something for him and do not want to get something from him, if you can show that you are offering something for his personal good, you immediately break down the wall between you. You are walking *with* him. Instead of trying to sell him, you are helping him to buy. And just that little difference in *attitude* makes the most tremendous difference in results."

"And how do we put the YOU-attitude into our products?" he concludes. "Every piece of material, every strip of brass, every piece of iron or steel wire, or brass rod, goes through tests to see that it is the standard that we can confidently talk about in what we say! The word *You* doesn't do it. It's the spirit back of the words."

Why Did the First Attempt Fail? A contractor wrote a letter to send to prospective customers. It appears on page 69 in the original, and as it was revised. Examine the two versions. Note their striking points of difference. You will sense the difference in emphasis.

THE FIRST DRAFT: "WE"

We wish to announce that we are in the sheet-metal business, using All-Weather Aluminex sheets and specializing in cottage and residence work, such as gutters, downspouts, roofing, etc.

We can give you immediate service with the best material and mechanics and will be glad to furnish you with an estimate.

We do not care how large or how small the job may be, for we can assure you that it will be handled satisfactorily. Please let us hear from you.

Of course, this attempt failed. A second, drafted by an expert who had analyzed the task and planned his appeals, brought in a pleasing number of inquiries that resulted in profitable sheet-metal contracts. Why was the second effort a success?

THE REVISED DRAFT: "YOU"

Do you know that rust eats away about as much sheet metal every year as is manufactured in the same period? It may prey on your new building from the moment it is completed unless you select lasting material that can stand against it.

All-Weather Aluminex sheet metal, which we use, is astonishingly durable. Tests in service have proved the lasting qualities of this material, resistant because it is pure and dense.

Quantities of All-Weather Aluminex sheets have been used in important buildings in which durability is essential. The Empire Building and the Washington Memorial Building are structures in which this material has proved its durable qualities and its handsome permanence over a period of many long and heavy-weather years.

With the best of material and mechanics, we can promise you immediate service. Whether your building is large or small, you'll find it an economy to get an estimate from us. All-Weather Aluminex service enjoys top rating for roofing, gutters, flashings, and similar metal work.

Why not dial Plaza 1-6398, or write us a line, today?

Why Did the New Version Succeed? The first message wrapped itself around the writer's point of view and failed to interest the reader, who was not acquainted with this product. The first message based its case on weak generalities. Even the clincher (that which aims to bring about favorable action) was vague: ". . . let us hear from you." When? Where? How? What telephone number?

The second version seized the reader's attention. An arresting fact about the colossal waste by rust, appealing to the reader's instinct

for economy appears in the first sentence. Then follows a challenging statement, representing another appeal to thrift. The message is
studded with concrete detail to make its statements vivid and convincing. Names of famous buildings are introduced as proof of
severe tests through which this product has been put. The final line
invites clear-cut action.

"Think Across" to Your Reader. If you "think across" to the
reader in terms of YOU, and get out of your own hard shell of *We*
and *Us*; if you fall naturally into the generous attitude of "How
would *I* like this to sound if *I* were going to receive this message?"—
if you do those two enormously important things when you prepare
to write or dictate to others, you'll have the gift that others strive
to find.

To make your writing effective, visualize the reader, put yourself in his shoes, see through his eyes, and try to appreciate his
feelings.

Summary

You will notice, as you review the discussion of Completeness,
Courtesy, and Consideration, that you have really been reading about
sound business policy, based upon the principle of thinking of others
first—the application of the Golden Rule.

The YOU-approach is sound business policy because it is based
upon the great principle which would, if put into practice, solve all the
problems of effective human relations: *Do unto others as you would
have others do unto you.*

Communication Problems

*Your instructor may designate the style of layout and punctuation that
you are to use in certain communication problems of this course. If not,
follow the layout and punctuation style illustrated on page 44 of Chapter 2.*

● **1.** You as Assistant Supervisor of Correspondence of The City
Bank of Detroit, Michigan, received an inquiry from Mr. Ronald
Cook, a student at State University. Mr. Cook gives as his address:
1013 West Chicago Boulevard, Detroit 21, Michigan.

Mr. Cook asks the following questions:

(a) What importance do you attach to the physical aspects and details of business messages?

(b) What do you consider to be the most important quality of a business message?

(c) What recommendations can you make to keep down the cost of a business message?

Directions: In several well-developed paragraphs, write an answer to Mr. Cook's inquiry. Be certain that your message is complete, courteous, and considerate of his interests.

● **2.** Revise the following message for improved order of points, YOU-attitude, positiveness, and conciseness of statement. It is from the Mark Book Company to Mr. Donald Schell, 12890 Birchcrest Drive, Grosstown, Michigan.

We regret to inform you that we do not have in stock the recent Hill book on report writing you ordered. We find that the cost of publishing this book is out of all proportion to sales volume. The added publication costs resulted in a decreased sales volume.

It is true that many copies of this book are now being used in schools that teach reports, but in each instance it is generally true that these copies were purchased long before rising costs prohibited us from publishing it to sales advantage. In place of the Hill book we now publish the Curtis text you mentioned.

Thank you for your inquiry of May 14 and for your interest in our books. We will be pleased to fill your book needs.

● **3.** The effective business writer makes generous use of *plus* words in his writing and avoids using *minus* words. *Plus* words are pleasant words—words people like to read and hear. *Minus* words are negative words—words to be avoided.

Directions: The following message exhibits an over-use of *minus* words. Read these paragraphs and pick out the *minus* words. After you have isolated the *minus* words, rewrite the message, making it more positive in tone.

Your recent note has been received in which you claim that the sofa you purchased from us must be cheap-quality merchandise because the springs in the cushions are beginning to sag. This is unfortunate.

The information you gave us is too meager to aid us in making an adjustment. You neglected to give us detailed information which we will need for our records.

You are wrong in stating that the merchandise you purchased is inferior. We are more inclined to believe that perhaps you have mistreated your purchase. We do not like to be blamed for a customer's negligence.

If you will fill out the enclosed claims form to supplement your sketchy report, we will send an adjuster to your home to settle this dispute.

● **4.** The following inquiry was sent out by a retail store asking for a reply to a previous message mailed to a customer who had submitted a claim.

Directions: Rewrite this inquiry, changing it from the I-attitude to the YOU-attitude.

        We do not appear to have received an answer to our letter
of June 1, regarding a claim you filed with us in early May
to replace a silk lamp shade that you claimed was damaged when
you received it.

        We are rather at a loss to understand why you have failed
to answer our letter. Perhaps our letter did not reach you
asking you to furnish us with your order number.

        We would certainly appreciate hearing from you in order
that we may get this claim settled on our records.

        As soon as we hear from you, we will be most happy to
adjust the claim. Write us immediately and give us the information we want. Your cooperation will help us to adjust
promptly.

        I wish to assure you that we stand ready to give you and
all our customers the fine service for which we have been
known for more than 30 years.

● **5.** Secure from business sources three *personally dictated* business letters. Analyze these three letters for their weak points in terms of completeness, courtesy, and consideration. If your instructor directs you to do so, exchange your three analyses with another member of the class and reanalyze his examples for weak points that he might have overlooked.

● **6.** Effective writers of business messages should indicate to their readers the relative importance of ideas expressed in sentences. Emphasis in writing may be secured by subordination—playing up the important and playing down the unimportant.

Directions: Indicate the relative importance of the ideas in the following compound sentences by changing them to complex sentences.

a. The equipment is all new, and it meets our every need.

b. The report to be sure is neat, but it is in error in many places.

c. Good lighting is a must in every business office, but few office managers are aware of its importance in reducing fatigue.

d. The service of this company is at your disposal, but please make use of it.

e. Your recent request has been received, and your claim is being granted.

f. We are sorry that your order arrived in a damaged condition, but we assure you that we are replacing the merchandise at once.

● **7.** The writer of effective business messages makes a strong point of avoiding business jargon, commonly referred to as "commercialese" or "gobbledygook." In striving to do so, however, he has hit upon what has been called "reverse gobbledygook." Where ordinary, run-of-the-mill business jargon is multisyllabic and drawn out down to the last dullest word, "reverse gobbledygook" is characterized by short, hard-hitting words and sentences. Its proponents refer to it as "shirt-sleeve" English. The following memorandum from a sales manager to his staff is a good example of this so-called "down-to-earth" language.

Date: January 1, 19--

From: Sales Manager, Western District

  To: Sales Representatives, Western District

  I shall not waste words but get right to the point. The time has come for me to step out from behind the trees into the plain view of the forest and to put my cards on the table. It is my duty to let you know straight from the cuff what the plain, cold, hard facts are that are facing this organization.

  In straight English and without mincing any words, the sales of this company in the Western District are slipping--have been slipping fast for the past month. If this condition continues for any length of time, each of you will have good cause and justification for crying into the old bucket. I feel that it is needless for me to say that bonuses come from the things sales are made of.

  The old song and dance that there is a general business slump has been heard too often. The crux of our present position stems straight from a lack of the old team spirit in our sales force. This is it in a nut shell--take it or leave it!

  Instead of pulling together toward our common goal, the sales force in the Western District appears to be pulling in their own direction. Let me remind you that no winning team is better than its individual members--members all running in the same direction toward a common goal. Our goal is $$$.

  These $$$ depend on your sales, and these sales depend upon the three E's. What are they? Enterprise! Energy! Earnestness! In these attributes I find a majority of our sales force lacking--sorely lacking! So what to do? Let's show the old home office that we have a winning team. Our sales quota for next month is $100,000!

  Let's ALL "shoot the works!" You can do it, and I'm depending on you.

Directions: Study carefully the message given above. In a series of well-organized paragraphs, analyze and give your honest impression of this particular style of writing.

● **8.** You are a correspondent in the Order Department of a company that carries a line of goods for sports, hunting, fishing, picnicking, and related activities. The following order (signed by L. R. Brock, 2749 Oak Street, Phoenix 2, Arizona) has come to your desk.

Your company is glad to receive this order, but the clerk is having difficulty filling it. The Sure-Lite Embossed Cigaret Lighter comes in a choice of designs: mallard, pheasant, horsehead, or trout rising for fly. The choice was not indicated in the order.

```
The Sportsman, Inc.
502 Third Street
Duluth 2, Minnesota

Gentlemen:

Please send me the following items:

    1 Folding Picnic Table #382               $12.95
    1 Fitted Picnic Case for Six #2165          36.50
    1 Sure Lite Embossed Cigaret Lighter #1437   8.25
                                     Total     $58.70

I understand that these articles will be sent postpaid.  My
check for $58.70 is enclosed.

                     Yours very truly,
```

The correct total amount for the order is *$57.70* instead of *$58.70.* You could, of course, send Mr. Brock a check for the $1 overpayment. It is possible, however, that he intended to order flints for the lighter, which are listed as #1720 and sell at 50 for $1.

Compose a reply to Mr. Brock that will gain the needed information.

Directions: Thank him for his order. Promise prompt shipment. Explain the need for additional information and make it easy for him to reply.

Suggestions: Avoid any impression that you are criticizing him for carelessness. Such statements as "You failed to state the design" and "You made a mistake in figuring the amount" irritate the reader.

A business reply envelope (for which no stamp is needed) would help. Some writers set up a space on their inquiries with blanks to be filled in and ask the reader to return the sheet to the company. This procedure makes it easy for the customer and helps the writer obtain the specific information that is needed.

The oversight might have occurred because Mr. Brock may have been unusually busy at the time he sent the order. He might appreciate the extra help that you can give him and remember it the next time he is ready to place an order for any goods that your company carries.

PART II

Chapter 4　　　　　　　*The Positive C-Qualities (Concluded):*
Clearness; Conciseness;
Concreteness; Correctness

Thursday

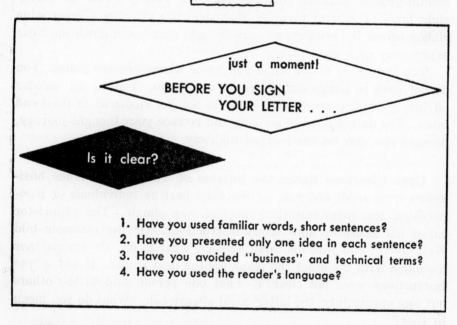

Clearness

just a moment!
BEFORE YOU SIGN
YOUR LETTER . . .

Is it clear?

1. Have you used familiar words, short sentences?
2. Have you presented only one idea in each sentence?
3. Have you avoided "business" and technical terms?
4. Have you used the reader's language?

What a Management Executive Seeks. A member of the personnel management group of a large subsidiary of the Bell Telephone Company considers as many as two hundred applications for jobs each week.

"Clearness," he says, "is a quality we demand. We can hire any number of people who can write something that can be understood. But the people we are after are those who can write something that cannot be *mis*understood."

The Aim of the Pages Ahead. The coming pages will give you some suggestions on how you can create swift-running messages, developed under the guidance of a crystal-clear plan by a mind that knows what it wants to say and how to say it.

A good many generations ago Lord Chesterfield set up a guide that became famous throughout the writing world. "Every paragraph," he suggested, "should be so clear and unambiguous that the dullest fellow in the world will not be able to misstate it, nor be obliged to read it twice in order to understand it."

Clearness Flows from a Well-Built Plan. The rock-foundation of clearness is good planning. Thought flows easily down a clear mental groove. Just as your car may roll swiftly down the six or eight lanes of a great turnpike that stretches away in a great wide ribbon across the country, so your thought may speed down the clear expressway of a good plan.

You simply go faster when you know where you are going. You do not have to puzzle out the route as you go. You do not wander off into confusing crossroads. You do not get ensnared in dead-end lanes. You do not have to go back and retrace your thought-journey, because you stay on the marked highway.

Upon Clearness Hangs the Success of Your Firm. When businesses were small and run for the most part by individuals or partnerships, the communication problem was simple. The proprietor called his assistant and issued instructions. Or the manager told Walt, Jerry, and Bill, his three helpers, what to do. Or one partner discussed with the other the plans for the next month. If any of the instructions were not clear, if what one person said to the others left any uncertainty, the latter could always ask, "What do you mean by that?"

Then firms began to grow. Employees in many businesses began to number in the hundreds and then thousands. No longer was there time enough in the day for the manager to talk to everyone on his payroll, let alone tell each one individually what to do. Instructions had to be put into writing. Ever since that day business has had to grapple with the problem of clearness, because upon clearness hangs the success of your firm.

Personal Power from Two Directions. Clearness gives you personal power in two ways. First, your effective use of language helps you to make an excellent impression on those with whom you deal.

A firm control of language is your hallmark of distinction. Second, ease in speaking and writing is a strategic kind of power that conveys clear ideas to others in order to persuade them to think or act as you wish them to think or act.

"What Are You Trying to Say?" Until you can give the right answer to this question, do not start to write anything. Otherwise your expression will be muddy because you will have tried to express an idea while you were still groping in a mental fog.

Contrast the following wordy paragraph with the simplified paragraph at its right. From the first version twenty surplus words have been removed, and the paragraph has been cleared up.

WORDY
(*34 Words*)

We believe that by giving these independents an opportunity whereby they can have the same functions and weapons of attack that have been developed by the packers, they too will succeed in the trade.

SIMPLIFIED
(*14 Words*)

The independents will succeed if they are given the same weapons as the packers.

How a Management Executive Tests Clearness. The clearer the plan, and the simpler the language, the more quickly your message will reach other people's minds. So that readers may not have to grope through a dark maze of confusion, light up your reader's path with clearness. Make his way easy.

A vice president of the Goodyear Tire and Rubber Company,

Bouquet or Brickbat?

LAKEWOOD, N. J. (AP)— Bouquet or brickbat? A letter from the Lakewood Board of Education thanking Mrs. Eugene Axelrod for a cake has her wondering. Seems Mrs. Axelrod recently gave the cake to board members for a post-meeting snack. The thank-you letter commends her cooperative spirit—"of which your cake was concrete evidence."

Not Quite Clear!

who handles legal matters, suggests one test: "I never," he says, "send out a contract or communication I have written until I allow some one or two other persons in the organization to read it. If that person questions the thought at any place, I rewrite that sentence, for I know a slight vagueness to anyone right here will quite likely become a serious misunderstanding to a stranger, and misunderstandings cost both time and money."

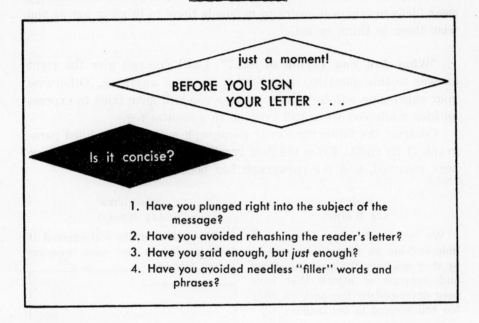

Conciseness

just a moment!
BEFORE YOU SIGN
YOUR LETTER . . .

Is it concise?

1. Have you plunged right into the subject of the
   message?
2. Have you avoided rehashing the reader's letter?
3. Have you said enough, but *just* enough?
4. Have you avoided needless "filler" words and
   phrases?

The "Dollars and Cents" of Conciseness. You can sometimes win twice the comprehension of your message in half the time if you use a sharp economy of words. And TIME, as the old saying goes, is money. It is, in business. Hence comes the demand for chiseled messages that, with completeness, courtesy, and consideration, tell *all that needs to be told.*

Behind this call for conciseness is powerful "cost-cutting" pressure. The characteristics of modern business organization—machine tools, assembly lines, standardization, chain-store distribution, accelerated transportation, automation, and swift communication—demand the stern economy of conciseness, test the mettle of your expression.

"How Long Should Your Message Be?" Ten lines? twenty lines? thirty lines? No expert can give you the answer in figures, because the answer does not lie there. Although it has been told countless times, Abraham Lincoln's story is still the best answer. When President Lincoln was asked how long a man's legs ought to be, he replied, "Just long enough to reach to the ground."

A message should be just long enough to do its job. By this test many messages are too long. On the other hand, some, in an effort for brevity, sacrifice completeness and achieve only curtness. The good letter strikes the happy medium. It fuses completeness and conciseness. Conciseness guarantees that the message will be pruned to the logical minimum. Completeness guarantees that the message will be transmitted in full. No gaps are left in the thought; nor is the thought obscured under a smother of useless words.

The aim of language is to communicate complete thought in as few words as possible. Conciseness not only expands the force of the message but also saves money.

Streamlining, Century by Century. Down the years from the days of Shakespeare, great writers have created sentences progressively superior in structure of phrase and clause, and in concise economy of words—superior, indeed, in every quality to any sentence written before their time. The improvement, century by century, has been demonstrated not only by the observation of expert readers, but also by the research of trained scholars. Today modern management men, taking full advantage of this streamlining progress, have in some cases cut their communication costs in half.

Don't Overdo a Good Thing. You can of course overdo briefness and destroy valuable good will that may have taken years to build. Why is there this danger? Because only a step separates brevity from curtness. If the object were merely to transmit a message and to do nothing more, the thought might be expressed in perhaps forty words instead of sixty-five. But machinelike curtness, carrying brevity to an extreme, may endanger good will.

Beware of too much emphasis on saving three words in this sentence and seventeen words in that paragraph. Beware of statements like "Short messages are better than long ones," "Use short words instead of long ones," "Short letters will be read first." Such statements do not furnish a safe guide. To follow them blindly may injure both your message and the manner in which you write it. Brevity should not be gained at the expense of courtesy, completeness, and clearness. The classic, and almost the final, statement on this point is without doubt Napoleon's famous *Maxim of War*: "Begrudge every word you put in an order; but never sacrifice clearness for brevity."

Conciseness in Dramatic Parallel. Management men have found that with attention to compactness they can cut down the length of their communications from one third to one fourth without sacrificing completeness or courtesy. Contrast the two messages illustrated in parallel on page 80.

THE ORIGINAL MESSAGE
(246 Words)

Dear Sir:

We have your kind favor of the 7th inst., and wish to state that we have very carefully gone over its contents.

In reply to your statement that you received a consignment of nine NX-211 Whirlwind Aviation Motors without the latest style valves, wish to state that is in no sense a shortage. You state that you cannot understand why same were not packed with the engines in original shipment and that something must have gone wrong in our shipping department. Beg to advise that the latest style valves do not come as standard equipment. You probably did not know that these are special and not covered in the original price of the motors as quoted to you in our letter of April 19th.

In other words, you ought to specify more carefully on your orders that you want the latest style valves on your orders, in any case where you want us to supply you with this extra equipment. If you will use a little extra care in this direction, we shall always do as you request. Of course you must remember that we will have to add an extra charge of $190.00 each for every job. In addition, if you want these for the jobs you just ordered, you will have to send us another order.

Trusting our explanation as outlined above is entirely satisfactory, and awaiting your further favors which will always receive the best of service and attention, we remain

THE SAME MESSAGE REVISED
(86 Words)

Dear Mr. Manville:

Apparently our catalog was not available at the time you ordered the nine NX-211 Whirlwind Motors mentioned in your letter of May 7.

On page 26 of the enclosed catalog will be found the latest style cam-and-roller valves, specified as extra equipment ($190 each, net). These valves could not, of course, be included at the unusually low price you obtained.

May we send you the valves? Simply telegraph us collect, and we will rush nine sets by air express, billing them net.

This blank space dramatically represents wasted effort at the left, intelligent economy on the right.

A Dramatic Contrast in Conciseness

Note in the short message (1) the startling contrast in compactness, (2) the pruning out of stock phraseology, (3) the revision of sentence structure for simplicity and brevity, (4) the avoidance of phrases that might anger.

You will also note in the short message (1) interested directness (Go directly to the point), (2) courteous brevity (Say it and quit), and (3) unmistakable friendliness (Be ready to serve).

Examine another startling contrast in the art of deflating surplus wordage. It is hard to believe that the two sentences say the same thing.

WORDY	CONCISE
(*42 Words*)	(*7 Words*)

Assuming that you are in search of valuable information that may increase your earning capacity by a more complete knowledge of any subject in which you may be interested, we desire to state most emphatically that your wages increase with your intelligence.

You earn more as you learn more.

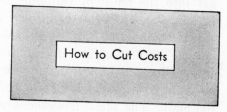

How to Cut Costs

"—And All They Did Was Bend the Handle." Packing the maximum of thought into the minimum of words economizes time and gets attention. Concise writing cuts straight through nonessential verbiage. You can *train* for conciseness by noting how others get it. Study the compactness and word economy of the following message about the Stillson pipe wrench:

```
        --and all they did was bend the handle.

        Four brawny boys in our research foundry once put a
pipe on the end of an 18-inch Stillson and swung on it--to
see what would happen.  The wrench handle bent, as tough
steel should.  The heavyweight committee got tired and fell
off.  But the Stillson never budged a tooth.

        A real Stillson always bends before it breaks.  It took
four big men to bend this one.  Any mechanic who risks his
neck on high scaffolding knows what that means.

        But most men look for the Stillson trademark (on the
top jaw) just to make sure of getting a husky tool that will
turn anything and will probably last until their grandchil-
dren need it more than they do.
```

"This is the age of condensation," writes Kenneth Collins, former sales executive. "Many newspapermen used to be paid for the amount of space they filled in the paper. Today they are rewarded for their ability to boil down news and ideas to their very essence. The great editorial writers and the successful advertising writers have this talent. It is what makes their copy so readable, their message so vivid. They cut directly to the core."

Your Bus Driver Is a Good Critic: Try It Out on Him. A sales management executive who won remarkable results with direct mail was asked, "How do you do it?" His letters were sent to people of from low to medium income. Each message brought a gratifying response. His answer was simple. He never, he said, sent a letter to a large number of people without first trying it out on his friend, the bus driver.

"I have often boarded a bus to ride to the end of the line with the driver in order to read him my letter. I found that those fellows get into the habit of thinking clearly and dealing in short, direct statements. They taught me the fine art of cutting out superfluous words. Often, too, I have read these letters to the janitor who cleans out the office at night. He has given me splendid help, unknowingly, in the line of simplifying my thoughts. That is why the drafts I send out now are mighty crisp and to the point. Some think they are too plain. The facts, however, are that they bring me the business." The fact that his "close-cut" style of writing "brings him the business" is, in his case, the final proof of effectiveness—the acid test.

The simple way of saying things is usually the better way. You gain simplicity by going directly to the point, by saying in a courteous way what you have to say, and by being friendly from beginning to end. The motto of the modern correspondent should be: "Say it courteously and quit."

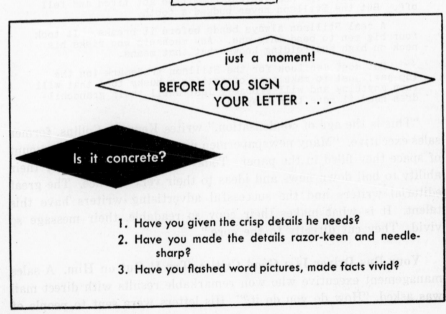

Concreteness

just a moment!
BEFORE YOU SIGN YOUR LETTER . . .

Is it concrete?

1. Have you given the crisp details he needs?
2. Have you made the details razor-keen and needle-sharp?
3. Have you flashed word pictures, made facts vivid?

 craftsmen buy <u>More</u> tools

4 1/3 hammers per reader

Home Craftsman readers aren't content with one claw **hammer**.
They also buy soft-face, riveting, flooring, planishing,
ball-peen, upholsterer's, magnetic and others.

3 9/10 planes per reader

Home Craftsman readers aren't content with one smooth plane.
They also buy fore, jack, block, finger, jointer, rabbet,
model maker's, corner rounding, edge and others.

9 9/10 screw drivers per reader

Home Craftsman readers aren't content with one standard
screw driver. The also buy square-blade, stubby, cabinet,
parallel, offset, Phillips and others.

—Home Craftsman Magazine

Turning the Abstract into the *Concrete and Specific*

(a) Not just a hammer, but SEVEN KINDS of hammer;
(b) Not just a plane, but NINE KINDS of plane;
(c) Not just a screwdriver, but SIX KINDS of screwdriver.

Flash Your Pictures with Concreteness. Concreteness is the opposite of abstractness and generality. We speak of the Thunderjet Rocket Plane that "climbs like a homesick angel." We speak of an edge as "razor-keen," a point as "needle-sharp," a light like "a flaming skyrocket against an ink-black sky,"—vivid comparisons because they refer to concrete objects. See what it does:

CONCRETE AND VIVID	DULLED BY ABSTRACTION
A thousand star points of Christmas Eve twinkle on the firs.	Trees are lighted on Christmas Eve.
The new eight-lane 200-foot turnpike stretches away like a giant ribbon from Chicago to New York.	It is a wide cement road.
Multiplies itself in lather 250 times.	This soap gives generous lather.
A shower of eerie-blue sparks sputtered and crackled across the high-tension gap.	We saw sparks at the break in the electric line.
Four General Double-Tread tires stop this 2-ton car, from 60 miles an hour, in 317 feet.	These tires stop the car within a short distance.
Like a huge bullet the Vulcan-Rocket, its cyclone jets whining, thundered overhead at 5,000 miles an hour.	The jet rocket roared overhead.

Build Power with Concreteness. Now let us apply the technique of concreteness to some simple problems. A real estate firm prepares a message in which this sentence occurs:

> Come out where trees abound, where fresh air is cool and plentiful, where children play undisturbed. (*Abstract and Generalized*)

In that sentence are three arguments for buying. Not one of them is pointed. The firm apparently wants to sell "abounding trees." Would you buy them? Probably not. What kind of trees are they? How big are they? How old are they? The firm wants you to buy cool air. How cool? The children are undisturbed. Undisturbed by what? An expert changes the sentence like this:

> Come out where there are from three to ten giant oaks, a hundred years old, on every lot; where the year-around temperature is seven degrees cooler than downtown, so cool that residents had to sleep under blankets seventeen nights in August; where not a single child has been injured in five years by passenger car or truck. (*Concrete and Factual*)

A famous electrical equipment manufacturer writes about some of its products. Suppose the message had said:

> On our product list are such items as electric irons, generators, motors both big and little, elevators, sodium lamps, spinning buckets, watt-hour meters, Mazda bulbs, washing machines, refrigerators, ranges, etc. We make everything electrical, and of the highest quality. (*Abstract and Generalized*)

What the manufacturer actually wrote was this:

> ". . . A Company proud of its products. Its electric irons press Vionnet gowns in penthouse apartments and red flannels in dude-ranch laundries. Its generators provide the current to run chippers in Canadian pulp mills and air drills in Arizona copper mines. Its motors drive ponderous steel slabbing mills in Braddock, Pennsylvania, and the so-called "one-mouse power" electric razor that subtly shears off your beard. Its elevators kite you sixty-five stories in forty-seven seconds in Rockefeller Center's R. C. A. Building. Its sodium lamps flood airport runways at Akron, Ohio, and Grand Island, Nebraska. In southern textile mills its spinning buckets twist rayon filaments into thread, and in fifteen million homes its watt-hour meters tick off the line load consumed by its Mazda bulbs, its washing machines, its refrigerators, and its ranges. . . ." (*Concrete and Factual*)

Concreteness and vivid word choice multiply and magnify descriptive power. You can develop descriptive power through the skillful use of words that picture facts, situations, events, and actions in colorful terms appealing to the senses of seeing, hearing, feeling, touching, and tasting. Words that stimulate these senses transform dull generalities into the colorful vividness of the concrete. Management executives will tell you that they are constantly on the lookout for people who have the gift of concreteness.

Correctness

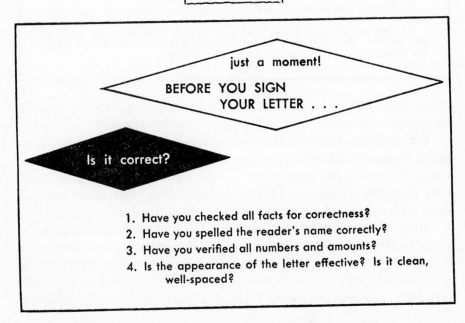

just a moment!
BEFORE YOU SIGN YOUR LETTER . . .

Is it correct?

1. Have you checked all facts for correctness?
2. Have you spelled the reader's name correctly?
3. Have you verified all numbers and amounts?
4. Is the appearance of the letter effective? Is it clean, well-spaced?

Management Men Pay for Accuracy. Give It to Them! "Paying attention to the simple little things that most men disregard as unimportant makes a few men rich." This statement, ascribed to Henry Ford I, is one for the notebook. A similar thought appears in the suggestion by L. M. Hodges in the *Philadelphia Evening Bulletin* that a new kind of degree should be awarded, that of *M.L.T.*— Master of Little Things.

"This degree is not honorary," the suggestion concludes. "It is earned. It is not now conferred by any college or university. It is a gift from self. No outsider can bestow it. In the daily conduct of

GIVE 'ER ANOTHER 100, ALBERT

WASHINGTON (U.P.)—Oil deliveryman Robert Harding couldn't understand why he didn't hear any "tank full" noises.

So he and his truck driver, Albert Green, yesterday pumped another 100 gallons of fuel oil into the intake pipe outside the two-story house.

But he still didn't hear any of those old familiar "tank full" whistling noises that tell the veteran oil deliveryman it's about time to stop pumping.

So Harding and Green pumped in another 100.

By then the oil truck gauge read 385 gallons. But the order called for filling a 135-gallon tank.

Then Harding noted another thing about that order: it called for delivery of oil to 323 34th St. NE. and—what do you know—the number on this house where he was delivering the oil was 223 34th St. NE.

Harding and Green left to consult higher authorities at Griffith Consumers Co. Mrs. Charles Gober of 223 34th St. NE. arrived.

The house seemed to smell of oil. Mrs. Gober investigated. She found 385 gallons of oil five inches deep covering the floor of her cellar recreation room.

Obviously there was some mistake. The Gobers don't have an oil burner. The tank was removed eight years ago. Only the old intake pipe remains.

---

duties from affairs of state to the most humble of tasks, *profitable management depends upon a mastery of little things."*

For example, the president of an American Telephone and Telegraph Company subsidiary, hiring a university graduate, put it this way: "You have fine expression . . . the right timbre . . . you speak your thoughts crisply . . . I'll hire you. Give up your other job and come with us. You have the kind of precision I want."

Many a worthy effort is ruined by a touch of carelessness, by some slight inattention to an important detail. For example, a well-designed letterhead on sleazy paper, a good report under a wrong title or with a misspelled name . . . a thousand and one errors, large and small, lurk always around the corner ready to slip unnoticed into your work.

Little Acorns of Error Grow into Towering Oaks of Trouble. A small mistake in an office may become a giant mistake a thousand miles away. The error may be in figures or words: the wrong addition or subtraction of a unit or a cipher, the omission of a vital phrase, the blunder of a misleading statement. Many can write a message that can be understood. Few can write a message that cannot be misunderstood. Hence, strive to write so that you *cannot* be misunderstood; and guard against misunderstanding by being courteous.

Imagine, for example, the difficulties that might beset a utility company operating electric lines and electric railways:

1. If a customer were recommended the wrong size of motor, and after purchase the motor proved too small to drive the machinery.
2. If a farmer were to find that the contract price for the extension of an electric line to his farm turned out to be three times as much as he was quoted.
3. If an extra cipher were, in error, added to the amount involved in the settlement of a $1,000 claim.
4. If a trainman's instructions from the dispatcher's office told him to take the siding at 2:10 p.m. instead of 2:01 p.m. and he continued for nine minutes on the right-of-way when he should have been on the siding. In this instance the dispatcher might prevent the wreck, and probably would; but the high risk would still have been there.

"NOTHING PERSONAL ABOUT THIS, ARGYLE!"

—Dale McFeatters and
Publishers Syndicate, Inc.

Anyone can realize what such cases might cost a company. Nor are such errors impossible. In cases on record, exactly such errors have occurred. In most instances they have been caught before expensive trouble has developed. But even the *correction* of errors is costly—as adjustment managers so well know.

Ninety-Thousand Waybills Become Waste Paper. A now famous management expert confesses a bitter lesson early in life. As a youthful clerk employed by a great express company, he made out an order for 10,000 waybills. In error he added one extra cipher, calling for 100,000 waybills. The enormous shipment arrived, the error came to light, and the company had on hand 90,000 surplus waybills which, for the most part, had to be used for waste paper.

A Quarter of a Million Messages into the Wastebasket. A magazine decided to send out a series of form letters to increase circulation. Each envelope was, of course, addressed to an individual, but no matching "inside" address was put at the top of the letter because to do so would add heavily to the expense.

In the first mailing a quarter of a million pieces went out. At the end of each was a paragraph which contained this one sentence.

Just initial this letter and return it to me, and I will send you the January issue.

Nine thousand letters came back neatly initialed. *But there was no way by which the company could know to whom the initials belonged.* The fact that the letters bore no addresses was overlooked. So the 9,000 initials were valueless; the 9,000 possible subscribers were mystified as to why they never got the magazines requested, and the expensive campaign was a fiasco—all because someone failed to make the all-important final check of details.

Pure Carelessness Reaps Heavy Damage. A study of 3,237 letters reveals a startling number of careless omissions and mechanical mistakes:

Misspelled words 907
Company names misspelled 766
Messages with wrong address 578
Wrong initials or none at all 354
Messages with defective address 283
Duplicate messages received 95

Out of 303 letters addressed to one individual, his name was spelled 32 different ways, he was given 54 different combinations of initials, and on 19 different occasions the name appearing on the letter and in the salutation was a totally different one from that shown on the envelope.

Someday YOU Will Pay Taxes for This!

22,685,940 letters to the Dead Letter Office and its branches in one year.

511,687 parcels to the Division of Dead Letters and Dead Parcel Post and its branches.

286,238 of these parcels wrongly addressed.

225,449 of these parcels found loose in the mails or with wrappers so badly damaged that the parcels are undeliverable.

100,000 letters mailed annually in *perfectly blank envelopes*, 30 per cent of these containing enclosures of money, checks, drafts, and other valuable papers.

---

*—Courtesy of the First Assistant Postmaster General,
Division of Dead Letters and Dead Parcel Post.*

Pure Waste

It may startle you to learn that errors of this kind are so commonplace and so costly. You may rightly be disturbed by these disclosures because it will be **your** tax money, or your consumer dollars, that will "pay the freight" for the costly carelessness out of which such errors arise.

Don't Blunder into the Dead Letter Office. Proof of careless error is the Dead Letter Office of the United States. Mail inadequately addressed and requiring return or dead-letter service suffers expensive delay. The cost of the Dead Letter Office and its service runs into added millions.

POORLY ADDRESSED LETTERS

SERIOUS PROBLEM FOR U. S. POSTAL SERVICE

WASHINGTON. — (AP) — The United States postal service has one problem as old as itself—poorly addressed letters. A postal official estimated today that careless handwriting costs the government about $1,500,000 a year. There is no telling what the people pay for it individually, he added.

The similarity of city names almost drives the clerks out of their cages. Take Cleveland, for instance. The nation has 26 besides the one in Ohio. And there are 28 Troys, and 12 Birminghams. Cities causing a lot of trouble right now are: Homestead, Pa., and Honesdale, Pa.; Chino, Calif., and Chico, Calif.; Macon, Ill., and Macomb, Ill.; Dillon, Mont., and Dillon, Mo.; Winona, Minn., and Winona, Miss.

It's hard to believe, but more than 100,000 Americans didn't put any address on letters last year. They didn't, in fact, write anything on the envelopes—just mailed them blank.

Errors Become News!

The division of Dead Letters and Dead Parcel Post could be abolished with the saving of vast sums if each piece of mail carried an accurate return address and if each parcel were wrapped in stout paper and tied with strong cord. Every man knows at least his *own* address. He should use it on every piece of outgoing mail for which he is responsible.

The tens of thousands of letters and the thousands of parcels that end their useless journeys in the Dead Letter Office each day are examples of dead loss. But probably an equal number of messages, even though they reach their destinations, make such damaging impressions as a result of their mistakes that the loss is equally great. The waste wrought by negligent errors is appalling. Poorly addressed mail, a chronic problem for the United States Post Office Department, requires special service. Often the mail must be returned to the sender for a new address. If the sender has supplied no return address, the mail goes to the Dead Letter Office . . . and probably to oblivion.

Don't Derail the Thought Train. You send a message that you hope will be read attentively. So, perhaps, do fifty other writers whose letters may reach the same desk the same morning. What will your reader do?

1. *His eye scans the lines.* If the message is well typed, the wide and ample white margins will lead his eye to the proper point, the first sentence.

2. *He looks for the core idea.* "What is this all about?" he inquires. His eye scans the paragraphs for the message "gist."

3. *He formulates his reply.* He pencils his notes in the margin and goes on to the next message.

For each message he has a limited time. That time can usually be counted in seconds. If there are no hurdles to leap, he will get the points forcefully. With every error hurdle in his way, he has less attention for the essentials. Each error distracts attention from the subject. Poor spelling, careless message layout, haphazard punctuation, defective grammar, all clog the flow of thought because they stop the eye, through which the thought is picked up. Too many errors may befog attention, derail the thought train, and wreck your entire effort.

Don't Let Your Reader Laugh at You! Gross errors may amuse or irritate your reader. The first is the more dangerous. If they amuse him, he is laughing at you. Your message loses its dignity. It draws an ironic smile and perhaps the comment, "I thought he knew better than that." And when anyone says about you, "I thought he knew better than that," look out!

Don't Let Your Reader Ridicule You! If your errors irritate him, then you suffer not only criticism but also ridicule. He may forgive you for your bad grammar, your faulty punctuation, your careless spelling. But you do not want him to take time to forgive you. You want him to put his time on the message. And you cannot rely on his ignorance. He himself may make many mistakes—but that fact will not prevent his noticing yours!

Correctly English-- In Only Five Lessons

TAIPEI, Formosa (AP)—Just about everyone in Formosa is studying the English language. Bookstores are crammed with textbooks.

Private teachers advertise widely. One says, "Correctly English in five lessons."

They Better Get Together

COLUMBUS, Miss. (AP)—A new sign at the east end of the bridge identifies the river as the Luxapalilla. The new sign at the west end says it's the Luxapalillia. The state highway department's own maps agree with other authorities that it's really the Luxapalila.

Costly Mistakes Are "Management" Problems. "Mistakes in English cost the company more than mistakes in engineering," states a management executive of the Westinghouse Electric Corporation. He points out that, if messages and specifications from sales offices or from within the East Pittsburgh Works are incorrect, incomplete, or ambiguous, the result may be prolonged correspondence and sometimes wrong designs and shipments. In the engineering division, he accepted the tradition that it was the engineers who made the mistakes. But he said he finds that the communicators can make mistakes too. "And," he added, "unless these [mistakes] are watched and avoided, they offer a constant threat of unnecessary operating expense and intolerable rising costs."

Clear Away the Error-Blocks. Clear away the error-blocks that clog the flow of thought. Haul away the hurdles that derail the thought train. Clear the track for close attention—through accuracy. *To cut management costs, to economize the reader's attention, and to focus it on the message, be correct.* An executive's letter should be like a sheet of plate glass, clean and polished, permitting the light of the message to pass through with limpid clearness. It should be accurate enough, and therefore transparent enough, to let the reader grasp the message instantly. Like plate glass, the language should be flawless.

> **"ME MISPELLUM WORD, ME ERASUM"**
>
> A tourist spotted an Indian sending up smoke signals in the desert. He had a fire extinguisher strapped to his side.
> "What's the idea of the fire extinguisher?" asked the tourist.
> The Indian replied, "If me mispellum word, me erasum."

> Leading men of business have great need of a highly trained power of clear and convincing expression. . . . Businessmen need, in speech and writing, all the Roman terseness and the clearness of the French. The graces and elegances of literary style they can dispense with, but not with the greater qualities of compactness, accuracy, and vigor.
>
> —*Charles W. Eliot, noted educator*

Is This Example Some Kind of Joke? Now and then you will run across writing so bad that you seriously wonder whether it may be some kind of joke. Read the critical analysis on page 92. It raises the question: How bad *can* writing be? Then read on page 93 the "message that might have been."

This Effort Wasted *Not Less Than* **$1.50** from the Company Treasury

(Communication Is a "High Cost" Activity)

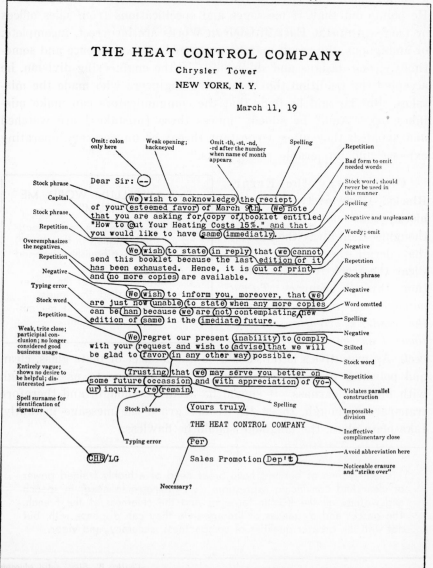

THE HEAT CONTROL COMPANY

Chrysler Tower

NEW YORK, N. Y.

March 11, 19

Omit: colon only here — Weak opening; hackneyed — Omit -th, -st, -nd, -rd after the number when name of month appears — Spelling — Repetition — Bad form to omit needed words

Dear Sir: (--)

Stock phrase

Capital

Stock phrase

Repetition

We wish to acknowledge the reciept of your esteemed favor of March 9th. We note that you are asking for copy of booklet entitled "How to Cut Your Heating Costs 15%," and that you would like to have same immediately.

Stock word, should never be used in this manner

Spelling

Negative and unpleasant

Wordy; omit

Overemphasizes the negatives

Repetition

Negative

Typing error

We wish to state in reply that we cannot send this booklet because the last edition of it has been exhausted. Hence, it is out of print, and no more copies are available.

Negative

Repetition

Stock phrase

Stock word

Repetition

We wish to inform you, moreover, that we are just now unable to state when any more copies can be han because we are not contemplating new edition of same in the imediate future.

Negative

Word omitted

Spelling

Weak, trite close; participial conclusion; no longer considered good business usage

We regret our present inability to comply with your request and wish to advise that we will be glad to favor in any other way possible.

Negative

Stilted

Stock word

Entirely vague; shows no desire to be helpful; disinterested

Spell surname for identification of signature

Trusting that we may serve you better on some future occassion and with appreciation of your inquiry, re remain.

Repetition

Violates parallel construction

Impossible division

Stock phrase

Yours truly,

Spelling

THE HEAT CONTROL COMPANY

Ineffective complimentary close

Avoid abbreviation here

Typing error

Per

CHB/LG

Sales Promotion Dep't

Noticeable erasure and "strike over"

Necessary?

Summary of analysis: (1) Message filled with unpleasant negatives. (2) Weak and trite opening and closing sentences. (3) Numerous stock phrases. (4) Repetition. (5) Entire message built around the big "WE" and "OUR COMPANY" point of view; little thought or consideration for the one making the inquiry. (6) Wordiness and hackneyed expressions; weak, uninteresting, and costly message. (7) Errors in spelling, typing, and grammar; omission of needed words. (8) Not a hint of present helpfulness in the whole message. **Result:** This effort (1) injures the reputation of the company; (2) chills the interest of the man who made the inquiry, (3) ruins the opportunity for an effective follow-up, and, hence, (4) loses possible business that might have resulted. Business goes where it is invited and stays where it is well treated.

Top Management Knows That Accuracy Cuts Costs
(This Is How the Letter Might Have Looked)

THE HEAT CONTROL COMPANY
Chrysler Tower
NEW YORK, N. Y.

March 11, 19

Mr. J. R. Neilson
2250 Seventh Avenue
New Rochelle, New York

Dear Mr. Neilson:

It is a pleasure to send you at once, in reply
to your request of March 9, a copy of an interesting
mimeographed report on heating problems.

From these sheets you can get a first-rate idea
of the actual savings that may be made in operating
a 24" fire box, the size you mention. The booklet,
"How to Cut Your Heating Costs 15%," has enjoyed such
an unusually heavy demand that all available copies
are at this moment exhausted. When further copies
become available, we shall see that you get one.

You will find much of the same information in
the several sheets enclosed. After you have examined
especially pages five and six, will you not write us
more fully about your problem?

Just as soon as you are able to give us further
details on your heating installation, we shall be
glad to put before you the long experience of our
five expert heating engineers.

Thank you for your inquiry.

Very sincerely yours,

THE HEAT CONTROL COMPANY

C. H. Becker

Sales Promotion Department

CHBecker:LG

Enclosure

Summary of analysis: (1) Message written in a pleasant, positive tone. (2) A courteous opening sentence, full of pleasing action—action in favor of the one who has inquired. A courteous closing sentence. (3) No stock phrases. (4) Variety in word choice. (5) Entire message built around the big "YOU" and "YOUR INTERESTS" point of view; in every paragraph, thought and consideration for the one making the inquiry. (6) Economy of words, fresh phraseology, interesting concreteness. (7) Clean, technical accuracy throughout. (8) Entire message showing active interest in supplying helpful, concrete information. **Result:** This effort (1) builds up the reputation of the firm, (2) warms the interest of the man who made the inquiry, (3) creates an excellent opportunity for an effective follow-up, and, hence, (4) may win future business.
Business goes where it is invited and stays where it is well treated.

Summary

What are the tested ways through which executives have made their writing cost-saving and forceful? Let us put them into seven guide signs:

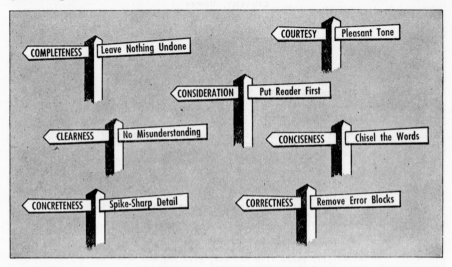

Completeness is essential so that the full picture may be given, avoiding further inquiries; *Courtesy*, so that the message may find a pleasant hearing; *Consideration*, so that the reader may be truly helped and his wants truly understood; *Clearness*, so that the way shall not be clogged; *Conciseness*, so that the attention shall not be wearied; *Concreteness*, so that every fact may be definite, informative, vivid, and interesting; and *Correctness*, so that costly delay and misunderstanding shall not occur.

Taken together, the Seven C's are tested guides, important to apply and easy to remember. You will find them of the highest usefulness in the interesting situations that lie ahead.

Communication Problems

● **1.** Miss Victoria Lambert's automobile insurance policy includes a reimbursement feature for costs of starting and towing. Yesterday she had to call a service garage to have her car towed to it. Write the request for reimbursement.

Directions: Make up an address for Miss Lambert and a name and address for the insurance company, directing your request to a local agent from whom Miss Lambert purchased the policy. State the situation. Enclose the receipt for service. Give the policy number, which is 81SC73190. Request the reimbursement.

● **2.** You are the program chairman for an Annual Awards Dinner given by a college organization (a club, fraternity, sorority, religious group, etc.). Your committee has the responsibility of inviting a guest speaker for this occasion. Prepare a written invitation in which you ask a prominent person to speak to your group.

Directions: Use your organization campus address, or your home address in the heading. Select a person to receive your invitation who has earned recognition in your community. Mention a reason for your interest in him. Perhaps you or a member of your committee has heard this person speak on another occasion or has read a book or an article he has written.

Extend the invitation. In case the recipient is not familiar with your organization, describe it briefly. Set the date for the dinner at least two months in advance, and give the time and the place. Select a local hotel or a campus building used for such occasions. Assume that the members will bring guests. Tell how many persons are expected to attend and whether the group will be made up of all men, all women, or both men and women. If men and women will be present, extend an invitation to the guest speaker's wife—or husband—or to a guest whom he or she may wish to bring. Indicate whether the dress will be formal or informal.

Tell other plans for the program. Assume that the dean of your school or college will make the presentation of awards. State that fifteen minutes have been allotted for this part of the program and forty-five minutes for the main speech of the evening. Suggest an appropriate topic, but leave the way open for the speaker to tell you his wishes concerning any modifications. A discussion period might be planned for fifteen minutes, but this is optional depending upon the topic selected.

Offer to answer any questions that may arise, and express the hope that he may be able to accept your invitation.

Suggestions: The person you invite might be one of the following: author, banker, business or industrial leader, doctor, educator, engineer, governmental official, journalist, lawyer or judge, minister, officer of a trade or professional association, national officer of your fraternity or sorority if this person is living in your area, scientist, radio-television commentator, or sports personality. The financial and fraternal pages of your newspaper will describe activities of leaders who might be glad to speak to a college group.

Work for a courteous, friendly tone. Avoid such cumbersome statements as "It will be appreciated if you will accept our invitation"; and such rude implications as "Please limit yourself to forty-five minutes"; or the curt, abrupt sentence, "Please bring your wife."

Comments: Sometimes it is possible to invite a speaker by telephone or by calling at the person's office. The written invitation, however, is a courtesy to the person because it gives him the pertinent information in written form and allows time for him to think it over before making his decision. Writing can often save extra effort for busy people.

● **3.** Rate the following message for the seven C's of good writing. Use in your analysis the Comprehensive Communications Appraisal Form on page 97 of the text.

Dear Sir

Your order of February for some copies of our typing textbook to be used by your school has been received and entered. Delivery aught to be made sometime shortly, we hope.

It is indeed a sincere pleasure to complement you on the very very excellent standards of performance that you require of your graduates in typing upon his leaving your school. The type of student you turn out might well have employers in your community saying "Send us all of the graduates you can." This is a real feather in your cap and which you should be proud of and I know you are saying "you are".

This book which you buy from us will help you to learn your students all there is to know about up to date typewritting. There is no better book on the market. Indicentally, this is what many users say.

Thanks in advance for this order.

HOW TO USE THE COMPREHENSIVE COMMUNICATIONS APPRAISAL FORM (Page 97)

This is an objective rating chart for scoring the relative effectiveness of a business message.

1. For each message appraisal lay a fresh strip of paper over the vertical checking columns at the right.

2. Score the message by checking *Yes* or *No* at the points on the paper strip corresponding to the points on the columns in the Appraisal Form.

3. Balance the number of spaces in which you have answered *Yes* against the number in which you have answered *No*.

4. On the basis of the evidence of your check marks, determine the "Rating of Over-All Effectiveness" by selecting one of the four words (at the base of the chart) which best expresses your judgment. Note that each of these four rating words carries its corresponding letter grade.

5. At the top of your paper strip write your Rating Initial and Word [Thus: *A (Distinguished)*] which in your best judgment most nearly describes the rank of the message you have rated.

6. Clip or pin this rating slip to the message it evaluates. Other judges may, in turn, evaluate your rating by laying your rating slip again over the vertical columns of the Appraisal Form. In this manner others may judge whether their critical opinion agrees with yours.

COMPREHENSIVE COMMUNICATIONS APPRAISAL FORM	CHECK	
Is the Message:	√ Yes	√ No
1. Guided by Completeness? a. Does the message fully answer all the questions asked? .... b. Does it give all facts needed to fulfill its purpose? .... c. Does it give enough background for clearness?		
2. Toned with Courtesy? with Positive Attitude? a. Does the message observe ordinary good manners? .... b. Are the expressions of courtesy handled skillfully? .... c. Do the expressions of courtesy sound sincere? .... d. Does the tone seem positive and pleasant? .... e. Does the tone preserve and develop good will? .... f. Is the message free from irritating words, antagonistic phrases, negative expressions? .... g. Does the message show a helpful attitude? .... h. Will the message draw the response desired?		
3. Guided by the YOU-Attitude, or Consideration? a. Does it center the message around the reader? .... b. Does it show appreciation of the reader's problem? .... c. Does it talk the reader's language? .... d. Does it "see John Smith through John Smith's eyes"? .... e. Is the **spirit** of the message "YOU"?		
4. Guided by Clearness? a. Does its structure reveal a plan? .... b. Does the thought flow smoothly from beginning to end? .... c. Is the subject clearly announced? .... d. Are the paragraphs appropriate in length? .... e. Are the paragraphs clear in structure, easy to read? .... f. Are the sentences varied in structure, pleasant to read, easy to understand? .... g. Are the words chosen with exactness?		
5. Chiseled with Conciseness? a. Does it say just enough and quit? .... b. Does it avoid the danger of curtness? .... c. Does it use the simpler word when there is a choice? .... d. Do the short words carry the correct shade of meaning? .... e. Has needless repetition been avoided?		
6. Lighted with Concreteness? a. Does it give sharp, informative facts? .... b. Does it give figures, data, to support claims? .... c. Does it use fresh, specific words?		
7. Featured by Correctness? a. Is the message free from slipshod erasures, smudges, strikeovers? ... b. Is the message free from punctuation, spelling, and grammatical errors? .... c. Is the message free from conspicuous omissions? .... d. Do all facts seem truthful and accurate?		
8. Attractive in General Appearance? a. Is the layout like that of a picture in a frame? .... b. Are the margins even and well adjusted? .... c. Is the typing regular and even? .... d. Does the message win a favorable first impression?		

RATING OF OVER-ALL EFFECTIVENESS:

Select the word which best expresses your final rating.

A (Distinguished)   B (Good)   C (Commonplace)   D (Rejected)

● 4. This problem is based on the message you rated for the seven C's in Problem 3. Referring to your appraisal before you begin this problem, rewrite the message. Strive in your own revision for a strict observance of the seven C's.

In your revision assume that 150 copies of the typing text were ordered on February 12 and that shipment can be made immediately.

● 5. The following message was sent out by a retail furniture store to one of its rural customers:

> Answering yours of March 15, I have attended your request to ascertain shipping date of your order of March 1.
>
> I wish to corroborate that said shipping date in accordance with a check of our order department index indicates shipment via Railway Express on March 3. Our shipping department also substantiates this date.
>
> We are at a loss to understand why you have not received shipment. Kindly execute the enclosed claim form and return it. In the interim we will initiate a tracer. If we are not successful in locating shipment, immediate shipment in the way of a replacement will be in order upon due receipt of said executed claim form.

The one who received this message was puzzled. He wrote back:

> Dear Mister:
>
> I got your letter. If I only knew what you meant, I would be happy to do it.

The first writer violated clearness. Rewrite his paragraphs striving for clearness in your choice of words. Keep in mind that the simpler your language, the more quickly your message can be comprehended by even the dullest reader. You must see to it that your reader not only understands you, but that he cannot misunderstand.

● 6. A common writing fault that adds to needless wordage and message length is *tautology*, the needless doubling or repetition of words of the same or similar meaning.

The following paragraphs err in regard to tautology. Rewrite them, eliminating the repetition of words of the same or similar meaning.

> I am most grateful and most appreciative to be able to have this chance and opportunity to write and to submit to you the data and information enclosed herewith.
>
> I stand ready, willing, and able to cooperate and assist you in whatever way, shape, or manner you wish.
>
> I am always happy and glad to be of help and service in advising and counseling our clients and patrons.
>
> Your patronage and business is appreciated.

● 7. The chart below indicates how difficult or how easy it is to "read and understand" your writing style, your reports, and your other forms of expression. This chart is based on a scale for measuring reading difficulty developed by Rudolph Flesch and adapted for use at The Prudential Insurance Company of America. The scale is explained in detail in *The Art of Plain Talk*, published by Harper and Brothers.

These factors are involved:

1. The more words in a sentence, the more difficult it is to read and understand that sentence.

2. The more syllables a word has, the more difficult it is to read and understand that word.

3. The more personal references in a passage, the easier it is to read and understand that passage.

The *standard* writing level is easily understood by most persons.

Reading Level	Very Easy	Easy	Fairly Easy	Standard	Fairly Difficult	Difficult	Very Difficult
Average Sentence Length in Words	8 or less	11	14	17	21	25	29 or more
Syllables Per 100 Words	127	134	142	150	158	166	175
Personal References Per 100 Words	19 or more	14	10	6	4	3	2 or less

Directions for Using the Scale: Select several samples of your writing (about 100 words each), preferably not from the introduction or conclusion. (Examples: two or three paragraphs from a report, or part of a letter.)

1. Count the words in the samples. Then count the sentences. Divide the number of words by the number of sentences. Count contractions and hyphenated words as one word. Numbers and letters separated by spaces should be regarded as single words. In counting sentences, tabulate each unit of thought as a sentence even though it is set off by colons or semicolons rather than periods.

2. Count the syllables in the samples. Divide the total by the number of words and multiply the result by 100. The result is

the number of syllables for each 100 words. This, of course, is a rough measure. A more detailed test is described in *The Art of Plain Talk*.

3. Count the personal references. Divide the total by the number of words and multiply the result by 100. This gives the number of references per 100 words. There are three types of personal references:

Personal Pronouns: I, you, he, she, them, me, himself, ourselves, yourselves, etc.

Names of People: Count the entire name, including any title, as one reference.

Words Referring to Human Beings or Human Relationships: Count only the following: aunt, baby, boy, brother, child, cousin, dad, daddy, daughter, family, father, fellow, folks, friend, gentlemen, girl, husband, lad, lady, lass, madam, mamma, man, miss, mister, mother, nephew, niece, pal, parent, people (*not* peoples), sir, sister, son, sweetheart, uncle, wife, woman. Count as one personal reference combinations of these words such as: baby boy and girl friend; combinations using grand, great, step, and in-law.

Suggestion: Following the directions given for using the "writing yardstick," select at random or as directed by your instructor a letter or several letters that you have written and determine the level of reading difficulty for each.

PART II

Chapter 5

The Message Itself: Applying Brain Power To Word Power

How Do the Experts Power Their Writing? Have you wondered how the experts reach out and snare your attention? What magic do they put into their words to make you stop in your tracks and to concentrate your attention on them? How do they manage to seem to reach out, take hold of your coat lapels, and say "Listen!"? What is the secret of their power to do these things? Suppose we analyze what they do and discover the secret.

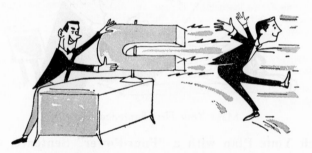

The Experts Magnetize Your Attention

Study Human Nature. First of all, these experts study human nature. They discover what makes people act and react. They determine what makes people "tick" and what seizes their attention. In short, they find out what *you* are interested in, what *you* are thinking about, what will make *you* pay attention.

Use "Talk" Words. Next, they put these discoveries into simple, everyday words, fairly short and easy words, that attract your eye and that slide into your mind. Before you know it, you have read, you have understood, and possibly you have even acted on their first sentence. That is what they wanted you to do. How did they do it?

Be Natural—Be Yourself. Here is what the experts will tell you: Let your first sentence be as natural and fresh and interesting as if you were talking to a friend across your desk. Many an executive has made his correspondence strong by developing natural, conversational first sentences that express his personality.

101

"The Headline": Your First Sentence

For example, each news story in your daily paper carries a headline. The headline attracts attention, tells what the story is about. Veteran news writers try to make each headline strong, brief, and dynamic.

The most prominent place in a parade is the head of the column; at a public gathering, the platform; at a banquet, the speakers' table; at a theater, the stage; *in a message, the first sentence.* Upon these places attention is centered. Make the first impression count!

Make Your First Sentence Glow

Launch Your Plan with a "Four-Power" Sentence. Your first sentence powers your whole message plan. It should do four things:

1. Show courtesy.
2. Identify the subject.
3. Refer, *in a subordinated position*, to the date of the previous message (unless yours is, for example, an original inquiry) so that the reader may refer to the carbon copy; refer briefly, *in a subordinated position*, to the subject of the previous message if such reference is needed.
4. Show action in favor of the reader, if appropriate.

Test Yourself. Now for a test: Let us suppose that you are on the staff of the Citizens Bank. A customer sends in a deposit totaling $385.36 and asks for an acknowledgment. How will you answer him? What will be the central or core idea of your reply? Clearly the core idea is the $385.36 remittance and what has been done with it.

Caution: don't let the *apparent* simplicity of this situation fool you. Simple as it appears, it demands care if it is to be handled *well*. You have identified the core idea. Now you are ready to meet and solve the problem of the first sentence.

What should the first sentence do? Reviewing the four steps, you find that it should be courteous; announce the subject; refer in an incidental way to the date of the previous message and its subject; and, if appropriate, show action in favor of the reader. Following these steps to the decimal, you write the first sentence:

```
    Thank you for the deposit of $385.36 enclosed in your
letter of April 23; we are pleased to credit it to your
account.
```

But it is not necessary to assume that there is only one right way to write an opening sentence. Usually you can find another good way. For example, you could have said:

```
    We are pleased to credit to your account the deposit of
$385.36 enclosed in your letter of April 23.
```

Now look back at these first sentences and see how they performed their functions.

The First Example
Did It This Way

The Second Example
Did It This Way

Both examples are successful and effective solutions of a business problem that many executives and students make complicated and difficult; that, in fact, many executives and students bungle badly.

Flash the Meaning: Tell the Reader What He Wants to Know. The first sentence is your opportunity to headline the news, to flash the meaning. Word it so that it becomes the key to the message.

Let us picture your reader. He is likely to be even busier than you. Confronting him is a pile of mail. The bigger it is, the less attention he will pay to each message. He will read rapidly. His eye will sweep down the page, searching for the answer to the insistent question, "What's this all about?" Your message will be read as one of many, each a different problem. For each, his mind must adjust itself anew. For each, he may have to prepare a swift reply that will, he hopes, tell you exactly what you want to know.

Before every new problem ask yourself, "What does he want to know first?" And, again, "*Exactly* what does he want to know first?" This question is the starting point for the construction of a clear plan. When you have correctly answered your own question, you have found the central idea. It is this central idea that you will strive to transmit.

"Exactly What Does My Reader Want to Know *First?*"

"The Flying Start." To make a favorable impression, show action in favor of the reader. Of all styles of openings this is probably the most effective.

You want a two weeks' vacation with pay during the Christmas season. You ask your employer, in a written memorandum, whether you may have the vacation. What more pleasing and effective first sentence could you read than that in the following note you receive from him:

> It is a pleasure to grant your request of December 3 for two weeks' vacation with pay. Your record has been of such faithful character that you have earned the privilege. Your vacation runs from December 16 to December 30, inclusive.

Even in routine matters action makes a favorable impression. Action implies decision, energy, and alertness. Most of us like to

Applying Brain Power to Word Power

Every person in this busy office is concentrating on the universal problem: how to turn intelligent ideas into clear and forceful words. You, too, will face this problem throughout life.

have our requests treated with decision, energy, and alertness. Note how, in these examples, action makes a favorable impression:

EXAMPLE 1

Promptly upon receipt of your telegram we telegraphed our Cincinnati distributor to release the shipment specified in your note of May 25.

EXAMPLE 2

We can furnish Boron Octane, as called for in your inquiry of January 3, at the following price schedule:

The Man Who Forgot What the Reader Wanted to Know. A dealer wrote a manufacturer of containers, expressing his intention to use a large quantity of a special kind of container. He received this reply:

Your request of May 1, addressed to our New York office, has been turned over to this office inasmuch as your city is in our territory. We enclose a few samples of our beautiful bags, which we believe would be just the thing for your store. Our bag is distinctive in color, yet strong. People carrying it would be a walking advertisement for your store. It would be recognized as coming from your establishment.

We suggest you tell us the quantity you would purchase. We shall be glad to quote you prices.

Although the customer was in a hurry to get the bags, he was disappointed because the message gave no information that would justify him in ordering. "The thing I wanted to know," he said, "was the price of the bags. I wanted quotations on 1,000, 5,000, and 10,000 lots. This reply fails to tell me."

The customer was right. Which is more important here: (1) the price of the bags in large lots or (2) the fact that "Your request . . . has been turned over to this office"? This case is a well-defined example of waste. Because the test question "What does he want to know first?" was not answered promptly, two extra messages had to be written.

No one will deny that it is old-fashioned and wasteful to use fifty words to say something that could be said better in twenty. Yet many communicators of this modern day, up to the minute in every other detail of their daily life, remain citizens of a bygone century in their first and last sentences. Note the following contrasts. Each of the paragraphs in the left column maddens the reader with a cloud of verbiage, while the paragraphs in the right column give the needed information with crisp brevity.

THE OLD WAY
(57 Words)

We desire herewith to acknowledge the receipt of your note of January 25, in which you inquire whether you are fully protected under our policy No. 2-40378, and we wish to advise that an examination of our records shows that your policy is in force and that you are protected according to the terms and stipulations therein.

THE NEW WAY
(17 Words)

Your policy No. 2-40378, our records indicate, is still effective, along with endorsements that have been attached.

IRRITATING WORDINESS
(53 Words)

We beg to acknowledge receipt of your kind favor of the 15th inst. and wish to state that we appreciate the interest you have shown in our present situation. In the matter of your inquiry relative to your illustrations, we beg to advise that they have had our attention and are enclosed herewith.

CRISP INFORMATION
(37 Words)

Here are the illustrations you requested in your note of October 15. Thank you for giving us a chance to see examples of your work. You have made it easier for us in placing our future orders.

Increase Your Sentence Power by Four Steps. The first impression counts most. Get away to a flying start! Used singly or in combination, the four steps at the right will stamp your openings with character and originality and give you *first-sentence power.*

1. Show courtesy

2. Identify the subject

3. Tie down your reference

4. Show action

The Closing Sentence

Closing Sentences Make the Final Impression. Your goal is to leave your reader with a favorable impression. The beginning and the end of anything, because they are the most conspicuous, are positions of emphasis. The skipping eye of a rapid reader leaps from paragraph to paragraph. Anything that stands out, that serves as an eye-stopper, will get a little more of his fleeting attention than the rest. Make your closing sentence do these three things:

1. Round out the letter plan
2. Bring to a focus the action desired
3. Leave an echo of courtesy

Beware the Participial Conclusion. The participial conclusion is old-fashioned. Do not use it. An example: "Trusting that you will give this request your prompt attention, we remain." Expressions like this are out of date and much too weak to justify their use as closing sentences. Yet many who pride themselves on possessing the latest equipment for their business offices persist, strangely enough, in closing their messages with this most horse-and-buggy claptrap of all—the participial conclusion.

The participle is, in fact, the weakest form of the verb. The participial construction, introduced by *thanking, assuring, hoping, trusting, believing,* or the like, hinging its weight on a participle, is the weakest verbal construction in the English language. Never use it to express important ideas. An idea important enough to hold the closing position is important enough to deserve full strength. Full strength comes in a definite statement that rounds out the plan, focuses attention on the action desired, and leaves an echo of courtesy. Study the contrasts at the top of page 108.

SAY IT THIS WAY (GOOD):

Thank you for the care with which you have handled this request. We hope to return the courtesy soon.

Your business is most deeply appreciated.

Although we are unable to fill your exact requirements, may we serve you in other ways?

We shall appreciate it if you will act promptly upon this request.

We thank you for your order and are confident that it will reach you in excellent condition.

NOT THIS WAY (POOR):

Assuring you in advance of our appreciation for your kind attention, and hoping that we may have the opportunity to return the same, we are

Hoping this is O.K., and thanking you for past favors, we are

Regretting our inability to comply with your demand, we beg to remain

Trusting you will give this request your prompt attention, we remain

Thanking you for your order, and assuring you of our careful attention, we remain

Do Not Thank People in Advance. Always thank people for their services. But let the thanks be expressed after the service has been performed, not in advance.

The expression *Thanking you in advance* is a poisonous stock phrase, worn and weary

---

Sleigh Before the Reindeer

A little girl, writing a letter to Santa Claus, was counseled by her mother to end the letter by thanking Santa for the gifts on her list.
"Why should I thank him?" the little girl wisely asked. "He hasn't brought them yet!"

---

with overuse. It suggests that the writer is taking for granted that his request will be approved or some other service rendered, and no one likes to be taken for granted. Furthermore, the person who thanks in advance leaves the impression that he wants to save himself the trouble of expressing his appreciation later.

Expanding the Main Thought

The Main Thought Is the Heart of the Message. A message is built around its main or central thought. If, for example, you plan to talk about copper flashings and gutters, the statement "Copper Lasts Longer" may be the central thought. If you are talking about electric refrigerators, such statements as "The Sealed-in-Steel Unit Saves You Money," "The Meter-Miser Cuts Costs," or "The Silent Gas Flame Freezes More Cubes," may be the central thoughts. These core ideas, packed into tight cartridges of condensed thought, are concise summaries of your message.

Get Quickly to the Heart of the Message. The subject or central thought of the message is called the *corethought*. The corethought is the commander that gives orders to the pieces of material out of which the body is built, and that marshals the ideas into a well-planned unit. The corethought is the subject you are writing about, the heart of the plan. It must be in supreme control. You must identify the corethought before the ideas can be put into right relation to one another. After you have identified the corethought and have decided *exactly what it is*, you can put the essential ideas of the message into the proper order to make sense and to bring about the result you wish.

How to Develop the Body of a Message—Example 1. What is the corethought of the following message, sent by a large corporation to several thousand businessmen in all parts of the country?

> Would you like to see one hundred years of business history in a three-foot chart?
>
> On this chart you may study the ups and downs of the past century of business activity. You may view the interplay of wages, prices, real-estate values, and the stock market, all clearly shown.
>
> We shall be glad to send you one of these charts as our small contribution toward business progress. If you would like to have one, please return the attached card; and we shall see that you get one at once. No charge.

The corethought of this message is announced like a trumpet call in the first sentence. You cannot mistake it. You cannot misunderstand it. The corethought defines itself in sixteen little words. "Would you," it inquires, "like to see one hundred years of business history in a three-foot chart?" The subject is (1) an offer, (2) of a chart (3) three feet long (4) showing what has happened to business (5) in the last hundred years.

We have identified the corethought and have decided exactly what it is. We can now see how the essential ideas, all of them perfectly simple, are put into the proper order to make sense and to bring about the result the writer wishes. Once the subject is announced, the rest of the message tells (1) what may be done with this chart, (2) what advantages may come from its use, (3) the reason for its distribution, and (4) how it may be had.

How to Develop the Body of a Message—Example 2. Let us try another test with a longer message. The problem is this: The Remington Arms Company, Inc., manufacturer of firearms, ammunition, cutlery, and targets, wishes to send a letter to boys between the ages of fifteen and eighteen years, in answer to inquiries about Remington .22-caliber repeating rifles.

How should the Remington Arms Company solve this problem? What should be the corethought of the message? How should this corethought be expanded in order to stimulate a lively interest in what the company has to offer?

First, of course, the company must decide exactly what the subject should be. The one who develops the plan must study the inquiries and determine what particular .22-caliber repeating rifle would best suit the needs of those who have inquired. He can then assemble all the material in a large pile of unassorted but essential ideas in the following manner:

> Features of the Sportmaster Remington: good for small game; accurate target rifle; durable; built of wear-resisting materials to stand hard usage; double-locking lugs; larger barrel, heavier-gauge steel; husky, man-sized stock; fore-end semibeavertail in effect; new peep sights; eight sighting combinations; Lyman No. 422 Expert telescope sight optional at additional charge; genuine walnut stock of selected wood; special tempered-steel barrel; expert Remington workmanship; prices to be quoted; now lowest in past five years; apply for further information to dealer; handle gun; try it, test it, sight it.

Notice the sharp, concrete detail in these features he has brought together. Now (1) he studies them; (2) he puts the material into the right order to make sense; (3) he assorts the ideas into related groups; (4) he organizes each group into suitable paragraphs; (5) he prepares his final draft.

The message he writes is shown on page 111.

In fewer than thirty words you are told precisely what you are going to read about. You cannot mistake the corethought. You cannot misunderstand it: the new Sportmaster Remington, Model 341, .22-caliber bolt-action repeating rifle. The next five paragraphs describe this specific model.

The opening paragraph, in two sentences, expresses courteous thanks for the inquiry and directs attention to the enclosed Sportmaster folder. The subject once launched, the rich fact-supply is marshaled in effective order to explain (1) the uses for the rifle, (2) the needs it will fill, (3) the convenient special features that may be had, (4) the way in which to test it, and (5) the favorable prices. The facts have been put into marching order and have been brought together into related squads. That is how the body is built.

REMINGTON ARMS COMPANY, INC.

NORWOOD 12, OHIO

June 6, 19

Mr. Jack Swanson
2906 Northcut Street
Columbus 7, Ohio

Dear Mr. Swanson

    Thank you for your letter asking about the Remington .22-caliber bolt-action repeating rifle. Enclosed is a folder telling all about the new Sportmaster Remington Model 341.

    The Sportmaster is the rifle you want for small-game hunting in season and for accurate target shooting. Built for hard service, the Sportmaster replaces the famous Remington Model 34 repeater. It has all the same advantages, including double-locking lugs, and in addition it has many fine new features.

    Read about the new rifle in the folder. Notice the man-sized stock with wide semi-beavertail fore-end, and the larger, heavier barrel. Notice, too, the new Remington peep sights giving eight sighting combinations.

    Read also about the Lyman No. 422 Expert telescope sight, which you may buy with the Sportmaster if you wish. This polished telescope sight, although moderately priced, is of high grade, in keeping with the superior quality of this rifle.

    See your favorite sporting-goods or hardware dealer, and ask him to show you the Sportmaster Model 341. Handle this rifle. Bring it to your shoulder. Compare it with other rifles at or near the price. Notice the fine workmanship and materials--the high-grade steel barrel, the genuine walnut stock.

    Buy your Sportmaster now while the price is low. If your local Remington dealer does not have it, he will get it for you.

                      Cordially yours

CD:FL   REMINGTON ARMS COMPANY, INC.

Enclosure

A Message with the Corethought Well Expanded

Drive Home the Main Thought

A stationery company faces this message on a sales promotion blotter.

Identify Your Subject, Select What Is Important, and Reject the Rest. Perhaps you remember in *Aesop's Fables* the story of the monkey who tried to take a handful of sweetmeats from a jar with a small neck. But he was greedy. He seized such a large handful that he could not draw his hand out of the jar. Many who write are like the monkey. In their haste to cover the subject, they seize too big a handful. Failing to identify the corethought, they talk about things that do not matter; they ramble along about trivial side issues; they smother the significant facts and the important arguments in a cloud of inconsequential details. Their discussion remains foggy and nebulous. It never comes into sharp focus. The rule is: Choose the chief point you want to make, and stick to it.

Developing Well-Planned Paragraphs

What a Paragraph Is. The body of a message is a planned series of well-constructed paragraphs. A *paragraph* is a sentence or a group of related sentences expanding a thought. Logically it is a thought group impressing itself as a unit on the mind of the reader. Mechanically it is an effective way to break up masses of material, to give a "breather" to the mind and to the eye, and to offer a change of pace.

Reasons for the Paragraph. The paragraph, largest unit into which a small block of writing is divided, was originally a mechanical device for the convenience of the reader. In the time of William Caxton, a famous printer of the fifteenth century, it was discovered that unbroken masses of type tire the eye and make it hard for the reader to follow the thought. Printers, therefore, experimented with devices to break up the page into smaller units in order to provide comfortable resting places for the eye and for the mind. In early times these resting places were indicated by the paragraph mark (¶). Today, in business messages, paragraphs are indicated by double spacing between paragraphs and, in some styles, by indenting the first line of each paragraph.

The Business Paragraph Drives Toward a Goal. The typical business paragraph is on its way to get something done, or to help to get something done. It does not enjoy the expansive leisure in which other types of writing may revel. It cannot indulge in entertaining experiments, in decorative furbelows, or in musical cadenzas and melodic flourishes. Instead it drives straight for the mark.

Modern business rush and pressure call upon you to make reading easy. For this reason the paragraphs in most types of business writing average less than a hundred words. Such frequent division breaks the page in a way to invite the reader's eye. Hence a message made up of a few crisp paragraphs is more readable than one containing a solid mass of composition.

Experienced business writers keep the opening paragraph short. A two- to five-line opening paragraph, easy to see, easy to grasp, speeds its subject into the reader's mind. Later paragraphs may well vary within the normal length of four to ten lines.

Avoid Long Paragraphs and Overparagraphing. Long paragraphs should be avoided, except in special cases where unusual length is used as a device for emphasis and contrast. Four paragraphs of six lines each or five paragraphs of five lines each are easier to read than a solid paragraph of twenty-five lines. The eye measures the length of paragraphs, and the mind appraises the difficulty of understanding them, in part, by how "solid" they look. If they are oversolid, the eye and the mind shy away as from an obstacle too high to climb.

At the other extreme is overparagraphing. Nothing is more tiresome and irritating than a long sequence of "snippet" paragraphs averaging two lines or so in length. Paragraphing carried to an extreme soon loses its effectiveness. Overparagraphing destroys unity of thought and dulls the eye by overstimulation. It is easier to read four paragraphs of six lines each than twelve paragraphs of two lines each.

Adjust Paragraphs to Fit the Reader. *Occasional* short or long paragraphs are emphatic because of their contrast with normal-length paragraphs. The shorter the paragraph, the quicker the pace, the brisker the air. The longer the paragraph, the slower the pace, the more deliberate the feeling.

To some extent, therefore, you may adjust paragraphs to the people who will read them. To professional men and women and similar highly educated groups a well-developed paragraph containing a balanced statement of facts will be appropriate and acceptable. But for inexperienced readers and those with less training, paragraphs of simplicity and moderate length are best.

Central Thought of the Paragraph. The central thought of the paragraph is the guide that aids unity. The central thought may be expressed in a topic sentence, which often opens the paragraph. The rest of the paragraph develops the central thought. Sample topic sentences are:

> The form of a business message is highly important in creating a good first impression.
> The content of a business message reveals the nature of the mind of the man who dictated it.
> Present developments suggest business improvement in the next quarter.

Ways to Develop the Central Thought. The central thought of a paragraph, often expressed in a topic sentence, may be expanded in the following ways, or by any combination of them:

1. With facts, details, or particulars
2. With reasons
3. With specific instances or with concrete examples
4. By narrative (telling the events of a happening in the order of occurrence)
5. By comparison
6. By contrast

In business the first three methods are most used.

General to Particular. The paragraph may be expanded by opening with a general statement and then supporting it with facts, details, particulars (Method 1), with reasons why the opening general statement is true (Method 2), or with specific instances and concrete examples (Method 3). The procedure from the general to the particular is called the *deductive*.

> The instinct of possession is one of the most deep-seated instincts in human nature. [*Corethought and topic sentence*] For example, in a certain store a sale of rugs was planned by offering a reduction of "20 per cent in price." Before this plan was carried out, someone conceived the notion of printing a rough facsimile of a $20 bill to represent in physical form approximately what such a reduction could mean. [*Expansion by example (Method 3)*]

A picture-diagram of the preceding paragraph illustrating the method of the general to the particular appears as follows:

CORETHOUGHT
(OR TOPIC
SENTENCE)
IN INITIAL
POSITION

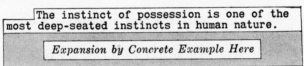

The instinct of possession is one of the most deep-seated instincts in human nature.

Expansion by Concrete Example Here

Particular to General. The reverse order, from the particular to the general, is often used with striking effect. This is called the *inductive* order—opening with facts, details, particulars, with reasons, or with specific instances and concrete examples, and closing with a summary, or general statement.

> Some years ago a bakery in Chicago tried an interesting experiment. It inserted in the city buses a card that gave only the name of the baker. After the first day, the card was changed daily. The statement on the card was always brief. It did not state what the proposal was, but in varying ways it referred to the original card by such statements as . . . [*numerous detailed statements*]. This was kept up for some time until finally . . . so much curiosity and interest were aroused that the campaign became a common topic of conversation. Thus is illustrated the tremendous underlying power of the basic instinct of curiosity. [*The final sentence gives the corethought or topic sentence in a summary or general statement.*]

A picture-diagram of the paragraph above illustrating the method of the particular to the general appears as follows:

CORETHOUGHT
(OR TOPIC
SENTENCE)
IN CLOSING
POSITION

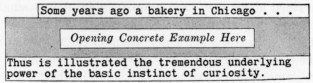

Some years ago a bakery in Chicago . . .

Opening Concrete Example Here

Thus is illustrated the tremendous underlying power of the basic instinct of curiosity.

Paragraph Order. Paragraphs must be put together in the right order. For example, the first paragraph in your letter to a hardware dealer may list the different sizes of Stillson pipe wrenches you can supply. The next paragraph may counsel him to stock the ten-inch size because you have found it the most popular. The final paragraph describes the tough and dependable qualities of the Stillson wrench under the hardest service.

The topic of each paragraph:

1. The sizes of Stillson wrenches
2. Ten-inch, the most popular size
3. Superior qualities of the Stillson

In proper order these paragraphs appear in picture-diagram as follows:

CORETHOUGHT (OR TOPIC SENTENCE) OF PARAGRAPH 1	Stillson pipe wrenches are available in ten graded sizes. *Method 1: Details and Particulars*
CORETHOUGHT (OR TOPIC SENTENCE) OF PARAGRAPH 2	Of the several available sizes of Stillson pipe wrenches the convenient, yet rugged and durable, ten-inch size is the most popular. *Method 2: Reasons*
CORETHOUGHT (OR TOPIC SENTENCE) OF PARAGRAPH 3	The tough and rugged qualities of the Stillson pipe wrench show up best under the most gruelling service tests. *Method 3: Concrete Examples*

This picture-diagram visualizes the three paragraph corethoughts or topic sentences, each playing its respective part in bringing into proper order the series of three paragraphs. The sequence of paragraphs is satisfactory and is logical in flow of thought.

Paragraph Unity. The sentences of each of the three paragraphs illustrated above now bear unmistakably upon a single, easily recognized, and important point in the message; hence each paragraph has unity. A paragraph has unity when all the sentences in it are related to the common subject announced in the corethought (topic sentence). Furthermore, the three topic sentences in the picture-diagram above carry the thought *forward* in a logical and organized way. A persuasive flow of thought is assured by the proper unity and order of the paragraphs.

A paragraph may also have a *unity of function:* unity in *what it does.* For example, in a sales message, one paragraph may be devoted to attracting attention, another to stimulating interest, a third to developing desire and belief, and a fourth to impelling action. Each paragraph thus performs a single function—*does one thing.* Of course, sometimes more than one paragraph will be used to expand each of these functions.

Paragraph Coherence. Coherence in the paragraph is the quality that makes all the statements hang together and carries the reader smoothly from one to another. Right construction and right connection are the means of assuring coherence. The writer must establish a close relation between his statements by arranging the ideas in a natural order according to one of the methods suggested for developing the corethought.

Each type of business message—whether it is a routine item, a note of congratulation, an acknowledgment, an adjustment, a message of credit or collection, an application, or a sales message—has a certain natural order in which its ideas and paragraphs should be arranged. The special sequences of these types are the subjects of later chapters in this book.

The writer should guide the reader from sentence to sentence. The reader's mind should glide along the current of thought like a canoe on a stream. To assure smooth progress, sentences must be connected.

Such connection would be easy if the sentences were like a continuous railroad track. But they do not always lie end-to-end like rails. One sentence may turn the thought a little to one direction; the next may slant it a degree to another direction. To link the sentences together, good writers use linking devices to inform the reader how the sentence he is reading is related to the one he has just finished. Signals like *for example, consequently,* or *on the other hand* make the paragraph and the whole message easier to grasp. They steer the reader's thought in the right direction.

The three methods by which the writer helps the reader to make the logical connection between sentences are:

1. By the repetition of important words
2. By the use of pronouns
3. By the use of link words and phrases

By the Repetition of Important Words. Coherence may be assured by repeating important words that join one sentence or one paragraph to the next. In the following illustration the italicized words are the coherence device:

> Models are equipped with newly designed, self-cooling, *total-contact power brakes. These total-contact power brakes* are instantly responsive to the gentlest tip-toe pressure.

By the Use of Pronouns. The personal pronouns *he, she, it, they,* and the demonstrative pronouns *this, that, these, those, the former, the latter, the one, the other,* are valuable coherence devices.

> He received this morning several airmail letters. *These* were the rush messages for which he had been waiting.

By the Use of Link Words and Phrases. A selected list of connectives is presented below. Connectives, from their nature, slow up the reading rate. Do not use them unless there is a need. They are guides, not thought-carriers. Use them only when and where a guide-post is called for.

at any rate	for instance	truly, in truth
at least	indeed	really
in particular	naturally	in fact
especially	of course	although
specifically	certainly	yet
for example	surely	nevertheless
in spite of	quite as necessary	accordingly
notwithstanding	equally important	consequently
on the contrary	not so obvious	therefore
on the other hand	more effective	hence, so, thus
besides	in contrast to	first
moreover	for this purpose	second (etc.)
then, next	keeping this in mind	besides
too	in this way	again
after	to this end	further, furthermore
still	with this in view	lastly
another	to bring about	finally

Paragraph Emphasis. Emphasis in the business paragraph is the quality that gives force. Emphasis adds thrust to a paragraph already clear. In a business message each of the paragraphs should deal with an easily recognized thought (unity); everything in the paragraph should fall into place without befogging the meaning (coherence); where possible, added thrust should guide the meaning into even the most reluctant mind (emphasis). In your writing make those shifts in paragraph structure that put the important elements in the most important places.

Seven Ways to Emphasize. Emphasis can be given to a most important idea by:

1. Awarding it prominence in position: putting it at the beginning or the end of the paragraph.
2. Giving it extra space.
3. Repeating it in a number of forms.
4. Repeating significant words or phrases.
5. Compressing the idea into a strikingly short paragraph.
6. Packing the idea into a dynamic slogan.
7. Resorting to mechanical methods, such as underlining, the use of a red ribbon, extra-wide margins, and the like.

Choice of position is the most useful of the seven methods of emphasis. The most important position is the beginning of a paragraph; the next in importance is the end. These points reach out for the reader's glance. Use them to expose important ideas to his eye.

Position of Corethought. Since the beginning and the end of a paragraph are positions of emphasis, normally the corethought (topic sentence) of the paragraph will assume one or the other of these positions. Occasionally the corethought is stressed not only at the beginning but also at the end in order to make a still more emphatically rounded-out unit.

When, in conversation, you hear a speaker put special stress on certain sentences and expressions, you know that he regards these as important. You *hear* him emphasize. But emphasis in writing must be *seen.* Spoken words emphasized by vocal stress are, in writing, made emphatic by *where they are put,* and by other methods listed at the top of this page.

Putting Paragraphs Together into a Complete Message. Let us now suppose that you are a communications supervisor for a large enterprise. You are about to draft a set of instructions, to be published and distributed to the company dictators as a bulletin on the topic, "The Vital Role of the First Sentence in Successful Business Communication." Let us *picture-diagram* the possible expansion of this topic into a complete statement. Watch the logical thought-flow and the unfolding paragraph order. Note the underscored expressions that link the paragraphs into a continuous thought-chain.

CORETHOUGHT
OF THE
INTRODUCTORY
PARAGRAPH

> The first sentence of a business message plays a vital and strategic role in the success with which the message reaches its objective.

CORETHOUGHT OF
PARAGRAPH 2

> In contributing to the success of the message, the first sentence performs four important functions.

CORETHOUGHT OF
PARAGRAPH 3

> The first function of the opening sentence is . . .

CORETHOUGHT OF
PARAGRAPH 4

> Equally important is the second function of the opening sentence, which . . .

CORETHOUGHT OF
PARAGRAPH 5

> Not to be overlooked in its favorable effect on the reader is the third function of the opening sentence, namely . . .

CORETHOUGHT OF
PARAGRAPH 6

> Fourth in the list of functions to be discharged by the opening sentence is . . .

CORETHOUGHT OF
PARAGRAPH 7

> Let us now illustrate how these four functions can be built into different yet equally effective opening sentences. First . . . Second . . . Third . . .

CORETHOUGHT OF
THE SUMMARY
PARAGRAPH

> In summary, then, those opening sentences that effectively discharge the four major functions will go far to assure . . .

Keeping in mind this *paragraph-picture method,* you can now easily construct your own paragraphs for the messages you will write or dictate in solving business situations in the coming chapters.

Communication Problems

● 1. This problem is based upon the situation in Problem 2 of Chapter 4, page 95. Assume yourself to be the person who received the invitation to speak to your group. Prepare the message of acceptance that would be written to the chairman of the program committee.

Directions: Make up an appropriate heading for the letter. Say that you will be glad to talk to this group. Indicate your interest in the organization and your pleasure in looking forward to their dinner. If you are using the information in Problem 2, tell your travel plans so that a hotel reservation can be made for you.

● 2. Using the situation in Problem 1, prepare a written message declining the invitation.

● 3. Select a "Letter to the Editor" from either your school newspaper, the local newspaper, or a popular magazine. Evaluate it in terms of corethought, unity, and coherence.

Tell in your own words what you believe is wrong with the message (if anything *is* wrong). Make a list of constructive criticisms illustrating the possible areas of improvement, but be sure you offer suggestions that will make the message both readable and understandable. Do not, of course, belittle the person who wrote or the ideas that are earnestly and sincerely expressed.

Points for discussion may include:

    a. The effectiveness of the first and last paragraphs.
    b. Methods of emphasizing important points.
    c. Unity and coherence.
    d. Orientation of the reader.

● 4. You are a member of a campus organization—social or professional fraternity or sorority, band, vocal group, service club, etc., and there is a current drive on for new members. You, as well as every other member, have been asked to write to a campus friend who would be eligible and interested. Write your friend, explaining your organization and telling him why you believe he should join.

    a. Emphasize important ideas by at least two of the "Seven Ways to Emphasize" listed on page 119. Indicate the methods or devices you have used to impress him.
    b. Rewrite your message, using a different technique of emphasis. Point out, again, the methods you have used.
    c. What other methods could you use?

Suggestion: Remember, the most important position for emphasis is located at the beginning of the paragraph; the next important position is at the end. Unity and coherence are, of course, always important considerations.

● 5. Write to a prospective student of your school. Assume that he is interested in the same general field of studies as you are now pursuing and that his background is similar to yours. Tell him about your school and why you believe he will profit by attending.
  Pay particular attention to the following points:

    a. The Heart of the Message
    b. The Corethought of Each Paragraph
    c. The Coherence of the Message (that is, the logical following of one paragraph by a succeeding paragraph)

Suggestions: A message of this type will vary from writer to writer, just as a sales presentation will vary from one salesman to another and from one customer to another. Points that you may want to bring out could include such matters as availability of part-time work, campus social organizations and functions, placement of graduates, current need for graduates in the field, and housing. Accessibility to nearby recreational facilities such as beaches, mountain resorts, professional athletic events, or good music are other important attractions. Use your judgment and write according to how you feel and to what you believe the reader will be interested in hearing.

● 6. Collect and analyze at least ten business messages. Follow the steps given below in making your analysis:

    a. Make a list of the link words and phrases used.
    b. Decide whether the words are correctly used; if not, show how improvement can be accomplished.
    c. Show how link words can be added, if appropriate, to improve interest and readability.

Suggestion: Writers often use a great many short, simple sentences. The resulting impression is that the reader is being shot at with a machine gun geared to short word blasts . . . and the reader's interest is killed just as dead as if real bullets had been used. Link words may, therefore, help an otherwise uninteresting message to become alive and significant.

PART II

Chapter 6

Effective Human Relations:
The Psychology of Tone

The Way You Feel Toward a Person: The Emotional Factor

The Business that Runs "As Smooth As Silk." One of the first great problems of management is to put together an organization and weld it into a team that "clicks"—that runs "like a fine watch," and "as smooth as silk."

To bring about this result is by no means easy. It requires skill in handling many diverse kinds of people. It requires insight into their natures and whims and quirks. It requires an understanding of human relations and how to generate incentives for close teamwork. In short, it requires management "know-how."

Every large organization is made up of specialized departments, each run by specialists. If you were a top management man, one of your first tasks would be to weld your specialists and their specialized departments into a smooth-running team by means of a common language through which they can clearly understand each other. This common language—we might call it "layman's language"—cuts across all the specialized fields and transmits "clear-as-crystal" meaning that *everyone can quickly understand*. In this way the production engineers can talk to the market researchers; the engineers can talk to the lawyers; the purchasing agent can talk to the accountants; and the salesmen can talk to the boss.

Keeping Human Relations Cordial. Every executive who writes or dictates messages creates an intermingled pattern of fact and feeling. It can hardly be otherwise because that is what life is made of: facts and feelings. Hence, he often finds himself in an intricate web of human relations bound together by strands woven of emotions, sentiments, and factual data.

Intertwined in complex and powerful ways, facts may have a heavy impact upon human feelings. Human feelings, in turn, may heavily affect a man's attitude toward facts and how he decides to deal with them. Obviously, if we can keep the human feelings cordial, the decision is far more likely to be favorable, the outcomes pleasant and constructive. This is true right down the management line—in production, sales, finance, engineering, public relations, industrial relations, economic research, and all the rest. So, keep human relations cordial.

Facts and Feelings Can't Be Kept Apart. You cannot separate facts from feelings because you can never be quite sure where one set ends and the other begins. Facts and feelings intertwine, interact, merge, and mix. This mixing goes on ceaselessly in every kind of human-relations message.

For example, when we say, "They closed the deal," we know that at least two people, and perhaps several more, got together, exchanged ideas, had a meeting of minds, and came to an agreement, usually put in writing in contract form. This kind of a negotiation almost always involves a complex mixing of cold facts wrapped around with various kinds of feelings and attitudes. These feelings and attitudes are *emotional* in nature—offshoots of the factual transaction. If these feelings and attitudes are largely favorable, then we say, "They closed the deal." In that case you may be sure that a problem in human relations was met and properly solved.

"The Way You Feel Toward a Person. . . ." As you will note in the coming pages, many types of communication require the sensitive transmission of emotions and sentiments along with the facts. The way in which these are combined and expressed is, in almost every case, quite as important as—and sometimes much more important than—the bare facts themselves.

In one important sense, therefore, we are something like personal TV sending and receiving stations. We transmit impressions of ourselves on *our* particular personal telecast channels. We receive impressions of others as they reach us on *their* personal channels. If you steadily send out a good impression, you are building yourself up. If you continually send out a bad impression, you are tearing yourself down. Whether you like it or not, there is nothing you can do to avoid this steady exchange of impressions. Whatever may be your desires, this transmitting and receiving goes on day in and day out as you form your opinions of others and they form their opinions of you.

Transmit a Good Impression on Your Own Personal TV Channel!

How Do You Make Your Decisions? How you *feel* toward another person is often far more important in bringing you to some decision than how you think about him. You may, for example, have admiration for another person, or respect for him, but *feel* no liking for him. You may sense the prestige and dignity of another but *feel* no friendliness toward him. How we *feel* closes at least as many deals as how we think. A *feeling* of dislike, distrust, uncertainty, or irritation is an obstacle—an emotional obstacle—that blocks success. A *feeling* of trust, confidence, liking, or pleasure is an incentive that assures success.

Emotions: Powerful Friends, or Implacable Foes! No matter how determined you may be to reason things out, emotions constantly pull and haul you around. You may believe that you have reached a certain decision by calm, cool reasoning. Don't fool yourself! The practicing psychologist knows that your decision was the result of a complex tussle of mingled emotions, feelings, attitudes, desires, prejudices, and reason, aided a little by past experience.

"Why are clever people so often blind?" asks Lord Tweedsmuir, the late Governor-General of Canada. "The only explanation I can give," he suggests, "is that they are too clever. They overintellectualize the world. They are too logical. . . . They don't allow for the unseen accident. . . . They work wholly by intellect and are lacking in instinct."

In thousands of actual cases a message, "intellectually" perfect in content, gave the wrong emotional impression and highly displeased the person who received it. Indeed, a message can be clear, concise, complete, and pointed—but so faulty in tone, so defective in its attitude, that it antagonizes everyone.

Are Spoken Words "Safer" than Written Words? When you talk, the person who hears you is a partner in a conversation. He can interrupt you when he does not understand. He can ask a question to clear up a potential misunderstanding. He can, if he wants to, switch the talk into a different channel. He judges your words and sentences not merely by what they mean, but by your tone of voice, your accent on special points, the gestures of your head and hands, your facial expression, and, in short, your whole *manner*. He "sizes up" the conversation and decides whether he is pleased. If he is not pleased, you have at least a chance to overcome his displeasure.

Here is how you do it. You watch him for clues as to how your words strike him. You note a frown of disagreement, a shake of the head, a gesture of denial. So, if you are trying to persuade, you re-phrase your argument to iron out the disagreement. You also note signs of pleasure, a nod of the head, a gesture of approval. This evidence may mean that you have won your point.

Try to Anticipate the Risks. In a conversational give and take you can adjust your words and phrases to avoid irritation. If you see signs of it, you can adjust your expression to other words that may invite agreement. In a written message, on the other hand, a single sentence that seems all right, that seems free enough from any word that may offend, sometimes leaves an unintentional hurt. Many a company by such an unintentional slip has lost good will without ever knowing why. To offset this risk, experienced executives use frequent courtesy words, such as *appreciation, approval, enjoy, helpful, satisfying, splendid, willingness, thank you.*

The Words You Write Must Stand Alone. Without the help of your personal gestures, physical presence, or smile, your written words must stand alone as a permanent record of what you have said. Hence you must try to mold these written words so that they will carry pleasant overtones of feeling to take the place of the gestures and the facial expressions you would use if you were speaking face-to-face.

The "Television Typewriter" That Is Not Yet Invented. Suppose every typewriter carried a two-way television attachment as standard equipment. You could then watch the effect, on your reader, of your words as you put them on paper. Today you use your own judgment as a "stand-in" for the not-yet-invented television attachment. Your judgment, like the needle on a speedometer, tells you whether your words strike too fast or too slow, whether they arouse antagonism or cement friendship.

Once Your Message Is in the Mailbox, It's Hard to Change Your Mind. If you ever mail a message and then wish you hadn't, don't expect to wait at the corner box and ask the mail collector to hand it over. He won't. Legal interception is far more complicated than that.

If you were indifferent, thoughtless, tactless, sarcastic, even angry, the record of your mood is there in black and white. It cannot be erased. You cannot be with the reader to excuse yourself or expunge your error or soften his anger. "The moving finger writes and having writ moves on. Nor all thy piety nor wit shall lure it back to cancel half a line."

But if you were thoughtful, tactful, helpful, and courteous; if you gave the facts requested; if you showed your desire to cooperate as a business friend—then you have nothing to worry about. Drop your message in the mailbox with no regrets.

Climb into the Envelope and Seal the Flap. The good writer "climbs into the envelope and seals the flap." Having traveled the journey, he steps out of the envelope and delivers his message. Later with the coming developments in television, what natural interviews we may enjoy with our associates; how direct and informal will be the conversational exchange! Every good writer strives for this outcome:  to make his words take him into the envelope and bring him out again when he reaches his reader.

When some of the 600,000 words in the unabridged dictionary are brought together in a certain way, they mirror the character of the person who has used them. He rises out of the typewritten lines, steps off the page, and delivers his message. We may lay the message down on the desk and think, "There's a man I should like to do business with. He's a fellow to be trusted. I like his style." What we mean is that we like his character and his personality as they are projected through his words.

Make Your Words
"Step Off the Page"

"I Like His Style." "The force and personality of individuals **are** expressed in their communication skill," concludes a top-rank management executive. "Those who possess and make use of this facility in sensible and graceful manner shine in any company.

"When we speak of men having fine personalities, we are thinking of their ways of expression rather than their physical attractions. In the personal force and manner of his use of the language in writing and speaking," he summarizes, "lies the difference between the man of failure and the man of success."

Fact Messages and Power Messages. Much of our writing has one of two main purposes: (1) to convey factual information **or** (2) to arouse emotion and to move or impress with power.

Fact writing, to convey matter-of-fact information, is found in business reports, direction books, summaries, statistical reports, abstracts, catalogs, fiscal reviews, quarterly reports, and the like. In documents of this kind, clearness, exactness, and accuracy are important. Attention and interest are less vital matters because they are supplied voluntarily. Fact writing, dealing with matter-of-fact material, uses a simple, direct, and explanatory style. This style is illustrated in the Union Carbide letter on page 129. The tone is matter of fact and calm.

Power writing, to arouse emotion and to move or impress with power, is found in sales work and in similar forms of promotional writing, in which the aim is to stimulate lively interest and to move the reader to favorable action. The manner and the tone are persuasive, imaginative, alive, and powerful in their appeal to human desires, passions, and emotions. Notice in the Robert Gelczer letter on page 129 how the vivid, picture-making words build up a gripping appeal founded on an emotional, dynamic tone.

Fact Writing: To Convey Information

Power Writing: To Move to Action

Letter 1:

MORSE G. DIAL
President

UNION CARBIDE CORPORATION

30 EAST FORTY-SECOND STREET

NEW YORK 17, N.Y.

TO OUR STOCKHOLDERS:

I thought that you might like to have a copy of the attached booklet, "Hot-Metal Magic," which describes an important activity of our corporation. This booklet gives a glimpse of some of the romance of alloy making, one of the most basic of all American industries, and tells about the everyday miracles that alloys are performing for all of us.

"Hot-Metal Magic" was written primarily for educational purposes, and you will find that the story is presented briefly and simply. It is hoped that it will bring about a better understanding of an industry that affects nearly everything around us, yet that few people are aware even exists.

This is the third booklet on a specific phase of the Corporation's work that has been mailed recently to our stockholders. You may recall receiving last year the "Mesa Miracle" booklet describing UCC's role in the mining and processing of uranium ores, and also "Research at Union Carbide" which was published to interest graduate students in a career with the corporation. I was gratified to receive many favorable comments from stockholders on both these booklets.

I hope that you will enjoy reading "Hot-Metal Magic." If you wish additional copies for any of your friends or associates who you think might find the booklet informative, I shall be very glad to send them to you.

Sincerely,

President

Letter 2:

Robert Gelozer & Associates

Merchandising Counselors

Los Angeles 14, California

5460 Wilshire Boulevard

DUnkirk 5-5556

August 19, 19--

Mr. Norman L. Dean
1100 Fountain Street
Minneapolis 15, Minnesota

Dear Mr. Dean

ENDANGERED!

In every city of the country, retail merchants today feel the tightening grip of severe competition. Welded link by link, the threat of cut prices is sinking into the flesh and blood of normal profits.

Panicky and fearful of the future of his business, many a dealer has tried to fight his way to success by wiping out his own profit with cut prices or, worse still, by reducing the quality of the articles he sells.

Both methods lead only to destruction.

Let's have a heart-to-heart talk about this serious situation. There is a way out for you, and we want to help you find it. First of all, let us make this point clear: We have organized our entire merchandising program for the single purpose of helping every retail merchant to increase the efficiency of his store. If we accomplish that purpose, we assure ourselves an expanding market for our products. Thus we all win!

Take heart! The small merchant is not going to have to go out of business. Provided both he and the manufacturer from whom he buys are prepared--through mutual cooperation and understanding--to establish their business methods on the solid rock of rapid turnover and small inventories, then a bright new future of better profits is already assured!

Our next letter will go into further details. Meanwhile don't lose your nerve. You have us with you through the current difficulties. YOU ARE GOING TO WIN! With our organization and ample capital we are going to help you win.

Sincerely and earnestly yours

ROBERT GELOZER & ASSOCIATES

VS/ck

What Tone Will You Use?

The Tone Scale of the Written Word. You can give the written word more tone shadings than you can find in a color chart. Some words are formal, reserved, conservative—or jocular, cajoling, buoyant, sprightly, and jaunty. Some words are curt, blunt, sharp, insolent, boastful, stern, insistent, convincing, and persuasive. Some are wheedling, meek, humble. Some are lofty, superior, aristocratic. Some are straightforward, earnest, confident, courteous, and considerate of the welfare of others.

For Better Human Relations, Use the Considerate Tone. There may have been a time when big corporations, in the minds of many, were simply big, distant, and impersonal. But that time has vanished. Top managements use great care in fitting their organizations into the community of which they are a part. Sometimes, indeed, they display delightfully subtle skill in handling their human relations problems. They show a mastery of considerateness in tone and act.

Consider, for example, the Pigott Construction Company, Limited. These large-scale Canadian builders were erecting, in the beautiful city of Montreal, a huge new hotel adjoining the Canadian National Railway Central Station at the intersection of Mansfield Street and West Dorchester.

Squarely at the intersection at the exact point of heaviest pedestrian travel was the subtle "human relations" sign—the sign that instantly took all the sting and annoyance out of the construction inconveniences and barriers. Here is what the sign said:

> WE ARE SORRY TO CAUSE ANY INCONVENIENCE.
> PLEASE LET US SHARE THE SIDEWALK WITH YOU.

The world's greatest diplomat could hardly do better than that!

The Sincere Tone Vs. the Sham Tone. So much "Commercialese," so much false "pep," so much cheap vocabulary, so much trite wordage is likely to creep into the day's work that you should always be on guard against this kind of poisonous infection. Beware of shoddy language and a threadbare vocabulary.

In the box on page 132 is the famed original text of Lincoln's Gettysburg Address. Note how the powerful simplicity of the original has been smothered and lost in the cheap version alongside it.

The Positive Tone Vs. the Negative and Neutral Tones. The positive tone is dependable, constructive, and cooperative. The negative tone is dangerous, destructive, and antagonistic. The neutral tone is on dead center, informative, machinelike, often statistical, always emotionless.

USE THE POSITIVE TONE	*NOT* THE NEGATIVE TONE	USE THE POSITIVE TONE	*NOT* THE NEGATIVE TONE
accuracy	carelessness	honesty	trickery
adjustment	complaint	initiative	slothfulness
ambition	laziness	level-headedness	irritability
assurance	fear	neatness	slovenliness
calm	anger	pleasure	displeasure
cheerfulness	discouragement	satisfaction	discontent
confidence	uncertainty	security	insecurity
cooperation	refusal	success	failure
courage	cowardice	tact	bluntness
courtesy	curtness	thoughtfulness	egotism
desire to serve	disinterestedness	triumph	defeat
diplomacy	insolence	trust	suspicion
generosity	selfishness	understanding	obstinacy
happiness	unhappiness	willingness	hesitance

Work for the positive tone. It is a priceless jewel. Cultivate its use. But beware of what you have written while you are irritated or excited. Never mail it until the next morning. You'll be glad you waited . . . because then you'll probably not mail it at all.

Twenty Winning Messages Used These Words. A contest to discover some of the best writing of the year was held some time ago under the supervision of a consulting organization. In commenting on the twenty winners, the judges were deeply impressed with *the spirit of optimism that ran through them.* "The writers," they observed, "drew up words so gracious, so genuine, so sincere that the readers would say, 'these are men we would like to do business with.' Such words cannot be ignored. *They are like friendly handshakes . . . signs of good will.*"

Here are some of the words in the twenty winners the judges ranked at the top:

appreciation	effective	good folks	loyal	splendid
approval	enjoy	grateful	satisfying	thank you
best wishes	excellence	helpful	serve you	willingness
clean slate	genuine	honestly	smile	your confidence

Fourscore and seven years ago our fathers brought forth on this continent a new nation, conceived in liberty, and dedicated to the proposition that all men are created equal.

Now we are engaged in a great civil war, testing whether that nation, or any nation so conceived and so dedicated, can long endure. We are met on a great battlefield of that war. We have come to dedicate a portion of that field, as a final resting place for those who here gave their lives that that nation might live. It is altogether fitting and proper that we should do this.

But, in a larger sense, we cannot dedicate—we cannot consecrate—we cannot hallow—this ground. The brave men, living and dead, who struggled here have consecrated it, far above our poor power to add or detract. The world will little note, nor long remember, what we say here, but it can never forget what they did here. It is for us, the living, rather, to be dedicated here to the unfinished work which they who fought here have thus far so nobly advanced. It is rather for us to be here dedicated to the great task remaining before us—that from these honored dead we take increased devotion to that cause for which they gave the last full measure of devotion—that we here highly resolve that these dead shall not have died in vain—that this nation, under God, shall have a new birth of freedom—and that government of the people, by the people, for the people, shall not perish from the earth.

Back in 1776 our fathers founded a new nation based on the proposition that all men are born equal.

Now we are engaged in a great civil war, the aim being to save the Union. We are met on a great battlefield of that war to dedicate a portion of that field as a cemetery for those who have made the supreme sacrifice. This is a good idea.

Of course, the brave men, alive and dead, who fought it out here have consecrated it better than anything we can do. [Give the size of our army here.] It's not so much what we say. It's what they did that counts. It's up to us to carry on the unfinished work which they who fought here brought so far along. It is also up to us to dedicate ourselves to the real job ahead of us—namely, to be brave and true, to support the Constitution of the U. S., and to carry Old Glory to the heights, from the rock-ribbed coast of Maine to the sun-kissed shores of California.

The Gettysburg Address in Two Tone Styles

The Twenty Big Winners Did NOT Use THESE Words! Now look at the other end of the scale. Here are some words that were nowhere to be found in any of the twenty winners:

abuse	like a deadbeat	we take issue
alibi	mildly ridiculous	why have you ignored
blame	not our responsibility	why not be fair
crooked	simply nonsense	wrong
dispute	suggests the chiseler	your complaint
exaggerate.	surely you don't expect	your insinuation
frankly, it seems to us	we are surprised	your neglect
fraud	we do not intend	your own carelessness
ignorant	we must insist	you should know

These are "chip-on-the-shoulder" words. With insulting folly, they leer and swagger and create hosts of enemies for the misguided writers who use them. To anyone sensitive to psychological tone, they grate on the nerves like grains of sand between the teeth.

A Quick Success—Out of a Flat Failure. Express positive ideas first, if you want to be in the winners' column. A finance company sent out a follow-up message to those who had received, upon their own request, an elaborate booklet. The company planned to get action by requesting the return of the book after two weeks had passed without an order. The results from this message were sharply disappointing. Then, *without any other change whatever*, the second paragraph was put first and the first paragraph was put second. The results increased 40 per cent.

A FAILURE—THE ORIGINAL VERSION
Study the First Impression.
(Negative)

If you have decided not to accept the invitation to ownership in this company, please return the book that we sent you twelve days ago in response to your request. Postage for the return is enclosed.

If you have decided to accept our invitation, you will still be in time to obtain one of the ownerships allotted to your state. Your application should be mailed promptly upon receipt of this letter.

A SUCCESS—THE REWRITTEN VERSION
Returns Increased 40%.
(Positive)

If you have decided to accept our invitation, you will still be in time to obtain one of the ownerships allotted to your state. Your application should be mailed promptly upon receipt of this letter.

If you have decided not to accept the invitation to ownership in this company, please return the book that we sent you twelve days ago in response to your request. Postage for the return is enclosed.

May 15, 19--

Mr. Donald Holmes
3470 Brotherton Road
Toledo 9, Ohio

Dear Mr. Holmes

On the 5:15 to Westport the other night I was reading
over the final proof of the enclosed book. Suddenly
I realized that my next-seat neighbor, a well-known
advertising man, was reading over my shoulder. "I
couldn't help being interested," he apologized. "Do
you mind if I read along with you?"

When we'd finished reading together, he said, "Roy,
that's the most understandable exposition of _why_ the
NBC-TV, 'Tuned to the Stars,' is the Number One Network
buy for advertisers that I've ever seen."

We know that you, too, will find this story interesting
and well worth the few minutes to read from cover to
cover.

And now we turn you over to Abdullah!

Cordially yours

Roy Witmer

Roy Witmer:RH

Enclosure

Conversational Tone

This informal narrative is phrased in attractive TALK-language.

How to Refresh and "Warm Up" the Tone. A bank acknowledges the receipt of a deposit. Watch the tone shift:

(1) DULL, WORDY "COMMERCIALESE"

We have your letter of May 6, and we hereby acknowledge the receipt of the deposit enclosed. We wish to state that we have duly credited this deposit in the sum of $164.55.

(2) SLIGHTLY IMPROVED—"COMMERCIALESE" CUT OUT

We acknowledge receipt, in your letter of May 6, of a deposit totaling $164.55, which we have credited to your account.

(3) EXCELLENT—PLEASANT, BRISK TONE

Appreciation First:

Thank you for your May 6 deposit of $164.55. Your account has been credited for this amount.

or

We are glad to credit to your account today the deposit for $164.55, received with your note of May 6.

Action First:

We have promptly credited your deposit totaling $164.55, received today, to your account.

In the original the tone is dull, the expression wordy. In the improved version the "Commercialese" is corrected, but the action is still hidden. In the final versions the tone becomes positive through the expression of courtesy or action in the opening words. Simple though these tone shifts are, literally thousands fail to understand them and remain forever incapable of putting them to practical use. You now have your chance to stay out of the latter group—by "reaching always for the positive."

Instead of Saying "NO," Say "YES" to Something Else

Look for the Bright Spots. While building construction was going on, the scaffolding on the thirty-eighth story of a New York hotel caught fire. The firemen had plenty of trouble in smothering the flames because of the great height of the building. But the fire did not spread, and the huge building was saved. The next day the management announced that the fire would not interrupt construction. Then it concluded, "And so is proved in a spectacular way that the Park Plaza is fireproof." A fire in any building is bad news. But the alert writer located the bright spot!

A customer some time ago sent to a mail-order house an out-of-town order for a space heater that could not be shipped for three weeks. But the weather was still mild and was seasonally expected to remain so. Under these circumstances what would you do? What kind of a reply would you make?

WHY SAY IT THIS WAY . . .	WHEN YOU CAN SAY IT THIS WAY?
Negative Disappointment	*Positive Satisfaction*
We regret that we are absolutely unable to fill your order for three weeks. We are simply stacked up with a lot of orders that came in ahead of yours.	Thank you for your order of an Acme Automatic De Luxe Space Heater. We shall be able to send it to you in plenty of time for installation before cold weather.

The first reply, a stark disappointment, emphasized what the company could *not* do. Here we see pure negativism without excuse. The one who dictated this message committed a classic blunder: he failed to use the excellent positive alternate that was instantly available "right in front of his nose."

On the other hand, the revised answer was highly pleasing because it showed that the company was thinking of the customer's interests. What was the difference? *The second writer located the bright spot—and emphasized it.*

How to Lose a Customer: A Case Study in How NOT to Write. A patron of a city bank, a man who had done business with the institution for years, asked for a loan. Someone in the bank, unfamiliar with his account, wrote him a letter. It was just a routine message. In fact, when you read it, you may say to yourself, "Why . . . that isn't bad . . . what's so wrong about it?" It is shown at the top of page 137.

This message tripped the trigger and lit the fuse! Our friend, the customer, came up to the desk of one of the bank officers with the letter clenched in his hand. He was choked with anger and ready to close out for good his long-standing connections and his profitable account.

What Angered Him? All the facts were true. The practice of all good banks is to keep their financial statements up to date, and never to consider loans to persons about whom they have insufficient credit information. But because this ordinary request was made in such an untactful and repellent tone, a good customer was angry enough to

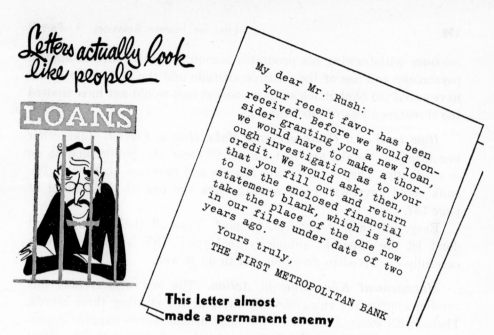

Letters actually look like people

This letter almost made a permanent enemy

How to Lose a Customer and Make Him Angry

My dear Mr. Rush:

Your recent favor has been received. Before we would consider granting you a new loan, we would have to make a thorough investigation as to your credit. We would ask, then, that you fill out and return to us the enclosed financial statement blank, which is to take the place of the one now in our files under date of two years ago.

Yours truly,

THE FIRST METROPOLITAN BANK

This letter extends a friendly hand

How to Win a Customer and Make Him a Friend

Dear Mr. Rush:

I was glad to learn from your letter of May 10 that you have another loan for us. It is about two years since you made out a financial statement, I believe, so I am enclosing another blank.

Just as soon as you fill it out for us, I'll see that the loan goes at once before the loan committee.

Sincerely yours,

Jefferson C. Thomas

Jefferson C. Thomas
Vice President
THE FIRST METROPOLITAN BANK

consider withdrawing his profitable account. A little skill in applied psychology and use of the positive attitude and the right tone would have saved the bank much embarrassment and would not have invited the threatened loss of business.

How to Win a Customer and Make Him a Friend. Like other organizations, banks are in business to serve the public, and to do so efficiently. They want to win friends and generate good will. The bank could have written a message like the one at the bottom of page 137.

Easy, informal, courteous, simple? Yes—all these things. But don't let the *apparent* simplicity fool you! This brief message is carefully contrived to do a job and to do it well.

Management Know-How in Action. The one who creates this version applies the rule, *courtesy first*, in the opening three words. Then—with exceptional tact—the next fifteen words express appreciation to the customer for bringing his loan business to The First Metropolitan Bank: "I was glad to learn . . . that you have another loan for us." Note the YOU-attitude. ". . . YOU have another loan for *us*." That is, "YOU deserve the credit for bringing in some new business to *us*, and we want you to know that we appreciate it."

Then, in an incidental way, the next twenty words refer to the two-year time lapse since the last financial statement and the customary routine of filling out the enclosed blank. But note: *this* time there is no implied doubt about the present status of the customer's credit standing ("Before we would consider granting you a new loan . . ."). This time there is no implied challenge, no discourteous implication that the customer may fail the test of investigation (". . . we would have to make a thorough investigation as to your credit.").

Finally, the last twenty-two words are filled with pleasant tone, the suggestion of action—not just ordinary action, but quick, efficient action. The customer, having had a long record of past successful loans with the bank, has reasonable justification for reading between the lines that the action will again be favorable. Here is how it sums up:

POWERFUL OPENING:

  COURTESY FIRST: "I was glad to learn . . .

POWERFUL CLOSE:

  ACTION IN BEHALF OF THE CUSTOMER:
  "Just as soon as . . . , I'll see that . . . "

People Can Be Positive and Negative, Too. Even people are created with a positive or a negative "twist." You may have acquaintances who are cheerful and buoyant and others who are morose and sullen. There are always some, fortunately, who are pleasant and tactful, in contrast with some who were simply "born cross." A nationally famous basketball coach, because of his self-centeredness, could keep only a small circle of friends. A suspicious professor, because of his belligerency, irascibility, envious nature, and infantile lack of self-control, became known on his college campus chiefly for his capacity in making hosts of enemies. And the secretary of an association of commerce, because of dictatorial curtness, antagonized his associates and destroyed all chances of teamwork. Thousands of written paragraphs, carrying the vicious faults of the basketball coach, the professor, and the secretary, never accomplish what they set out to do.

Illustrating the positive-negative on a broader scale, Ralph Ingersoll, newspaper editor, writes: "We are against fraud and deceit and greed and cruelty. We are for people who are kindly and courageous and honest. We respect intelligence, sound accomplishment, open-mindedness, religious tolerance. We propose to crusade for those who seek constructively to improve the way men live together."

"A Friend in Need." And in the example below you hear the tone of comradeship, cooperation, sincerity, and a desire to help—all of which play a part in forming the positive tones in life. In the face of the strife that afflicts humanity, this appeal glows in contrast:

AN APPEAL WITH A POSITIVE TONE

"A friend in need" is an old adage we quote frequently, and here is a chance to do something about it. Your friend and ours, Bill Page of Lowe Associates, is confined to his home because of illness; and it may be quite a while before he will be back on the firing line.

We who are his competitors (as well as his friends) need business, but we do not want it at the expense of a fellow worker in the field who is temporarily out of the race.

You who are his customers (as well as his friends) can help by loyalty to his organization, which will carry on during his absence. They will give you the same careful attention and service as in the past.

So let's all pitch in and do our little bit to keep Bill's business going as usual. You can't tell--you may need a friend yourself some day.

The Executive's Guide to Message Analysis

		Yes	No
1. Is your message attractive?	....	☐	☐

It is human nature to be attracted by the beautiful and repulsed by the slovenly. Make the body of your message assume the proportions of the sheet upon which it is typed.

2. Have you been unselfish? .... ☐ ☐

Consider the reader's viewpoint. Put yourself in his place, and you will exert one of the strongest forces at your command. Say the things that you would want said if you and your reader exchanged places.

3. Have you been sincere? .... ☐ ☐

Tell no untruths. Remember that half-truths and polite misstatements work their own undoing.

4. Have you been courteous? .... ☐ ☐

Courtesy means neither flattery nor insincerity. It means straight-forward consideration of the other man's point of view. Courtesy costs nothing. It pays thousands in dividends.

5. Is your message clear and logical? .... ☐ ☐

Think straight. Tell your story in simple language.

6. Have you TALKED directly to your reader? .... ☐ ☐

Write as if you were sitting across from your reader and talking to him carefully. Project your personality through your words.

7. Is your message interesting to the reader? .... ☐ ☐

See the problem through his eyes. Write not to please yourself but to interest him.

8. Have you made every line count? .... ☐ ☐

Strip off the excess whether your message takes five lines or six pages. Carve away the surplus.

9. Is the first sentence the headline? .... ☐ ☐

Find out what the reader wants to know and tell it to him—first.

10. Have you written paragraphs and sentences moderate to short in length? .... ☐ ☐

If long paragraphs are necessary (as in technical discussion), place them between shorter paragraphs for "change of pace."

11. Have you used simple words? .... ☐ ☐

Use a simple word when it is as accurate in its shade of meaning as a longer word.

12. Have you used the positive tone? .... ☐ ☐

Thought comes before action. Make that thought positive. Be helpful and considerate. See the bright spots! Tell him what you CAN do.

Communication Problems

● 1. Write a memorandum to the members of your office staff, reminding them of the necessity of keeping cordial human relations with present and prospective customers. Stress, with specific illustrations, points of similarity and contrast between written and spoken communication. List what you believe to be the four or five most important factors involved in the tone of business writing. Impress upon each employee the need for evaluating each communication situation carefully so that a considerate, positive, helpful message can be prepared.

● 2. Oftentimes a communication problem may be solved by either a factual or a power message. When such an option exists, the purpose of the message will determine the type of writing to be used. The business writer should be able to write either type of message well.

Assume that you are to answer an inquiry from a prospective student who has written to ask about the cost of attending your school. The writer has specifically asked for the actual dollar costs for one year of study. He has not asked about any advantages that your school might offer—advantages not reflected in the cost.

Write a factual answer to the prospective student's inquiry. Give the student a detailed breakdown of the costs of attending your school. Be certain to include such costs as tuition, books, room and board in school dormitories, and student activity fees. Remind him of possible extras—laundry, fraternity or sorority dues, entertainment, recreation, and the like. Be factual, complete, and clear.

● 3. Using the situation described in Problem 2, write a "power" message to answer the inquiry. Give the reader facts, but appeal to his emotions so that his choice of school will be based not only on dollar cost but also on other values and advantages.

Be honest in your statements. Do not exaggerate, belittle another school, or criticize. Appeal to pride, prestige, and other intangible values which graduation from your school will provide.

● 4. Rate five business messages according to "The Executive's Guide to Message Analysis" on page 140. Use examples that you have not evaluated before. Let your first impressions influence your decisions.

Make for each message a list of constructive suggestions for improvement.

● 5. You are a student officer in a campus organization and have been asked to talk before one of the local high school Career-Day groups. You are qualified to talk on the subject suggested, and you would like to meet with the students.

The date the high school has set aside for Career Day is, however, also the first day of mid-term examinations. You know that it would be unwise for you to accept the invitation since it might affect your grades.

Write to the principal of the high school, expressing your regret at having to decline the invitation. Offer to come to talk to the group on another day if that is convenient and agreeable to him. Try to keep the door open for further talks by you and other students from your school. Make it easy for the principal to reply.

● **6.** It is true that the NOMA style "simplifies" by dropping the traditional salutation and complimentary close. The originators of this style, however, would not be happy with this very narrow concept of simplification. More important than these mechanical details of simplification, business writers should concern themselves with a complete simplification of the language used in the body of the message itself. It is important that communicators write in a language style that can be understood. Every effort should be made to avoid using any needless words, hackneyed expressions, and technical jargon which tend to confuse readers, clutter language, and rob messages of their individuality. An excellent example of "how *not* to write a simplified letter" is given here:

> May we take this liberty to acknowledge receipt of your esteemed favor of the 10th inst. enclosing your kind order for shipment of 20 doz. white towels. The writer is truly grateful for your esteemed patronage and wishes to inform you at this writing that the merchandise ordered herewith will be forwarded in due course.
>
> The undersigned asks permission to take this sterling opportunity to again thank you for your business.
>
> Hoping it may be our humble pleasure to serve your other needs at an early date, we beg to remain

Directions: Analyze these paragraphs for words and phrases that would sound out of place if heard in conversation, and then rewrite the message in whatever form you choose. Your revision should incorporate the following points:

1. Acknowledgment of the order
2. Disposition of the order
3. A good-will close with a sales note

PART II

Chapter 7

Effective Human Relations: Through the Power of TALK-Writing

Generating Teamwork. The seasoned management executive will tell you this: one of the most important aims of management is to generate teamwork in the organization. In every person management adds to its staff, it seeks the team spirit.

Team spirit will always be the foundation for effective human relations—the human subject of how we all live together, earn our way in life together, and get along successfully together. Almost from the moment we put our first words and sentences together, whether in spoken or written form, we learn of *human relations*, our interdependence, the relationships of small enterprises to large enterprises, and again, their interdependence, one on the other now and in all our future. What is the lesson here? The lesson is this: We are never working alone.

Success in Human Relations Depends on What You Say and How You Say It. In a successful organization we start with the assumption that the people in it are in the main honest, that they are people of integrity, and that they carry out their promises *by doing what they say they will do.* These qualities are the ones that make a winning team. They are the qualities you strive for, and if you possess them, then your future success in human relations depends for the most part on what you say and how you say it. You will build your success with the words you use and the way in which you use them.

> **WANTED**
>
> **Director of Public Relations**
>
> A large corporation employing 15,000 people and doing a world-wide business needs man of experience. This man must be able to write simply and forcefully. He must know when to write and what to say. He must sense situations. His personality must be pleasing and he must be able to cooperate. Salary commensurate with this important position. Address O B 290, Tribune, and give full particulars of experience and background.

". . . must be able to write simply and forcefully. . . . He must sense situations. . . . His personality must be pleasing."

At this Moment: How Well Do YOU Know "How to Say It"?
Rutgers University in New Jersey has made a change of policy that
may prove revolutionary in American collegiate education. *Hence-*
forth, students who cannot express themselves clearly in the English
language will be denied diplomas.

Rutgers has a freshman course known as English 101. It is simply
a course in the fundamentals, presumably similar to the English A
course of the University of Cali-
fornia. Some students apparently are unable to master the
course, even in the four years
they spend at Rutgers. From
now on such students will not
get degrees, no matter what
their performance may be in
other courses.

> **Vocabulary and Success**
> "How forcible are right words."
> —Book of Job.
> "The selection of the right word
> calls for the exercise of man's
> greatest faculty—that of judg-
> ment."—Alexander Hamilton.
> "With words we govern men."
> —Disraeli.

**Shall We Deny Diplomas to Those Who "Don't Know How to
Say It"?** Commenting on this major policy shift, a prominent newspaper editor writes: "At *The Herald* we receive letters every day
from college graduates who are obviously unable to express themselves clearly. This situation forces us to conclude that our colleges
should certainly refuse a degree to people who can't handle their
native language adequately, who can't make known their ideas well.
Otherwise, what value does a degree have?

"And since colleges grant degrees by authority of the state, the
state should make sure its authority isn't abused. *Awarding a degree*
to a student who is so badly educated that he can't communicate
properly is as phony as putting a sterling silver hallmark on a cheap
piece of silverplate."

Top Management Men Support the Editor. If you think the editor has used rather strong language, listen to this statement by
R. N. Hilkert, Vice President, Federal Reserve Bank of Philadelphia:

"In matters of promotion, other things being equal, the man who
can write has a significant edge on the man who cannot. He is more
valuable to the organization, and he will climb more rapidly to the
management levels because he can clearly and forcefully express his
thoughts and because he can persuasively and tactfully present his
points of view. As management material he is more valuable to the
organization because he is *articulate*. This is one of the facts of
business life.

"A management executive is supposed to be an idea man. If he is not a man of ideas, he is out of place in his post. Having ideas, he must transmit them to others—perhaps to the board of directors, perhaps to his boss, perhaps to his colleagues or his subordinates. If he has the ideas but is so inarticulate that he does not know how to transmit them, then we tag him with the old expression, 'He knows his stuff, but he can't get it across.' And if he 'can't get it across,' he may not be an executive for long."

Can He "Get It Across"?

Says G. M. Loeb, managing partner of E. F. Hutton and Company, "In business itself we must realize that we are in a changed world. The problem of effective human relations grows ever more complex, depends ever more heavily on articulate communication. And communication, which is the lifeblood of business, is faster than ever before. Master it, if you would succeed."

For Better Human Relations, Use TALK-Language

Use Conversational Words. Have you ever heard of the "five-syllable" disease? This is the disease that most seriously afflicts those people who get all wound up in big words. The three-to-five-syllable people, as they are often called, hide their normal, natural, human selves behind strange masks of big words and old-fashioned phrases. The task is to tear away these masks and to show the friendly persons who may be there. But for those who have become infected with the big-word habit, the task is not easy.

"Please Tell Me in One-Syllable Words What You Mean." A well-known management executive tells the following story: "A few days ago one of our dictating staff showed me a reply that had just come in. It read, 'Please tell me in one-syllable words what you mean.' I directed that that reply be circulated to every one on our dictating staff. For every one of us it packed a powerful lesson!" The lesson? Loosen up your writing with simple, natural words.

Let TALK-Language Flow Into Your Sentences. Use TALK-words when you express yourself. Here is how to do it: Go through each line and underline each word that sounds "upstage" or superformal. Then bring the stilted words down to an easy TALK-level by translating each one into its TALK-equivalent.

Simplify . . . Simplify . . . Simplify! Shun big words when simpler words are just as good. The English language has a forceful one-syllable word for many three-to-five-syllable words. Often the one-syllable word "packs the heavier punch." Suppose we try the actual experiment. The following pairs, although not in all cases strict equivalents, are close enough to be often interchangeable. They illustrate the principle of *how to simplify.*

28-38 Clinton St.
Zanesville, N. J.

Dear Sir:

I have received your letter. If you will explain what you mean, I will try to do what you ask.

Yours truly,
Henry Blane

Simplify!

"If you will explain what you mean . . ."—in words of one syllable.

WHY SAY THIS?	WHEN YOU CAN SAY THIS?	WHY SAY THIS?	WHEN YOU CAN SAY THIS?
Formal	*TALK-Language*	*Formal*	*TALK-Language*
approximately	about	inquire	ask
ascertain	find out	obtain	get
assist	help	participate	share
conclusion	end	permit	let
construct	build	procure	get
contribute	give	provided	if
demonstrate	show	purchase	buy
difficult	hard	render	give
initial	first	sufficient	enough

Investigate can become *probe*; instead of *difficulty* we run into a *snag*; instead of *frustrate* or *circumvent* we can *foil* the enemy; a *division* or *disagreement* can become a *split.* Words like *go, slay, flay, pact, foe, wed, hop, bid, tilt, bloc, scan, dig, snag, foil,* and *split*—

all of them are simple and direct and carry two or three times as much "punch" as their multisyllable equivalents.

From Chicago comes this example of a public sign written in a language you might describe as "Municipalese." Because there have been so many accidents at the dangerous triple street intersection of Logan, Milwaukee, and Kedzie Avenues, the street department put up signs that warn:

"Pedestrians Please Cross at Signalized Intersections." Ask a seven-year-old what this means and he may not be able to tell you. But if you say, "Cross at the Lights," he'll know what you mean.

WHY SAY IT THIS WAY . . .	WHEN YOU CAN SAY IT THIS WAY?
When reporting a conflagration, caller will please specify the site of conflagration with precision.	When you report a fire, tell exactly where it is.
Here is a common species of that feathered creature belonging to the general classification of gallinaceous biped, and noted for its egg-laying propensities.	Here is a hen with a fine record for laying eggs.

Lincoln's writing, many believe, reached its climax in the Gettysburg Address. This masterpiece contains only two hundred sixty-five words. Of these, *one hundred ninety-five are of one syllable.* Forty-three are of two syllables. Most of the remainder are of three. In total length the Gettysburg Address is less than three quarters of an ordinary typed page.

Simplify Your Phrases to the TALK-Level. Just as it is wise to use simple TALK-words when they are as clear and as accurate as formal WRITE-words, so it is wise to simplify phrases. The following contrasts (close enough to be reasonably interchangeable) will illustrate:

WHY SAY THIS	WHEN YOU CAN SAY THIS?	WHY SAY THIS	WHEN YOU CAN SAY THIS?
Stuffy	*Natural TALK-Words*	*Stuffy*	*Natural TALK-Words*
at all times	always	in the event that ...	if
at the present time..	now	in the near future ..	soon
costs the sum of	costs	in view of the fact	
due to the fact that..	because	that	since
enclosed herewith for		owing to the fact that	because
your information..	enclosed	report to the effect	
first of all	first	that	report **that**
for the period of a		under date of	on
year	for a year	until such time as ..	until
for the month of June	for June	we would ask that	
in the amount of ...	for	you	please

Of the 8,630,000 share-owners in the country today, no fewer than 4,453,080 — 51.6 percent — are women. And we say more power to them!

There's only one thing that bothers us, and we have to say it at the risk of offending not only the 4,453,080 share-owning women in the United States but also the other 80,000,000 or so who don't own stock.

What bothers us is that women in general know less about the stock market and share-ownership than men do. There are exceptions, of course, but on the whole it's true if our experience is any criterion.

Why? Well, that's anybody's guess. Maybe they're too busy being wives and mothers and career women. Maybe the Victorian idea that women should be kept in the dark about financial matters still prevails in some quarters.

One thing we know for certain. It isn't for lack of interest that most women know less than men do about investing. They're just as much concerned as the menfolk about planning and budgeting for the future — about travel, a house in the country, and all the "extras" that careful investment can help to make possible. Then too, many of them realize that the whole problem of family finances may some day fall into their hands.

Any way you look at it, it's a good idea for the distaff side to know something about stocks and bonds and how the market operates.

What should you do if you want to brush up on investing — you or anyone else you know?

A good place to start would be right here at Merrill Lynch. We've always considered education a basic part of our job. You'll find your account executive, for instance, willing and able to answer questions about investing, no matter how elementary they may be. Or you might be interested in some of our standard educational booklets: "How to Invest," "How to Buy Stocks," "How to Read a Financial Report." A good starter is "What Everybody Ought to Know About This Stock and Bond Business," the simplest and most basic of all our publications.

If you'd like a copy yourself, or if you'd like copies sent to friends of yours, just use the other side of this folder to give us the names and addresses. There's a business reply envelope enclosed for your convenience.

MERRILL LYNCH, PIERCE, FENNER & SMITH

TALK-Language in an Easy, Conversational, Natural Format, with Humorous Matching Illustrations

A skillful message written in natural talk.

When you are "wound up" in your words and are struggling to untangle yourself, put this question: "What are you really trying to tell him? In easy talk, how would you say it?" Then choose the little words—*as long as they are accurate and convey the right shade of meaning.*

At the same time avoid long, involved sentences. Godfrey Dewey, in an analysis of 100,000 words chosen from forty different kinds of writing, found that the average sentence length was a fraction over nineteen words.

A Three-Point Guide to TALK-Level Simplification

Remember: **1** The more syllables in a word, the harder it is to read.

2 The more words in a sentence, the harder it is to read.

3 The more personal "human-relations" references there are in your message, the more "talk-conversational-natural" it will be.

Fit Your Words to Your Reader

Visualize Your Reader and Make Him "Comfortable." Write straight to your reader in simple words fitted to his outlook and interests. Write to him as an individual. Use terms that are familiar to him, that he will understand, and that will make him comfortable. Think of him as a living person with human likes and prejudices. You will then be more likely to approach him in a natural way, choosing words that make him feel "at home." You win him over when he thinks, "This writer talks my language. Let's see what he has to say."

Match Your Terms to the Right Groups. To a person who doesn't know much about factories, it will probably be useless to talk of driving fit, sliding fit, and running fit. To a woman who has never seen a college or professional football game, it may be useless to talk of a hand-off, or a draw play, or a tailback, or an off-tackle smash, or an end-around. To a man who has never "socked" a golf ball in his life, it may be useless to talk of a number three wood off the tee, of using a wedge to blast out of a sandtrap, or of reading the breaks on a rolling green. So fit your words to your reader. Remember this guide: Only to those groups of people who understand them as familiar everyday language will terms, such as those used in this paragraph, be clear. We all agree that the terms of the factory, the football field, and the golf course are vividly descriptive and highly concrete. But to understand them, we need the right experience and background.

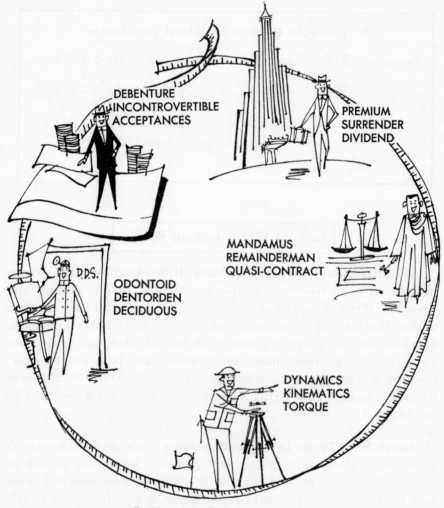

Fit Your Words to Your Reader

Use legal terms to lawyers, financial terms to bank executives, electrical terms to electricians, scientific terms to scientists, medical terms to medical men, etc.

Power Your Words for Future Progress

You Can Predict Your Own Success. We now have plenty of evidence that *word power*—a wide and accurate vocabulary, a command of language—is closely linked with management leadership.

The Human Engineering Laboratories tested and measured the vocabularies of twenty men who had left school at the age of fifteen and who had worked their way into major positions. In the case of these twenty men it proved to be their vocabularies that were important rather than their formal school education. Since their large vocabularies were not the result of schooling—at least not the result of training within the walls of a classroom—it was evident that the direct connection between their vocabulary and their success was significant in itself.

"A high degree of worldly prosperity"—in other words, a substantial salary—is the dictionary definition of one accepted meaning of success. Without arguing whether this is a worthy definition, let us follow the demonstrated facts to their conclusion. "The measured English vocabulary of an executive correlates with his salary," declares Johnson O'Connor, Human Engineering Laboratories director. "This does not mean that every high-vocabulary person receives a large salary, but the relation between the two is close enough to show that a large vocabulary is one element, and seemingly an important one."

"An extensive knowledge of the exact meanings of English words accompanies outstanding success in this country more often than any other single characteristic which the Human Engineering Laboratories have been able to isolate and measure," writes O'Connor ("Vocabulary and Success," *The Atlantic*).

"Why do large vocabularies characterize executives and possibly outstanding men and women in other fields?" asks O'Connor in summarizing the connection between vocabulary and success. *"The final answer seems to be that words are the instruments by means of which men and women grasp the thoughts of others and with which they do much of their own thinking. They are the tools of thought."*

Words Are Like a Bank Deposit. Your personal set of words is like a bank account. Every time you deposit a new word, you increase your account and it bears more interest. Every new word is another deposit on personal success, a tool for winning friendship.

Can you summon the one word you want when you need it most? The English language offers you three million. A million of these are basic terms. The other two million are grammatical variants. This treasure house lies between the covers of the unabridged dictionary, ready to serve you.

> "Clarke . . . had a gift of knowing instantly the right word. His deft touches lifted stories out of the ordinary. He never hesitated; when he wrote a headline, it was a *Sun* masterpiece. He handled the living language, and was not afraid to use a word or a phrase merely because it was unusual. His pencil slew a million clichés."—Stanley Walker, *City Editor.*

How Professional Experts Make Their Writing Glow. Expert professional writers have the gift of Clarke (described above), city editor of the *Sun*. They know the right word. Their expert touches make their stories glow. Here, for example, is an expert writing for the NBC Television Network. Watch as the descriptive power unfolds:

> No magic Carpet of Bagdad . . . carrying the wishful traveler to that never-never-land of vanished dreams . . . was ever half so wonderful as the daily miracles wrought by modern television. With the flick of a dial the fireside voyager is borne across the atmosphere to those silent, remote kingdoms of eternal snows . . . another flick brings him instantly to a land of Black Magic— where a lemon-colored sun beats mercilessly down upon trackless green oceans of primeval jungle.
>
> NBC-TV invites you to become a member of two unusual expeditions sailing to those lands of mystery beyond the horizon's farthest rim. From one, you can hear the throbbing of native drums beating their cryptic messages through the stifling night . . . or else, you can tune in on the grind and crash of ice floes, as a trim three-master holds a northerly course below the low-hung sun of midnight. Join these two intrepid explorers simply by tuning in your favorite NBC-TV station.

A Space-Age scientist, after discussing giant space stations, orbiting satellites, and massive, rocketing interplanetary space ships, describes with *powerful picture-words* the probable state of affairs on a distant planet:

> These Alpha Twins are so close to their sun that in the constant terrific heat the seas are boiling cauldrons. The land must be a chaos of roaring volcanoes lashing the hot, humid air with giant whips of flame.

When an earnest but awkward sports enthusiast is referred to as playing "Bumble-Puppy" tennis, we picture an almost incomparable exhibit of sheer clumsiness.

An observer watches the great International Cup Race between an American and a British racing yacht:

> Two towering pyramids of canvas, heeled to the breeze, dipping and rolling as the slim hulls under them breast the lazy Atlantic ground swell, sweep across the starting line.

Adapted with factual changes from the *Monsanto Magazine* is this paragraph of sheer picture-power:

> It happens nearly every day now—experimental planes outdazzling the high cirrus, spreading brilliant vapor plumes at speeds in the range of 5,000 miles an hour. Yet it seems only short years ago that the first airman ripped through the sound barrier to record the first official supersonic speed mark. Colonel Horace A. Hanes of the U. S. Air Force, at the controls of his red-hot Satellite Sabre F-500-F zoomed to smashing victory in the Space Age Thompson Trophy Race. Electronic timers clocked his historic flight. For more about the F-500-F Satellite Sabre see "Air Force's Hottest Manned Missile," page 5 of this Air Issue.

A great hotel invites you to use its services. Every word is easy and natural:

> We've made the Sandman night manager in each of our hotels. At bedtime your nightlamp is turned on . . . everything ready for you to slide between the crisp, snowy-white sheets. A bit of chill in the air? Then tuck the fluffy, virgin wool blanket around you—it's featherweight, yet warm as toast. Snap off the light, and sink down into your soft pillow. Take a trip to our own special Land of Nod.

What is the one common thread that runs through all these writings? Whether it be night editor, NBC-TV writer, poet, scientist, essayist, race commentator, foreign reporter, business analyst, or executive, the one common thread that runs through their professional writings is *vivid descriptive power through an expert choice of picture-making words*.

Work for Vivid Picture-Power. Words may be dull or diamond-brilliant, may soothe or may smart like vitriol; may be as downy as ermine or as sharp as needles. Words will project these effects for you—*if* you develop the "Know-how."

> "For me words have colors, form, character . . . moods, humors, eccentricities . . . tints, tones, personalities.
>
> Because people cannot see the color in words, the tints of words . . . Because they cannot hear the whisperings of words, the rustling of the procession of letters . . . Because they cannot perceive . . . the frowning and fuming of words, the weeping, the raging and racketing and rioting of words . . . Because they are insensible to the phosphorescing of words, the fragrance of words . . . the tenderness and hardness of words . . .
>
> Is that any reason why we should not try to make them hear, to make them see, to make them feel?"—Lafcadio Hearn.

The following rugged narrative of an engineering triumph projects the feeling of massive labor. Here you sense throbbing energy and dynamic movement.

> On this, the world's longest petroleum pipe line built as a single construction job, the U. S. and British building crews turned in one of the smoothest jobs of pipe laying ever seen. They had to build camps, dig water wells, run water lines, telephone and telegraph lines. Huge 18-wheel trucks carried the 12-in. pipe in 40-ft. lengths over some of the world's worst terrain. An automatic ditch-digging caterpillar tractor scraped out the 3-foot trench; compressor drills took care of the rock; Texan welders joined the "firing lines" of six or eight lengths; Sudanese painted and poured boiling asphalt over the section, wrapped it in brown paper and lowered it into the trench; and another tractor shoveled the dirt back.

A sleek Diesel-electric locomotive stands, like a lonely giant, in dark silence. To bring this unmoving mass of steel and motors to life requires explosive force in the cylinders. What power is to the locomotive, enthusiasm is to a man—the driving, explosive force. In business writing the vital force that drives a message home is a *live* vocabulary.

Power Your Writing with Colorful Verbs. In the rugged engineering narrative you are carried along with picture verbs like *poured, shoveled, scraped, painted.* Vivid verbs head the list of power-makers.

If you choose the right verb, you may not need the adverb. *Very,* used to intensify, often weakens instead of strengthens the word to which it is linked. For example, in the sentence, "The machine runs very smoothly," you gain no power over that of the sentence, "The machine purrs smoothly." In the latter sentence the verb says it all.

The English language is rich in verbs, hundreds of them dynamic. Note how color fuses into action in the following picture-painters:

alarm	clutch	glare	munch	sling
ally	dangle	glimmer	probe	slip
badger	dare	glitter	pry	snip
beguile	dash	gleam	rake	soothe
caper	dip	glow	ransack	surge
carve	drag	juggle	rivet	swoop
cheer	drive	loaf	rummage	tickle
chill	fidget	lock	skimp	track
chisel	flog	lug	slice	tremble
clang	floor	lunge	slide	wring

Make Your Words Specific. A specific word is one that is definite and explicit in its particular use. For example, an executive of the Goodyear Corporation, stressing the value of *specific* word accuracy, writes:

> The young machinist learns with a jolt that *sliding fit, running fit,* and *driving fit* are not synonymous terms to be used to avoid monotonous repetition, but words describing accurately and specifically a special relation one machine part should bear to another. He learns with a jolt, too, that failure to use each word for its particular, specific purpose is disastrous.

Sliding fit, running fit, and *driving fit* are examples of specific words—words that are definite and explicit in their particular use.

Paint Word-Pictures with Figures of Speech. Figures of speech, founded on concreteness, drive ideas home. They fire the imagination by creating lively pictorial images.

> We cannot find the magic words that will make the spirit march forward off the page and into your Season's joy. We cannot word-mirror the leaping flames that warm the hearth and paint a rosy tint on the deepening twilight. We cannot make our plodding language foretell the dainty jingle of reindeer bells, nor the pearly twinkle of distant stars . . . .

Your attention fastens on the lively movement in the figurative expressions *march forward, word-mirror, paint, plodding, foretell, jingle, twinkle.*

GENERALIZED, ABSTRACT, DULL	FORCEFUL FIGURES OF SPEECH
Let us discuss the fundamental factors involved here.	Let's get down to *bedrock*.
Many new roads will be built.	The country will be *ribboned* with new highways.
The clock showed that it was getting close to midnight and that another day was almost over.	The clock hands closed *like scissor blades* on midnight, *snipping* off another day.
When you reduce it simply to the essential facts. . . .	When you *boil it all down.* . . .

Vivid "comparison" figures of speech generate force in these sentences from a business report of the Westinghouse Electric Corporation:

> The most delicate meters made by Westinghouse use wire *like the strands of gossamer:* .0008 of an inch in diameter, or about *one fourth as thick as a human hair.* The wheels turn on pivots *ten times as sharp as a sewing needle.* Wheels and bearings are gold-plated *like a treasured cup* to prevent corrosion in the delicate gears of the registering mechanism. Our meters can measure almost any level of electrical energy, from an output *as tiny as one tenth of a fly-power,* to a gigantic rush of energy *as huge as that of the entire Boulder Dam.*

Develop Your Own Vocabulary. How many words does the average person use? How large is his "talking" vocabulary? How many words can be understand when he reads? In Dr. Silverthorn's study * a High Frequency Business Vocabulary Word List of approximately 5,000 of the most frequently used words was compiled from among 11,564 different words in 300,000 running words (total occurrences of all words) occurring in business communications. Here are the results:

1. The 10 commonest words (in the order named) are *the, of, to, and, in, you, a, for, we,* and *your.*

2. The total occurrences of the first 50 words accounted for approximately 45 per cent of the occurrences of all words.

3. The total occurrences of the first 500 words accounted for approximately 70 per cent of the occurrences of all words.

4. The total occurrences of the first 5,000 words accounted for approximately 95 per cent of the occurrences of all words.

* James Edwin Silverthorn, *The Basic Vocabulary of Written Business Communications,* Ed.D. Thesis, Indiana University, June, 1955.

An adult with a small range of information can understand three thousand words when he reads; a businessman or a skilled technician, ten thousand; a college graduate, twenty thousand. So concludes the editor of a leading dictionary.

How to Multiply *Said* 220 Times. One of the more frequently used words is *said*. Would you suspect that it really represents not less than 220 other words? You can translate *said* into not less than 220 vivid substitutes, each of which is descriptively more specific and more powerful than its mother-word! Here are a few of the 220:

VIVID OFFSHOOTS OF THE VERB *SAID*

announced	cried	exclaimed	grumbled	promised
argued	declared	explained	hinted	recommended
blurted	denied	exploded	insisted	responded
burst out	drawled	faltered	maintained	whispered
conceded	droned	growled	predicted	yelled

(and there are one hundred and ninety-five more!)

You can quickly build your own word power if you try this "breakdown" exercise on other words you often use.

Never Poison Your Writing with "Commercialese"

With the huge surge in the American population, thousands upon thousands more people are writing today than ever before. Each business day breeds a new crop of employees, most of whom have never had any training and perhaps never will have any training in the stern requirements of effective communication.

Today, for example, in New York City alone, a hundred brand-new correspondents are sitting down to new jobs in a hundred offices writing messages *poisoned* with "Commercialese" and reeking with the musty smell of "We are in receipt of your esteemed favor of the 10th inst. and in reply wish to state . . ." Why does anyone write like this?

Where Does "Commercialese" Come From? The New York Life Insurance Company suggests one explanation: "We believe that 'Commercialese' is still widely used because, as business and industry have grown, more and more people are called upon to do the writing

that business and industry demand. Most of these people are un-
trained and unskilled, perhaps even unsuited for the work. People
with little or no training or experience are still being encouraged to
write messages and reports for business and industry. The language
they use is 'Commercialese' either because they have learned it in a
misguided school or because they have discovered it in the company
files. Seeing it in the files and thinking it 'sounds businesslike,' they
poison themselves with the old 'Commercialese' infection." And so
the disease flourishes, choking off progress to better communication,
better management, and better human relations.

"Commercialese" Poisons Messages. The office door is open. Our
ears catch a droning voice dictating:

> Gentlemen: In reply to your favor of the tenth instant, comma,
> in which you give facts to support your claim for credit with us,
> comma, we beg to advise you that same is inadequate from the
> point of view of our company, period, paragraph.
> Although we regret that the information given us makes it
> impossible to grant credit as requested, comma, we will fill your
> order provided check is sent in advance as specified per our quo-
> tation of recent date, period, paragraph.
> Trusting this arrangement will be entirely satisfactory, and
> regretting that we are unable to extend credit on an open account
> at this time, comma, we beg to remain, comma. . . .

And the voice drones on. If this message were not so typical of
many still being dictated, its hopelessly old-fashioned phrases would
seem a laughable travesty. But there is also a second defect. The
tone of the message is so offensive that it would not be surprising if
the reader were never to place another order with the concern. This
dictator is an active "business-killer" through his use of faulty language and negative tone.

The poison of "Commercialese" (the stock phrase) is one that
has been passed down from father to son. A century or two ago it
was both polite and correct for gentlemen to write to one another
in elevated and artificial language. Today the remaining evidence
of this early style is the hackneyed jargon illustrated in the dictated
example given above.

Mumbo-Jumbo Jargon: KILL IT OFF! Unless you use your
own TALK-language in your own natural way, you may fall into the
mumbo-jumbo trap of such laughable expressions as *beg to advise*
and *trusting this meets with your approval*—expressions still to be

enclosed herewith
hoping to hear
from you soon
in reply we
wish to advise
thanking you
in advance
trusting this is
satisfactory
ultimo, proximo,
instant

Get Rid of "Commercialese" in Your Messages!

found in messages of miserable quality. Such kinds of "Commercialese" are sometimes called "boilerplate," possibly because their cast-iron jargon makes any message slightly ridiculous. To get rid of only the stock phrases would cut the length of the average message a third—so calculated one management executive after a study of carbon copies of messages sent from his company.

WOULD YOU APPROVE THIS?

In reply to your inquiry of the 26th inst., wish to advise that the writer is contemplating a trip to your city December second or third, and will then call on you.

We also wish to state that we have a very nice line of textured fabrics and feel quite certain that we will have what you want in our line of sketches.

Thanking you for your inquiry, we beg to remain,

This message is smothered in a mass of dull wordage. Its writer missed a great chance to highlight his coming. His task was to make the reader want to see his sketches.

THIS IS HOW IT WAS ACTUALLY SENT

Thank you for your letter of November 28, inviting me to come over to show you some of our interesting fabrics. I expect to reach York on December 2 or 3. Just as soon as I arrive, I'll arrange to call at a time convenient to you.

Our distinctive work in textured draperies, in which you have expressed interest, will please you. I shall also bring along my illustrated brochures and some hand-drawn designs.

Your invitation is indeed appreciated.

Conversational Warmth. How many banking officials this very day may be dictating stiffly
some such "Commercialese" as this? "We hereby
acknowledge your remittance of April 23 in the
amount of $377.45 and wish to state that it has
been duly credited to your account." Cold . . .
frigid . . . zero.

Many modern bankers are just as warm, just
as approachable, as businessmen in other fields. Like other business
groups, they have learned that business is friendship, not warfare.

They have learned, further, that one secret of
power is to *use simple words in* TALK-*language.*
So they write: "Thank you for the remittance
of $377.45 sent in on April 23. We take pleasure
in crediting it to your account." Or, with equal
simplicity and warmth of tone, "We take pleasure in crediting to your account the remittance
of $377.45 sent in on April 23."

"Power" Your Openings. Use one of these three strong types of
openings:

1. Show action that has been taken.

> Mr. C. T. Allenby, our treasurer, has just reported to
> me the figures on the excellent showing you made in your
> recent regional sales program.

> The Directors, after conferring with our departmental
> executives, have decided to accept your recommendation of
> April 5.

2. Express pleasure or regret.

> We are pleased indeed to hear of your favorable action
> on the Intertype Contract.

> Thank you for your May remittance of $350.

3. Make a specific statement.

> The first group of officials from our company will
> arrive at your office at noon, July 25.

> The profit margin for February, about which you inquire
> in your note of March 10, is 3%.

You will add power, variety, and originality through the use
of these three procedures, or a reasonable combination of them.

AVOID THESE "OBSOLETES"

How NOT to Open a Message

Replying to your inquiry, we would say
We have your inquiry, and in reply will say
Referring to [*or* Answering] your inquiry
Yours received and contents noted and in reply

NATURAL, DIRECT	"COMMERCIALESE"
We are glad to send you the information asked for in your inquiry of June 21 about the current Continental program.	We have received your inquiry of June 21, in which you ask about the current Continental program. In reply we wish to state that we shall be glad to give you the information requested.

"Power" Your Closings. Your closing gives the final impression. An experienced trial lawyer, in making his closing argument, may end on a crashing crescendo of emotional appeal or may lower his voice to a whisper. These skilled men stage their endings. They want their parting words to clinch their efforts. Messages, too, should end with force. But if they are to end with force, every stale, hackneyed, and commonplace expression must be sheared away.

Closings, like openings, attract "Commercialese." Any participial conclusion (an expression beginning with *thanking, trusting, hoping, assuring, believing,* or the like) is "Commercialese" (a stock phrase). NEVER USE IT!

The Golden Secret: "Be NATURAL." The golden secret of good writing is to *be natural.* "It's always a pleasure to meet new friends," writes an expert management executive as the first sentence of a message welcoming new customers. "You feel it in business just as you do in everyday life." That writing is good because it is natural talk. Address the reader as if you were speaking to him naturally. Visualize him as an interesting visitor sitting on the other side of your desk. Then simply *talk* to him—using your words carefully.

"I am talking to my reader as if he were now with me *right here,*" you say to yourself. "The only reason I am putting my words down on this paper is that his distance from me requires it. He's not actually here, I know—but I'm vividly visualizing him exactly as if he were."

"There's a trick to visualizing," says a sales management executive. "When I'm about to write to a dozen of my customers, I choose one I know well. Then I turn to my secretary and I say, 'Miss Ainslie, I'd like to talk to Jack Trimble about our color television line for next season.' Then I picture Jack Trimble sitting across from me . . . and I just have a little *talk* with him for a few moments. Of course I know—before I start—what I'm going to say. But when I do start, I *talk* to Jack . . . I don't write an essay. It's as simple as that."

The Short Guide to Success. Top management constantly looks for people—carefully trained, intelligent, promising people—who know how to use the powerful tool of conversational, well-planned talk, put handsomely on paper; who, in short, know how to apply the seven steps to success set forth at the left. If you can master

1. Write in TALK-language.
2. Use familiar words.
3. Use action verbs.
4. Fit your terms to your reader's experience.
5. "Red-pencil" all needless words.
6. Work for simplicity.
7. Keep sentences reasonably short, but use variety and change of pace.

these seven basic steps, if you can "TALK-write" with the same personal force and conversational directness that guide an interview between two people on opposite sides of a desk, your road to success is assured. It is assured because you will have learned how to deal with people in friendship and understanding through the use of expertly chosen talk-words. This ability you will find priceless throughout your career.

Communication Problems

● 1. Sportswriters are often required to seek descriptive words that will enable them to avoid repetition in recording game results. In baseball season, for example, we find the following typical sports headlines:

Cubs *Win* 4th Straight	Nats Rally to *Defeat* Bosox
Giants *Belt* Dodgers	Braves *Stop* Philadelphia
Tigers *Rip* Tribe	Redlegs *Hang Setback* on Pirates

Directions: Study samples of your own writing or examples from your business message collection. Underline each commonplace, colorless verb; then, substitute a vivid, forceful word or figure of speech. See how well you can change drabness into concrete, picturesque writing.

Make a list of the colorless, commonplace verbs. In a separate column opposite the first list, make a list of the new words or phrases you substituted.

● **2.** The following message is full of hackneyed words and expressions that should be avoided because they rob the message of individuality. Furthermore, they contribute nothing to the effectiveness of the writing.

Directions: Read the message carefully and underline all the hackneyed words and expressions; then, rewrite it, striving for individuality of expression. Set the material up in whatever style you wish. Supply any needed elements to make the form complete.

In compliance with your request of the 9th inst., we wish to advise you that a copy of our latest catalog is being mailed to you in due time by parcel post. Upon receipt of same you will want to take advantage of the values noted by placing your order in the near future.

May we take this liberty of inviting you to visit our store at your earliest convenience. Our Mr. Quill will be happy to show you our fine line of merchandise and help you with reference to your needs.

Please be assured that we look forward to the privilege of your patronage. The writer also wishes to state you will find our merchandise different from that of most competing firms.

Trusting to be of service to you, I am

● **3.** A major heading in this chapter reads, "For Better Human Relations, Use TALK-Language." Following that is a paragraph heading which reads, "Please Tell Me in One-Syllable Words What You Mean." Check the following paragraph of a message from one of the major universities in the United States.

Many more examples could be given of the willingness of nations and of individuals to work for a better world, even though there is not complete agreement as to the best methods to use. Each one of us has his own notions; but in order to reach valid conclusions, we must have adequate background information, and an opportunity to test out the conflicting ideas. A summer session offers a wonderful opportunity to propound your theories in free discussion with your classmates, in an environment conducive to the acquisition of new ideas and free from the harassments of the daily job that can so often destroy one's perspective. The School of Education offers many opportunities for such discussions, together with a full program of courses, activities, and workshops in over twenty different departments. A copy of our summer bulletin is yours for the asking; merely fill out and mail the enclosed postcard. PLEASE NOTE! If you intend to enroll in any of the 19— Summer Sessions of the School of Education, be sure to ask for a copy of the special instructions on registration procedures. If you live more than fifty miles from New York City, you may complete registration by mail.

Does this letter use TALK-language? Obviously not. Many of the words are multisyllable and of a general nature.

Directions: Rewrite the paragraph. Try to make the illustrations and expressions more concrete. Make the paragraph more concise. Bring in the YOU-attitude. Strive for clearness. Try to be conversationally persuasive.

● 4. Study the section entitled "Toward a More Picturesque Speech" in several issues of the *Reader's Digest*. Note how writing can be made vivid and colorful by the mere turn of a phrase or the adroit use of a picturesque word. Then reread the illustrative paragraphs on pages 152, 153, 155, and 156 of this book to see how figures of speech and descriptive words can be used to paint word-pictures.

Directions: (a) Make a list of the picturesque words and expressions used to paint word-pictures in the business messages you have in your collection.

(b) Study some of the paragraphs and messages you have written. What words or expressions have you used that would qualify as picturesque or picture-painters?

(c) Rewrite one of the messages from your collection. Use words that will cause the reader to stop, recognize, and appreciate your word-pictures. Submit both the original message and your revision of it to your instructor.

● 5. Revise the following sentences taken from actual business messages. All are examples of poor human relations.

a. Since you completely ignored my last note, I am going to demand an explanation of the extra charges as shown on my payment record card.

b. As an ordinary agent you would not find it profitable to handle this class of business, so we have decided to restrict its sale to our combination agents.

c. The sale was made to you in good faith and we have gone to considerable expense in connection with the sale and delivery of this order to you.

d. Naturally we are extremely anxious to retain all our charge customers and we dislike to enter into any controversy over the matter, but we think we are entitled to the courtesy of an explanation of your silence.

e. We are always ready and willing to rectify our mistakes, but we like to know that they are our mistakes.

f. Your complaint indicates considerable misunderstanding—either of our reply or of marketing procedure.

g. It seems that within the past year or two, our customers have taken an unfair advantage of our liberal policy.

h. You say you have had several complaints but that is nothing for us to go by, so please let us know what ads were left off and what ads were misspelled or misplaced and we will be glad to make these corrections.

i. We are sorry to learn of the difficulties which have been encountered and are sorry that we are unable to help you further in this complaint.

j. Really, Mrs. Adams, we are as embarassed to write this note as you will be to receive it.

PART III Effective Dictation: Vital Management Tool

Chapter 8   *How to Dictate a Business Letter*

The Power of TALK-Writing

Top Management Calls for Expert Dictators. Talk to any top management executive. He will tell you this: "Show me a person who knows my business and *who is an expert dictator*, and I'll hire him on the spot. And the salary I'll pay him may be bigger than he expects!"

What *makes* a dictator an expert? First of all, he obviously must know something about words—not *big* words, not long words, not pompous words, not polysyllabic words, not sesquipedalian words, not "nine-dollar-and-seventy-five-cent" words—but simple, clear, accurate, tested, clean-cut, *conversational TALK-words that anybody can understand.*

Next, he must know something about people—what kind of feelings they have, and how they react to the words used. He must feel a normal friendliness toward people, be ready to show considerateness, be constantly alert to see the other fellow's point of view. As one management expert puts it: If you don't like people, *don't dictate!*

COME DOWN OUT OF THE CLOUDS

Not Pompous Words, Not "$9.75" Words!

Come down out of the clouds and use simple TALK-words that anybody can understand.

Be Yourself When You Dictate. Would you like to find out how you can learn to dictate forcefully? Would you like to discover the hidden secret of powerful dictation? Would you like to discover what kind of magic the experts put into their dictated words to get their successful results? Would you like to find out what they do to build up such high word power? The secret is this: they follow the magic guide words: "BE YOURSELF."

This "magic" really sounds quite simple when you put it down in black and white and tell exactly what it is, step by step. But a word of caution: It isn't quite so simple as it sounds, even though the experts make it seem so. In fact you may have to practice the art of being your "informal self" for quite a while to "get the hang of it."

The Curious Case of Bill Wright. Bill Wright is as nice a chap as you'd want to meet. He has a warm, outgoing personality. He is respected for his integrity, his thoughtfulness of others, and his business keenness. As an insurance man he is moderately successful. People buy from him because they like him. His way of doing business is to sell himself first and his insurance second. But the other day Bill had an experience that brought him up short.

A large department store in his city brought in a new manager. Reading about it in his newspaper, and trained to be alert to this kind of development, Bill immediately wrote to the new man, asking for an appointment.

Silence. No reply. Naturally, Bill was puzzled. Then a week later he met the new manager face to face at a Chamber of Commerce luncheon, and the two got acquainted. The manager was immediately at ease with Bill and obviously liked him. A little farther along in the visit, he said:

"I have a confession to make. You wrote me a letter recently, asking for an appointment. I guess it was rude of me, but I didn't answer it—on purpose. I hope you won't take this the wrong way, but when I read that letter I thought, 'He must be a stuffed shirt.' It wasn't what you said—it was just the *tone* you used. Now that I've met you I know I was mistaken. I'll be glad to get together with you. It was just that your letter gave me a false impression of you." [Adapted from an actual case in the files of the New York Life Insurance Company.]

Bill's problem is a common one with inexperienced dictators. It is also a problem with a great many veteran dictators who ought to know better!

Dictation—Have You Checked Yours Lately? The people of Johns-Manville Corporation put it excellently in a handbook entitled "Letters—Have You Read Your Own Lately?": "Give him a typewriter, and a gal to punch it, and the average nice guy can manage to sound like the most pompous, thundering bore who ever lived. Meaningless and confusing phrases roll out, and out, and out—and some poor reader has to unscramble them."

Yet all the "average nice guy" has to do to get *started toward* effective dictation is to use the same language you use with people in your own home— the unadorned, common-garden variety of language you use in your daily life, the simple straightforward words that sound like you, and that people easily understand. But, as Bill Wright discovered, this is not an easy thing to do.

> *"Except ye utter by the tongue words easy to be understood, how shall it be known what is spoken? For ye shall speak into the air."*
>
> CORINTHIANS I — 14:9

Why? Because, lurking around the corner ready to trip you up and make you fall on your face, are such ancient dictation wheeze-boxes as *beg to state, contents duly noted, has come to hand, in answer to same, in conclusion would state, please be advised, trusting to receive same,* and *thanking you in anticipation*—and all the other ancient horse-and-buggy claptrap that no one would dream of using in ordinary conversation.

In dictating that way, inexperienced beginners convey to their readers a false "stuffed shirt" impression of themselves—exactly like Bill Wright, who almost cost himself an interview and a good prospect. Remember this: the person to whom you dictate doesn't know whether you handle hundreds of letters every week on the same subject in your company. He doesn't care either. He is interested in just the one piece of dictation he gets from you. He forms his picture of your company, your methods, and your interest in him as he reads, line by line, the words you dictated. If all he gets from you is a lot of rumbling logwood—similar to the ancient wheeze-box examples in the previous paragraph—he will certainly put the wrong tag on you and your company. You will both lose.

Dictate Your Way to Better Human Relations

Top Management Experts Call for IMPROVEMENT in Dictation. In calling for vast improvement in dictation practices, the top management experts do not "pull their punches." C. B. Larrabee, President and Publisher of *Printers' Ink*, writes: "How many millions of dollars are wasted each year because of poor, fuzzy, incoherent communication, it's impossible to estimate. Executive direc-

tives are not carried out properly because the man who makes them has not explained himself well enough so that his associates understand his wishes clearly.

"Busy executives at the end of busy days find themselves drowsing over memoranda of the greatest importance, because the men who wrote the memoranda express themselves with a dull ponderousness that can be found only in business communication. Stilted, overdone, outworn phrases continue to crop up.

"Today a few large companies conduct courses in communication for minor executives. *Nobody quite has the boldness to suggest similar courses to top brass. Yet in many companies the men at the top try to communicate with their immediate associates and with the people on the lower levels of the organization chart in language that is dull, opaque, and time-and-word wasting.*

"The art of clear, coherent communication," concludes experienced authority Larrabee, "will advance in great strides once executives realize that *the prolific writers of today* are not the professional staff and free-lance writers for the business press but *the men who dictate the letters and memoranda that are an essential part of the modern business operation."*

An Experienced Dictator Tells How He Does It. A top management executive, veteran of many years of dictation, describes his procedure:

> In beginning dictation I make a statement indicating to my reader that this letter concerns something in which he is interested. Reference to the date of his letter and to the subject is subordinated and brought in incidentally.
>
> Before beginning, I spend a minute or two mulling over the circumstances, the idea I wish to convey, the probable attitude of the reader, his interests, what will appeal to him, and so on. I visualize him at his desk or wherever he is likely to be when he reads my letter; my visualization includes his surroundings and his associates.
>
> Since I desire his complete attention, I speak so that at the moment my letter is more important to him than anything else. I consider what I would say to him if I were greeting him in his office or home and talking to him face to face. This keeps me from writing something that would sound foolish and silly if spoken to him in person.
>
> At some point in my thought I find myself ready to dictate. At once I start speaking. Note that I do not start dictating until I have clearly in mind what I am going to say. The silent pause may seem embarrassing to the stenographer, but since I am not writing to her, that aspect is unimportant. Nevertheless, I have had the experience many times, when dictating, of having the stenographer herself answer some question I have dictated, just as though I were speaking to her. I have been told that this is the highest form of praise a dictator may receive. I do not know. I do believe, however, that if what I say sounds natural to the stenographer, it will sound natural to the reader.[—*Bulletin* of the American Business Writing Association.]

Number Your Letters to Save Time. Number your letters and save dictating time. Experienced executives, going through the morning's pack of mail, number letters that require an answer. Then, instead of consuming time dictating the names and addresses of persons to whom letters are to go, the dictator says, "Letter No. 1," and follows immediately with the appropriate salutation and message. Then he continues with "Letter No. 2" with salutation and message. As he completes his dictation of each message, he hands to the secretary the letter he is answering. If he is using a dictating machine, he places the numbered letter in the proper order in his dictation folder. · When the secretary transcribes the dictation, she simply takes the names and addresses from those incoming letters. So—number your letters and save everybody's time.

Speak Clearly! Whether your words are being recorded by the flying pen or pencil of a secretary or by the high-fidelity mechanism of a dictating machine, *speaking clearly is at least half the art of dictation.*

Enunciate each syllable distinctly. Do not slur. When dictated material is no longer fresh, the transcriber must rely wholly on symbols for sounds, just as she must rely wholly on the clearness of your articulation on a machine. Hence the effective dictator must strive to pronounce distinctly, to utter each vowel and syllable with care, to speak slowly, and to gather the words into intelligible groups. Paragraphs and special punctuation should be indicated. Proper or unusual names should first be pronounced and then spelled. In brief, everything possible should be done to ease and smooth the path of the transcriber.

Here Is What Can Happen! Some of the errors that spring out of dictation-into-transcription are amusing, some amazing, and some unbelievable.

Between such words as *affect-effect, accept-except, access-excess*, and the like, confusion is easy. You can help to cure this confusion with super-clear pronunciation and better secretarial training. Anyone with office experience will understand the Boston *Transcript* language-confusion story of "The Misconstrued Phrases." The original was, "It rained here." Of three listeners, the first heard "a trained deer"; the second, "the train, dear"; and the third, "a trained ear."

—*Dale McFeatters and Publishers Syndicate, Inc.*

"Very good, Miss Frilly. Only five misspelled words—now let's look at the second sentence!"

Look at these before-and-after examples:

WHAT THE DICTATOR SAID:	WHAT THE STENOGRAPHER TYPED:
He *acceded to* these restrictions.	He *exceeded* these restrictions.
Archimedes said . . .	*Our committees* said . . .
If possible, find a *fifteen-inch* ruler.	If possible, find a *fifty-ditch river.*
This will *enable* us to close the deal.	This will *unable* us to close the deal.
I can *heartily* reciprocate your good wishes.	I can *hardly* reciprocate your good wishes.
It is not wise to *mix* type *faces.*	It is not wise to *skip* type *spaces.*

Dictate at an Even Rate and Group Words Naturally. Dictate at an even rate of speed. Avoid spurts and rushes intermingled with long pauses. If you first think your sentence through, you can then deliver your words evenly. Let your sentences fall into their natural phrases and word groups in order to help your transcriber get the logical sense. Note the natural word grouping of the following sentence, just as it is dictated:

The Electronic Drive/ of the Simplex Imperial/ about which you ask/ in your inquiry of May 10/ can be easily inspected/ by releasing the clamps/ on the ends of the inspection plate/ and slipping the plate to one side.

The hesitation between word groups may be so slight as not to be noticed. Without in any way interrupting the continuity, you give just enough rhythm to indicate the sense.

TALK Your Writing onto the Page. Some of the most natural, most conversational messages ever prepared were made so because they were *talked.* The sender *talked* his words conversationally onto the paper. He "saw" his reader in his mind's eye and talked directly to him as if he were sitting just over there on the other side of the desk.

The secret of good dictating is careful talking based on clear, straight thinking. Approach every dictating situation in a *talking* frame of mind. Of course, *simply dictating a message does not assure you that it will be conversational.* It merely helps. Contradictory though it may seem, some of the most cast-iron boiler-plate messages ever composed were dictated. On the other hand, some of the freshest and most naturally conversational messages were first carefully written in longhand.

The act of *talking* a message makes it natural and easy only if your attitude when you dictate reflects the same natural warmth that your personal conversation does. Naturalness and conversational ease come not from any physical act of your tongue, teeth, and lips, but from the attitude of relaxed friendliness toward the person who will soon read your words. If you can translate your natural friendliness into simple and unassuming words, you'll gain conversational ease.

How to Put Straight Thinking on Paper. The executive who dictates effective messages knows something about straight thinking and how to find and use the tools by which he can put straight thinking into the secretary's notebook or onto the recording mechanism of a dictating machine.

To put straight thinking into dictation, you must use certain tools, too. These tools have been tested by experts so many millions of times that they are known to be absolutely essential in the equipment kit of every dictator, every secretary, and every management executive.

The basic parts of speech—nouns, verbs, adjectives, and all the rest—are the basic tools by which you put straight thinking into effective dictation.

You will also use other equipment such as sentences, the "thought carriers"; punctuation, the "traffic control"; and paragraphs, the "thought groupers."

In your unabridged dictionary you own a treasure house—a rich reservoir of 600,000 words. When you bring some of these words together in related order, you make them reflect your personality. Your character "comes off the page." You emerge from the words. You step out of your dictated lines, and you deliver your message with personal force.

Dictating Teamwork. Superior dictating ability is something that top management demands. Consider some parallel examples: You want your car to be serviced by a mechanic who knows the difference between a radiator and a crankshaft, between a water pump and a fuel pump, between a throttle arm and a cylinder head. You want your office desk to be repaired by a carpenter who knows the difference between a brace and bit and a crosscut saw. You want your typing done by a typist who knows the difference between lower-case and capital letters, between tabulator key and margin set. By the same reasoning top management wants dictation to go down on paper through the expert service of dictators and secretaries who know the tools of good expression and who have been trained to put these tools to expert use.

"I Dictate the First Paragraph. Then I Listen Back." A successful executive was asked why his dictation "pulled" so well. "I dictate the first paragraph," he said. "Then I listen back to see whether I have got off to a fresh, fast start."

If every writer "listened back" to his dictated opening paragraph, he might often decide to burn his first attempt and start over. If this were done, more messages would hit the bull's-eye and fewer would hit the reader's wastebasket.

—Dale McFeatters and Publishers Syndicate, Inc.

". . . And in taking this letter, Miss Filbert, please don't ad lib!"

How Experienced Dictators Do Their Work

The Eight Secrets of Powerful Dictation. To follow the procedure of experienced dictators, here is what the experts will tell you to do:

1. Organize your materials
2. Make marginal notes
3. Gather needed data
4. Visualize your reader
5. Kill off "Freeze-up" and "Dictatoritis"
6. Dictate in simple TALK-language
7. Be positive and helpful in tone
8. Dictate with an occasional "color-flash"

Now let us take a closer look at each of these eight suggestions, to see exactly how each one may be applied to make dictation results more successful through greater power.

(1) Organize Your Materials. To save your own time, your secretary's time, and your reader's time, organize your materials. First, see what facts are actually needed, how the facts should be arranged, and what should come first and last. Organize your facts into related groups and put them into thought units, each of which is clear in itself and in relation to the other thought units.*

As a dictator you will deal with two chief classes of correspondence: (1) messages to be answered and (2) messages that you yourself originate. The amount of planning and organizing needed to handle a given message depends on the set of facts with which it deals.

(2) Make Marginal Notes. Make marginal notes at points where these guides will prove

The Dictator's Plan Chart

1. What is the purpose of the message? Decide before you write what you want to accomplish—just what the actual message is.

2. What correspondence has gone before? What is the background of the message? Will it help to read over the file of correspondence?

3. What idea can you find to begin your message that will immediately arouse your reader's interest? Some aspect of the situation will make a good opening wedge. Can you find it?

4. What is likely to be the recipient's attitude? Are you asking something he will want to do? Must he be persuaded? How much does he know about it?

5. Why is it to his advantage to do what you want him to do? Some advantages always exist in a given course of action. Can you pick out concrete advantages to the reader in this case?

6. What information does he need to make his decision? He may not know as much about the subject as you do. Can you give him enough information to bring him to a decision?

7. What final "hook" can you put in the message that will help to arouse the recipient to immediate action?

helpful. In answering incoming letters, you will find it helpful to make marginal notes on items to be included, topics to be covered, and points to be emphasized. Such penciled marginal notes make certain that you will cover all the important points. For example, if you are answering a request, you may jot down brief notes on each of the points you plan to make in your reply. You may also find it convenient to pencil these in the margin in the order of their importance. If you are answering an inquiry, you pencil a guide note of perhaps half-a-dozen words that will remind you to tell your reader in the first sentence what he wants to know. (For example, in the margin: "Tell Richards we'll bring both portfolios and ten Verifax copies.")

---

* You will have interesting opportunities to put this procedure into practice in the projects and cases at the end of this chapter.

With each new task you become more familiar with analyzing dictating situations and with sizing up the type of people to whom you are "letter talking." You thus improve your grasp on your materials and gradually are able to retain in your mind most of the points to be covered, instead of jotting them all down in the margins. But until you have reached this point, you will find it most helpful to continue your marginal guide notes as dictation guides.

An interesting modern development is the use of marginal notes as a dictator-shortcut, particularly useful in handling within-the-company correspondence. Note the five steps in the shortcut:

1. The original communication comes in.
2. The reader pencils his reply or comment in the margin.
3. An exact duplicate reproduction copy (using Verifax or a similar copying device) is then made, showing the original message and the penciled marginal comments.
4. The *Verifax copy* is returned to the writer of the original letter.
5. The original message, with its penciled marginal reply (or comment) is permanently filed at the receiving office.

This "marginal note" exchange comprises the entire correspondence file.

(3) Gather Needed Data. The next step is to gather needed data —the information you will need at your desk in order to dictate complete replies and to prepare original messages of your own.

Suppose, for example, you have to stop in the midst of your dictation to search for more information. Or suppose reference sheets containing essential names, dates, or figures are incomplete or missing. Because of such interruptions you are forced to have your dictation "repeated back" so many times to remind you of what you have already said that your sentences are liable to emerge loose and ill-constructed. If, on the other hand, you have gathered all the essential data and have jotted down adequate marginal guide notes, you can "hold the letter-talking mood," call at will upon the correct facts, put them in the right order, and compose fluent and conversational sentences in your own natural manner.

(4) Visualize Your Reader. Sometimes dictators have too little knowledge of the people who are to read their words. Naturally they have trouble communicating with people they do not know. Not only are such messages hard to dictate, but they are also usually impersonal and cold.

To dictate a warm, friendly, effective message you need to know something about the reader, his characteristics, his needs, his wants, and his interests. In each case your dictation should be based on what you know about the individual. You can often learn something about him before you begin talking with him—from letters he has dictated to you, from reports about him that have come to you from field salesmen, from magazine or newspaper articles about him, or from your own company files. Often you can learn his age, his occupation, whether he is married, and if he has a family. When you have points of identification like these, you can personalize your reader and create, from your facts, a real "three-dimensional" person.

As you learn more about each of the persons with whom you correspond, you file this information systematically. Many good dictators who follow exactly this practice report that dictation is much easier and that they can power their words more accurately as they accumulate this information and develop a closer understanding of each individual correspondent.

Visualize your reader as you dictate. Use his name occasionally in your dictation. To do so helps to focus your thoughts directly upon him. Picture how he looks. View him in your mind. *There he is*—see him? He's sitting across from you on the other side of *your* desk. He's interested in what you want to tell him. He's listening carefully, attentively. *Talk* to *him* as a flesh-and-blood person.

Build up his picture in three dimensions. Glance at him now and then while you are dictating. The more you practice visualizing, the more real it becomes, and the more naturally and easily you dictate. This is really what you do every time you pick up your telephone. The moment you hear the voice at the other end of the line, you start visualizing an image of the person behind that voice. Then you talk to that image you've pictured. Do the same thing when you dictate.

A Westinghouse Electric Corporation bulletin sets up an interesting parallel: "Suppose," it says, "that you are going to telephone to a distant customer. It's your final opportunity. You won't get another chance. Your customer is in a last-minute rush, impatient of every interruption. So time is precious.

"Before you lift the receiver, you plan just what you are going to say, you plan how to make every word count. You try in your first words to show your customer that your message is important to him, gives facts that he needs. As far as you can, you anticipate questions

he may ask, by giving him the answers. Your language is conversational, courteous, and friendly. You are 'saying it with a smile.'

"Perhaps," says Westinghouse, "some of our letters might be improved if we would dictate exactly what we would say if we were talking by telephone to a busy man, at $2 a minute, with the understanding that we would not get another chance."

(5) Kill Off "Freeze-Up" and "Dictatoritis." A typical affliction of the young executive about to dictate his morning's grist is the "personal freeze-up" when he starts to speak. This "freeze-up" may hit him or descend upon him or roll over him with the icy blight of a glacial chill. All this may happen the moment he starts to speak to the stenographer or into the microphone of his dictating machine.

He gets a bad case of dictator's jitters and microphone fright. He *freezes*. Has it ever happened to you?

What do you do to combat that old devil, "Freeze-Up"? The remedy is simple: You ask yourself, "What am I trying to say?"

"What do I want to tell him?" "How would I say it if he were standing right here with me and we were just 'shooting the breeze'?" "How would I put this thing if I were just saying it to a pal?" Then say it that way and keep on saying it that way. You'll never suffer from microphone freeze again.

If you have a tendency to get all wound up in "stuffed-shirt" words—and what a painfully common affliction this is—then you are suffering from the insidious disease of "Dictatoritis."

"Dictatoritis" sneaks up on you. You think you're doing fine. You "barrel" along with *therefores* and *thereafters, hereinbefores* and *hereinafters, hereins, whereins,* and *thereins*—not to mention a few *to-wits* and *please be adviseds.* How all this stuff does roll out in a fine baritone or even a smooth mezzo-soprano! The thought may not keep up— but the words sound fine. That is, they sound fine until you look back over them to figure out what it is you said. Or maybe you're a lucky one, free from all that rattling claptrap, and you wouldn't be caught dictating such silly stuff. But maybe your type of "Dictatoritis" is that you RAMBLE.

Some beginners, failing to organize their materials and to make marginal notes, ramble in endless circles and lose themselves in the dark forests of their own verbiage.

What should you do to combat this fault? The answer is supremely simple: *Think each sentence through to its end before you begin to dictate.* Keep each sentence short. For example, try ten or twenty words. Then stop. Put a period there. Start a new sentence. There's your cure. You're rid of rambling.

(6) Dictate in Simple TALK-Language. Say to yourself, "There's a friendly acquaintance across from me. He's sitting right there just a short distance from me. I'm just going to carry on an easy conversation with him. I'm not going to be afraid to use the same easy words I use every day: morning, afternoon, and night. I think he'll like that."

Just as you get more natural power using TALK-words, so you'll get more natural power dictating TALK-language. Remember once again that friendly acquaintance a short distance from you. You're talking to him in simple, natural language— the kind he's used to. Power your dictation with conversational language that is natural to you. Then you can safely wager that it will be natural to

TALK WORDS ONTO THE PAPER

him because your words will seem warm and comfortable. Send *yourself* along with your dictation. Then when your message reaches its goal, your easy words will bring you out of your envelope and off the written page—almost in person—to talk to your reader.

Some modern dictators *talk* their salutations in a highly effective way:

Yes, Jim:

We still set up our personnel interviews as we used to do when you were here. . . .

Use TALK-language . . . yes . . . but NOT careless talk. Good dictation keeps all the virtues, but avoids the faults of easy conversation. As you know, the common fault of hasty conversation is its incomplete expression of ideas, its careless organization of thought, its haphazard and sometimes fragmentary handling of phrases, clauses, and sentences. All these faults good dictation avoids through the use of sustained and well-phrased intelligent thought units. In brief, expert dictation avoids the conversational fault of "looseness," retains the conversational virtue of naturalness.

WHY WRITE IT THIS WAY
*Negative Tone—Stilted, Frozen
Language*

In reply to your favor of the 10th instant, in which you give facts to support your claim for credit with us, we beg to advise you that same is inadequate from the point of view of our company.

Although we regret that the information given us makes it impossible to grant credit as requested, we will fill your order provided check is sent in advance as specified per our quotation of recent date.

Trusting this arrangement will be entirely satisfactory, and regretting that we are unable to extend credit on an open account at this time, we beg to remain. . . .

WHEN YOU CAN *TALK* IT THIS WAY?
*Positive Tone—Conversational,
Natural, Friendly, Helpful*

Thanks for your November 10 order and for enclosing credit information and references.

You ought to feel happy about the many complimentary opinions we've had of your character and ability. Your associates certainly build you up. Congratulations!

There's one risk in your financial position. Your asset-liability ratio shows that you just don't have enough capital. You need about $5,000 more. We think you can get it, too, because of your favorable location and your good management record.

Look into this matter, won't you? Meanwhile, we'll be glad to take care of all your current needs with our most favorable cash terms. That will also give us a good basis for getting better acquainted.

(7) Be Positive and Helpful in Tone. Never waste valuable time moaning on paper, or in dictation, about how bad things (or times or circumstances or situations or people) are. Moaning and pessimism are both completely futile and completely negative. They damage you. They damage your reader. They damage you both because they generate gloominess. And if you want to defeat yourself at the very outset, if you want to roadblock the very purpose for which you are dictating, all you have to do is to deal in gloom. Gloom is your sure road to failure, in dictating as in anything else.

When you dictate, strive *to say something positive, constructive, and helpful.* What, for instance? Here are three positive, constructive, and helpful things you can do, one of which is always suitable and ready for your dictating use:

The Expert Dictator:
1. Gives definite information by making a definite statement.
2. Expresses pleasure (or regret) as a form of normal courtesy.
3. Shows clear-cut action.

COMFORT AGREEABILITY CORDIALITY
ENJOYMENT FRIENDLINESS SATI
PLEASURE GRATIFICATION GLADN
HAPPINESS FREEDOM RELAX
COMFORT AGREEABILITY CORDIA
ENJOYMENT FRIENDLINESS S
PLEASURE GRATIFICATION GLADI
HAPPINESS FREEDOM RELAX
COMFORT AGREEABILITY CORDIAL
ENJOYMENT FRIENDLINESS S
PLEASURE GRATIFICATION GLAI
HAPPINESS FREEDOM RELA
COMFORT AGREEABILITY CORD
ENJOYMENT FRIENDLINESS S
PLEASURE GRATIFICATION GLADNESS
HAPPINESS FREEDOM RELAXATIO
COMFORT AGREEABILITY CORDIALITY
ENJOYMENT FRIENDLINESS SATIS
PLEASURE GRATIFICATION GLADNES
HAPPINESS FREEDOM RELAXA
COMFORT AGREEABILITY CORDIAL
ENJOYMENT FRIENDLINESS
PLEASURE GRATIFICATION GL
HAPPINESS FREEDOM RE
COMFORT AGREEABILITY C
ENJOYMENT FRIENDLIN
PLEASURE GRATIFICATION

Be Positive in Tone: Look for the Bright Spots

You want to give some definite information? "Here is the good news: the blueprints and floor plans will be ready in 48 hours." You want to express normal courtesy? "Thanks for your cordial invitation. We're looking forward to being at your Conference." You want to show clear-cut action? "Just ten days from now, on September 23, we'll announce our plans; we think you'll like them."

Finally, *always look for the bright spot*. At first it may seem there isn't a one around. But the experts will tell you this: there's always one somewhere, if you will look for it. The experienced dictator recommends, "Don't say 'no'—say 'YES' to something else!" "I wish I could send you the brochure you want—but it's out of print. In its place I'm sending you our annual report that contains the same material. It may give you exactly what you want."

(8) Dictate with an Occasional "Color-Flash." A touch of color now and then is relished by the best of men. The Reverend Ralph W. Sockman, New York minister whose "National Radio Pulpit" sermons are broadcast over a hundred stations each Sunday morning, puts it this way: "I have learned, in thirty years of broadcasting, that delivering an effective sermon by radio is much harder than preaching from a pulpit to a congregation." Then, he concludes, "You have to use colorful words, words that the listener can 'see' in his mind, together with a light touch now and then." Dr. Sockman might have been discussing effective dictation. The problems are identical.

Many people tend to write in monotones—in relatively grey, drab, uninteresting, and unimpressive fashion. Mill-run writing is notably lacking in sparkle and emphasis. Important words and passages are not made to stand out from the rest of the text, but are permitted to melt into the background.

In good dictation you have your chance to correct this trend. You can give your dictated words occasional flashes of color just as you do in conversations with your friends:

   (1) Use contractions now and then. "I'll be glad to come to your Conference." "You'll find the information on page 3." "We'll plan on your arrival Thursday." "Don't worry about that. We'll take care of it."

   (2) Don't be afraid of a few natural idioms occasionally. "We're sure you'll make it in a breeze." "We're betting you'll coast home 'way out ahead of your competition." "The statistics are running neck and neck with the same figures for last year." "By all means, shoot your questions along. . . . We'll do our best to answer the whole bunch."

   (3) Use personal names when it's natural. "As far as we're concerned, Joe, it's OK." "Go ahead, Bill, any time you're ready." "We'll try to make it next time, Ralph—sorry, we're tied up now—but thanks, anyway, for the appreciated invitation."

A Dozen Don'ts for Dictators

What the Experts Recommend

1. DON'T dictate too fast.
2. DON'T dictate in rushes and spurts. Dictate at an even rate.
3. DON'T "run on and on." Group your words naturally.
4. DON'T mumble your words. Enunciate distinctly.
5. DON'T let your voice "trail off." Keep a full, sustained tone to the ends of sentences so that your secretary can hear without straining.
6. DON'T wander around the room. Stay put. Your voice will then register from one spot in a clear, steady tone.
7. DON'T ask for constant "read-backs." Plan and organize your thoughts before you start to speak.
8. DON'T guess where you're going. Make marginal notes. Gather needed data before you start.
9. DON'T dictate into the dark. Visualize your reader.
10. DON'T "soar into the blue." Avoid high-flown, highfalutin, high-nosed, "$9.75" words. Use simple TALK-language that any friend would understand.
11. DON'T ramble into long, loose, overloaded sentences. Keep them clear, clean, fluent, and readable.
12. DON'T make your secretary guess. Spell out rare words when you have to use them. Clear up rare references when you have to make them. Put a dictionary within her easy reach, and keep one on your desk. Use them as a team.

Top Management Depends on Effective Teamwork

From the Spoken Word into the Written Word the dictation power line guides and outlines executive decisions.

Using Dictating Machines. The executive who uses a dictating machine should have his ideas so well in mind and should make his phrasing so clear that correction and repetition will be largely avoided. Paragraphs, internal punctuation, and periods should be indicated. All difficult words, the names of cities and states, all given names and surnames, and all other strange or unusual expressions should be spelled and, if necessary, explained or described at the point where the word occurs on the recording device.

All instructions of any character whatsoever, including instructions for special handling, "Rush," extra carbons, insertions, and the like, must naturally be given at the *beginning* of any block of dictation, in order that the operator may take them into proper consideration in finishing the work.

Dictating machines using cylinder, disc, belt, wire, or tape recording mechanisms have certain advantages. They save the time of the secretary for other duties while the dictating is being done. They make it possible for the dictator to take care of his correspondence at hours when the secretary may not be available. On the other hand, dictating to the secretary or stenographer has certain advantages if the dictator and stenographer have learned to work together as a team. An alert stenographer may supply the word you are groping for. She may serve as a sounding board for phrases you hope will mollify a difficult customer. "How does this sound to you, Miss Rogers?" is the type of question that may bring out suggestions to make your dictation more effective.

Top Management's Guide for the Dictator

Dictate Less—Delegate More

1. Develop effective interchangeable form paragraphs and use them wisely to handle your repetitive situations.
2. Dictate only the basic ideas and let your subordinate compose the message.
3. Delegate responsibility for routine correspondence to your subordinates.

Get Your Facts Faster

1. Encourage your subordinates to sort, open, read, route, and deliver the mail.
2. Route incoming mail through the files so that necessary information and correspondence can be assembled and delivered with your incoming letters.
3. Use interoffice memos, check lists, forms, or telephones to gather the information you need for dictation.
4. Keep a file near your desk if you need technical or confidential information quickly.
5. Glue an index inside your large folders so that you can find correspondence quickly.

Minimize Your Interruptions

1. Conduct a survey of the number and kinds of interruptions to discover your best time for planning and dictating correspondence.
2. Schedule a "quiet hour" each morning so that you can plan and dictate without interruption.
3. Find an isolated room where you can plan and dictate without distraction.
4. Use "rereading" or "playback" as little as possible. Concentrate.

Help Your Secretary Help You

1. Encourage a mutual exchange of suggestions with your transcriber.
2. Provide a check list so your transcriber can indicate which of your dictation practices cause difficulty in transcription.
3. Help your transcriber become thoroughly familiar with your company, its functions, its departments, its products, and its terminology.
4. Develop a complete and accurate job description to inform your transcriber of her responsibilities concerning your correspondence.
5. Be sure you provide all necessary instructions and directions prior to dictating a message.

Help Your Secretary Help You (Continued)

6. Standardize your basic transcription instructions and put them in writing for your transcriber.
7. Develop simple code words to indicate transcription instructions. [Example: CANIO, in one company, indicates to the transcriber that a carbon copy and an appropriate notation is to be sent to the Indianapolis office.]
8. Hand incoming letters and previous correspondence to your transcriber so that she may check the completeness and accuracy of the dictated replies.
9. Number your incoming letters to avoid having to dictate names and addresses which your transcriber can simply copy from the letters.
10. Complete your dictation early to avoid rushed transcription.
11. Regulate your dictation speed by watching your secretary's hand as she writes the shorthand symbols.
12. Be sure you understand all of the possibilities and limitations of the dictating machine you use.
13. Know how to make changes and corrections in machine dictation and how to indicate these to your transcriber.

Plan Before You Dictate

1. Jot down and arrange a few notes prior to dictating.
2. Use a simple outline to separate the "what to say" from the "how to say it." Having planned the "what," you can concentrate on the "how" during dictation.
3. Avoid writing extensive longhand drafts prior to dictating. It is often easier and faster to dictate the first draft. Then, if you find it necessary, you can edit your transcript.
4. Plan and dictate your reply immediately after reading the incoming letter—if you have all the facts you will need.

Continue Your Progress: Coach Yourself

1. Collect and review carbon copies of your most effective dictation.
2. Learn more about the individuals who read your messages.
3. Keep informed on company policies and procedures so you can easily interpret them to your readers.
4. Encourage your transcriber to help you edit your dictation *for accuracy.*

—*Adapted from a Research Study, Courtesy of Professor Ray W. Arensman, School of Business, Indiana University; based upon interviews and visitations with 81 management executives, and a comprehensive study of materials used by 73 organizations in the training of dictators.*

The Executive and His Secretary Are a Team. Would you like to be a member of a Championship Team? Most people would. And you can be, if you wish. How do you do it? Simply practice intelligent teamwork. The executive and his secretary are a team. They are concerned with one common aim: to produce effective letters. You can instantly recognize two outstanding qualities in a letter produced by an expert dictator-secretary team:

1. Attractive form
2. Effective content

Your stenographer can make or break the effectiveness of any dictation. No matter how carefully you dictate to her, no matter how thoughtfully you line up your ideas, no matter how forcefully you use your words, she can ruin the whole effect in the twinkling of an eye with a few ill-chosen strokes of the typewriter. Yet, if she has an eye for symmetry, for proportion, for balance—if she knows how a picture ought to look in a handsome frame—she can give your dictated message every advantage you can possibly hope for. If your message is powerfully dictated, it gains still more power with a handsome layout. Your task is to make your dictation good. Your stenographer's task is to make her transcription good. Each one of you is a part of the Championship Team.

If you are blessed with a capable secretary, perhaps you may want to encourage her to sort the mail and to draft answers for routine situations with which she is familiar. Or you may prefer to outline the message and have her compose the draft to express your ideas. Either way, as Professor Ray Arensman correctly concludes in his study, cited earlier, you are upgrading your secretary, saving dictation time, and freeing yourself for higher-level work.

Expert Dictators Are a Part of Every Management Team. In carrying out your daily responsibilities, make your language so natural, so conversational, so direct that it generates easy acceptance and a feeling of friendly confidence among all your readers and associates. By all means recognize the top importance of outlining, mentally or on paper (preferably the latter), what you want to say *before* you jump into dictation and are confronted with the question of how to say it.

Retaining the virtues and avoiding the faults of natural conversation, cultivate the art of well-phrased thought units. Practice the technique of suspending one part of your thought while you are formulating the rest of it. Speak with the utmost clarity, at a fairly even rate, and pronounce and enunciate with precision. Do these things, and you will make yourself not only an effective dictator but also an essential part of the management pattern. Expert dictation is, in fact, an inescapable part of successful executive action and of efficient top management.

Communication Problems

● 1. Assume that your closest male relative enjoys watching football and that you have never met his boss, George W. Salat. Prepare to dictate (in class) a message to your relative inviting him to your school's next home game. Prepare to dictate another message to your friend's boss inviting him to come to the game with your relative. Which is the easier message to dictate? Why? What information would be helpful in dictating the more difficult message?

● 2. Find a business message that requires an answer. Secure an actual letter received by a local business or select one from your book. Jot down any brief pencil notes you would need to make a complete reply. Using these brief marginal notes, dictate your reply to the class.

● 3. Executives who have capable secretaries frequently delegate simpler correspondence to their secretaries. These executives read the incoming message, jot down a few simple instructions on how the matter should be handled, then ask their secretaries to compose the answer. Select one of the message examples in this book and assume that you have actually received it. Write a few brief notes you think would enable a capable secretary to compose a good reply if you handed her the message.

● 4. Assume that you are to dictate a message to a local businessman asking him to come to your class to describe his dictation procedures. In class, dictate the first paragraph of your message. Ask your classmates to evaluate the tone of your first paragraph and give reasons for their responses.

● **5.** Select one of the inquiries in this book (see pages 188 and 190). Assume that you are to dictate a reply to this inquiry. Make a list of all the data or information you would need to prepare for dictation. Which of this information could a capable clerk or secretary assemble for you? Which of this information would you probably need to assemble personally?

● **6.** From your book, choose what you believe to be a highly effective business message. On a piece of memo paper, jot down the core-thought of each paragraph. Use only three or four words for each corethought. Then, using these corethoughts as notes, dictate your version of the message. Phrase these thoughts naturally in your own words—make no attempt to parrot the words or phrases in the original.

● **7.** From a few short notes, dictate a message without dictating paragraphs or punctuation. Then dictate the message again, indicating all punctuation and paragraphs. Some executives believe that dictating paragraphs and punctuation helps them organize their ideas and verbalize them into natural thought groups. As a result of your brief trial, do you agree or disagree with these executives?

● **8.** A group of forty-four Indianapolis executives recently agreed unanimously that the dictator and the secretary must work as a team. What can the dictator do to promote this team feeling and secure the sincere interest and cooperation of the secretary? Limit your answer to specific suggestions.

● **9.** With the assistance of your instructor, arrange to visit a local businessman to review and discuss some of his incoming correspond-ence. Then, with the businessman's cooperation, collect several of the simpler problems. Ask him to give you enough background to enable you to understand the situation well enough to dictate the answers to these incoming messages. Quickly plan and outline your dictation and, again with the businessman's cooperation, arrange to dictate your responses to his secretary. Arrange also for his secretary to transcribe the dictation on the company letterhead and to indicate your name and a fictitious title in the closing lines. Ask both the businessman and his secretary to comment on your dictation practices and the quality of your completed work. Bring these transcribed messages to class, exhibit them to the class, report on the business-man's and secretary's comments, and ask the class for their evaluation of your efforts.

● **10.** Ask a local businessman to bring some of his incoming corre-spondence, some of his company's letterheads, and his secretary to your class and to demonstrate how he plans his messages and dictates them to his secretary. Arrange to have a typewriter in the room and ask the secretary to transcribe the dictation—one or two letters—on the company letterhead. In what ways did the dictator help the secretary? How did the secretary help the dictator? Ask the dictator and secretary to discuss other practices which each uses to assist the other with his or her portion of their responsibilities.

CHAS. PFIZER & CO., INC.

ESTABLISHED 1849

Manufacturing Chemists

630 FLUSHING AVENUE

BROOKLYN 6, N.Y.

PLANTS & LABORATORIES
BROOKLYN, N.Y.
GROTON, CONN.
TERRE HAUTE, IND.
MAYWOOD, N.J.

SALES OFFICES
BROOKLYN
CHICAGO
SAN FRANCISCO
ATLANTA
DALLAS

December 29, 19--

Mr. George Liddell
2128 Central Boulevard
El Paso, Texas

Dear Mr. Liddell:

Thank you for your letter asking us about samples of Pfizer
products. Viterra Tastitabs, a vitamin-mineral supplement
marketed by our J. B. Roerig and Company Division, were
mailed to our shareholders last year. A similar packet of
Viterra is being mailed to you.

We are glad that you took the opportunity to inquire, and we
shall be happy to add your name to our list to receive future
samples.

Very truly yours,

S. M. Low, Manager
Institutional Public Relations

SML/mf

**This Reply to an Inquiry Courteously Stresses
Immediate Favorable Action**

LIFE

540 NORTH MICHIGAN AVE.
CHICAGO 11

PUBLISHER OF
TIME, FORTUNE, LIFE
SPORTS ILLUSTRATED
ARCHITECTURAL FORUM
HOUSE & HOME

January 30, 19--

Dear LIFE Reader:

For some time we have mailed you copies of our
semiannual index. We are glad to continue doing so
if you find the indexes useful, but it may be that you
no longer need them.

We would appreciate your letting us know if you
still wish to receive LIFE indexes. Just initial the
enclosed reply card and mail it back to us. If we do
not hear from you by April 1, we will automatically
remove your name from our index list.

Of course, this in no way affects your subscription to LIFE Magazine.

Sincerely,

L. I. Peters
LIFE Magazine

**This Simple Inquiry Makes Reply Easy
Through the Reply-Card Enclosure**

PART IV Simpler Types of
Management Messages

Chapter 9   **Inquiries and Replies;**
Notices, Announcements, Invitations, and Appointments;
Orders, Remittances, and Acknowledgments

Executive Action in Its First Stages. One of the simpler forms of executive action is to issue an announcement. Another is to make an appointment. Another is to prepare a responsible inquiry of importance to company management, or to make an equally responsible reply on the part of the company management. Scores of similar basic executive actions are taken in the course of the business day.

Successful executive action vitally depends upon the power of the written word. Three management executives, Messrs. Batten, Goodrich, and Toogood, wrote an entire book upon this subject and concluded, "There is in the world today . . . virtually no phase of human activity which is not influenced, directly or indirectly, by the power of the written word." In this and later chapters we shall aim at three major targets: (1) to understand other people; (2) to learn how they act and why they act as they do; and (3) through the written word, to win a favorable response from them. For let it be remembered: every purchase, every sale, every contract, every financial transaction, every constructive management outcome, depends upon the word "Yes" from some human being.

Management activities call for the transmission of questions and answers, orders and acknowledgments, announcements, factual data, and know-how information. Over the rails, through the air, by teletypewriter, by radio facsimile, billions of messages reach their destination to inquire, reply, announce, invite, appoint, order, remit, acknowledge, apply, adjust, collect and sell.

Inquiries and Replies

Inquiries. Inquiries are messages that ask for information: price quotations, terms of payment, folders, catalogs, articles, services, particular knowledge, special data, and the like. Your inquiry should indicate exactly what you want.

Clearness is vital. Word your questions so clearly that even a dull reader will not fail to understand what you want to know. If your inquiry involves several points, paragraph each one or list them in numerical order. Use this plan:

1. State the subject of your inquiry.
2. Add explanatory material, specific details, definitions.
3. Give the reason for your inquiry; make it clear why the inquiry is addressed to the reader.
4. End with courtesy.

If the answer to your inquiry will be a favor to you, enclose a stamped, self-addressed envelope of convenient size or clip a loose stamp to your letter. The latter procedure is recommended when your inquiry goes to a business, because the business may prefer to use its own stationery. When an inquiry is about a matter of mutual interest or when it is sent to someone with whom you have regular dealings, it is not necessary to enclose a stamp or a business reply envelope.

AN INQUIRY

May I ask what kind of typewriter you use in your office and why you prefer that machine?

Our company expects shortly to move its offices into new quarters with entirely new equipment. In the stenographic department forty-five new typewriters are to be installed. I have been asked to choose the make.

Your wide experience with the leading typewriters makes your advice most valuable in guiding me to a selection. Will you please tell me:

1. What make of typewriter you use?
2. Does the machine stand up well under constant use?
3. Does it produce clear, sharp stencils?
4. Which of its special service mechanisms do you find most useful?
5. Does the manufacturer give satisfactory service in repairs and replacements?

I, as well as my company, will deeply appreciate your help.

Requests for catalogs, booklets, or samples and inquiries for general information on timetables and the like may be brief.

Do you have available for distribution publications on stock control systems for retail sporting goods stores?

If you have such publications, will you please give me their titles and indicate the price of each.

Answering Inquiries. Handle inquiries courteously whether the desired information is supplied or withheld. The exact information, if available, should be given in the briefest form. Study the following answer to the inquiry given earlier on selection of typewriters:

ANSWER TO AN INQUIRY—ITEMS NUMBERED

It is a pleasure to answer your inquiry of August 19. We are using the Electronic typewriter. Our preference is based on these superior features:

1. Each unit is easy to adjust and clean.
2. The touch is remarkably light and fast.
3. The service mechanisms are simple, and their uses can be learned quickly.
4. The touch-control, repeat-key, page-gage, and tabulator mechanisms are particularly useful.
5. The Electronic produces clear-cut stencils.
6. Repairmen are efficient, dependable, and prompt.
7. The company allows a good "turn-in" rate.
8. The Electronic is extraordinarily rugged. On this point we have convincing comparative statistical records.

If you have further questions on other office equipment, let us have them. We are glad to help.

The numbered listing of questions and answers helps to keep the inquiry and the answer clear and brief. But tabulations like these are not always necessary. Well-judged paragraphing is also effective. Note in the following reply how the first paragraph shows courtesy; the second discusses the Excel; the third, the Duplex; the fourth, the Multiplex; and the last extends a courteous invitation.

ANSWER TO AN INQUIRY—ITEMS PARAGRAPHED

We are glad to tell you, in answer to your May 1 inquiry, of our experience with duplicating machines.

For several years we have used the Excel duplicator for interoffice and interdepartmental notices. We found, though, that clear-cut copies were difficult to make from the blue stencils that are recommended for use with this machine. The A-B stencils that we now use produce far better copies.

The Duplex machine that we use for our shop orders is quite satisfactory. We can make about twenty clear copies from a single Duplex carbon. By using a Duplex ribbon on the typewriter, it is possible to make about fifty good copies from the original.

We use the Multiplex machine for our direct-mail work. By using a ribbon on the machine in preference to the ink roller, we are able to fill in the address and the salutation either with the typewriter or with the addresser.

If you will call at our office before making your selection, we'll gladly demonstrate these three machines for you.

Stress Favorable Action. "Action First" is a particularly effective rule in answers to inquiries. Every reader is interested in action. Things in action are good. People in action are better. If suitable, make the first sentence an action headline.

STRESSING "ACTION FIRST" AND COURTEOUS TONE IN A
REPLY TO AN INQUIRY FOR INFORMATION

Action First *with Courtesy*	We are pleased to send you the three copies of Socony-Vacuum's Cruising Guides that you requested in your letter of June 7.
Explanation *of Material* *and Comment* *on Enclosures*	The complete series consists of five guides, four of which cover coastwise cruising from the Bay of Fundy to Cape Henlopen, Delaware. Guide No. 4 carries a small scale outline of the Intracoastal Waterway, showing distances and government charts necessary in making the cruise from New York to Florida. The fifth guide covers New York Inland Waterways, Lake Champlain, Lake Ontario, the St. Lawrence River, and adjacent Canadian Waters.
Courteous *Good-Will Close*	You should find this "Friendly Service" of real value in planning your pleasure cruises.

Note, also, these favorable action openings:

Here's our airmail "Thank You" for your congratulatory note of July 12 about our current issue of <u>Dividends</u> . . . and, as you requested, here is also a reprint of the article "How to Get to Be President."

* * *

Immediately after your long-distance call this morning, telling us of the shortage in your Kardex order, we sent the three items by air express.

* * *

We shall find out at once why your Order No. M-405 has been delayed. Just as soon as we get the report, we shall wire you.

Be Positive in Your Replies. Hold the positive tone in answering inquiries. The positive tone means (1) clearness, (2) active willingness to serve, (3) courtesy. The following brief, but positive-toned note wins good will with every word:

We are pleased to send you the copy of "Executive Action" requested in your note of June 4.

Along with this publication we are including a copy of the later issue entitled "The Management Guide." We believe you will find it equally helpful in your work.

Here is a "before-and-after" contrast in positive tone:

THE NEGATIVE ORIGINAL

Impersonal tone, poor structure, stock phrases, elementary errors, favorable elements hidden.

Dear Madam:

In reply to your favor will say that we have this ring on Order, the reason it is taken longer is that we waited for the Salesman instead of ordering right away, thinking he might have one with him, however he did not, so we have it on Order and just as soon as it arrives we will send the same to you. Trusting this will be satisfactory, we are

Respectfully yours,

CROWN SILVER COMPANY

P. S. Imported Rings sometimes take longer.

THE POSITIVE REVISION

Cordial tone, clear structure, fresh vocabulary, favorable "action first," tactful explanation, careful detail, courteous close.

Dear Miss McLain:

Your beautiful ring is on its way from Europe, and we shall forward it at once upon its arrival.

It had been our hope to fill your order at once; but since our salesman did not have your choice on hand, we ordered direct from our foreign agent.

Our rings are imported from Switzerland, where they are hand-wrought by craftsmen noted for fine workmanship.

Thank you for your order. We know the ring will please you.

Take Prompt Care of Inquiries. When, after spending thousands of dollars in promotion, a concern succeeds in getting inquiries from many prospective buyers, these inquiries should be handled in a way to win the largest possible amount of business and good will. Inquiries that may lead to valuable orders should be answered at once. Inquiries that involve the consulting of files, the tabulation of figures, or the preparation of estimates, consuming several days' time, should be acknowledged at once with a statement of progress and the probable date on which the information can be sent.

AN ACKNOWLEDGMENT

Your appreciated inquiry concerning the new "Slimline" color-TV cabinets was referred immediately to our styling staff. Preliminary sketches are now being made, and we shall send you our recommendations within the next five days.

Let us now suppose that a prospective buyer requests a booklet, a catalog, or other purchasing information. Would you send merely the impersonal booklet or catalog? Management experts say "No!" Leading concerns send with the booklet or catalog a carefully prepared sales message to fan the flame of interest and to stimulate purchase.

Show courtesy by a prompt reply. If you answer promptly, you say in effect, "By this prompt answer I want to show you that I appreciate your inquiry, value your approval, and hope to win your patronage."

Delays Can Be Ruinous. A startling quantity of mail is always late. Inquiries calling for an immediate answer fail to be identified. Yet no matter how fine a message may be in conciseness, courtesy, or action, it is not worth a nickel if it comes too late.

Case I. To test the matter, one investigator wrote businesses, asking for information on articles offered. These were the results:

> 64 of the inquiries were NEVER ANSWERED.
> 1 came two months and five days late.
> 3 were a month late.
> 12 answers arrived twenty days late.
> 65 came in on the eleventh day.
> Only 10 answers came back within five days.

Case II. In another investigation an inquiry went to 119 automobile manufacturers. Straggling in over a period of thirty days came 97 answers. Forty of the companies misspelled the inquirer's name although it was engraved on his letterhead. Sixty of the replies had no value because they were merely stereotyped—like impersonal "rubber stamps."

INTERNATIONAL, INC. ● **Correspondence Instructions**

Refer To_____ Date_____

Indicate Purpose by Check Mark:

☐ RUSH—Immediate action desired
☐ Your comments, please
☐ Please note and see me about this ——AM ——PM
☐ Please answer, sending me copy of your letter
☐ Please prepare reply for my signature
☐ To be signed
☐ For your information
☐ Please note and file
☐ Please note and send to main files
☐ Please note, initial, and return to me
☐ Please note, initial, and route to:

1_____   2_____

3_____   4_____

Remarks_____

_____

Signed_____

An Interoffice Memorandum Form for Speeding Up Executive Action

This type of memo sheet is often used to speed up replies to inquiries. Note especially the first seven entries.

Case III. A third study found that it took a group of firms 11.89 days on the average to get their replies into the hands of the inquirers. The range of time ran from two days to fifty-two days. Not more than a fifth of the inquiries were answered promptly. Only one in ten used a follow-up.

"Received—but Not Read," an article in *Nation's Business*, suggests that eleven out of twelve firms lose business and good will by failure to reply, or by failure to reply promptly and completely.

The delayed reply is the greatest single communication fault. Tardy answers cost each year immense sums in good will alone, not to mention canceled orders and lost sales. Yet, curiously enough, the positive cure to this widespread fault of delay is always at hand: (1) promptness in handling the mail, and (2) sending courteous acknowledgments when delay is unavoidable.

How to Change Negatives into Positives. Let us now turn to another situation. You receive this message: "Gentlemen: We are planning to build. Please send a copy of the booklet you mention in your advertisement in the LIFE issue of August 20." There are two ways to handle this situation—one bad and one good.

(1) The Negative Way. The request lies on the desk for a week or ten days. When the correspondent does answer it, he may write something like this:

> Referring to your inquiry of August 25, in which you ask for a copy of our booklet *70-Degree Temperature in Arctics or Tropics,* wish to advise that the last edition has just been exhausted, and we are unable to advise when other copies will be available inasmuch as no new edition is planned. Regret our present inability to comply with your request.

(2) The Positive Way. The answer to the inquiry goes out, if possible, on the same day, certainly within not more than two days from the day on which the inquiry was received. Remember that buyers, too, want to save time. That is why they respond to the advertisements. They seek information that they can study in their homes or offices, and they want it *while the fever of interest is upon them.*

Promptness is never more necessary than in the case of an interested person who has asked for information. If the answer is to be written at all, it will be most effective when the impulse that prompted the inquiry is fresh and alive. When interest has waned, when the psychological moment of lively inquiry has passed, a reply two weeks late is only a "cold potato." And so, *shortly after the inquiry is received*, the following reply is written:

> We are glad to send you, in response to your August 25 inquiry, a copy of an interesting, lithographed summary of the superior qualities of Arcto-Tropic paneling.
>
> This summary will give you much of the information presented in our Booklet <u>70-Degree Temperature in Arctics or Tropics</u>, copies of which are just now exhausted because of an unexpectedly heavy demand. If further copies become available, we shall forward one to you at once.
>
> You will find on pages 27 to 30 of the summary the heart of the paneling story. Note that these figures support our statements about Arcto-Tropic paneling.
>
> Our information center will gladly answer your specific questions as they arise.

This message reflects courtesy through promptness and develops good will through a desire to serve. *Always show a desire to serve.*

Say the "Courtesy Word." When helpful replies to inquiries are interchanged often—when, in other words, the obligations are kept about even—letters of thanks are unnecessary. But when a reasonable sense of gratitude calls for it, say the "courtesy word." Examples:

> Thank you for your exceptionally fine reply to our recent inquiry. We are glad that the divided page, the definitions, and the careful treatment of familiar allusions have pleased you.
>
> Your suggestion that some device be adopted for supplying purchasers of the dictionary with later information in the form of supplementary pages is being studied carefully.
>
> We shall welcome any other suggestions you may have.
>
>   *   *   *
>
> Thank you for sending us the material that won top honors at the International Meeting of the United Nations Commission. Reprints will be sent to you as soon as the material has been edited.

Notices, Announcements, Invitations, and Appointments

Notices and Announcements. Certain situations require messages of notice, announcement, or information. Often these functions are combined in one message. A company calls a meeting of its stockholders. A new business opens. An office is moved to a new location. A committee meets. A store expands into a new building. A new president is elected. One firm absorbs another. For examples, see pages 197 and 198.

More formal announcements may be printed on cards, or they may be embossed in a handsome type face on heavy paper. Other

AVON PRODUCTS, INC.
30 ROCKEFELLER PLAZA
NEW YORK 20, N. Y.

NOTICE OF SPECIAL MEETING OF STOCKHOLDERS
To Be Held November 5, 19—

October 15, 19—

To the Common Stockholders of
Avon Products, Inc.:

NOTICE IS HEREBY GIVEN that a Special Meeting of Stockholders of Avon Products, Inc. will be held at the offices of the Corporation, 30 Rockefeller Plaza, New York, N. Y., on Monday, November 5, 19—, at 3:00 p. m, for the following purposes:

(1) To consider and vote upon a proposal recommended by the Board of Directors of the Corporation that the certificate of incorporation of the Corporation, as heretofore amended, be further amended so as to change the present 1,800,000 authorized shares of Common Stock of the par value of $5 per share, including therein the 1,401,183 issued shares of such Common Stock, into 3,600,000 shares of authorized Common Stock with a par value of $2.50 per share; and to authorize the execution and filing of the certificate required by the New York Stock Corporation Law to effect such change in capital stock; and

(2) To consider and act upon any and all other matters incidental to the foregoing purpose that may properly come before said meeting.

The stock transfer books of the Corporation will not be closed, but only the holders of the Common Stock of record at the close of business October 15, 19—, will be entitled to vote at the meeting.

Stockholders who do not expect to attend in person and who wish their stock to be voted are urged to sign and return the enclosed proxy in the enclosed self-addressed stamped envelope.

By Order of the Board of Directors,

LOUIS W. JAEGER,
Secretary

GAYLORD CONTAINER CORPORATION
GENERAL OFFICES
ONE HUNDRED NORTH FOURTH STREET
St. Louis 2 Missouri

EDWIN J. SPIEGEL
PRESIDENT

November 23, 19—

TO GAYLORD STOCKHOLDERS:

You will be interested to know that the merger agreement between Gaylord Container Corporation and Crown Zellerbach Corporation was approved yesterday at a special meeting of stockholders.

Votes cast by shareholders owning 88.9% of all outstanding shares were in favor of the merger and 00.04% were against.

It is thus apparent that an overwhelming majority of stockholders agree with Gaylord management and directors in the conviction that this merger is in the best interests of all concerned.

The merger becomes effective November 30, 19—, and very shortly thereafter you will be informed of the method of exchange of your Gaylord stock certificates for those of Crown Zellerbach Corporation.

May I express to you, on behalf of the management and directors, our deep appreciation for your cooperation and interest in the affairs of your company.

Sincerely,

Edwin J. Spiegel

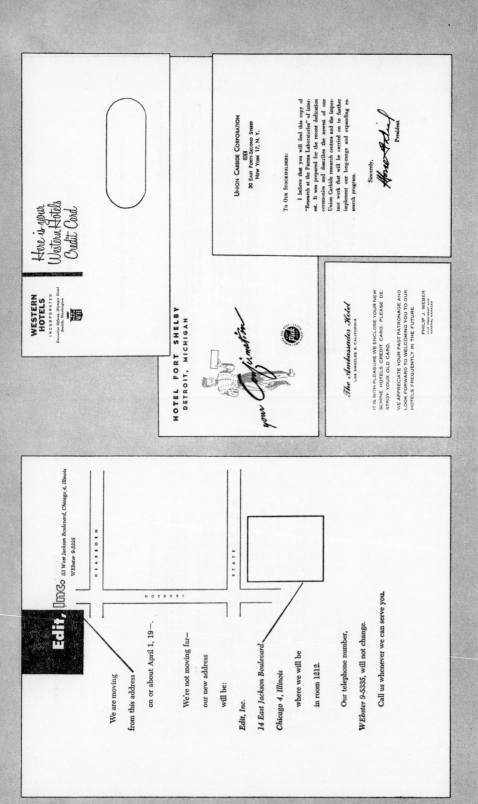

An Announcement of a Company's New Location

Interesting Variations in Forms of Announcement

variations of announcements are sometimes imprinted (a few words or a sentence) on the face of the envelope carrying related material such as credit cards, confirmations of room reservations, and the like. For examples, see page 198.

A newly elected president of a famous nationwide corporation sends the following announcement-greeting to his widely distributed organization.

AN ANNOUNCEMENT-GREETING

For the first time I greet you as President of your Company. I hope before very long I will have shaken the hand of every member of our organization from Minneapolis to Dallas, from New York to San Francisco. You and I have a great deal in common. We have a rich heritage to live up to and a great future to strive toward.

I am proud to be your President--grateful for the trust, appreciative of the challenge, humble in the honor, and confident that with your help our Company, as you and I, will continue to progress. I pledge to you 100 per cent of my time at all times. Your ideas, your suggestions, and your cooperation are needed. We can go just as far as we will. Let's go forward together.

Invitations. Like announcements, business invitations may be formal or informal.

INFORMAL BUSINESS INVITATION

June 20, 21, and 22 are the "Red-Letter" days for the business executive who wants to do more business. On these three days the Direct Mail Advertising Association and its two affiliated bodies, the Better Letters Association and the Association of House Organ Editors, will hold an annual convention and exposition in Cleveland, Ohio.

The purpose of this three-day institute is to create a better understanding of how to use and apply direct mail, to study the solution of distribution problems, and to make it possible for you to exchange experiences with others.

This letter is your invitation to come. When you read the enclosed program, you'll see that you certainly should be on hand!

Accepting Invitations. If you find it possible to accept an invitation, do so with prompt courtesy. Use care to confirm the time and place.

ACCEPTING AN INVITATION

I am happy to accept your invitation to deliver the graduation address to the officers of the Management School of the U. S. Naval Postgraduate School at 10 a.m. on June 7.

Your invitation does me great honor. I shall present to your graduates some ideas on management that I have formulated through the years as a consultant to many business firms.

You are invited . . .

The Home Savings and Loan Association cordially invites you to a special preview, for its members only, of the new Beverly Hills branch office building at 9245 Wilshire Boulevard, on Thursday, March 15, 19—, from 10 a.m. to 4 p.m. We are proud of the new building, and feel that it is an outstanding example of a modern business building which combines efficiency and function with unusual beauty of design and materials.

A Printed Card Invitation

Declining Invitations. If you find it necessary to decline an invitation, again do so with prompt courtesy. Cushion your action with an expression of thanks for the invitation and with other appropriate "positives."

DECLINING AN INVITATION

Thank you for inviting me to attend the Centennial Celebration of your organization to be held May 20.

Much as I would like to be with you and my other friends on this happy occasion, it will not be possible for me to join you. I shall be in the East at that time on a business trip.

In my absence, please accept these written greetings and best wishes for all members of your splendid organization on its 100th anniversary.

Appointments. The statement of appointment on page 201 differs from an announcement chiefly in that it goes to one person.

A SIMPLE STATEMENT OF APPOINTMENT

I should like to appoint you a member of the Municipal Planning Commission to succeed Mr. Raymond Allen, whose term has expired. I hope you will find it possible to accept this important post.

As a courtesy, the appointee should acknowledge the notice of his appointment and promptly accept or decline.

NATIONAL BROADCASTING COMPANY, INC.

A SERVICE OF RADIO CORPORATION OF AMERICA

R.C.A. Building, Radio City, New York 20, N.Y.

CIRCLE 7-8300

May 21, 19--

Mr. Louis J. Albers
435 Enright Avenue
Chicago 16, Illinois

Dear Mr. Albers

With genuine pleasure we announce the appointment of
John F. Corbin as NBC Central Division Spot and Local
Sales Manager with headquarters in Chicago.

Mr. Corbin will supervise the local sales for Stations
WMAQ and WENR, as well as national spot sales for the
nine additional stations that are programmed by NBC--
WJZ and WEAF, New York; KOA and KPO, San Francisco;
WRC and WMAL, Washington; WGY, Schenectady; WTAM,
Cleveland; and KOA, Denver.

Prompt and efficient attention will be given to all
your radio requirements by Mr. Corbin who comes to
Chicago with a rich background of experience and
achievement, having been Spot and Local Sales Manager
for our Eastern Division out of New York.

Mr. Corbin and his staff will be glad to serve you.

Sincerely

Sidney N. Strotz

Sidney N. Strotz

SNS:RM

OFFICE OF THE VICE PRESIDENT

WASHINGTON

June 24, 19--

Dear Dr. McHenry:

On behalf of the Vice President, I wish to
acknowledge your letter of July 16 expressing your
support of Senate Concurrent Resolution 12 and House
Concurrent Resolution 72 and 80.

If these measures should reach the floor of
of the Senate before adjournment, the Vice President,
as Presiding Officer, will not have an opportunity to
vote, except in the case of a tie. However, you may be
sure he will appreciate your interest in writing to him,
and I shall certainly bring your letter to his attention.

I know that the Vice President would want
me to extend his best wishes to you.

Sincerely,

Robert L. King

Robert L. King
Assistant to the
Vice President

Dr. Lee C. McHenry
3169 Neeb Road
Providence 3, Rhode Island

Orders, Remittances, and Acknowledgments

Orders. An order message (written when an order blank or purchase order form is not available) requests the shipment of goods or the giving of service, either in exchange for an agreed payment or under some special arrangement. Chief requirements are clear arrangement and accuracy of specifications. Delay, financial loss, or perhaps legal entanglement may result from a misinterpreted order. Hence, every detail should be checked.

Essentials of an Order. The order should specify the following facts. Each item should be placed on a separate line. All items should be tabulated to show the total value.

1. *Quantity:* Give the number of feet, yards, dozens, ounces, pounds, tons, gross, reams, or the like. For example: "6 copies *Space Travel to the Planets.*"

2. *Catalog number:* The catalog number is the short cut to the exact identification of the article. When no number is available, every possible item of identification, such as size, color, material, weight, finish, quality, or style, should be supplied.

3. *Price of each article:* Supply the price of each article.

4. *Method of shipment:* Unless there is a fixed agreement between the buyer and the seller on shipping methods and routes, specify whether the shipment is to go by freight, express, or parcel post, and if necessary indicate the route.

5. *Destination of shipment:* This information is necessary if the goods are to be sent to an address different from that of the one placing the order.

6. *Desired date of shipment:* This information indicates whether the goods are to be held for later delivery or must be delivered by a certain date. Need for haste should be given special note.

7. *Order number:* Concerns doing a large volume of business number all orders as a method of control.

8. *Method of payment:* This information is necessary if the method is not understood and agreed upon, or if the buyer is not a regular customer with credit terms.

Order Blanks. Use order blanks if they are available. The printed order form helps to save time and typing. The blank spaces on the printed form are your automatic guides indicating the information needed. Illustrated on page 203 is a purchase order form. It may be readily adapted to fit the needs of any organization.

```
                                                          PURCHASE ORDER
         J. E. Stevens & Company                            No. 183
                "Super" for Service and Reliability
                         967 Third Street
                          Philadelphia

   Laboratory Manufacturers, Inc.
   111 Madison Boulevard              Date    September 10, 19--
   Toledo 7, Ohio
                                      Terms   2/10, n/30

                                      Ship Via Allied Lines, Inc.
```

QUANTITY	DESCRIPTION	PRICE
100	Packages Filter Paper	15.00
3	Magnetic Needles	1.65
1	Compass	1.00
15	Bar Magnets	3.00
5	Glass Funnels	1.10

By *Robert C. Brooks*

A Purchase Order Form

Remittance Letters. Remittance letters indicate the amount of the remittance and the form in which it is sent. The debtor may also specify how the money is to be applied. This information is important in case he has more than one account, owes a note, or is delinquent on an overdue remittance. Unless the debtor specifies to what item the money is to be applied, the creditor may apply it as he sees fit. Remittances, except checks, should be acknowledged. Canceled checks are their own receipts. Remittance letters should indicate enclosures by a reference line (*Enclosure* or *Enclosures 2*).

Simple Acknowledgments. Occasionally there will be situations in the business office that call for messages of simple acknowledgment. Oftentimes, for example, an executive may be out of his office visiting the divisional offices of his company. From past experience he knows that on each business day certain pieces of mail will come in that only he can answer. But he does not want his mail to lie unattended on his desk during his absence. Accordingly, his secretary is instructed to acknowledge the incoming mail. An example:

```
    Thank you for your note of September 20, addressed to
Mr. A. C. Hobson.  Mr. Hobson telephoned me this morning that
he will be back in his office on September 28.  Immediately
upon his return I shall be happy to bring your note to his
attention.  I know he will be pleased that you wrote.
```

Sutter near Grant   *San Francisco*

To_ Mrs. R. D. Bateman _____

We acknowledge with pleasure the opportunity to number you among our friends and are placing your name on our books today.

It is our sincere hope that we will be able to assist you in all your home furnishing needs. We especially welcome any calls you may want to make on the unusual services we are prepared to give our patrons.

W. & J. Sloane

A Formal Acknowledgment and Welcome to a New Customer

It is a pleasure to send you the

enclosed material in response to

your recent request.

AMERICAN MANAGEMENT ASSOCIATION
1515 BROADWAY • TIMES SQUARE • NEW YORK 36, N. Y.

A Courteous, Printed Acknowledgment

This reply to an inquiry, emphasizing favorable action and courtesy, is attractively printed in the form of a card or slip and neatly attached to the transmitted material.

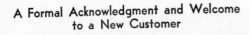

An excellent example of a formal acknowledgment much used out of Washington is illustrated on page 201. Note other types of acknowledgments on this page and page 216 of Chapter 10.

Order Acknowledgments. An order should, if possible, be acknowledged on the day it is received. In the handling of (1) orders from new customers, (2) large orders from regular customers, and (3) defective orders, personally dictated replies are necessary. Other orders that can be filled in full and without delay are acknowledged on a printed form, sometimes carrying spaces for filling in information.

1. The New Customer. When an order from a new customer is received, a personal acknowledgment is sent on the same day. It should be appreciative and definite. Observe the following plan:

1. Thank the customer and welcome him.
2. Restate the order.
3. Make clear exactly how the order is being handled and shipped.
4. Express your cordial interest in serving him.

WELCOMING THE NEW CUSTOMER

We appreciate the order you gave to our representative, Mr. Ramsey, on February 3. It is a pleasure to have you as a user of our cut-and-copy service.

The contract provides that service is to be supplied for a period of one year, but you are to have the privilege of cancellation after two months if you are then convinced that the service will not prove profitable to you. Plates of the November release of the service are being shipped to you by express today.

Our service should prove of the greatest value to you in building up your patronage.

2. A Large Order from a Regular Customer. In accepting large orders from regular customers, follow the same outline. Expand 4, however, to include vigorous sales material to center the customer's attention on the selling points of the goods. The fact that the customer has sent a large order for your goods indicates that you have favorable ground in which to cultivate enthusiasm and to show a lively interest in his side of the transaction—the profits he will make.

ACKNOWLEDGMENT OF A LARGE ORDER FROM A REGULAR CUSTOMER

It was pleasant to hear yesterday from our representative, Mr. Britton, that you are placing an exclusive contract with us for the current year, covering your entire requirements of kegs and barrels. He has asked us to forward to you for your signature two copies of this contract, one to be retained for your files and the other to be returned for ours.

You can rely on us to give your orders our most prompt and careful attention. We shall observe your usual stipulations as to methods of shipment and routes until you give further notice.

Perhaps the fact that you have awarded us the contract for your entire year's requirements is evidence enough that you have had ample proof of the ruggedness and durability of our products. Under the most bruising conditions of service during long periods, Ironclad kegs and barrels with the corrugated steel-lock bindings stand the gaff.

For two reasons we hope that your consumption of barrels and kegs will be larger than ever this year. A larger consumption will indicate good business and profits for you, and it will give us more chance than ever to prove the economy of using Ironclad products.

We are glad indeed to be supplying your needs again this year as we have for so many years past.

3. Handling Defective Orders. In handling defective orders, lacking in necessary data, never make the customer feel at fault. Ask tactfully for the additional information needed. Point out that the

A "Card-Form" Order Acknowledgment

added information will prevent delay and assure accuracy in filling the order. Follow this plan:

1. Thank the customer.
2. Ask tactfully for additional information. Never suggest that the customer is at fault.
3. Show that your request is made in order to serve the customer well.

HANDLING A DEFECTIVE ORDER

The Negative Way	*The Positive Way*
We have received your order for six Bulldog Grip pipe wrenches but can do nothing until we get more information.	Thank you for your order of November 23.
You failed to state in what size or sizes you want us to send these wrenches. Naturally we can't guess at this, and we will have to hold your order up until you give us the necessary sizes. Trust you will correct this error at once.	The sizes in which you want these six Bulldog Grip pipe wrenches were not mentioned. We stock 8-inch, 10-inch, 12-inch, and 14-inch in the regular heads.
	If you will indicate the exact sizes you want, we will see that your order goes out at once.

Acknowledgments to Bridge Unavoidable Delays. An acknowledgment note should without fail be sent in those situations in which some delay is necessary.

Thank you for your inquiry [*or* order *or* suggestion, etc.]. Just as soon as we can gather the necessary facts [*or* data *or* figures *or* reports *or* estimates, etc.], we'll write you promptly.

206

Part-Shipment, Out-of-Stock, and Deferred-Shipment Acknowledgments. At times in every business only a part of an order can be shipped at once because of an unexpected demand that has exhausted the particular item called for. Sometimes deferred shipment is necessary when new stock is in production but has not yet been finished for shipping. Such situations call for suitable acknowledgments. Too often messages concerning exhausted stock mention only delay, inconvenience, disappointment—exactly the matters which should not be emphasized. In their place should appear:

1. Appreciation for the order.
2. Businesslike speed in filling it at the earliest possible moment.
3. A cordial request to the customer for cooperation in overcoming the present difficulty.

AN EFFECTIVE DEFERRED-SHIPMENT MESSAGE

Thank you for your confirmation of order No. 261, given to our representative, Mr. Osmer.

Complete shipment of your order can be made about May 1. Style No. 907 could not be placed in process as anticipated, and we do not as yet have a run of B width. We believe you would prefer to have us hold your order on file until that time. If, however, you wish us to send ahead by express the 18 pairs of Style No. 322, and the 5 pairs of Style No. 108 in D width, please let us know.

You have our warm wishes for a profit-making spring.

Declining Orders. Established merchandising policies, exclusive agencies, and restricted territories sometimes make it necessary to refuse orders that come to the wrong offices. National manufacturers selling exclusively through local dealers, for example, usually decline orders that come to the factory, itself, as some orders do. The correspondent who handles this type of message must develop and maintain a positive, willing-to-serve, assuring attitude, which tactfully handles the customer in such a way as to induce him to finish the transaction through the proper channel. Such a message calls for:

1. A statement of appreciation for the order.
2. Complete information.
3. Definite directions as to what the customer should do next.
4. A closing sentence courteously suggesting the proper action.

Note the examples on page 208. The first shows how an order is refused in the wrong way; the second, how the business is tactfully saved by rerouting it through the local dealer.

THIS REFUSAL EMPHASIZES THE CUSTOMER'S IGNORANCE

We are sorry that we are unable to take care of your request of March 17. Perhaps you did not know that all merchandise advertised by us in Chicago newspapers is intended for the residents of Cook County only. Outside of this territory we sell only through home-furnishing dealers.

Martin and Kline of Council Bluffs have a copy of our latest catalog and can show you what we offer. Perhaps you can find a satisfactory model by consulting them, and we can then take your order through them in due course.

THIS POSITIVE REVISION TACTFULLY SAVES THE BUSINESS

Thank you for your inquiry of March 17. We are glad to help you get the hi-fi speaker cabinet you want.

For the convenience of our customers living outside the Chicago area, we supply their needs through home-furnishings dealers in their home cities. In Council Bluffs our dealer is Martin and Kline. They have a copy of the latest catalog in which our complete line of hi-fi speaker cabinets is illustrated. We have written them to call on you so that you can look over the catalog to determine the model you prefer. You can then place your order with them.

From the information in your inquiry, we believe you would especially like the new, graceful lines of the Criterion model, illustrated in color on pages 29 and 30 of the catalog.

We shall be pleased to fill your order through Martin and Kline.

Summary

Mastery of the basic messages enlarges management power. Daily transaction messages—the types discussed in this chapter—are instruments in constant use during each business day. The art of dictating a concise inquiry or reply is by no means as simple as commonly thought. Nor are well-constructed announcements, business invitations, and appointments as numerous as might be hoped. The discussion of orders, remittances, and acknowledgments carries value for everyone. Almost every person has to order something in writing at some time. He also needs some knowledge of handling remittances. Tactful acknowledgments, which often play an immense part in building priceless good will, are part of the lifeblood of the successful management operation. To these basic forms of daily expression the future management man must therefore first apply himself, in order to assure his ready mastery over situations that will face him the first day he goes to work.

Communication Problems

● 1. J. H. Taylor has purchased an automobile liability insurance policy from the Mutual Automobile Insurance Company. He wants to be sure that he fully understands the coverage. He wishes to know if the policy covers his personal loss in a collision—for example, clothes—as well as assumes his liability. He wants to know if his wife is included as the named insured even though her name does not appear on the policy. From time to time he drives cars belonging to other people. Is he covered in these cases? Taylor has a 17-year-old son who drives the car occasionally. Is the insurance in force when his son is driving? Assume that you are J. H. Taylor and write this inquiry.

● 2. Mrs. Tom Bennett, 1021 Avenue O, Denton, Texas, types themes, theses, and dissertations for the students at North Texas State College. She has been using a reconditioned Royal typewriter for the past three years. She thinks that if she had an electric typewriter, she could make more money because of its increased ease and speed of operation.

She heard by radio that the Central Typewriter Supply Company at 105 Main Street, Dallas 3, Texas is offering special prices on their new and reconditioned typewriters. She feels that since her old reconditioned typewriter has given good service, another reconditioned one would be sufficient for her work.

Write an inquiry for Mrs. Bennett to Central Typewriter Supply Company asking if they handle reconditioned electric typewriters. Include any other questions you think Mrs. Bennett would like answered in order for her to decide about going over to see the typewriter.

● 3. Reply to J. H. Taylor's inquiry about his automobile liability insurance policy (Problem 1). The policy automatically includes the wife even though her name does not appear on the policy. The son is also protected, provided he is living at home. In other words, the policy includes all members of the household, and they are covered while driving the family car or when driving a car belonging to someone else.

If the son is away at school, the policy can be extended for a nominal cost to include him.

This liability policy includes collision, comprehensive, and medical payments. It does not cover personal belongings. For a small cost, however, coverage of personal effects can be made a stated part of the policy.

● 4. You saw an advertisement in your church magazine for a summer companion for a slightly crippled young person about your age. The advertisement indicated all expenses paid for an enjoyable summer in the person's home in Boston and at a summer home on Cape Cod, plus other possible travel opportunities. You answered the advertisement. You receive a long reply from the father, asking for a great deal of detailed information. You can see that this long reply was used to weed out those persons who answered out of curiosity and those who felt they might be able to get something for nothing.

The message states that the person wanted is someone who can sincerely take the place of a sister (or brother)—someone to give advice or suggestions; someone to help with simple household chores; someone to share friends. As in any family relationship, not all of your time would be required in companionship; whole days at a time you might be on your own.

Following this explanation, you are asked to submit your qualifications under these five headings:

1. *Background and Breeding:* Tell pertinent facts about your childhood, your family, your education, and your work experience.

2. *Health:* Serious illnesses, general physical condition, athletic participation.

3. *Point of View:* Are you naturally conservative and conventional? Or do you believe in "speaking your piece"? Can you discuss any topic calmly and without giving offense? Do you readily accept the new? For example, in clothes, in entertainment, in cars, in music?

4. *Tastes:* Do you prefer sedentary and intellectual occupations? Or do you prefer rigorous activities? What are your preferences in literature, fiction, music? What kind of social affairs do you like—formal or informal, large or small parties? What is your favorite pastime, hobby?

5. *Disposition and Personality:* Are you usually gay and high spirited? Are you sociable and chatty? Are you easily discouraged? Are you emotionally well-balanced, easily adaptable? Are you practical in almost all things?

This opportunity and challenge appeal to you. Respond by giving the detailed information. Make up a name and address.

This analytical, critical self-analysis may serve you well when you begin job finding. It is not too soon for you to begin to think about what you have to offer a prospective employer. Make notations (thinking as objectively about yourself as you can) for reference when you study applications and later when you begin an actual job campaign.

● 5. You are correspondent for TV Antennas, Inc. Mr. John Rose has ordered your #A2307 television antenna selling for $27.50. He enclosed his check for the antenna and $2.70 shipping charges. You determine that Mr. Rose lives in a fringe area. The antenna he ordered is suitable only for local reception. Your #A3500 fringe area antenna is $5 more than the one that Mr. Rose ordered. Write him that the #A2307 would not be adequate in his area. Try tactfully to switch him to your #A3500 model. Tell him that you will hold his check until you hear from him.

● 6. As Sales Manager for the Farrell Manufacturing Co. of Oklahoma City, you personally try to acknowledge all orders that cannot be filled promptly. Today you received an order from J. B. Jones, Manager of Jones Department Store in McAlister, Oklahoma, asking that the following goods be sent and charged to his account:

> 3 dozen No. 35B 1337 Men's rayon and cotton short sleeve sport shirts; tan, green, and blue; one dozen each of size small, medium, and large @ $36 .... $108
>
> 3 dozen No. 35B 1304 Men's combed cotton short sleeve sport shirts; red, charcoal, and blue; one dozen each of size small, medium, and large @ $33 99
>
> $207

You can send the rayon and cotton sport shirts right away, but the combed cotton sport shirts will have to be delayed. The combed cotton sport shirt has been such a popular seller that you are now three weeks behind in your current orders. This shirt has the authentic ivy styling with the button-down collar, button at back of collar, and the center box pleat. Tell Mr. Jones of its wrinkle-resistant qualities that will appeal to the women doing the buying, and tell him about its square cut "in-or-outer" bottom that is the accepted style today. Try to convince Mr. Jones that it is to his advantage to wait, and, at the same time, try to keep him as a regular customer.

● 7. *Lead* Magazine is sponsoring a nationwide puzzle contest. First prize is $10,000. The initial 120 puzzles appeared weekly in leading newspapers. As Contest Editor for *Lead*, you have discovered that contestants found puzzles Nos. 81, 96, 106, and 116 the more difficult. Thousands of persons who entered either missed one of these or dropped out of the contest entirely.

Write an announcement to the contestants who submitted correct solutions to the initial puzzles. The tie-breaking puzzles with complete instructions will be mailed within a week or two.

● 8. As President, you want to tell the members of your Mutual Savings and Loan Association about the change in telephone number as well as report on the progress of your new building.

Since telephone service has been unsatisfactory, Mutual Savings has taken advantage of the switchover to new numbers by providing a switchboard and additional trunk lines on a rotary system. This will eliminate "busy" signals, which you feel possibly has been a disadvantage to you and to your members when they have tried to call.

Give your members your new telephone number. Tell them work on your new building is going right along ("Yes, the work does seem slow. You're even more anxious than they are, you imagine. But, as they know, time is needed to build a first-class building of first-class materials.") Add any additional information you think will keep your members happy with their selection of a savings institution.

● 9. You are a photographer. You have just received an inquiry from Mrs. Edward Barnhart, 1111 Lovers Lane, Tucson, Arizona, concerning the pictures you made at her wedding two months ago. She said, "I have not received the pictures I ordered. I have my canceled check which I sent in payment for the pictures."

You search your files and find that your assistant who resigned three weeks ago was supposed to have mailed the pictures but failed to do so. Send Mrs. Barnhart the pictures with an explanation.

● 10. As owner-manager of the Carpenter Lumber Company, Bridgeport, Texas, you have received an order from Mr. Rush Wages, Route 1, Paradise, Texas, for 100 rough oak boards, 2″ by 12″ by 18′. He included his check for $203 ($2 for each board and $3 for delivery). You have only 75 of the boards and will not have the other 25 until July 12, two days after the requested delivery date.

In an acknowledgment to Mr. Wages, ask if he would prefer to have you send all 100 of the boards at the same time (two days late), or deliver the 75 oak boards on the specified date and the other 25 when they arrive and at no extra cost. You can finish filling the order with 26 smooth oak boards at an additional cost of $6.25.

Remind Mr. Wages that these oak boards are guaranteed to have no more than three knotholes each. Moreover, even though you charge for delivery, Mr. Wages will no doubt find this less expensive and surely less trouble than if he had to provide the transportation.

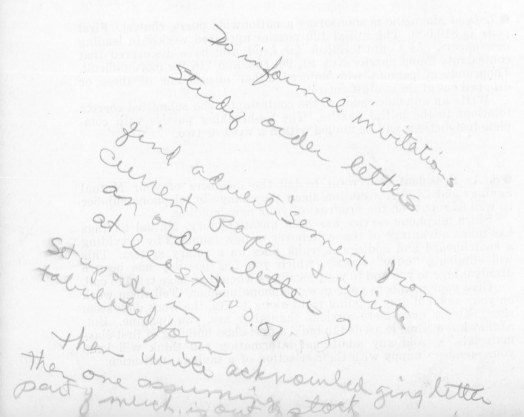

PART IV

Chapter 10
Human-Interest Messages:
Asking, Granting, and Declining Favors;
Appreciation, Congratulation, and Praise;
Introductions and Recommendations

Executive Action in Its Developing Stages. Early in your career you will be called upon to deal with situations involving important personal feelings. These situations will often present special kinds of "human relations" problems that may have emotional overtones. To handle such situations, you will need to develop and learn to apply some new kinds of executive action. In the following pages, therefore, we shall explain and illustrate some of these more advanced procedures, reflecting executive action in its developing stages.

Successful Handling of Personal Feelings. Many messages deal with sensitive personal feelings. Suppose, for example, that you now hold a good junior executive post with your organization. Let us say that you ask for a certain privilege that, although a little out of the ordinary, has been granted to others on several occasions.

If your chief says, "OK . . . your request is fully approved," and adds a verbal pat on the back for good work, you will almost certainly bask in a glow of satisfaction. On the other hand, if you get a curt note saying, "Request refused," that brusque message will surely involve your sensitive personal feelings in quite another way. It goes without saying that neither you nor anyone else can expect to go through life having all requests granted like a warm breeze. But one thing is certain: when they can't be granted—when they have to be refused—they can be handled with courtesy and cushioned with tact.

Asking, Granting, and Declining Favors

Asking Favors. In carrying out necessary executive action, as well as in one's own personal activities, asking others for favors or for various kinds of cooperation is often required. No matter whether the favor is great or small in importance, you should prepare each request as persuasively as possible in order that you may be sure it receives a favorable reception. Here is an illustration in tactful words.

ASKING A FAVOR

Clear-Cut Request
  { May I have your permission to keep my report, "Methods Used by the University Student Employment Bureau to Accomplish Its Purpose"? This was our Commerce 200 assignment for December 12, 19--.

Explanation and Background
  { I plan to give this report to Miss Arlene Ford, a co-worker at the Student Employment Bureau, who is leaving for a position at Midland University after her graduation in June. She hopes to convince the Regents at Midland of the value of such a bureau and to help establish one there.

Courteous Close
  { If my report will aid Miss Ford in any way, I should be happy to give it to her. We shall both appreciate your approval of this request.

Be Positive in Tone. Make your request interesting to your reader. Put yourself in his place. Use the positive approach.

A SUCCESSFUL, POSITIVE REQUEST

Subject
  { As part of my work in the American School of Administration, I am asked to report on the quality of written communication sent and received in the state of Massachusetts.

Request
  { Do you have any business messages of the following types (carbon copies will do), for which you have no further use? The examples may be good, average, or poor in quality.

Inquiry; answer to an inquiry
Asking a favor or granting or refusing one
Acknowledgment
Application
Report

Explanation
  { If you wish to retain these pieces of correspondence in your files, may I make copies of them? I shall make copies without revealing the name of either the sender or the recipient if you prefer.

Courteous Close
  { I shall appreciate any help you can give me.

Don't Ruin Your Effort with Negative Suggestion. Suggesting that someone may try to block the request, or that the action your reader may take is liable to be unfavorable, or that your suggestion is unlikely to be a success, or that you know the reader is busy, is negative through and through and will defeat the proposal before it can "get off the ground." A typically negative and clumsy appeal goes like this: "I know that you are extremely busy, and I further realize that you are bothered a great deal by people who want to sell

you kitchenware. I know also that you have some connections which
have undoubtedly proved satisfactory to you. But I want to explain
. . . " etc. This writer was beaten before he began!

Asking Cooperation. How would you handle this management
case? The vice president of Roycrofts, Inc. notices that his store is
suffering an increasing loss caused by customers' returning goods
taken out on approval. The loss is due to the fact that goods taken
out on approval are kept for several days before being returned.
Through agreement of all the stores in the city to restrict to 48 hours
the privilege of returning goods, the evil may, in some degree, be
reduced. Such an agreement requires cooperation. Accordingly, he
writes to the managers of other important city businesses:

ASKING COOPERATION

Tactful
Opening

     The question of placing a 48-hour limit on the
privilege of returning goods will be discussed at a
luncheon meeting at noon on Friday, October 29, at

Specific
Invitation

the Portland Club. As a businessman of long experience and keen interest in all problems of store
management, we should like to have you attend.

Supporting
Material
Urging
Cooperation

     The meeting will be attended by the managers
of the leading department stores in our city and
others interested in this question--of vital importance not only to the merchants but also to our
patrons.

     All who have discussed the matter with me
believe that only at such a meeting can we weigh
the question frankly and reach a solution.

Courteous
Close;
Action Made
Easy

     Your wise counsel will do much to make this
meeting a great success. I shall appreciate your
signing and returning the enclosed card to let me
know that you will be with us.

Granting Favors. To grant favors should be the easiest thing
in the world to do. It should be "child's play" to find cordial language
for such a message. Yet surprisingly enough, many messages are
ruined by a grudging consent. To give grudging consent is to destroy
the whole spirit of willingness. A request should be granted cheerfully and cordially—or not at all!

A FAVOR GRANTED CHEERFULLY AND CORDIALLY

     We are glad indeed to fill your request for a copy of
Space Age Ahead? Six months from now this book will be
entirely out of print--as a matter of fact, we have a meager
supply of a half-dozen copies in stock.

     I can think of no worthier mission for this book than
to have it permanently filed in your library. It is, therefore, with great pleasure that we send a copy to you in a
separate package.

GREY ADVERTISING AGENCY·INC

166 West 32nd Street · New York1, N.Y. · Chickering 4-3900

January 25, 19--

Mr. Kenneth K. O'Neal
1682 Arbor Boulevard
Fresno, California

Dear Mr. O'Neal

We are pleased in 117 ways to have you
ask for a copy of our study entitled
"117 Shortage-Tested Ideas."

Your copy is going to you with this note
and with it goes our earnest hope that in
its pages you will find perhaps specific
help and, if not that, then at least an
imaginative prod.

Cordially

Lawrence Valenstein

Lawrence Valenstein
President

LV:q
Enc.

General Motors takes pleasure in making
available to you this material. We hope
that it will prove interesting and contribute in some measure to a better understanding of the subject matter presented.

PUBLIC RELATIONS STAFF
GENERAL MOTORS
DETROIT 2, MICHIGAN

Granting Favors

Replies to inquiries may be typewritten or attractively printed in the
form of cards or slips. The replies
shown here emphasize favorable action
and courtesy and are neatly attached
to the transmitted material.

Here is another example of granting a favor. This message with
ungrudging and sincere cordiality, begets the full measure of good
will it so highly deserves. Note, too, the courteous tone and the
evident desire to help:

COURTEOUSLY GRANTING ANOTHER FAVOR

Pleasing Action First; Comment on Material

Here is a complimentary copy of the portfolio
of our spring promotional program, including our
salesmen's aids, store material, and other merchandising services. The portfolio is self-explanatory.

Expression of Interest

We are pleased to have students ask us for
help because improvements in methods rest largely
with young people who are now training themselves.
The merchandising field needs well-trained people.

Courteous Close

Your interest in our merchandising services
is appreciated. We shall be glad to help you with
any of your other training needs.

Often favors are granted by telephone. In these instances it is
usually desirable to confirm the telephone conversation and to give
additional information. For example:

It was a great pleasure to "OK" your request, made
yesterday afternoon in your long-distance call. The plans
as you described them seem first rate. I will be in your
office at 9 a.m. Monday, March 9, to discuss them further.

Declining Favors. When you are forced to decline a request for
a favor—and such a case is not infrequent—use the positive tone.

216

Mention first what you can do, if anything, rather than what you cannot do. *Instead of saying "No," say "Yes" to something else.* Follow this opening with a frank statement of what cannot be granted, giving the reason if you believe it should be given. Impersonal reasons for refusal (fixed company policies, regulations laid down by the board of directors or the like) reduce and may entirely remove the possibility of irritating the reader. Under no circumstances give a curt refusal. Tact in choice of words and courtesy in tone are vital.

Decline with Courtesy and Tact. To find a needle in the haystack is almost easier than to find a man who can refuse a request and leave the reader in almost as pleased a frame of mind as if he had granted it. The following examples are skillful in developing the positive and helpful attitude. Each, however, refuses the request. Study the plan, the choice of words, and the use of the courtesy tone.

A BANK VICE PRESIDENT DECLINES TO SUPPLY MATERIAL

Cordial Opening
{ Your interest in our campaign portfolios is very much appreciated.

Definite Reasons for Declining Request
{ The portfolios that you wish to examine were so successful that we received many more requests for them than we could fill. We no longer have sufficient materials to make up additional copies.

Concrete, Helpful Suggestions
{ Several firms supplied the materials from which our portfolios were made. A number of them are willing to supply copies of the original materials to others who want them. The enclosed list gives you the names and addresses of those firms whom you may write for these materials.

Concluding Suggestion for Alternate Help
{ Another excellent source of material of this type is the United Agency, of Chicago, who until this year developed our campaigns for us. There is also some excellent syndicated material available for a reasonable fee.

A COMPANY CONTROLLER DECLINES TO RELEASE A FINANCIAL STATEMENT

Positive Opening; Pleasant Tone
{ I wish it were possible for me to grant your request of April 14, but our directors have passed a resolution prohibiting the distribution of financial statements to anyone but stockholders.

Careful, Clear-Cut Explanation
{ This curtailment was necessary to protect the holders of our stock from unscrupulous individuals who, profiting by the information in our statements, were often instrumental in causing stockholders to dispose of their holdings at unfair prices.

Courteous Offer of Other Help
{ Why not come in to see me at your convenience? I can then give you such information about our company as will fully answer your purpose.

A PERSONNEL MANAGER DECLINES TO RAISE A SALARY

Positive
Opening;
Careful
Explanation
{ The substantial increase in your salary, given just six months ago after a year of service with our company, is still too recent to allow the additional increase requested in your memorandum of June 1. The policy of our company is to start all employees at an average salary with the understanding that increases will be considered on a yearly basis.

Encouraging
Tone; Positive
Close
{ Your work is very much appreciated. We carefully note the output of our employees, and we find your work quite acceptable. Mr. Daniel, your department head, reports that your attitude is praiseworthy and your work promising. Keep up this standard, and the advances will come.

Emphasize What You CAN Do. Almost every situation, however dark it may seem at first, has some feature, faint perhaps, that may carry favorable emphasis. Look for that feature. Give it prominence. Put a spotlight on it.

A customer of a finance company asks a favor, but what he asks is neither feasible nor desirable from the viewpoint of the company. The company can, however, suggest something that will fairly well meet the customer's original wishes. An executive writes: "I have had clerks who would begin with a blunt refusal and then, several paragraphs later, intimate that, after all, something might be done. . . . If the answer had stated first what could be done, and the least emphasis possible had been laid on the refusal to do exactly what was asked for, the whole tone and effect would have been different. The reply would have indicated a desire to meet the wishes of the correspondent. If it had been worded well, it would, quite likely, have presented a solution entirely satisfactory. The refusal to do exactly what had been asked would have been lost sight of in the earlier gratification of learning that something *would* be done."

EMPHASIZE WHAT *CAN* BE DONE

What CAN
Be Done;
Favorable
Action First
{ We are glad to send you a copy of <u>Executive Action</u>, which we hope will be helpful in planning your campaign. We have found the book of exceptional value. The success of our recent campaign was due to this practical volume.

The Refusal
{ In our type of business requests to examine our management methods are so numerous and the expense involved in keeping the material open for inspection is so great, that it has been necessary to decline all such requests.

Courteous
Close
{ We appreciate, however, your interest in our campaign and are glad that you liked it enough to inquire.

In Asking, Granting, and Declining Favors, Courtesy Pays Off!

"I do not know of a more certain key to success than courtesy," writes a famous top management man. "It will carry you further in this world and cost you less than any other single quality you could possess. If I could talk in twenty languages, I would preach courtesy in all of them!"

The "Stupid" Refusal: A Classic Case. A member of the staff of a certain university accepted the leadership of a part of the drive for collecting money for charity. Others on the staff normally helped in the drive to bring it to success. The following request to one of them drew the refusal shown in the right column.

COURTEOUS REQUEST	CLUMSY REFUSAL
Accompanying this note are several cards of the United Appeal. Can you arrange to take care of them or delegate an individual in your department to do so? I shall be glad to call someone personally to help you if you wish. The cards are so few in number that I am taking this informal means of reaching your department with them. You may be sure I shall appreciate your help.	I found on my desk this morning a bunch of United Appeal literature with a memo from you asking me if I would take care of the matter for the department. I have never done any soliciting, and I do not intend to begin now. Consequently, I shall refuse to help you in this matter. I do not want to start a thing of this kind, for it would result in a volume of such work being shifted to me. Ask somebody else.

In the refusal, note the curt and tactless expressions: " a bunch," "I do not intend to begin now," "I shall refuse to help you," "I do not want to start a thing of this kind." These are unwise and short-sighted in their irritability, and ruinous, of course, to good will. One can well imagine the dilemma in which this man will find himself when the situation is reversed and he wants some help from the man he so untactfully refused.

How to Win or Lose Friends and Business. Whether they are granted or refused, requests that are tactfully handled often lead to pleasing and friendly outcomes. The following instructive contrast shows how an order for fifty books was lost and how it might have been won through skill, courtesy, and tact.

THIS VERSION LOST THE ORDER FOR FIFTY BOOKS

You write us asking for a copy of *The Egotist,* which you state is wanted as a desk copy. Would state that if we were to furnish copies free of charge for all requests that we have, we would be pretty busy, as many requests come in each day.

We supply desk copy if asked for if an order is received for the book; that is if a quantity of books are ordered, we willingly furnish the teacher with desk copy, but we do not think we should be called upon to furnish said copy unless accompanied by an order.

Trusting you can see your way clear to order stock.

THIS VERSION CORDIALLY INVITES THE BUSINESS

We shall be glad to send you a desk copy of *The Egotist* free of charge if you will accompany your request with an order for ten or more copies.

The Egotist is attracting much attention today, and we have hundreds of requests every month for desk copies. For this reason we have found it necessary to limit our free copies to instructors using the book as a text in the classroom. It is our custom to furnish the desk copy free of charge with every order for ten or more copies.

As soon as we receive your order, a desk copy will be sent promptly.

The man who asked for the desk copy declared, "That 'scolding' discourteous reply has lost that company a sale of just fifty books. I was going to use their edition anyhow, without seeing the desk copy, but now I wouldn't use their book, no matter how good it may be!" Through blundering ignorance of human nature, lack of tact, and failure to see through the eyes of the other person, the sale of fifty books—a sale *almost completed*—was lost.

In the negative "scolding" reply the writer indulged in the expensive pastime of "dressing down" his reader and of telling him testily why he was wrong. The revision at the right (1) suggests favorable action in the opening paragraph; (2) gives a tactful explanation of policy in the second paragraph, with a note on the high-volume success of the book; and (3) concludes with a courteous invitation to order.

How to Say "No"—and Still Keep Friends and Customers

1. Put your "No" on an impersonal basis.
2. Make it clear that—if you could—you would like to say "Yes."
3. Make it evident that you have given the request careful thought.
4. When you say "No," show what needs to be done to get a "Yes."
5. Finally—and most important of all—say "No" in the warmest and most courteous way you know how.

Appreciation, Congratulation, and Praise

Appreciation. *To intend* to write notes of appreciation, congratulation, and praise—tomorrow, or next week—is typical of human nature. Yet how often the time lengthens into—never. And how often someone performs unusual services for us that we allow to pass unpraised, taking courtesy and helpfulness for granted.

Showing appreciation for service given is a part of good manners. Appreciation for service well done, like recognition of an achievement well won, is on the whole rare. Yet, to fail to pass along the good word for good work is both bad manners and poor business policy. An executive tells of a grizzled old salesman, a man who would never be suspected of caring a snap of his fingers for compliments, but who nevertheless grieved deeply over the fact that repeated good work brought forth no word of positive praise from his chief.

Good Taste. No matter how illustrious, no matter how humble he may be, every man likes to know when he has done well. Of course, he wants the recognition to be genuine. He will detect the differ-

THE OVERLAND ROUTE

March 27, 19

Dear Mr. Newkirk:

We're happy to have had the opportunity of serving you recently on the Overland Route.

Your patronage is genuinely appreciated and we extend to you our sincere "thank you."

We hope your trip was thoroughly enjoyable and that you will soon travel again over the Union Pacific Railroad.

Cordially yours,

Omaha, Nebraska

UNION PACIFIC RAILROAD

Notes of Appreciation Create Good Will

ence between sincerity and "eyewash." Express warmth and friendship. But to preserve their genuineness express them with restraint.

GENERAL ELECTRIC COMPANY

ONE RIVER ROAD, SCHENECTADY 5, NEW YORK . . . . . TELEPHONE FR 4:2211

August 27, 19--

Mr. Ronald C. McDonough
McDonough Manufacturing, Inc.
9027 Ferguson Road
Louisville 8, Kentucky

Dear Mr. McDonough:

Mr. Cordiner wants you to know that he is grateful for your cordial comments on our recent Employee Relations News Letter. Your enthusiastic response, along with that of so many more of your fellow share owners, has been most encouraging to us.

As you requested, we have sent you one dozen additional copies of this publication for your use, and I hope you have received them by now. We are confident that this type of active support by people like yourself should go a long way toward creating a climate of public opinion in which business can operate in the balanced best interests of all concerned.

I should be most interested to learn of the reaction of your acquaintances to the News Letter, and if you or they can use additional copies, please let me know.

Very truly yours,

C. S. Scott

Manager
SHARE OWNER RELATIONS

CSScott/j1
Enclosure

330 EAST 22 STREET LIFE CHICAGO, ILLINOIS

May 18, 19--

Dr. George K. Nantz
Doctors' Building
189 Central Parkway
Grand Rapids 7, Michigan

Dear Dr. Nantz

Thank you for expressing your interest in the special article published in the May 8 issue. The questions you have raised in your letter of May 15 are so important, in our opinion, that we have made plans to deal with them at length in a subsequent issue.

Accept our appreciation for your thoughtfulness in writing and for giving us the valuable benefit of your research.

Sincerely yours

W. K. Wills
For the
Editorial Board

WLWills/rr

Appreciation Expressed in a Brief, Effective Note

Some people should never attempt to write a note of appreciation because they are unable to put themselves into a generous frame of mind. The humiliating truth is that too many individuals find their chief pleasure in discovering weaknesses in others. Acutely aware, perhaps, of the many faults of which they themselves are guilty, they unconsciously defend themselves by searching hopefully for even more numerous faults in their associates. Something that can be criticized wins lively attention; something worthy of praise earns only jealous silence. The mails are sprinkled with complaints. That is why firms have correspondents who specialize in nothing but adjustments. But rare is the message praising good work.

Occasions that call for appreciation, congratulation, or praise are:

1. Appreciation for a favor granted.
2. Acknowledgment of special consideration shown.
3. Praise for a good record; for example, a strict devotion to duty during a difficult period.
4. Congratulations for success well earned.
5. Commendation for a public-spirited act.

Such messages show generosity of thought and interest in the welfare of others. As a by-product such messages cool the world's friction points and generate good will.

Can You Do as Well as These? The following are appreciative messages selected to illustrate typical occasions for use. Note their (1) tone, (2) expression, (3) good taste and restraint.

APPRECIATION FROM A MANAGEMENT EXECUTIVE

Your thoughtful comments on our recent survey certainly added to its value, and I sincerely thank you for your help. Please count me at your service when I can return your courtesy.

APPRECIATION FROM A MANUFACTURER TO A POLICE CHIEF

A few days ago our company had occasion to confer with Lieutenant Reardon regarding a traffic problem at our North Avenue plant. Let me express our appreciation for the prompt way in which Lieutenant Reardon and his department handled this matter. Your cooperation has helped to reduce a dangerous traffic hazard.

APPRECIATION FROM A PRINTER

The staff in our composing room are still feeling pretty fine over that note you sent them about the last job on the bulletins, which you felt came out so well. All they usually hear is kicks. They just wanted me to tell you that they appreciate the contrast.

A Printed Card of Appreciation   **A Window Envelope Expresses Appreciation After the Message Has Been Removed**

The normal relationship between individuals may be wholly in the realm of business. But business association offers many a chance for messages that cement cordial friendships. However far removed from business the messages of appreciation may seem, they give rise to friendly understandings that may profoundly affect the later course of important transactions.

With the postal service collecting and delivering one or more times a day in every community, it is hard, indeed, to understand why anyone should deprive himself of a business friend or a personal friend that is his for the asking.

Personal Messages of Appreciation: They Are More Important Than You Think. The line between business appreciation and personal appreciation is often so thin that it cannot be discerned. You cannot tell where one leaves off and the other begins. This is as it should be. The businessman, the professional man, the public servant —all of us—owe an eternal debt to those who have constructively shaped our lives. We should never forget our debt.

"We were a group of friends in the midst of an after-dinner conversation ten years ago," writes the Reverend William L. Stidger of the staff of the Boston University School of Theology. "Because Thanksgiving was just around the corner and prosperity wasn't, we were talking about what we had to be thankful for." He continues:*

That started us. One of us said: "Well I, for one, am grateful to Mrs. Wendt, an old schoolteacher who 30 years ago went out of her way to introduce me to Tennyson." She had, it appeared, awakened his literary interests and developed his gifts for expression.

"Does this Mrs. Wendt know that she made such a contribution to your life?" someone asked.

* William L. Stidger, "Must You Keep Your Heart in Cold Storage?" in the *Christian Advocate*, November 27, 1941; and as condensed in the *Reader's Digest*, November, 1942. Quoted by permission.

"I'm afraid not. I've never taken the trouble to tell her."

"Then why don't you write her? It would certainly make her happy, if she is alive, and it might make you happier, too. Far too few of us have developed the habit of gratitude."

All this was very poignant to me, because Mrs. Wendt was my teacher, and I was the fellow who hadn't written. My friend's challenge made me see that I had accepted something precious and hadn't bothered to say thanks.

That evening, on the chance that Mrs. Wendt might still be living, I wrote her what I called a Thanksgiving letter.

My letter was forwarded from town to town. Finally it reached her, and this is the note I had in return. . . .

> I can't tell you how much your note meant to me. I am in my eighties, living alone in a small room, cooking my own meals, lonely and like the last leaf of fall lingering behind.
>
> You will be interested to know that I taught school for fifty years and yours is the first note of appreciation I ever received. It came on a blue, cold morning, and it cheered me as nothing has in many years. . . .

My first Thanksgiving letter had proved so satisfying that I made a list of people who had contributed something deep and lasting to my life, and planned to write at least one every day in November. I sent out 50 letters. All but two brought answers immediately. Those two were returned by relatives, saying that the addressees were dead. And even those letters expressed thanks for the little bit of thoughtfulness.

Perhaps the most touching answer came from Bishop William F. McDowell, whose wife had once cared for me with such motherly thoughtfulness that I never forgot it—but I had never written her a letter of thanks. Now I remembered and, knowing that she was gone, wrote my Thanksgiving letter to the bishop, telling him of my memory. I received this in response:

> Your letter was so beautiful, so real, that as I sat reading it in my study tears fell from my eyes, tears of gratitude. Then, before I realized what I was doing, I arose from my chair, called her name, and started to show it to her—forgetting that she was gone. You will never know how much your letter has warmed my spirit. I have been walking about in the glow of it all day long.

For ten years I have continued to write my Thanksgiving month letters, and I now have more than 500 of the most beautiful answers anyone has ever received.

A Thanksgiving letter isn't much. Only a few lines are necessary. But the rewards are so great that eternity alone can estimate them. . . . Thanks to the rebuke of a friend, I have learned a little about gratitude.

Congratulations and Praise.

Messages of congratulation and praise offer you the chance to show pleasure in the success and good fortune of others. To send a note of congratulation that rings true, you must of course feel true pleasure in the good luck about which you write. If you do not, or if your feeling is tinged with envy, you will do better not to write. Insincerity always shows itself. Look for sincere opportunities to congratulate a friend on some piece of good fortune. Your effort may give you as much pleasure as it does him.

Pat Him on the Back with a Note of Congratulations!

Note the firm tone, the warm sincerity, and the good taste in the following examples:

A BRIEF CONGRATULATORY NOTE

    This brief note is to tell you how pleased I was to read, on page 196 of the <u>Bulletin</u> for February, of the honors you received last November from the National Association of Technical Schools. My congratulations are most sincere because I know that the honor is well deserved.

A CONGRATULATORY MESSAGE FROM A TOP MANAGEMENT EXECUTIVE

    Let me congratulate you on your advancement to vice president of your firm. The promotion is well merited, and I am glad to know that your top people are recognizing your fine services. You have been doing wonderful work that reflects energetic, resourceful, and capable administration. I am glad to see it recognized.

PRESIDENT COOLIDGE WRITES BIRTHDAY CONGRATULATIONS
TO THOMAS A. EDISON

    I am glad to have an opportunity to join with your friends throughout the world in extending hearty congratulations upon your eightieth birthday. To your energy, courage, industry, and strong will the world owes a debt of gratitude which it is impossible to compute. Your inventions, placing the forces of nature at the service of humanity, have added to our comfort and happiness and are a benefaction to all mankind for generations to come. I trust that there are in store for you many more years of health and usefulness.

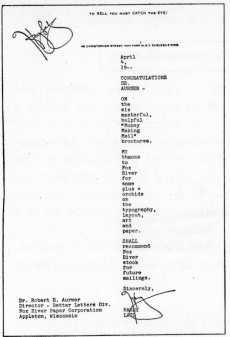

Message of Congratulations	Message of Praise and Appreciation

Note the unusual arrangement.

Sympathy. The true meaning of expressions of sympathy comes only from the reality of the misfortune that brings them forth. But sorrows may be softened through the sympathetic expression of good friends. Probably the most celebrated of all notes of sympathy—and one of the world's most famous—is that of President Lincoln to Mrs. Bixby.

> MESSENGER OF SYMPATHY AND LOVE
> SERVANT OF PARTED FRIENDS
> CONSOLER OF THE LONELY
> BOND OF THE SCATTERED FAMILY
> ENLARGER OF THE COMMON LIFE

"Messenger of Sympathy"

Inscription engraved on capstones of U. S. Post Office, Washington, D. C.

I have been shown in the files of the War Department a statement of the Adjutant General of Massachusetts that you are the mother of five sons who have died gloriously on the field of battle. I feel how weak and fruitless must be any words of mine which should attempt to beguile you from the grief of a loss so overwhelming. But I cannot refrain from tendering to you the consolation that may be found in the thanks of the Republic they died to save. I pray that our heavenly Father may assuage the anguish of your bereavement and leave you only the cherished memory of the loved and lost, and the solemn pride that must be yours to have laid so costly a sacrifice upon the altar of freedom.

Introductions and Recommendations

Introductions. Especially helpful in establishing business and social contacts are introductions. Let us suppose you are taking a position in Cleveland, Ohio. You have no acquaintances in that city, but your present employer has business connections there. As a courtesy to you, he gives you an unsealed written introduction to one of his friends in Cleveland. When you arrive at your new location, you present the introduction in person to the one addressed. He may help you to make acquaintance with others—and you will be off to a good start.

In writing the introduction, you make a statement about another, telling who he is and why he is being introduced. Use the following plan:

1. Introduce the person.
2. Give your reason for writing the introduction.
3. Supply brief information about the person introduced.
4. Express appreciation for any courtesies.

This example follows the plan suggested:

Introduction and Identification   It is a pleasure to introduce Mr. Carl Benet, who has until the first of this month been on the staff of Consulting Associates, Inc., New York City, as vice president in charge of accounts.

Reason for Writing   Mr. Benet has been commissioned to open and take charge of the Chicago office.

Information About the Individual   I have known Mr. Benet for a number of years. He is energetic, full of enthusiasm and leadership, and among the best of community citizens.

Appreciation for Courtesies Shown   Any aid you can give him in making some desirable contacts in his new location will be personally appreciated.

When the occasion is simple, a substitute for a letter is a business card bearing the words, *Introducing Mr. Benet*.

The envelope carrying the written introduction should be addressed in the usual manner. In the lower left-hand corner add a notation similar to the following one:

                          Introducing
                          Mr. Carl Benet

Recommendations. A recommendation may be (1) *specific*, addressed to a particular individual, or (2) *general*, intended for anyone interested. The specific recommendation carries more weight because it contains more detail. It is often written to cover an inquiry from an employer who is following up a reference given in an application. The following examples give *specific* recommendations to the inquiries:

AN INQUIRY

What can you tell us about Miss Christine Lowry, who is an applicant for the position of office manager in our organization? Your comments will be of great help in filling the position.

THE REPLY: A SPECIFIC RECOMMENDATION

Miss Christine Lowry, for whom you requested a rating in your note of May 19, can capably fill your office managership. In expressing that opinion, I believe I speak conservatively.

The record shows that in her preparatory training she turned in the type of creative work that reflects initiative, careful and thoughtful planning, and the ability to assume responsibility in carrying out a series of related projects.

Miss Lowry appears to have sound technical abilities and the temperament and background to make effective use of them. But aside from her technical preparation, about which I understand she has given you full information, she is fortunate in having a pleasing personality. In the kind of position for which she is applying, these attributes would seem vital. A part of her personal pattern is the quality of tact and the ability to work with others.

If I were filling the type of position you now have open, I should give careful consideration to Miss Lowry. She has reached the point at which she will develop into a valuable junior office executive.

*   *   *

AN INQUIRY

Mr. Marshall T. Simpson has applied for a position in our Engineering Department. He has given your name as reference. We shall appreciate it if you will let us have your impression of Mr. Simpson's character and ability.

THE REPLY: A SPECIFIC RECOMMENDATION

Mr. Marshall T. Simpson, about whom you ask in your inquiry of November 6, was employed in our Engineering Department from 19-- to 19--. Before coming to us, he spent three years in marine and stationary engineering work. During the time he was here, he developed into a capable draftsman.

The experience he has in stationary and marine engineering work from the operating standpoint is of great value in boiler and power plant engineering. Mr. Simpson is industrious, of high character, and of superior ability. He is a man who made a definite place for himself in our organization.

During a slump, while he was temporarily laid off, he secured another position and made a change. We were sorry to lose him and should be glad to employ him again, if the chance came.

The *general* recommendation, intended to be read by anyone interested, customarily carries the opening address: "To Whom It May Concern."

A GENERAL RECOMMENDATION

Mr. Louis Frank, bearer, has been in the employ of the Lawton Company since 19--. During the last eight years he has been in the Department of General Superintendence.

Mr. Frank is thoroughly reliable and is a man of good habits. He has given us entire satisfaction, and we consider him a capable workman. He is an excellent man to handle a crew.

A general recommendation is valued at little more than a certificate of good standing. Much more valuable is the specific recommendation giving definite information.

Handle Psychological Overtones with Care. Human decisions and relationships continually involve actions of asking, granting, or declining requests. Hence, the practical suggestions of this chapter, showing how these actions may be carried out to the advantage of everyone concerned, are most important.

Relatively few people have enjoyed the interesting experience of writing appreciative or congratulatory notes. Such messages are comparatively rare. The majority of people are too self-centered, and their reserve supply of unselfishness is too small, to permit such messages to become numerous. In spite of the caustic truth, however, it is worth while to practice writing such messages. Because messages of praise and sympathy involve a structure similar to those of congratulation, these forms have also been discussed. These strictly human-interest notes bring into play psychological overtones involving one's personal feelings in a most sensitive fashion. For that reason they should be handled with great care. One prediction may confidently be made: once you learn how to handle human-interest writing, you will possess a management tool that will serve you well throughout your life.

Communication Problems

● 1. Mr. and Mrs. Carl Brown who live in a Midwestern state are moving to Seattle for the summer months. Since they have never been there, they have decided to write the Seattle Chamber of Commerce to learn what rent expense to expect for a moderate, nearly new, three-bedroom home in a newer neighborhood. Learning something about the climate would help them decide what kind of clothes to take. They are also interested in recreational activities offered and in points of interest. (The Seattle office of the company Mr. Brown works for will help them find a location, but the Browns would like to do a little investigating on their own). Write the request for information that the Browns will send.

● 2. Mrs. Carrie Roberts' billfold has disappeared. In it she had three Charga-Plates from Oklahoma City stores. Not knowing what happened to her billfold and whether she is likely to recover it, she wants to write each of the three stores for a new Charga-Plate. To forestall possible use of the lost Charga-Plates by someone else, she wants a name-and-address change. Her charge accounts are in the name of Mrs. Carrie Roberts, 915 West Ninth Street, Tulsa 6, Oklahoma (her permanent address). She wants the name changed to Mrs. Monroe Roberts, 2013 West Ridge, Norman, Oklahoma. Write the request for Mrs. Roberts.

● 3. J. L. Forrest has applied for the position of Secretary-Manager of the Chamber of Commerce in your city. As Chairman of the Selection Committee, it is your job to write to Mr. Forrest's references asking their opinion of the ability of Mr. Forrest to fill satisfactorily such a position.

Of course, you are interested in the applicant's personality since your organization has an important public relations function to perform for your city. Tact is an important qualification. In meeting others and discussing affairs with them, does Mr. Forrest have any tendency toward antagonizing them? How did the applicant stand in the respect of his fellow workers? Does he have an open mind? Since he will assume responsibility for the supervision of Chamber affairs, how would the respondent rate the candidate's basic intelligence? Does he possess initiative and resourcefulness?

Write to Dr. B. L. Little (one of the references), a college professor in another state, inquiring about Mr. Forrest. You do not know Dr. Little.

● 4. The Arrowhead Council of the Boy Scouts of America needs a camp site for this year's roundup. The Gulf Oil Company's Dallas office has a beautiful section of land on Lake Grapevine that would be perfect for the one-week encampment, attended by about 200 boys. The boys will be well supervised by counselors.

As scout executive for the Arrowhead Council, write to Harry McMill requesting the free use of the Lake Grapevine site. The scouts will assume all responsibility for damages.

● 5. In a reply to Mr. Carl Brown, give him the information about Seattle. (Refer to Problem 1.)

● 6. You are Harry McMill, Division Manager for Gulf Oil Company, Dallas. You cannot grant the scouts' request (Problem 4). True, the land at the Lake Grapevine site is in the name of Gulf Oil, but credit for the development of the site goes to the division employees. For many weekends, the employees contributed their labor toward the building of a clubhouse and boat dock and in beautifying the area.

It was decided early in the effort to limit the use of the facilities to Gulf employees, and even they are restricted to some extent.

Employees must make reservations and each reservation is limited to three days. The policy has proved to be a satisfactory one, and the site is so popular that reservations are usually booked weeks ahead.

Mindful of the worthy purpose prompting the request and of the good will that could be generated through granting it, you still must refuse. Write the refusal.

● 7. Assuming you are Dr. B. L. Little, write a recommendation for Mr. J. L. Forrest (Problem 3). You recall Mr. Forrest very well. For one reason, in the classroom he seemed to carry a chip on his shoulder; he was argumentative about every point. You sometimes felt this indicated a pugnacious quality; yet you tried to give him the benefit of the doubt by thinking it indicated an inquiring mind, since Mr. Forrest was a capable student. Yet he frequently questioned his grade, thinking it should have been higher. You wondered whether he could do even better work if he would relax and concentrate on learning rather than on arguing about grades.

Outside the classroom, Mr. Forrest was pleasant to talk with and seemed to be well liked by his fellow students. You learned through talking with him that he commuted about 200 miles round trip three days a week to attend classes. He was punctual and regular in attendance. In your opinion, this long-distance commuting indicated initiative, determination, and dependability.

Since you believe Mr. Forrest capable of the Secretary-Manager position, you want to give him a favorable recommendation. Yet in fairness to the applicant, to the inquirer, and to yourself, you want to mention not only desirable qualities but also those that you feel might possibly be a drawback. Give emphasis to the favorable and, through subordination and space adjustment, minimize the unfavorable to whatever degree you feel is just.

● 8. With her last payment on her Twenty Pay Endowment at Age 65 Policy for $1,000, Mrs. Mae Bettis Jackson sends a note asking, "Am I supposed to do anything now except wait until I'm 65 to collect my insurance?"

You are the Manager of the Policyholders Service Department for the insurance company. Write a congratulatory-explanatory reply to Mrs. Jackson, 911 Avenue J, Orlando, Florida.

Mrs. Jackson had two riders attached to her policy. The double-indemnity benefit rider will terminate on the paid-up date (the 12th). Mrs. Jackson may, however, make a new arrangement for its being continued. She cannot as heretofore pay this premium on an annual basis, but she can extend this benefit to age 65 by paying one single premium of $26.58. (This is equivalent to about $1.25 a year since Mrs. Jackson's endowment policy will not mature for about twenty more years.) Enclose the form for applying for the extension and tactfully urge her to complete it and return it with her payment.

The automobile-accident benefit rider also will terminate on the paid-up date, and there is no provision by which it can be continued.

Mrs. Jackson was prompt in her premium payments for twenty years. Encourage her to ask about additional life insurance needs—your company issues a form of policy to meet every need, for all ages, and at premium rates lower than is usual.

PART V Effective Applications: A Personnel Management Problem

Chapter II   *Preparing to Write an Application*

Your Success Will Depend on One Word: "Yes." Naturally you hope to be successful in getting your first job. Or you hope to be equally successful in making a change from your present job to a still better one.

> JUNIOR-EXECUTIVE CORRESPONDENT—rapid dictator; good language command; able to meet people well; college course in communications desirable. State education and experience fully. Address P H 387, TRIBUNE.

In either of these hopes you will aim at three vital—and now familiar —targets. First mentioned in an earlier chapter, they continue to play an important part in executive action in its first stages. Do you recall those three targets? Here they are, more vital than ever in assuring you a successful application:

1. Aim to understand other people.
2. Aim to learn how they act and why they act as they do.
3. *Aim, through the written word, to win a favorable response.*

For let it again be remembered, every day of your employed life, that every purchase, every sale, every contract, every transaction, every application to personnel management, and every other constructive management outcome *depends upon the word "Yes" from someone.* This fact is ten times true of applications, because when you ask for a job, someone—probably a personnel management man —will have to say "Yes" (or "No") to you. And so it is easy to see why applications often present special kinds of "human relations" problems that may have emotional "side effects" or "overtones" either joyful—or the opposite.

Follow the Experts' Rules. Personnel experts will tell you that the most successful applications are prepared according to tested rules that experience, hard and practical experience, has proved sound. Remember that rules for preparing good applications are not imposed to cramp your originality but to guide it. Rules are simply concise statements telling you how the most successful people prepared applications that won jobs.

233

Follow the Experts' Rules

Such rules have gone through the fire of experience. They have worked. Properly used, they will work again. You use them as guides to steer your thinking and your preparation. You really need these guides. The fact is that only a few people ever succeed without strenuously studying them. And these "rare birds" do succeed only because they *instinctively* follow the rules without having to think about them.

If you can prove that you are of this "gifted" class, then you can fling rules to the stars and go your own inspired way. But if you cannot prove it, you will be far wiser to drive according to the "application road signs." In fact the only person who can disregard rules is he who has mastered every one of them and knows what he is doing when he violates one.

You may hear now and then of a "born" football star, a "born" basketball or tennis or golf star. These rare people may indeed run ninety yards through a phalanx of opposing players and cross the goal line standing up; or shoot impossible one-hand baskets with their backs to the hoop; or make service "aces" with sizzling bullet-like drives across the net; or drive a golf ball 220 yards straight to the green across 200 yards of blue ocean water and boiling surf at the Sixteenth Hole at Cypress Point.

But for each of these brilliant and gifted persons you will find tens of thousands who find they have to learn the rules, drill on the fundamentals, and time their follow-through and their pitch shots and their drives by endless and patient practice. The chances are that you are one of these. And so you are most likely to succeed by learning and following the rules. This and the next chapter will present the rules for you.

What Management Men Will Tell You. Personnel management men, the men who hire and fire or who make important recommendations to those who do hire and fire, have nothing but the most merciless condemnation of the "mill-run" applications they currently receive. Anyone who, like a personnel management officer, is forced to read hundreds of applications, will not long doubt the need for intensive study of the subject.

As they are currently prepared, the majority of applications are painful exhibits of miserable mediocrity. "I have just read more than two hundred applications," comments a personnel management executive, *"and not more than three out of the two hundred were worth my attention.* They all seemed to come out of the same old 'model-book' mold. These cursed so-called 'application model-books' that purport to give misguided persons a 'model' that they can copy verbatim are pernicious abuses that mislead the ignorant hopefuls into personal dishonesty, and lose for them any chance they have for the position they want. I can spot a 'model-book' application," he concluded, "almost before my secretary has it out of the envelope. In fact I sometimes believe I can detect it by its peculiar smell!"

Personal-Use Value High. No document ranks higher than the application in terms of personal-use value. Everyone admits this fact, but not everyone has the will power to master the application art.

Most placement directors, men whose professional management duty is to find positions for those who want them, conclude that an astonishingly large number of job hunters do not have the slightest knowledge of how to prepare an application that will advance their chances of getting work. Many of these applicants have good educations. Yet, from their products, one is forced to the conclusion that they were taught nothing whatever about applications for personal use; or else they have forgotten everything they once knew.

A management executive puts it this way: "One thing we cannot overemphasize: If the applicant has the best education in the world and is unable to sell it, it is worth exactly nothing from the standpoint of income."

A personnel director comments, "Apparently, instruction in applications is lacking in many colleges and universities. To my way of thinking, practical knowledge of this type is of the utmost importance in preparing students for their future lives."

Surveys reveal that personnel executives want facts: the complete story, told interestingly, without high pressure, and *keyed* to the needs of the position.

Applicant-Rating Guide

An employer looks for qualities like these in the application, in the interview, and after the position has been won.

1. How does the applicant rate on the following points:

Industry	Reaction to correction
Accuracy	Punctuality and attendance
Rapidity in work	

2. (a) How long has the candidate been employed?
   (b) For what reason was the connection with the firm ended?
3. Would the conduct of the applicant entitle him to the confidence of his employer?
4. Underline the qualities in which you consider the applicant strong; cross out any in which you think him weak.

Pride in quality of work	Mental alertness
Thoroughness	Versatility
Ambition	Common sense

Applications Vastly Important as "Career Tools." Overwhelming evidence shows the huge importance of applications in winning job interviews. "The letters a candidate writes probably have most weight," concludes a recent survey, "in securing him an interview and a job."

From the *Reader's Digest*: "Winifred Tarwood was just out of school, looking for her first job. She haunted agencies, she answered want ads; once in a while she got an interview—but never a job. Yet after she had discovered the key . . . she received 34 answers to a batch of letters of application, finally was offered two jobs, in spite of the competition of experienced girls."

Significant to every person who will ever need a position is an item that appeared in a New York financial publication. It offered an exceptional opportunity for a sales executive. The man, said the notice, must have a personality that will enable him to get the full cooperation of his associates and to inspire confidence in his subordinates. Then the notice continued:

> This man must be old enough to have had the experience which will qualify him for this position and still be young enough to work with an aggressive organization.
>
> The man securing this position must be of a caliber and ability to command a salary of at least $25,000 a year to start.
>
> WRITE A LETTER giving in detail your qualifications. Your application will be treated in strictest confidence. Address Box CC87.

You will notice that, although this invitation was directed to men who believed they were competent to handle the executive burdens of a $25,000-a-year position, it asked them to write a letter of application. Employers looking for men of this caliber still want to examine qualifications *before* they grant interviews.

YOU, Personified on Paper. Your application is, in one important sense, a YOU-selling message. Specifically, and as persuasively as you can, you present your training, skill, knowledge, service, and ability in the most intensely personal form you will ever use in business. Your effort will represent you as it reaches your prospective employer's desk; in one sense it will be you. It will be as if you said: "This, Mr. Employer, is my accredited representative, my chief ambassador. This letter shows you what I think I am, and gives you my own picture of myself. By it I am ready to stand or fall!"

Of course you will be in the midst of competition. Prepare yourself to compete with other applicants who, just as earnestly as you, will want the same job you do. They too will send their accredited representatives. Like you, they will depend on a piece of writing that pictures themselves as well as they know how. Your task is to make yourself more skillful than they in order that you may put your case more adroitly. The competition is keen and fair. To win, you must prove yourself the better applicant.

The compelling reason for mastering the art of application is this: prospective employers in every business like to "size up" applicants ahead of the interview. They want to determine in advance whether the applicants are worth taking the time to see. Whether they are worth taking the time to see depends almost entirely upon the impression their letters of application make.

Jobs Are Always Available—If You Know How to Apply for Them

The Teeth of These Two Gears Should Intermesh with Fine Precision
Can you put them together and make them fit?

Show How "What You Can Do" Fits "What Must Be Done."
Take any two men, equal in training and ability: the one who has
better knowledge of application procedure will get the position. He
wins it for two reasons: (1) He knows how to state to advantage
what he can do, and (2) he has the all-essential knack of showing how
"what he can do" measures up with "what the employer wants done."
He fits together the teeth of two gears—"what he can do" gears into
"what must be done"—and shows to his prospective employer how
these two gears might work well together.

**To Win a Position, Study (1) Yourself, (2) the Job You Want,
and (3) Techniques of Showing How the Two Fit Together.** When
you prepare to sell yourself, you study yourself to determine your
actual abilities. You get ready to put into persuasive words a description of your training, your skill, and your knowledge. You study the
services you can perform in order to be able to put these services
vividly on paper. In brief, you give yourself a realistic analysis and
an objective appraisal.

If you want to sell a product, you study it to discover its superior
qualities and its valuable uses. You next study the market to find out
who are your prospective buyers, where they live, what their buying
habits are, what features and qualities they want, and what appeals
will prove strongest in directing these buyers to your product and
in linking your product to their needs. You follow the same process
in preparing to win a job.

What Kind of Person are You?

Analyzing "Yourself" (as the Product). An applicant's self-analysis is a thorough self-examination designed to show the essential details of (1) what you are and (2) what you can do.

How to Analyze Yourself

I. Outline the basic requirements of the type of position in which you are interested.

II. Show how your education fits these requirements.

III. Show how your experiences fit these requirements.

IV. Add personal qualifications and items of human interest.

Supply Sharp Detail: Be Concrete. For eight months Tony Morosini, a young delivery truck driver, had hunted in vain for a job. He had references praising his "loyalty" and "efficiency" and "faithful work," but these somehow had failed to impress other employers. Then Tony met an expert. The expert asked questions. How many accidents had he had? Tony's black eyes flashed. "Not a fender dented in six years!" Had he made many mistakes? "You know Indian Point?" Tony countered. Yes, the counselor knew Indian Point was a mass of unnumbered houses. "Well," continued Tony, sticking out his chest, "in those six years I never made a wrong delivery on Indian Point!" "All right," said his adviser, "from now on you begin by asking every employer you call on how he would like a delivery man who hasn't dented a fender in six years or made a mistake on Indian Point." Four days later Tony had a job.*

The same procedure works for college graduates. Arthur K., who had worked his way through college by clerking in an athletic-goods store, found upon graduation that mention of this experience alone did not impress employers. Prompted by expert counsel, he focused his approach on specific points. He had made a certain brand of socks best sellers in the college by inducing six prominent students to wear them; he had doubled the sales of a sweater by displaying in the store window photographs of it worn by coaches and athletic stars. He went back to employers, submitted those simple but telling details, and soon had a job.

"At least 50 per cent of the applications we receive," writes a personnel officer, "are ineffective because they lack details. Time will not permit us to ferret out the facts that are missing and write for further information."

* The *Reader's Digest*, Vol. 36, No. 214, p. 18.

"Most letters of application do not give sufficient information. Ours is a large organization," points out another executive, "and there may be a vacancy other than the one the applicant has mentioned. Often, however, we can take no action because the applicant has not given enough information to disclose whether he can do more than one type of work."

> "You told me how good you were when I hired you three months ago," said the boss to the new employee. "Now, tell me all over again. I'm getting discouraged!"

In preparing your Basic Data Self-Analysis, let your slogan be this: *Specify. Give Details.* In all your application materials strike out every generality and substitute a fact. Tell concretely, factually, vividly what you have done that was well done. Your prospective employer wants to know in sharp and concrete detail what you can do *for him*, and he wants as complete a picture of you and your characteristics as possible, including background, education, knowledge of your field, and the kinds of work you most enjoy.

Two Successful Self-Analyses: How Will Yours Look? On pages 241 and 242 appear two successful self-analyses. See how they provide the needed basic data. Note the care with which they develop detailed information.

Your Future Employer: Who and Where Is He?

Location and Character of Your Possible Employer (Market Analysis). In hiring you, your future employer must have something in return for his money. Just as in selling a vacuum cleaner the sales representative first studies his product, then analyzes the need of his prospect, and finally fits them together, so you apply these principles when you campaign for a job. Yet an appalling number of applications sound like the wailing of lost souls in the wilderness. Their theme: "I want a job. I want a job because I need that pay check." "I've got to have a job. I've got to have a job because my shoes are getting thin!" All the time their wails are howling across the industrial scene, these unhappy lost souls may, ironically enough, have qualifications that would *get* them jobs, if they knew where to look for prospects and how to state their qualifications in the right way. To learn this right way and its basic requirements is a personal necessity in the face of modern competition.

Case I. Applicant's Self-Analysis for an Accounting Position

I. My Understanding of Requirements of Position

A technical and theoretical accounting background.
A knowledge of all phases of accounting.
A knowledge of business phases, techniques, and operations related to accounting.
Specifically applicant should be able to:

1. Audit accounts under supervision.
2. Maintain control accounts in accordance with prescribed rules, regulations, and procedures.
3. Do accounting work on field audits of major scope under specific directions.
4. Analyze tax and other returns of partnerships, individuals, and fiduciaries.
5. Determine tax or other financial liability.
6. Verify returns and compile accounting data as directed.
7. Assist in the construction and installation of systems of accounting suitable to the needs of co-operative associations and public utilities, and subdivisions of the state, county, or municipal governments.
8. Prepare contract and disability claims.
9. Keep general ledger accounts for a large department.
10. Reconcile accounts with detail.
11. Carry out routine accounting work in accordance with prescribed classification of accounts.
12. Audit the allocation of disbursements to funds and set up adjustment accounts.
13. Work on inventories and other related duties.

II. How My Education Fits These Requirements

Four years of study at Western University as an accounting major.
Have a proficiency in operating Monroe and Marchant calculators.
Specifically, also have:

1. Become acquainted with the organization of partnerships, fiduciaries, co-operatives, and corporations.
2. Studied various systems of cost accounting.
3. Become accustomed to the handling of records and statistical data.
4. Become acquainted with the preparation and adjustment of inventories.
5. Made audits of depreciation accounts.
6. Become acquainted with contracts and disability claims in courses in general insurance and fire and casualty insurance.

III. How My Experience Fits These Requirements

Treasurer and bookkeeper of a student co-operative for two years.
Summer jobs as stock and sales clerk in a large grocery supermarket.
Operator of bakery route at a summer resort.
Payroll clerk at Scott County headquarters.
Bookkeeper in County Agent's office.
Accounting clerk in State Senate under direction of Chief Clerk.

IV. Personal Qualifications and Items of Human Interest

Worked as farm hand during early summer vacations.
Accounting clerk in the State Legislature for the 39th Biennium.
Earned 75% of my college expenses while carrying full academic load; earned the other 25% in summers.

Case II. Applicant's Self-Analysis for a Wholesale-Grocery Salesman's Position

I. My Understanding of Requirements of Position

Sell fruit, produce, and dry groceries such as sugar, candy, beans, rice, and cheese to grocery stores, hotels, and restaurants, to be delivered by truck a few days later.
Make collections from customers.
Make adjustments of customers' complaints.
Make weekly reports.
Act as host for visiting manufacturers' salesmen and take them along on the route.
Help retailers (my customers) with suggestions and merchandising ideas.

II. How My Education Fits These Requirements

Understand the workings of a wholesale house. As a graduate of the University of Florida, have also taken:

1. Psychology courses—Introductory, Applied, and Abnormal Psychology—all have helped me to understand others, meet them, and sell to them.
2. Courses in investment, money and banking, accounting. Statistics have shown me many of the grocer's financial problems.
3. Courses in marketing, advertising, and merchandising, which will aid me in giving the dealer good display helps and keep me alert to inform the sales force of their value.

My reports will be neatly presented and easily read as a result of my report training.
Social experience at the University will make it easier for me to introduce the manufacturer's salesmen.

III. How My Experience Fits These Requirements

Have had three years' work in a grocery store, meeting and talking with salesmen.
For two years was doing a good deal of the buying in this store.
Have had one year of successful experience in selling wholesale dairy products.
Have sold bread and pastry at retail for six months.
From experience I know many of the grocer's problems and attitudes.
Know the importance of maintaining good feelings with dealers.
Have worked in the commissary of a large transient camp; am acquainted with commissary report forms.
Have experience in merchandising, card lettering, and window display.
My experience in helping to set up a credit system in a small-town store has given me useful background.

IV. Personal Qualifications and Items of Human Interest

Like people, like to sell, and enjoy changes of scenery.
Can work cooperatively.
Do a great deal of my own car and truck repair work.
My study of psychology and my experience in dealing with 500 "hobos" in the transient camp mentioned above have given me insight into human behavior.

How to Build Your Prospect List. Your next step, then, after completing your Self-Analysis, is to comb the market and search out prospective employers who might need the kind of ability you can offer. The person who lacks the initiative to analyze himself and his prospective market will, perhaps, send a few half-hearted messages to a haphazard collection of addresses—and promptly be lost in the shuffle of competition. Therefore:

1. Make a mailing list of likely prospective employers. Find out what companies are showing net earnings. (Don't waste your energies on companies that are laying off men.) The sources given below are useful in making a list of prospective employers.

Sources for Making a List of Prospective Employers

Accountants' Index
Art Index
Ayer's Directory of American Newspapers and Periodicals
Bradford's Survey and Directory of Marketing Research Agencies in the United States and the World
Chemical Engineering Catalog
Custom House Guide
Engineering Index
Fitch Statistical Service
Guide to American Business Directories
Industrial Arts Index
Insurance Year Book
Kelly's Directory of Merchants, Manufacturers, and Shippers of the World
McKittrick Directory of Advertisers
The Mercantile Year Book and Directory of Exporters
Moody's Manual of Investments, American and Foreign

Oil and Petroleum Yearbook
Polk's Bank Directory
Poor's Register of Directors and Executives
Public Affairs Information Service Bulletin
Rand McNally's Bankers' Directory
Readers' Guide to Periodical Literature
Reference Book of Dun & Bradstreet
Security Dealers of North America
Standard and Poor's Facts and Forecasts
Standard Corporation Records
Survey of Current Business (U. S. Department of Commerce)
Thomas' Register of American Manufacturers
U. S. Census of Manufactures
U. S. Government Organization Manual
Wall Street Journal
Who's Who in Commerce and Industry
World Almanac

---

2. Watch rentals, leases, and incorporations in order to be among the first to apply to a new organization.
3. Talk to secretaries of chambers of commerce, both local and regional, in order to be among the first to hear of industrial developments.
4. Talk to secretaries of trade associations for the same purpose.
5. Talk to local bankers to keep abreast of business developments in your area.

These sources may give you not only a valuable mailing list but also helpful information on individual companies and their executives. A personal knowledge of an executive is useful. Through such knowledge you may "slant" the selection of your facts and personal data to fit the expressed interests of the executive himself.

Your prospect list should be well developed, so that your returns will be adequate. You are organizing a "sharpshooting" mail campaign. Ordinary direct-mail returns commonly range between 2 per cent and 20 per cent, with the norm perhaps between 5 per cent and 10 per cent. Aim to make your returns far better than any of these figures. Remember—you are "sharpshooting" to a highly selected *personal* list of prospects. Hence your returns should be far better. Perhaps it hardly needs to be repeated as a blanket precaution; but it does no harm to state again the one basic rule of *what not to do*: NEVER BROADCAST A MIMEOGRAPHED SHEET TO HUNDREDS OF POTENTIAL EMPLOYERS!

Study Your Prospective Employer. To analyze the character of companies and their products or services requires systematic research. Use the following procedure:

(1) Check the resources of your library; (2) talk to people who know your field; (3) if there is a branch office of the company nearby, arrange a visit; (4) find out about the man who does the hiring; (5) familiarize yourself with current marketing, distribution, mercantile, and industrial problems by keeping abreast of magazines in your field, e. g., *Business Week, Printers' Ink, Sales Management, Chain Store Management,* the *Nation's Business, Fortune,* and others; (6) read the house organs and trade papers of the mercantile or industrial field in which you are interested. Then you can write your application and talk in your interview from a wealth of background material.

Gathering Information about the Position. You are now ready to gather data regarding the position. Include even the minor points. Use the following procedure:

(1) Determine the specific needs of the position; (2) determine whether the company is conservative or aggressive, whether the major executives are young or old; (3) determine the nature of the product or line of products, or the type of service; (4) determine the position of the company within its industry or field; (5) determine, as far as possible, what qualities the employer will look for in the applicant: initiative, ability, precision, conscientiousness, tact, etc.; (6) determine who really runs the show; (7) determine how the company is thought of in the community; (8) find out how the product is accepted; (9) get the answer to the question, "What's the reputation of the management?"; (10) find out the employee turnover rate; finally, (11) find out, if you can, what former employees say about the company.

How One Individual Analyzed the Market and the Prospective Employers and "Made" a Position. A stenographic expert decided one day that if she were to open an office of public stenography, she could earn far more than in the secretarial position she already held. But there was risk in the venture, as she well knew. Good positions were scarce. She hesitated to give up the one she had until she was reasonably sure that the prospective venture was sound. To make sure called for a *market analysis*.

Selecting a medium-sized office building in Chicago as a field for her survey, she copied from the lobby directory the name of each tenant in the building. There were 102. To these she sent the following questionnaire-letter:

> Would a high-grade, complete stenographic service, right here in the Mid-State Building, help you solve some of your office problems?
>
> Several executives in this building have asked me to open an office here. They feel there is room for a public stenographer in the building. I would sincerely appreciate your opinion.
>
> Could you use: 1. High-grade dictation service?
> 2. Typing service of all kinds?
> 3. A notary public service?
>
> A candid reply from you in the enclosed stamped envelope will help determine whether this service comes here or not. Any suggestions you make will be appreciated.

The letter went out on a Friday evening. By the following Tuesday morning, she had 39 replies. Of these, 20 were so favorable that they decided the question for her. Two months later she had all the business she could handle and was earning twice as much as in her previous job. She had determined the possibilities of her business venture with a market analysis that cost her less than fifteen dollars. [*Bulletin* of the Direct Mail Advertising Association.]

Completing the Steps. Let us assume that you have now found out where the prospective employers are located, when they do their interviewing, what opportunities are open, and what qualifications are needed for handling these jobs.

You now put yourself back on the examining stand and determine whether the qualifications you have are those the employer wants. If your product and market analyses disclose that your qualifications fit those required by the employer, you proceed to the third and final step—*use of the proper contact*, discussion of which will appear in the next chapter.

┌─────────────┐
│   Summary   │
└─────────────┘

In this way you complete the preparatory market research that gives your application the advantage over its pressing competition. For competition you will have, and plenty of it! To meet it, you must make every preparatory step count. The simple outline of your study will look somewhat as follows:

1. *The product:* yourself, your skills, your abilities.
2. *The market:* prospective employers whose locations, job opportunities, and needs you have studied.
3. *The contact:* your application—one of the most personal documents you will ever write.

A Six-Step Plan for Landing the *Right* Job

(Steps used by 20,000 successful job-seekers)

1. **Analyze yourself.** Begin by writing an experience record of jobs held. Put down how well you handled each job, whether you made any contribution to your employer's interests, and what the results were. Compare your assets and liabilities. Draw honest conclusions.

2. **Determine what service you have to offer.** What can you do best? What do you most want to do? By the process of elimination, settle on one specific job.

3. **Make a list of prospective employers.** Do some research on them. Then decide how you can best reach them: by letter, by personal contact, through mutual friends or business associates, by advertisements, or through employment agencies.

4. **Prepare your material.** First, a resumé of what you can best do. Slant it directly toward the job you want. Major rule for the resumé is: Keep it brief. Prepare your master application to use in getting your interview.

5. **Never assume you are going to get a job because you need it.** The employer cannot afford to consult your needs. But show that you can be an asset to his business and you will get the job.

6. **Aim for the specific job.** Never ask a prospective employer, "Have you any jobs open?"

—*Reader's Digest, Vol. 55, No. 330, pages 88-89*

Communication Problems

● **1.** Write a job description of the position you want. Assume that you really want this job and that your application will have to compete with other excellent applications. List what you believe your competitors will stress in their applications. What other characteristics would you expect to find in your competitors' applications?

● 2. Many companies, and particularly larger firms, have prepared special folders, booklets, and other informational materials to familiarize college students with career opportunities in these firms. Professional and industrial associations have also prepared useful materials to inform college graduates of job requirements and career opportunities in various fields of work. Examples include:

Career Opportunities, Glidden Company
Opportunities with the Dow Chemical Company
Your Opportunity at Western Electric
Employment Opportunities, Socony Mobil Oil Company
Opportunities for College Graduates in the Bell System
Job Opportunity Descriptions, The Texas Company
Job Opportunities at the Northern Trust Company, Chicago, Illinois
Employment Opportunities, Swift & Company
Careers in Red Cross, American National Red Cross

Directions: Because these materials will be highly useful in your job-hunting campaign, collect them for the type of work or the industry in which you are actually interested. For each booklet or piece of material you collect, list the title, the source, and a brief summary of the contents.

Possible sources of such materials include libraries, placement offices, guidance officers, vocational education departments, and your major faculty advisor. Trade journals, business magazines, and company offices are other possible sources. Because many large firms distribute these booklets and materials, you may be able to obtain many of them by writing directly to the company and indicating specifically how these items will be used.

After you have reviewed your collection of items, indicate which companies or which jobs interest you most and explain how these materials influenced your decision.

● 3. Arrange for interviews with persons who are now working at jobs for which you are preparing. You may wish to interview two or three people who are working in similar jobs but in different firms. On the other hand, you may prefer to interview two or three people who are working in different jobs within your area of specialization. Your instructor or major professor will be able to help you find persons—perhaps recent graduates—who will be willing to talk with you about their respective careers.

Before you ask for these interviews, plan your questions so that you will include the following topics:

Nature of the position
Duties and responsibilities
Usual starting point or initial position
Special training required
Favorable features of position
Unfavorable features of position
Opportunities for promotion
Places where this type of employment is likely to be found
General information about salary at various levels

Add any other topics that are of interest to you and that will help you make a good analysis and comparison of these various jobs or types of work.

Directions: Arrange and conduct your interviews. Then write a brief report of these topics, reviewing the information you have gathered from each person interviewed. For the second part of your report, indicate which of the positions has the greatest attraction to you. Explain your preferences.

● 4. Outline in detail the type of job you would like to have ten years after graduation, and specify the company in which you would like to work. Gather all the information you can about the position and the company. Use the appropriate sources of information listed on page 243. See the eleven points listed on page 244. Present your findings in a well-organized report.

● 5. In connection with Problem 4, assume that a casual friend now works for the firm in which you want to work and that he has offered to "tell you anything you would like to know about the company." Write him an informal inquiry and enumerate any questions about the firm you would like him to answer.

● 6. After completing Problem 4 above, make a complete list of your qualifications for this job. Your list should be a frank self-analysis and should include phases of your education, experiences, or interests which might be considered favorably by the hiring official who will interview you. Your analysis should be similar to the examples on pages 241 and 242.

● 7. Again consider the requirements of the position you outlined in Problem 4. List your specific qualifications, detailed accomplishments, and concrete experiences, or personal interests which might be helpful or interesting to your interviewers. Be specific.

● 8. Interview the hiring executive of a large organization in your community, and get his opinions and comments on "How to Write a Successful Application." Compare his points with those listed in this book, and report to the class on your findings.

● 9. Find an example of a poor application, or get an actual example from a businessman. Disguise the name of the applicant and tell why you think it is a poor application.

● 10. Select a blind announcement from the "Help Wanted" columns of a newspaper. Choose a job in which you have some actual interest. Assume you want the job. List the reasons why it would be difficult to write a good application in response to this blind announcement.

•
•
•
•
•
•

PART V

•
•

Chapter 12   *Creating a Successful Application*
                                    to Personnel Management

Personnel Managers Are Human. The impression sometimes gets around that personnel management people are like watchdogs at the gate. They sit at their desks guarding the interests of the company— and keeping outsiders from getting a job.

Of course such an impression is ridiculous. Nothing could be further from the truth. Personnel men are as human as all the rest of us. They have an important job to do. To test this statement, ask yourself these questions: "Why do *they* hold *their* jobs? Why do *they* sit at *their* desks? Why do *they* invite you to come in so that *they* can talk to you?" The answer to all these questions is the same: They are the "selectors." They are the experts through whom the company selects its future employees. If they are lax, the company hires someone it doesn't want. If they are overrigid, the company may lose someone it should have hired. Like all other people, personnel managers sometimes make mistakes. But in the main they do an effective job. They select qualified people whom the company will welcome into the "family." Perhaps you will be one of these.

Now Comes the "Pay-Off." There is more to the job-getting process than a period of anticipation and an exhibition of hopefulness. You may indeed be most sincere and earnest in your preparation. But preparatory steps are only that—preparation. Now comes the "Pay-Off." (1) Can you put on paper—persuasively—what you know about yourself? Then (2) Can you fit these facts precisely to the employer's needs? You will recall those two famous "gears" mentioned on page 238: the first entitled "What You Can Do," and the second, "What Must Be Done." Can you fit them together?

Applications Fall into Two Types. You will recognize two broad types of applications: (1) *solicited applications*, written in answer to general "announcement of job opportunities" (often called "want ads" when they appear in newspapers), and (2) *unsolicited applications*: the type written by an applicant who hopes that there may be an employment opening or who happens to hear of a vacancy.

But more commonly the unsolicited type is written at the suggestion of a third person who may know the prospective employer or who may know of a specific position. The third person may be a representative of an appointment bureau, of an employment agency, or simply a friend.

The greater number of applications are drawn by "want ads," in answer to which sometimes hundreds of replies will pour in. Hence, your application, if it is to get more than casual notice, should seek to stimulate attention and interest through its tone, expression, and appearance.

Answering "Masked" Announcements. A "masked" or "blind" announcement is one in which the employer's name is not revealed. The requirements of the job are also mentioned only in general terms. Hence the success of your reply will depend somewhat on luck. Since you know in advance that your application will be only one of perhaps hundreds, some simple distinction like a long envelope or a lightly tinted envelope may help to single your reply out of the pile.

When You Don't Know to Whom to Write. "To whom shall I send my application when I'm not able to determine the name of one of the company officers?" asks a puzzled graduate accounting major. "Should I address the application to the head of the company, the treasurer, chief accountant, comptroller, employment department, or to whom?"

Firms differ in their hiring procedure, and they may place the responsibility for employing and dismissing personnel upon any one of these officers or department heads. When you know no officer by name, you may safely address your letter to the *Personnel Director.* Your letter will then be routed promptly to the hiring office if the firm has no personnel director. Mention of the office of Personnel Director compliments the firm if it is not large enough to have such a specialized officer. You should try, of course, to determine, in advance of applying, the name of the hiring officer and his correct title. If you use the man's name, then for his sake *and yours,* spell his name correctly! If your inquiry fails to bring the information, you lose no advantage. And your inquiry may possibly supply some incidental points of information you can later use to advantage.

Answering "Complete" Announcements. An "announcement of a job opportunity" that offers facts enough so that the applicant can make a study of the opportunity and can fit his abilities to the needs of the employer is called a "complete" announcement. In general—though this rule does not always hold—complete announcements offer opportunities for more desirable and better paying positions than do blind announcements. Hence you can afford to put more effort into studying the employer's needs and showing how you can fill them.

The Application

Planning the Application. A plan for anything as individual and personal as an application must be adaptable to many circumstances. Sometimes a man of rich personality and engaging expression can win a position with an application that seems to have little plan and less structure. In his case he wins the job, not because of lack of plan, but in spite of it. His personality and his power of expression more than offset the structural defects of his effort. The tested plan developed in the following paragraphs can be shaped to express individuality without sacrificing power.

What Personnel Officers Say About Applications

Any deficiencies or careless errors tend to cause an employer to judge the applicant accordingly.

* * *

A well set-up application with good grammar and spelling, as well as good presentation, gives the applicant an immense advantage.

* * *

We try not to be too greatly influenced by these factors, but subconsciously we are swayed by them far more than we realize.

* * *

Often these factors determine whether an applicant will receive the consideration of an interview.

* * *

If an applicant were appearing personally for his interview, he would naturally shine his shoes, brush his hair, put on well-pressed clothes. That application of his is going in his place. *Its* appearance is just as important as *his* appearance would be.

Make the First Impression Favorable. When an employer glances over a pile of from 25 to 200 applications, he may select not more than 10 or 20 of the best-looking applications for examination. A neat, accurate, and handsome draft has far more chance of favorable attention than its less attractive competitors. Employers know by experience that a poor letter usually means a poor applicant. They turn their attention to the fine-looking letter, knowing that it usually means a superior applicant. Handsome appearance is doubly essential in applications responding to "masked" advertisements because it is the sole means by which you can gain distinction.

Buy a few sheets of good-quality bond paper with envelopes to match. The paper should be white, and the size should be the standard business sheet of 8½ by 11 inches. Avoid social, club, hotel, fraternity, or fancy stationery. To use any of these is to run the risk of raising a prejudice against yourself. Do not use the letterhead of the business with which you are now employed.

When you prepare for a personal interview, you are careful to dress attractively and in good taste. The message by which you hope to get the interview should be equally attractive. Make your message command respect. Its strength will be tested by "how it looks." Make it symmetrical through proper arrangement. Frame it like a picture in the same proportions as those of the sheet upon which it is placed. Let every detail be perfect.

Type Your Application. A typed application will have a strong competitive advantage over the large number of others that will come in handwritten. By contrast your application will stand out. Typewriting may mean the difference between winning and losing the job.

If the advertisement asks you to submit the application in your own handwriting, do so—but send along an excellent typewritten copy. Your prospective employer will then read the typewriting, and may do no more than glance at the handwriting. Thus you follow the employer's literal instructions without losing your competitive advantage.

Follow the Six Steps. An application should attract favorable attention, arouse interest, stimulate desire, get action. These functions translate themselves into the six steps of application shown below.

The Six Steps in an Application

1. **Establish a point of contact** (attract favorable attention).
   a. Physical appearance and arrangement (discussed in the preceding paragraphs)
   b. A direct opening statement: nature and purpose of the message

2. **State your understanding of the requirements of the position** (arouse beginning interest).

3. **Show how your education and experience fit these requirements** (sustain interest, and stimulate desire for a personal interview, as your qualifications begin to appear valuable).

4. **Give personal qualifications with flashes of "human interest"** (strengthen desire for a personal interview that will check your "written" personality against your actual presence).
   a. Your interest in the employer's type of business
   b. Reasons for leaving your present connection
   c. Personal desires and chief aim or interest
   d. Why you feel you can fill the requirements

5. **Give references** (strengthen the employer's desire to look further into your qualifications).

6. **Ask for an interview** (the result you desire).

Step 1. Your Point of Contact: the Opening Sentence. Your point of contact, the opening sentence, shows the purpose of the application and tells where you learned of the position (through an advertisement or otherwise) or mentions the name of the person with whom the prospective employer is acquainted and who has suggested that you write. Your opening sentence should be followed by a statement that you *are* applying. The fact that you are applying should not be left to suggestion or implication. It should be said outright. Apply in clear-cut terms: "Please consider me an applicant." "I should like to apply for this position." "May I be considered an applicant?"

① *Point of Contact*	Mr. George Reston, Personnel Officer of the American Trust Bank of Chicago, has told me that you have a vacancy in your Research and Statistical Department. May I be considered an applicant for this position?

Step 2. Your Understanding of the Requirements. If you are making your first application, your understanding of the needs of the employer will come from general knowledge and what you learn from friends. If you are a mature person of considerable experience, this part offers you a chance to show your understanding and capacity.

② *Understanding of the Requirements*	I understand that you want a young man with a working knowledge of statistical techniques. He should also have a thorough understanding of the application of mathematics to statistical procedure, a background in business and economics, and be able to assume the responsibility for preparing monthly reports and analyses.

Step 3. How Your Training Fits These Requirements. Base your statement of your education and experience upon selected facts from your career. This part of the letter may also be enlarged by use of a data sheet, discussed and illustrated in later pages. Sift these facts several times until you have found the ones that bear on the employer's needs. Take the YOU-attitude. Assume the point of view of the employer. Try to see how what you can do fits into what he wants done. Imagine that you have two maps of the same size and shape. The one below is what the employer wants done. The one above is what you can do. Your task is to fit the two together so that the lines meet as closely as possible. From your education and experience choose and sift until you find the facts that focus on the employer's needs. In the words of one expert who employs thousands, "The approach should reveal something about the applicant that is of value to us."

Even the largest companies want applications to be personal. "If an applicant is interested in our industry," says one executive, "he should make a sufficient study of that industry to know for what specific company he wants to work, and why."

③
*How Your
Training
Fits These
Requirements*
{ A June 19-- graduate of Central University in
the College of Business Administration, I majored
in statistics and economics. Through other courses
studied, I obtained a background in business law,
finance, insurance, accounting, communication in
business, and marketing methods.

How You Select the Main Points. You naturally select, from the list of your qualifications assembled in your Self-Analysis, those that directly meet the requirements and that focus most brightly on the employer's needs. These are your main points. For example, suppose that the job calls for a knowledge of market research procedure and business report organization. If you have this knowledge, that is the strong point to stress.

CASE I. A university senior chooses the main points from his education and experience:

In June of this year I will be graduated from Oregon University with a marketing major. To aid and give understanding to my marketing work, I have taken such courses as communication in business, money and banking, investments, accounting principles, and other related courses (listed on the enclosed data sheet).

Your records will show that I worked in your employ for sixteen months. Twelve of these were spent in your laboratories testing pulp and paper. The remainder of the time I spent in the mill doing varied jobs from night watchman to fourth-hand on No. 8 paper machine.

CASE II. A graduate student, about to apply for a position, offers a still more advanced case: "Out of my practical experiences in retail management I have sifted the data until I am certain I have the selected points on which to base my application. The person to whom I am applying is a management consultant, and uses as the basis for his operations a budgetary procedure that he has evolved and perfected. The stores that he supervises are primarily of small sales volume ($500,000 to $2,000,000) and are scattered from coast to coast. I have found out enough about this executive to be sure that the following experience-entries, taken from my basic data, and representing some of my field work, are the strongest points:

1. Four years at the Walgreen Drug Company as a salesman.
2. Four years at the L. S. Ayres Company as office manager, purchasing agent, manager of stock, marking and receiving departments, traffic auditor, and supervisor of inventories.
3. Several months at the Schuster Company as floor superintendent, customer service and adjustments, and personnel and sales training follow-up.
4. Several months at the Hirsch Company as assistant to the general manager and the personnel manager.

"Have You Had Any Experience?" The applicant who lets himself be stopped by the common rejoinder, "But you have had no experience," must share a part of the blame if he fails to go out and gather some experience under his own power, without pay if necessary. You can always find a newspaper in the local community, several printers, a men's tailor shop, a women's dress shop, and other stores. There may even be a manufacturing plant. Some of these people can probably use you, part-time or by the hour. These are some of the channels through which you can find the answer to the question, "What shall I say about experience—when I haven't any?" *Go out and get some.* Or, if that is not feasible, say nothing. Stress other things.

Employers Want People with "Get Up and Go!" Roy Dickinson, veteran editorial writer, watching the industrial scene from the vantage point of his staff position on the magazine, *Printers' Ink*, points out that employers scan the horizon day in and day out for young people with ideas who are willing to go out and "make their own experience" under their own power.

He cites the case of a "self-starting" applicant who studied specific companies, discovered one sharp fact valuable to a specific employer, and who then reported on the item:

> . . . I have discovered this fact about your own business that you may find helpful.

Editor Dickinson, in the following words, describes one actual case:

> I remember a young man from a New England college who wrote me what looked like a form letter. I didn't answer it. He followed me up later. Finally I made an appointment. When he came in, I said: "I suppose you're looking for a job." "No," he replied, "I want you to tell me which one of eight you think I ought to take!"
>
> That was a startling statement, so I looked into the matter. This young self-starter had taken the trouble to investigate the sales in the New England college town where he was a student, of sixteen different products ranging from corn flakes to belt buckles and shaving soap. He found out, through calling both on the people who sold these items and on many users in the college community, just what they thought of the merchandise, what any objections might be, whether the packages could be improved, and so on. He then wrote a personal letter to the sales executives of these companies and to the top management of their advertising agencies.

In each case he made a simple, concrete suggestion based upon his investigation of the product itself. From the thirty-two letters he sent out asking for an appointment, he received so many opportunities to meet either the agency men or the manufacturer that he didn't have time to cover half of them during his Easter vacation. But he came back to see the rest after June, and I had the pleasure of helping him choose one out of eight jobs that he had been offered.

Generate Power with Concreteness and Convincing Detail. Put "golden nuggets" of concreteness, detail, and human personal experiences into your paragraphs. Never be satisfied with a "glossy surface draped around a vacuum." Concreteness is based upon convincing details that reflect what activities you have been engaged in, what your major interests are, what types of work you have a natural aptitude for, where you have gathered your past experience, and perhaps some of the little individual happenings and accomplishments that mirror your personality.

What are some of the convincing concrete details that make applications strong? Read this passage, taken from a recent application:

> For one year I was employed as instrument man for general survey work by Davis and Cole, Consulting Engineers. During this time I did a wide variety of instrument work--

We interrupt for a moment and ask you to note how weak and unconvincing the statement would have been, had the applicant stopped at the dash. But he did not stop there. He continued with this sharp detail:

> --such as run levels, cross-sectioning, precise traverse, water-power survey, primary triangulation, and solar observation, besides running a final location for the key spur of the Green Bay and Western Railway Company at Iron Mountain, Michigan.

CASE I. A senior answers a magazine advertisement:

> I wish to apply for the position of assistant laboratory technician noted in your advertisement in the February issue of the Electric World.

A later part of his application reads:

> Our work consisted of pole setting, stringing of drop wire, poling conduit, pulling in cable, and office survey work. In the last-named projects we laid out and designed a cable line and made a drop-wire survey of Des Moines.

CASE II. A mechanical engineer, a graduate of the Federal Technical University of Zurich, Switzerland, applies for a job in America. He knows the value of concreteness and sharp details:

```
      Experience:  Calculations in dynamics and thermodynamics,
heat transmissions, temperature of furnace walls, strength of
materials; measurement of the temperature of gases.  Calcula-
lation of steam turbines, Diesel engines, and heat pumps.
```

CASE III. A young woman applies for a job in a public library, with sharp details that give a definite picture of her background:

```
      As a library worker, I have been a Jack-of-all-trades.
Some of my tasks were mending books, keeping registration
records, taking charge of the contingent fund, and acting as
reference librarian in the periodical room of the library.
```

The mind "wraps itself around" a sharply defined idea chiseled in concrete terms, but it slides off a vague, smooth idea cast in empty generality. Project your trained preparation so clearly that it cannot be missed. Power your paragraphs with concrete detail.

Step 4. Personal Qualifications: Use Flashes of "Human Interest." At this point in your application, you enjoy the chance to light up your paragraphs with flashes and touches of "human interest"— items revealing your human side. Sometimes the flash of one phrase or even one detail may floodlight some odd little corner of your personality or background enough to make your prospective employer remember you and your application out of the entire shower of those that lie before him.

Of course, if you happen to be lucky enough to be selected a member of the American Olympic ski team, as did one applicant not long ago, you enjoy a tremendous hook through which to seize attention, a brilliant flash of human interest. Although his membership in the squad could not, in any direct way, indicate his ability to perform in the job for which he was applying, it did reflect the desirable qualities of good physical condition, stamina, courage, alertness, coordination, and probably some measure of leadership. Such indirect proof of human qualities is spectacular and enormously convincing—but simply not available to most people, because most people don't make the American Olympic squads. Yet that fact shouldn't discourage you.

Little Things May Tip the Balance in Your Favor. Curiously enough, your most obvious accomplishments may not be rated the most important. "Jobs hang on strange hooks these days." Little things may tip the balance in your favor. Some item that you consider of small moment may, in the eyes of a certain prospective employer, set you off from the crowd. The winning item is *entirely unpredictable*. Will it be speaking experience? Travel? House-to-house selling? Secretarial skill? Stamp-collecting? Speedboat model-building? Winning the Inland Lakes Regatta Gold Cup in the E-Boat Class? Working in the Indianapolis Speedway racing pits? Six years in the U. S. Marines? Color photography? Or any one of a hundred other extraordinary sidelines? Or will it be working as a member of a road construction gang? Lifeguard at Atlantic City? Page boy in the United States Senate? Tree cutter on a forest reserve?

The answer? No one knows. Your prospective employer himself could not tell you. *He has to wait to read what you have to say.*

"A Western Union messenger," reports an airline executive, "had kept a record of the sums we had paid the telegraph company for delivery of tickets. He suggested that by employing him to make ticket deliveries, we could save money and give better service. *He got the job.*"

Another case: A finance executive tells of a graduating senior who couldn't be fitted into his firm. "After talking with him, I found he had been busy, after school hours, in supervising about twenty others who distributed newspapers. I suggested immediately that he call on a large news distributing company and tell them that he knew how to distribute their goods in a relatively small way and that he wanted a chance to do it in a big way. *The company hired him.*" *

In presenting your personal qualifications, tell why you are interested in the employer's kind of business and why you feel that you can do the work that the prospective employer wants done.

④
*Personal
Qualifications;
Human
Interest
Details*

> I believe I have developed the ability to make myself of value to you. During my last two high school years, I worked in the school office several hours each day to supplement the commercial training offered in classes. I was also employed part time in this office for three summers following my graduation. This practical background--and that gained by holding offices in several university organizations--has given me some administrative experience and the ability to get along with people.
>
> Research is also of great interest to me. My aptitude tests and my experience with several statistical term reports indicate that I have the persevering patience and exacting temperament required of statisticians. My chief aim is to put these qualities to work, if possible, with your organization. As a result of my training, I hope I can justify my personal confidence that I can serve you well.

* These last two examples are from "Two Million Men Wanted" by Don Wharton, *Reader's Digest*, Vol. 36, No. 215, pages 11-12.

Step 5. Give References. References are something like guaranties. They increase the employer's confidence in your ability. Give at least three references with correct and exact addresses, and make clear that you give these references with the permission of the persons named. The following expressions are suitable and courteous: "I have permission to refer . . ." "I refer by permission . . ." and "[place names here] have permitted me to refer . . ." Choose references that represent both business and personal character.

⑤
*References
and Mention
of Data Sheet*
{
Mr. W. D. Rand has kindly permitted me to use his name as a reference. On the enclosed data sheet are further references and additional information concerning my qualifications.
}

Step 6. Ask for an Interview: the Closing Sentence. Your closing sentence should (1) suggest action for an interview and (2) make that action as easy as possible. Make a direct request for an interview. Tell how and when the prospective employer may reach you. Use different kinds of closings. Practice variety.

⑥
*Request for
Interview*
{
May I have a personal interview at your convenience? You can reach me by telephone at MAin 1-3478 or by mail at 610 Rowe Avenue, Chicago 27, Illinois.
}

Put It All Together—and You Have a Winner. Now let us see how the whole application looks and sounds when it is put together in one piece. The complete unit is reproduced on page 261. It was successful in winning a new job for the senior who wrote it. Logical and well developed, the message emphasizes facts that the employer wants to know.

The Top Man Likes Your Application!

He's about to lift the telephone and say to his secretary, "Miss Lane, I like this application you handed me. Please invite this man in for an interview."

Tone. Tone must strike a balance between two dangers. On the one side is the danger of arrogance, vanity, and self-conceit. On the other is the danger of timidity, diffidence, and

610 Rowe Avenue
Chicago 27, Illinois
January 25, 19--

Beamer Market Research, Inc.
378 South Clark Street
Chicago 5, Illinois

Gentlemen:

    Mr. George Reston, Personnel Officer of the American Trust Bank of Chicago, has told me that you have a vacancy in your Research and Statistical Department. May I be considered an applicant for this position?

    I understand that you want a young man with a working knowledge of statistical techniques. He should also have a thorough understanding of the application of mathematics to statistical procedure, a background in business and economics, and be able to assume the responsibility for preparing monthly reports and analyses.

    A June 19-- graduate of Central University in the College of Business Administration, I majored in statistics and economics. Through other courses studied.I obtained a background in business law, finance, insurance, accounting, communication in business, and marketing methods.

    I believe I have developed the ability to make myself of value to you. During my last two high school years, I worked in the school office several hours each day to supplement the commercial training offered in classes. I was also employed part time in this office for three summers following my graduation. This practical background--and that gained by holding offices in several university organizations--has given me some administrative experience and the ability to get along with people.

    Research is also of great interest to me. My aptitude tests and my experience with several statistical term reports indicate that I have the persevering patience and exacting temperament required of statisticians. My chief aim is to put these qualities to work, if possible, with your organization. As a result of my training, I hope I can justify my personal confidence that I can serve you well.

    Mr. W. D. Rand has kindly permitted me to use his name as a reference. On the enclosed data sheet are further references and additional information concerning my qualifications.

    May I have a personal interview at your convenience? You can reach me by telephone at MAin 1-3478 or by mail at 610 Rowe Avenue, Chicago 27, Illinois.

Sincerely yours,

William R. Tebbens

William R. Tebbens

An Effective Application That Won the Writer a New Job

This logical and well-planned application follows the six steps in an application (given in detail on pages 253 to 260.)

self-abasement. Between these dangers the applicant must make his precarious way. The desirable tone is that of *rational and modest confidence in one's ability.*

How to Handle the Pronoun *I*. You have nothing to be afraid of in the first-person singular pronoun *I*. You are talking about yourself. You are giving information about your training and experience. You are conveying some idea of your personality and your individuality. If the general tone of your letter is modest, there is nothing objectionable in using *I* when you need to. To avoid *I* by elaborate circumlocutions may make the tone of the message seem artificial and insincere.

At the same time the unpleasant repetition of any word should be avoided. A little attention to the phrasing will disclose ways of keeping the *I's* down to a reasonable number without straining to hide them. As a general rule, try to begin alternate paragraphs with some word other than *I*. The beginnings of paragraphs, as we have seen, are conspicuous. If the same pronoun opens each paragraph, it may, through emphasis and repetition, gather unpleasant attention.

For example, instead of saying, "After I took four years of work in business administration, and after I graduated with a B. A. in Commerce, I worked for two years . . . ," say: "After completing the four-year requirements for my B. A. in Commerce, I worked for two years, following my graduation. . . ." Instead of saying, "I shall be glad to send you further references," say: "Let me know if you wish further references." Through a thoughtful use of these shifts of pronouns, you will soon master the knack of soft-pedaling *I-emphasis.*

Avoid Negative Suggestion. Certain recurrent negative suggestions tend to creep into applications. Guard against them. (1) Do not let your letter sound like a wholesale broadcast. It should be tailored to fit the specific situation. (2) If you have had no experience, do not mention experience at all. To say, "Although I lack experience in your type of business," or "I regret that I have no business experience," is to put yourself on the defensive. Use the space to tell what your positive qualifications are and leave the rest of the matter for discussion in the interview. (3) Defer a discussion of salary, if possible, until the interview. It is at least unwise to write, "Salary is unimportant," "I care nothing about salary," or "I am willing to start at almost any wage." Such a statement may paint an unfair picture of you; it may cause the prospective employer to dismiss you from consideration as unambitious.

Never Copy Others. . . . It's Poison! The one great and fatal error is to attempt to express your individuality in the words of another. To borrow the phrases, the sentences, the paragraphs, or even the entire draft of another is only to masquerade in the costume of someone else—to "strut in borrowed plumage." You misrepresent yourself and endanger your chances. You instantly earn a reputation for depending on somebody else's "crutch." You put yourself under the well-known classification headlined with the dubious words, "This person is a *crutch-peddler*."

Two applications came to an executive in a firm located in Chicago. You may find this hard to believe, but in sober fact the two were identical from beginning to end, without so much as the variation of a comma. The first paragraph of each read:

> You probably have been swamped with applications, both personal and written, for positions with your company. Probably each and every one of those applicants thinks that he is essential to your success. And probably you are tired of reading applications, but here is mine.

Each application, of course, killed the other. And to make the situation even worse, a tone of negative suggestion ran through the "master model" from which these letters were copied. The executive, disgusted, dropped both applications into the wastebasket. "There," he said, "are two applicants who will 'probably' never get positions with this firm!"

The applications you have read in this and the previous chapter are illustrations of how certain individuals presented their cases. They are *not* "models." So personal is an application that it must be the individual effort of each writer. There should be as many different applications as there are people to write them. *Avoid borrowed plumage.* "Crutching" along on models written by someone else is doubly dangerous. First, the plagiarism may be discovered; and second, the "crutch" itself may, ironically enough, be much poorer than your own draft.

Stamped, Self-Addressed Return Envelopes. Opinion is divided on the desirability of enclosing stamped, self-addressed return envelopes in applications. Such enclosures may speed replies and may possibly under certain circumstances increase their number. But those opposing the practice object that such enclosures may be considered presumptions on the ground that a favorable reply is assumed. Each applicant must decide this matter for himself. In either case his target is clear: "Get an interview!"

15 DON'Ts for Applicants

1. DON'T brag.
2. DON'T use superlatives.
3. DON'T use flowery words.
4. DON'T use horse-and-buggy wheeze-box language.
5. DON'T sound stiff and insincere and artificial.
6. DON'T play on sympathy. "I support my family."
7. DON'T assume a know-it-all attitude.
8. DON'T use your company letterhead, if employed.
9. DON'T use social, club, hotel, fraternity, or fancy stationery. Use plain, fine, white bond.
10. DON'T use a postcard. (It has been done!)
11. DON'T let your application sound like a wholesale broadcast. Sharpshoot for one job.
12. DON'T generalize. Be specific with spike-sharp facts.
13. DON'T be dull. Use a flash of "human interest."
14. DON'T make a statement you can't back up in an interview.
15. DON'T copy an application from a "model book" unless you want to take a short cut to failure.

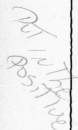

The Data Sheet

The Data Sheet and Its Advantages. The purpose of the data sheet is to provide classified personal details and tabulated general information. Its use relieves the letter itself of a mass of routine detail, lifts from the letter the weight of a great many cataloged facts. Most successful applicants use a data sheet, attached to their letter of application.

The purpose of the letter itself is to give a well-rounded impression of the background and the ability of the applicant. The letter is the place to show personality, individuality, and capacity. The data sheet, on the other hand, is the place to classify the assembled information in tabular form. It serves as a compact summary for quick reference. Many a letter of application has been saved from oblivion by a workmanlike data sheet. Employers may file the letter but detach the convenient data sheet and keep it on the desk for further examination.

Data Sheet Headings. The data sheet's tabular form makes it easy to consult for quick reference. Clip the data sheet firmly to the letter.

Applicants should adapt headings (such as those in the Data Sheet Guide on page 266) to suit their requirements, making omissions or adding new headings where appropriate. The data sheet shown on page 272 was attached to a letter of application for a position in an accounting firm.

Large Concerns Have Their Own Data Sheets. Large concerns, hiring employees by the scores, have developed the data sheet to the fullest degree. To each applicant is given a printed information blank to be filled out in great detail. Page one of a typical blank of four pages is reproduced on page 271.

Data Sheet and Applicant's Self-Analysis Record. The applicant's self-analysis record, discussed and illustrated in the preceding chapter, provides your raw material. From this raw material you sift and choose the facts you consider important enough to go on your data sheet and into your letter. The letter stresses the vital and central points of human interest. The data sheet carries a tabular summary of all other points felt worthy of mention. Hence, only a portion of the material gathered in the basic data self-analysis will appear at the final stage. The finished application uses only the "cream."

Like the letter itself, your data sheet performs a definite function. It has an organic relation to the letter. If your letter is written with a data sheet in mind, it enjoys advantages that it is forced to sacrifice

---

What Personnel Officers Prefer on Data Sheets

The letter may be less than a page in length, but the data sheet should be complete in every detail. This second sheet conserves time because its carefully prepared outline of qualifications can be quickly scanned.

* * *

To include a data sheet outline makes it much easier for a personnel man to review a candidate's qualifications.

* * *

I personally prefer a letter with an attached data sheet. I am willing to go further and say that every personnel man I know has the same preference.

Data Sheet Guide

if the data sheet is not used. In summary, the data sheet is simply a concise adaptation of the elaborate printed information blanks used by many large organizations in recording data about new applicants.

A Personal Art. The creation of an effective application, with its data sheet and its follow-ups, is a personal art. It should be so approached. The acid test of your final product will be, "Did it get you a job?"

"I thought you might be interested to know," writes a former student, "that I have been offered a job with J. Walter Thompson. I'm now doing office detail, but in a week or so I'll be given a chance to write some copy. Incidentally, the personnel manager said he hired me on the basis of my application. He said it was the most complete he had ever seen."

The Interview

How Do You Make the Interview Successful? Get Ready for It! If you make adequate and intelligent preparation for the interview that—you hope—will follow your application, you will find it not an ordeal but a pleasant visit. This is literally true. Many a successful applicant has found it so.

In simplest terms, your interviewer—perhaps the personnel director or one of his assistants

—has a job he wants to fill. He wants to know whether you, the applicant, are the best person he can get to fill it. He first reads your application and studies your data sheet to judge whether he wants to see you at all. If he decides that he does, he gives you a definite interview appointment. When you appear at the exact time specified, you have reached the point in the procedure where you have to show that you are really the kind of person your application has represented you to be. His invitation to you to appear for the interview is a clear indication that up to the moment all impressions have been favorable ones. It is now up to you to see that these impressions are not changed when you appear in person for the final checkup.

Nervous? Take It in Stride. The trained personnel executive expects that you may reveal a certain degree of nervousness. Don't let that bother you because he won't let it bother him. From long experience he'll expect it and take it in stride. So should you. Skilled interviewers are almost always sympathetic and realize that what to them is a routine matter may be to you a great adventure. They want to put you at your ease so that you feel free to talk. They want to get acquainted with you, to find out what sort of a person you really are. Like all human beings, personnel directors will have their share of vagaries and prejudices and preferences—just as you yourself have—but in the main they will not permit their prejudices and preferences to interfere with making a sound appraisal of your usefulness. You'll get fair treatment and a fair chance.

—Dale McFeatters and Publishers Syndicate, Inc.

"I'm not particular—I'll start in any kind of executive job!"

—Saturday Evening Post

"No I don't have any experience; but I can offer you Ambition, Initiative, Enthusiasm—stuff like that."

Appearance Will Count. Your interviewer does not expect a Beau Brummel or a glamour girl. But he does rightly expect you to be well-groomed. The natural rule is simply to use the same care in preparing yourself for an interview that you use in preparing yourself to have a photograph taken. Another simple and natural rule is to wear the correct daytime office attire that would be expected of you if you were appearing at the office as a member of the staff.

Be Yourself: Don't Try to "Make an Impression." You have already submitted adequate written material telling about your background, abilities, and skills. The interviewer has seen this material. But no amount of written material will reveal much to the interviewer about your actual personal characteristics. These he wants to know. He wants to see you personally. He wants to look at you, talk with you, and try to "size you up." He may make this process easy for you with a cordial handshake, a pleasant invitation to sit down, and perhaps a friendly comment about the weather or your college or university football season.

You are bound to be aware, of course, that you are "on display." But again: take it in stride. Remember that you are in the hands of a friend—one who would like to know you better.

Helpful Interview Check Lists

Major, Minor, and Related Courses	Occupational Preferences
(Enter *1* for *Major*, 2 for *Minor*, *3* for *Related Courses*)	(Enter *1* for *first choice*, 2 for *second*, etc. Limit choice to five.)

Major, Minor, and Related Courses	Occupational Preferences
Accounting .... ( )	Accounting, Private .... ( )
Actuarial .... ( )	Accounting, Public .... ( )
Advertising .... ( )	Advertising .... ( )
Auditing .... ( )	Banking .... ( )
Banking .... ( )	Credits and Collections ...... ( )
Business Administration ...... ( )	Foreign Service .... ( )
Business Law .... ( )	Foreign Trade .... ( )
Credits and Collections ...... ( )	General Business .... ( )
Economics .... ( )	Industrial Relations .... ( )
Finance .... ( )	Insurance .... ( )
Foreign Trade .... ( )	Investments .... ( )
Insurance .... ( )	Marketing Research .... ( )
Investments .... ( )	Merchandising .... ( )
Labor .... ( )	Personnel .... ( )
Management .... ( )	Production .... ( )
Marketing .... ( )	Purchasing .... ( )
Personnel .... ( )	Real Estate .... ( )
Production .... ( )	Retailing .... ( )
Purchasing .... ( )	Sales .... ( )
Real Estate .... ( )	Secretarial .... ( )
Retailing .... ( )	Statistics .... ( )
Sales .... ( )	Teaching .... ( )
Statistics .... ( )	Traffic Management .... ( )
Transportation .... ( )	Transportation .... ( )
Other: _____ ( )	Other: _____ ( )

Be Prepared to Talk. At some point during the interview it is likely that your interviewer will offer you one or more openings for you to pick up the discussion. He does this with a double purpose: It helps him to "size up" your ability to express yourself and to adapt yourself

A young man, just graduated from college with the idea that his degree would make life easy for him, had presented himself to the personnel department of a large corporation.

"What sort of position did you have in mind?" asked the personnel officer.

Replied he, "A sitting position."

to unfamiliar situations. And he knows that it helps to put you at ease to talk a little. One of his favorite questions will be, "Why did you decide to apply to us for a job?" Be sure you have a *good* answer for that one! Make your discussion a frank, direct, cordial, and personal visit. Let it be a give-and-take affair.

To illustrate the "wrong-way-to" approach to an interview, consider the following comment. A representative of one of the country's largest manufacturing firms, an executive who has interviewed thousands of college job-seekers, makes this critical statement: "In so many interviews the college senior assumes the attitude of *daring* us to find out something about him. We want him to talk—not too much, but enough. We want to see how he handles words, how he expresses himself, whether he's articulate, whether he can think on his own feet, how he handles his ideas." A second experienced personnel executive puts it this way: "Too many college seniors act during an interview as if we were the Grand Inquisitors—something like super District Attorneys—and that they must answer a simple 'Yes' or 'No.' They've got it wrong. We want to get a line on their personal adaptability in human situations like an interview. We want to make a direct 'size up' of their personality traits. Every college job-seeker should be prepared to help us do this."

When the Interview Is Over. Your interview may not last more than fifteen minutes, or in special circumstances it may be considerably longer. You will know when it is over. If you are attentive, you will sense when the interviewer has no more questions and wishes to end the discussion. He may rise and thank you for coming in. After thanking him in turn, you may properly inquire whether you will be notified when a decision has been reached. Then take your prompt departure.

The Follow-up Letter. Comparatively few jobs are closed at the first interview. The choice will usually be narrowed down to a few applicants, and then the final selection will be made. The follow-up may, therefore, be of importance. Follow up your interview promptly with a letter thanking the prospective employer for the interview and reviewing points of special interest to him. If you were told to send in the application form which may have been given to you, the letters on pages 271 and 273 are illustrative of one that may be sent with the filled-out form.

Sometimes a second follow-up letter may be advisable a week or two after the first. If no action has taken place within a reasonable time, a brief note is not out of place. The second follow-up merely reminds the prospective employer of your having filed an application and may express willingness to return for another interview. Like the original application and the first follow-up, the final note should present a well-framed picture.

5846 Andersonville Road
Salt Lake City 3, Utah
March 16, 19--

Mr. Edward R. Morris
Conners, Morris & Todd
Consulting Engineers
6589 Southgate Parkway
Salt Lake City 7, Utah

Dear Mr. Morris

Thank you for the interview you gave me this morning. Because of my specialized training, I feel that I can do accurate, competent work in the drafting office, and that I can meet the high standards of your firm. I hope for the opportunity to prove my worth.

Enclosed is the application form you gave me, together with a fairly recent photograph. A second copy of the data sheet that you asked me to send is also enclosed.

I am available for work at once. You may reach me at my home, telephone Dixon 1-6850.

Sincerely yours

Lawrence R. Cole

Lawrence R. Cole

Enclosures

CONNERS, MORRIS & TODD · Consulting Engineers

APPLICATION FOR EMPLOYMENT

DATE _____

NAME _____
Last   First   Middle

ADDRESS _____
Street   City, Zone   State

AGE _____ DATE OF BIRTH _____ BIRTHPLACE _____ TELEPHONE _____

IF FOREIGN BORN, ARE YOU NATURALIZED? _____ IF SO, GIVE DATE _____

HEIGHT _____ WEIGHT _____ PHYSICAL CONDITION _____

LIST PHYSICAL DEFECTS (IF ANY) _____

SOCIAL SECURITY NUMBER _____ MARITAL STATUS _____

SPOUSE'S OCCUPATION _____ NO. OF CHILDREN _____ OTHER DEPENDENTS _____

RELATIVES EMPLOYED BY THIS FIRM _____ Name (s) _____ Relationship _____

WHO REFERRED YOU TO THIS FIRM? _____ DATE YOU CAN BEGIN WORK _____ FOR WHAT POSITION ARE YOU APPLYING? _____

INSERT APPLICANT'S PHOTOGRAPH HERE

EDUCATION	Name and Location	Attended From	To	Diploma or Degree	Major
HIGH SCHOOL					
COLLEGE/UNIVERSITY					
GRADUATE SCHOOL					
BUSINESS, MILITARY CORRESPONDENCE, ETC.					

HONORS WON, SCHOLASTIC SOCIETIES _____

OTHER SCHOOL ACTIVITIES _____

FOREIGN LANGUAGES, SPEAK _____ READ _____ WRITE _____

HOBBIES, TALENTS _____

OUTSIDE INTERESTS, AFFILIATIONS _____

PREVIOUS EMPLOYERS	Address	Employed From	To	Salary Received	Duties	Reason for Leaving

(OVER)

3434 Columbia Drive
Buffalo 21, New York
April 11, 19--

Van Brinton & Brewster
Tax Consultants
253 Third Avenue
New York 4, New York

Gentlemen:

Because I am deeply interested in public accounting, I want to secure a position with an organization carrying on this kind of work. Professor C. R. Blair, Head of the Accounting Department of Western University, speaks highly of your firm. At his suggestion I wish to apply for a position with you.

Upon completion of my high school course in 19--, I entered Western University where I am now a senior and shall graduate with a Bachelor of Business Administration degree in June.

At the University I specialized in accounting, taking every course offered. Among the courses were Auditing, C. P. A. Problems, Income Tax Accounting, Cost Accounting, Accounting Systems, and Governmental Accounting. In addition, I have studied courses allied to accounting and have read extensively from books and periodicals devoted to the subject. These readings and other personal information are given in detail on the enclosed sheet.

During the past two years I have been doing accounting work for three small firms. With them I have had complete charge of the books and income tax returns. I feel that this experience has been valuable to me in broadening my point of view.

Mr. C. R. Blair, who is also the senior partner of a local firm of tax consultants, has kindly allowed me to use his name as a reference in regard to my character and ability. I also have permission to use the names on the enclosed sheet, of men who have known me as a student or employee.

If you will write me at 3434 Columbia Drive or telephone me at Trenton 1-9087, I shall be glad to furnish you with further particulars of my experience or any personal information you may want.

Sincerely yours,
Frank W. Rockwell
Frank W. Rockwell

Enclosure

An Application That Scored a Victory

FRANK W. ROCKWELL

PERSONAL INFORMATION
Address: 3434 Columbia Drive, Buffalo 21, New York
Telephone: Trenton 1-9087
Age: 24 years
Marital Status: Single
Birthplace: Utica, New York
Height and Weight: 6'1" - 180 pounds
Physical Condition: Excellent

(Applicant's Photograph in This Space)

EDUCATION
Central High School, Buffalo, New York
(Graduated in June, 19--)
Western University, Buffalo, New York
(Bachelor of Business Administration degree in June, 19--)

Accounting Courses Studied:
Elementary Accounting, Applied Accounting, Cost Accounting, Advanced C. P. A. Course, Income Tax Accounting, Auditing, Accounting Systems, Governmental Accounting

Courses Allied to Accounting Studied:
Business Law, Corporation Law, Mathematics of Investment, Theory of Economics, Corporation Finance, Investments, Money and Banking, Credits and Collections, Factory Administration, Business Communication, Marketing Methods, Sales Administration

Books Read on Accounting and Allied Subjects:
Noble and Niswonger, Accounting Principles
Karrenbrock and Simons, Intermediate Accounting
Kennedy, Financial Statements, Advanced Accounting
Culey and Bauer, Auditing
Matz, Curry, and Frank, Cost Accounting
Stockton, Business Statistics

EXPERIENCE
Two years of bookkeeping, Norval's Pharmacy, Buffalo, New York
Accounting work, 19-- to 19--, with three Buffalo stores

EXTRACURRICULAR ACTIVITIES
Beta Gamma Sigma honorary, Captain of the Western University basketball team, Treasurer of the Senior Class, Advertising Manager for the Western University Record (a student newspaper)

REFERENCES
Professor C. R. Blair, Head of the Accounting Department, Western University, 990 Central Avenue, Buffalo 4, New York
Mr. Lee K. Jones, Treasurer of the Citizens Bank, State Building, 9010 Lawton Avenue, Buffalo 6, New York
Mr. John R. Norval, Norval's Pharmacy, 830 W. Main Street, Buffalo 8, New York
Reverend M. O. Townes, 346 Beech Avenue, Buffalo 16, New York

The Data Sheet (Enclosed with the Application)

3434 Columbia Drive
Buffalo 21, New York
April 17, 19—

Mr. John K. Brewster
Van Brinton & Brewster
Tax Consultants
253 Third Avenue
New York 4, New York

Dear Mr. Brewster:

Thank you for your letter of April 15. I am enclosing the application blank, filled out as you requested.

I had intended to find a permanent position soon after graduation. If, however, some definite arrangement can be made whereby I can join your organization early in the fall, I shall be very well satisfied to find temporary employment for the summer.

As to location, I prefer to work in New York although I should not be unwilling to go farther west, if necessary. I prefer this vicinity because my home and friends are located here, and I would have an opportunity to see my parents more often.

Although I have no definite ideas as to the compensation I should merit, I would as a general statement suggest that $420 to $440 would be a fair initial salary.

I shall be very glad to furnish you with any further information necessary to a satisfactory arrangement.

Yours very sincerely,

Frank W. Rockwell

Frank W. Rockwell

Enclosure

VAN BRINTON & BREWSTER

Tax Consultants

253 THIRD AVE · NEW YORK 4 · LEXINGTON 2-2616

April 21, 19—

Mr. Frank W. Rockwell
3434 Columbia Drive
Buffalo 21, New York

Dear Mr. Rockwell:

I am pleased to inform you that, on the basis of your satisfactory letter of April 17, you have been employed by Van Brinton & Brewster.

Your work will start in our New York office on July 1, at a beginning salary of $425 a month. We believe that you will show the kind of progress justifying a higher salary within a reasonable time. Congratulations!

Cordially

John K. Brewster
Vice President

How Well Do Applications "Pull"? What success can you expect from your application efforts? The "pull" of applications is, of course, as widely variable as the skills that go into their preparation. Some applications get (and deserve) no returns at all. Others pull with almost phenomenal force. Some classic examples: CASE I. An application, sent at a time when jobs were almost nonexistent, pulled 45% returns—32 replies from 72 letters sent. A follow-up message pulled 68% returns—27 replies from 40 letters sent. From this effort came five offers of jobs, all from excellent companies located more than a thousand miles away from the applicant—*a fact that put the full burden on the applications themselves.* CASE II. A second application, of which 54 original drafts were sent, brought 14 interviews and 7 offers of good jobs. CASE III. A third application pulled 60% returns—36 replies from 60 applications sent—and resulted in *6 concrete offers of employment!*

Two Successful Case Histories

How Frank W. Rockwell Won Himself a Job. The application and its data sheet, shown on page 272, were written by a young man trained in accounting. The application was addressed to a firm of public accountants with offices in New York and other cities. Note how the student unfolds his story with a carefully designed plan, essential concrete detail, and effective tone. Observe, too (Paragraphs 3 and 5), the important cross reference to the data sheet.

A prompt reply from the junior partner of the firm, Mr. Brewster, expressed an interest in the application but requested additional information, which was supplied by the applicant (page 273).

The sequence ends to everyone's satisfaction. The successful conclusion is shown by the final message of the series in which Mr. Brewster employs candidate Rockwell (page 273).

"Here's the Way I Found a Job." The second of our case histories also has features of extraordinary interest. James R. Hare, the successful candidate, tells the story of his campaign in an article entitled *A Business of Your Own* [The Reader's Digest Association]. Suppose we let Mr. Hare give his own interesting recital of what he did and how he did it:

I received my honorable discharge from the Army just before the end of 1945. Before the war I'd been a small-town newspaperman in Virginia,

1. James R. Hare   East 23rd Street   New York 10

DO YOU HAVE A JOB FOR ME?

A five-minute check list to save the time of busy editors, advertising managers, and personnel managers.

Do you need a man who: Check here

1. Can write fluently in a plain way   ☐

2. Can do rough editing, copyreading, proofreading   ☐

3. Can make rough advertising layouts   ☐

4. Has lots of ideas, some good, some bad   ☐

5. Can write trade-paper advertising, or edit house organ   ☐

6. Can prepare publicity and simple direct-mail pieces   ☐

7. Can do research, if not too technical   ☐

8. Can make abstracts or condensations   ☐

9. Knows a little about type, printing, paper   ☐

10. Is willing to do detail work   ☐

11. Will study hard to learn the business he enters   ☐

Portion of Page 1 of Mr. Hare's Check-List

and had always wanted to live in New York and work in a book publishing firm; as second choices, I wanted to be with a trade magazine or an advertising agency. Demobilization left me free to start anew, so, when I put on civilian clothes again, I went to New York. I was convinced that I could find the kind of job I wanted *if I tackled the problem of job-hunting systematically and put some originality into it.*

First, I asked myself what abilities I had to offer an employer, and listed them on a sheet of paper. The next step was to find the logical market for these abilities. From the public library I obtained the addresses of all book publishers, trade magazine editors, and advertising agencies to whom I would write a letter.

Now came the tough problem: what kind of letter would attract attention and get interviews? I worked several days on an unusual but simple way to present the gist of my story on one sheet of paper. The result was the *one-page check-list* reproduced in this article. Then, to supplement that, I wrote *three pages of details* about the items on the check-list.

I mailed 135 copies of this four-page letter—55 to book publishers, 41 to advertising agencies, and the remainder to trade magazine editors and other business firms.

The response amazed me. First there arrived two telegrams asking me to come for an interview. Many other replies followed in the next few days; among them were 14 more invitations to come around and talk about a job.

From these interviews I received five definite job offers, and several tentative offers which I didn't follow up *because by that time I had found just the job I wanted—in the advertising department of a large book publishing company.* Two of the offers I didn't accept seemed equally good opportunities; one was in an advertising agency and the other was on a trade magazine.

A systematic campaign like the one described here may be the answer to your job problem, no matter what field you want to enter. A clear presentation of your story to all possible employers in a specified locality is accomplished quickly and effectively by this method. An effective presentation by letter will open doors which otherwise might be barred by various circumstances if you simply called in person.

Originality and clarity are appreciated by employers. The letter I received from the executive editor of one trade magazine said: "Anybody who can produce a resumé like yours can get 15 minutes of my time any day. Call me for an appointment." I was flattered that the general manager of a book publishing company began his reply: "Have *you* time for an interview?"

Anyone who wants to use this method might follow these steps:

1. Decide what kind of job or jobs you want, and are qualified for.

2. Decide in what locality you want to work.

3. From trade directories, classified telephone books, and such sources, make a list of all possible employers in that area.

4. Decide what you have to offer in education, experience, and talent. Make a one-page list of schools attended, jobs you have had, your service record, and your abilities. Number each item. Keep the items as brief as possible (I confined each of mine to one line). Then, on not more than three other sheets of paper, write a brief paragraph of details explaining a little about each of the numbered qualifications on your one-page list. Revise all this information until it is as orderly and brief an account of your capabilities as you can make it.

If you are an expert at your job, it may be best to leave the matter of salary for the personal interview. But if you are trying to get started in a new field, or are primarily interested in a job with a future rather than in immediate earnings, it may be best to state a definite wage on your check-list, making it as low as you reasonably can, because you will be serving what is virtually an apprenticeship.

5. Proofread your letters and *make sure* that any errors are corrected before you send out a single one.

6. Have a good sales talk ready for interviews. When you learn just what job is open, and if you want it and could make good in it, emphasize your qualifications for that particular job.

7. Don't be too quick about accepting the first job offered. You've gone into this job-hunting program to look the field over; stick to that idea. The next offer may be even better. Explain that you have several other people to see, and ask that the job be held open for a few days. Most prospective employers will do this. After all, they want you to be satisfied with your job.

This worked with me. Here's good luck to you!

ADDITIONAL INFORMATION

1. WRITING ABILITY AND EXPERIENCE.--I always have been greatly
interested in writing. Sold more than a dozen stories to pulp
magazines while in college. Have written several novels since,
but never tried to have any of them published, as I realize
they are not good enough.

Was feature writer and reporter on the MORGANTOWN (W. VA.)
DOMINION-NEWS. Wrote a series of articles on the need of a
water-softening plant which resulted in the installation of a
$40,000 system. That was my only newspaper crusade. Later, I
worked for a weekly newspaper published by the same company
at Martinsburg, W. Va.

Next, I worked for P. T. Atkins, who published a rather well-
known weekly at Norton, Va. I did all sorts of chores on this
paper--wrote editorials and straight news; wrote and sold
advertising; collected subscription money with a series of
letters which were reproduced in trade journals as examples of
original, effective work.

I wrote a personal column for two years. One of the large
oil companies reprinted several thousand copies of an editorial I wrote on the place of advertising in American life.

I left this interesting job because I was offered more money
to write and sell advertising for the NORTHERN VIRGINIA DAILY,

Portion of Page 2 from Mr. Hare's Four-Page Application

Communication Problems

● 1. In Problem 4 of Chapter 11, page 248, you outlined in detail the
type of job you would like to have ten years after graduation. Then,
in Problem 6, page 248, you prepared a self-analysis with a view to
getting ready for the interview. Expand this self-analysis into a complete personal data sheet following the format listed on page 266.

● 2. Review your personal data sheet prepared in Problem 1. Outline
what you frankly believe to be your strong points. Then outline your
weak points. Explain in a written statement how you will minimize
or explain these weak points if they are brought out during the
interview.

● 3. Refer to the complete personal data sheet you developed in
Problem 1. Select three items from your education or experience
which "focus most brightly on the employer's needs" in the job you
have considered in Problem 4 of Chapter 11, page 248. Indicate in
writing which of these three items would be most advantageous to
stress as your "central selling point" in an application; and explain
the reasons for your choice.

● 4. Again referring to Problems 2, 3, and related problems, write
one of your references asking him to send your prospective employer
a specific recommendation. Specify the kind of information and detail
you would like this person to include in his recommendation. How
can you persuade your references to submit specific information which
will support your data sheet and your application?

● **5.** Having completed Problems 2-4 and related problems, you have done all the work required to write an excellent application. Write the best application you can, type it neatly, fold it carefully, address and mail it to your instructor.

● **6.** Assume that your original application (Problem 5) has not been answered. Write a good follow-up application which will again call attention to your major qualification and repeat your request for an interview. Be persuasive without showing any irritation.

● **7.** Again referring to Problem 5 and related problems, assume that you have had an enjoyable interview, that you were offered the position, and that you declined it. Now write a brief note of appreciation thanking the company for the interview and the opportunity offered.

● **8.** Again, refer to Problem 5 and related problems. Assume that you were offered the position and that you quickly and happily accepted. Now write a brief note to one of the persons who wrote an excellent recommendation for you. Tell the person your good news and thank him for the major role he played in your success.

● **9.** Refer again to Problem 5 and related problems. Assume that after your interview, you accepted a better offer from a competitive firm. Although the duties and opportunities were comparable, you accepted the later job because it was much more attractive financially. Write the first company expressing gratitude for your interview. Explain the situation. (Should you tell why you took the other job?)

● **10.** The New York Life Insurance Company in an excellent booklet entitled, "Your Job Interview," reports a survey made by Frank S. Endicott, Director of Placement, Northwestern University. This survey lists 93 questions frequently asked during employment interviews in 92 companies. Here are the first twenty of these frequently asked questions. How would you answer them?
1. What are your future vocational plans?
2. In what school activities have you participated? Why?
3. How do you spend your spare time? What are your hobbies?
4. In what type of position are you most interested?
5. Why do you think you might like to work for our company?
6. What jobs have you held? How were they obtained?
7. What courses did you like best? Least? Why?
8. Why did you choose your particular field of work?
9. What percentage of your college expenses did you earn? How?
10. How did you spend your vacations while in school?
11. What do you know about our company?
12. Do you feel that you have received a good general training?
13. What qualifications do you have that make you feel that you will be successful in your field?
14. What extracurricular offices have you held?
15. What are your ideas on salary?
16. How do you feel about your family?
17. How interested are you in sports?
18. If you could start college again, what courses would you take?
19. Can you forget your education and start from scratch?
20. Do you prefer any specific geographic location? Why?

PART VI Effective Sales Messages: A Function of Marketing Management

Chapter 13

*Using Business Promotion Messages,
Follow-Up Systems,
and Form Systems*

With each of its successive years, the Twentieth Century marks its path with ceaseless industrial expansion and a steadily increasing complexity in its human enterprises. Nowhere is this truth more evident than in today's business organizations.

Top management responsibilities become greater. The span of management control tends to widen. Executive action has to deal with more and more people as enterprises multiply in number and become larger in size. To keep in frequent touch with more people, management executives depend increasingly upon the power of the written and spoken word. And to win the favorable response of more people, executive action—in the form of Marketing Management— turns to Business Promotion, Follow-up Systems, and Form Systems, which are forms of effective sales messages with special characteristics.

Business Promotion Messages

The straightforward purpose of business promotion messages is to bring about the sales of products and services—in other words, to "promote business." But there is one great difference: the business promotion *often seems to sell nothing at all.* It simply strives to make helpful suggestions. In so doing, it accomplishes its purpose in an indirect way. Its message looks primarily to the interests of the customer and offers suggestions to enlarge his profits or to advance his personal comfort and welfare.

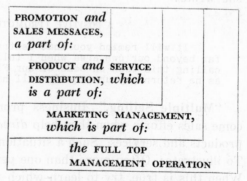

PROMOTION *and* SALES MESSAGES, *a part of:*

PRODUCT *and* SERVICE DISTRIBUTION, *which is a part of:*

MARKETING MANAGEMENT, *which is part of:*

the FULL TOP MANAGEMENT OPERATION

Sales Effort Is the Business Dynamo

Promotion and sales are part of the power plant of the nation's business, and a powerful tool of top management.

Some Uses of Business Promotion. Stores use business promotion messages (1) to inform customers about new merchandise, (2) to offer special-delivery services for holidays and after-store hours, (3) to offer storage privileges for valuable garments and furs over long vacation periods, (4) to remind parents of coming birthdays of children and to suggest the purchase of suitable gifts, (5) to remind husbands of approaching wedding anniversaries and to suggest the purchase of appropriate anniversary presents, (6) to offer Christmas-gift counsel and expert gift-buying advice to busy Christmas shoppers.

Similar messages are likewise used by banks (7) to offer gift envelopes and holiday containers in which crisp new bills may be folded; by sporting goods shops (8) to invite customers to view a demonstration by a visiting tennis star, Olympic ski-runner, or golf champion; by professional men (9) to suggest that clients should, for their own welfare, come in for a regular conference, interview, examination, or the like; and by manufacturers (10) to offer help to their dealers and to suggest practical ways in which their dealers can increase their sales.

Special Opportunities for Business Promotion. Opportunities for business promotion come from many unexpected quarters. A secretary to the president of a motor freight company handles his incoming mail while he is out of town. She would have lost a promotional opportunity if she had written negatively, "I regret that Mr. Wilson is out of his office, and therefore his reply to your inquiry must be delayed for several days." Here, instead, is the positive way in which she wrote:

A POSITIVE (PROMOTION) REPLY

It will remind you that Central Motor Service extends far beyond our own area when I tell you that Mr. Wilson is calling this week on some of our Florida shippers. As soon as he returns, your inquiry will have his prompt attention.

"Multiple Selling." Business promotion messages virtually become sales efforts when they help *directly* to bring about the sales of products and services. Such a situation is found in "multiple selling." To illustrate: Often more than one person is involved in a purchase. When this is true, try to learn which person will initiate the buying and concentrate effort on that person, sending supporting (promotion) material to others who may also play an influential part in making the final decision.

For example, assume that you are selling a money-saving device for use in factory operation. Logically (1) the superintendent or works manager will initiate the buying of such equipment and so your primary effort is directed to him. Since the actual order will be placed by (2) the purchasing agent, it is advisable to send him information more closely identified with his function—descriptive details, weights, sizes, prices, etc. And since the equipment is money-saving in character, it may be a good plan to send (3) an "economy" series to a higher officer—probably the treasurer, who is in charge of all budgets—acquainting him with the economy features.

If this course is followed, you will be developing three well-informed persons in the company, all having a voice in the buying decision. The more support you can win, the better your chances of success.*

Two Main Classes of Promotion. The two main classes of promotion are: (1) messages from the merchant to the customer and (2) messages from the manufacturer (or other source) to the merchant, or to key executives.

(1) Promotion to the Customer. In any normal business a certain number of old customers are falling away from active buying. They may have become dissatisfied—a major cause of lost patronage. Unless the unspoken grievances are drawn out, inactive-customer lists grow. In recognition of this fact many businesses exert special efforts to draw answers telling what the trouble is. When the cause for the grievance has been brought into the open, proper steps can be taken to remedy it. A personal message may then convey the right adjustment and win back further business. Whether customers become dissatisfied, or competitors lure them away, they can in both cases be won back.

The Hecht Company of Washington, D. C., produced excellent results with this message:

> There must be an important reason why you have not used your account at The Hecht Company for over a year. If it is important enough to cause you to stay away from us, it is important enough for us to make an effort to find the reason.
>
> Won't you help us by answering the enclosed questionnaire and returning it in the envelope provided?

A haberdasher mailed the following appeal to 1,200 men who, though once good customers, had not purchased from him for at least

* *Letters as Business Builders* (Cleveland: Addressograph-Multigraph Corporation), pp. 44 and 45.

④ DON'T BRAG

it isn't the whistle
that pulls the train

... call GArfield 1-5530

The Pownford Stationery Company · 422 Main Street · Cincinnati 2, Ohio

we're not bragging - just want
to let you know we are only a
phone call away to offer you
a complete printing service ..

---

⑤

DATE	CHARGE	CREDIT	BALANCE
			PREVIOUS BALANCE ▶

Roses are red,
Violets are blue,
It's been a long time
since we last
saw you.

Perhaps you didn't know of the Gammill
1-2-3 plan · Purchases made now
will be billed in March, then pay only
1/3 ... 1/3 in April and 1/3 in May.

Gammills

THIS ACCOUNT IS PAYABLE 1% MONTHLY ON OR BEFORE
THE 10TH TO THE MONTH. IF YOU WOULD PREFER TO PAY
THE ENTIRE BALANCE THE AMOUNT IS SHOWN IN THE
LAST COLUMN.

Don't Forget
VALENTINE'S DAY
February 14th

Roy E Gammill · clothier · haberdasher · hatter · importer · 1005 STATE STREET · SANTA BARBARA

CODE: 1) CH. CHECK. 2) CS. CASH. 3) MR MERCHANDISE RETURNED. 4) GC. GIFT CERTIFICATE.

---

⑥

Because of television's exciting coverage of sporting events
we are sometimes inclined to overlook the wide variety of
entertainment being offered daily to the television audience.

The attached reprint is the first in a series stressing the great
range of television programs now available to viewers —
programs which guarantee to advertisers large enthusiastic
audiences on the NBC Television Network.

George N Frey
Director of Network Sales

---

②

Memo

From the desk of
Chas. E. Snell

It's a real pleasure --

-- to furnish you with this helpful
booklet on home decorating, which
you requested. You will find it a
handy guide to color harmonies,
furniture arrangements and proper
carpeting to fit in perfectly with
your tastes in decorating.

If you wish any further cooperation
please feel free to have one of our
carpet experts call at your home ...
without any cost or obligation ...
to discuss decorating and carpeting
with you further. By seeing your
home and types of furnishings, I am
sure we can make helpful suggestions
... and we serve many homeowners
right "In the home" every week in
the year.

Take advantage of this popular, free
SERVICE!

Cordially,

Chas E Snell

W & J SLOANE
216 Sutter Street
San Francisco 8, California

---

③

SAVE BY MAIL
THE EASY CONVENIENT WAY

SAVE TIME AND EFFORT
TRAFFIC CONGESTION
PARKING PROBLEMS

---

①

Dictaphone Corporation
420 LEXINGTON AVENUE
New York 17

LLOYD M. POWELL
PRESIDENT

May I please
have your opinion?

One of my associates has just written a book on the extremely
important subject of executive communication.

I should like to send you a copy with my compliments, to see
if you find it as helpful as I did, and also whether you agree
that most executives could read it with decided profit.

It's called "Writing Out Loud" and contains 36 pages of up-to-
date and refreshingly presented pointers on one of the most
important parts of your job and mine—dictating.

I think you'll get a real kick out of it. It's not the least bit
technical, takes only a comparatively few minutes to read,
will almost certainly help you save a considerable amount of
your dictating time.

May I send it? Simply fill in and mail the enclosed card and
I'll see that it reaches you promptly. And thank you very much
for letting me "try it out" on you.

Sincerely,

Lloyd M. Powell
President

Interesting Variations in Forms of Promotion to the Customer

(1) Promotion on executive stationery; (2) a promotion "form" acknowledgment; (3)
"window-envelope" promotion; (4) promotion on the back of a blotter; (5) a promotion
reminder imprint on a bill form; (6) a printed promotion.

Have We Done Something You Don't Like?

Today I'm checking up on myself. You haven't been here for some time, and I am eager to know why. As president of LAMSON MOTORS, I feel personally responsible. I want you to stay in the "family," and I can assure you that we'll try to make it worth your while.

We at LAMSON MOTORS work day and night trying to please our customers, and I have been wondering if anyone here has done something to keep you away. If so, won't you please get in touch with me—by telephone, letter, or personal visit—*and help me check up on myself?*

Fred Lamson — LAMSON MOTORS, INC.

A Brief "Post-Card Promotion" Appeal

four months. There was a return of 60 per cent—730 people replying, either by purchasing goods or by stating their reason for discontinuing their account.

THIS APPEAL "PULLED" A 60 PER CENT RETURN

If you should discover that a good friend of yours, to whom you had given the best in the way of friendship, courtesy, and understanding, had suddenly stopped visiting you without apparent cause, you'd want to know why, wouldn't you?

This business--representing twenty years of hard work-- is the biggest thing in my life. My customers are, in every sense of the word, my best friends for they make my success a reality. You are one of them.

Nearly a half year has passed since you were in this store. Being human, I quite possibly have done something or sold you something with which you are not thoroughly satisfied. If that is the case, won't you come in and tell me about it, just as one good fellow to another? Even now, if you are not satisfied with that last purchase, I will make things right.

This is no suggestion that you need to buy anything. I should appreciate, though, an opportunity to talk the matter over with you.

Holding Old Customers. To keep old customers on the books is much easier than to bring in new ones, although both activities must be kept up. Through promotion the store manager keeps in touch with his customers and informs them of new features. A retail men's clothing store, using the ten-payment credit plan, sends every customer who completes a contract satisfactorily the following thank-you note. A cordial business promotion like this, sent out on Friday by one store, caused 23 out of 77 customers to reopen their accounts on the following Tuesday.

THIS PROMOTION "THANK YOU" REVIVED 23 OUT OF 77 CUSTOMERS

Thank you for the prompt way in which you paid your recent account. We want you to know that we appreciate such reliable patronage.

Come in any time you want to use your credit privilege. It will be waiting here for you, already established. You won't have to fill out any card again--just step over to the Credit Department and have it approve the payment plan on whatever you buy. Come in soon!

The following message adds the personal persuasion of the sales-man who last served the customer.

THIS PROMOTION EFFORT CAUSED ONE OLD CUSTOMER TO BRING
IN FIVE NEW ONES

It was a real pleasure for me to help you select your suit last March, and I'm eager to help you again this year in selecting your new spring apparel.

Style and color in suits and sportswear are changing this spring. You will be especially interested in the new wrinkle-resistant fabrics featured in our new line.

Please come in and look over our complete and attrac-tive array of men's wear. I would really like to serve you again. May I?

(2) Promotion to the Dealer. Promotion to the dealer emphasizes that the goods will sell well and that the sales will be profitable to him. Stress is laid upon advertising that is under way or about to be released, evidence that the article will sell. Emphasis is placed upon the margin of profit the dealer will receive from each unit sold, and the quality of the product, which will assure the customer's satis-faction. Any retail dealer can supply samples of such promotion messages.

A famous manufacturer of electrical appliances keeps in close touch with its retail outlets and supply distributors through promo-tion like this:

PROMOTION TO DISTRIBUTORS

Multiply your sales of the JET Automatic Dishwasher!!! We'll help you with attractive folders and booklets like the samples enclosed. The attached sample letter can also be multigraphed on your stationery. Sign it, enclose a folder, and mail it to every name in your prospect file.

Attractive advertisements for your local newspaper are also yours, free on request. Outline your advertising cam-paign. Then write for the JET portfolio. Use the materials suggested, follow up with telephone calls and vivid demonstra-tions, and you will soon build a growing and profitable busi-ness--because our research shows that the potential market for the JET Automatic Dishwasher is immense.

FORBES LITHOGRAPH MFG. CO.

DESIGNERS AND CREATORS OF COLORFUL ADVERTISING

P. O. BOX 515

BOSTON, MASS.

June 23, 19--

Mr. Louis T. Paulson, President
Paulson Manufacturing Company
298 W. 66th Street
New York 22, New York

Dear Mr. Paulson

We've got a hunch about you.

We have a feeling that, like many other successful business-men, you're a fact-minded person. For that reason, we believe the attached advertisement will interest you.

In it, you will read how Forbes Litho, working closely with its clients and clients' agencies, is developing some of the most impact-packed merchandising material in the industry. The reason? Facts.

Forbes keeps ideas sharply aimed and up to date by means of a special facts service available to clients. This facts service consists of an ever-growing accumulation of pertinent facts about merchandising material that helps Forbes clients enjoy the sales benefits of the right displays, the right packaging, the right promotions to keep goods moving.

If you would like to know how Forbes facts can help you, please drop us a line and we will send the Man from Forbes to see you.

Sincerely

Paul L. Butze
Sales Promotion Manager

PLB:S
Encl.

HOME OFFICE AND FACTORY P.O. BOX 515 BOSTON, MASS.
BRANCH OFFICES NEW YORK CHICAGO CLEVELAND ROCHESTER

VESTA Heating & Air Conditioning Inc.

7141 THACKER DRIVE, CHICAGO 16, ILLINOIS • RANDOLPH 6-8921

WHEN A PROSPECT ASKS:

"Will this gas furnace heat those back bedrooms of mine that are always like barns--and will it eliminate all of that dirt and soot that accumulates now?" What is your answer?

DO YOU TELL HIM.--

that the gas furnace can't compensate for an under-sized furnace and faulty heating system--that you can't con-scientiously recommend a gas-furnace installation if he is having heating trouble now?

OR DO YOU SAY SOMETHING LIKE THIS:

"Frankly, Mr. Jones, your heating system needs more than a gas furnace to provide comfort and convenience. You need a forced air-conditioning unit to clean the air, force it up to those hard-to-heat rooms, and keep an even tempera-ture in every room. The air conditioner will increase the efficiency of the gas furnace, too, because it uses all of the available heat."

AS A MATTER OF FACT,

the progressive gas-furnace dealer doesn't wait for his prospects to ask those "tough" questions. He anticipates them by explaining that a gas furnace and a conditioner are needed for complete heating comfort and convenience.

LET VESTA HELP YOU

get new customers and keep your old ones. A port-folio of literature, with technical data and sales promotion material, is yours for the asking. Just return the enclosed business reply envelope--it requires no postage.

Yours very truly,

James R. Milane
Sales Promotion Manager

JLM/ck
Enclosure

A hosiery company, in a tone of friendly interest, makes a cordial offer of cooperation in building profits for the dealer:

PROMOTION TO A DEALER

We're ready right now to help you develop your PHOENIX hosiery business into ever-greater profits. For your inspection and approval, here are the latest styles and colors for Milady's hosiery wardrobe.

Our research agency has proved that these samples have excellent market possibilities. After you have examined them, decide on those you think will sell best and order from the enclosed price list. When buying from PHOENIX, remember--Service is our middle name!

Making New Dealer Contacts. Many companies, having discovered the importance of getting dealers off to a good start, greet each new dealer with a promotion message. Amity Leather Products sends a short greeting to all new accounts opened either by sales representatives or by mail.

ASSURING STRONG DEALER SUPPORT

Thank you for the courtesies shown our representative, Mr. Gordon, during his recent visit and also for the initial order you gave him. We appreciate this first opportunity to serve you and are confident that it is just the beginning of a happy business relationship. We'll strive to serve you in such a way as to merit your good will and patronage.

Our merchandise and our merchandising plans have all been set up to help you increase your sales of leather goods. We're continuously on call to help you!

The L. E. Waterman Company sends a good-will note when the salesman has installed all displays and promotional material.

WELCOMING A NEW DISTRIBUTOR

Welcome to a friendly group--this family of Waterman dealers you've just joined--a family that welcomes you with enthusiasm and bids you make yourself at home.

You'll find us congenial, but more than that you'll find us always at your service. We are here to answer any questions and cooperate with you in any way you may desire. Available to you is a great source of advertising and display material, as well as the advice of any department in our company--from manufacturing to sales.

Incidentally, do us a favor and let us be the first to hear about any dissatisfaction with our service or products. You'll see how quickly we can correct the situation.

If you are ever in New York or Newark, drop in on us and let us show you the family home grounds.

"Daily" Promotion Paragraphs. Promotion paragraphs inserted into daily correspondence sometimes far outpull all other kinds. Here are some interesting examples.

A CAR AGENCY REMINDS A PATRON TO APPLY FOR NEXT YEAR'S
CAR LICENSE, THEN GOES ON:

By the way, you'll find our new branch, LENOX MOTORS,
located in your neighborhood at 432 Denton Lane. LENOX's
skilled mechanics have the latest equipment to service all
your car needs.

AN INTERIOR DECORATING FIRM, DISCUSSING A SUBJECT RELATED
TO HOME FURNISHING, INSERTS THIS NOTE:

Incidentally, we can now get you the shade of plastic
flowered chintz you wanted for your shower curtain. Just
telegraph collect, and we'll put the order in for you.

THE VICE PRESIDENT OF A BANK WRITES:

Thank you for your rental of one of our safety-deposit
boxes. I want to extend our welcome to you.

I notice that you paid the rental with a check on the
National State Bank. Perhaps it would be more convenient for
you to carry a checking account here now that your home is
somewhat closer to us.

A PUBLISHING HOUSE MAILS A CUSTOMER THE FOLLOWING NOTE
SHORTLY AFTER SENDING A BILL FOR A SET OF CHILDREN'S BOOKS:

Will you please tell us which stories in Volume I of
THE CHILDREN'S STORYBOOK your youngsters have most enjoyed?

Your comments on the enclosed questionnaire would be of
the utmost interest to us. Simply return the questionnaire
when you remit the monthly payment.

The suggestion in the last paragraph of the publisher's note stimulates prompt payment and at the same time gathers helpful information.

The Dramatized (Novelty) Message. The dramatized message has compelling attention value. If the dramatic feature emphasizes an important selling point, it may also help to convince and to lead to action. Unusual folds, mechanical cutouts, and peculiar shapes of the sheet or of the typewritten material on it are frequent.

The risk is that the peculiarity of the novelty shape or features may unduly distract attention from the message. In the examples illustrated on pages 288 and 289, the novelty features have a clear connection with the theme of the messages and therefore strengthen them.

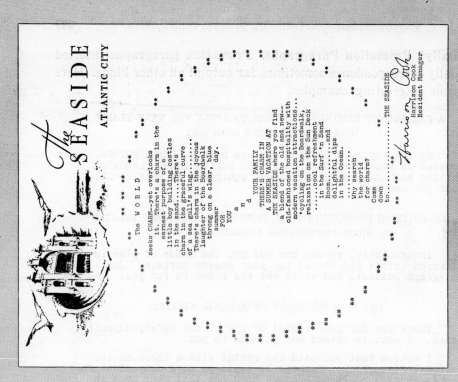

Dramatizing with a Novel "Map" Layout—The First Page
of a Four-Page Illustrated Folder

The Novel Opening of This Promotion Message Compels
Attention and Emphasizes an Important Selling Point

AMERICA'S MOST COMPLETE
DIRECT MAIL SERVICES

BUCKLEY-DEMENT is a house of many services . . . each obtainable by itself or in combination with the others. Knowledge of advertising principles . . . unified control of production . . . and familiarity with postal rules make B-D services effective, fast and economical.

PRINTING . . . IMPRINTING	PHOTO OFFSET . . . PLANOGRAPHING	TYPEWRITING . . . ADDRESSING	PROCESS LETTERS OF ALL KINDS	GUARANTEED MAILING LISTS
ALL MAILING OPERATIONS	MACHINE ADDRESSING	COUNSELING AND CREATIVE SERVICES	SAMPLING BY MAIL	CONTEST ADMINISTRATION

Marketing Management by Mail

This printed message is a promotion piece outlining business promotion.

Dramatizing with Illustrative Features

This promotion piece is printed in facsimile typewriter type. Note the illustrated heading and the novel thumb-print signature.

Illustrated Four-Page Folders. Illustrated four-page folders have the marked advantage of being able to tell a more elaborate story than can possibly be presented on one page. The multiple device is often used to promote a new product or to present new features of an already established product. Here are its advantages:

1. The message on the first page is physically attached to the expanded sales material on the following pages. The four pages are a unit, typed and printed on one sheet commonly measuring 17 by 11 inches, folded the long way, making an 8½- by 11-inch four-page folder, with the fold at the left edge.
2. The processed or individually typewritten message on the first page is more personal than a printed folder.
3. Inside and back surfaces (pages 2, 3, and 4) may carry illustrations and headlines and subheadlines in colors. All the ingenious devices of promotional layout, including pictures and blocks of printed copy, may be brought into play.
4. Four times as much space is available for the message. If additional folds are used, the space may be increased to six or eight pages.
5. Novel folds and illustrations may give compelling attention value.
6. The entire layout may be designed to lead the eye directly to the "action device," usually a business reply card clipped, tabbed, or perforated so that it can be torn out.

Follow-Up Systems

The follow-up system is a planned campaign of sales messages, or of sales messages and mailing pieces in combination, one following another like links in a chain, and organized in a related program for the accomplishment of a defined sales objective. The parts of the system are written with a definite relation to one another, are mailed at calculated time intervals, and are put to these chief uses: (1) following up inquiries about products, (2) stimulating inquiries, (3) selling by mail to a prospective customer, (4) bringing prospects to retail stores to buy, (5) holding the customer's good will, (6) preparing a prospective buyer for the call of a salesman, (7) introducing improvements and new models.

Three Types of Follow-Up Systems. The three common types of follow-up are (1) the campaign system, (2) the wear-out system, (3) the continuous system.

The *campaign system* is prepared in full before the first mailing and is sent, piece by piece, during a definite period of time. The number of pieces, the time between the mailings, and the total length of the campaign are planned ahead. The system is cumulative in force. Each mailing piece advances the sales campaign another step.

The *wear-out system* keeps "everlastingly at it." Each mailing piece carries its own complete sales presentation. One piece after another is sent until returns are no longer profitable. The mailing list is then "worn out."

The *continuous system* is indefinite in length. To established customers, sales messages may be sent at intervals, often with monthly catalogs or weekly price lists. To prospective customers, messages may be sent at longer time intervals, as in the spring and fall.

The Campaign System. The over-all plan of the campaign follow-up system is developed as carefully as the individual mailing pieces. The higher the price of the article, the wider the margin, the better the mailing list, then the larger the number of mailings that may be sent. For new and unfamiliar articles the system must be long to develop confidence. For an article costing a hundred dollars or more, like an encyclopedia set, a system of six to ten mailings with elaborate enclosures has proved profitable. On the other hand, the margin of profit on one ordinary volume would not justify even four mailings under ordinary circumstances. Hundreds of low-priced articles, interesting and distinctive enough in character to be sold by mail, have only enough profit margin to justify one mailing and no campaign.

Campaign Appeals and Emphasis. Throughout the campaign one central selling point, the dominant value of the article, is kept foremost. This plan keeps the chief feature prominent. The whole campaign, whether two or eight pieces, holds attention and interest through variety in appeals. Variety of appeals freshens the customer's interest and stimulates it anew. The material is so handled that the early mailings ensnare attention and develop interest, and the later ones present powerful offers to induce action. The progress is from attention through interest to desire and favorable action.

Intervals between mailings may be a week, ten days, or two weeks. Action is invited at the close of the first mailing, and at the close of each following mailing. The reader may be convinced and ready to buy long before the campaign is complete. To secure his order by early action saves the rest of an expensive series. With each succeeding mailing the action urge increases and reaches its climax in the final message. The Encyclopaedia Britannica letter on page 379 offers an excellent example of final action in a campaign.

Mechanical Setup of Sales Messages. Studies on the mechanics of style in sales messages, particularly in follow-up mailings, reveal interesting practices. The most valuable of these studies analyzes two hundred sales messages sent to hardware, paint, sporting goods, automotive accessories, and department stores. The study was made to determine prevailing practice in the physical aspects of campaign construction. The introduction says:

> It is not suggested that the most common practice is the correct practice, or that the uncommon practice is the one to avoid. The medium is too fluid to be bound by inflexible rules; too susceptible of individuality. Writers of sales messages, however, may be interested in having some basis of comparison against which to check their favorite salutations, closings, and other component elements. ["Sales Letter Style," *Printers' Ink Monthly*, Vol. 38, No. 1, p. 10.]

Some of the briefed results are these:

Inside Address: Of the two hundred sales messages surveyed, only fifty-nine bore inside addresses. Here the cost of fill-ins is the deciding factor. Several messages with poorly matched fill-ins would have been improved had the fill-ins been omitted.

Salutations: Eighty-four of the messages bore the salutation, "Gentlemen." Forty-six carried no salutation. Ten were written "To All (name of product) Dealers." Four went "To the House Furnishings (or Window Shade, etc.) Buyer." Three used "To Our Customers." Three more used "To the Trade." The rest were widely scattered variants.

Special Headings: About 25 per cent of the messages (51 messages to be exact) made use of a special heading of one kind or another. The special heading (or "running head") is often used as a substitute for the salutation. It has no standard placement, appearing sometimes at the left, sometimes at the right, sometimes in the center. Specimen headings: "Sales-Tested Values Are Your Best Christmas Investments," "Proving a Cardinal Principle of Merchandising," "An Important Announcement to Retail Jewelers," "A Spring Sales Campaign for Hadley Dealers." *

---

* "In spite of all the advantages of personalizing messages," writes G. Lynn Sumner, "it is better to use an intriguing well-phrased running head arranged in the form of a salutation than to risk bad handling of a considerable percentage of the names." See "A Business Man's Reactions to His Mail," an address before the Direct Mail Advertising Association, briefed in the *Advertiser's Digest*, Vol. 8, No. 1.

Paragraphing: Block paragraphing is the most popular style, leading the indented style, 115 to 82.

Complimentary Closes: Almost as varied as salutation forms are the styles of complimentary closes revealed in the study. Whereas 46 messages failed to carry a salutation, only 7 omitted the complimentary close. The percentage of traditional closes is high.

The "From" Style of Introductory Address for Follow-Ups. One device for gaining uniformity in introductory addresses and salutations is shown at the right. This arrangement is much better than a poor fill-in.

```
From Paul S. Hart
Circulation Manager
BOOK-OF-THE-MONTH CLUB

Dear Reader:
```

"Sky-View Towers"—All Its Apartments Filled—by Mail. The Wilshire Company, a real estate firm, was commissioned to rent several apartments in a new apartment building called SKY-VIEW TOWERS. After determining the market they desired to reach, they used a follow-up campaign of two mailings, each with an instructive enclosure to reinforce the message. The first mailing directed attention to the enclosure: "Pictured on the enclosed sheet is. . . ." The action paragraph went right to work: ". . . Send now for the illustrated brochure. . . ."

THE FIRST MAILING IN THE "SKY-VIEW TOWERS" CAMPAIGN

Attention { Pictured on the enclosed sheet is SKY-VIEW TOWERS, the first co-operative apartment building in this city.

Interest and Desire (Note buying points) {

Located on Seacliff Boulevard at Vista Lane, SKY-VIEW TOWERS offers a new way to buy a home without paying the homeowner's penalty of worry and bother. Close to bus transportation and only a few blocks from the university, SKY-VIEW TOWERS is in the heart of the restricted residential district that borders Auburn Heights.

Here is a new kind of apartment--one that you can buy outright at a low cost with easy terms and one that becomes your permanent property. A sum of $500,000,000 has been written into the successful investment record of co-operative apartments. You are further safeguarded by the integrity of the Wilshire Company, which has brought the project to its completion.

Action { The plan is simple. Send now for the illustrated brochure, SKY-VIEW TOWERS. Your copy will come to you with no obligation.

After an interval of one week the second mailing, with a group of carefully selected *new* facts and with an enclosure of a typical floor plan of one of the apartments, was sent:

THE FINAL MAILING IN THE "SKY-VIEW TOWERS" CAMPAIGN

Attention
{
Last week we were pleased to send you the architect's drawing of the nearly completed SKY-VIEW TOWERS--this city's first co-operative apartment building located on Seacliff Boulevard at Vista Lane.
}

Reference to Important Enclosure
{
Enclosed you will find a typical floor plan of one of the ten distinctive apartment-homes, a number of which are still available.
}

Interest and Desire (Note Concrete Detail)
{
You may choose from the four- or five-room size. The entire building is of fire-resistant material-- the basic structure being concrete, brick, tile, and steel. The interior bears the delightful stamp of quiet and refined homelikeness, with distinctive fittings and interior design.

Each of the apartment-homes is most modern in conveniences such as GE refrigerators, dishwashers, Disposall, built-in cupboards, private storage rooms, metal weather strip, and plenty of electric outlets and base plugs. Intercommunicating and call button systems are part of the building equipment. Even in the details of hardware and electric fixtures, harmony is assured.

Utmost consideration has also been given to sound deadening to insure the quiet, peaceful atmosphere of a true home. For this purpose the famous Acoustex System has been installed at a cost of over $5,000--the first installation of this type in this city.
}

Action
{
So that you may read the entire story of our new homeowning plan and the details of its economical operation, just return the enclosed reply card and we shall send you the free illustrated brochure, SKY-VIEW TOWERS, A Co-operative Apartment Project.
}

The inquiries for the booklet were followed up by a personal call of a representative of the company. The results: the campaign filled the apartments.

Form Systems

Forms. Messages of identical wording, based on a master draft, and sent to one or more persons, are called *forms*. The number of copies mailed may be 1, 10, 100, 1,000, 10,000, or 100,000—more or less—depending on the task to be accomplished.

Advantages of Forms. The form enjoys three advantages:

1. *It multiplies skill.* An expert can prepare master forms, adapt them to specific situations, and tell exactly how to use them. Then less experienced communicators, having an expert guide as to which forms to choose, can cover scores of situations with skill, speed, and economy.

2. *It multiplies coverage.* Large numbers of forms may be machine-produced and sent out at the same time over a large area, with the "sharpshooting" advantage, however, of being sent to one individual at a specified address with a tailored-to-fit message.

3. *It is economical.* One master draft may be duplicated without limit at very low unit cost. Instead of costing $1.50, as might be the case if the message were individually dictated, the form-guided message may cost only the postage plus a few cents.

How Forms Are Used. Some important uses of forms are (1) as single sales messages, or as units in a follow-up system; (2) to answer inquiries; (3) to acknowledge orders; (4) to acknowledge remittances; (5) in business promotion; (6) to handle the simpler types of adjustments; (7) as units in a collection follow-up procedure; (8) to ask for references on job-seekers; (9) as announcements from management to a particular group (Examples: chain-store employees, mail-order house customers, corporation stockholders).

Three Types of Forms. Forms are of three types: the complete form, the guide form, and the paragraph form.

(1) *The complete form* is prepared in advance to cover a definite situation. It may be "processed"—that is, the entire unit may be imprinted on letterhead paper in one impression, usually by the multigraph or by typewriter type set up in a printing shop. When the form is to be individually typewritten for use in place of a dictated message, it is given a key number. The communicator then specifies (a) the key number of the form to be used and (b) the addressee. The stenographic assistant does the rest.

(2) *The guide form,* likewise prepared in advance to cover a definite situation, is more flexible than the complete form because the dictator uses it only as a guide and alters its phrasing to fit each new individual.

(3) *The paragraph form* is a group of paragraphs, related in nature, carefully drafted in advance in such a way that they may

be chosen and combined to meet different situations. Experience in correspondence reveals after a time what kinds of paragraphs are most often needed. These may then be fitted so closely to the individual needs of the average customer that they give the effect of personal dictation. Because form paragraphs may be put together in endless combinations, they too are more flexible than complete forms. But they require more judgment on the part of the communicator. Messages produced from form paragraphs are individually typed.

Building a Message from Form Paragraphs. Form paragraphs (as well as complete letter forms) are grouped in a *dictaform* (a form book). Each paragraph is keyed by the number of the page on which it falls, and by a letter of the alphabet, the paragraphs being grouped under subject headings such as routine types of messages, sales, credits, collections, adjustments, thanks and appreciation, and so on.

FORM BOOK INDEX	
Subject Heading	*Page*
Routine Messages	1–5
Sales	6–15
Credits	16–20
Collections	21–27
Adjustments	28–33
Thanks and Appreciation	34–37

Each subject heading may have a certain number of pages reserved in the book, as shown at the left.

Each page carries a group of form paragraphs. Each paragraph is designated *A*, *B*, *C*, etc. The dictator leafs through the form book, selects the paragraphs he needs, and constructs a complete message by jotting down the symbols as: *7A, 9C, 11D, 12E, 14F*. The stenographic assistant then copies the paragaphs out of the form book in the order indicated.

How Management Dictates with Code Symbols: A Concrete Example. From the code symbols used, you can tell by a glance at the form index that this executive has constructed a sales message. Pages 6 and 7 of the form book contain a group of "points of contact" for securing *attention* (the first sales function). From this group he selects *7A* (Paragraph A from page 7) because it best fits his purpose:

> **7A** Findex Calculators stand ready to demonstrate in two short weeks that profit lies not in the volume of business done but in the efficiency with which it is handled.

Pages 8 and 9 of the form book contain a group of sales paragraphs designed to arouse *interest* (the second sales function). From the group he selects *9C* (Paragraph C from page 9):

> 9C
>
> The firm that shows its volume in SIX figures and its profit in only four, is smaller by far than the firm doing HALF this amount but--through Findex Calculator Control--so systematized that its costs of doing business are held down to a minimum and a substantial profit is shown each month.

Pages 10, 11, 12, and 13 of the form book contain a group of sales paragraphs aimed to stimulate *desire* (the third sales function). From the group he selects *11D* (Paragraph D from page 11):

> IID
>
> To illustrate the true nature of efficiency in business management, check the methods of the most prosperous organization located nearest you. Seven times out of ten you are likely to find it governed by the foolproof simplicity of Findex Calculators, rather than by expensive-to-operate systems of cost-finding, estimating, and billing.

His judgment suggests that he strengthen his appeal with *desire-belief* material from *12E* (Paragraph E from page 12):

> I2E
>
> Because the controller's department is--in the final analysis--the key to net profits, and the strongest bulwark against insidious leaks through which profits slip away, it is vital to your business to handle cost-finding, estimating, and billing at the lowest possible cost without risk of error. This is precisely what Findex Calculators can do in the simple, low-cost Findex way.

Pages 14 and 15 contain a group of paragraphs designed to get *action* (the fourth and final sales function). From this group the dictator selects *14F* (Paragraph F from page 14):

> I4F
>
> Findex Calculators, fully described in the enclosed illustrated brochure, cut $1,700 off the operating costs of the Royal Company in the first three months after installation. Why not see if they can do as much for you? There is no charge for a 14-day demonstration. Simply return the enclosed reply card, and one of our representatives will arrange to call on you at your convenience.

THE FINDEX CALCULATOR CORPORATION

1000 FINDEX BUILDING

WILMINGTON, DELAWARE

June 13, 19--

Mr. John T. Spencer, President
Spencer Manufacturing Company
465 Carondelet Street
New Orleans 4, Louisiana

Dear Mr. Spencer:

Findex Calculators stand ready to demonstrate in two short weeks that profit lies not in the volume of business done but in the efficiency with which it is handled.

The firm that shows its volume in SIX figures and its profit in only four, is smaller by far than the firm doing HALF this amount, but-- through Findex Calculator control--so systematized that its costs of doing business are held down to a minimum and a substantial profit is shown each month.

To illustrate the true nature of efficiency in business management, check the methods of the most prosperous organization located nearest you. Seven times out of ten you are likely to find it governed by the foolproof simplicity of Findex Calculators, rather than by expensive-to-operate systems of cost-finding, estimating, and billing.

Because the controller's department is--in the final analysis--the key to net profits, and the strongest bulwark against insidious leaks through which profits slip away, it is vital to your business to handle cost-finding, estimating, and billing at the lowest possible cost without risk of error. This is precisely what Findex Calculators can do in the simple, low-cost Findex way.

Findex Calculators, fully described in the enclosed illustrated brochure, cut $1,700 off the operating costs of the Royal Company in the first three months after installation. Why not see if they can do as much for you? There is no charge for a 14-day demonstration. Simply return the enclosed reply card, and one of our representatives will arrange to call on you at your convenience.

Very sincerely yours,

James C. Van Dyke

JCVD:mc   James C. Van Dyke, Sales Manager

A Sales Executive "Dictates" This Message from Paragraph Forms

(See pages 294 to 299 for a discussion on how it is done.)

The executive dictates the index symbols, *7A, 9C, 11D, 12E, 14F*. The transcriber turns to the form book, locates the symbols, and writes the paragraphs in the order indicated. The final result appears on page 298.

Enclosures in Forms. On first-class mail every stamp may carry a full ounce of material. Yet a single letterhead and an envelope weigh only a fraction of an ounce. Hence many businesses insert an enclosure to use the postage margin to good purpose. Enclosures may be used to answer inquiries because they can explain through pictures many points that would be difficult to present otherwise. Enclosures reflect many styles, folds, and colors.

Multiplying Management Power with High-Speed Machines

"Automation" Comes to the Modern Office. Today's top management uses high-speed machines to keep the gears of business humming smoothly. An executive of the Addressograph-Multigraph Corporation comments:

> Our research men have discovered that *good management and good control depend upon a good communications system.* Increasing numbers of copies of instructions, orders, and reports are required to keep the wheels of modern commerce, finance, and industry going. Some of the required information is statistical in nature. The business machine simply gets the information on paper once—directly on the master sheet—and from then on we can produce just a few or hundreds or thousands of copies as required.

Multigraphing. A multigraphed imprint made *through a ribbon* gives the effect of a typewriter at a fraction of the expense. The ribbon impression closely matches ordinary typewriting. The multigraphing looks "personal," yet it can be multiplied to many without losing its individual attractiveness. The printing is done from facsimile typewriter type. If the ribbon that inks the type properly matches that of the typewriter, the later "fill-ins" of address, salutation, and other items can hardly be detected. Printing directly from facsimile typewriter type (without "ribbon effect") is also attractive.

Mimeographing. For impersonal messages mimeographing may be used by typing the copy upon the specially prepared waxlike surface of a stencil. This stencil is then placed on a drum, inked, and

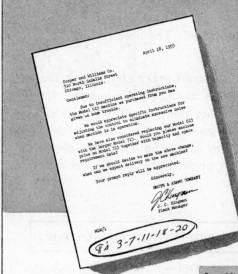

A Typical Letter — Answered the Easy Auto-typist Way

Look at the letter shown at left. Those multiple questions look like sure dictation, don't they? But note the circled group of figures written in at the bottom of the letter—each number indicates a specific pre-composed and perforated Auto-typist paragraph containing the correct answer to each of the questions asked. After these paragraphs are quickly selected and noted on the letter, correspondent merely hands letter to the Auto-typist operator—his work is done!

Here's What Auto-typist Does

Girl slips letterhead in her Model 3054 Push Button Selector Auto-typist, manually types heading and salutation, and touches selector buttons 3—7—11—18—20. Auto-typist automatically picks out these paragraphs on record roll, in order, and accurately types them 2½ times faster than the fastest human typist—without further attention from the operator except for short manual "fill-ins." Here's what the finished letter looks like.

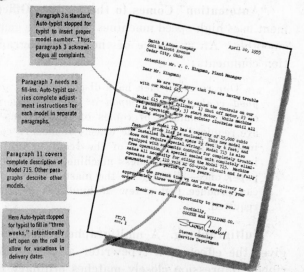

Paragraph 3 is standard. Auto-typist stopped for typist to insert proper model number. Thus, paragraph 3 acknowledges all complaints.

Paragraph 7 needs no fill-ins. Auto-typist carries complete adjustment instructions for each model in separate paragraphs.

Paragraph 11 covers complete description of Model 715. Other paragraphs describe other models.

Here Auto-typist stopped for typist to fill in "three weeks," intentionally left open on the roll to allow for variations in delivery dates.

The above example shows the ease and speed with which Auto-typist can answer even complex letters. Using Auto-typist, correspondent can dispose of a whole morning's dictation in less than an hour. Then your typist can turn out a full day's work before noon!

—*American Automatic Typewriter Co.*

A Typical Letter—Answered the Easy Auto-typist Way

A correspondent can dispose of a whole morning's dictation in less than an hour by using Auto-typist.

Automatic Typewriters

These tape-controlled machines can be adjusted to stop automatically, permitting the typist supervisor to insert special material at any desirable point.

used to run off several hundred copies. As a rule, mimeographed messages are not filled in with an address and a salutation because the mimeograph process does not closely enough match actual typewriting. The outlines of letters, made by forcing ink through the openings cut in the stencil, are not so clear as they are in ribbon-multigraphing.

"Automation" in Typing: The Automatic Typewriter. Controlled by a mechanism similar in principle to that of a player piano, the automatic typewriter operates from a "master record" made from the original draft of the message. Copies may be prepared at great speed. You may thus send an individually typed message to a large list. Some companies, specializing in this work, operate a battery of automatic typewriters under the supervision of an attendant who moves from machine to machine feeding in new sheets, filling in addresses and salutations, and setting the machine in motion under its automatic control. Without further attention the machine completes the copy. Or, if the name of the addressee or some special information is to be inserted at a given point in the body, the machine automatically stops at this point, the attendant inserts the name or the information, and the machine then automatically starts again.

Addressing Machines. Imprinting through plates that are fed through the machine one at a time, addressing machines are used to address envelopes and sometimes to imprint inside addresses and salutations.

Addressing machine models range from portable hand-operated machines to large, high-speed automatic machines that can produce several thousand impressions per hour. Addressing plates are kept in trays similar to the one illustrated.

Addressing Machines and Plates

The plates are also highly useful for automatically *selecting* groups of names. For example, a department store may classify all of its charge customers on the basis of their past buying, as revealed by their charge account records. A list of 5,000 names may be subdivided according to such classifications as (1) men and women who have purchased house furnishings, (2) women who have purchased silks and other fabrics as yard goods, (3) men and women who have purchased electric appliances, and so on. Names and addresses of all charge customers are then recorded on plates. Each of these plates is "tabbed" with a colored metal tab designating in which of the above purchasing classifications the customer belongs. A mechanical device selects only those names that belong to a particular classification.

Is Your Mailing List "Perfect"?

The "Perfect" Mailing List. A mailing list in its ideal form is a *constantly revised list of correct names and addresses* of living people, located in a given trade territory, and, by reason of their careful selection, logical prospects for the purchase of a particular article or a particular service.

Mailing Lists Can Swiftly Sag into "Wastebasket Promotion." Anyone not familiar with a mailing list can scarcely believe how

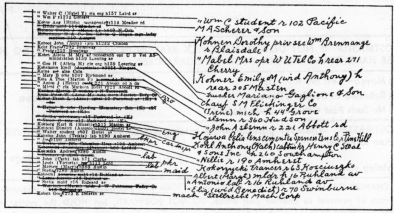

—*R. L. Polk & Co.*

Section of a Corrected City Directory

Dramatic proof that "one of the most changeable things in the world
is a mailing list."

rapid is the shift in names and addresses. The average active mailing list becomes 20 per cent *wrong* in a year. In some cities the
figure is much higher. The postmaster of Chicago estimates that a
mailing list based on his area *depreciates*, on an average, *42 per cent
in a year!*

An executive of R. L. Polk & Co., directory publishers, writes: "The average city directory will be *65 per cent incorrect at the end of the first year and over 80 per cent incorrect at the end of the second year.* Because changes are so numerous and so rapid, we make every directory a new publication from the ground up, with new informa-tion taken and the type set afresh."

WHAT HAPPENED TO A THREE-YEAR-OLD LIST OF 1,000 NAMES
410 people had changed ad-dresses
261 had moved to parts un-known
124 had already purchased the advertised article
83 had already purchased a competing article
7 had died
1 had gone to jail

I resent evidence of carelessness and waste in mail material that comes to my desk, and particularly in sending mail to people who are no longer in our organization. The responsibility for cutting out this waste rests upon those who prepare and send out these mailings. . . . Another kind of care-lessness in mail is the mangling or misspelling of the name itself. Remember that a man's name is his proudest possession, the one thing exclusively his. How he hates to see it misused!

—*G. Lynn Sumner, outspoken critic of mailing waste*

POSTMASTER: IF NOT DELIVERABLE, CHECK REASON IN SPACES BELOW. DO NOT USE HAND STAMP. RETURN POSTAGE GUARANTEED.

☐ Moved—Left No Address   ☐ Refused
☐ Returned at Sender's Request   ☐ Unclaimed or Unknown
☐ No Such Post Office in State Named

POSTMASTER: Whenever possible where catalog is a duplicate, DO NOT DELIVER but return to sender.

                                                     Return Postage
Catalog same as_____*Guaranteed*

IF CHANGE OF ADDRESS ON FILE, notify us on FORM 3547 postage for which is guaranteed. In case of removal to another post office, DO NOT FORWARD, but HOLD the matter and state on FORM 3547 amount of forwarding postage required, which we will promptly furnish.

How Mail-Order Houses Keep Their Catalogs from Going to Waste

Accuracy Essential. An inaccurate mailing list is a liability. Enlightened firms realize this and take extraordinary precautions to keep lists correct.* An investment service checks its mailing lists with a double post card carrying this copy:

> They addressed him as John T. Williams, but his name was John P. Willetts. Then they made this prize error: They addressed him at 235 Beechtree Street, and the address should have been 253 Peachtree Street. And what he wanted never reached him. Of course, he didn't like it. So we're making doubly sure of your correct name and address by sending you this double post card.

"Return Postage Guaranteed." First-class mail carries the return privilege if it is undeliverable. On mailing pieces in other classes that do not carry this privilege, most firms place the printed phrase, "Return postage guaranteed." Then all misdirected and unclaimed pieces are returned and checked against the mailing list, and the dead names are removed. The small postage cost of the return is money well spent, for returned mail is one of the best known ways of keeping the list "clean."

Mailing List Sources. A firm may secure a mailing list, valuable to its particular line of business, by either of two methods: (1) by buying the list ready-made from a mailing list company; (2) by compiling its own list from suitable local sources.

---

* *LIFE* magazine gets about 127,000 address changes every month. And every year one family in fifteen in the United States moves to a different county, and one in six moves to a different house. Other equally surprising figures on the constant mobility of the U. S. population are available from the *Population Housing Division, Bureau of the Census.*

Sources of Names for Mailing Lists

Directories:
 Telephone
 City
 Street
 Trade
 Mercantile

General sources:
 Newspapers
 General advertising
 Salesmen's reports
 Canvassing

Social registers
Rating books
Contests

City records:
 Voting lists
 Tax lists
 License records
 Vital statistics
 Incorporations
 Auto licenses
 City employees

County employees
Permit records
Labor reports
Real estate transfers
School lists

Organization membership lists:
 Club memberships
 Payrolls of firms
 Labor unions
 Church organizations

Lists Bought Ready-Made. A firm may buy a ready-made mailing list for any line of trade from companies specializing in this service. One organization keeps 4,000 trained men in the field collecting list information. It publishes an annual catalog, containing more than 8,000 national mailing lists.

An Example of Specialized Lists

Mailing list companies will also compile special lists. You may have the names and addresses of all the hardware stores in Dallas, Texas, or of all the drugstores in Portland, Maine, or you may secure a list of all department stores in the United States with annual sales of $100,000 or more.

Sources of names for mailing lists are given at the top of this page.

Good Marketing Management Calls for "Sending to the Right People." Effective marketing management tailors its messages to fit individuals who fall naturally into a group and who *are known to have a need for and a possible interest in* the article or the service presented. Form messages sent haphazardly to an unselected and unclassified list of names hastily thrown together from nowhere in particular are probably worth less than scattered handbills tossed on front porches. On the other hand, well-prepared forms *sent to the right people* have proved themselves immensely powerful.

The "directness" of a promotion effort depends on its words, rather than on its form. If the message talks about something in which the receiver cannot possibly have an interest, it is not direct, no matter how personal its matching and other details of preparation. Conversely, it is direct if the article or the service has an obvious relation to the needs of the person to whom the announcement is sent.

The single most important advantage of mail communication to marketing management executives is that it can be made to appeal more specifically to the interests of a limited group and that it can be more direct and personal than any other form of contact short of an actual visit.

Communication Problems

 1. The Sales Manager of the Model Department Store has discovered that 1,500 of the 6,000 names of out-of-town customers having charge accounts at the Model Department Store have made no purchases on their accounts for at least the past six months. Most of these customers live seventy miles or more from St. Louis, where the store is located, and probably buy from the store only on those special occasions when they visit St. Louis in person.

The Sales Manager believes that a good promotion message sent to these 1,500 out-of-town inactive customers might cause many of the accounts to become active again.

The Model Department Store maintains a Personal Shopping Service that promptly fills mail orders; and many of the store services such as money-back guarantee, gift advice, and approval purchases are available by mail. The store has attractive lounges where visitors may meet and rest, and as a service to all patrons, the store will cash checks for any person having a charge account at the store.

Prepare a form message for the Model Department Store which can be sent to these inactive out-of-town charge account customers. Extend a welcome to the customer to visit the store again during the next visit to St. Louis and also mention some of the services the store offers that might make the customer's next trip to St. Louis easier or more pleasant. In addition, mention ways in which the store can serve the customer by mail.

2. The Timepay Jewelry Store, 18 Ocean Drive, Santa Barbara, California, sells jewelry, small appliances, tableware, and gifts on the installment plan. Customers may pay for merchandise in equal installments over a period of a year. Regular collection messages are mailed to customers who fail to keep up their payments, but the store previously has sent nothing to those persons who were prompt and dependable with their payments. The customers who pay regularly, however, are usually the better credit risks; the store would prefer to deal with such customers because collection costs and credit losses are lower.

Write a business promotion message that the Timepay Jewelry Store can mail to each installment-plan customer after his account has been paid in full. While the message will be a form, it will be sent only to those customers who were prompt in payments throughout the year and who have thereby established a good credit reputation with the store.

Write in a cordial, friendly tone. Point out to the customer how his dependable payment record places him among the list of preferred credit customers. The customer now may make additional credit purchases from the store at any time. No further credit checks or references will be required. You may also wish to mention that the store will be glad to act as a credit reference for the customer at any time.

● **3.** The Heat-Rite Appliance Company plans to sell by mail the Heat-Rite Automatic Steam Iron. This iron is made of polished aluminum alloy with a heat resistant, high-impact plastic handle. A heat control on the handle is marked to indicate correct heat settings for various natural and synthetic fabrics. The iron is easy to fill and holds enough water for about an hour's ironing. A 1300-watt heating element provides steam in about two minutes. The iron weighs six pounds and has a 72-inch electric cord. While similar quality steam irons sell for $14 to $18 in retail stores, the Heat-Rite Iron sells for $11.95, postpaid, and carries a six-month guarantee. The Heat-Rite Iron is sold only by mail.

The company owns an up-to-date mailing list of housewives living on farms and intends to use this list for its mailings.

Write a memo to the sales manager of the Heat-Rite Appliance Company in which you explain to him the various follow-up systems this company might use in selling the Heat-Rite Steam Iron to this particular list of prospects. In the memo, suggest advantages and problems the Heat-Rite Company might encounter with each type of follow-up system, and then recommend the system you believe to be best for the company to use under these circumstances. Be sure to explain clearly the reasons behind your recommendation.

● **4.** The staff of the Hometown Department Store, 1841 Sharp Street, Canton 7, Ohio, must write many routine messages covering different circumstances. These messages may be answers to inquiries, acknowledgments of payment, notification that an application for credit has been approved or a request has been granted, and similar favorable situations. You may assume the department store offers the usual services of large stores including credit and delivery, and that the store carries in stock the wide variety of merchandise usually associated with such retail outlets.

(1) Write five different "daily" promotion form paragraphs which the executives of the Hometown Department Store may instruct their secretaries to insert in such messages when appropriate. In writing these units, remember that the same paragraph may be used in several different situations. Likewise, probably no more than one of these "daily" promotion paragraphs will be used in any single message mailed by the department store.

(2) On an 8½- by 11-inch sheet of paper, write a short report to the correspondence supervisor of the Hometown Department Store. In this report, explain briefly to the supervisor how he might use the complete form, guide form, or paragraph form for the various kinds of promotional work that must be handled by his department. In the report, suggest specific types of communication problems for which the complete form might be more appropriate than the guide or paragraph forms.

● 5. The Reliable Brokers, Inc., Chicago, wish to expand their list of active customers by selling small quantities of stocks listed on the New York Exchange to persons who have never purchased stocks before. While stocks listed on the exchange range in price from less than $1 to more than $100 a share, purchases made by the broker on the exchange usually must be for units of 10 or 100 shares. The broker handling the purchase charges a commission for his services.

The Reliable Brokers firm has devised a plan whereby anyone may purchase stocks of their choice in small quantities by agreeing to make definite purchases of no less than $20 a month. Details of the plan are complex, but in general the investment plan allows small investors to buy shares or partial shares in the corporations listed on the exchange without having to invest large sums of money at any one time.

Reliable Brokers believes that investments in stocks provide a type of protection against inflation; trends in the market indicate that as price levels go up, the value of an investment in stock also tends to increase. Regular purchase of stocks is a form of savings. Stocks may be sold on the exchange at current prices at any time the investor needs to have money available. Many stocks pay regular dividends to their owners, and these dividends often are greater than the amount of money paid as interest on popular bonds or on savings accounts in banks.

The details of the stock purchase plan have been printed in a booklet which the Reliable Brokers, Inc. will mail to any interested person.

Prepare the first mailing in a campaign system, announcing the new stock purchase plan. The letter should be designed principally to develop some interest in the plan on the part of the prospect. Near the close should be a request for action, asking the reader to write for the booklet explaining the plan in more detail. Those persons who write for the booklet will later receive several additional mailings from the campaign system.

PART VI

Chapter 14

Opening Steps in Sales Writing: Studying the Product and the Sales Potential

Good marketing management is founded on a careful study of the product and its sales "potential"—that is, its sales possibilities. The sales executive of an automobile manufacturer, for example, will—with the help of his market research staff—make the most exhaustive study of the potential sales of the new model. He has to make this painstaking study in advance in order to project the probable number of cars he can sell in the coming year and to determine what share of the existing market his company can expect to enjoy. In carrying out his part as a management executive in the marketing division, he furnishes vitally necessary information to the management executives of the production division who, of course, have to know in advance about how many cars to build.

Studying the Product

The Basic Data Study. A basic data study is a systematic analysis of a product or service in order to determine basic facts about it of vital importance in the later sales effort. In the following discussion the term *product* is used to refer to a *product or service* in order to avoid the repeated use of the combined expression.

The basic data study has three aims:

1. To discover, classify, evaluate—to *know*—the essential features and characteristics of your product.
2. To *differentiate* its features and characteristics from those of competing products.
3. To key these basic facts to the *needs* of the prospective buyer.

Gathering Basic Facts. You need to know important facts about your product as compared with competing products. Through close comparison you can then determine the buyer-advantages of your own product. Some of these advantages may be: wide use, high quality, low price, low operating cost, famous reputation, precision manufacturing methods, excellent maintenance service, good credit terms, immediate delivery, etc.

309

Suppose, for example, that you have been hired by a publisher as an executive assistant to help in sales promotion. As one of your assignments, you are asked to draft a sales message for a book like the one you are now reading. What are the problems before you? To write intelligent copy, you will want to know (1) something about the book, (2) how it is better than its competitors, and (3) facts about the publisher and his policies. The starting point is always a basic data study of the product and the company behind it. The facts you will gather will be of two types: those to stimulate *general demand* and those to stimulate *selective demand*.

> **Basic Data Guide**
> 1. The Product: Type, Advantages
> 2. Materials and Construction
> 3. Method of Operation
> 4. Design and Appearance
> 5. Uses and Performance Facts
> 6. Differentiating Features
> 7. Service Facilities
> 8. Prices and Terms

General-Demand Stimulation. Facts needed to stimulate a *general demand* (without reference to direct competition of similar products) characterize efforts like these: (a) co-operative promotional program of the airlines of the United States; (b) the promotional campaign of the Association of American Railroads; (c) the joint campaign of the Association of Travel Agencies to "See America First"; (d) all other types of demand stimulated for products of one kind competing for a part of the consumer's dollar against products of an entirely different kind such as the demand for a new car as against the demand for an oriental rug.

Selective-Demand Stimulation. Facts needed to stimulate a *selective demand* in direct competition against like products characterize the appeals, for example, of (a) Imperial vs. Cadillac; (b) the New York Central vs. the Pennsylvania Railroad; (c) United Airlines vs. American Airlines vs. Trans World Airlines; (d) Royal vs. Underwood; (e) Tide vs. Rinso; (f) any selective demand for products of one kind competing for a part of the consumer's dollar against products of the same kind, as the demand for an RCA color-television set against the demand for a Zenith color-television set of similar console style. *Competitive selection* is the key.

The Basic Data Study Chart. The basic data study chart illustrated on page 312 "visualizes" important features such as (1) points that differentiate your product, and (2) points in which your own

$155.

- 3½ Rm. apartment $155
- Additional Bedrooms $20 each
- 3 year lease • 1 Mo. Security
- New beautiful 9 stories
- Bldg exteriors in pastel colors
- Simple layout uncluttered spacious
- All Glass cheerful rooms
- Large square living rm. 25'x 20'
- Only 4 apartments per floor
- Each a corner apartment
- With two exposures
- 20' balcony every apartment
- Private planted garden on balcony
- Sliding glass walls master bedroom
- Built-in Swedish glass bar
- Large storage roomette
- Tracy kitchen in color
- Stainless Steel counter & sink
- G.E. deluxe elect. range turquoise
- G.E. newest wallhung refrig. turquoise
- Japanese translucent sliding panels
- Kitchen easy service to balcony
- Swedish walnut privacy screens
- Briggs deluxe duo-bath 2 basins
- Maticork waterproof tile floors thruout
- Automatic laundries alternate floors
- Westinghouse newest electronic elevator
- Bethlehem Steel Fireproof Structure
- No ugly fire escapes • no congestion
- Private parking areas free

- Location very close to Manhattan
- Off Belt Pkwy near Whitestone Bridge
- At the waters edge
- Long Island's North Shore
- Waterviews E. River & L. I. Sound
- Private residential neighborhood
- Extensive gardens & trees
- Private Luxurious Clubhouse
- Permanent art exhibit
- Club dining room overlooks river
- Superb cuisine—Dancing Fri. Sat.
- Private white sand beach
- Cabanas & beach snack bar
- 3 magnificent swimming pools
- 3 fast drying tennis courts
- Private boat basin and docks
- Speed boats for fishing water skiing
- Billiard, ping pong, card rooms
- Television Theatre
- Private club barber
- New Schools • Bus to Subway
- 1, 2, 3 bedrm. apartments
- Moving dates now until Jan. 19—
- Models open to 9 P.M.

YOU MUST COME TO SEE IT!

Levitt
HOUSE INC.

DIRECTIONS: Belt Parkway to Utopia Parkway exit near Whitestone Bridge—
160th St. to 10th Ave. Right to models. Open to 9 P.M.

Phone: IN 3-4700

A Brilliant Example of Studying the Product and Analyzing Its Basic Features

This example of a basic data study appeared in a recent issue of the **New York Times.**

Basic Data Study Chart							
Product	Materials and Construction	Method of Operation	Design and Appearance	Uses and Performance Facts	Differ-entiating Features	Service Facilities	Prices and Terms
(Your Own Product)							
(Competing Products)							

product is equal or superior to others. You naturally stress a feature that no competitor has publicized. If you are the first to announce that feature, then (even though competing products likewise have it, or later include it) you have gained important market leadership.

The basic data study chart should be drawn up in a size large enough to accommodate the basic data. For some products a separate chart may be used for the "differentiating" features. For example, in the case of electric refrigerators a supplementary chart may include columns for such features as cubic-foot capacity, freezing capacity, freezing speed, automatic defrost control, type of finish (interior and exterior), and color.

A Basic Data Study of Paper. A publishing company commissions a laboratory to make a comparative study of several samples of book paper. Excerpts from the analysis are shown below.

Basic Data Study of Book Paper

Procedure: Samples of sheets torn from our own book and from all competing books and marked with code numbers have been turned over to the testing laboratory.

Basic Test Data: The test for weight is self-explanatory. The other tests need some explanatory comment:

1. The Pop Test: Measures the bursting strength in pounds per square inch.

2. The Tear Test: Measures the resistance of an instrument that swings on a pendulum and tears the paper as it strikes. The resistance to tear is measured in terms of grams, with the grain and across the grain.

3. The Folding Test: The paper is creased and stretched at a tension. It is then folded back and forth at a tension until the paper breaks. The tests are measured in terms of the number of times that the sheet will withstand the action of the testing machine.

4. The Opacity Test: The test for opacity is conducted by placing a sheet upon a light-absorbent background and then measuring the light reflection. Opacity should be 100 per cent in a perfect sheet.

Basic Data Study for the AIR-FILTER CLEANER

Product: Type, Advantages

1. Cylindrical air filter using water as the medium.
2. Dust and house dirt drawn through the water; traps dust and dirt in a water container; clean air ejected back into room.
3. Full efficiency of motor assured because it does not have to draw through cloth bag—just a water film.

Materials and Construction

1. Cylinder above water container houses motor; attached to base by two simple clips.
2. Motor—one-half H.P. Black and Decker suspended in live rubber mountings.
3. Shockproof—every electrical unit in machine fully insulated by live rubber insulation—U. L. A. tested.
4. Aluminum alloy—light; weighs twelve pounds.
5. No wheels or skids—wide base slides directly on floor.
6. Attachments—all chromium finished with air-tight joints.
7. Power—positive pick-up of anything that will enter attachment opening.
8. All moving parts enclosed—bearings sealed in oil; no belts or gears.

Method of Operation

1. Two-button positive-action switch on side of motor—tested for long life; completely insulated.
2. Attachments anchored directly to water container outlet—ratchet locks attachments in place.
3. Simple operation—child can use machine.
4. No bags; just empty water base and replace.
5. Attachments cleaned by using hose.

Design and Appearance

1. Compact all-cylindrical machine—13" high with a 13" base.
2. Chromium handles, clips, name plate; never tarnish.
3. Cordovan-satin finish.
4. Easily stored in small closet or cupboard.

Uses and Performance Facts

1. Complete cleaning from floor to ceiling.
2. Attachments: (a) aluminum arm, (b) extension arms, (c) carpet nozzle, (d) furniture brush, (e) sprayer.
3. Cleans 2,500 cubic feet of air per minute; conditions at the same time. Menthol or fragrant odors can be put into water to scent the ejected air.
4. Can be used for: (a) cleaning rugs or furniture, (b) scrubbing floors and conditioning rugs, (c) spraying wax or paint, (d) cleaning stairs, (e) cleaning furnace.

CHECK LIST OF
50 WAYS
IN WHICH DIRECT MAIL CAN HELP YOUR BUSINESS

IN YOUR OWN BUSINESS . . .

- [ ] Correcting present mailing lists
- [ ] Securing names for special lists
- [ ] Announcing price changes
- [ ] Presenting new models or patterns
- [ ] Securing new dealers
- [ ] Building low volume territories
- [ ] Securing orders direct
- [ ] Developing territories not covered at present
- [ ] Promoting sales to special groups
- [ ] Selling other items not ordinarily sold, offered or stocked
- [ ] Getting product specified
- [ ] Following up inquiries
- [ ] Winning back inactive accounts
- [ ] Driving home sales points
- [ ] Selling new type of outlets
- [ ] Bringing prospect to showroom
- [ ] Bringing dealers to group meetings

INCREASING BUSINESS OF PRESENT DEALERS . . .

- [ ] Educating dealer as to superiorities of your line
- [ ] Educating clerks in selling strategy
- [ ] Helping dealers make more sales
- [ ] Selling your sales program to the dealer
- [ ] Securing specialized information from dealer
- [ ] Referring inquiries to dealer
- [ ] Checking results of selling efforts
- [ ] Sales contests to dealers' salesmen

DIRECT MAIL TO THE CONSUMER . . .

- [ ] Creating a demand for your line
- [ ] Building volume of present users
- [ ] Opening new charge accounts
- [ ] Inviting customers to visit store
- [ ] Promoting special sales
- [ ] Exploiting seasonal merchandise

DIRECT MAIL WITHIN YOUR OWN ORGANIZATION . . .

- [ ] Increasing employee morale
- [ ] Pepping-up the sales force
- [ ] Paving the way for the salesman
- [ ] Securing inquiries for the salesman
- [ ] Teaching salesmanship to salesmen
- [ ] Keeping customer contact between salesmen's calls
- [ ] Pre-selling prospects ahead of sales call
- [ ] "Clinching" mailings after the salesman's call
- [ ] Welcoming new customers
- [ ] Acknowledging orders, etc.
- [ ] Collecting accounts
- [ ] Securing data from customers or employees

MISCELLANEOUS DIRECT MAIL USES . . .

- [ ] Fund raising for organizations
- [ ] Research for new developments
- [ ] Distribution of samples
- [ ] Building good will
- [ ] Announcing changes of policy
- [ ] Announcing new addresses, phone numbers, etc.
- [ ] Calling attention to other advertising

—Buckley, Dement & Co., Chicago

A Famous Direct-Mail Company Makes a Basic Data Study of Its Own Services

This check list also serves as a convenient summary of the various channels available to marketing executives in solving various types of management problems.

Studying the Market

Market Analysis: To Determine "Sales Potential." A market analysis is a systematic study of the market for a given product in order to determine sales possibilities and other facts of importance to marketing management. The market analysis has four aims:

1. To find out (a) the buyers and users of the product; (b) where they live; (c) under what circumstances they live; (d) their buying power; (e) what they want; and (f) under what terms and conditions they want the product.
2. To determine, classify, and evaluate other features and characteristics that may prove significant in the potential market.
3. To differentiate the characteristics of the present market from those of other markets not under consideration.
4. To bring together the results of (a) the *market analysis* and (b) the *basic data study*.

Market Analysis Interlocks with Basic Data Study. Just as a basic data study is an analysis of the product, so is market analysis, similarly, a study of consumers, buyers, and users of the product. The two forms of analyses interlock.

General Motors Customer (Market) Research, for example, gathers facts on consumer preferences that reveal not only the new features that car buyers want, but also the things that motorists like, dislike, or do not understand. The results serve as a guide for the management of the production division in designing new cars, and for the management of the sales division in stressing features in which prospective buyers are interested.

Bringing Together the Customer and the Product. What we are exploring in this chapter are ways and means to bring together "the consumer-and-the-product" and "the buyer-and-the-market." Note carefully that the consumer and the buyer may be *two quite different persons*. The consumer of a product may not be the buyer. The buyer may not be the consumer. You differentiate between these groups in completing the market study, because such differentiation will affect your choice of appeals for sales messages, the preparation of which will be based upon the dual foundation of basic data and market studies.

Two Kinds of Market Analyses. Two chief types of studies are in use in marketing management. The first is called the *economic*

6 1/4 pliers per reader

𝒥𝒥𝒥𝒥𝒥 ●

Home Craftsman readers aren't content with one slip-joint pliers.
They also buy side-cutting, combination, long-nose, diagonal,
compound leverage, flat-nose, end-cutting and others.

20 1/10 wrenches per reader

ͼͼͼͼͼ ͼͼͼͼͼ ͼͼͼͼͼ ͼͼͼͼͼ ◟

Home Craftsman readers aren't content with one monkey wrench.
They also buy adjustable, set screw, Stillson, open end, socket,
Allen, box, chain, hook spanner, key chuck and others.

Sharp-Cut, Concrete Buying Features to Inform and Interest the Prospective Tool Buyer

A magazine about tools and "do-it-yourself" craftsmanship uses concrete detail
in product and market analysis.

market analysis; the second is called the *psychological market analysis*. They are sometimes combined.

Economic Market Analysis. Facts commonly assembled in economic market surveys are those concerned with (a) buying power; (b) distribution of income into rent, food, and clothing; (c) geographic trading areas; (d) income groups; (e) age groups; and (f) other facts of population—its urban and rural distribution and its occupations. Such study is vital as a basis for planning production, distribution, and marketing procedure.

Psychological Market Analysis. Psychological market surveys are consumer analyses on the psychological level. The psychological market survey attempts to answer first the general question: What are the buying habits of the public? It then attempts to answer such specific questions as the following: (1) What are the buying habits of the public in relation to a certain kind of product? (2) What are the possibilities of shifting the buying habits of the public in regard to a certain kind of product, or in regard to a specific brand? (3) What are the chief barriers to be surmounted in altering fixed habits? (4) What types of appeal are likely to be most effective? (5) Why do so many more or so many fewer people use one kind of product or avoid one kind of product rather than other kinds? (6) How and where do people buy certain types of products? (7) What kind of distribution ought to be used in the light of this buying behavior? (8) How is the public likely to react when a new product is presented? (9) Will the new product be accepted? (10) What appeals will induce greatest acceptance?

The following paragraphs from a report, "Recent Scientific Techniques in Measuring Distribution," presented by Dr. Henry C. Link

316

and Dr. Rensis Likert at the Sixth International Congress for Scientific Management, in London, point the trend toward modern market management:

> Our research uses a "psychological yardstick"—the buying habits of comparable groups of consumers. Periodically in nationwide interviews, people are asked, "What brand of coffee did you buy last?" "What soap did you use last for washing dishes?" etc.
>
> The "psychological brand barometer" is a measure of customers. Its unit of measurement is not dollars—but people. Its purpose is to reveal whether more or fewer people are buying a given article and to show such trends in relation to competing articles in the same group. These reports are derived from nationwide surveys. Such groups as automobile tires, gasoline, automobile lubricating oils, automobiles, cereals, canned soups, flours, dentifrices, teas, and soaps are included and about 500 different brands are recorded. Each study is based on calls in 4,000 homes (different homes each time) made in the same 47 cities and towns.

How These Surveys Are Applied. Such surveys bring answers to questions like these:

1. The kinds of people who buy a given product.
2. The manner in which buyers are divided into geographical and city-size groups.
3. Where the dealers who sell the product are located.
4. The types of media that reach the buyers most effectively.
5. Consumer buying habits relative to the product.

Under the heading of buying habits, the surveys reveal:

1. Why people buy the product.
2. Why others do not buy the product.
3. Why those who formerly bought no longer do so.
4. Why people do and do not buy competitive products.

Famous Users of Market Research. Among famous management users of market research are: American Telephone & Telegraph Co., Bristol-Myers Co., Coca-Cola Co., DuPont, Eastman Kodak Co., General Electric Co., General Foods Corp., Goodyear Tire & Rubber Co., Lever Bros. Co., Procter & Gamble Co., Standard Oil Co. of New Jersey, and Swift & Co.

Professional Market Research Cuts Costs. To help cut marketing costs, professional research groups investigate such special areas as: (1) Factors influencing brand choice; (2) Consumer likes and dislikes, and consumer opinions of what can be done to improve a

—*Milwaukee Journal*

A Nationally Famous Market Analysis

This consumer analysis of the Greater Milwaukee market has been an annual management guide for many years. Information in this market study is gathered by means of a comprehensive questionnaire, sections of which are reproduced on page 321.

product; (3) Pricing; (4) Public's buying habits; (5) Brand name and package selection; (6) What people think of store service; (7) Discovering new markets; (8) Measuring effectiveness of appeals.

The field forces of some research groups operate from coast to coast and are equipped to obtain personal interviews with consumers, dealers, jobbers, and others. The research executives define the marketing problem, develop methods for getting the facts, and evolve a sound interpretation of the results. These are then used for developing improved consumer-relations, cutting costs, increasing margins, and for the solution of other management problems.

"Manufacturing" New Customers Through Market Studies. To aid in locating, identifying, and winning new customers, is a function of market analysis. A top management executive of the Stewart-Warner Corporation asserts that the most hazardous and speculative manufacturing process any company has to deal with takes place outside the factory—the process of "manufacturing" customers.

For example, when a hundred pieces of sheet steel are put through a press, the factory knows that it will get one hundred finished products (barring some technical error). But management also knows that the enterprise must locate and develop one hundred *prospective* customers—to get only five to twenty "finished products"—*actual* customers. Moreover, if the "new-customer-manufacturing department" is not in steady operation, it makes small difference how well the factory itself is functioning or how well the products are designed and made. *Unless there is a steady flow of new customers, no company stays in business.*

"You Sell to a Parade." The market is dynamic, ever-changing, in ceaseless shift and flux, like the roll and curl of sea waves. A half million college seniors, graduating in a current year, change one phase of the market. A thousand and one other shifts occur to change the nature of other parts. The eternal ebb and flow of human lives and destinies and hopes and wants and desires is set forth picturesquely in the following paragraphs.

4,000,000 AMERICANS NEVER SAW AN ELEPHANT!

That's why the circus will come back next year. Same old stuff, you say—same stunts, same clowns, same animals, same ballyhoo you saw when you were a kid. Yes, largely true of course, but since that same old elephant stalked through the streets a year ago, four million new Americans will have arrived in this country—four million *more* people who have never seen an elephant.

And in that same interval, a couple of million boys will reach the girl-crazy stage and start shaving the fuzz off their chins for the benefit of another couple of million young women suddenly become acutely clothes and cosmetic conscious. Another four million folks will up and get married—start new homes, buy new furniture, new dishes, new linens. Yesterday they "weren't interested," today they are—and tomorrow other people will be.

That's why the same old elephant walks around serenely confident that among every bored group of people who say, "That's just an elephant," some eager voice will shout, "Oh—*that's* an elephant!"

When you promote your product, you are not talking to a *grandstand*, but rather to a parade that is constantly on the move with new faces—new buyers—coming into the picture every day.

Customer Needs Arise Overnight: Problem—Find Out When and Where. After a short eight months in his new home, a proud owner discovers that there are hosts of things he still needs: (1) new rugs, because the rugs he brought over from the old house don't fit the new room sizes as well as he hoped they might; (2) a few new pictures, now obviously needed for the new wall spaces; (3) new furniture to fit into the decorative scheme of the living room; (4) a new armchair for the master bedroom; (5) new lamps for the whole house; (6) four more electrical outlets in the recreation room, and two more on the outside porch . . . you finish the list. Market study helps to find out when and where these sudden needs spring up in the ever-changing world. Always and forever you "sell to a parade."

"Sharpshoot" to the RIGHT People. If a message presents a product in which your reader cannot possibly have an interest, it is not direct, no matter how personal and intimate its form. For example: (a) a mailing piece extolling the merits of Kopper's coke sent to people who burn oil for heating, (b) swatches of cloth sent by custom tailors to men who habitually buy ready-made suits, (c) a mail message announcing a sale of silks sent to housewives who buy all their dresses ready-made. These errors are examples, not of "direct mail," but of *misdirected* mail. Such waste can be avoided by a preliminary market study.

Questionnaires As Fact-Finders

Questionnaires in Market Studies. Questionnaires are useful tools in getting facts. Observe these rules: (1) Frame questionnaires with great care, (2) Give them a preliminary test, (3) Make them easy to answer, (4) Avoid leading questions, and (5) Word questions so that answers can be easily checked.

To illustrate why it is necessary to frame questions with care, to run an advance test, and to make answers easy, consider the following case. One question in a coffee-buying-habit survey read (before testing) as follows: "About how much coffee do you use each week?" Sample testing revealed that the housewife had trouble answering this question. To make the answer easier, the question was rewritten in the form of two new questions: "How often do you buy coffee?" and "How much do you usually buy at a time?" The results were then satisfactory.

Equally important is to avoid leading questions. Leading questions are those that suggest a given answer. "Slanted" returns from leading questions that influence answers have ruined many investigations.

WRONG: LEADING QUESTION	RIGHT: FACTUAL QUESTION
Don't you think that the Omega Typewriter is the best you can buy?	What kind of typewriter do you now own?

Finally, questions should be so worded that the answers can be checked rapidly and the results treated statistically.

AN "EASY-TO-CHECK" QUESTION

Was your use of business promotion in 19—, (a) smaller? ☐
    as compared to 19—, ... (b) equal? ☐
                                            (c) greater? ☐

QUESTIONS ON THIS PAGE TO BE ANSWERED BY THE HOUSEWIFE

Do you do any home canning? ☐ YES ☐ NO

What brand of jar do you usually use? ....
BRAND

What brand of lid do you usually use? ....
BRAND

Do you own an incinerator for burning garbage or rubbish? ☐ YES ☐ NO .... MAKE
(Do NOT include furnace or outside rubbish burners.)

Please check whether it is: ☐ Gas ☐ Electric

Did you see last Sunday's Milwaukee Journal? ☐ YES ☐ NO

Please check which sections you read and those that you did not read. (If you looked at any part of a section, check the "read" column.)

	READ	DID NOT READ
Main News		
Local News		
Classified		
Comics		
Editorial Section		
Home Section		
Men's and Recreation		
Roto (Picture Journal)		
Sports Section		
This Week Magazine		
TV Screen		
Women's and Society		

Within the past 30 days, have you bought anything at the BOSTON STORE? ☐ YES ☐ NO

Within the past 30 days, have you bought anything at CHAPMAN'S—
DOWNTOWN STORE? ☐ YES ☐ NO
CAPITOL COURT STORE? ☐ YES ☐ NO

Within the past 30 days, have you bought anything at GIMBELS—
DOWNTOWN STORE? ☐ YES ☐ NO
SOUTHGATE STORE? ☐ YES ☐ NO

Within the past 30 days, have you bought anything at SCHUSTER'S—
3RD ST. STORE? ☐ YES ☐ NO
CAPITOL COURT STORE? ☐ YES ☐ NO
12TH ST. STORE? ☐ YES ☐ NO
MITCHELL ST. STORE? ☐ YES ☐ NO

Within the past 30 days, have you bought anything at SEARS—
NORTH SIDE STORE? ☐ YES ☐ NO
SOUTH SIDE STORE? ☐ YES ☐ NO
BAY SHORE STORE? ☐ YES ☐ NO
WEST ALLIS STORE? ☐ YES ☐ NO

QUESTIONS ON THIS PAGE TO BE ANSWERED BY THE MAN OF THE HOUSE

Do you own a television set? • ☐ YES ☐ NO .... MAKE

What size screen does it have? ....
SIZE SCREEN IN INCHES

Was this television set bought NEW in 19—? ☐ YES ☐ NO

Can you get channel 19 on your set? ☐ YES ☐ NO

Do you own more than one TV set? ☐ YES ☐ NO .... Make of Second Set

Do you own a color TV set? ☐ YES ☐ NO .... MAKE

How is your home heated?
(Please check PRINCIPAL fuel.)
☐ Coal or Coke ☐ Oil ☐ Gas

If oil, what brand? ....
BRAND

What make of heating unit do you have? ....
MAKE

Do you have an electric garbage disposer in your sink? ☐ YES ☐ NO .... MAKE

Is there anyone in your household looking for a full time job? ☐ YES ☐ NO

How many in your household have full time paid jobs? ....

Is there more than one married couple in your household? ☐ YES ☐ NO

Do you have any roomers (other than your own children) in your household? ☐ YES ☐ NO .... HOW MANY?

Please check approximate YEARLY family income BEFORE TAXES. •
(Include total income of ALL MEMBERS of your family living in your household.)

☐ Under $2,000 ☐ $3,000-$3,999 ☐ $5,000-$6,999
☐ $2,000-$2,999 ☐ $4,000-$4,999 ☐ $7,000-$9,999
☐ $10,000 and over

Do you read a daily newspaper regularly? ☐ YES ☐ NO   Check whether it is delivered by carrier:
....   ☐ YES ☐ NO
NAME OF PAPER
....   ☐ YES ☐ NO
NAME OF PAPER

Do you read a Sunday newspaper regularly? ☐ YES ☐ NO   Check whether it is delivered by carrier:
....   ☐ YES ☐ NO
NAME OF PAPER
....   ☐ YES ☐ NO
NAME OF PAPER

—*Milwaukee Journal Survey Department*

Portions of a Consumer Questionnaire

This questionnaire is used for gathering facts on consumer preferences.

```
IDENTIFICATION (Circle appropriate year) . . . 1, 2, 3, 4, Grad

    1.  Do you prepare written              Usually  ☐
        assignments on a              Occasionally  ☐
        typewriter? . . . . . . .           Never  ☐

    2.  If you do, is your          Personally owned?  ☐
        typewriter . . . . . . . .          Rented?  ☐
                                          Borrowed?  ☐

    3.  How many people besides
        yourself use the typewriter
        that you use? . . . . . .      _____

                                           As a gift  ☐
    4.  If you own a typewriter,      Purchased new  ☐
        how was it acquired? . .   Purchased rebuilt  ☐
                                Purchased secondhand  ☐

                                       In this city  ☐
    5.  If you own a type-          In your home town  ☐
        writer, where was      From a mail-order house  ☐
        it purchased? . . . .       Elsewhere_____

    6.  What kind of a type-       MAKE_____
        writer do you use? . .
                                MODEL {     Portable  ☐
                                      {     Standard  ☐

                                TYPE SIZE {    Elite  ☐
                                          {     Pica  ☐
                                          { Other_____

    7.  In typing, do             The touch system?  ☐
        you use . . . . .  The "hunt and peck" system?  ☐

    8.  Name three makes of type-    _____
        writers in the order of      _____
        your personal choice.        _____
```

Typewriter Questionnaire Addressed to College Students

A Top Expert Comments on Questionnaires and Market Studies.
The late Henry Grady Weaver, Customer Research Staff expert for
General Motors Corporation, made the following penetrating com-
ment on the difficulties of constructing a *foolproof* questionnaire.

The more I do of this work the more I realize how little I know about
it. For one thing, we've got to make our questionnaires easy to answer—
for another thing we've got to make sure (or at least as sure as we can) that
the answers reflect the true facts.

Getting enough answers—and getting the correct answers—these are
the big problems.

It's not so difficult when we are seeking viewpoints regarding a mechanical feature of motor car design which can be reduced to simple, straightforward "yes" and "no" replies.

But when we get into the kind of thing dealt with on the attached sheet it's far from simple because there are dozens, if not hundreds, of possible answers and we know we are not smart enough to think of them all. And if we don't include all of them, then the ones not listed will not "get a good run for their money," and our conclusions may be erroneous. By way of illustration, suppose we were getting out a questionnaire on color preferences and forgot to include red as one of the choices—naturally that would tend to reduce the number of votes that we would get back for red. Even a person who was partial to red might check off blue or brown if there was nothing there to remind him of his favorite color.

"Why then," you ask, "why not just ask the question—leave a lot of blank space and let each respondent write in his own answer—'tailored to his own measure' so to speak?"

Well, that's the usual way of doing it and it might be all right except that it cuts down the number of answers—it calls for far too much effort. Most people don't like to write. When you ask them to write out something in longhand it's hard to get more than 8% or 10% replies—and you are never sure that the limited number who do answer will reflect a true cross-section of those who do not answer.

By designing the questionnaire so that a person can easily check off his answer without having to write out anything, we can get 30, 40, 50, and sometimes even as high as 75% returns.*

Interviews

Personal Interview and Direct Contact. For anything with a general appeal like foods, books, magazines, shirts, socks, and ties, every man on a mailing list of executives would be a possible prospective purchaser. Each one wears, uses, or consumes these products. But note the sharp difference when the product is a Delco or Kohler electric power plant for farms: What kind of farms will be the most likely prospective buyers? For what uses do they need this equipment? What features of the product will interest them most? Which of the optional sizes will they prefer? On what terms will they expect to buy? These and other facts about the prospective buyer form the basis for a successful sales program.

* H. G. Weaver, "A Questionnaire on Questionnaires," Thought Starter No. 3 (Detroit: General Motors Corporation), pages 2-3.

One of the country's most successful sales executives, after studying his product to determine the class of people to whom the offer should be addressed, then finds one or more individuals who are typical of these logical prospects and talks with them in an informal way. He makes no effort to sell. His aim is to collect vivid impressions. "I am successful," he observes, "because I *know* my prospective purchaser." *

Another executive, whose responsibility is to sell products used on the farm, drives into the country to spend weekends among farmers. He has also spent whole vacation periods in rural communities. He is a frequent reader of farm journals. Thus he learns to know his audience, their needs and desires, their buying habits and buying motives.

A manufacturer sends his sales executive into the sales territories at intervals to set up contact with dealers and their salespeople and to understand better their problems and preferences, their likes and dislikes, and their trends of thought. Meeting the customers of these dealers, he becomes better acquainted with the character of his market—those who read what he writes.

One retailer, showing ingenuity, acquaints himself directly with the families of his customers. Much to the astonishment of his competitors he often makes his own deliveries for the purpose of learning where and how his customers live. His weekly bulletins reflect, in their informal tone, a friendly grasp of his market developed from what he observes on his delivery trips. Through direct study of the prospective buyer he and the others cited in the foregoing paragraphs intimately know the market they serve.

A Typical Market Study: The Case of Mirror-Shine Car Wash, Inc.

Taking you behind the scenes, the following case discloses how a local market is put under a microscope. The president of Mirror-Shine Car Wash, Inc.—the leading car-wash service in a city of 100,000 people—knows that if sales can be increased, his operating cost percentage can be cut. At his request an expert analyzes the market and makes these recommendations:

---

* This and the following examples are adapted from *Letters as Business Builders*, 2d ed. (Cleveland: Addressograph-Multigraph Corporation), pages 9-10.

I. The Service: What Do We Have to Sell?

1. **Car wash:** Equipment is specialized. The employees are highly skilled. The wash is divided into three phases:
   a. *Chassis wash:* Performed by two men using streams of heated water under pressure.
   b. *Body wash:* The car is enveloped in lathery suds and swabbed with long-handled brushes and sponges. The top is thoroughly cleaned.
   c. *Drying and polishing:* The body is dried with chamois skins; all chromium is polished.
2. **Lubrication:** Using the most modern automatic-pressure lubrication apparatus.
3. **Body polish:** Brilliant-Shine, a semipermanent body polish is applied with power-buffers.
4. **Vacuum cleaning of the car interior:** A good-will service.

II. The Market: Who Will Buy Our Service?

Two classes of car owners may be approached: (1) The man who washes his own car and performs other services for it. He may be shown how time-saving and thorough a job can be done at the car wash. (2) The man who takes his car to another garage. Demonstrate the faster and more specialized service given here.

III. The Medium: How Shall We Reach Prospective Customers?

Because of the location, newspaper advertising is impractical. Much of it would be wasted on car owners who live too far away to be prospects. The solution to the problem is direct mail. Our recommendations are:

1. A mailing list of 1,000 car owners on the east side (including business-men) should be compiled.
2. A four-page illustrated letter—to be printed on 28-pound substance two-text paper, and folded once to the size of the regulation business letter (8½ by 11 inches)—is to be prepared. The advantage: the front page (bearing the letterhead of the company and the multigraphed letter) has a bond surface of high-grade texture. The inside of the letter, however (see enclosed sample), is coated and presents a fine printing surface for small-screen halftones.
3. A strong human-interest appeal is to be used. Mr. Carr, your president, is an exceptionally good personality that can be used in bringing in and keeping customers. Mr. Carr is a pleasant and likable man. His picture, showing his smile, will be featured.
4. Now comes a description of how M-S washes the car and a list of the more important services given.
5. The city survey made by Miss Roberts furnishes the company with an effective mailing list for future promotion. Every name on the list represents a prospective customer.

The cards can be sorted into any number of selected classifications: territory, year, model, and kind of car; customer or good prospect. *Each effort can be made personal because we now have specific knowledge about each customer.*

IV. Sales Program Recommended to Management

Mailings:

1. Telling of the convenience offered by Mirror-Shine Car Wash, Inc. should be sent to the people living near the company.
2. Telling about "call-and-delivery plan," which brings the service as near as the telephone, should be sent to people who live at greater distances from the company.
3. Should be sent telling owners of new cars how Mirror-Shine hard-gloss service protects the original brilliance of their cars for years.
4. Should be sent telling owners of cars driven several seasons of the possibility of restoring the original brilliance of the finish through M-S service.
5. Should be sent using testimonials of satisfied M-S patrons.
6. Should be sent reminding former customers of the thorough servicing done by experts at the M-S shop.

Note the plan of this market study. The service is analyzed in logical sections, the character of the market is defined, and six clearcut recommendations are given.

Through the use of intelligent product and market studies, prepared in the forms outlined in this chapter discussion, sales-executive action effectively solves the complexities and responsibilities of dynamic marketing management.

Communication Problems

● 1. When you get ready to draft an effective sales message, you must be thoroughly prepared before beginning your task. As a part of that preparation, you must (1) know your product well, (2) know competing products, and (3) understand who the prospective buyer is and what his needs are. The sales message then provides an opportunity for you to interpret the product in terms of how well it fits the needs of the particular consumer being reached.

Because in some cases you may not be well acquainted with the product, you must first assemble as much helpful information about it as possible. At times this preliminary but essential preparation requires more time than does the actual drafting of the message itself.

Assembling basic data about your product can be accomplished more quickly when you follow a systematic approach.

Prepare a two-page report telling how you plan to assemble a basic data analysis for a small home appliance of your choice selling for $25 or more. You do not need in this case to gather the information about the product. Instead, you are to describe step by step how you will gather the information and how you will assemble it to be of greatest use to you in preparing sales messages. Be sure to explain the need for adequate information about the product you plan to sell, and show also the need for information about competing products.

On a sheet separate from the report, draw a form which can be used for presenting the basic data analysis of the product.

● **2.** You have been asked by the Riteway Distributing Company to help them make preparations for a mail campaign designed to sell an electric fence charger to farmers. The product is a device which when connected to an electric line and then attached to a fence will place a strong electric charge in the fence wires. Animals touching the wires are shocked and quickly learn to stay away from the fence even when the electricity is not turned on. The shock, while strong, cannot burn and is harmless to animals and human beings. The device needs no batteries and operates on regular 110-volt Alternating Current. The charger is priced at $31.95. It can be installed by anyone in a few minutes.

A principal advantage of the fence charger is that farmers can effectively enclose areas with a lower-cost fencing when the electrical charger is used. The device is particularly helpful to farmers who must set up temporary fencing for enclosing pasture areas.

A major market for this electric unit is among operators of small farms where some livestock—cattle, horses, ponies—may be kept.

Write a short report to the Riteway Distributing Company in which you explain (1) how they may go about gathering the market information needed to analyze their mail-order market for this product. In your report (2) suggest ways whereby the company may obtain the information needed, and (3) outline the specific types of facts that may be required by the Riteway Distributing Company in order to prepare a careful analysis of their market for the electric fence charger.

Note that it is not necessary for you to gather the facts about the market for this product. Instead, explain what facts are needed, how they may be obtained, and how the economic analysis may be carried out.

● **3.** The management of the Keystone Products Company—a firm that manufacturers and sells by mail a variety of products—is considering the manufacture of a new product. An inventor has approached the company with plans for an inexpensive disposable toothbrush, designed in such a way that the brush contains just enough dentrifice for one cleansing. After use, the brush can be thrown away.

Preliminary cost estimates show the company can profitably manufacture the product to sell at a price of $3 for a package of 100
brushes. Machinery for manufacturing the product, however, must
be designed and the investment required for going into production
runs into many thousands of dollars. The executives believe that the
product will produce many repeat orders after its first sale. They
believe the profit possibilities of the idea are highly favorable.

Before making an investment in equipment to manufacture the
product, however, the company wishes to answer certain specific
questions about the buying habits of customers and their attitudes
toward the acceptance of this product. Among the questions for
which answers are needed are those listed in your book in the section
labeled "Psychological Market Analysis" (page 316).

After lengthy discussions the company executives have decided to
conduct a psychological market analysis through the use of questionnaires mailed to 1,000 persons carefully selected as a representative
sample of the market the company hopes to reach.

Review the discussion of questionnaires in your book. Then draw
up a questionnaire that may be used by the Keystone Products Company to collect the information needed in a psychological market
analysis. Test each question with two or three of your friends to see
whether they interpret the questions in the way you intend. Make
the questions easy to answer: word them so that answers can be
rapidly checked and the results easily tabulated.

● 4. You have been hired to write sales and promotion material for
Askenfind Research, Inc. in New York City. Askenfind Research,
Inc. is a professional research group that draws up questionnaires
and conducts personal interviews to determine (1) factors influencing
brand choice; (2) consumer opinions of likes and dislikes about
products; (3) brand name and package selection; and (4) the effectiveness of various appeals. Askenfind Research, Inc. is prepared to
conduct nationwide surveys and offers professional skill, experience,
accuracy, and cost savings to any company using its services.

Askenfind Research, Inc. plans to conduct a direct mail campaign
aimed toward executives of the leading automatic washing machine
manufacturing firms in the United States, in which Askenfind will
introduce and sell to these company executives the research services
of the agency. They plan to use a campaign system of follow-ups
for their personalized sales mailings.

Write the first message of the campaign system (see Chapter 13),
to be used by Askenfind Research, Inc. in promoting its services to
the manufacturers of automatic washing machines.

The first mailing in the campaign system should (1) explain
briefly how market research can add to the effectiveness of any sales
promotion plans the company may undertake. It should also (2)
explain briefly the type of information Askenfind can obtain and
show how this information can be useful to the manufacturer in his
promotion plans. The close should contain (3) a request for the
executive to write for additional information about the research
services of the agency.

● 5. To aid him in planning future promotions, the owner of a retail clothing store in the town in which your college or university is located wants to know (1) how much money each student spends for clothing during the academic year; (2) what percentage of the clothing expenditure is made in the student's home town, in the college town, and in other towns; (3) whether suits, dresses, and shoes are purchased in the college town or elsewhere; (4) whether most of the clothing purchases are made in department stores or specialty stores (such as dress shops, shoe stores, men's clothing stores, hat shops); and (5) about what percentage of all money spent by the student during a year is spent for clothing items.

He has asked for your help in the preparation of such a market study, based on information obtained from personal interviews. For this case you will conduct interviews with six of your student friends.

First, prepare a list of questions you plan to ask during the interviews. These questions should be worded carefully in order to provide the exact information you need for the market analysis of the clothing store. After you have prepared the list of questions, conduct a "test" interview using the questions you have written. Conduct the test interview with your roommate or a close friend so that you can determine whether the questions you have drawn up will bring the information you seek.

After the test interview, revise the questions as you think necessary and conduct individual interviews with six of your student friends. Be sure to write down the answers as the interview is being conducted. Because the study deals with money expenditures, you may wish to explain to the students you interview that answers to the questions you ask will be held in confidence and will not be identified in any way with the student himself.

When you have completed the six interviews, (1) prepare a summary of the results in a systematic fashion. (2) In a paragraph or two at the end of the presentation, explain how this information might be of special value to a clothing retailer as he makes his plans for future sales promotions. (3) As a part of your solution of this case, submit the list of questions you asked.

THE KIMBALLS OF OSHKOSH   Fall, 19--

When it's Christmas in Ohio

Your Christmas Cards will be excitingly different this year -- they'll feature your own state...your own town...your own address!

Look at the sample. You'll see that the lovely cover design is a scene symbolic of your state. Inside is a map of the state. On it, at the location of your home, a star is printed in raised frost-white together with the words: "It's Christmas in (Your Town)."

See how the theme is carried through into the message to read: "It's Christmas at (Your Address or Estate Name) where the (Your Family Name) are wishing you the Merriest Christmas of All." Your first names follow.

You want your Cards to be like this-- warm in spirit, friendly in every way and completely personal.

Your Greetings will be just like the sample...entirely done in distinctive raised frost-white that contrasts so strikingly with the soft green antique finish paper. You'll send this fine Greeting to your friends with a warm glow of pride.

We're so sure you'll be pleased that we unconditionally guarantee your enthusiastic satisfaction or your money back

forward, please

---

two

Most of all, you'll like the price. How much would you expect to pay for a Greeting like this, completely tailor-made for you? 25¢? No, you'd pay that much for an ordinary run-of-the-mill imprinted card. 35¢, then? That's more like it, considering the costly raised frost-white and the fine quality of the antique paper.

Well, be ready for a pleasant surprise. Your price is only 12¢ each for 50 Cards. It's even less when you order more.

This unbelievable price is possible only because this offer is made by mail directly to you.

One thing. We do need time for the careful preparation of your Greetings, since they are made to order especially for you. Won't you use the order form on the back of this letter right away? Show us on the map where you are located.

For only 95¢ additional we'll print your return address on the back flaps of your Greeting Card envelopes.

Mail your instructions now and then sit back, ready to send out the most unusual Cards your friends have ever seen.

Sincerely yours,

Albert Kimball

PS--For individual rather than family use, just tell us on the order form your full name ("where John Jones is wishing...") and omit first names.

A Gay Holiday Appeal "Personalized" to Home Town and Home State

One of a series of Christmas promotion pieces issued by a highly successful mail order firm.

—Miles Kimball Company

PART VI

Chapter 15

Capturing Human Interest in Sales Presentations

The vice president in charge of sales, the sales manager, the assistant sales manager, and the staff working under their direction, are all a part of the marketing management team. Their primary responsibility is to develop demand for the products or services of their company. When this demand materializes, the resulting orders for the products or services will come in through such channels as: the U. S. mail, the telephone, over the counter in sales offices and branches, through field salesmen and their order books, and by various other means.

When an order comes in, it sets in motion a long series of management activities including, perhaps, the enlargement of sales into related fields, the extension of credit, the making of adjustments, the management of time-payment contracts, and the collection of overdue accounts, all of which are topics discussed in the following chapters.

The dynamo, the generator, the central source of "locomotive power" that sets in motion the series of management activities we have listed is the sales program. The sales program is the direct power that brings to the customer the products and the services he wants.

"What Does the Customer Want?" Your customer is the natural starting point for a discussion of modern sales management. From whatever direction you prefer to approach the matter, your key question is always, "What does the customer want?" To gain sales acceptance—that is, to meet the customer's needs, desires, and preferences—is the simplest definition of good marketing management, as manufacturers, wholesalers, and retailers have proved to their own satisfaction. In former times, following a now outmoded and discredited theory, some sadly misguided groups tried to steamroller the market, tried to crush sales resistance, tried to "strong-arm" the buyers. But today's sales managers constantly consult the customer and *ask him what he wants*. Then, working together as a close-knit

331

team, sales and production management give the customer what he asks for. General Motors' Customer Research Department (mentioned in Chapter 14 in connection with studying the market) is a dramatic example of this kind of activity, through which management avoids sales resistance and gains sales acceptance.

To win sales acceptance, the sales manager launches two projects, product analysis and market analysis—terms now familiar to you from our discussion in a prior chapter. Having completed these projects, he "matches" the results. Then he can plan and create an effective and intelligent sales program.

Developing Demand

Do Products Sell Themselves? Never! The most fabulous product in the world will gather dust in an unknown warehouse, the most skillful service in recorded history will go unsought unless someone has the initiative to *find* the buyer who needs and wants that product or service. No matter how much you, the seller, may want to sell, no matter how much your buyer may want to buy, no possible exchange can take place until each one of you knows the wish of the other.

The aim of good sales management is to bring buyer and seller together for their mutual benefit.

Developing demand is another term for (1) finding buyers, (2) telling them that products they have asked for are now available, and (3) causing them to want to buy. The American system is one of incentive, individual initiative, and free enterprise. Under this system, someone finds the buyer and informs him about the features and qualities (the buying points) of the articles and services offered. However fine the product or service may be, you can sell it only with controlled effort and careful planning.

Marketing Functions

Transfer of Ownership
1. Developing demand
2. Assembling inventory: placing goods where and when wanted by customers, in proper quantities, qualities, and varieties

Shipment and Handling
1. Transportation
2. Storage

Other Aids to Transfer
1. Financing
2. Risk taking
3. Standardizing

Main Methods of Developing Demand. Three main methods are used to develop the desire to buy:

1. *Use of the Article.* The prospective customer tries the product. He likes it better than others of its type. As long as he can conveniently get it at a price he believes fair, he buys it in preference to any other. But the product must be conveniently available. He must be able to find it without using up his energy hunting for it.

2. *Personal Solicitation.* Salesmen travel from office to office, or from buyer to buyer, with information about the product and the advantages of its use.

3. *The Written Sales Message.* This most widely used method of developing demand takes the form of the sales letter, the advertisement, and the related forms of television, radio, pictures, and other media requiring the preparation of written script or comment.

This chapter discusses the written sales message, the third of the three main methods for developing demand.

The Sales Message

Definition. To establish a desire to buy and bring about a decision to act upon that desire, management uses salesmanship, often in the form of sales letters. These are written selling messages carrying persuasive business information that stimulates a desire to buy. A common defect of old-style sales letters is that they try too hard to "sell" (to force something upon) the reader instead of causing him, through lively interest and keen desire, to want to buy. If you can truly grasp this vital distinction, you already have the key to success. You have the secret.

Abercrombie, Inc., sells shirts and collars by mail. Company success rests not only on the quality of the product but also on the skill with which news about the product is brought to the attention of potential buyers. However fine the quality of the product, shirts and collars do not sell themselves through the mail. Those neat boxes will gather dust in the warehouse unless a sales executive of Abercrombie, Inc., energetically seeks out, by written messages, the customers who want his product.

Every Message "Sells." Even if the message is not selling a product or a service, it builds reputation. Whether it answers inquiries, acknowledges requests, sells, adjusts, or collects—it can help to turn people into friends and make them loyal customers. If the writer is gifted with a touch of imagination and a feeling for tact, the chance to make hundreds and thousands of personal contacts each year by written message is full of creative possibilities.

Capturing the Precious Treasure—Good Will. Every written message and, of course, every other kind of contact has its effect upon a company's reputation. Discussing the subject with his staff, a National City Bank executive puts it this way:

> To me, it is just as important to have properly written letters go out from an organization as it is to produce the best goods and to have the best salesmen sell them.
>
> At the close of each year's business we have prepared for our stockholders a balance sheet. The inventories, the plant, the working capital, the other items have for a number of years shown an increase of sound intrinsic value in our assets.
>
> But we have never listed what in our judgment is the most valuable item of all—the goodwill of this company. Now every dealing that we have with a customer has its effect upon this company's goodwill. Every letter has its effect. A man will write letters to a great many more people in a day than he can call upon. A customer will receive more letters from us in the course of a year than calls from our salesmen. This is why the man who writes letters has a big responsibility.
>
> Through your letters the reader knows the City Bank.
>
> Our company's standing is in a very great degree placed in the hands of the men who dictate its letters. The company's policies, its ideals, the esteem in which the company is held by the American public, are affected by the hundreds of letters which, every working day in the year, are going to almost every city and state in the Union.

Many famous firms have entrenched themselves in the public favor through the development of business friendship. Some of them value this good will in millions on the balance sheet. Such good-will figures mean that certain organizations have won in the minds of customers a "good feeling," a desire to "come back and buy some more," a solid regard for the offerings and for the reputation of the company.

Advantages of the Mailed Message. The "sharpshooting" mailed message enjoys certain advantages over more general media. The mailed message is to the advertisement, for example, as the rifle is to the shotgun. If the message is well aimed, it pierces the bull's-eye. An advertisement—a general message to many—diffuses itself with less force over a larger area.

Writing a sales message to a given list is a far different procedure from writing an advertisement. A sales letter is a personal message

Why Management Uses the Sales Letter

1. **More personal** than any other form of message.
2. **Highly selective.** "Sharpshoots" more directly to the interests of a limited group than can the more general messages.
3. **Flexible and elastic.** Can reach few or many without waste. The message can be long or short.
4. **Wide variety of forms.** Permits broad choice of designs and colors.
5. **Privacy.** Covering envelope assures privacy of the message.
6. **Mailability.** May be sent to home, office, or wherever the addressee will be most receptive.
7. **Timing.** May be timed for the most opportune moment.
8. **Highly adaptable** to a broad scale of uses; has been successfully used to market products costing as little as $5 or less, as much as $5,000 or more.
9. **Economical.** Costs about 3 per cent of sales. In contrast, services of salesmen cost about 10 per cent. Except for postage, a letter has no traveling expenses and no hotel bills.
10. **May be checked and traced for exact results.** The mailing list shows where each message went.

sent to an individual at a specific destination. An advertisement is a general message broadcast to many individuals over a general area. Hence, merely to slip an advertisement into an envelope, seal the envelope, and stamp it does not transform the advertisement in any sense into a sales letter, because the advertisement still appeals to the mass—in or out of an envelope.

The sales letter offers the retailer, for example, a chance to control the lists of persons addressed, the methods of distribution, and the form and the cost of enclosures. The retailer may single out as few or include as many persons as he desires, and he may fashion his messages to suit the special task at hand.

As the manager of a small store, you and your sales force can enjoy personal talks with all your customers—pleasant, conversational contacts. But as your store becomes larger and more successful, your customers increase in number. Finally you find it physically impossible to have a personal talk with even a tenth of them. You then turn to the sales letter as a close approach to personal talk. You give it human qualities—courtesy, naturalness, logic, interesting manner, and enthusiasm. Through them you extend yourself and multiply your personality. You now talk not to one customer but to perhaps a thousand at once. Your letter multiplies *you*. In effect you can now be in a thousand different places at the same time.

Disadvantages of the Mailed Message. Some disadvantages are these: (1) high cost per unit; (2) rapid deterioration of the mailing list; (3) expense of keeping the mailing list up to date; (4) over-selectivity, too sharp and narrow a focus for general announcements; (5) annoyance to persons addressed; (6) offensiveness through careless mailings to the wrong people such as letters to a successful executive urging him to augment his income by taking up sign painting or railroad telegraphy; and (7) costly preparation.

Eight Steps to Success. The experienced sales writer completes eight tested steps before he starts to write:

> **What the Sales Expert Asks Himself Before He Starts**
>
> 1. What do we have to sell?
>   (BASIC DATA STUDY)
>
> 2. Who will buy it?
>   (MARKET ANALYSIS)
>
> 3. How shall we reach him?
>   (CHANNEL FOR THE MESSAGE)

(1) *Complete the Basic Data Study—What Do We Have to Sell?* Study the product (or the service). Learn what materials go into it, how it is made, what its advantages are, what its uses are.

(2) *Complete the Market Analysis—Who Will Buy It?* Study the market for the product. Study the person to whom your message is to go. Consider where he lives, what his buying habits are, whether he is an old or a new customer, and whether your message is to answer an inquiry or to stimulate inquiries.

(3) *Determine the Aim of Your Message.* If the customer has not inquired, decide whether you want to persuade him to visit your store, to order your product by mail, to try your product for a few days, or to take some other definite action.

(4) *Determine How Interested Your Reader Is.* How much interest has your reader in your product? How much does he know about it? Only when you have the right answers to these questions can you choose the right appeal.

For example, if he has never heard of an air-conditioning unit, it would be futile to outline the advantages of your air-conditioning unit over competing units. But if he has a strong interest in air-conditioning for his home, and if he has the money to buy it, you will not need to explain to him what is meant by air conditioning.

Again, if the customer has never heard of a natural gas heater, you will have to describe it to him in order to develop his interest. If he knows all about it and its usefulness, you can assume his interest and go on to list the superior features of your particular brand.

(5) *Determine Whether the Results Will Justify Writing.* This point must be decided by past records and experience. If a similar effort to a similar prospect under similar conditions has been successful, this one probably will be. A favorable answer is assumed for this step.

(6) *Choose the Central Buying Point (Selling Point).* The central buying point of the product is identical with the central selling point: the feature best designed to make the strongest impression and to make the product most wanted by your reader.

(7) *Assemble the Supporting Facts.* Choose those of strongest appeal to your particular reader.

(8) *Organize Your Selected Facts According to an Effective Plan.* This plan will be outlined in later pages. In general, (a) begin "where the reader is" and swim with the reader's stream of thought; talk about what he wants; (b) end by talking about what you want; close with a strong inducement for action.

The Four Stages. Your sales message will reflect four stages:

Attention ....Attracting favorable attention.
Interest ....Arousing interest.
Desire ....Stimulating desire and convincing the mind.
Action ....Getting action.

*Attention,** once favorably secured, arouses interest. *Interest,* once aroused, leads into *desire,* belief that the product is worthy, reasoned conviction that it has satisfactory value, and a growing enthusiasm over the idea of ownership. Belief and conviction are the twin fires

---

* A survey by a direct mail agency discloses that seven out of every ten businessmen, and practically all housewives and other home dwellers open their own mail. That is one reason why the initial point of contact between sender and receiver is so important.

"The most critical and potentially decisive moment in the career of a direct mail piece," concludes the survey, "is the flick of time when its recipient's eye first rests on the letters of his own name (the most interesting print he ever sees), and on the envelope which carries it." The *Curtis Courier,* Vol. XI, No. 3, page 14.

AIDA IS A TRIED FORMULA FOR WRITING EFFECTIVE

Sales Messages

ATTENTION

Opening Paragraph: First sentence (headline) should get desire as well as attention. Five points to remember in planning headlines:

1. "Sell the sizzle—not the steak"—Sell the smell, not the rose. Appeal to the imagination.
2. "Don't write—telegraph." Telegraph your thoughts. Cut out the useless words.
3. "Say it with flowers." Be nice. Don't use objectionable words.
4. Don't ask "IF"—ask "WHICH." Try to make it a "WHICH" proposition, not an "IF" proposition.
5. Watch your bark. Don't growl at your prospects. Be nice to them—flatter.

Either ask a question or make a statement.

If a question—ask one which cannot be answered "yes" or "no," so reader can't brush you off quickly. If you cannot avoid it—make it a "yes" question.

If you make a statement, it should contain a fact which is (a) new, (b) different, or (c) interesting.

INTEREST

You must make your messages so interesting that they will overcome the natural laziness of the reader and really compete with others who are trying to get his dollars.

1. Inspirational lead in—appeal to the emotions.
2. Give a clear concise definition of the product or service.
3. Be Positive. Say what you mean positively and avoid unnecessary explanations.
4. Special features. What are the special features about the product or service which will be of help to the person reading the message.

DESIRE

Appeal to the emotions. Be dramatic. What we feel about a product, a service, or a cause influences us to spend our money. Very few people spend money because of what they think.

1. Give some little success story about the use of the product or service.
2. Testimonials and endorsements are still good.
3. Statements of value—a definite statement of value to reader.

ACTION

Tell prospect what to do. When you get down to the most important part of the message (action closer) do not forget why you are writing. Do not leave the reader hanging out on a limb—tell him what to do . . . Sign order blank, fill-in inquiry card, initial letter, send check, make reservation, etc.

☆ ☆ ☆

P. S. The most important part of a successful message is the P. S. The message with a P. S. usually outpulls the one without it. The P. S. should rephrase the headline or first paragraph. Or high spot some one important point of your offer.

BLUE PENCIL—use freely on (1) Useless words that don't count toward final effect desired. (2) Dubious words ("I," "we," "our," "us," "me," "my" and phrases preceding and including "that"). (3) Incorrect expressions of thought. (4) Improper arrangement of words. (5) $5 or Sunday words—use every day words—one syllable words preferred. (6) Hackneyed expressions from horse-and-buggy days, "In reply to," "we beg to state," "we beg to remain," etc.

BEST FORMAT for return pulling copy—a. Letter. b. An informative circular. c. An order form. d. A business reply envelope.

Compiled from talk by Henry Hoke, Editor and Publisher of The Reporter and other sources by John J. Patafio, President of Ambassador Letter Service Co., New York City.

that ignite enthusiasm. The merging of these factors into desire to buy leads toward *action*.

Few messages express these four aims with equal emphasis. But when one dominates, the others are implied. For example, sales writing answering inquiries may assume that attention and interest already exist and may proceed at once to stimulate desire and convince the mind.

Of course, you do not box the four stages off in separate compartments. Although you study them separately for your convenience in discussing and practicing them, you will recognize that they flow together in forward-moving thought. In brief, the four parts "shade into one another like the colors of a rainbow," the thought stream flowing smoothly ahead from one part to the next until it reaches final action.

The written sales message follows the principles of personal salesmanship. How close the parallel is, you may see from what every good salesman does:

1. Attracts attention.
2. Maintains interest by giving plentiful facts showing the value of the article.
3. Stimulates desire and convinces the mind by demonstrating the features that make the article valuable to the buyer.
4. Closes, that is, secures favorable action.

How an Expert Did It. Now suppose we watch an expert go to work. The tested letter shown on page 340 sold more than one hundred thousand dollars' worth of books.

In the first line a gripping concrete fact seizes your attention. The first two short paragraphs place you in the midst of a little drama and whip up curiosity. Now come two paragraphs of factual material to develop and sustain the interest. The next two paragraphs then swing around to *you*, showing how you, too, may master the same methods that brought such success to the general manager. These two paragraphs develop desire and convince the mind. Finally come two brief paragraphs to stimulate the desired action and make it easy.

This expertly constructed sales message—just a piece of writing sent through the U. S. mail—produced a tenth of a million dollars in sales. Soon you will have a chance to look more closely at each of the four stages in order to understand better how they work, and how the experts use them so skillfully to produce such powerful results.

SANFORD PUBLISHING COMPANY
230 South Clark Street   Chicago 5, Illinois

March 3, 19--

Mr. R. A. Dean, President
Business Research Associates
1335 Merchant Boulevard
Chicago 11, Illinois

Dear Mr. Dean:

$22,267.64 from a single letter!

The General Manager was amazed. He hadn't the remotest idea that he could write a letter that would bring in more than $20,000 worth of business. But there are the returns to prove it--order after order from his circular-letter campaign to win back 1,305 old customers.

Was this $22,267.64 letter pure luck?

Not exactly! For when the General Manager heard of our unusual publication on business communication, containing the special working methods of Dr. J. C. Harvey, the well-known expert, he was among the first to send for a copy. A few weeks later, he wrote us: "I must say that I never knew there were so many fine points in business letters as I found in Dr. Harvey's Effective Business Writing Techniques. Below are the detailed results of my circular-letter campaign to win back 1,305 old customers. I most certainly owe the unusually good results to your publication."

Business received from first letter.....$22,267.64
Business Received from second letter.... 1,829.62
    Total................................$26,147.31
Average invoice......................$82.74
Average business for each name.......$20.03
Percentage of returns from first letter.....17.9%
Percentage of returns from second letter....10.7%

This is the frank statement of the treasurer and general manager of an important concern in San Francisco, California. Seldom has there been such a whole-hearted endorsement of a publication. None the less interesting, however, is the experience of W. W. Mays of Albany, New York, who after reading the part dealing with the power a letter can develop, wrote one that made a $1,200 sale. As soon as Whitley Supply, Inc., heard of the publication, they bought a copy and later reordered five copies. Hundreds of concerns are using this book to increase sales, collect slow accounts, and soothe disgruntled customers. Their letters are becoming more human, more compelling, more effective.

Mr. R. A. Dean
Page 2
March 3, 19--

Now, in Effective Business Writing Techniques, the same methods that have been so helpful to these concerns are offered to you. Here in this new 650-page book by J. C. Harvey are explained, illustrated, and applied the basic principles behind all letters including those that win orders, bring delinquents to time, and build up good will.

This remarkable book shows how to judge the weight of the work a letter must do, how to express feelings or ideas in words, how to overcome indifference or opposition, how to make your meaning clear, how to make your message get action, how to make it grip attention, how to plan letterheads, how to organize correspondence work, how to test letters, how to find and use ideas for letters--650 pages on preparing business-winning messages. (See the circular enclosed.)

Will you examine a copy? Send no money now. The book is yours on approval for five days, free examination. If you are entirely satisfied with it, remit according to the terms on the card enclosed. Otherwise return the book.

The sooner you get this book, the more quickly you can profit from its use. So send the convenient examination card today--now!

Sincerely yours,

Wilson T. Elliott

Wilson T. Elliott
Sales Manager

jo

Enclosure

Sales Appeals to Buying Drives

Psychological Drives. People *act* in certain ways when they buy. Modern sales messages shape themselves to fit this "buying behavior." The alert writer watches how people act. He finds that people are triggered by motives, called psychological *drives*, that cause them to do the things they do. The expert writer touches off the psychological trigger that impels the customer to buy. When the right appeal is directed to the whole mind * and energizes the drive (want) lying there, it touches off this trigger.

Buying drives (wants) are a set of feelings or inclinations within the buyer's mind that press him toward the purchase of a given product or service.

Sales appeals are sparks that set off the buying drive. Appeals are not, themselves, the direct cause of action, but the "activators" which, when brought into play, trigger the buying drives.

Now review the process: (1) normal people respond to certain basic drives—the desire for success, the desire for attractive personal appearance, the desire for health, the desire for gain and many others; (2) if, by purchase of the product or service, they can win success, improve personal appearance, assure health, or save money, they may buy that product or service; (3) the correct buying drives must be aroused by properly selected selling points; (4) if these selected selling points sufficiently arouse the correct drives, the prospect acts.

Basic Human Drives (Wants). As a general guide, a list of psychological drives used in practical sales work is given on page 342.

In this list the drives have been brought together into related groups. When you apply these drives, take these two simple steps:

1. Make a list of possible drives that you may use in selling your product or service.
2. List for each drive those sales points that will energize that drive.

Motivational Research. To study the "triggers" that impel people to buy—the motivations that cause them to act as they do—we now have Institutes of Motivational Research. These organizations devote

---

* The mind is *considered as a whole unit* in its reaction to the given appeal. The human mind, it should be remembered, is an organic unit—not a slot machine.

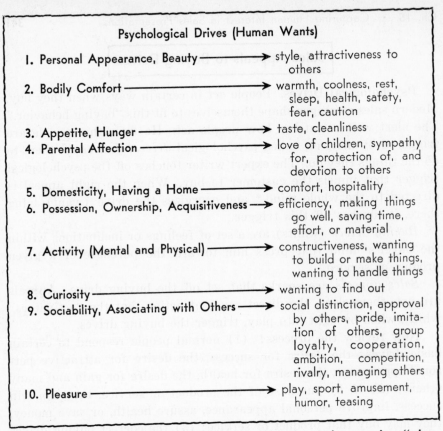

Psychological Drives (Human Wants)

1. Personal Appearance, Beauty ⟶ style, attractiveness to others
2. Bodily Comfort ⟶ warmth, coolness, rest, sleep, health, safety, fear, caution
3. Appetite, Hunger ⟶ taste, cleanliness
4. Parental Affection ⟶ love of children, sympathy for, protection of, and devotion to others
5. Domesticity, Having a Home ⟶ comfort, hospitality
6. Possession, Ownership, Acquisitiveness ⟶ efficiency, making things go well, saving time, effort, or material
7. Activity (Mental and Physical) ⟶ constructiveness, wanting to build or make things, wanting to handle things
8. Curiosity ⟶ wanting to find out
9. Sociability, Associating with Others ⟶ social distinction, approval by others, pride, imitation of others, group loyalty, cooperation, ambition, competition, rivalry, managing others
10. Pleasure ⟶ play, sport, amusement, humor, teasing

their study to "consumer motivation." This is an impressive "nine-dollar" phrase that may be defined in simple words of one syllable as "What makes folks buy?"

Indeed, Vance Packard, in a book entitled *The Hidden Persuaders*, suggests that we are entering the "Age of Manipulation," an age in which hidden urges, fears, frustrations, and wish fulfillments are probed, analyzed, and used to part people from their money.

Most lists of psychological drives rarely run over sixty different motives. But recent researches have discovered a total of nearly six hundred that do not overlap each other. These drives have been entered on tabulator "punched cards"—a procedure that makes it possible to tabulate the information in any way desired. For example, it is now possible to assemble all the reasons that motivate the consumer in buying any one particular product, whether it is gasoline, vacuum cleaners, or breakfast food. Moreover, it is possible to determine from the punched cards which buying motives have been triggered by each selling activity—such as store planning, store displays, pricing, advertising, sales clerk training, or other marketing management actions.

"Special Occasion" Appeal

Buying drives are based on pleasure of major events, style, attractiveness, personal appearance, social distinction, and approval by others—with a pleasant background tone of excitement and anticipation.

A Selective Sales Message to Management Executives

Psychological appeals, on the Christmas seasonal theme, to convenience, ease, comfort, distinctiveness, efficiency, and time-saving. (Note the "running head" used instead of the conventional salutation.)

Our "Hidden" Motives. Our basic motivations for buying (as well as for many other social activities) are often wholly unconscious. Our final decisions are often made not on reason or logic or even prudence, but on the desires and drives and frustrations that retain their stubborn influence beneath the surface of the mind.

Our first researchers, a good many years ago, were *objective*: they merely reported such easily observable facts as who was buying, what was being bought, and when and how. Our next researchers moved to the *subjective*: they wanted to know *why* people buy. They used the technique called the sample survey, in which a representative cross-section of the population is questioned directly by interviewers. But even this method left something to be desired, because people will not confide everything to the interviewer. Instead they often tell him things they think sound good rather than the actual truth. Then, too, the individual himself sometimes hardly recognizes many subconscious and half-realized reasons for buying.

To uncover these concealed or "hidden" motivations, researchers then turned to tools the clinical psychologists had developed, often called "projective" methods. For example, instead of asking a person why he buys or doesn't buy, they now ask *why he thinks other people do, or what sort of people they are*. In his answers he "projects" his own attitudes and feelings in such a way that they become easily available for evaluation, measurement, and study.

What Do YOU Really Want? Hidden motives can play many tricks. Sometimes the tricks are costly. Consider the extraordinary case of the two automobile makers. One company asked the public "What kind of a car would you like?" Most of the answers indicated that the buyers wanted a shorter, more easily handled car. The company acted accordingly. The other car maker made a similar survey about the same time but asked a much shrewder question. After asking the usual question—"What kind of a car would you like?"—he then inquired, "What kind do you think your neighbors would prefer?" "Oh, them?" was the invariable answer, "they want a long, low sleek car with chrome and gadgets, just for show."

The first car maker built the car that the public *said it "wanted."* The second car maker built a car *for everybody's neighbors*. Car 1 was a spectacular failure that almost plunged the company into bankruptcy. Car 2 won the largest sales its company had ever had. The simple fact was this: the car that "everybody's neighbors wanted" was the car that everybody wanted!

Thus does motivational research reveal the hidden and deeply underlying motives of the subconscious that play their powerful part in controlling buying decisions.

"Don't Sell Me *Things*. Sell Me Ideals." Discussing motivation and psychological drives, *Forbes Magazine*, the business publication, puts it this way:

"Don't sell me clothes. Sell me neat appearance, style, attractiveness.

"Don't sell me shoes. Sell me foot comfort and the pleasure of walking in the open air.

"Don't sell me furniture. Sell me a home that has comfort, contentment, cleanliness.

"Don't sell me books. Sell me pleasant hours and the profits of knowledge.

"Don't sell me tools. Sell me the pleasure and profit of making fine things.

"Don't sell me *things*. Sell me ideals, feelings, self-respect, home life, and happiness."

Applying the Psychological Drives. To put our list of drives (page 342) to the test, let us apply them one by one to you and to your daily life.

(1) You like to have people think you good-looking, and you would rather be in style than out of it.

(2) You are cautious in traffic and in avoiding disease and infection, for the sake of safety and health and because of fear. You complain with everyone else about the heat and the humidity, or about zero weather and slush. You dislike frostbite as much as you do severe sunburn. And at about the same time each night you yawn with sleepiness.

(3) About three times a day you are hungry. You enjoy the taste of delicious things, but you must have confidence that they are clean. You instinctively prefer living in cleanliness to living in dirt.

(4) Among the precious things in life to you are your mother, father, brother, and sister; and if the last-named are little, you take part of the responsibility in shielding them from harm. If you are normal, you feel sorry for others when they are in trouble, and you try to help them.

(5) You like to have your home a place where friends may come and have a good time.

(6) You like to have things of your own—each one of us has his pet likes and possessions—and yet you like to save up a surplus for the future.

(7) For the "fun of it" you do many things not in the academic calendar. You may have a special skill at editing a student publication, at designing or building scenery for a play, or making models of objects. Doubtless you enjoy driving a car, a motor boat, or possibly an airplane.

(8) There will never come a time when you will not instinctively want to follow the roaring fire trucks, lights flashing, sirens screaming, as they rocket by in a thundering clamor.

(9) You want people to invite you to social events in which you would be glad to stand out as a center of attraction, approved by all. If such distinction seems not immediately possible, you tend to imitate someone who holds the focus of attention, whether you consciously do so or not. You are without doubt loyal to your group; well mannered in public and, it is hoped, in private; ambitious to hold a class office or a managership or a chairmanship. If you have the instinct of leadership, you unquestionably have the trait of ambition. You back your athletic team against all comers, triumph with it in victory, and support it in defeat.

(10) You want to do things that are fun and to be in things that are interesting. From student activity, political, social, forensic, or athletic, you get pleasure, sport, or amusement.

Reread carefully line by line the ten paragraphs given above. Identify as many appeals as you can. How many do you find? How many of them apply to you?

The Right Psychological Tone. Use an active, pleasing tone that impels reading. Choose words that arouse pleasant images, that suggest desirable situations. Even when you use appeals to safety, fear, and health (as in selling insurance, safety devices, and the like), strike the positive note of protection.

The zestful holiday atmosphere is created with much skill in the following Christmas letter:

EXCELLENT TONE, PLEASING DETAIL, DELIGHTFUL ATMOSPHERE

Attention
>   Tingling thrills await you at The White House, in the most exciting of the year's indoor sports-- Christmas shopping!
>
>   Of course, you're ready to plunge into the midst of it, and we'd have you know that we're ready, too, to make this year's adventure the most satisfactory you've ever known.

Interest and Desire
>   Who is on your list--the Prime Minister? The newspaper boy? The most sophisticated of debutantes? The problem is solved in this store of a million-and-one wonders.

Action and Festive Atmosphere
>   We do hope you'll come in soon and often, and that you'll enjoy shopping at The White House for your home, family, or other special occasions--not only during this festive Christmas season when the store is so gloriously gay and cheerful, but through all the year--for the true Christian spirit of good will is ever present here. Please come and share it with us.

> ## The Central Buying Feature (Selling Point)

Finding the Central Buying Feature. The feature of your article that will make the strongest impression upon the prospective buyer is its *central selling point*. Through the buyer's eyes, this same feature is the one most likely to make him buy. To find the central feature, review (1) what the reader wants and (2) what the article can give, and then bring these two areas together. You determine the central point by studying the features of the product in relation to the needs and the desires of the reader. You sift the qualities of the product. Then you draw forth the one central point that most powerfully harmonizes the product with your buyer's chief need.

To become familiar with important buying features, salesmen in training are often sent into the factory to study with their own eyes how the product is made, what materials go into it, how it takes form on the assembly line, or how it is put together on the production floor. When these salesmen begin to sell, they can, with confident accuracy, tell the prospective buyer exactly what quality of material and what painstaking skill went into the design and construction of the air-conditioning unit, what kind of mahogany is used in the dining-room set, what kind of parchment in the ivory lampshade, what kind of waterproof varnish is on the office desk. They can also describe precisely how each article has been put together, why it has strength, durability, long life, what its other advantages are, and the important ways in which it may be used.

The Case of Mr. Adams and the Paper Mill. The story is told of a young man named Adams, who was sent to write copy to sell the output of a paper mill. Did he begin to dream about paper, to imagine what it was like, to consider descriptive phrases that might apply to paper? He did not. Instead, he began to study paper by reporting to the paper mill:

> The paper-mill president asked him if he thought bond paper could be advertised successfully. Adams replied that he couldn't tell until he knew more about the mill and the product. He had to have the facts. He was given a guide, and for the next two days he fairly wallowed in paper. He found that this mill's paper was made of selected white rags; that the purest filtered water was used in the making; that it was dried in a clean loft; and, most surprising of all, it was gone over sheet by sheet and inspected by hand. . . . [Robert R. Updegraff, *Obvious Adams*]

Like the salesman who reported in overalls to learn the raw materials and the factory methods, and like young Adams who first reported to the mill before he wrote a line, so should each sales writer first know his product intimately before he sets pen to paper.

Keep the Customer's Point of View. See the product through the eyes of the customer. "If I were the buyer," ask yourself, "what would *I* look for in this product, and what features would make *me* want to buy it?" In this way you apply the YOU-attitude discussed in an earlier chapter. Not always, of course, can you match the buyer's feelings, because your background and outlook may be far from his. But you can apply the YOU-attitude by searching for the features your buyer will want.

For example, what questions should you ask in selecting the central buying point for an automatic washer? To satisfy the modern buyer, you should try to find the answers to questions like these:

THINGS THE CONSUMER MAY WANT TO KNOW ABOUT
AN AUTOMATIC WASHER

1. What is the capacity of the machine?
2. Are controls conveniently located?
3. Are rinsing and drying fully automatic?
4. Is the machine quiet?
5. Will it handle fine laundry as well as heavy work?
6. Is its height convenient? other measurements?
7. Will it fit into the space reserved for it?
8. Can it be easily cleaned?
9. Are operating directions clear?
10. Is there a variety of colors available?

Here are ten searching questions on which the prospective purchaser *may* want information. The list reveals the large amount of material from which to select the central point, as well as the most forceful supporting facts.

Check Your Facts for the Central Buying Point. Suppose you have gathered these facts about the following products:

Woman's Purse: Leather in peacock or kid, or of silk pique in *Tucktite* construction; white only; leather types washable, all types easy to clean; contains coin purse and mirror; envelope, strap, and zipper type.

Can of Peaches: Sun-ripened, picked ripe from trees; sorted, peeled, and packed in cans by machine, untouched by human hands; cooked by clean live steam, sealed air-tight; can contains 12 full-bodied halves in natural syrup.

Tire Chains: Molybdenum steel, toughest known, for cross chains, case hardened; heavy four-ply rubberized strap, long wearing, waterproof, tested to 1,400 pounds; nonslip wedge-lock keeps chains from slipping around tire; positive grip buckle, designed so that strap passes back through loop to prevent fraying.

Here you have facts about (a) raw materials, (b) manufacturing methods, (c) construction, (d) method of operation, (e) design and appearance of the finished product, and (f) uses. Possible central buying points for each are shown at the right.

Manufacturers Develop Central Buying Points. In order to differentiate a new

Product	Central Buying Point
Woman's Purse	*Tucktite* construction, easy to clean
Can of Peaches	12 full-bodied halves in natural syrup, sealed airtight
Tire Chains	Molybdenum for cross-links, super-tough steel

product from others already on the market, the manufacturer incorporates in the design a striking feature that sets it off from all other products of its type, and that makes it particularly desirable to the market. Examples:

Ball-Point Pen. A pen manufacturer produces a new type of ball-point pen with an excellent polished-iridium point, a large-capacity refill cartridge, streamlined construction, attractive finishes and colors, and a firm clip. But the feature that differentiates it and makes it stand alone is a positive, patented feature that makes possible an ironclad guarantee that *the pen will never smear.* The unqualified nonsmear guarantee is the central buying point. This pen manufacturer based an entire season's campaign of magazine messages on this one central buying feature. He showed his pen lying on white linen tablecloths, on an ermine wrap, on white kid gloves, on a white silk purse—always to emphasize the central buying feature.

Automatic Inner Tube. A tire manufacturer produces a safety inner tube. It has all the qualities of competing inner tubes: rugged, durable, tough in resisting damage, and will last as long as competing tubes. But the feature that sets it apart is now determined: with this tube a tire blowout at high speed cannot tip the car over because *a tube within a tube* prevents the air from escaping in a rush, supports the car until it rolls to a safe stop. This is the central buying point. Motorists are seeking safety from high-speed blowouts.

Comfort

Introducing the Central Buying Feature (Selling Point) of a Wardrobe Trunk

Wardrobe Trunk. A trunk manufacturer produces a new trunk. It has all the qualities of competing trunks: rugged in construction, with sturdy chromium plated Yale locks, attractively finished in several two-tone combinations, striped in the modern fashion, air-travel light, yet strongly braced with welded magnesium frame. But one outstanding feature differentiates it and sets it apart from other products of its type. *It turns on a turntable engineered into the bottom.* This is the central buying point. Travelers have been seeking a trunk which, like this revolving turntable wardrobe, will make all garments quickly accessible.

Fan. An electrical appliance maker markets a new electric fan. It has all the qualities of competing electric fans: handsome in appearance and finish, efficient in operation, operates in three speeds, delivers huge quantities of air, silent motor. But it needs no safety guard because *its blades are made of harmless rubber.* Near this fan small children may play in safety. This feature is the central buying point. Buyers are seeking a safe fan.

Aim the Spotlight on the Buyer's Wants. Your study of the buyer may disclose an important want that can best be filled by your product. Your object is to select the one feature that best satisfies your buyer's chief need. Thus you bring the product into line with the buyer. The two are harmonized. When you have selected the central point in harmony with the buyer's chief need—the turntable revolving trunk, the smearproof ball-point pen, the double-construction inner tube, the rubber fan blades, you have found the one point about which everything else turns. This strong feature, most likely to draw favorable response, is given the spotlight.

The Central Buying Point Shifts as the Buyer Shifts. The class of buyer determines the central buying point. For example, to motorists the central buying point of the inner tube is that it offers positive protection against dangerous blowouts; to dealers, the central buying point is that it sells faster than other inner tubes in the same price class and therefore gives them more profit through more rapid turnover; to industrial users, who operate fleets of trucks and salesmen's cars, the central buying point is that it makes the outer casings last longer, prevents expensive blowout-accident damage, and reduces car-costs.

Or again, to the careful mother the central point is the harmless rubber blades of the fan; to the electric-appliance dealer the central point is that the fan sells faster than competing fans in the same price class and therefore will give him more profit through faster turnover; to a purchasing agent buying fifty fans for a company with a large office, the central point may be that the fan costs no more than competing types and needs little adjustment or repair.

Support the Central Buying Point. Concentrate on the central point. Then add concrete facts that support it, seeing that they are sharp, definite, and detailed. For example, you may want to tell the buyer that the new model rubber-bladed electric fan is streamlined and crinkle-finished in soft shades of brown, green, or ivory; operates for two hours at a cost of one cent; has three speeds from zephyr to whirlwind; delivers by test 25 per cent more air volume than any earlier model; and has an improved Silent-Night motor with bearings permanently oiled and sealed for long life.

Capturing Human Interest. "What does the customer want?" we ask ourselves as we continue our study of sales procedure and its techniques. From our review of the foregoing pages we have found that the customer is the natural starting point for discussion of modern sales management. To capture his interest, to win his patronage, to gain his "sales acceptance" of our products and services—that is, to meet his needs, desires, and preferences, and to do so on a friendly, human basis—is the simplest definition of good marketing management.

How these management experts approach the customer has been the subject of this chapter. The next chapter discusses how the experts apply their skills and how they get their results.

Communication Problems

● **1.** Skillful sales executives, responsible for creating effective sales material, use appeals directed toward basic human drives. A mailing selling a weight control plan to women, for example, may begin by saying: "Here's the way to a lovelier, more beautiful you . . ." and would be directed toward the psychological drive or human want of Beauty and Personal Appearance. Executives preparing successful sales material select an appeal that is appropriate and strong in triggering response from the reader.

You are planning a sales promotion to stimulate sales for an electric automatic hot water heater. (1) From the ten psychological drives listed on page 342, select one that you think may be appropriate in a mailing designed to sell an electric hot water heater to home-owners. Then write an opening sentence in which you use a sales appeal directed toward the psychological drive you have selected.

(2) In the same manner, list an appropriate psychological drive and write an appropriate opening sentence for each of these products:

Quiet-running electric outboard motor to be sold to fishermen.
Distinctive matching purse and hat to be sold to women college students.
Large frozen food storage chest to be sold to farmers.
Life and accident insurance to be sold to married men with families.
New record album to be sold to high-fidelity fans.

● **2.** Most consumers buy products for the satisfactions the product will deliver. Persons buy air conditioners to be comfortable, for example, rather than simply to own a one-horse power motor and compressor. The writer of an effective sales presentation for air conditioners, then, must explain how product features such as motors, size, construction, and so on, can satisfy the wants of the prospect.

Select any product with which you are familiar and obtain the specifications for as many of the physical features of the product as you can: size of the product, weight, materials or ingredients, average length of life, price, method of construction, workmanship, design.

(1) Prepare a list of at least ten specific features of the product you have selected. Arrange the list in a column on the left side of a sheet of 8½″ by 11″ paper. (2) In a column on the right side of the page, write the consumer satisfaction or benefit that the product feature should deliver to the prospective buyer. Be sure to list the consumer benefits opposite the appropriate product feature, as in this example:

FEATURES AND BENEFITS OF COLDAY AIR CONDITIONER

Product Feature	*Benefit to Prospect*
1. 7.5 ampere motor	1. Economical to use; saves money on electric bills.
2. One-ton capacity	2. Keeps you cool and comfortable even on hottest days.
3. Operates on 110-volt, 60-cycle Alternating Current	3. Plugs in anywhere; no costly installation; saves money because no special wiring required.

● 3. The central selling point used in sales promotion material must be appropriate for the product and must also be appropriate and strong in reaching the group of prospects selected. Because mailed material can be keyed to the specific interests of each prospect, the writer of effective sales messages must be particularly aware of the needs of the persons he wishes to reach. A central selling point appropriate for one group of prospects may not be strong in reaching a different group of prospects even though the product is the same in both cases.

You are planning a series of promotion messages for the Super Airsafe Automobile Tire. The tire is manufactured in all sizes, is distributed by tire stores and filling stations located throughout the United States, and is priced competitively with tires sold by the major mail order houses. The Super Airsafe has a special tread design that gives traction in mud, sand, snow, and ice, yet runs quietly on dry highways; a special inner layer of plastic and gum seals itself and makes the tire punctureproof; rugged tests prove the tire is virtually blowoutproof even under severe conditions; special rubber and tread design gives up to 3,000 more miles per tire than from competing brands; installation is free, and dealers throughout the country offer free tire service for the first 5,000 miles; outsells all other brands of tires in its class; dealer profit is about the same as for competing brands; tire is advertised nationally and manufacturer cooperates with local dealer in preparing and paying for local advertising.

Select a central selling point to be used in a mail promotion for the Super Airsafe tire, and to be mailed to farmers who must drive on back roads and in fields. Explain briefly the reason for your choice of central selling point.

In the same way, select a central selling point and briefly explain your choice, to be used in promotions designed to reach each of these groups of Super Airsafe tire prospects:

Business executives with expensive new personal cars.
Retailers who plan to sell Super Airsafe tires.
Elderly women who drive principally in town.
Parents of teen-age children.
Traveling salesmen who must pay their own expenses.
Owner of a fleet of taxis.

● 4. Select a sales message that has been mailed by a business firm to a list of prospects. This may be a form message you have received about insurance, magazine subscriptions, encyclopedias, or other products; or it may be a mailing received by one of your friends.

Prepare a concise analysis in which you present the following information along with appropriate explanations to support your opinions:

(1) To what general group of prospects is this message addressed? Why do you believe this particular group of prospects was selected?
(2) To what basic psychological drive is the message aimed? You may discover that the writer has appealed to more than one of the basic human wants or psychological drives listed in the chapter.

(3) What is the central selling point?
(4) In your opinion, what one other basic psychological drive and central selling point might have been appropriately used in selling this same product to the same group of prospects?
(5) Name an entirely different group of prospects to whom this product might be sold, and suggest an appropriate psychological drive and central selling point that could be used in a message addressed to these prospects.

You may write your analysis in outline or in sentence and paragraph form. Be sure, however, that your analysis is clear and does not require reference to this problem in order to be understood. Submit, along with your assignment, the sales example you have analyzed.

● 5. The Terry Cover Company manufactures Cool-Terry Automobile Seat Covers with these features:

> Made from absorbent terry cloth, the material used for bath towels; special elastic bands and ties make one size of the cover fit snugly on all cars; covers can be installed or removed quickly; guaranteed washable; soft and comfortable, cool in summer and warm in winter; available in styles for solid-back or split-back seats; front seat only; white color; price is $3.50, postpaid, with money-back satisfaction guarantee.

(1) Prepare a sales promotion message for Cool-Terry Seat Covers, designed to sell these seat covers by mail. This message should appeal to a strong psychological drive (such as fun, comfort, sociability, or possession) near the opening. The message should throughout provide plenty of specific facts to support the central selling point. The close should ask for the order.
(2) At the bottom of this message, identify the psychological drive which has been triggered, and write in one sentence a summary of the central selling point.

● 6. You are the sales manager for a nationally known manufacturer of all kinds of tables for the home. Your company regularly places advertisements in the leading magazines devoted to home decorating. These advertisements carry a form for requesting the company's booklet describing its tables and their correct, decorative uses.
Since you made it easy for people to respond, you receive many requests for your booklet. To follow through on your sales promotion—to make the prospective customer feel your response is a sincere desire to be helpful—you want to send an invited sales message along with the booklet.
You want to make your reply say more than the routine "Thank you for requesting our booklet." Emphasize the necessity for tables as a complement to home attractiveness and comfortable living.
Because you want to send the booklet and the sales message the day the request is received, you plan to omit the inside address and the salutation and to use only the printed company name in the signature. But you feel that the "form" effect can be minimized through an enthusiastic, sincere, *what-tables-can-do-for-you approach*. Compose the reply designed to turn many of these requests for the booklets into sales for your tables.

PART VI

Chapter 16　　　　　　　　　　　　　*Capturing Human Interest in*
Sales Presentations (Concluded)

"Capturing Human Interest" Is an Art of Many Skills. Perhaps no one knows better than the sales executives at the top how important it is for business management to maintain warm, human relations with its customers. To win these warm customer feelings, these favorable customer attitudes, is the responsibility not merely of the sales department but of the entire company management and staff.

"During the next several weeks," writes the executive editor of an eastern investment service, "many hundreds of messages to stockholders will be going out of corporation offices all over the country. Some will be notices of annual meetings, others will accompany copies of annual reports, and still more will carry other kinds of management messages."

Then he notes that all these management messages will inevitably sell—something. How well they sell will depend on the impressions they make on the thousands of stockholders who receive them. What impressions *will* they make? That depends upon their "sales tone." Take the following pair, for instance. Each is quoted word for word.

How NOT to Talk to a Stockholder. If you were an assistant to the secretary, an assistant to the treasurer, an assistant to the president—in other words, a responsible member of the management team at any level, whether or not connected with the sales department —you would strive to capture human interest through friendly words, if you were writing the company stockholders. It is certain you would *not* write like this:

> Notice is hereby given that, pursuant to the provisions of the By-Laws, the Annual Meeting of the Stockholders of THE NEGATIVE COMPANY will be held . . . [Signed in cold print by the Clerk]

How the Expert Executive Talks to His Stockholders. The expert management man knows the incalculable value of capturing human interest and good will, whether he is the vice president in charge of sales, or whether he is the president and chairman of the board. With human understanding of the opportunity before him, he writes:

> It is a pleasure to invite you to attend the Annual Meeting of Stockholders of THE POSITIVE CORPORATION. The meeting will take place . . . [Signed in facsimile by the President]

Then, in the concluding paragraph, the President adds:

> I hope that you will be able to attend because it is always a pleasure to meet and become better acquainted with our share owners. If you cannot be present, I would appreciate your signing and returning the enclosed Proxy promptly so your vote can be recorded.

Which of These Management Approaches Is the Better "Selling"? Expressing his reaction to these two types of management approach, the executive editor, himself a management man, remarks, "No figures are available, but I would be willing to bet a good deal that the percentage return of proxies was a lot higher for the second of these corporations than the first. Also, I am sure that the 'taste' left in the minds of all stockholders was much better in the second case. Time after time it is the 'sales tone' that wins."

Let us now turn our attention to the management experts and find out how they apply their skills and how they get their sales results.

Part I—Attracting Favorable Attention

"When New York Blacked Out." It all happened out on Cape Cod. The Second World War was raging at its height. One afternoon a magazine executive, spending his vacation at the Cape, simply could not believe his eyes. He looked again. Yes . . . no question about it . . . it *was* true—he saw a German submarine lying off the Cape shelling an American tug and a string of barges.

Later on, the story goes, he mentioned the startling episode to a friend. The friend retorted skeptically, "You must be dreaming! Enemy submarines operating off the American coast . . . that's a bunch of eyewash!" And to his surprise the Cape Code vacationer couldn't find one person who remembered the incident. So, in collaboration with another, he decided to write an article about it. He did. It came back from magazine after magazine with one rejection slip after another. Then the story continues:

> One day he met a couple of successful authors and told them the incident. They looked the article over, picked up a few paragraphs in the middle which described the near-hysteria caused in New York, moved them to the lead, put on a heading "When New York Blacked Out"—*and Collier's bought it for $600.* Same story. Same incidents. Same words, pretty much. Just a different arrangement.

> *Collier's had turned it down before. Why did they buy it the second time around?*

> The story about a German submarine shelling the coast of Cape Cod left them cold. But the story about New Yorkers with their lights out, their shades drawn, their subways hailed as bomb shelters—that sold them! [As reported in "Dividends," Ketchum, Macleod & Grove, Inc., Vol. 6, No. 1, pp. 1-2.]

Drop Your Reader Squarely into the Middle of the Action! ". . . picked up a few paragraphs in the middle . . . moved them to the lead . . . put on a heading 'When New York Blacked Out' . . ." Note those words. A sales letter is much like a short story, or a hundred-yard dash. To make it win, get it off to a fast start. Keep up the pace to the final spurt. "Write a first sentence," says a short-story expert, "that will drop the reader squarely into the middle of the action and make him read on to find out what piques his curiosity."

Swing Aboard Your Reader's Train of Thought. The skillful sales writer "swings aboard the reader's train of thought." He draws the reader's attention from side distractions and centers it upon what *he* has to say. He does so by announcing an arresting fact, or by asking a question, or by making a pleasant and agreeable statement. He puts the reader into an attitude of assent that will make him say, "Yes, I've often thought of that myself," or, "No question about that; it's true." Such openings incline the reader to say, several paragraphs later, "Yes, I am certain that I want this article."

Fifteen Ways to Seize Attention. To intercept the reader's attention, sales writers use the following methods:

(1) Flash a "Short-Short" Story:

> She gets more letters than a movie star!
> They saw Europe on dimes.
> Somewhere west of Laramie. . . .
> How twenty men won a fortune. . . .
> Why the Troy Company signed—the other contract!

(2) Paint an Action Picture:

A snap of the wrist . . . the line sailed out over the stream, the reel hummed merrily . . . a strike! [For a letter on fishing rods and reels.]

A flash . . . a flame . . . a puff of smoke . . . and precious papers gone! [For a letter on safe deposit boxes.]

(3) Offer a Miniature Testimonial:

"*Torsion-Aire Ride* has given my car and me the most velvety travel I have ever enjoyed," remarked one of our owners recently. "How did you invent it?" That is the story we want to tell you.

(4) Ask a Question:

How long does it take you to read a movie title?

Are you a genius size?

Could you obtain a blank piece of U. S. bank-note paper? No, because each sheet is registered and guarded.

Have you a hungry wastebasket?

(5) Flash a Piece of News:

You can make color a King in your home!

A milk so rich it whips like cream. . . .

Now you can buy a 30-inch color-TV, with full-automatic remote control!

This year, over a million quarter-inch drills will be sold—not because people want quarter-inch drills, *but because they want quarter-inch holes.*

(6) Strike a Parallel:

In the Bay of Fundy everything afloat rises and falls fifty feet every 24 hours. But the up-and-down cycle of business in Canada and the United States is much slower than the Fundy tide.

(7) Supply a Startling Fact:

$22,267.64 from a single letter!

Sixty per cent of merchandise is bought on or after the salesman's fifth call. But only 12.7 per cent of the salesmen make a fifth call.

The letter that lighted two million lamps!

(8) Use an "If" Opening:

If we should place in your office an electric typewriter and show that it would save you 40% of your daily typing cost, you would chuck your old machines out fast!

(9) Make a Pleasant and Agreeable Assertion:

The life of a bubble is fleeting seconds.

You readily pay a few pennies for a newspaper. But for this booklet, much more interesting than a newspaper, I believe you will willingly pay several pennies more.

(10) Use a Quotation:

"If at first you don't succeed, . . ." was carried to the seventh degree by the famous old Scottish warrior.

(11) Refer to Current Events:

This morning the President, the members of his Cabinet, the nine members of the Supreme Court, and the 531 members of the Senate and the House of Representatives are receiving their copies of . . .

(12) Use a "Power"-Phrase That Compresses the Point:

The Scottish woolen weavers want to present you with a $20 bill. [For a letter stressing a reduction.]

(13) Use a Flash of Human Interest:

Andrew Carnegie's recipe for a poor man to get rich: Save $1,000 and then begin prudent investing.

(14) "Thumb-Nail" a Situation:

While I was waiting at the Cypress Point Golf Club's famous Sixteenth Hole, where the ball must sail 200 yards out over the Pacific Ocean, I watched a Foursome trying to make this tee shot.

(15) Make Your Reader Hungry:

Would you like to make mouth-melting pies: lemon chiffon, old-fashioned pumpkin, brandied mincemeat with hard sauce, southern pecan, deep-dish apple, strawberry angel, fudge cake . . . ?

Arrest Attention with Action-Pictures. "A window with something moving in it attracts dozens of people. The same window without the moving feature passes unnoticed," comments a display expert. "Let me give you an illustration. One of our toy windows had a moving train in it. There was a crowd four deep along the entire length of this 20-foot window. As an experiment we stopped the train. Inside of ten minutes there were only two people left. The train was again turned on, and very shortly another large crowd was again looking in the window." *Action always gets attention.*

Test yourself on these action pictures:

This morning Mr. Talbot startled me with the announcement that he had on his desk the twelve most extraordinarily fascinating stories that had ever come into his hands. I thought, "Something special must be done!"

* * *

Yesterday we got the enclosed "Rush" message from Madame Vediér, now busy scanning styles on the Rue de la Paix. Since then she has excitedly cabled. . . .

Seizing Attention by Facsimile Handwriting

Facsimile handwritten messages, high in attention value, are directed, as a rule, to feminine audiences.

What NOT to Do in "Openers." Avoid these errors in opening sentences:

1. *Meaningless generalities:* "We would like to tell you something about our products." "Let us give you some information we think you will find valuable in your daily work."

2. *"Scare" openings:* "Beware!" "Wanted at Once!" "Danger Ahead!" "Look Out!" etc.

3. *Trite questions:* "Have you ever stopped to think . . . ?" "Wouldn't you like to hear some great news?" "Don't you enjoy being surprised?"

4. *Negative suggestions:* "We know that you are beset on all sides by people wanting to sell you things, but we, too, should like a moment of your time." "Maybe you won't find this message at all interesting, but we hope otherwise after you've read what we have to say."

5. *Emphasis on "we" and "our company."* "We feel that we have an important message concerning our company's success. Accordingly we would like to tell you what our company has succeeded in doing during this past year."

6. *Unconnected and irrelevant beginnings:* "Captain Ace's round-trip flight to Cape Town, South Africa, in four hours may be fast but so is our speed in getting the latest styles for fall."

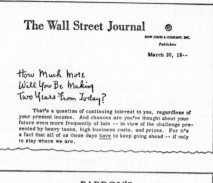

Seizing Attention and Arousing Interest

The message at the left "dramatizes" its material into high attention through its physical arrangement into an "echelon of items"—a diagonal column of concrete details. Note the instant opening appeal to economy. Both messages at the right are high-attention devices with powerful appeals to (a) the desire to "get ahead" and (b) the desire to invest wisely.

Parts 2 and 3—Expanding Interest and Desire

Arousing Interest. The first sentence of the message switches the reader's thoughts away from the business engaging them and gets his undivided attention. The subject then has a chance to gain a clear field, to make a forceful impression, and to arouse sustained interest.

Interest, leading directly into desire, is aroused by facts, specific information, and concrete detail. As the facts become clearer and the details more vivid, the reader begins to visualize the article, see what it can do, appreciate his need for it. His interest mounts steadily higher until, by imperceptible shift, it becomes desire.

Stimulating Desire and Convincing the Mind. Materials for interest and desire can rarely be separated into "sections." Like quicksilver they run together, each reinforcing the other. The difference between interest and desire is largely a matter of (1) degree and (2) appeal to emotions.

```
    Here's your invitation for a joyful Thanksgiving of
restful relaxation--no hot ranges, no time-consuming dinner
details--we'll do it all!  Ready for you, from 1 to 7 p.m.
. . . another wonderful buffet "traditional" with all the
old-fashioned, home-flavored delights of your well-loved
delicious favorites. . . .

    Fresh grapefruit in claret, creamy oyster soup, a wide
choice of crisp salads . . . Irish potato, whipped to a snowy
fluff with hot milk and butter; sweet potato golden glazed
with butter and brown sugar; old-fashioned Hubbard squash;
creamed tiny onions!  Then young Tom Turkey, stuffed, basted,
and roasted as our mothers did it, lovingly watched until
done to a tender, juicy "T," with rich, smooth gravy, tender
giblets; whole, fresh cranberry sauce. . . . And, of course,
our famous pastries . . . hot, light yeast rolls . . . and the
grand finale of mouth-melting pies, taste-joys of pumpkin,
tender mincemeat, and lemon chiffon; and that most famous of
all, the fudge cake Royal!

    Be our guest . . . we'll expect you!
```

In this vivid physical taste description interest swiftly shades into desire as the fabulous feast is appealingly set before the reader.

Factual and Emotional Persuasion. What is a persuader? The dictionary tells us that he is one who (a) induces a person to *believe* something, (b) prevails upon a person to *do* something. Sales managers persuade America, for example, to want to eat better, dress better, live better, enjoy more good music, and do more traveling. In one sense the power of persuasion has been a potent instrument in helping the American people to a way of living that the entire world would like to enjoy.

Effective persuasion is based upon facts and a lot of them. Every person who buys your product or service wants plentiful facts before he makes his decision to buy. But your task is to convey more than facts alone. To win success, you must also appeal powerfully to the emotions. You must make your prospective buyer "hanker" for what you offer. Successful sales writing translates product and service facts into vivid benefits that cause a prospective buyer to "hanker" for what you have to sell. The expert managers know, therefore, that the final secret of effective selling is to give the prospective buyer the convincing answer to his ever-present question: "What will this offer do *for me*?" To give the convincing answer, sales experts use physical and emotional description. Each type must be given concreteness and vividness through sharp detail.

Foreign Travel Service

2001 MICHIGAN BOULEVARD

CHICAGO 4

"LURLINE" SOUTH SEAS and ORIENTAL CRUISE

September 1, 19--

Mr. Fred V. Grayson
3950 Frederick Avenue
Chicago 10, Illinois

Dear Mr. Grayson

Appreciating your interest in the new and unusual developments in
the realm of travel, we take pleasure in bringing to your attention
an event which we unhesitatingly recommend as one of the outstanding travel opportunities of 19 --the South Seas and Oriental Cruise
of the new $8,000,000 luxury liner "Lurline."

This modern white giant of the Pacific--a sister ship of the popular
"Mariposa" and "Monterey"--will begin her de luxe "Coronation
Tour" at New York on January 12, next. From San Francisco
January 27, and from Los Angeles January 28, she will continue on
a sweeping circle tour of the Pacific, calling at nineteen fascinating
ports in the South Seas and Orient. Direct calls at primitive Bali
and Port Moresby are included, with famed Angkor Wat available
as an optional tour.

It isn't often that the "fundamentals" so essential to the success of a
major travel project are so perfectly balanced as in the case of the
Lurline Cruise. Ship, season and itinerary are in ideal combination.
And the prices are surprisingly low when measured against the cost
of "wintering at home." These factors, coupled with the outstanding
successes of previous cruises under the Matson-Oceanic Line management, warrant our strongest endorsement of the Lurline Cruise as an
exceptional travel opportunity.

The enclosed folder gives only a sketchy outline of the prominent
features of this de luxe tour. If you will return the card, it will
be a pleasure to forward more comprehensive details.

Cordially yours

Vincent K. Beckman

Vincent K. Beckman, Agent

Encls.

I am interested in the
"Lurline" South Seas and
Oriental Cruise, and would
like to have additional
information.

Name_____

Street No._____

City_____

Factual and Emotional Description for a Travel Cruise

Informative facts, concrete detail, emotional description, low-pitched tone, and colorful
word-choice . . . all of these are provided in the message
along with the enclosed folder.

Factual Description. All the objective details of the nature and exterior of an article make up physical description: length, breadth, height, size, shape, color, scent, sound, texture, taste, and the like. Your physical description stimulates dawning interest. It may tell of the huge tractive power of a massive, four-unit, diesel locomotive, the brute load-hauling capacity of a compound double-duty tractor, the satin finish of a gleaming aluminum sheet, the high tensile strength of a steel girder, the incredible speed of a diamond drill. Or it may tell of the petal delicacy of Alençon lace, the velvety texture of fine cloth, the rich and vibrant tones of a Steinway Grand, or the haunting scent of an exotic perfume.

Emotional Description. The joy, the satisfaction, the pleasure your buyer will gain in using your product or service to fill his wants—highly vivid pictures of your article in satisfying use—are presented through emotional description. Emotional description arouses higher levels of desire. It vividly translates the diesel locomotive, the compound tractor, the aluminum sheet, the steel girder, the diamond drill, the Alençon lace, the velvety cloth, the vibrant Steinway, and the haunting perfume into uses that fill human needs and powerful wants.

An Example to Show the Difference. A color-TV console, pictured by physical description, may be of handsome burled walnut, measuring 17″ x 48″ x 48″, finished in blond "satin-rub," with full-automatic remote control channel-changer, and refined electronic remote tuning. But the same color-TV, by emotional description, suddenly becomes a Magic "Color" Carpet by which one can vault the hemispheres and see around the earth, can watch from his armchair the tossing waves of the Atlantic, can see from his living room the British Prime Minister addressing the House of Commons, can witness the thunder of a giant missile taking off from the launching pad at Cape Canaveral.

Illustrated on page 366 is a description of a consumer product that skillfully weaves together both physical and emotional appeal.

Kinds of Evidence. Following are the kinds of evidence most useful to arouse interest, to stimulate desire, to induce confidence and belief, to convince the mind, and to give proof of product value:

1. *The product in use:* Picture the product in use—not merely the air-conditioning cabinet, but a "living room of cool comfort through summer heat."

2. *Savings and economies resulting from purchase.*
3. *Explanation of construction:* How the product is built.
4. *Facts and figures.*
5. *Tests* by the maker, laboratory, dealer, and customer.
6. *Samples:* Sometimes enclosed with the letter.
7. *Trial Use.*
8. *Testimonials:* (a) expert testimony of scientists or authorities; (b) user's testimony showing satisfaction.
9. *References* such as a list of satisfied owners.
10. *Warranties.*

Example. A management executive is accustomed to methodical reasoning. He will be interested in any article—a dictating machine, a calculating machine, a duplicator, a tabulator—if you can supply evidence, facts, figures, definite *proof* to show that he can make more money, cut his costs, increase his output, simplify his routine, or increase his sales. These centers of interest call for plentiful facts, sharply and concretely listed. Present such facts, and you tap his centers of interest and desire, and you successfully move toward favorable action. You supply him with the factual material on the basis of which he will form his judgments and on which he will make the favorable decisions you are trying to win.

Here is an example that presents details of construction carefully selected to highlight attractive features and to convince the reader with proof of value:

LUXURY "TRADITION" TIME PIECES

Lifetime Mainspring

Perma-life unbreakable TRADITION mainsprings are the finest obtainable in Switzerland. The Perma-life Mainspring is guaranteed to last a lifetime. Anti-magnetic hairspring and balance wheel.

Jeweled Lever Escapement

In every TRADITION Watch only superhard red rubies are patiently set by master craftsmen in the one exact position necessary for precision performance and maximum accuracy. Expensive styling too, at each price level.

Incabloc Shock Protected

Each TRADITION is designed with the finest Swiss-type shock protection. The springs are scientifically engineered to take up shock . . . to help prevent breakage of jewels or staff. TRADITION Watches are actually *armed against damage!*

30-Day Trial Offer, Guarantee

Guaranteed 1 full year against defective materials or workmanship, 30-day Trial offer. If not completely satisfied with your TRADITION, return to us within 30 days for a full refund of purchase price.

Scott, INC.

411 EAST MASON STREET   PRODUCT DIVISION   MILWAUKEE 2, WISCONSIN

April 28, 19--

SPECIAL
REPRESENTATIVES

GENERAL ⊛ ELECTRIC
ROOM
AIR CONDITIONING

Patience !
Patience !
PATIENCE !

Doctor, yours is a profession requiring a great amount of patience.

So comfort for you -- your nurses -- and for the sick who depend on you, is so important!

We're in the business of supplying one of your most vital comfort needs -- low-cost, efficient air conditioning ... engineered and guaranteed by one of the greatest names of all, General Electric.

Perhaps you already have a unit installed in your office. If so, you know how wonderful it is to have cool working quarters on the hottest, muggiest day. You know the value of dust-free, filtered air. You appreciate being able to flick a switch at any time and clear your examining room of the odor of anesthetics in a jiffy.

But if you are without this wonderful invention, why do without it any longer! The cost is not high, installation is simple, and operation is as reliable and quiet as an electric fan.

Efficient filters, built-in, give great relief to hay fever, asthma, and other respiratory disease sufferers -- and this feature of a room air conditioner works the year 'round.

We supply homes, too -- and General Electric will be a tremendous boon to your family when the sun beats down.

Now is the time -- before everyone wants refreshing coolness at the same moment -- to insure air-conditioned comfort for yourself this year.

The postage-paid postcard -- or a 'phone call -- will bring a trained air-conditioning specialist to your office. Or an actual demonstration can be arranged any time at our showroom, conveniently located at 411 East Mason Street, Suite 305.

Harry H. Scott

Harry H. Scott, President

Scott, INC.

Come in and tell me more about
GENERAL ⊛ ELECTRIC
Room Air Conditioners

Phone for Appointment ☐   Come in anytime ☐

Name_____

Street_____ Phone_____

City_____

We'll thank you for mailing this card even though you already have an air conditioner. Please check where:
    ☐ Home   ☐ Office

• DALLAS • DAYTON • DENVER • DES MOINES • LOS ANGELES • MINNEAPOLIS
IA • PITTSBURGH • PORTLAND • PROVIDENCE • ST. LOUIS • SAN FRANCISCO
IN CANADA . . . HALIFAX • MONTREAL • TORONTO • VANCOUVER • WINNIPEG

Proof of Value Through Performance Facts, Design and Construction Details, Description of Product in Use, with Demonstration Offer

The "action-card" is attached to the message with a paper clip.

366

How to Gather Your Evidence

- **Get Performance Facts . .** What the product will do for the buyer

    Increased production or convenience   Lower upkeep
    Improved economy   Longer life

- **Get Design and
  Construction Details. . .** How it is built to give this performance

    Good materials   Rugged construction
    Careful workmanship   Unique features
    Simple design   Reliable tests

- **Outline
  Service Facilities. . . .** How the manufacturer aids its use

    Performance guarantees   Repair service
    Trial installation   Delivery

Help the Customer Convince *Himself*: Give Him "Rationalizing" Evidence. The customer often deeply wants an article but cannot, through any logical reasoning, justify the purchase. He hesitates. If, at this point, concrete proofs of value are put forward, these points of evidence may support him in deciding to go ahead and buy. The "value proof" gives him good reasons to *justify* his purchase. His first impulse was possibly actuated by purely emotional appeals. His purchase itself is, however, finally justified on the basis of cool reasoning and on the solid evidence of product value. Thus the reader rationalizes his decision to buy. This thought process is called *rationalization.*

"Rationalization" appeals are used in presenting products (1) that are in the semiluxury or luxury class, and often of high price, or (2) that gratify purely instinctive or emotional wants, the purchase of which the buyer may somewhat guiltily feel he shouldn't make unless he can justify it on solid grounds of true value.

Cold facts alone may leave your reader unmoved until he sees that they have a particular application to *himself.* To stimulate desire, the words *must fit the article to the reader's needs by picturing it in use or by showing the advantages of its use.*

For example, you'll remember the sales executive who "dramatized" his company's quarter-inch drill by writing, "This year, over a million quarter-inch drills will be sold—not because people want quarter-inch drills, *but because they want quarter-inch holes.*" If you were an assistant in the sales department of a manufacturer, you would wisely ask yourself whether you are giving enough thought and study to *what your product will do* to satisfy—perhaps dramatically—your customer's wants and desires, rather than merely how it rates as "something packed in a carton."

Ask yourself: "What will my product do that my customer wants done?" "How can I fit my product to my reader's needs?" "How can I dramatically show its advantages?" "How can I dramatically picture it in use right now?" If you flash a dramatic *use*-picture, then you arouse your customer's interest, you sharpen his desire, you convince his mind, and you put him into the buying mood.

The following little drama is directed toward women:

The Reader Steps into the Center of This Little Drama

> It's a swank style shop . . . all about you are beautiful things. . . . You may be wondering (and who hasn't?) whether the fabulous gown that looks so "right" in the fitting room mirror will look equally so at the Junior Prom . . . whether a really breathtaking hat would be a better investment. . . .

In the following paragraph note the high level of attention, the atmosphere of narrative suspense (the heart of good short-story writing), and the "dramatized" setting.

Attention Through Dramatic Suspense

> It is the end of the chapter. The pens of the distinguished adventurers, novelists, philosophers, critics, who fill the pages of <u>World Magazine</u>, are still. They are waiting for you to speak. . . . The whole famous company pauses. Your subscription has expired, and they are waiting to present you the best of new things to come.

Add Power with Vivid Pictures. "Dramatizing" usually gets much of its power from vivid situations and word pictures. Suppose we look at some examples. "We're Saving a Vice President's Salary in the Mailroom!" runs the dramatic, attention-getting opener of a strong sales message for the Pitney-Bowes Mail Inserting Machine (on page 370). "Give me the next 5 minutes or less, and you'll know about . . . [facts and details here]. Five minutes from here, I believe you'll agree we've made a fair exchange. See for yourself!" So runs the "time picture" of a sales message from *American Heritage,* dramatized into an eye-stopping "capsule" (on page 370). And "Abel Cable" becomes a TV dramatic actor in the following vivid story situation presenting a TV cable service for TV viewers too far from TV stations to get good signals otherwise.

Attention

> Will you let me come to your house for Christmas . . . and stay forever? I'm Abel Cable. You'll find that I take very little space. You can keep me for only a few pennies a day.

Interest, Desire

> And what will I promise you in return? I prom-
> ise to keep you entertained and happy. In your own
> living room, week after week, I'll bring you
>
>   --the brightest stars of entertainment
>   --the best in Broadway plays
>   --hot, dramatic news events
>   --fun, laughs, and frolic for the kids
>   --all the new, wonderful, exciting TELEVISION
>   enjoyed by millions of Americans in New York,
>   Hollywood, and millions of homes including
>   your neighbor down the street.

Action

> What a sparkling Christmas Eve I can give you
> . . . if you'll only let me! Remember, I'm Abel
> Cable, and I can work miracles! I'll move a new TV
> right into your living room along with your Christmas
> tree, I'll make all the connections, I'll
> I'll guarantee you . . . right now . . .
>
>   The Merriest Christmas Ever!

How Would You Handle This Management Case? How would *you* generate vivid picture-power and dramatic suspense in this situation? You are now the assistant manager of the safe-deposit department of the Fidelity Trust Company. You are preparing a sales appeal to increase the number of rentals of safe-deposit boxes. How will you proceed?

First you would probably make a simple service and market analysis:

1. *The Service:* A safe-deposit box rental for one year for the positive safeguarding of valuable papers.

2. *The Market:* Persons of sufficient means to have papers or valuables important enough to need safeguarding.

3. *The Medium:* A sales message with a descriptive enclosure.

Next you select the central selling point—safety, protection against thievery, and freedom from worry and loss. Then you assemble supporting facts, and decide on a narrative appeal to the reader's desire to protect his papers and other valuables. Finally, you might write copy like one of these:

GRIPPING ATTENTION FROM A "FLASH" DRAMA

And then--

"There was a crash, and the room was plunged into darkness.
I turned and fired at a masked figure silhouetted against the
open window--"

Now go on with the story in "Security," the folder enclosed
with this letter. This has probably never happened to you, and
we hope it never will. But it did happen to . . . [etc.]

AMERICAN HERITAGE

551 Fifth Avenue, New York 17, N.Y.

July 19, 19—

Dear Reader:

Your history is visible in your mirror.

And you don't have to be handsome or pretty to be grateful for what you see: one of the best-educated, best-informed, best-fed, best-groomed, least afraid — <u>and proudly free</u> — faces ever mirrored on earth.

You're lucky. Most of us Americans are. In due humility, we usually credit our "luck" to our truly miraculous heritage — to a short, violent period of history, to a soaring idea, and to a lot of ordinary people who somehow rose to greatness when their call came. What people? See your mirror, with its shadows of your predecessors.

Give me the next 5 minutes or less, and you'll know about

- the first map ever drawn of the New World, and how you can own a true copy,

- the look, via a dozen full-color pictures, of one of the world's most beautiful series of books,

- the only magazine that no one ever throws away, because it gains in value with age (and has no ads),

- an item for your conversation — says the St. Louis Globe-Democrat, "The success of so unorthodox a venture has amazed the publishing world" — and

- a rare good buy.

Five minutes from here, I believe you'll agree we've made a fair exchange. See for yourself.

An Eye-Stopping Dramatic "Capsule" Opener

This message "drops you" into a little time drama beginning a skillful four-page selling appeal for a magazine-type book.

PITNEY-BOWES, INC.
STAMFORD, CONNECTICUT

ORIGINATORS OF THE POSTAGE METER AND METERED MAIL ◄|))◄ WORLD'S LARGEST MANUFACTURERS OF MAILING MACHINES

March 19, 19—

"WE'RE SAVING A VP'S SALARY IN THE MAILROOM!"

"How do we do it? Let me show you: the actual saving is in the mailing — with Pitney-Bowes' new Mail Inserting Machine. PB's Inserter cuts costs as much as $7 per thousand pieces on some mailings. . . does as much work as eight girls formerly did. . . shaved mailing-room overtime 'way down! Now we no longer need to hire, beg, or borrow crews of helpers. It's the best buy in office machines we ever made!"

That's a fair composite "batch" of testimonials we've received from users of the PB Model 3100. And why does Model 3100 gather all these orchids? Here's why: The "3100" gathers, nests, and stuffs into envelope as many as four assorted enclosures. It closes, seals, counts, and stacks envelopes at speeds up to 6,000 per hour! You can hook up an optional postage meter machine that will simultaneously imprint metered mail postage, either first or third class.

NINE TREMENDOUS ADVANTAGES... COUNT 'EM:

- Speed—capacity up to 6,000 an hour. Available in 1- to 4-station models.
- Accuracy—automatic detection of errors before envelopes are filled.
- Simplicity of setting—can be adjusted to any job in minutes.
- Feeding—is friction type, handles wide variety of material from invoices and statements to checks and tabulating cards.
- Ease of operation—all controls handy on one side.
- Versatility—handles widest range of envelope sizes—from 6 by 3¼ inches up to 12 by 6 inches.
- Compact design—with straight-line, self-centering feed.
- Preferred metered postage (1st or 3rd class) is provided by an optional hookup with a PB postage meter.
- Backed by Pitney-Bowes service from 102 branches, coast-to-coast, in the U. S. and Canada.

With only one large mailing a quarter, your Model 3100 will quickly pay for itself in costs and time saved, and your mailings will get better and prompter schedules.

Ask your nearest PB office for a free demonstration... and for free illustrated folders including the actual "PAY-OFF" case studies of proved savings. Or drop the enclosed postage-free reply card into the nearest mailbox—because we've got a valuable chart of postal rates with parcel post map and zone finder reserved for you.

YOURS FOR "VP SALARY SAVING!"

Charles J. Lawrence

Executive Vice President

"Dramatizing" the Powerful Economy Appeal

Note the use of sharp, concrete, trenchant, convincing facts and figures.

POWERFUL PROTECTION APPEAL

This morning the 27 great expanding bolts on the 17-ton
dynamite-proof steel door of our massive new vault caught my
eye with special force. I turned to my boss, the manager of
this Department, and exclaimed: "You know, this department
is really offering our customers fire insurance without any
premium!"

Yes . . . it's true . . . we guarantee the return of your
papers and valuables when you call for them . . . not merely
payment for their assessed value after they're destroyed!

Your wife's bracelet heirloom, perhaps the ring grand-
mother bequeathed to her granddaughter, your stock certificates,
your contracts, your insurance policies--all will be safe in
our massive new vault. For pennies a day you can place your
valuables behind heavy concrete bastions reinforced with thick
walls of bent railroad iron and battleship steel.

Before red tongues of flame sear into ashes the precious
documents you would not lose, think and--ACT!

Powerful safety (positive) appeals are normally better than vivid
fear (negative) appeals. But when the product or the service is one
of protection to human life or property—as in the case of safe-
deposit boxes, life and fire insurance, automobile chains, firearms,
inspection services, alarm equipment, and the like—appeals to the
motives of fear and self-protection are convincing and effective.

The "Test-It-Yourself" Approach. Similarly, a powerful device
to seize attention and to stimulate interest and desire is this: Suggest
that your reader himself do something to test the article, to try out
the product, to put it through its paces. This is called *test-it-yourself*
suggestion. The suggestion is usually made in the body of the message, although it may appear in a postscript or on an enclosure.

Here are some vivid illustrations of "Test-It-Yourself." Compare
them with others you will find in your current reading.

(1) The E. W. Bliss Company asks you, "What Do You Want to
Do with Metal? Want a machine to work at high speed? To deliver
enormous pressures? To check and correct itself as it works? Whatever way you'd like your machine to carve or shape metal, we'll come
up with the answer. Then you can roll it, stamp it, forge it, shear it,
coil it, level it, straighten it, draw it, punch it, edge it, turn it, slit
it, temper it, flange it, galvanize it, extrude it . . . you name it! Try
it! Test it yourself!"

(2) The United States Plywood Company encloses a card to
which is attached a small sample of its plastic, *Kalistron,* and a tiny
metal nail file. To the buyer: "Kalistron is tough! Take the little
nail file and *try* to scratch it, scrape it, scuff it! It won't mar—the
color's always there."

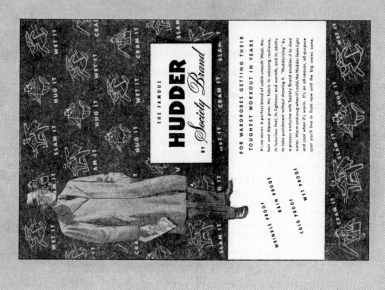

Joseph M. Eways

IMPORTER OF ORIENTAL RUGS AND CARPETS

213 North Fifth St. Reading, Pa.

Dear Mr. Smith:

Just two little pieces of yarn -- but what an important story they tell you.

Pull the ends of the red yarn and notice how the strands separate and fray easily. Now pull the blue yarn and notice the difference -- it will not fray.

The red yarn was spun by machine. The blue yarn was spun by hand in far-off Persia.

Genuine oriental rugs are made only with hand-spun yarn. The wool for this yarn comes from the backs of sheep which graze most of the year in the warm, sunny pastures of lands across the sea. It is the extra strength of this wool and the skill of the hand weaver which enables the genuine oriental rug to hold its beauty for centuries.

I would like you to see the exceptional oriental rug in my shop which was hand-woven so firmly that there are as many as 400 knots to the square inch, compared to 200 knots in the average oriental rug.

I would like to show you some of the genuine Orientals which have journeyed thousands of miles across oceans and continents to reach my shop from far-off lands. I can promise you one of the most pleasant half hours you have ever enjoyed, just "talk-ing rugs" ... telling you some of the truly romantic legends behind these rugs and showing you the magnificent pieces which will add charm, distinction and character to your home.

Of course, you will not be under the slightest obligation. Either stop at the store the next time you are downtown or telephone 2-3446 for an evening appointment.

Sincerely yours,

Joseph M. Eways

Joseph M. Eways

JME:A

This Dramatic "Test-It-Yourself" Message Doubled Sales

On the original, the two pieces of yarn—red and blue—were stapled into position under the letterhead.

This Enclosure Urges You to "Test It Yourself!"

Note the imperative suggestions in the background; "WET IT," "CRAM IT," "SLAM IT," and "HUG IT,"

(3) The Syntho-Fibre Corporation sent its stockholders a sample of glass cloth with the following invitation: "Touch a lighted match to this fabric. It will not burn!" Along with a dividend check, the glass-cloth sample was inserted inside a folder telling where and how the cloth is used. The results surpassed all expectations! Not only did stockholders try the match test, but they also started telephoning the company before ten o'clock the day the sample was received, asking where the fabric could be bought. The market simply "created itself" out of a dramatic "test-it-yourself" appeal.

(4) A famous rubber company attaches a small sample of sponge rubber about the size of a nickel to the upper left corner of the message. The opening sentence: "A little piece of ordinary sponge rubber like the sample attached gave our tire engineers their first clue to a revolutionary discovery for adding months to the life of a tire tread." At the bottom is a second sample, a tiny strip of the new tread rubber, which you are invited to detach: "Notice how smooth it feels. Bite it. See how live and springy it is. Take it in both hands and stretch it. Pull hard! Try to break it! It's the toughest tread rubber ever known!"

What Happens in a "Test-It-Yourself" Trial? When you perform trial actions and make tests for yourself, three psychological outcomes follow: (1) you build up a mental association on one strong buying feature or you do something that dramatizes a central point that the seller wants to highlight, (2) your interest is aroused, and (3) you are put into a receptive attitude for further favorable action.

Enclosures Multiply Power. Leaflets, folders, pamphlets, testimonial letters, samples, an order blank, a business reply card or envelope, and similar material may be enclosed in various combinations. Enclosures are especially important when one mailing is to be used with no follow-up, because here

> **TEST AMAZING VARLAR YOURSELF, FREE!**
>
> VARLAR, Inc., Dept. F118
> Merchandise Mart, Chicago 54, Illinois
>
> I accept your challenge! Please send me my free sample of Varlar Stainproof Wall Covering and I'll test it for myself.
>
> Name_____
>
> Address_____
>
> City_____Zone____State____

they carry the greater part of the load. Enclosed material makes possible the use of large display type, headings, illustrations, and color.

The sales writer should refer to the enclosed material. The reader should be urged to examine and act upon those enclosures, which, of

Addressograph-Multigraph Corporation

SIMPLIFIED BUSINESS METHODS

1200 BABBITT ROAD, CLEVELAND 17, OHIO

TELEPHONE: REDWOOD 1-8000 • CABLE ADDRESS: ARDMULCOR

October 6, 19--

Mr. Ralph W. Gelsey
Gelsey Brothers, Inc.
6895 Stettinius Avenue
Cincinnati 27, Ohio

Gentlemen:

Wouldn't you like to have the most successful collection men and women in the country explain their methods to you, show you copies of the forms they use, and tell you how they have effectively and economically solved some of their important collection problems?

We did just that this summer. We visited wholesalers and retailers - factories both large and small - great department stores - clubs and associations - correspondence schools and banks. We went where collections were being made for goods and services sold under various installment plans.

We took pictures, got samples of forms. And we have now put the whole story together in a book we would like to send you with our compliments. It is called "Turning Accounts Receivable Into Cash" and no matter what your business, you will find helpful suggestions in it.

If you will send us the enclosed post card, we will mail you this book. You will find it attractive, well illustrated, exceptionally well planned, and very complete.

Sincerely yours,

G. L. Harris

G. L. Harris
Sales Manager

GLH/jc
Enclosure

"If you will send us the enclosed post card. . . ."

Mailed to 102,000, this "customer-lead" message pulled 7,705 replies. Replies were referred to field representatives who called personally on the prospective buyers.

---

pioneer investors savings and loan association

499 ALVARADO STREET, MONTEREY, CALIFORNIA   FRONTIER 2-7514

SAN JOSE:
Downtown
Willow Glen
Steven Creek

SAN FRANCISCO
SUNNYVALE
LOS GATOS

OAKLAND
SAN LEANDRO
HAYWARD
MONTEREY

Dear Friends:

We'd like you to accept, with our compliments, a free dollar.

Yes, we are enclosing a passbook showing a credit of $1 to a new Savings Account in your name at the Monterey Office of Pioneer Savings. This free $1 is yours if you open your insured Savings Account with us on or before November 29, 19--. There is no obligation, other than your starting the account by adding $25 or more to the free $1 we are giving you.

We hope you'll take advantage of this opportunity to get acquainted with the higher earnings and insured safely afforded your savings here at Pioneer — Northern California's oldest, largest savings and loan association.

At Pioneer, your funds earn the high rate of 4% per annum; that's one-third more than the interest paid by many savings institutions. Your savings are insured to $10,000 by an instrumentality of the Federal Government and further protected by Pioneer's great strength of over $90 millions in resources and largest reserves of any savings and loan association in Northern California.

Remember. More people place their savings with savings and loan associations than with any other type of savings institutions in America. And more people place more money with Pioneer than with any other savings and loan association in Northern California.

We suggest you start right now to put your savings dollars to work earning the highest interest with insured Safety. Come in . . . or mail in the enclosed Savings Passbook to us with your check (be sure to write your address on the passbook). Or call us and we'll be happy to arrange to transfer your funds for you.

Drop in . . . let's get acquainted!

Yours most sincerely,

Ted T. Fehring

Ted T. Fehring
Manager, Monterey Office

TTF:cw
Encl.

". . . mail in the enclosed Savings Passbook. . . ."

The enclosure is a passbook showing a credit of $1 to the reader. Action request: "Return the enclosure." Note the powerful psychological appeal to thrift.

course, are included for this very purpose. Note how the messages illustrated on page 374 direct attention to the enclosures and move swiftly toward action.

Testimonials. "Testimonial" enclosures are effective *when properly used*. Although the extent to which testimonials are abused has sometimes caused skepticism of their truth, there is much natural force in a testimonial delivered by a competent and trustworthy individual. Honest testimonials by qualified persons are powerful forms of evidence. The experience of others sways us in making our own decisions.

Copies of testimonials made by the photographic, photostatic, or facsimile process, are often enclosed with sales mailings. Note these two types: (1) user's (or ordinary) testimony and (2) expert (or authoritative) testimony. The second type is stronger because a recognized expert can be more accurate, more certain, and more authoritative in his statements.

Part 4—Getting Action

Action Is What You Want. To turn interest and desire into a favorable decision is the purpose of the action close. Your aim is to clinch success by getting the action for which you are working. People must be urged. The action close prods human inertia, overrides procrastination, offsets delay, and urges decision. The best time to spur action is the moment when the reader's interest and desire are keenest and when his buying impulse is at its peak.

Buyers rarely rush into the market to buy a brilliant new invention. Unless they were given the news facts and urged to act, buyers would scarcely know the invention existed, still less turn a finger to possess it! Thirty years passed before the Singer sewing machine really hit its stride. It may be hard for you to believe *now*, but it took four years of pioneering, uphill effort against vast public disinterest to convince the nation that there was any particular merit in the electric refrigerator.

How to Get Action. You can turn to three tested methods to stimulate your reader to favorable action:

1 Offer him certain inducements
2 Make it easy for him to act
3 Suggest that he act at once

The two chief blocks in your path to the favorable decision are "putting it off" (I'll wait and order it tomorrow) and everyone's quite natural dislike for parting with money. Let us now examine at greater length the three ways by which you can get around these blocks—each of the three tested action methods.

Offer Your Buyer Inducements. Here are the inducements you may offer your buyer:

1. Send no money in advance.
2. Examine the article for five days on approval.
3. Your money will be promptly refunded if you are not satisfied.
4. You have our unqualified warranty.
5. Pay for the article in installments, or use our deferred-payment plan.
6. This offer is open only until [a limit date].
7. Send your money in by [time limit] and get this additional premium. [Example: "If your order for the Seventh Edition of the 20-volume *Century Science Guide* arrives by June 1, midnight, we shall include, free of charge, our handsome 700-page *Science Glossary.*"]
8. You will receive a special 20% discount if you send your order at once, and an additional 2% discount if you send cash in full.
9. The price of this identical article will go up $10 after September 1.
10. There are only 250 copies of this edition left, and at $29.95 they are going fast. Act now before the supply is exhausted.
11. Order now—pay in 30 days.
12. Use the product without obligation for five days. [Trial offer, no money down.]

Make It Easy to Act. Make it easy for your buyer to act. Here are the things the experts have tested and that they recommend:

1. *Enclose an order blank.* Keep the blank simple. Plan it so that the customer can check squares or spaces to show his choice. Some companies even suggest to the customer, "If you prefer, just check off right on this letter the items you want, sign your name, and mail back to us." Listed at a convenient point are the items with a square or space for a check mark before each item.
2. *Enclose a business reply card or business reply envelope.* A certain percentage of buyers will have neither stamps nor envelopes at hand. The business reply card and the business reply envelope leave nothing for the reader to do except check, sign, and drop in the mail. Under postal regulations postage is due on business reply cards and envelopes only if they are returned.
3. *When money is to be sent:* state to the exact detail in what form you want it (cash, check, draft, money order, stamps). Examples: "Use the enclosed convenient coin card," or "Fold a dollar bill and place it in the enclosed currency folder; slip the folder into the enclosed business reply envelope; then just drop it in the mail." "Send check or draft with your order, and we'll add three extra copies to your subscription."

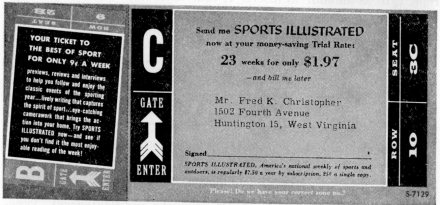

Both Sides of an Effective "Action" Business Reply Card

Suggest That Your Buyer Act at Once. Urge immediate action. The experts use these three tested and successful methods:

1. *The Definite Command:* "Check the easy order blank and send it today." "Mail the card now." "Sign the card and drop it in the mail at once." The "command" may arouse antagonism unless carefully phrased.
2. *The Persuasive Suggestion:* "Signing the enclosed card is all you need to do to obtain your copy of this book." "Why not mail the order blank now, and let us send you a set of these attractive samples?"
3. *The Brisk Action Request:* A favored type, suggesting the force of the definite command while retaining the courtesy of the persuasive suggestion. Examples: "Check the word *yes* on the handy card now and get your set of valuable road maps free." "If you'll print your name and address on the enclosed blank, place the blank in the business reply envelope, and drop the envelope in the mail at once, we'll stamp your name in 24-carat gold on the flyleaf of each of these handsome portfolios."

Action Devices. Illustrated above is an effective business reply card. Note the expert use of features that may induce the reader to act, and that make it extraordinarily easy to do so.

The Encyclopaedia Britannica letter on page 379 is an example of a sales message concentrating on action. This message depends on previous mailings and on separate enclosures to carry out the previous three functions of attention, interest, and desire. Enclosed with the letter were (1) an announcement of a limited-time sale, (2) a sheet picturing two Britannica bindings in color and actual size, (3) two different order blanks presenting two different offers, and (4) a business reply envelope.

The Guardian letter on page 379 illustrates the use of the action reply card as an address insert. It calls immediate attention to itself by its unique position. Furthermore, the first paragraph of the letter refers to it to create action in the letter beginning.

How to Use Emphasis to Get Action

Emphasis helps to get action. The experts apply emphasis in these three ways: (1) short units (paragraphs and sentences), (2) mechanical helps, (3) prominent postscripts.

Emphasize with Short Units (Paragraphs and Sentences). Typographical experts like to "let daylight" into a printing job. They leave enough white space around the edges and between the lines so that the eye can more easily find its way into the lines of type and begin to read. Printers call these open areas "breathing space," "elbow room," or "daylight."

In the same fashion experts break up their typewritten sales messages into short units. Short paragraphs, for example, help the buyer to see the featured points because they stand out. Several short paragraphs make the message easy and quick to grasp.

For the same reason experts use relatively short sentences in sales work. An over-long sentence may strain the reader's attention, may be obscure, and may fail to carry its point. Short sentences carry the reader along. He doesn't have to carry them. They "move." They suggest life, zest, and brisk action.

Emphasize with Mechanical Helps. Sometimes you will want to stress certain special sales points. To do this, you may call on one of the mechanical devices on page 380 that guide the eye to the point you want to hammer home.

This message devotes itself to action from beginning to end. Note the emphatic short paragraph units and the various mechanical-emphasis devices.

ENCYCLOPAEDIA BRITANNICA

Founded [logo] in 1768

LONDON
60-to-Regent Street

NEW YORK
342 Madison Avenue

January 19, 19--

NOW AS NEVER BEFORE
YOU NEED IT!

We made you the unusual offer, two weeks ago, of a set of the Encyclopaedia Britannica at a sharp reduction in price.

Now--as a final surprise, we enclose a special order-form from which will enable you to buy the Britannica, in dark blue cloth binding, on a payment basis of only $5 a month if you wish.

May we now remind you that orders for this greatest knowledge book in the world, under the special sales-price reduction, must be sent in promptly.

This offer--with its attractive saving to you--is of such exceptional nature that (as we explained in our first letter) it is, and must be, only a short-time privilege. To gain the substantial advantage of this Short-Time Sale, you must act quickly.

More than 60,000 families own sets of this brilliantly illustrated and richest harvest of practical information ever published. Thousands of unsolicited letters tell us that all users of the new Britannica, whether their ages be 8 or 80, find it to be an unfailing source of helpfulness.

Now as never before you need it! And now, for a brief period, you may buy it at an extraordinarily low cost. But you must be quick.

We, therefore, cordially urge you to take advantage of this inviting offer and to send in your order now.

Additional information is enclosed--with an order blank for your immediate use.

Don't miss this splendid opportunity.

Sincerely yours,
K. E. [signature]
Vice President

IES/bja
Enclosure

The "window" draws attention to the reply card for an illustrated road guide, while the rest of the message appeals to the reader's future retirement plans.

The GUARDIAN Life Insurance Company OF AMERICA

ESTABLISHED 1860 UNDER THE LAWS OF THE STATE OF NEW YORK

50 UNION SQUARE, NEW YORK 3, N. Y.

JOHN C. SLATTERY
Second Vice President

REPLY CARD

Mr. Walter A. Kumpf
3650 Cresthill Drive
Ann Arbor, Michigan

You are cordially invited to mail the post-paid card in the window above and receive a gift copy of the new Rand McNally ILLUSTRATED ROAD GUIDE. It's perfect for the glove compartment of your car and is a wonderful aid when planning pleasure or vacation trips.

The Guide gives important road maps and motoring data for each state and Canada ... shows the dates and locations of all important festivals and fairs, contains 600 pictorial illustrations of our National Parks and major tourist attractions.

With this gift you will receive information about our flexible Retirement Income Plan which is currently assuring comfortable and secure futures to thousands of men and women.

This plan provides a way to guarantee a monthly income at 55, 60, 65 or 70, which you cannot outlive. And with Guardian's flexible plan, you can select the starting date later--when you know what is best for you.

With the lifetime income which this plan provides, you can look forward confidently to the fruits of your working years ... to take life easy or travel to your heart's content.

Simply mail the post-free card in the window above for details and your complimentary Rand McNally ILLUSTRATED ROAD GUIDE. Your signature is not needed and there is no obligation other than your willingness to look over the information when it reaches you.

Cordially yours,
[signature] Slattery
Second Vice President

JCS:RI

1. Exclamation points.
2. Dashes.
3. Circles (for encircled words), stars, other special marks.
4. Unexpected blank spaces.
5. Underscoring.
6. Capitalization.
7. Heading (capitals or small letters), as the title of a chapter; sometimes a "running head" instead of a salutation.
8. Wide margins.
9. Wider inset margins for one or more paragraphs (contrast emphasis).

> A sales message will attract and hold your reader far longer if it has a good, "easy-on-the-eye" layout. Hence, work in some of the tested "eye-hooks." Use a headline, a subhead or two, an indented whole paragraph, a second color, a postscript, underscoring, an occasional word or sentence in capital letters, facsimile handwritten words in the margins, and check marks or dashes or circles around words.
>
> *—Management Methods*

10. A check mark or a few handwritten words, a pointing finger, or similar devices in the margin.
11. Using red ribbon typing for several words or sentences.
12. Direct parallel: two short columns of contrasted facts, typed side by side (powerful contrast of each column with the other).
13. "Split" paragraphing: breaking a sentence in the middle; showing the break by a *dash* at the end of the first paragraph and one at the beginning of the second.
14. Indention, special indention, or extension of first words of a paragraph beyond the regular margin.
15. A short *double-spaced* paragraph in the body of a *single-spaced* letter (contrast emphasis).

Emphasize with Prominent Postscripts. A *planned* prominent postscript is emphatic. Its separate "setoff" makes the postscript stand out and draw attention to itself. In sales work an important point is often featured in a postscript.

The publishers of *Time* magazine announce a special offer. A facsimile-handwritten postscript emphasizes the saving thus: "This Special Offer puts $3.50 back in your pocket."

A department store writes to a select list of its women charge customers announcing a three-day white goods sale. The following postscript emphasizes the sale dates: "You can buy at these low prices only on November 6, 7, and 8."

Newsweek uses this postscript in its sales message: "Read the enclosed reprint from 'Periscope'—just one of our 18 departments. See for yourself some of *tomorrow's* news in the making!"

Experts use postscripts for still another purpose: Many people, the experts know, skip through a message, reading only a sentence or two in the main body. *But their eyes are almost always caught by the postscript,* which may whet their curiosity and prompt them to go back and read carefully.*

Don't WASTE Emphasis. The great Egyptian pyramids seize the imagination because they rear themselves out of the level sands of the Sahara. But drop those same pyramids among the peaks of the American Rockies and no one would know they were there! Build a *contrast*—then you emphasize!

When you read a message in which every seventh word is capitalized and every other paragraph is underscored, in which dashes and exclamation points are peppered all about, you may assume that the writer was trying for emphasis. But he was wrong. He over-emphasized. He defeated his own purpose. The altered shape of letters (CAPITALS LIKE THESE) or a line under a group of words (underscoring like this) keep their power only if used at climaxes. No natural force exists in fist-pounding or in a mass of capital letters in a solid line.

If a political candidate shouts from beginning to end of his harangue, he tires out his audience, wears down their nerves, leaves them disgusted, and probably doesn't get elected. But if an effective speaker talks in a conversational, well-modulated tone and only now and then raises his voice for the emphasis he needs, he wins and holds attention. *Use mechanical emphasis only when you need it.*

Are You a Good Craftsman? Effective sales messages cannot be "dreamed up." In a finished and powerful sales message the vibrant, glowing, moving, fact-packed sentences are created—not by dreamy dallyings in the realm of the floating imagination—but through patient effort by an honest craftsman who has painstakingly prepared for his task. There is sometimes a peculiar and completely erroneous idea that dynamic writing is something you can create (1) only "when you are inspired," (2) only "when the big idea hits you," (3) only "when your mind is hitting on all twelve," and (4) only "when your idea-furnace gets hot." Not so! Dynamic writing comes from just one simple source: *hard work.* Work with intense concentration—and the ideas will flow.

* Henry G. Weaver, the late head of the Customer Research Division of the General Motors Corporation, found that in most cases footnotes received higher attention than an identical passage in the main text. So it is with postscripts. (Query: Did you read this footnote first?)

Pulling Power

What Is Sales "Pulling Power"? The success with which a sales message brings in returns is called its *pulling power*. The pulling power will vary between wide extremes, depending on such factors as the nature of the product, the character of the market, the kind of offer, the action asked for.

The reliable method of testing the effectiveness of a sales message *before* it is put to wide-scale use is to run a preliminary small-scale test on a *correct sample* of the market to be reached. Mere estimates of what the pulling power is likely to be are worthless unless they are based on records of a number of similar mailings used under similar circumstances. Even then the estimate may often be wide of the mark because it is subject to the many unpredictable influences of a changing market.

An expert using a preliminary test on a correct sample of the mailing list (the list of those to whom the sales message is to be sent) can, however, predict within small limits of error what the results will be as to

1. Approximate cost of the mailing (percent of sales).
2. Approximate volume of sales in dollars.
3. Percentage of replies in relation to the total list.
4. Number of replies received.

In department stores, for example, mail programs produce returns ranging all the way from literally nothing at all to as high as 25 per cent or more. A message and an enclosure issued by a metropolitan store to a selected list of customers numbering 10,000 names, and presenting a popular garment at an important price reduction, produced sales to the number of 3,000 pieces. On the other hand, the same retail organization sent out a mailing piece to a list of 16,000 homes and made only eight sales. Among retail establishments using considerable amounts of direct mail, the average returns range from 2 per cent to 5 per cent of the total number on the mailing list.

Suppose that you are an assistant manager of the Sales Promotion Department. You are presenting a short memorandum report to show cost ratios on a typical mail campaign. This is the way your figures might look: "1,000 pieces, each with an enclosure, have been prepared at a cost of $90. They produce a 3 per cent return, or 30 sales. The average of these sales is only $3. The resulting income is only $90, or exactly the amount spent to prepare the mailing. A second campaign, however, is of such a nature that the average sale amounts to $30. Accordingly, the total resulting sales are $900. The cost of the mailing on this basis is 10 per cent."

Experts of long experience point out that direct-mail programs, in order to be worth undertaking, must produce sales of not less than five times, and an average of ten times, the cost of the effort. Direct mail succeeds best when used to sell or *to help sell* goods of high unit value. Sales messages are often used to carry *part* of the selling task that the salesman himself completes when he makes his personal call.

Increase Pulling Power with Color and Pictures. Tinted stationery in pink, buff, or blue, and illustrations in one or several colors are not uncommon in sales work. A manufacturer tested two mailings, one on white and the other on tinted paper. The returns from the white were 10.5%; those from the tinted, 19.2%. He then tested two more messages, adding to each an illustration. The illustrated white mailing drew returns of 20%; the illustrated tinted, returns of 34%. For normal direct-mail offers, responses as high as these are not to be expected. For some offers a 2% response must be considered satisfactory.

The *American Paper Merchant* presents an account of another test. The replies to a message addressed to 11,000 carefully selected prospects totaled 4%. Dissatisfied with the result, the manufacturer called in a sales management expert who approved the copy but planned a new letterhead. He divided the mailing into a number of color combinations and prepared the mailing in such a way that one half of the messages carried an illustration of the product and the other half did not. The same 11,000 persons were circularized again, this time in 11 groups of 1,000 each. This test revealed that illustrated letters written on pink, canary, or green stationery and mailed in blue envelopes were—for this particular campaign—the most effective. The results of this test demonstrated the power of distinctive color combinations under certain conditions. Distinctive paper tints are successfully used, of course, only under circumstances in which they are appropriate.

Summary. We now look back over the pages of this chapter and find that our outline of the four-part sales procedure is now complete. Sales management, and its staff of people, strive for:

Attention, which concentrates the reader's train of thought upon the message.

Interest, which, with clear detail, with facts and figures, arouses interest in the article, reveals its merits, and shows that the article is good in itself.

Desire and belief, which, with persuasive material and forceful psychological appeals, shows the reader how the article fills his need.

Action, which, with suitable phrasing and with helps like business reply cards and envelopes, makes favorable decision easy.

The first three of these functions lead logically to the fourth—*action*—upon which the final success must hang. People in the mass have little self-propulsion. Vigorous initiative is limited to the few. Hence the writer of a sales message designed to get action must *ask* for that action, must make it *easy* to take, and must *urge* it with emphasis, if he expects to get it.

Will the reader act favorably? Will he retain information that will lead him to act favorably at a future time? To bring about a favorable decision now, or to give information that will eventually lead to such a decision, is the aim of effective sales management.

Six Tests for Your Sales Message

1. **Will your mailing be opened?** Some messages give out an air of "this is too important to be thrown away."

2. **Will it be read?** To make sure that your message will be read, make it attractive in appearance.

3. **Will your message be understood?** Only the seven C's can insure quick understanding: Completeness, Courtesy, Consideration, Clearness, Conciseness, Concreteness, Correctness.

4. **Will it be believed?** Be suspicious of superlatives. If in doubt, understate. Then offer proof.

5. **Will your message be agreed with?** Cast the message in the reader's mold. Tie up with his interests. Present your position, make your statement, put forward your argument in pleasant words. Meet objections before they occur.

6. **Will your reader act favorably?** You must chalk up the final score on the basis of this test if your message calls for action. No matter how excellent a writer you have been in the preceding five tests, your "percentage of pull" must be within the norm to assure your success in the final "action" test.

Communication Problems

● **1.** You have been asked by the manager of the National Radio Manufacturing Company to write a sales promotion message to be mailed to college students living in cities with FM broadcasting stations. The purpose of the message is to sell the National AM-FM Table Model Radio that has these specifications:

> Six tubes plus rectifier for long-distance reception; two 5-inch speakers for good tone quality; separate knobs for volume control, on-off and tone control, and dial tuning; dial is lighted for easy visibility; printed circuit cuts need for expensive repairs; approved by Underwriters Laboratory as safe appliance; brown plastic cabinet fits color scheme of most rooms and cleans easily; 7 inches high, 14 inches wide, and 5 inches in depth; has built-in antennas for AM and FM stations; operates on standard 110-volt, 60-cycle Alternating Current; built so that standard record players can be plugged in without additional attachments; FM stations are almost static-free; most standard broadcasting stations are AM. Price is $49.95. Radio compares in tone and quality with AM-FM sets costing $60 or more. Guaranteed for one year against defects in workmanship and materials; tubes guaranteed 90 days.

(1) Select any five ways to seize attention (see the list of fifteen ways, pages 357-359) and write opening pararaphs for five different sales messages about the National Radio. For each, use a different method of gaining attention. (Refer also to the list of *What* NOT *to Do in "Openers,"* page 360.)

For this case you need not write the complete draft. Instead write only enough to capture attention and tie in with the National Radio.

NOTE: Retain a copy of each of the opening paragraphs for use in Problem 6 (page 388).

(2) Write a concise summary statement, addressed to your instructor, in which you explain which of the five openings you have written is strongest, in your opinion, for reaching the college student prospects. Show clearly why you believe as you do.

● **2.** You have been asked by the manager of the Artstock Gift Company, 1313 North Hampton Road, Ames, Iowa, to write a complete sales message for the Artcraft Musical Jewel Box. Some of the features of the product are:

> 5 x 8 inches, 4 inches high; made of unbreakable, transparent Lucite plastic ¼-inch thick; has four silver-plated legs ¼-inch high; two silver-plated hinges to match legs; stain, scar, burn, scratch resistant; imported Swiss movement visible in side compartment plays "Blue Danube Waltz" when top is opened; plays two minutes with one winding; packed in attractive gift box; price is $3.50, postpaid, cash, check, or money order; no C.O.D. orders accepted. One silver-plated initial, to match legs and hinges, mounted on top of box for additional 50 cents.

(1) On the first page of your solution: (a) include a statement describing the market you plan to reach with a sales message designed to sell the Artcraft Musical Jewel Box by mail; (b) list the principal selling points you believe would be appropriate to sell this item to the market you have selected.

(2) On the second page of your solution write a complete sales message to sell this product to the market you have selected. Be sure the message fits the requirements listed below. If you wish, you may tie in with some seasonal promotion such as Mother's Day, Christmas, Graduation, or Valentine's Day.

The manager has decided that one silver-plated initial will be mounted free of charge on all jewel boxes ordered during the next ten days. Include this information in a planned postscript.

Review the fifteen mechanical devices for achieving emphasis (pages 378, 380) and the section explaining problems of wasted emphasis (page 381). Then, in the material you have prepared for the Artcraft Jewel Box, use with good taste four of the fifteen mechanical-emphasis devices listed in your book. In the margin identify neatly the emphasis devices you have used.

● 3. Alex Thomas, student in a large university, has drawn up arrangements to operate a personalized birthday cake delivery service. About two weeks before a student's birthday, Thomas plans to write to the student's parents explaining that for a nominal charge he will deliver a decorated birthday cake to the student on the correct day. Thomas has made arrangements to purchase the cakes from a local bakery which has agreed to sell the decorated cakes to him at a wholesale price. Thomas has also compiled a mailing list, from university records, showing the name of each student, date of birth by month and day, campus address, and home-town address.

He offers chocolate or angel food cakes in three sizes—small (serves about 12), large (serves about 16), and giant (serves about 24); chocolate or vanilla icing; and decorated with the words "Happy Birthday" and the student's first name.

(1) On one page: (a) list the main selling features of this service, (b) state the central selling point you would use to promote the service to parents, and (c) prepare a list of appropriate appeals.

(2) On another page, draft a form sales message that Thomas will use to sell this birthday cake service to parents of university students.

(3) Prepare a concise order blank that can be enclosed with this mailing. Make the blank easy to use (perhaps with answers to be checked off by the customer), simple, and clear. Be sure the order blank asks for all the information Thomas will need for filling the order promptly.

● 4. The promotion manager of *Young Executive Outlook*, a monthly magazine of interest to junior executives in management, plans to conduct a mail campaign designed to obtain new subscribers. The magazine subscription rate is $6 a year.

The publishers have purchased a list of 100,000 names and addresses of persons who might have an interest in such a magazine, and a professional expert has prepared two different mailing promotions, either of which could be sent to this list. Printing and production executives have calculated that either mailing can be printed, stuffed, addressed, and mailed at a cost of $85 per thousand. The mailings are designed to sell one-year subscriptions. The publisher believes he can at least break even and thus incur no loss of profits if he spends as much as $2 to secure one new subscription order.

Write a concise report to the promotion manager of *Young Executive Outlook* in which you (a) explain a method by which he might conduct a test to determine which of the two mailings would be more profitable to use; (b) state how he can estimate the cost of the 100,000 mailing as a per cent of sales after the initial test mailings have been conducted; and (c) point out the minimum percentage of returns the magazine must expect on the mailing of 100,000 in order to break even.

● **5.** You have been hired as a sales promotion consultant by the World Mail Order Sales, Inc., a company that promotes to sell a variety of products by mail to the consumer. World Mail Order Sales has made a special purchase of 5,000 Sno-Breeze Electric Fans with these specifications:

> 12-inch; 900 cubic feet per minute capacity; 3-speeds; 60-watt motor; gray enamel base and cadmium-plated guard grill; felt pad on base; slot in base for easy wall mount; one-year guarantee by manufacturer. The fan is built to retail for $16.95; while supply of 5,000 lasts, World Mail Order will sell for $11.45, postpaid.

(1) Prepare a basic data study chart in which the features of the Sno-Breeze fan are compared with features of two competing fans. You may find specifications for other fans in advertisements, catalogs, or from local dealers. (Review Chapter 14 for details about the basic data study chart.)

(2) Prepare a market data analysis, listing as much information of value as you believe would be appropriate for this product. As a summary statement in the market analysis, explain the market you would choose to reach for this product, the timing of the promotion, and suggestions for obtaining names for the mailing. If you do not have access to market information you believe would be helpful in the analysis, explain the type of information needed and suggest ways in which the data might be obtained.

(3) Prepare (a) a list of psychological drives that would be appropriate appeals to use in reaching the market you have selected; (b) list the main selling points of the product that would be appropriate for this market; and (c) state clearly the central selling point to be used in a direct mail promotion.

(4) Assume the mailing will cost $90 per thousand and the company will receive a profit margin of $3 on each electric fan sold. (a) What percentage of returns must the company produce in order to pay the cost of the mailing? (b) Write a concise report in which you propose a method for testing the mailing on a small scale to determine its cost in relation to returns. (c) Assume for your report that the test mailing produced 2 per cent returns. How many messages should be mailed in order to sell all 5,000 electric fans?

(b) Write a complete sales message to sell the Sno-Breeze Electric Fan by mail. You may assume that an illustrated leaflet describing the fan will be enclosed.

● 6. This case is based on the National AM-FM Table Model Radio described in Problem 1 (page 385).

(1) On the first page of your two-page solution: (a) Outline briefly what you believe a college student wants from a table model radio. You may assume the student lives in a city with both AM and FM broadcasting stations. (b) Using the information about the National Radio in Problem 1 as a guide, explain briefly the ways in which this radio does and does not fit the needs of the college market as you have analyzed that market. (c) Select an appropriate strong central selling point for the radio and give reasons for your choice.

(2) On the second page of your solution, draft a sales message to be mailed to college students, in which you gain attention and build interest and desire for the National Radio. Use both factual and emotional description as appropriate. In closing the message, ask the reader to write for a free booklet about the radio and details on how he can purchase one for a limited time at a discount of 30% from regular price.

PART VII Adjustments, Credits, and Collections: Functions of Finance Management

Chapter 17   *The YOU-Approach in Adjustments*

The Art of Adjustment Management. To win and to hold the favorable response and regard of more customers, executive action—in the form of *adjustment management*—is especially alert to handle every kind of trouble with the utmost speed, courtesy, and tact.

Adjustment experts know that there is nothing quite so delicate and perishable as customer good will. Such good will is staunch when it flourishes on satisfactory products and services and company policy, but it can perish if the words in an adjustment are irritable.

Look again at those words of a top executive: "Whether you like it or not, the customer has a picture of your company in his mind. It may not be the picture you think it is. It may not be the picture you want it to be. But whatever that picture is, it has a lot to do with the success or failure of your business. Your customers are interested in something 'behind the scenes'—something delicate, intangible, and priceless. That 'something' is tied up now and forever with the character and personality of your company. You build this by the way you handle your customer relations."

Excellent customer relations are protected largely through expert adjustment management based on the YOU-approach. The very heart of the YOU-approach is *courtesy*.

Can You Answer "Yes" to These Key Questions? Customer-centered (or "YOU-attitude") courtesy has been properly called the lubricant that cools the world's adjustment-friction points. In one of his most famous cartoons the great John T. McCutcheon put it this way: "When there's trouble around, politeness is the world's greatest trouble lubricant. It makes everything easier

Adjustment Courtesy lights up this Message

ONE WORD FOR ALL: COURTEOUS!

and pleasanter. Courtesy is positively 'catching,' and we should all be glad to 'catch' it."

You can test your adjustment skill right at the outset with these key questions: (1) Are you building a courtesy feeling between your company and your customers? (2) Are you giving your customers the desire to return to your house again and again because they like your tone and tact and customer-centered willingness to serve? (3) Do you let cheerful, trouble-smoothing friendship play its natural part in getting and holding more customers who return again and again to patronize you? (4) Do you build ever-mounting good will into your adjustment messages through the power of your thoughtfully written words? If you can answer yes to these questions, then your trouble-smoothing management already carries the stamp of success.

The YOU-Approach: "A Soft Answer Turneth Away Wrath." You can scald yourself or you can bless yourself with the written words you put on paper, if they are words that your customer will eventually see. When you are handling trouble, remember this: each line you write will be on the record. If you write in anger and irritation, you may destroy friendship or endanger good will. But if you speak softly and focus your energies on *curing* the trouble, you will "turn away wrath," win added friendship, and retain good will. In thousands upon thousands of instances, *it is not what you say but how you say it that counts*. The fortune-building success-secret is in the HOW! Note the courteous tone of the following adjustment.

> Another complimentary copy of the painting of the Queen Elizabeth is on its way to you today.
>
> We are sorry that the first copy arrived in such damaged condition. Perhaps the Post Office will be more gentle in its handling this time! If not, please let us know and we will work out a safer method of forwarding.

No One Wants Trouble. No one wants to make mistakes. No one wants trouble. When mistakes and trouble happen, they are simply necessary evils that interfere. Errors are obstructions that clog the even flow of transactions. The purpose of effective adjustment management is to remove error-obstructions, to repair the damage they cause, and to restore the smooth flow of the business stream.

"Mind Your Speech a Little, Lest It Mar Your Fortune." If human beings never *said* the wrong thing, never *wrote* the wrong thing, never *did* the wrong thing; if they knew how to reach perfection, business would make no mistakes, customers would make no mistakes, transportation agencies would make no mistakes, and we

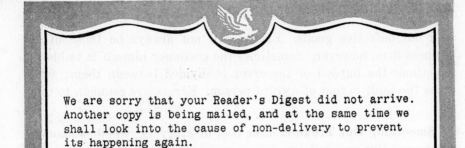

We are sorry that your Reader's Digest did not arrive. Another copy is being mailed, and at the same time we shall look into the cause of non-delivery to prevent its happening again.

As all copies are mailed from our printing plant, it may be a week or so before you receive the one now being addressed.

m   THE READER'S DIGEST

THE READER'S DIGEST ASSOCIATION · PLEASANTVILLE, N. Y.

A Famous Magazine Adjusts Promptly, Holds Subscriber Good Will

would live in a beautiful, errorless world. Adjustment departments would vanish, and adjustment managers would look for other jobs. No one would need to ask the key question, "Where does the fault lie?"

Of course, no such millennium will ever arrive. Adjustment departments will be destined to the end of time to wage friendly warfare against human error: saying the wrong thing, writing the wrong thing, doing the wrong thing. Like Shakespeare's Hamlet they must ". . . take arms against a sea of troubles, And by opposing end them. . . ."

Says the top executive of a company catering to women: "It costs our company several dollars to get a customer. Furthermore, each customer has friends who are customers. We know of actual cases where other companies by dissatisfying one customer have lost the business of from ten to a score of her friends. It does not take long for ripples of discontent to spread pretty widely."

"To Err Is Human, To Forgive Divine" wrote Alexander Pope a few centuries ago. Of course he wasn't discussing adjustment management. He was suggesting a point of view about human nature. But this observation of two centuries ago carries a profound truth for twentieth-century trouble-smoothers.

Who Makes the Errors? A certain amount of trouble is bound to occur as long as business activity continues anywhere. Even the best firms will sometimes commit mistakes, suffer shipping delays, send out defective goods. Errors will not always be those of the business firm, however. Sometimes the customer himself is to blame; sometimes the burden of the error is divided between them; sometimes the fault is that of a third person. Errors are common to them all.

Smoothing Out Trouble. Like that of everyone, whether management executive or employee, your common problem is to hold errors down, to reduce them, and, as far as possible, to avoid them. No one has ever found customers' complaints pleasant to deal with; but experienced adjusters, skillful in the art of smoothing out trouble, know that if complaints are handled cheerfully, promptly, and fairly, they are powerful good-will builders—winners of customer loyalty.

Asking, Granting, and Declining Adjustments

How Should You Ask for an Adjustment? Suppose, first of all, we take the YOU-approach, "customer-center" ourselves, and see the problem through his eyes. When trouble happens to him, it looms large and black. He is liable to be bothered, worried, and irritable. Yet these are just the qualities he should not display when he makes his request for the correction.

"It relieves the pressure."

—*Saturday Evening Post*

An effective request for adjustment should reflect clearness, careful details, and avoidance of irritation. Follow this plan:

Subject first, requesting the adjustment ⟶ Explanation— reason for the request ⟶ Courteous suggestion for prompt action

Requesting an Adjustment. You recently ordered from a construction-hardware company a "De Luxe Art Aluminum" screen door with an automatic door-closer that prevents the screen from slamming shut. The closer proves unsatisfactory. How will you write the adjustment request? It might take this form:

EFFECTIVE REQUEST FOR AN ADJUSTMENT

Subject First, {   Can you supply me with a new compressed-air
with Request   door closer for the "De Luxe Art Aluminum" screen
for Adjustment   door (Model 27D) ordered from you on August 3?

Explanatory {   After fitting the door into place, I found
Detail   that the closer failed to operate, apparently due
                to a defect in the compressed-air valve. Because
                this door is used continuously, the closer mecha-
                nism is vitally important.

Courteous {   I'll gladly follow your instructions on the
Suggestion for   replacement of the closer mechanism. You may be
Prompt Action   sure of my appreciation for a prompt adjustment.

After you have analyzed the facts, determine the central subject, and place it first, as illustrated in the opening sentence of the request that you have just read. This is the *analytical order*. It is more direct—cuts faster to the point—than the *chronological order*, beginning "On August 3 I ordered from you a 'De Luxe Art Aluminum' screen door. . . ." The chronological opening tends to fog the subject, the central point. Make the request *first*; explain afterwards.

When Trouble Is More Involved. The more involved the trouble, the more details should be given and the more care should be taken to avoid irritation. The exact extent of the trouble should be defined. To show anger may result in possibly angering the reader and may defeat the adjustment. Charges of neglect, incompetence, or double-dealing should, of course, never appear.

EFFECTIVE REQUEST FOR AN ADJUSTMENT MORE INVOLVED

Subject First, {   May I ask for the correction of a $20 error in
with Request   my checking account?
for Adjustment

             For several months prior to June, 19--, I main-
tained an active checking account in the Brentwood
Branch of your bank. On June 8, 19--, I asked the
cashier for the exact amount of my checking account
balance. The cashier gave me the figure as $622.89.
I explained that I wished to close the account and
wrote my check accordingly for $622.89.

Explanatory   The monthly statement recently sent me (with
Detail Giving   the last entry on October 6, 19--) shows an actual
Reasons for   balance on June 8, 19--, of $642.89, leaving a $20
Making the   balance after the deduction of the check I wrote
Request   on that date.

             With the statement a "Charge" memo slip was
also enclosed, covering a deduction of $1 from the
balance because the account had remained inactive
over a certain period. Yet you will note every
necessary step was taken to close out the account.
Through an understandable error I was misinformed
about my correct balance and then charged for
account inactivity because of the misinformation.

Courteous
Suggestion
for Prompt
Action
{
        I am sure you will be glad to correct this
error, and your cooperation in doing so will be
much appreciated.

Be Confident, Positive, and Helpful. The confident, positive, helpful tone is your key to success. The positive tone suggests that your adjuster is fair and honest. It emphasizes remedies. The negative tone hints (sometimes through mere clumsiness) that the adjuster is unfair and dishonest. It suggests that you have been injured and feel it necessary to fight back. Curb personal feelings. Use the confident and helpful tone.

Make the Adjustment "Stick": Hold Good Will. Too often an adjustment is made, apparently to the satisfaction of the customer. The episode is forgotten—but the customer never comes back. Yet no adjustment is successful unless you hold on to good will. The adjustment may fail because of a tone fault or perhaps an inadequate explanation of how the error happened.

Many companies wisely check up on their adjustments. The adjusting officer does not stop with adjusting the mistake. He goes a step further. The customer gets a double government postcard on which he is asked if he is completely satisfied. Proof that the plan is worth while is found in the complimentary comments that come back.

Be Cheerful and Act Fast When Granting an Adjustment. Granting an adjustment, like granting a favor, should be the easiest message in the world to write. You are doing something pleasant which is going to satisfy somebody, possibly make somebody happy. The standing and still unsolved mystery is why an otherwise well-managed business will allow adjustments to be so granted that they "sound" almost worse than a refusal! If an adjustment is to be granted, it should be granted promptly and cheerfully—or not at all. An adjustment, like a favor, is ruined by grudging consent.

"Yes, We'll Correct This Trouble." It is clearly an inexcusable waste of opportunity not to gain from the adjustment every atom of good will. If, therefore, the business is going to say "Yes, we'll correct this trouble," it should take pains to make a

We are pleased to return the amount enclosed covering the deposit made by you at one of our public telephone coin boxes. We are sorry you were inconvenienced and wish to thank you for bringing this matter to our attention.

ILLINOIS BELL TELEPHONE COMPANY

A Printed Adjustment

Northern Falls
Iowa
October 10, 19--

Gentlemen:

Five days ago, I took my account book from the top drawer of my writing desk where it had been kept all these years, and intended to mail it to you. But it is lost. I can't find it.

The only reason that I can think of is that it got mixed up among a pile of old letters that I had been going thru, and which I put in the kitchen range to burn. I've been so distressed about it, I could hardly sleep.

It is not as if I had lost it outside my home where someone could find it. But even the done contract a book that has been reduced to ashes. Oh! I suppose it could, but I don't think it will happen in my case.

I had a little hard luck last November. On the 18th of June I was taken to the hospital in Davenport with a broken left hip. I was released on April 10. I have been very fortunate in recovery, as I am able to get around by using a cane. Under my right arm, I went eighty-four years old last Dec. 10. I have a good constitution, and I expect to live several years yet.

You will make me a new book won't you? And put in the front that in case of my death, the insurance is to go to my husband. I have not told my husband that I have lost the book. No need of both of us worrying.

I shall be anxiously waiting to hear from you.

Sincerely,
Nora Louise Calvin

Am I the only one who ever lost a book?

NEW YORK LIFE INSURANCE COMPANY
51 Madison Avenue, New York 10, N.Y.
SUPPLEMENTARY CONTRACTS DIVISION

October 13, 19--

AIRMAIL

Mrs. Nora Louise Calvin
Northern Falls
Iowa

Agreement and Account Book 968 521

Dear Mrs. Calvin:

Thank you for your explanatory letter. I am sorry you lost your book. But do not let it worry you any longer, for I am sure I can help you.

If you will complete the enclosed affidavit, answering the questions to the best of your ability, and mail it to me in the enclosed postage-free envelope, I will arrange to have another contract issued.

The form of book you lost is no longer used by the Company. These contracts are no longer in book form but look something like a small insurance policy. The terms of the new form are the same as the book lost.

If you want to receive the interest of $90 which is due December 6, write the following answer to Question 7 in the affidavit:

"Yes, Interest for 19--."

If you do this, then I will send you a check for the interest at the same time I send you the new contract.

I am glad to know that you have had a favorable recovery from your broken hip.

It has been a pleasure to be of service to you. If I can help you in any other way, please let me know.

Sincerely yours,
George H. Mullen
Superintendent

GHM:id
Encl.

What Would You Have Said to Mrs. Calvin?

Adjustment experts know that a tiny, even trivial bit of trouble may become monumental to a customer. Accordingly, they handle even little troubles with great care.

Here Is What a Top Executive Wrote

swift and cheerful concession. Always remember the "old saw," *You cannot sweeten a cup of coffee into which you have first poured vinegar.* Note the excellent tone in the printed adjustment message at the bottom of page 394.

The Prize Way NOT to Adjust is this: (1) "We are absolutely right"; (2) "You are all wrong"; (3) "We will, however, grant your claim." Follow this plan and you will defeat your adjustment and destroy its entire value. Here are two versions of the same adjustment, the first clumsy and irritable, the second skillful and pleasant. Which would *you* rather get? Which adjustment wins good will?

CLUMSY, GRUDGING, AND NEGATIVE

We certainly are astonished at this claim, regarding our very best line of waders. You know perfectly well we have sold thousands all over the country and have hardly ever had any trouble like this reported.

Your customer ought to know by this time that any wader has to be fastened snugly at the top. However, since your customer seems much disturbed, we have decided against our better judgment to grant your claim.

Why can't your customers read plain directions? We are enclosing another folder. If your customer can't read, we recommend that you read it to him. We're disgusted with this whole matter.

SKILLFUL, CHEERFUL, AND POSITIVE

Thank you for your claim of November 17. In appreciation, and as an aid to you in giving satisfaction, we are honoring it in full.

On the way to you right now is a new pair of waders. To insure future satisfaction, please tell your customers that these waders will give the finest service if they are strapped snugly according to the enclosed directions.

These famous hunter waders are of the finest design and rugged construction. They'll give long service. . . . [etc.]

NEVER Use Offensive Expressions. Harsh phrases carry bad associations. Never use them in adjustment work. Avoid these like poison:

(1) *You state, you say, you claim, you assert.* These expressions are dangerous. They suggest disbelief. Use, instead, *you report, which were reported.* When criticism floats in the air, avoid *you* because it tends to fasten an accusation upon the reader. Contrast the expressions on page 397.

SAFE, IMPERSONAL	DANGEROUS, ACCUSING
We were in error not to have made the matter clearer.	You never heard us make such a statement.
As size was not mentioned, . . .	You neglected to give the size.
The sample, which was not enclosed, . . .	You failed to enclose the sample.
There is a misunderstanding.	You are wrong in saying that.

(2) *We are utterly at a loss, we cannot understand.* Discourteous expressions like these suggest that the customer is ignorant or careless. They also suggest that the firm itself is incompetent and poor in its management.

PROMPT, COURTEOUS	HELPLESS, TACTLESS
Just as soon as you let us know what sizes you wish, . . .	We cannot understand why you failed to include the sizes.
A duplicate shipment of your order is on its way to you right now.	We are at a loss to know what has become of your order.

(3) *Your complaint.* A bristling, irritable, and generally disagreeable atmosphere surrounds the word "complaint."

(4) *If this is not satisfactory* or *we hope* [or *trust*] *this will be satisfactory.* Expressions like these suggest that the company itself is not sure whether its adjustment has been correct. If the company is uncertain, it is very likely that you will be too. Make your closing sentence "clinch" the action. An example: "Because we prize our business associations with you, we are glad to make this adjustment."

(5) *Never happen again.* A dangerous phrase indeed. The error is bound to happen again sometime. But it must not happen too often. A successful management is one that holds the good will of customers and, through careful supervision of its activities, permits only the fewest possible mistakes. You are safe when you say, "We shall be careful to guard against this error in the future."

Friendship Phrases Are Worth Their Weight in Gold. Just as there are harsh and dangerous phrases to avoid, so there are tactful and winning phrases to accept. The real skill in adjustment management lies in the expressions you use and the "turn" you give them. Some adjusters have the instinctive knack of knowing how to give a pleasant twist to an unpleasant subject. While they actually say "No," they come as near to saying "Yes" as could well be imagined. One man can take a situation and make it as bitter as gall. Another can take the same situation and make it almost as pleasant as a summer breeze.

The Adjustment Department. The purpose of an adjustment department is to take care of things that have gone askew and to set them right. The unavoidable mistakes that creep into the best-managed business, plus the bungling, discourtesy, and inefficiency, of which some firms are guilty, are what make adjustment departments necessary.

The right tone psychology ought to be applied in naming the department that handles trouble. It was the custom years ago to call it the *Complaint Department.* But "complaint" is an ugly, snarling word, bristling with irritation and resentment. As this fact was discovered, companies looked around for a word that more truly represented the function of the department. Today we deal more frequently with *adjustment departments.* The change is logical and most desirable. "Complaint" suggests only the trouble (negative). "Adjustment" suggests the *settling* of the trouble (positive).

What Makes a Good Adjustment Executive? A good adjustment manager is a person who knows human motives. He has an even temper. He knows the power of constructive appeals and how to use them. A customer bestows his loyalty and his patronage only when he feels that he has been well treated. Adjustment psychology aims to make the customer feel so. The adjustment department deals with men and women who are disappointed, disgruntled, and irritated over real or fancied wrongs. Accusation, discontent, suspicion—these are the attitudes that the adjustment department must face. It trains itself and its staff to meet negative mental attitudes with powerful positive ones.

Instead of Saying "NO," Say "YES" to Something Else. Some of our most successful adjustment managers have been former salesmen. Men with a selling background are able quickly to sense what customers really want. And what customers really want—not merely what they ask for—should, if possible, be given to them. Many a time an offer to render an alternative service is more valuable to the claimant than the adjustment for which he originally asked. The adjuster who senses this situation, and who offers what the customer *really wants,* generates extra good will. Hence, it helps to gather some selling experience, if you can, before entering the adjustment division. To a professional adjuster nothing is more valuable than calm patience plus the sales point of view.

The adjustment officer welds together business insight and a practical knowledge of human nature. Using this equipment, he confidently approaches trouble. The experienced adjuster knows, from the cases he has handled, how the shift of a word or two can completely alter the tone of his message, and how it is possible to choose in advance to be contentious and cantankerous, or calm and conciliatory, simply through the choice of words. His experience proves that adjustment management, and the handling of adjustment language, can be an exact undertaking, calling upon a special kind of word precision.

Adjustment Approaches: "Who Is at Fault?"

Four Main Types of Adjustments. The adjuster must first carefully determine where the trouble comes from before he can apply the correct solution. Hence he asks, "Who is at fault?" The answer to this question will tell him what he should do. The four main adjustment situations are classified according to the one who is at fault. Each calls for a tested plan varying according to these circumstances: (1) when the company is at fault, (2) when a third party is at fault, (3) when the fault is divided between company and customer, and (4) when the customer is at fault.

(1) When the Company Is at Fault. In this situation grant the adjustment at once. Use this order:

Grant the request → Explanation for → Close cordially to
with prompt courtesy   the action   invite future business

Case I. The Dull Razor Blades. Perhaps you will recall the customer who wrote to the safety-razor company:

> I know you can't make *magic* blades, and I know it's human to make a mistake—I just got a package of five of those mistakes —each one duller than the one before. Of course I didn't get the shaving mileage you intended I should.
>
> Enclosed is the guilty package so you can find out what went wrong—and I wish you luck.

This customer, you will probably agree, was courteous in the extreme. He could so easily have taken the bristling, snarling "What kind of an outfit are you?" attitude. But he didn't! He cushioned his complaint with courtesy. Now, someone back in the corner may be saying, "But the sale is only 25 cents!" That is true. But does the 25-cent sale have anything to do with it? The answer is *no*. A

THE ARROW BLADE CORPORATION

3002 Reading Road

PATERSON 15, NEW JERSEY

September 10, 19

Mr. Harry H. Marston
1000 Washington Boulevard
Cincinnati 21, Ohio

Dear Mr. Marston:

Thank you for your thoughtfulness in writing
as you did in your September 7 letter, and for
sending in the package that disappointed you.

The first thing we're going to do is to see
that you have some of the keenest blades in the
world to take the place of the ones you returned.

Enclosed is a package of 25's which will give
you five Super-Keen blades for each one you returned.
These are yours with our compliments and with the
hope that you'll enjoy new shaving luxury from the
feather-honed, high-chrome Swedish steel edges.

The next thing we're going to do is to see
what happened in the case of your purchase. You
may be sure we'll trace this down. Meanwhile let
us know, won't you please, how the new luxury blades
go?

Cordially yours,

THE ARROW BLADE CORPORATION

Robert A. Wiley

RAW:MB   Robert A. Wiley

Adjustment-Courtesy Glows in This Message

Note the concrete and convincing "resale" of the product in the
expression **feather-honed, high-chrome Swedish steel.**

mountain of experience and on-the-record "pay-off" proves that *no expression of complaint or customer dissatisfaction is ever too trivial for adjustment attention.* How can you tell the status of this customer? How do you know whether he is important or unimportant? You never know, and it makes little difference anyhow. He may, for example, be the president of his own corporation; yet he may be writing on his personal stationery. You never can be sure.

The action to be taken in this adjustment situation is crystal clear. You make a prompt and courteous adjustment. And you take special care to "light up" your prompt adjustment with courtesy. The solution to this interesting case appears on page 400, reproduced in the form of the finished message.

Case II. Adjusting an Invoice Error. In auditing its accounts, one firm found an error in one of the invoices sent it by another firm from which it made purchases. The necessary adjustment was requested thus:

REQUEST FOR THE ADJUSTMENT OF AN INVOICE ERROR

In auditing our vouchers, we find a discrepancy in your invoices covering our purchase orders No. 3015A and No. 6580. Both orders covered No. 1760 sections. On order No. 3015A you charged us $98.75 each, less 20%. On order No. 6580 you charged us $99 each, with <u>no</u> discount.

Apparently this error is the result of an oversight of both your billing department and our invoice department. We feel that you will want to send us a credit memorandum for $62 to adjust.

Notice the clearness with which the request tells (a) what the trouble is and (b) what the customer wants. The exactness of detail, the precise dates and order numbers, help to bring the desired results. The tone is courteous. Notice the appeal to fair play and the quiet assurance that the request will be granted.

Three days afterward came the following answer:

THE CORRECTION IS PROMPTLY MADE

Prompt Action First

Enclosed is our credit memorandum for $62 covering the discount asked for in your request of May 9.

Explanation

The correct list price on these files is $99, and the discount should be 20%. It was our oversight in not allowing this 20% discount on our invoice of March 15.

The list price of $98.75 on the second invoice is, of course, in error. Although we have no record, it is possible that the list price was misquoted. The correct list price for March is $99, and we are crediting your account on that basis.

Cordial   { Thank you for calling the error to our atten-
Close   { tion. We are glad to rectify it at once and to
             { assure you that we are ready for your next order.

Companies at Fault Often Take Extraordinary Action to Protect Customer Good Will. So valuable is good will that wise management protects it through every available means. Sometimes they go to extraordinary lengths to bring about the prompt adjustment of, or to express a vigorous apology for, trouble that might otherwise ruin the good will so painstakingly built up over the years.

Case III. The Company That Got Too Many Orders. Here is a piece of expert writing containing an energetic adjustment apology that explains itself.

```
TO A CUSTOMER WHO HAS MET WITH
DISAPPOINTMENT AT MY HANDS:

     I have in some degree upset your Christmas--and that of
hundreds of others of our good customers.  If you lack the
time or inclination to read this message, let me make clear
now that (1) I am sorrier than I could ever make you realize
and (2) at least you will not be the loser financially.

     Some of my staff point out that for every order delivered
late, we have delivered at least 150 on time.  But that isn't
much comfort to you whose orders were muffed.

     We just guessed wrong on how many orders we would get.
Here we were in our new and greatly expanded plant.  We knew
we could easily handle a 10% to 20% increase in orders, which
was all we ever expected.  What did we get?  We got 52% more
business than we ever had before!

     We just got too many orders!  It would have been a lot
better for us if we had got only the number of orders we could
handle smartly.  So we're mighty sorry.  We most earnestly
apologize!

     If you got items too late to be of any use to you, just
send them back at our expense, and we'll cheerfully refund
your money in full.
```

One of the company's customers wrote afterwards: "We were *really* sore at this outfit until we got this message. It melted us."

Case IV. A Telephone Executive Wins Good Will. With all their speaking facilities over the local and long-distance lines, telephone companies turn constantly to the written message to carry on their operations. A company executive makes a prompt adjustment:

A TELEPHONE EXECUTIVE WINS GOOD WILL

Thank you for your note of June 6 regarding your long-distance telephone call to Dr. L. M. Thornell, PLaza 1-3478, St. Augustine, Florida.

We regret the cut-off interruption you experienced and the misunderstanding regarding the call. We strive always to avoid these service difficulties. In view of the facts as you have so well reviewed them, we are promptly canceling the charge of $4.60, the unpaid balance shown on our records. You may consider the matter closed.

We appreciate your prompt and courteous replies to our inquiries. This kind of customer cooperation helps to keep our standard of service high.

(2) When a Third Party Is at Fault. An airline, a railroad, a trucking company—any carrier—may be at fault because of delay or damage in transit. If the carrier is shown to be responsible for either or both, the company's adjustment should explain the action the customer should take to protect the company in case of damage or to speed the delivery. The consignee (the one who receives the shipment) should make sure that there is no shortage or apparent damage before he signs the receipt acknowledging that the shipment was received in good condition. When goods have been damaged in transit, the consignee should be sure to have the freight agent make a notation of the damage on the freight receipt before it is signed. Afterwards the consignee may take the goods and make a claim against the carrier in the customary manner. No claim can be made against the shipper. He is not at fault.

Some alert companies—even though they may not be legally responsible for the safe delivery of a shipment by the carrier—gain great good will by making a prompt adjustment *themselves* and putting in their own claim against the carrier. When necessary, they obtain the aid of the customer. But they win his valuable good will by taking the weight of the responsibility upon themselves. The plan followed is the same as that which would be used had the company itself been at fault. The difference is that the customer, knowing the company is not obligated to act, doubly appreciates the help and may feel a double measure of good will.

An Adjustment with the Carrier at Fault. In the following case an alert company wins good will by assuming some of the customer's troubles caused by damage in shipment. The customer was unfamiliar with the steps to be taken. He was much distressed about the damaged shipment. He found it a welcome relief to have the company's specialists take over the responsibility and release him from the worry.

A COMPANY ADJUSTS A CARRIER'S FAULT

Prompt Action First

Already on the way to you is an exact duplicate of the TV Stand and Bookcase Combination #300 you recently ordered. You'll get it in time to present to your husband on his birthday. To make doubly sure of prompt delivery, we're using Air Express.

Explanation

The first shipment, we find, was damaged in transit. This fact normally throws the responsibility for the adjustment on the railroad. But railroad adjustments are slow. Knowing how much you wish to give this gift to your husband, we have been glad to duplicate the order via Air Express to see that it gets to you at the time you want it most.

Just leave the damaged stand in the hands of the railroad people. We'll enter an immediate claim with the railroad, and you won't have to give the situation another thought.

Cordial Close

Thanks for telephoning us so promptly. Your call made it possible for us to get the duplicate TV Stand onto the plane in plenty of time. Please wish your husband a "Happy Birthday" for us.

The customer was delighted to know that her gift was to arrive in time after all. The good will and the potential future patronage earned by the company paid many times the expense of handling the adjustment in the manner shown.

(3) **When the Fault Is Divided Between Company and Customer.** When the error is divided, first search for the positive elements and emphasize them. Follow this plan:

1. Be prompt and courteous.
2. Adjust at once your part of the fault.
3. Mention the customer's share tactfully and as impersonally as possible.
4. Give any necessary further explanation.
5. Close on the note of future satisfaction.

Here, for example, is a customer who writes a vigorous letter asking for an instant correction of what he thinks is the company's error. But he mentions that in the past he has had pleasant dealings with the firm. That fact is the bright spot you are looking for. Open with it: "We're always pleased to have our customers tell us of their many satisfactory dealings with us. We are then even more determined to keep up the good record."

An Adjustment with the Fault Divided. Customers can so easily do things wrong. In the following case, for instance, the customer may have been a poor gardener. But here was an excellent chance to capture good will at small cost by cheerfully and promptly duplicating the order. The first example was the original letter; the second, the revision.

HOW TO MAKE ENEMIES

We certainly fail to understand why your rose selections did so poorly last season. Ordinarily we get no complaints at all on these. Moreover, it is not usually our custom to replace orders of this kind. If we tried to guarantee them for this long, we would always be getting fake claims.

In your case, however, we have decided—against our better judgment—to replace the order. Be particularly careful in how you plant them this time. We definitely won't replace them again.

HOW TO WIN FRIENDS

```
      Just about everybody had a bad time last spring with
rose plantings.  The season was not a good one and was a
tough experience for gardeners everywhere.  We're optimistic
in believing that this spring will more than make up for last
year's results.

      By air parcel post we are sending you three new "Royal
Queen" bushes from our antique rose collection.  We're sure
you will be delighted with them.
```

(4) When the Customer Is at Fault. Unfortunately the disappointments arising from the customer's own faults do not make his grievances any the less real. Nor does he feel any obligation to keep his unhappiness to himself.

The customer is often at fault. For instance, he puts the wrong figure down. He forgets something. He omits the samples, seals the envelope, and sends it on, not noticing his error. He neglects to give the size, the color, the quality, or the serial number. He misunderstands the directions on the order blank. He may commit scores of other errors. Follow this plan in handling customer faults:

1. Put something pleasant first. For example, thank the customer for the order.
2. Courteously state the facts and make the statement impersonal. Avoid: "You failed to give the size." Use: "As the size was not given, ..."
3. Assure favorable action as soon as the customer's error is corrected. Stress future satisfaction.

An Adjustment with the Customer at Fault. Joe Hixon, of Liberal, Kansas, asked for an adjustment on his roofing almost three years after the roofing had been put on. He wrote to the president of the mail-order house from which he had made the purchase. The facts showed that Hixon was wholly at fault.

So serious was this case that the adjuster carefully summarized all the facts at the beginning of his adjustment. The task was to place the blame where it belonged and yet to hold the customer. Note the forceful clearness with which the adjustment officer writes:

AN ADJUSTMENT IS REFUSED: CUSTOMER'S FAULT

Courteous Neutral Opening
> Thank you for your letter of July 16 addressed to the president of this company, asking for a roofing adjustment. Your request has been referred to me for an answer.

Careful Review of All Facts
> For the benefit of all of us, to write clearly on this subject, and also to review the facts for you, I have gathered the following information from those who have handled the previous correspondence. Here is what happened:
>
> On October 25, 19--, we received your order for this roofing, and shipment was made ten days later. Two years after this purchase was made, your letter dated September 2, 19--, was received. It requested an adjustment on this roofing, which apparently was not giving satisfaction.
>
> Investigation was made to find the reason. It was discovered that the shingles, which should have been nailed at the apex of each triangular point according to directions, were also nailed at the sides. The necessary expansion and contraction of the roofing consequently tore holes in the shingles.
>
> In order to help you out of this difficulty, we offered (in our letter of November 3, 19--) to pay half the price of a new roof. This is the last correspondence up to the present time.

Decision
> We now renew our offer to you, subject to acceptance within ten days. After August 1, 19--, it will be withdrawn.

Cordial Selling Close
> Considering the lapse of time since our original offer, we're sure you'll agree that this concession is indeed liberal. We'll be glad to receive your order for the roofing in accordance with our offer. And, of course, we'll also be glad to serve you in all your other construction work.

The adjuster stresses the liberal steps that the company has taken to retain the good will of the customer. The firmness of the tone of the renewed offer is justified by the long delay of which the customer has already been guilty. Note the effective invitation in the cordial closing paragraph.

When You Refuse an Adjustment, Affirm Your Customer's Mood. "Getting in step with the customer" is vital in handling those adjustments you must refuse. To get in step with him means to stress those points on which the buyer and the seller are agreed. When you

A RESIDENTIAL COMMUNITY
QUEENS, LONG ISLAND, NEW YORK
Owned and Operated by New York Life Insurance Company

June 9, 19--

Mr. Allen Bailey
67-55B 193rd Lane
Fresh Meadows 65, Long Island

Dear Mr. Bailey:

Recently one of our special patrolmen picked up a wheeled
vehicle belonging to you--it had been left out in a public
area apparently through an oversight by some member of your
family.

We recognize that wheeled equipment is an important part
of family life. That is why, when our community was planned,
the architects included special rooms for the convenience of
residents, so that they might store these vehicles when not
in use. It has been estimated that Fresh Meadows families
own a total of 5,500 baby carriages, velocipedes, bicycles,
and other wheel toys. When any of these are left in public
halls, passageways, outside of buildings on paths, sidewalks,
or roads, they not only are a nuisance to other residents who
must walk around them, but more important, they create a real
hazard, for people have been known to trip over them. Such
accidents could result in serious injuries.

In a community like Fresh Meadows it is necessary that
all residents cooperate in the care of vehicles belonging to
their families. Our leases contain a provision concerning
the use and care of such equipment. As you may know, should
one of these vehicles cause an accident, the responsibility
would be the owner's.

Last year it was necessary for us to remove nearly 2,000
baby carriages and assorted wheel toys which were left out.
Because of this demand on our staff, we have found it necessary
to make a service charge of $2 each time equipment is removed
from a public area. No charge, however, is being made to you
for the pick-up this time. But we want you to know that we
will have to make a charge in the future if it is necessary
to perform this service again.

Out of consideration to your neighbors, will you help us
with this problem?

Sincerely yours,

L. W. Schmidt

jc   Superintendent

When the "Customer" Is at Fault

A tactful request for the correction of "customer" oversight and carelessness.

emphasize agreement at the beginning, you soften resentment and put your reader into a receptive mood. The quickest way to get in step with any person is to take the YOU-attitude. Center your thinking around *him*. You can get in step with your customer in the following ways. Use one of them in the first sentence:

1. Thank him for calling attention to the need for adjustment.
2. If the trouble is a serious one, express emphatic regret.
3. Take a sympathetic attitude toward him.
4. If you can grant part of the adjustment, do so at the beginning. This puts the reader into a receptive state of mind.

Which of these openings you will use depends on whether the adjustment must be wholly refused or may be granted in part. To affirm your customer's mood at the beginning is good diplomacy, no matter what you must do with the claim. It helps to establish friendly relations before you give your explanation and decision. "We certainly agree with you," begins a skillful adjustment, "that your shipment should have arrived long before this. We are taking vigorous steps to trace it and will wire you as soon as we have further information."

Affirming your customer's mood does not necessarily mean you will grant his wish. It merely helps to swing into step with him and to secure his confidence. It makes it clear to him that the firm is with him and not against him, that his interests will be guarded, and that fairness will control your final decision.

Once You've Won Good Will, Hang On to It. The following examples offer an instructive contrast in adjusting. Note the effect of each upon your own feelings. Try to visualize the man who writes it and the reaction of the one who receives it.

The first attempt is curt, blunt, tactless, sarcastic, and insulting. In the first sentence it thrusts a hopeless barrier of antagonism between buyer and seller. In the last sentence it takes a superior fling at the customer's ignorance. No effort is made to reclaim good will. Attitude and expression are ill-mannered throughout the message.

HOW TO LOSE A CUSTOMER

Your complaint of June 19 is entirely unjustified, although your dissatisfaction regarding the present state of your roof was not unexpected. We warned you definitely when you asked us to undertake the job that it was risky to try to lay octagonal asbestos half-thicknesses over that type of ridgework. Most of our customers have got onto the fact by this time that they can do better by following our 40 years in the lumber and roofing business than by trying to decide such questions for themselves. The only way we are to blame, as far as we can see, is in allowing ourselves to be guided by what you wanted.

We would suggest that in the future you follow the advice of someone who knows shingles.

The revised message is straightforward, courteous, tactful, genuine, sincere, and helpful. In the first sentence it affirms the customer's mood by stressing points on which there is complete agreement. The explanation that follows is packed with careful detail based upon convincing facts. It stresses positive elements. The closing paragraph, taking the customer's point of view, tactfully suggests the type of product required, makes a special offer with a discount, and suggests favorable action. The tone is sympathetic and courteous. A serious effort is made to reclaim good will.

HERE'S THE WINNING VERSION!

```
        You are 100% right in your belief that your roof has not
given you the service which most of our jobs are known to give.
Our understanding, however, was that you considered durability
to be less essential than low price and quick protection so
we rushed the work through in three days' less time than we
like to take.  Our foreman, you will remember, advised against
using half thicknesses over your type of ridgework.  He himself
did much of the work at the most difficult points.  Frankly,
your roof lasted longer than could well have been expected.

        The "Super-Tough Triple-Strength" is the shingle you need.
To show you that we appreciate your past patronage, we'll quote
you the "Super" at a full 20% discount.  When may we figure
the new job?  Just let us know when you want us to start.  Now,
at the slack season, is an excellent time.
```

How the Experts Solve Adjustment Puzzles

The Case of the Skillful Publisher. After buying a book from a publishing company, a customer claims that it is shelf-worn. He sends an irritable letter announcing that he is going to put the book on his desk with a sign on it telling the public about the kind of merchandise this publishing company foists onto its customers. How would you, as the company's adjuster, handle this situation? Would you assume a lofty air and chastise the customer for losing his temper? Would you humble yourself in a tearful apology, assenting to every slur he has made? Or would you take a sporting attitude, as did the adjuster in the following reply? Note how the executive gets in step with the complainant in the first sentence and vigorously affirms his mood.

"GETTING IN STEP WITH THE CUSTOMER"

Conversational, Sporting Answer

> You certainly have every right to rise up in wrath if that book is only half as bad as you report it to be. In putting it up on your desk with a big sign telling the story about your experience, you are doing the right thing. You are doing it because at the present time you are convinced that people cannot deal with us--without getting "stung."
>
> But as your only wish is to be fair--and we are sure of that--you must also tell on that sign what we did when you called to our attention our failure to give you 100% service.
>
> This is what we are doing: First of all, we are asking the shipping clerk to send a brand-new book, and heaven help him if he doesn't! Then we are going to say this: You can have your money back in addition to the new book, or we will do any other thing you want us to do that will convince you that we are a fairly decent lot of folks in this office.

This reply recaptured the customer's good will. The informal tone, just touched with whimsical humor, gives the impression that the writer is talking to his reader face to face. There shines through the lines the personality of a man who wants to work with others in the spirit of fairness. A few months later the customer called at the firm's offices and met the man who had written. The two became personal friends, and a once-lost customer was won back "for good."

The Department Store's Dangerous Puzzle. Two department store employees have blundered; they have been ill-mannered to a customer. As accredited representatives of the store, they have caused serious damage to the store's good name. Unless the damage is repaired, a valuable customer may be lost. Yet to dismiss the two people may cripple the personnel of the department and may not bring the customer back. How would you solve this puzzle? Here is how one executive handled it:

AN ADJUSTMENT EXECUTIVE SOLVES A "PUZZLER"

Courteous Apology and Action First

> We can't tell you how sorry we are to learn of the discourtesy shown you recently by two of our employees. The matter has been carefully investigated. Let us assure you there will be no further annoyance.
>
> With your fairmindedness we hope you will forgive the two individuals for their conduct. The two have apologized most sincerely. Please do not hold any ill feeling toward them or this organization.

Explanatory Material, Store Policy

> You have helped us greatly by bringing this matter to our attention because it has made it possible for us to guard against this kind of incident. Our hope is always to give service with courtesy. To perfect this system is our aim.
>
> You have placed great confidence in us in the past, if we are to judge by the amount of patronage that you have given us. Will you not overlook this episode and give us an opportunity to make good our policy?

Cordial Selling Close

> Recently a new feature has been added to our shopping helps. Miss Ann Carter, our professional shopper, will give you personal suggestions and assist you in selections. Ask for Miss Carter-- she awaits your request to serve.

It is wise to apologize at the outset when a situation is serious as in this instance. This reply does so. The positive elements of the customer's cooperation and the store's favorable policy are taken up in the third paragraph. Then follows appreciation for past patronage and finally emphasis on an interesting new shopping feature, which draws matters back into the normal channel of cordial relationship.

Using the "Light Touch": A Hint of Humor. Famous in the annals of adjustment is "The Case of Mr. Bannister and the Missing Hotel Blankets." Let us see what happened, and how it all came out. It all began when Mr. Harry Bannister, a former Detroit executive who is now a vice-president of NBC, having finished his business appointments in a neighboring city, checked out of a famous hotel. After his departure the hotel, in the usual routine checking, found that certain room equipment appeared to be missing. Shortly afterward, the following routine "adjustment" request went out to the former guest:

LETTER TO THE HOTEL GUEST REQUESTING AN "ADJUSTMENT"

Diplomacy and Conciliation in a Hotel Adjustment:
An Entertaining Exchange

Upon making the customary room inspection immediately after a guest's departure, our housekeeper reports that two brown woolen blankets, replacement value of $15 each, were missing from the room you occupied.

May we respectfully ask, if these articles are noted when unpacking your luggage, that you return them at once? Guests frequently, we find, in their haste inadvertently place such items in their effects and, of course, return them when discovered.

Allow us also to emphasize our appreciation of your patronage. We trust that we may have the pleasure of serving you often in the future.

Observe the respectful and conciliatory tone, the emphasis on over-sight and inadvertent error, the careful avoidance of even a hint of personal accusation, and the expression of appreciation for past patronage.

Mr. Bannister, somewhat disconcerted at discovering himself to be the object of this type of follow-up, replied in the following way:

THE HOTEL GUEST'S WITTY REPLY

I am desolated to learn, after reading your very tactful letter of November 1, that you actually have guests at your hostelry who are so absent-minded as to check out and include such slight tokens of your esteem as woolen blankets (replace-ment value of $15 each) when packing the other necktie and the soiled shirt.

By the same token, I suppose that passengers on some of our leading railroads are apt to carry off a locomotive or a few hundred feet of rails when disembarking from the choo-choo on reaching their destinations. Or, a visitor to a big city zoo might conceivably take away an elephant or a rhinoceros, concealing one or the other in a sack of peanuts--after remov-ing the nuts (replacement value of $.10).

In this particular case I may be of slight assistance to you in running down the recalcitrant blankets. As I had a lot of baggage with me, I needed all the drawer space you so thought-fully provide in each room. The blankets in question occupied the bottom drawer of the dresser, and I wanted to place some white shirts (replacement value of $5 each) in that drawer so I lifted said blankets and placed them on a chair. Later, the maid came in and I handed the blankets (same blankets and same replacement value) to her, telling her in nice gentlemanly lan-guage to get them the *!!@ out of there.

If you'll count all the blankets in your esteemed estab-lishment, you'll find that all are present or accounted for--unless other absent-minded guests have been accommodated at your emporium in the meanwhile. That's the best I can do.

P. S. Have you counted your elevators lately?

The assistant general manager of the hotel, luckily possessing a sense of humor, took his cue from the tone of the guest and replied in the same manner in the following paragraphs. But note that his careful apology in the last two paragraphs is preceded by four detailed paragraphs of serious explanation outlining a few of the tough administrative problems that give cause for the writing of guest "follow-ups." The qualities of adjustment conciliation and diplomacy appear in the hotel executive's reply in a tone-combination of the light and the serious.

THE HOTEL EXECUTIVE EXPLAINS, APOLOGIZES, AND
WORKS FOR FUTURE PATRONAGE

Thank you for one of the most delightful letters it has been my pleasure to read in my entire business career. My sincere congratulations to you.

> Yes, Mr. Bannister, we do a lot of counting around here. I've counted the elevators--and they're right where they should be, and operating, every one of them. What I want to count now is more important to me. I want to continue counting you as a friend of this hotel.
>
> You, in your executive capacity, must of necessity super- vise numerous counts of cash registers, or of survey figures, or of the like. I shall assume, therefore, that you have real- ized you were most unfortunately a victim of a machinelike routine that is made necessary by the very vastness of an organ- ization like this hotel.
>
> There are a lot of folk in this merry world that would, as you put it, "carry off a locomotive, hundreds of feet of rails, and pack away an elephant or a rhinoceros." Just put a few ash trays, towels, blankets, pillows, glassware, and silverware in your reception rooms and see what happens.
>
> Twenty-five thousand dollars' worth of silverware (actual auditors' replacement value) is carried away annually by our "absent-minded" guests. A similar total ("in replacement value") is cherished annually by sentimental guests who like our linens as a memento of their visits to the hotel. They even go religious on us and take along the Gideon Bibles to the number of several thousand yearly. Nothing is sacred, it would seem.
>
> And so it goes. We are sorry, Mr. Bannister, that you were bothered as a result of a maid's mistake. Her lapse of memory started a giant wheel of routine in motion. In a way, I am happy that the incident happened, because it has given me the chance to read your entertaining letter.
>
> So, as the popular song used to go, "Let's Call the Whole Thing Off." And then there was that other Hit Parade tune I hope you won't forget. It was entitled, "Can't We Be Friends?"

Delightful as is the "light touch" in giving a pleasant change of pace to adjustment management, it takes people with a high order of skill to make successful use of it. Hints of humor help when trouble is around. And, as the foregoing exchange shows, the light touch can lessen trouble when expertly used.

Resale: Rebuilding the Customer's Confidence

Rebuild the Confidence of Unhappy Customers. Customers who ask for adjustments are customers who are disappointed in what they have received. If the fault lies in the article, it may be returned. Or the error may be corrected without having the article returned. But meanwhile the customer's confidence in the article has been shaken. *At this point resale enters.*

An adjustment containing resale material literally "resells" the purchaser what he bought, shows him that he has done the right thing after all, and repaints for him the genuine value of the article or the service ordered. Resale paragraphs in adjustments are designed to refresh the desire to keep the article or continue to use the service, to keep the customer's confidence from being undermined, to prevent his estimate of the value of the article or service from shrinking unjustifiably. Resale material is especially forceful in reclaiming the wavering loyalty of a customer about to be lost.

The Case of Pearsons, Inc. Mr. C. D. Morrow notified Pearsons, Inc., that he was withdrawing his trade, amounting to several hundred dollars a year, as of July 1 because of careless treatment given to an adjustment request made by Mrs. Morrow. Mrs. Morrow had asked that a metal fitting on a recently purchased dressing table be replaced because of a defect that caused it to break a few days after it was put into use. Pearsons, Inc. blundered in handling the matter. There was a long delay. Mr. Morrow then wrote as indicated above.

At this point the situation was placed in the hands of the Adjustment Manager, James Carr. Mr. Carr, a skilled executive to whom the handling of all serious situations was entrusted, wrote as follows:

THE COMPANY WINS BACK A CUSTOMER WITH EXPERT "RESALE"

You are entirely justified in your expression of lack of confidence in our store service.

It appears that when Mrs. Morrow gave the metal piece to the salesman, Mr. Archbold failed to record properly the name and address. When the manager of our furniture department returned without being successful in replacing the broken part, we could do nothing but wait until we should receive a letter from the unknown patron. Mrs. Morrow told us on April 7, much more courteously and patiently than was justified, that we had not taken care of the difficulty.

In the beginning, the buyer of the furniture department took with him this piece of hardware to the Chicago Merchandise Mart and made a sincere effort to replace the broken piece but was unsuccessful; nor could he find anything sufficiently similar to it to be of use to you. When he returned, he made an effort to have a local metal worker repair it by welding but was told that, while it could be done, it would not be a permanent job because of the nature of the metal itself.

We have given you this lengthy explanation because we want you to know that we tried to give you the kind of service you have experienced with us in the past.

Our representative, Mr. Archbold, will call at your office tomorrow and will bring back with him, if you will permit it, the broken fitting, which will be replaced without charge.

More than anything else we regret deeply that you should have been so annoyed by the faulty service of our employees. We shall be grateful to you if you will make to Mrs. Morrow such explanation on our behalf as will erase the disagreeable impression she has received.

So pleased was Mr. Morrow with Mr. Carr's reply that he wrote thus:

MR. MORROW IS HIGHLY PLEASED

```
Your note reached me this morning--and at the same time
your representative, Mr. Archbold, called upon me with refer-
ence to the difficulty we have had in getting the dressing
table hardware piece fixed up.  Mr. Archbold's apologies were
so wholehearted that I was somewhat ashamed of myself for
having written such a stiff letter as I did.  I promised him
I would ask Mrs. Morrow to call upon him when she is next in
Chicago.  The situation has been ironed out.  We're happy.
```

Mr. Carr proved himself an expert adjustment officer. The plan of his reply was first logical, then chronological. Its tone was pleasing and courteous. He chose his material from the records of the transaction, citing facts that had important bearing on what he hoped would be the successful solution for the trouble.

The action he proposed was the correct one in this situation. The store should take the initiative in sending its representative to correct the error. Throughout the paragraphs appear expressions that aim to re-establish in the customer's mind an esteem for the store and a loyalty to it as a place to trade. This is the process of resale which, in adjustments, is so crucially important.

Especially well-chosen are the following expressions:

"You are entirely justified . . ."

"Mrs. Morrow told us . . . much more courteously and patiently than was justified . . ."

". . . we want you to know that we tried to give you the kind of service you have experienced with us in the past."

"Our representative, Mr. Archbold, will call at your office tomorrow and will bring back with him, if you will permit it . . ."

"More than anything else we regret deeply . . ."

"We shall be grateful to you if you will make to Mrs. Morrow such explanation on our behalf as will erase the disagreeable impression she has received."

The Case of the Pressure Valve. A valuable customer of a large plumbing supply firm purchased by mail a pressure valve (to be installed in a basement water heater through the use of a few simple fittings, sent along with the device). But the customer discovers that the fittings do not fit. Something is wrong with the screw threads. He requests new fittings. A correspondent in the adjustment department of the supply firm writes thus:

FIRST DRAFT WOULD LOSE CUSTOMER—BAD TONE, TACTLESS

We have your request concerning the pressure valve #700. You say you are having difficulty with the fittings.

We are at a loss to understand why you should be having this trouble. You must be trying to put the valve on in the wrong place. We are sure that the threads on the fittings you have are all right because they were inspected before they went out. Furthermore, we have sold thousands of these valves, and yours is the first complaint we have had.

Because you think the threads on the fittings are faulty, however, we have decided to send you a new set, which will arrive in due time. We cannot understand why this adjustment should be necessary. We suggest that you be more careful in putting on the new fittings.

This letter is reviewed and held up. The divisional adjuster rewrites it thus:

SECOND DRAFT WOULD HOLD CUSTOMER BUT LACKS RESALE

We have noted your remarks regarding the trouble you have experienced with pressure valve #700. We have sold enormous quantities of these, and yours is the first complaint we have had of this nature regarding the article. We believe, however, the threads on the fittings are not correct. We will therefore send you by parcel post, free of charge, two new fittings which we hope will arrive promptly. We hope that after replacing the fittings you will overcome the difficulty you have been having.

Notice that the second draft avoids the pitfalls of offensive language and tactless expression, but that it leaves the customer uncertain as to the value of the valve and in doubt as to whether he wants to keep it.

The chief adjustment officer writes this third and final draft:

FINAL DRAFT, STRONG IN RESALE

Favorable Action First; Resale
> We are sending you by parcel post, free of charge, two new fittings for pressure valve #700. We are confident that replacing the fittings will overcome the difficulty you report having.

Explanation
> A careful investigation based on the facts submitted causes us to believe that the threads of the fittings are not correct. The remedy we are supplying, we feel sure, will prove effective.

More Resale Material
> Thank you for your explanation. It gives us the opportunity of enabling you to obtain good service from this valve, which thousands of customers have told us they find excellent.

In this version the message is sent, the customer is happy, and the adjustment is completed. Notice the strong resale expressions:

(1) "We are confident that replacing the fittings will overcome the difficulty." (2) "The remedy we are supplying, we feel sure, will prove effective." (3) "It gives us the opportunity of enabling you to obtain good service from this valve, which thousands of customers have told us they find excellent." With every added expression the confidence of the customer mounts higher. The valve now functions as it should. He is sure he wants to keep it.

Most Customers Are Reasonable, If You EXPLAIN What's Causing the Trouble. When trouble arises, people don't like to be kept in the dark. They want to be told what's going on. They want to know what's causing the trouble. Telling them what's causing the trouble is often as valuable to them as a 100 per cent adjustment refund. An example illustrating this fact is the case of the company that got too many orders (on page 402 of this chapter).

Top adjustment experts apply this principle of adjustment every day. "I was in a strange restaurant yesterday, waiting for my luncheon order," writes Sydney J. Harris in his famous column, *Strictly Personal*, "when the waitress came over and said smilingly, 'There's a foul-up in the kitchen. One of the cooks took ill this morning. May I get you a newspaper to read?' With these rare words she won me for life, as I am sure she has won hundreds of friends for her employer over the years. For she understands that impatience thrives on ignorance. Most of us don't mind the trouble itself so much so long as we know what's causing it. It's the feeling of being neglected that breeds dissatisfaction in patrons."

An airline stewardess puts it this way: "Whenever we have a delay, I explain to my passengers exactly why. I make them feel they are sharing in the workings of this organization. It's surprising how this knowledge converts them from angry patrons to members of the team."

Summary: Your Adjustment Guide

The expert adjustment manager, whose professional job is trouble-smoothing, always bears in mind these success-guides:

1. *Analyze each situation for the right solution.* An adjustment is a delicate instrument.
   a. Determine what is best to do in the given situation.
   b. Make a plan.
   c. Choose tactful expressions. The man who complains is sensitive. Choose words to fit the delicate adjustment instrument.

2. *Be genuinely helpful in smoothing out the trouble.* Work for the next order. Many companies adjust generously because of what such policy may mean in future patronage.

3. *Be sure to satisfy as far as satisfaction can be carried*—with justice to both the company and the customer.

4. *Take each request seriously.* To the customer the smallest claim is important. What may seem to the company the tiniest trifle is to the customer perhaps mountainous in importance. Never underestimate.

Your Customers Are Your Friends. Customers are almost always willing to share in the problems of an organization having momentary trouble—*if* they are made to feel that they are an important part of the situation, and that their good will is a valued prize earnestly to be desired and energetically to be protected by the company. Keep them informed. Tell them the facts. Treat them as friends.

Communication Problems

● 1. Assume that you recently purchased a twelve-place setting of W. R. Walker Silver Plate table silver. One knife, you discover, has a small blister in the silvered handle.

Directions: In order to get the knife replaced as quickly as possible, write directly to the manufacturer, W. R. Walker, Inc., Trenton 6, New Jersey. Explain the problem, use persuasive tone, and confidently ask for a replacement of the knife. Mention that you will keep the defective knife until the replacement is received.

● 2. As the adjustment correspondent for W. R. Walker, Inc., answer the adjustment request in Problem 1.

Directions: To assure that requests for adjustments are on purchases made within the one-year guarantee period, your company has established the policy of having all claims submitted through the retail store in which the purchase was made. Therefore, thank the customer for his request, get in step with him, and courteously ask him to request the adjustment through the retail store.

● 3. On October 1 you purchased a new set of Smallwood men's golf clubs from a prominent sporting goods store in your city. While you wanted the clubs very much, you have been in the habit of waiting for sale days to make your purchases. Because the salesman, however, assured you that the clubs would never be marked down, you paid $80 for the set and left the store content with your purchase. It is now November 1, and in reading the store's advertisements for its Midwinter Clearance, you notice that the same clubs are offered for $59.95.

Directions: Write, explaining the situation and requesting an appropriate adjustment. For persuasive tone, emphasize the faith you had in the salesman's word.

● **4.** Now put yourself in the shoes of the manager of the sporting goods mentioned in Problem 3. The customer visits the store frequently and has been a good account. What he says about sale days is true—most of his major purchases were made in off-season sales. Your salesman's information was correct at the time. The manufacturer has come out with a new model, however, featuring a different design. He has suggested to all retailers that they clear out the old clubs for $60 and, in exchange, he will credit the dealer with $20 a set on an equal number of new model orders.

Directions: Write, granting the adjustment. Send the check, review the facts justifying the salesman's statement, and encourage further business.

● **5.** A compact message contains essential material expressed in the fewest words. The letters you write should be "loaded" letters— loaded with the maximum of ideas expressed in minimum words. A concise message is the result of planned thinking and terse writing.

Study in detail the following paragraphs. Determine the essentials; then organize these essentials into a more effective revision. Choose words that are positive in tone. Express your ideas concisely and courteously.

> Your complaint of January 5 is before me in which you claim that the glass goblets you ordered did not arrive on time and that three of them were broken beyond repair has been received and read by me.
>
> It most certainly goes without saying to write and inform you that I am indeed sorry about this particular shipment to you and to readily assure that my company will immediately replace the damaged merchandise that was shipped to you. We don't have to be told to do this. Give us sense enough to know how to satisfy our customers on claims like yours.
>
> I sincerely appreciate and thank you for bringing this matter to my immediate attention, and I hope you will be more than pleased by the fine quality of these imported goblets.

● **6.** As manager of the Northern Electric Appliance Center you receive a visit from an indignant customer. She hands you an electric coffee maker with the explanation that it doesn't work and has been used only for a few days. She also hands you the receipt proving that the appliance was purchased in your store two weeks ago. Because it is a busy sales day and the customer is in a hurry, she asks that you examine the appliance and send her a new one early next week. After she leaves, your repairman examines the appliance and discovers that the electric unit is badly corroded because the base of the maker apparently was washed by immersing it in water. The instructions accompanying the appliance warn against this practice and recommend that the item be cleaned without getting water on the electric unit. Your repairman can install a new unit that will make the appliance as good as new. The cost of this unit to you is $4.50.

Directions: Write to the customer explaining the cause of the difficulty and offer to install a new unit for the $4.50. Ask her to call giving you permission to go ahead with the replacement.

● 7. *The Case:* You have had the following trouble. It's June—and in June a year ago, you had a Cleburne, Texas, distributor install a Polar Queen air conditioner in your car. During the first week you discovered the air conditioner would not put out cold air after a few minutes' driving. Of course, you took your car back to the garage and told the seller about the difficulty. He assured you he corrected the trouble. But he did not. So, for a year, at intervals you have been going through the same procedure—you explain to the seller there is something wrong with the air conditioner; he works on it and assures you once more he has the trouble corrected.

You are not interested in going through another Southwest summer with a defective air conditioner, but you hesitate to return any more to the seller. He is by now implying through his looks and actions that he thinks there is something wrong with you and not the air conditioner. However, he continues to be courteous and anxious to please. You have no idea what the trouble is. You may have bought a "lemon," or it may be the seller simply has not located the fault, even though you figure he has had ample opportunity to make correction. And so far as you know, he has not road tested the car a single time he has had it in his shop.

The Polar Queen manufacturer is located in Fort Worth, about twenty-five miles from Cleburne. You decide to write to the manufacturer to ask what he suggests that you do. Should your car be brought to Fort Worth to have the air conditioner inspected? If so, should you bring it or would they prefer that the distributor bring it? When would they want the car brought over? Would they prefer to send a representative to Cleburne to work in conjunction with the local distributor?

You feel the problem of any loss involved is between the seller and the manufacturer, since you began asking for correction long before the 90-day warranty expired.

● 8. Reply to the inquiry about your air conditioner (Problem 7). The company will have a representative in Cleburne within the next week or two. The distributor will call you when the representative arrives, probably about the middle of the afternoon. It's likely they will want to keep your car at least the early part of the night to allow plenty of time to locate the trouble. Of course, there is no doubt they can correct the difficulty; and you will have a cool summer driving in the Southwest heat.

PART VII

Chapter 18   Enjoying the Credit Privilege

How's Your Credit? The scene is a famous jewelry store of a large American city. The customer, a man of medium height, age about 45, stands at a counter carefully selecting a jewel-studded pin as a 20th-wedding-anniversary present.

"Could you charge this for me?" he asks.

"I think we can," replies the sales clerk. "Won't you fill out this form, and while your pin is being carefully checked and inspected, we'll take care of the details." A few moments later the clerk returns with the jeweled pin in a small velvet case. "Would you like it wrapped as a gift?" he asks.

"You mean I can take it with me right now? But you don't know much about me."

"Perhaps we know more about you than you think. Have a most happy anniversary!"

The Credit Bureaus Know about You. The credit bureaus know all about you—or they soon will. What had happened while the customer waited? Swift events took place. The store had telephoned the city's central Credit Bureau. The signal light flashed along the top of a row of files. Through her headphones the file-girl heard the man's name, jotted it down, drew open the proper file drawer, pulled out the customer's record.

Here's what she found and reported over the telephone: "Home; prompt, five houses; stable." What did that mean? Translated, it meant that (1) the customer owns his own home, (2) he has credit accounts, *promptly paid*, with five stores, and (3) he is considered a man of dependability. Within minutes the jewelry store has learned —while the customer waited for his pin to be polished—that he is a safe charge customer for any reasonable amount.

How Credit Management Does Its Work. The Associated Credit Bureaus of America, with more than 1,700 member bureaus, maintain more than one hundred million credit records—including yours. Because these 1,700 credit bureaus are constantly flashing back and forth swift exchanges of information, your credit rating will follow you all your life, wherever you go.

One credit bureau alone, in a large metropolitan area, maintains records on more than 3,000,000 individuals and firms and answers more than 40,000 credit inquiries each month.

How Is Credit Information Put to Work? What are some of the ways in which credit information is used? The most important obvious way is to answer the main questions, "Are you a dependable person?" "Do you have integrity?" "Do you honor your obligations?" "Is it safe to extend credit to you, to let you 'charge it'?" Or, to put it in the bluntest possible form, *"Do you pay your bills, and do you pay them promptly?"* But there are other ways in which credit information is used. Professional, business, fraternal, and club organizations often consider credit-bureau ratings in judging a candidate's membership application. You want to rent an apartment? Don't be surprised if the apartment owner first gets a rating on you. You want to get a new job? Be prepared to have your prospective employer look up your credit record before he seriously considers you. Remember that many credit bureaus now offer ability-and-character reports as a part of their extended service. You want to marry the girl? Don't be surprised if her parents check your credit record as one reflection of your industry, your stability, your general capacity to manage your affairs.

Where Does Credit Management Get Its Facts? When you apply for credit, you are normally asked to fill out a credit application form. From this form credit bureaus draw their basic information about your age, parents, the schools you have attended, the jobs you have held, and the length of time you have spent in each job. Other vital information comes from former employers, from high school and college records, from vital-statistics bureaus, from fraternal groups or clubs, from the corner druggist, from news items about you that may bear in any way upon your credit, your character, or your integrity; finally, even from court records. There is little that escapes the attention of an alert credit management.

Credit Is a Valuable Privilege. If you can go to your bank, ask for credit, and get it, your bank is really saying, "You're OK—we believe in you." The word *credit* comes from the Latin word *credo*

LANZ
OF CALIFORNIA, INC.

6150 WILSHIRE BOULEVARD · LOS ANGELES 48, CALIFORNIA · Telephone: WEBSTER 3-9541

April 18, 19--

Mrs. R. L. Ratcliffe
514 Avondale Avenue
Los Angeles 49, California

Dear Mrs. Ratcliffe

We welcome you most heartily as a new LANZ charge customer. You will enjoy buying our original styles in the friendly atmosphere of LANZ.

Your charge account is now ready for your use at all our LANZ stores, and you will find it a convenience and a pleasure.

Come in soon, come often, and just say: "Charge it!"

Cordially

Edward L. Eyster
Edward L. Eyster
Credit Manager

ck

SHERATON CORPORATION
OF AMERICA
SHERATON BUILDING
470 ATLANTIC AVE., BOSTON 10, MASS.

Phone HUbbard 2-4250

ERNEST HENDERSON
President
ROBERT L. MOORE
Treasurer
GEORGE K HENDERSON
Vice President
PAUL BROWNE
Vice President

Here Is Your 19--
Sheraton Credit Card

May I suggest that you remove it from the glassine envelope and sign it now?

I think you'll find your Sheraton Credit Card a real advantage. For, not only does it entitle you to credit privileges in all Sheraton Hotels, but also in many other hotels and stores - as explained in the enclosed folder.

19-
Sheraton Hotels

SPECIAL CREDIT AND RESERVATION PRIVILEGES AND MEMBERSHIP IN
SHERATON DINING CLUB TO.

1 9 0 A 5 4 9

SIGNATURE:

CHAIRMAN OF THE BOARD

In addition, the card is useful as a means of identification when cashing checks, or for other purposes. And, of course, it has a certain prestige value, since it is representative of one of the largest hotel groups in the world. There are now 31 Sheraton Hotels coast-to-coast in the United States and Canada.

Mr. A. Pendery
1201 Markbreit Avenue
Cincinnati 9, Ohio

Accommodations in each of these hotels conform to the highest standards in hospitality and comfort. And with Sheraton's nationwide Teletype Reservations Service, you can have confirmed space in any - or several - of these hotels in a matter of minutes, at no cost to you.

Wherever business or vacation travel takes you in the United States or Canada, plan to stay at a Sheraton Hotel. I'm certain you'll find the accommodations, the food, and the friendly service second to none. And please make full use of your credit privileges. Your card is a Sheraton service and we want you to benefit from it.

Cordially,

Ernest Henderson
Ernest Henderson
President

EH/dr
Enclosure

meaning "I believe." If you are a store manager and can go to your wholesale supplier, ask for a line of credit, and get it, your wholesale supplier is really saying, "You're OK—I believe in you." Any individual or organization that extends credit is really saying, "I'm betting on this customer. I believe in his dependability. I'm betting that he'll be able and willing to pay for this order promptly when the payment comes due."

"You Can Have the Goods Now. Pay for Them Later." Credit is the privilege of getting the goods now and paying for them later. This privilege is valuable because it means that you can buy without putting cash "on the line." Credit is the company's faith, belief, and confidence in your ability to pay for goods within a specified time after they have been delivered. The specified time is usually 30 days; but it may be 60 days, 90 days, or longer according to the character of the business. Since sooner or later 98 per cent of all bills are paid, according to the seasoned opinion of credit experts basing their conclusions on the figures of normal periods, the American credit system is sound.

Credit Demand Rises and Falls. Demand for credit is sensitively related to the economic outlook, which in turn generates "business sentiment." The term "business sentiment" means "how you feel about your business this morning when you come down to unlock the doors." Business sentiment is largely psychological. It has been known to change overnight with violent abruptness. Fragile though it is, both business and the demand for credit rest upon it.

Credit Multiplies Business Volume. You may ask, "Why not do all our business on a cash basis? Credit extension is pretty costly." Here is the answer: The extension of credit multiplies the volume of business that can be done with a given amount of cash. Suppose that a merchant has $2,000 to use in stocking one department of his store. The markup (the difference between the wholesale price and the retail price) on the goods is 25 per cent, which will cover his cost of doing business and leave him a net profit. (The markup in this illustration is figured on cost, for the sake of simplicity. The modern method, and the better one, for figuring markup is to base it on the selling price.) He buys these goods from the wholesaler on terms of 2/10, net 30, meaning 2 per cent discount for payment within 10 days, the net amount due at the end of 30 days. Through good management the merchant sells these goods at retail prices in 25 days and therefore takes in a total of $2,500. But, as the net amount is not due the wholesaler until 30 days after the date of purchase, the merchant does not have to pay until the expiration of 5 more days. In short, he has made his profit without spending a single dollar of his own capital. In the meantime he has had this $2,000 of capital available for active use in a hundred other ways. But remember that he usually has to have the cash capital before he can get the credit. The possession of the capital simply *multiplies*, through additional credit, the amount of business the merchant can enjoy. Credit vastly expands our annual business volume.

Taking the Discount. The most efficient merchants take their discounts as a matter of good management. Under terms of 2/10, for example, they pay a bill within ten days from the date of purchase. They are then privileged to deduct 2 per cent from the amount of the bill and to remit the balance. They are credited with payment in full. Thus they make money (by saving it) besides the normal margin on the retail sale of the goods. A man who discounts his bills is never subject to collection pressure because he is never delinquent. He belongs to the gilt-edge credit group.

Potential Credit and Actual Credit. Credit is far more important than all the cash, silver, and currency in this country, rolled into one sum. Credit falls into two important phases: (1) potential credit and (2) actual credit.

Potential Credit. Potential credit is the power to obtain present goods (or services, or money) in exchange for a promise to render a future payment. This power rests in the prospective purchaser or borrower, is based upon his character, capital, and capacity, and is sensitively influenced by business conditions. The amount of "potential" credit the applicant actually possesses depends not only upon his willingness and ability to pay but also on the length of the credit terms he has been allowed.

Actual Credit. Actual credit is created as potential credit is used. For example, suppose that the manager of credit sales finds that the customer's income is considerably larger than the sum of his obligations and he therefore possesses potential credit, or the power to secure goods by promising to pay for them in the future. The manager now allows him to charge $75 worth of goods. Seventy-five dollars of actual credit has been created by this transaction, and the customer's potential credit has been for the time being lessened to the extent of $75. This sum of actual credit, viewed through the customer's eyes, is a debt and an obligation to pay. Looked at through the merchant's eyes, it is an asset on the account books and a right to demand payment.

To appraise a customer's potential credit, take into account the actual credit he is already using. If the customer has involved himself in too much actual credit or outstanding debt, he may have little or no potential credit left. Clearly the manager of credit sales, in controlling collections, must be concerned with the actual credit or outstanding debt of his customer. When faulty credit control allows goods to be sold on credit to people who have *exhausted all of their potential credit,* the so-called "credit" thus extended by the merchant is pure fiction. The buyer, whose use of actual credit has reduced and finally exhausted his potential credit, will not be able to redeem his promise: a promise to pay in future for goods secured in the present.

The cycle of credit is:

Potential Credit ⟶ Actual Credit ⟶ Potential Credit
converted into   *and reconverted into*   *once again.*

The potential goes into actual and back into potential credit as the indebtedness is paid off.*

The Power to Buy Without Paying Cash. We have pointed out that credit represents the customer's power to buy without paying cash. The credit officer determines whether the customer really has this power or only an imitation of it. Here, for example, is R. G. Firestone, who carries on a profitable department store business in a city with a population of 150,000. He has just erected an ultramodern twelve-story building. Investigation shows him to have adequate capital, a satisfactory stock turnover, sound policies of markup and markdown, and up-to-the-minute systems of stock control. He shows an impressive record of buying merchandise wisely and in large quantities. In a recent year he has done a business volume of $7,000,000. Does Mr. Firestone really possess the power to buy without paying cash? There can be no doubt about it. The credit man of the wholesale house recognizes Mr. Firestone's ability to pay within 30 days or 60 days. He approves the application.

* An excellent development of this concept of the cycle of credit appears in C. W. Phelps, *Retail Credit Fundamentals* (St. Louis: National Retail Credit Association), Chapter I, "Credit As a Business Force."

This Credit Information Form Takes the Place
of a Personally Dictated $1.50 Message

A Department Store Welcomes a Convention Visitor
and Encloses a Credit Card for His Convenience

SMART SHOES, INC.

914-924 TENTH STREET

OMAHA • • NEBRASKA

March 26, 19--

Citizens National Bank
732-738 Racine Street
Topeka, Kansas

Gentlemen:

We shall appreciate information regarding the integrity, responsibility, capital, and promptness of

Mrs. Lee Rowe, 567 Maple Drive

For this information, thank you. Enclosed is a self-addressed, stamped envelope for your answer.

C. A. Johns
Credit Manager

Please reply on this sheet

Credit information on: Mrs. Lee Rowe, 567 Maple Drive

We have the following credit information with which we are glad to supply you: Integrity and responsibility are

A-1. Capital is adequate.

FOR PURPOSES OF IDENTIFICATION, PLEASE SIGN THIS SHEET BEFORE YOU RETURN IT.

Harvey Nichols
Vice President

The HIGBEE Co.

PUBLIC SQUARE
CLEVELAND 13, OHIO

TELEPHONE
CHERRY 1-4000

March 25, 19--

Dear Mr. Templeman:

The Higbee Company department store joins with all Cleveland in extending to you a warm welcome as a visitor to the convention of the American Association of School Administrators.

We believe our store can help you get greater pleasure from your visit. We are conveniently located on Cleveland's Public Square. In addition to the usual departments that you find in a new modern department store, we devote our 10th Floor exclusively to hospitality for visitors. There you will find modern restaurant facilities and attendants who will be pleased to help you. Here also are private dining rooms, a Lounge and Auditorium having an aggregate seating capacity of upwards of 1,200 people, all of which are made available, without cost, to private groups upon application.

For your greater convenience we are enclosing a Higbee credit card. You or any member of your family whom you authorize may charge purchases made in our store by your signing and filling out this card and presenting it at time of purchase.

Cordially yours,

John P. Murphy
President

JPM:fh

Enclosure

The HIGBEE Co.

Cleveland, Ohio

Charge Account Identification

issued to

Charles F. Templeman

Street ....

City .... State ....

Valid during the 19-- Convention of the American Association of School Administrators.

Signature ....

Good only when signed by authorized purchaser.

I authorize the following persons to use my account:

....
....

Character, Capital, and Capacity. An account wisely opened is a collection half made. The credit man appraises every application for three factors:

1. *Has the applicant* CHARACTER? Is his record that of a man who is steady and dependable? Does it indicate integrity in the man behind it? In negotiations with others does the applicant show a sense of obligation? Is he honest, straightforward, aboveboard in his business dealings?

2. *Has the applicant* CAPITAL? Does he have enough money in his business to "turn around on"? Is he, in other words, adequately capitalized? What is the present ratio of his assets to his liabilities? of his assets quickly convertible into cash (quick assets) to his liabilities that must be met in the near future? What is his general financial status?

3. *Has the applicant* CAPACITY? Does his record show that he can carry on a successful business, that he has a business head? Is he making progress or losing ground? Has he chosen his location well? Has he chosen a business in which there are expanding opportunities? In general, does he show an aptitude for management and good judgment in meeting business situations?

Character the Most Important. Of the three credit C's, the most important is character. R. G. Firestone, owner of the department store mentioned on page 426, shows dependable character in his record of achievements. He meets his obligations promptly. He takes his discounts. He has a reputation for fairness. The figures show his capital to be adequate. Finally, his capacity is proved by his efficient management and by the growth of his business.

A famous financier, internationally known as one of the shrewdest men of his time, and an outstanding figure in his generation, was a relentless judge of character when it came to extending credit. His name was J. P. Morgan. The following excerpt throws a revealing light on the credit philosophy of the man who lent more money than anyone before him.

> Questioned before a Congressional Committee, J. P. Morgan commented, "I have known a man to come into my office, and I have given him a check for $1,000,000. And I knew that he had not a cent in the world." The Congressional questioning goes on:
>
> Question: "There were not many of them?"
> Answer: "Yes, a good many."
>
> Question: "Commercial credits are based upon the possession of money or property?"
> Answer: "No, sir; the first thing is *character*."
>
> Question: "Before money or property?"
> Answer: "Before money or anything else. Money cannot buy it."

Question: "So that a man with character, without anything at all behind it, can get all the credit he wants, and a man with property cannot get it?"

Answer: "That is very often the case."

Question: "But is that the rule of business?"

Answer: "That is the rule of business, sir."

Investigating Credit. A credit account may be opened in several ways. The customer may request credit in a letter. He may request it with his first order. He may simply send in the first order and leave the credit decision to the company. Or a merchant buying on a cash basis may show promising growth, and the wholesaler may offer him credit. No matter what the method, credit is granted only after investigation. In requesting information from the customer, emphasize that the facts requested form a part of the uniform requirements and routine procedure for extending credit. This statement avoids the suggestion that the customer's financial standing is in question.

Useful Credit-Information Guide

Credit information needed varies somewhat according to the type of business, but in general it should include the following:

1. How long have you known the customer?
2. Does he attend to business?
3. How good is his location?
4. What kind of progress is he making?
5. What is his competition?
6. How does his management compare with his competitor's?
7. Does he own real estate? What is his degree of ownership (equity)?
8. Has he ever been in financial trouble?
9. How do the local bankers rate him?
10. What does his whole record show?

The following message went to a retail customer who had asked to open a charge account.

REQUESTING CREDIT INFORMATION

Thank you for your note asking us to open a charge account for you. We enjoy having you as our customer.

In order to establish your charge account, we need certain references and information as a matter of customary credit routine. In your answer will you please include the name of the bank with which you do business, and the names and the addresses of two persons in the city to whom we may refer? From the length of time we have enjoyed your patronage, we judge that you have been for several years a resident of Auburn. Have you charge accounts at other department stores?

Coming in this week are some attractive patterns in table linen of the same quality as the piece you were considering on Friday when you asked about credit. Perhaps you will want to see them.

The following message handles the case of a customer about whom certain favorable information is available—enough, in fact, to warrant the extension of credit—but not enough to complete the records.

ASKING FOR ADDITIONAL CREDIT INFORMATION

Thank you for the opportunity you have given us to show the service we are prepared to offer. Your name now appears on our list of credit customers.

Your return of the enclosed card will supplement information from various agencies and will tell us of your interests and desires so that we can serve you more promptly. We look forward to a pleasant business association and to many future satisfactory transactions. Consider us at your service.

An eastern distributor writes to a manufacturing firm in Minneapolis, Minnesota, for information on the credit standing of a Minneapolis retailer. The retailer has given the Minneapolis manufacturer as a reference.

ONE FIRM WRITES ANOTHER, ASKING FOR
CREDIT INFORMATION ON A RETAILER

Please give us confidentially the credit standing of Mr. Lawrence T. Hooper, 3210 National Avenue, Minneapolis 12, Minnesota.

Is he a satisfactory credit risk? Is he prospering? Or is he slipping? Information on this man's character, capital, capacity, and methods of meeting his obligations will be appreciated. Enclosed for your convenience in reply is a stamped return envelope.

Between manufacturers, distributors, and similar firms, forms for securing credit information are in common use. The form illustrated on page 427 provides blank spaces in which may be inserted the desired data for credit inquiry and reply.

Granting Credit. A message granting credit follows the same plan as a message granting a favor (see pages 215-216).

When You Grant Credit:	1. Extend credit courteously.
	2. Express your wish for cordial relations.
	3. Refer to the value of the credit privilege (a commercial advantage to the businessman, or a convenience to the retail customer).

Many retail organizations simply send a printed card to welcome a new credit customer. Credit-granting announcement cards are illustrated on page 431.

1

Marshall Field & Company

CREDIT AND
COLLECTION DEPARTMENT

111 NORTH STATE STREET · CHICAGO 90
Telephone Fine 1·1000

February 17, 19--

Mrs. Donald P. Dihlmeier
3740 Brotherton Road
Chicago 8, Illinois

Dear Mrs. Dihlmeier:

Thank you for your recent letter.

Unfortunately we are unable to locate an account in the
name shown above. Perhaps it has been removed from
our files because of inactivity.

If you are interested in an account with us, please fill
in the enclosed application and return it in the envelope
provided. As soon as it is received, the information
will have our prompt attention.

We look forward to hearing from you.

Cordially yours,

M. L. Socha

MLS:nbs
Enclosures 2

Application for Charge Account

| mr. | | |
| mrs. | first name of husband, if married | initial | last name |

| address | | |
| city | zone | state | phone |

			wife's first name
			how long own ( )
			rent ( )

previous address
(if less than three years at present address, please show previous address)

name of business
or employer
if married, husband's employer

business or
employer's address.   position

if less than three years, please show
previous employment and address.   income

wife's employer
name

	address
	checking ( )
	special ( )
	checking savings ( )

name of bank

I have credit
plans with   Stevens's □   Mandel's □   Carson's □   Fair □
other stores with
whom I have accounts.

authorized buyers.

personal references.
use reverse side if necessary
state relationship

I agree to pay in full within fifteen days after date of statement

signature.   date

It is our policy to keep accounts open only if yearly purchases amount to $100 or more

Marshall Field & Company

2

𝒯 h a n k   y o u ...

for your new charge account
which is now open and
ready for your use at any of
our seven stores—san francisco,
oakland, san mateo, palo alto,
sacramento downtown, town &
country village—sacramento, reno.

joseph magnin
JM

3

GUMP'S

It is indeed a pleasure to
welcome you as a charge customer.

Your account has been
opened and we hope that there
will be many occasions for you
to enjoy its conveniences.

You may be assured that
everything will be done to make
your shopping with us both
pleasant and advantageous.

S. & G. GUMP COMPANY

(I) A Credit Officer Invites a New Credit Account by Enclosing an Application; (2) A Novel Card
Acknowledgment of Credit; (3) A Formal Announcement Card Granting Credit

Refusing Credit. A message refusing credit follows the same plan as a message refusing a favor (see pages 216-221). To refuse credit and still make a friend is one of the acid tests of a good credit officer. This is how he does it.

*When You
Refuse Credit:*

1. Thank your customer for his order, for his information and references, and for his cooperation.
2. Explain the situation, mentioning first the favorable factors, then the less favorable ones.
3. Suggest as a temporary solution that dealings be undertaken on a cash basis. Offer full cooperation toward reaching a satisfactory future credit basis.

Messages granting and refusing credit to retail customers are usually simple and brief. Of course they should always be cordial.

REFUSING CREDIT TO A RETAIL CUSTOMER

Thank you for the compliment you pay us in expressing your interest in our store. Your wish to become one of our charge customers is deeply appreciated. You may be sure that your credit application has been carefully considered. While at this time we cannot comply with the request, we are confident that, as matters develop, your situation may become generally more favorable for credit consideration.

As conditions change, it is quite possible that we may be able to take up this matter with you again. In the meantime we cordially invite you to let us serve you on a cash basis.

In the following message the writer refuses credit. But in doing so, he makes every effort to capture the good will of the prospective customer.

REFUSING CREDIT TO A BUSINESSMAN

Thank you for your order of May 21 and for your courtesy in enclosing credit information, your business statement, and references, all of which have been examined with care.

It should please you to learn that we have gathered complimentary comments about your personal character and ability, showing that you have developed an enviable reputation among those with whom you have done business. Our study of your balance sheet reveals, however, certain aspects that in our judgment might easily endanger your entire financial position. The ratio of assets to liabilities shows you to be at the moment undercapitalized. You need additional capital. This should not be difficult to get in view of the favorable business opportunities promised by your present location. We suggest as satisfactory a capital addition of $7,500.

You have our assurance that we shall cooperate to the fullest extent in any way that may lead to a satisfactory future credit basis. Meanwhile we'll be glad to take care of your current needs with our most favorable cash terms. You will, we think, find this arrangement satisfactory for the present and a good basis for becoming better acquainted.

As soon as we have your favorable answer, our first shipment will go to you at once.

The Art of Saying NO. "An executive of a large New York firm has a unique collection of letters," reports the New York Life Insurance Company, "each handsomely mounted in a leather album that he keeps close at hand as he runs through his mail each morning. Each item in the growing collection is a testimonial to his exceptional talent: his extraordinary skill in saying NO *and making a friend while he says it!*"

His "fan mail" was written to him in response to "turn-downs" he wrote for his company. These turn-downs took the form of *refusals* to extend credit, to grant discounts, to make adjustments, to contribute to causes not approved by company policy, or to lengthen contract terms under circumstances that made it clearly unwise to do so. Each of his original messages denied a request. Yet somehow each captured the good will of its reader. Here, as reported by the New York Life Insurance Company, are a few typical replies in his "fan-mail" collection:

> My first reaction when I read your refusal [of a discount] was to ride off in a cloud of dust and take my business somewhere else. But since thinking it over, I have decided to place my order with you anyway. You can credit for this the staff of psychologists you hire to write for you.

> No one has ever said NO to me before and made me like it!

> If more people would write as you do, there would be a lot less criticism directed toward the large corporations.

> You made your reasons for refusal very clear and understandable. Another business house might merely have said NO and let it go at that. But you went out of your way to clarify the circumstances. Thank you for having taken the trouble to do so.

How Do the Experts "Say NO and Make Him Like It"? Experts in credits, adjustments, and human relations in general have learned to say NO in certain carefully planned ways. Here is what they suggest:

1. Instead of saying NO, *say YES to something else.* Whenever you can offer an alternative, do so. And do it at the outset. Give him something positive to think about. Put your accent on what you *can* do.

2. Explain, with straightforward frankness, the reason for the refusal, if the reason is not confidential. Give your explanation in simple TALK-language. Don't beat around the proverbial bush. Say it—simply. If the reason is confidential, then stress, carefully, that his request has been painstakingly and deliberately considered—that it has not been dismissed offhand.

3. Let courtesy, considerateness, and your customer's interest shine through your words.

Helping Customers to Protect Their Credit Privilege. Every message from the credit office may carry information on the value of credit, the importance of building up a credit reputation, of paying promptly, of discounting bills, and of watching for chances to save.

Customers whose minds have been impressed with the importance of credit are inclined to treat obligations seriously and to value their credit privilege at its true level. The following statement is an excellent example of credit education:

Keeping Behind to Keep Up a Front

One of the most foolish and inexcusable of all human practices is that of making a false display on other people's money.

A man who still owes his tailor a balance on the bill for his last season's suit is dickering with an automobile salesman for a greater trade-in allowance on a more expensive car.

A hostess who has not sent her caterer a check since the month before last is entertaining lavishly in an effort to outdo one of her guests, whose affair of the other night was the talk of her set.

A young man with the habit of "forgetting his bills" manages to have money to lavish on his lady friends.

Mrs. A of unlimited means buys an expensive gown. She *can* afford it. Her neighbor, Mrs. X, decides she must have a gown just as expensive as Mrs. A's. She *cannot* afford it. But, with more envy in her heart than money in her purse and with still less credit, she buys the gown anyway.

Such people are keeping up a front socially by the unfair means of keeping behind financially. Sooner or later will come the reckoning. Credit —instituted as a convenience and founded upon man's faith in his fellowmen—is all too frequently abused as a result of our common desire to "keep up a front."

No one can long maintain a $700 pace on a $500 income.

Let us continue to use credit, but only as it *should* be used. Let us be sure our incomes are equal to our promises.

A famous business house prints on one side of its collection slips the items of credit education on page 435.

WHO IS IN THE WHO'S WHO OF CREDIT?

Not all of us have our names recorded in *Who's Who in America* or the Social Register, but all of us, whether in high or low estate, are cataloged in the who's who of credit—the records of the Retail Credit Bureau.

Here on a little card is kept the life history of your credit record—of how you meet your obligations or *of how you don't.*

PROTECT YOUR CREDIT!

No one can protect your credit but you. No one else can destroy it, for, always, your credit is what you make it. Your credit is one of your greatest assets. It deserves your highest protection. Keep your credit record clear!

Make Your Credit Messages "Sell." The credit message may be equally effective as a valuable sales message. It sells the privilege of credit. It offers good will and business cooperation. It offers friendship. Whether the credit application is granted or refused, the keynote is helpfulness.

Below is an example of credit education and promotion combined in one message. The situation is this: A large bank carries a customer for some time on a character loan, that is, a loan without collateral. This customer at present does only a minimum of his business at the bank. In fairness to others who bring in profitable business and who also need loans from time to time, the vice president feels that this particular customer should give more of his business to the bank in return for the loan privilege. With the closer contact thus made possible, the bank can keep all credit information fresh and up to date. Note how the executive first emphasizes the value of credit and then, by an easy transition, turns to his concrete proposal of opening a savings or a checking account.

COMBINATION CREDIT AND PROMOTION

It has been a pleasure to us to extend our credit to you for some time past, through a personal loan.

In these days of modern living, credit has become a valuable article, highly prized, much sought after. As you know, it is granted only to those who warrant our extending it to them because of their character, their capacity, and, above all, because of what we know about their financial ability and personal status. The more we know about a patron, the more soundly we can appraise his credit advantages.

Now, we should like to get better acquainted with you. We should like to see you come into this bank oftener. What we suggest is that you open a savings or checking account with us. We should like to see you maintain a balance with us that

will more fully justify your loan and that will strengthen
your personal credit.

Why not take this action today? If you will, we think
we can assure you a continuation of your loan under its present terms, even though the demand for credit is steadily
increasing among those already our customers in our other
departments. Please come in soon.

Credit Matters Can Be Personal and Pleasant. Forgetting that
the customer wants to be an individual, not a statistic, some persons
fall into the bad habit of quoting voluminously from "our records."
The following sentences are typical:

THE "OUR RECORDS" TECHNIQUE—INFERIOR, IMPERSONAL

Our records indicate the renewed use of your charge account.

We note from our records that you are a good credit customer.

Consulting our records, we find you have had an account with
us for many years.

The quickest way to reduce your customer to a "statistic," to an
impersonal nameless unit, is to make him a mere matter of "our
records." Like every normal human being, he would like to be thought
important enough to be something other than a routine record-entry.
Although your records are naturally the source of most information
about him, don't remind him of that fact, particularly in messages
that thank him for his patronage or for his fine credit reputation.
What a far more favorable impression you would make if you wrote:

CORDIAL AND PERSONAL

Thank you very much for your loyal patronage for the
past ten years.

It pleases us greatly that you have begun to use your
charge account again.

We appreciate the promptness with which you regularly
pay your account.

Keep "your records" in the background. Use the human touch.
Give each customer cordial recognition as an important individual.

The Bond of Faith. "I Believe" binds the world together. It
draws all its value and power from faith in others. In the world of
financial management credit is built on belief that others will live up
to their promises. The aim of the credit manager is to see that these
promises are punctually kept. Only when obligations are defaulted
does collection pressure begin. In the next two chapters we take up
the subject of collection management.

Communication Problems

● **1.** As Public Relations Director of the Western Savings and Loan Association, you are to prepare promotional materials to be sent to new homeowners in the community. Account holders use your firm as a credit reference, and you are frequently used as a credit source by the local Retail Credit Association. Your firm pays 4% interest on savings accounts and issues a preferred credit card with each account over $250. Your save-by-mail plan is a customer service.

Directions: Prepare a form message to be sent to all new homeowners in your community. Enclose the credit card which will be countersigned when the account is opened. Stress the advantages of credit standing in a new community.

● **2.** As Credit Manager of the Automotive Parts Manufacturing Company, you receive a $347 order for spark plugs, batteries, fan belts, and brake linings from Mr. Robert T. Tyre, Manager of Bob's Service, 698 Magnolia Street, Atlanta 6, Georgia. The routine credit inquiries reveal that Mr. Tyre is relatively new in Atlanta, his financial condition is adequate, and he has a "good-pay" credit reputation. Based on the size of his accounts payable, however, you decide that he cannot purchase more than $400 worth of parts from you in any one credit period of sixty days. Your terms are 2/10, net 60.

Directions: Write the message accompanying the shipment to Mr. Tyre. Open his credit account, but be sure to mention the credit limit. In order to encourage prompt payment, interpret his discount by indicating the exact amount of his possible discount saving and assure him of your desire to serve him.

● **3.** Eugene Baty, proprietor of the Mountain Radio-TV Service, for many years a customer of the Arnold Wholesale Electronics Corporation, always discounted his bills with the Arnold Corporation until a year ago. At that time he began to take the full credit period. During the past few months his bills have finally been paid, although the payment has been delayed well beyond the due date—from thirty to ninety days. He now has an unpaid balance of $200 in his account.

A new superhighway is being constructed to replace the street on which Mr. Baty's business fronted. Construction has made access to his property difficult. As a result, his business has declined. As Credit Manager of the Arnold Corporation, you are now considering an additional order from him. The only move available for you is to notify Mr. Baty that it will be necessary for him to pay cash for his purchases until all of his accumulated bills are paid.

Directions: Prepare the reply that should be sent.

● **4.** Shortly after writing Mr. Baty (Problem 3), you receive a credit inquiry about him from Western Electronics Supply Company. He has listed you as a firm with whom he has carried an account. The inquiry reads:

> Mr. Eugene Baty, owner of the Mountain Radio-TV Service, has applied to us for credit and has given your firm as a current supplier. Can you give us the benefit of your experience with the

firm? Is it financially strong? What are its paying habits? Any information you give us will, of course, be held strictly confidential. Simply write in the space at the bottom of this page.

Directions: Based on the information you have, prepare the comments to answer the credit inquiry.

● **5.** You are the Credit Manager of the Bali-Hi Swimsuit Company of Los Angeles, California, which sells to retail stores throughout the country. Many retailers misuse your discount privilege terms 2/10, net 30, by paying after the ten-day discount period and still deducting the discount. In an effort to eliminate much of this problem, you have decided to attach a printed note to the first invoice sent to each new retail outlet informing them that the 2 per cent discount period is ten days from the first day of the month following the purchase date. You want to make it clear that the discount privilege is extended to encourage prompt payment.

Directions: (a) Prepare a notice of not more than fifty words that can be attached to the first invoice to all new accounts.

(b) Prepare a form letter that can be used to discourage persistent violators of the discount privilege. Ask that the firm inform its bookkeeping department of your terms.

● **6.** Assume that your new home has recently burned. You lost everything. In looking for furniture replacements, you have seen a bedroom suite at A. J. Ericksen and Company in a nearby city that you want very badly. You learned that Ericksen's credit policy limits their granting credit to only those people with credit references. Since you were always able to pay cash before the fire, you have no references.

You look for a similar suite at other stores, but the one at Ericksen's is the only one like it you can find. Write the store asking that they make an exception to their credit policy. You have been regularly employed at a good-paying job for ten years, and you can give personal references.

● **7.** You are the Credit Manager for A. J. Ericksen and Company. You have received an out-of-town letter from J. D. Bergstrom, asking that he be allowed to buy an exclusive bedroom suite on credit (Problem 6). Answer Mr. Bergstrom's request. Tell him that you cannot open an account for him because of your credit-references policy, but you will be glad to hold the bedroom suite for him for several days while he arranges to get money to pay for it. Ask him to come in and show you which bedroom suite he wants.

● **8.** You are the owner of a feed and farm supply store in the city of a farm area. Mr. C. Y. Davis has been a good customer of yours for years, but last year he suffered a crop failure. He still owes $1,100. This morning you received a request from Mr. Davis wanting you to deliver cotton poison amounting to $300. Many of the other farmers are in the same trouble as is Mr. Davis. You have extended all the credit your capital will allow. Write to Mr. Davis and turn him down, but use care because you want him to pay you the $1,100 he already owes you; and you want to retain him as a customer.

PART VII

Chapter 19   Generating Collection Power

A Function of Finance Management: Successful Collection. In the prior chapter we have seen how the extension of the credit privilege greatly multiplies business volume. In fact, it is quite true that credit wisely and skillfully extended to the right people can make an otherwise small business a profitable enterprise of vastly greater size.

In the world of finance management, credit, as we have seen, is based on the understanding and assurance that others will live up to the promises they have given. The credit-collection manager is charged with the responsibility of seeing that these promises are honored and that they are promptly kept at the agreed time. Only when the promises are not carried out—only when the credit obligations are defaulted—does collection pressure begin.

What Makes Credit-Collection Management Good? The modern credit-collection officer knows that his part in finance management is a highly sensitive one. He knows that when he faces his daily quota of collection problems, he must approach them with insight, understanding, and expert tact. He must "handle them with gloves on."

For these reasons the credit-collection manager is a special type of executive. Along with his understanding of finance management,

---

Definitely Closed

After months of effort, the old merchant at the general store finally collected from a stubborn debtor.

"Say on my receipt," said the troublemaking ex-customer, "that I don't owe you a thing."

With painstaking care, the old storeman wrote: "Bearer don't owe the undersigned nothing—and ain't going to."

—*The Wall Street Journal*

---

he finds it immensely important to have a sales background. Sensitively guiding the extension of credit, carefully applying collection pressure only when it becomes necessary, he is alertly aware that, in the final analysis, his obligations are not less than three in number. First, he must strive to protect his company's financial interests. Second, he must help to hold customer loyalty. Third, he must help the company to make profitable sales. Yet he knows that it is futile to make sales unless the customer pays his bills. So, to protect the company's operating margin, he strives to cut bad-debt losses to the very minimum.

Applying rigid standards of selection, the credit-collection officer extends the privilege of credit to those whom he considers good risks. Through credit education he strives to train his customers to understand the seriousness of the credit obligation. The twin activities of selective credit extension and credit education help to cut to a minimum the losses his company must risk from bad debts. The wiser the credit extension, the lighter is the load of the collection system because fewer accounts become delinquent. To extend credit shrewdly is the best way to reduce bad debts.

In spotting good risks and detecting bad ones, even the keenest credit officer now and then makes a mistake. Working as he does with human factors, he cannot hope to make a perfect record. Changes may, and at times do, take place that injure the customer's financial status and credit stability, and that cause him to fall behind in meeting his obligations. To handle such situations, the collection system is put into operation.

How the Collection Officer Approaches His Work. The collection officer knows that the only effective collection effort is one that holds the good will of the customer while it brings in the payment of a past-due account. With an eye on the sales curve the collection manager strives to protect sales volume at the same time that he is collecting money owed the company. Although he is responsible for collecting delinquent accounts, he must, if he can, preserve friendly relations with customers.

Keeping the sales viewpoint, he must not offend the customer if he can help it. Yet he must get the money. If he is too drastic, he drives away business. This would do no harm if he drove away only the faithless individual who has betrayed his business reputation and who never intends to pay anyhow. Such a loss would be helpful. But unless the collection manager handles his appeals with great care, he sometimes finds that he has alienated some of his steady buyers who are good but slow pay. Yet he dare not forget the other side of the picture. If he is too lenient, his own company will face a shrinkage of its liquid capital and may fall short of funds to carry on its own business. Debtors, becoming familiar with his reputation for being easy, may let him wait for the money while they pay others who are more strict.

Credit Customers Fall into Three Classes. Credit customers are classified as those who are (1) good pay, (2) good pay but slow, (3) uncertain.

1. *Those who are good pay* are reliable. They pay when notified. They are anxious to keep their credit unimpaired and cooperate with the credit department when they delay a payment. This class is gilt-edged.

2. *Those who are good pay but slow* may prove reliable in the long run, but they cause the collection department most of its correspondence. These customers are careless but rarely dishonest. They intend to pay—eventually.

3. *Those who are uncertain* will creep into the credit list in spite of the shrewdest judgment of the credit officer. They are unreliable. Their unreliability may at first fail to come to light, even under careful investigation. Some of them are dishonest. They pay under pressure. When discovered, they are reduced to a cash basis. This class is a bad risk.

A poor credit rating is often not a sign of dishonesty but merely of bad habits. It is a fair estimate that 95 per cent or more of all delinquents are basically honest. But perhaps a lack of self-management ability, a lack of self-discipline, ordinary carelessness, or pure laziness causes them to "put it off" until collection pressure forces them to pay. People who wouldn't think of trying to beat you out of a nickel will let five or six installment payments pile up; then, under pressure, they come in and pay them all at once.

Stages of Collection Management

The Four Stages. Collections are usually written in a series with the pressure increasing from the first phase to the last. Collection procedure falls into four stages:

Reminder ⟶ Stronger Reminder ⟶ Discussion ⟶ Urgency

The four stages of collection procedure may, and sometimes do, include *more* than four mailings. In some instances more than one stronger reminder, more than one discussion, or more than one urgency message may be used.

The Four Stages Illustrated. Most customers pay when they receive a statement. If they did not, business could not be done on credit because the confidence that supports the credit structure would collapse. A customer is not delinquent until his bill runs un-paid past the date on which it was due. Collection pressure does not begin until after the first reminder is sent.

(1) Reminder. Collection reminders are memory helps. They keep the bills before the eyes of the delinquents. They may contain sales material suggesting reorders. They may carry an enclosure introduc-ing new goods. A news item of current interest may be used. The assumption is oversight. You assume that the customer has over-looked the bill and will pay as soon as he reads the reminder.

STAGE I: REMINDER (INCLUDING SALES MATERIAL)

Timely Contact	{ These are the days that bring you the solid enjoyment of the new GE Air Conditioner you bought from us some weeks ago.
Reminder	{ May we count on receiving promptly a check for $47.50, which is the balance due on your account?
Sales-Material "Softener"	{ Enclosed is information on the new GE Electric Dryer that exactly matches the GE Automatic Washer you bought from us last year. We'll be glad to demonstrate this new GE Elec-tric Dryer in your home. Just indicate your wishes when you send in your check.

(2) Stronger Reminder. The stronger reminder is a second mem-ory jog put in stronger terms. The news item or the sales material, which, like a shock absorber, cushioned the money request in the first notice, is now withdrawn, because attention must be concentrated on getting the check and balancing the account. The phraseology be-comes more definite, added pressure appears, and the request for the check is direct.

Courtesy is maintained. The assumption is again oversight. You assume that the customer has once more overlooked the bill and will pay as soon as he receives the second notice. Questions may be in-cluded to make sure that the goods are satisfactory and that the amount is correct.

STAGE II: STRONGER REMINDER (REQUEST MORE DEFINITE)

Direct Strong Reminder	{ You will note from the attached statement that our July bill has apparently been overlooked. We're sure that we may rely on you to make payment now in order to avoid the annoyance of further correspondence.
Making Action Easy	{ A stamped, self-addressed envelope is enclosed for your reply.

NOW, WHAT WAS IT... WHAT WAS IT?

What did I forget to do?

I locked the door.

I set the alarm.

I turned off all the lights.

Now I remember!

I forgot to pay the phone bill!

P.S.

People do sometimes forget. Bills do sometimes get misplaced. We understand. And if your payment is already in the mail, thanks very much.

Your Telephone Company

Modern homes have plenty of phones. Ask us about a handy extension.

—*The Cincinnati and Suburban Bell Telephone Company*

A Printed Collection Reminder for an Overdue Telephone Bill

Collection reminders of this type drew a surprising number of complimentary comments from customers who had received them, indicating that this approach is serving its purpose. Note, too, in the lower right-hand corner, the sales promotion of extension telephones.

(3) Discussion. In the discussion stage your aim is to get the check or to draw a reply. The customer has now ignored a simple reminder and a stronger reminder of his obligation, and his account has run perhaps several weeks past the due date. He must be made to send a check or to break his silence and tell what the difficulty is that prevents him from paying. It must be made clear beyond any doubt that it is now "his move."

You now bring into play the appeal to friendly cooperation. "Won't you tell us frankly what the trouble is?" The assumption is financial difficulty. You assume that the customer is in the midst of money troubles and has hesitated to tell you about them. Your request for a check or an explanation is now insistent. The customer must pay. Your tone is courteous, but you exert sharply increasing pressure.

STAGE III: DISCUSSION (GET THE CHECK OR DRAW A REPLY)

Contact: Restates Facts

> Can you help us out? Won't you tell us frankly just what the difficulty is? Six weeks have now gone by since your account, itemized on the enclosed statement, became due. To our notices of May 15 and June 1, calling attention to the evident oversight, we have had no answer.

Appeal to Cooperation

> As we have had no word to the contrary, we feel confident that the purchase made has proved satisfactory, that our records are correct, and that you are indebted for the amount indicated. We want to enjoy the most cordial relations with our customers. We want them to buy freely and to use their credit privileges to the fullest extent. But to make it possible for us to offer such services, we must have equal cooperation from our customers. We must have prompt payment of accounts when they are due.

Rehearses Credit Material

> Your credit privilege is valuable. Your credit record has been sound, and we want you to keep it that way because of the advantages it opens to you. For example, we are just now beginning to receive our new fall stock, fresh, beautiful, and promising splendid selections. We want you to be among the customers who will enjoy making advance selections. So we're anxious that you do not allow this current situation to prevent your taking advantage of your "advance selection" privilege.

Appeal to Fair Play

> You have already enjoyed a liberal extension of time. As a matter of fair play and in justice to other customers, we cannot longer permit a delay in payment. We hope you will let us know at once the difficulty that has caused the delay, and we urge you to retain your past good credit standing in our establishment.

Direct Demand

> If you are to do so, your check to cover the full amount of the statement must be in our hands by noon of June 21.

This discussion rehearses credit material and stresses the appeals of fair play and cooperation. Attention is called to the exact amount of the statement, the dates of previous notices, and the length of time during which the debt has been overdue. The message closes in forceful language with a direct, imperative demand for explanation and payment.

(4) Urgency. The urgency stage calls for force, delivering the ultimatum to the customer who has chosen to ignore two reminders and a third message inviting discussion. The urgency ultimatum should be promptly followed by the action it threatens to take. That concern is most respected which, with scrupulous promptness, lives up to its word. The assumption is that the customer must be made to pay.

The language of urgency is sharp and imperative. Leniency, offered in previous stages, is now out of place. The keynote is finality, an insistence on immediate payment. But the insistence must be in a reasoned phraseology that avoids show of anger. The threat of action to be taken in case of failure to pay may be to place the account in the hands of a collection agency or to institute a suit at law.

STAGE IV: URGENCY (THREAT OF OTHER ACTION)

Final Restatement of Facts

It is a matter of deep regret that our efforts in calling attention to your indebtedness and urging payment of your account have received no consideration. The attached statement indicates the exact amount of your account and the full period of its delinquency.

Appeal to Fair Play

You have already enjoyed an extension of time far in excess of that permitting a good credit standing. Justice to our customers makes a further delay of the payment of your account out of the question.

Appeals to Fear, Self-Esteem, Community Standing

We must now inform you that, unless your check for your account in full is in our hands by July 5, we shall be forced to consider that you do not want to cooperate with us. Your account will then leave our office and will be transferred to a collection agency. You are aware, of course, that such action will inevitably lower your credit rating in the community. We feel certain that you will prevent such an unfavorable situation by attending to this matter at once.

Final Action; Urgent Demand

Let us urge you to act immediately so that it will not be necessary for us to resort to this unfriendly method of protecting our interests. To forestall this more rigorous and unpleasant action, it is imperative that your check be in our hands not later than July 5.

Note how this ultimatum uses one insistent phrase after another to emphasize the necessity for action on the part of the debtor if unpleasant measures are to be avoided. Appeal is made to self-esteem, community prestige, fair play, and fear.

Time Intervals. The time interval between collection efforts depends on several factors: (1) the credit standing of the customer on the basis of the original credit investigation and his past record, (2) the fact that the customer has or has not been delinquent before, (3) the nature of the business of the company—whether usual credit practice allows long or short collection periods, (4) business conditions. Businessmen are not in full accord among themselves in regard to the proper time intervals. But they are in general agreement that the more serious and urgent the case, the shorter should be the time between efforts and the sooner the matter should go to legal action.

If the customer has always been known as good pay, the time intervals are liberal. If he has earned the reputation of being slow or uncertain, the time intervals are shortened. If he has been delinquent shortly before, it would be foolish to attempt to use the same series in the same order because he would know at what point his payment would be forced and would be inclined to wait for that point. The collection manager then uses surprise tactics by dropping out one or more of the steps, moving from first reminder to discussion, or beginning at once with a stronger reminder and then bringing matters to an abrupt conclusion by sending the last-chance urgency ultimatum.

Accepted custom in the trade also dictates the usual period allowable for bringing in slow accounts. The farm-implement business may allow credit terms extending over months with a collection period thereafter running for more months. At the other extreme a specialty manufacturer, selling a product in high demand and operating on small capital and fast turnover, may shorten his collection period to a matter of days from the reminder to final urgency.

How Timing Is Changed by Business Conditions. In flush times collections come in with ease. Everyone has money because everyone is enjoying prosperous trade. Everyone is optimistic. Under these conditions collections are prompt and systematic, and regular procedure is strictly enforced. On the other hand, in times of severe depression no one seems to have money because merchants are suffering subnormal trade, are making little if any profit, and are in an attitude of fear that worse things are ahead. They hoard what little

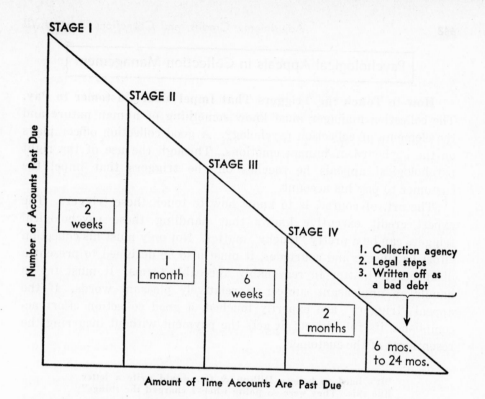

Illustrating Collection Time Intervals

Collection experience of companies varies widely. Some types of businesses clean up most of their slow accounts in Stage III, have few in Stage IV, and write off almost no bad debts. Others are forced to go through every stage. The diagram above is purely illustrative. It represents no particular company or industry.

resources they have. Under these conditions one cannot hope to make collections with normal promptness. Intervals between efforts are widened, and collection policies are modified to fit the situation while it endures.

In the collection follow-up procedure analyzed on pages 441 to 446, the interval between notices was approximately two weeks. The fan was bought on June 1. Under the terms of the store the bill became delinquent, and therefore subject to collection, after July 10. On July 15 the store sent what was in effect a sales message with a mild collection reminder tucked in. On August 1 the stronger reminder went out. On August 15 the discussion stage asked for an explanation and the check. On September 1 the five-day ultimatum was sent. Observe that a two-month period was allowed to pass before the threat was made of the collection agency and the resultant damage to credit standing. Such collection procedure is close. Good-pay accounts are permitted to run over greater periods.

Psychological Appeals in Collection Management

How to Touch the Triggers That Impel Your Customer to Pay.
The collection manager must know something of human nature and
the elements of collection psychology. A good collection officer plays
on the keyboard of human emotions. Through the use of the right
psychological appeals he touches off the triggers that impel the
customer to pay his account.

The art, of course, is to know how to touch these triggers. The
expert credit executive knows that handling these psychological
triggers can be a pretty "touchy" matter. Not only must his collection
effort be sincere and courteous, it must also be designed to present a
disagreeable matter in reasonably agreeable terms. It must try to
handle an unpleasant subject in relatively pleasant words. If the
appeal "triggers" are expertly touched, a good collection effort accomplishes its full object: it gets the payment without incurring the
resentment of the customer.

**"It's hard to believe Dillson & Co. would write a letter
like this. They were so polite when I charged the things"**

—Harry Mace, *Banking Magazine*

It should, of course, be understood that collection messages do not
always succeed in getting payment for the evident reason that these
efforts are not the only factor determining payment. For example,
a collection effort can be remarkably successful when the debtor is
willing and able to pay. If he is honest but temporarily unable to
pay, an expert collection effort will almost certainly draw a reply

THE OHIO RUBBER COMPANY
AUTOMOTIVE, MOLDED AND EXTRUDED RUBBER PRODUCTS

OHIO RUBBER CO.

FACTORY AND GENERAL OFFICES
WILLOUGHBY, OHIO

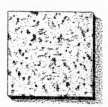

The Cleveland Container Company
10603 Berea Road
Cleveland, Ohio

Gentlemen:

That small square you see above is a sample of Orco Safety Flooring.

Try rubbing your thumb over it. Do you notice the resistance it gives? Well, imagine walking on an area covered with this material—you'd feel safe and it would be comfortable, too.

Your rubber heels have taught you that rubber is resilient—comfortable. You also know that you feel safe with them on as well. We combine those natural qualities of rubber with wear-resisting abrasive Norton Alundum for extra safety, add an attractive color, and we get Orco Safety Flooring.

It is the best insurance against accidents due to falls that we know of.

And speaking of falls, I hope that this request for payment of your past-due account for August, amounting to $15.00 does not fall into the discard. We imagine that our first request for payment slipped your attention. This bit of Orco Safety Flooring is to prevent that and perhaps to establish your interest in our new material.

May we expect your check soon and an inquiry regarding our new product?

Very truly yours,

THE OHIO RUBBER COMPANY

J. H. Winchester
Credit Manager

Combining Collections and Sales

A collection-reminder appeal (with sales material) is dramatized by affixing a piece of the product to the upper right corner and by using an action suggestion to "test-it-yourself" in the opening lines. This message **pulled 68% of payments in full within two weeks.** It also brought in a gratifying volume of new business.

and an explanation. But if the debtor is simply stubborn and unwilling to pay, even the most expertly planned appeals will fail.

You are safe in starting with the assumption that most debtors are honest. The vast majority of them are. Let that thought be foremost in your mind. From that thought will issue sincere and courteous words. If you will put them into easy, informal, conversational TALK-language, you will give your psychological collection triggers their finest chance to exert their power. To be sure, you may not always receive "cash on the barrelhead" by return mail. But you will earn the valuable good will and respect of the debtor who owes you. And as soon as he gets his affairs back into shape, he will have good reason indeed to place your bill at the top of his pile for first payment.

Power of Psychological Appeals. The extraordinary power of collection appeals is demonstrated in the following dramatic story:

When the financial world suddenly tightened up years ago, a wholesale dry-goods house found itself hard pressed for ready money. The credit manager wrote to the customers and begged them to pay at once. But the retailers were scared and stubbornly held their cash. Even the merchants who were well rated and whose bills were due played for time. The house could not borrow the money it needed, and almost in despair the president sat down and wrote to his customers.

It was no routine collection effort. It was a heart-to-heart talk, telling them that if they did not come to his rescue, the business that he had spent thirty years in building would be wiped out and he would be left penniless because he could not collect his money. He had the bookkeepers go through every important account, and they found that there was hardly a customer who had not, for one reason or another, at some time asked *him* for help—for an extension of credit.

The president dictated a personal paragraph to each customer, reminding him of the time when help had been asked for and granted. Then came the straight appeal: "Now, when the going is so rough for me, when I need help not merely to tide me over a few weeks but to save me from outright ruin, will you not strain a point, put forth some special effort to help me, *just as I helped you?*"

"If we can collect $20,000," he assured his associates, "I know we can borrow $20,000, and that amount will pull us through."

Here is what happened: The third day after his appeal went out, several checks came in. On the fourth day the cashier banked over

$22,000. Within ten days $68,000 had come in, several customers paying accounts that were not yet due. A few even offered to "help out the firm."

Sixty-eight thousand dollars was the sum collected within two weeks when money was almost invisible. Truly, appeals have power.

Selecting the Appeals. Select your appeals to match the collection stage that you have reached. In Stages I and II your appeals are mild; in Stages III and IV they are vigorous.

Important appeals are timed for use as follows:

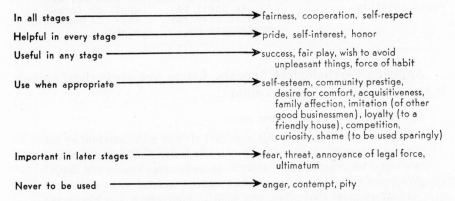

In all stages	fairness, cooperation, self-respect
Helpful in every stage	pride, self-interest, honor
Useful in any stage	success, fair play, wish to avoid unpleasant things, force of habit
Use when appropriate	self-esteem, community prestige, desire for comfort, acquisitiveness, family affection, imitation (of other good businessmen), loyalty (to a friendly house), competition, curiosity, shame (to be used sparingly)
Important in later stages	fear, threat, annoyance of legal force, ultimatum
Never to be used	anger, contempt, pity

You will recall that credit customers are classified as (a) good pay and prompt, (b) good pay but slow, and (c) uncertain, perhaps bad, pay. To these three classes may be added (d) special cases. We all act or react because of certain fundamental human drives. In the case of paying bills, we act because we want to be honest, because of force of habit, because of a desire to be systematic, because of fear, or because of several motives listed above.

After we have classified customers, our next step is to determine what motives are most likely to influence each to pay his account. For example, the motive of fear would doubtless be effective with good credit risks, but it would be undesirable to use the motive of fear because it would be inappropriate, and it would dangerously antagonize individuals who pride themselves on paying bills with regularity. On the other hand, the motive of habit is a useful one for good credit risks but not at all effective for uncertain and bad-pay risks.

After we have determined what motives are most likely to influence each debtor to pay his account, our third step is to select the specific appeals that can be used to play upon those motives. The information we have now assembled can be tabulated in a form similar to that of the following chart:

Guide for Selecting Appeals in Collection Stages

	"Good Pay" Customers	"Good Pay But Slow" Customers	"Uncertain, Bad Pay" Customers
Effective Motives	Force of habit	Self-interest	Fear
Specific Appeals	This statement has doubtless escaped your attention.	If you can let us have your payment of $50 by May 30, we shall be able to give you preference on . . .	Unless we have your check by noon of June 22, we shall be forced to take the usual legal steps . . .

Applying Psychological Appeals. Let us now apply these appeals to the three main classes of debtors.

(1) *To those who are good pay.*

Have you overlooked this account? Is our memorandum of the account correct? May we have your check for $77.50 in order that we can close accounts by Friday? Is there some reason for delay? We know that this statement has merely escaped your attention; and we suggest that when you send in your check you also make a trial order. [followed by sales material]

(2) *To those who are good pay but slow.*

Self-interest (reselling the customer the value of the goods originally ordered; reinstating in his mind how the goods looked when they arrived; suggesting concrete ways in which he has been benefited). Pride. Good will. Cooperation. Fair dealing. Honesty. Good nature. Wish to avoid annoyance. Reputation. Success. Family affection. Imitation. Competition. Value of keeping credit undamaged. Are you short of capital? Are your own collections slow? Our salesman, Mr. Fraser, tells us business is pretty slow in your locality. How about a time draft? Won't you tell us why your account has gone unpaid? If you will only give us the details of your present situation, perhaps we can arrange a partial-payment plan. Fear, phrased gently. Mild threats, growing stronger.

(3) *To those who are uncertain, perhaps bad, pay.*

Appeal to the discouraged delinquents through pride, imitation of other successful merchants, shame, fear, and threat of a lawsuit. Appeal to dishonest delinquents simply through fear, threat of a lawsuit, and direct legal steps.

The collection officer determines into which class the debtor falls. He then selects the set of appeals he believes will be most effective in energizing the act of payment.

Tone in Collections. Nowhere is tone more important than in collection work. It should be kept friendly up to the final legal break, after which the customer himself must decide whether he wishes a resumption of friendly relations. Courtesy is possible even in urgency ultimatums.

FORCEFUL, BUT NEUTRALLY COURTEOUS

We do not want to embarass you with legal action. Right now it is more than ever necessary for businessmen to exchange confidence in order to help each other in weathering present financial conditions. We want to help you if we can, but only the frankest, immediate statement from you will make this possible. Otherwise we shall have to turn the matter over for final action.

Are you going to let us help you? Or will you force us to go ahead in the other way? See that your answer gets to me personally and at once.

* * *

You will realize, Mr. Barnes, that we regret the need for placing this matter in the hands of our legal department. Yet, in fairness to our other clients, we must take this step if we have not received your check by noon of August 6.

In these illustrations the tone is freighted with finality, but the undertone is courteous. Collection efforts never need to make themselves offensive with rudeness, insulting phraseology, or peremptory command. The iron hand, sheathed in the velvet glove, can still exert its final, relentless pressure.

MAY LOSE THE CUSTOMER

The gasoline tax effective May 1 forces us to advance 9¢ per gallon in cash to the state for all of our credit customers.

This makes it impossible for us to carry an account not paid in full by the 10th of every month. We are therefore obliged to ask you to pay cash until the enclosed account has been properly taken care of.

We trust you appreciate our position in this matter.

WILL HOLD THE CUSTOMER

The gasoline tax effective May 1 forces us to advance 9¢ a gallon in cash to the state for each of our credit customers.

Yet, if we ourselves were to advance the tax money on all accounts not paid up on the due date (the tenth of each month), our risk swiftly rises to unsound levels.

With this explanation, we are confident you will pay the enclosed bill at once. Meanwhile, we'll be glad to serve you on a cash basis.

ILL-MANNERED

Your note for $300 has been past due for one week.

We certainly cannot understand your attitude in this matter. We were courteous enough to grant you this loan on the understanding that you would take care of it when due.

If you expect to borrow money from us, Mr. Locke, you will have to report here on the day the note is due.

Kindly come in immediately and settle this matter.

INSISTENT, BUT COURTEOUS

When we made you a loan of $300 on February 7, we did so willingly because we were sure you would meet it on the day it was due. But your note has now been past due for one week.

We extended you a courtesy. We look for a return of this courtesy in prompt payment. Only through meeting obligations with promptness can a man expect to retain the privilege of getting loans when he needs them.

Please come in immediately and take care of your obligation.

In the first pair, the same object is achieved; namely, informing the customer that he has been placed on a cash basis until he pays his account. In the example at the left he is told that he will have to pay cash until he has settled his account. In the one at the right he is told that he will be served as always, with a temporary change to a cash basis until the check arrives. Between the two is a basic difference. One letter is negative; the other is positive.

Dangerous Are Tones of Anger, Contempt, and Insult. Many violations of correct procedure are found in collections. A survey will disclose examples that are unwise in tone, that quite properly may seem, to the debtor, to be arbitrary, insulting, condescending, or blunt. Rarely, however, does one come across such an extreme illustration of how to lose friends and kill customers as the following:

ARBITRARY AND INSULTING

I am sure you are aware of the fact that your payment of $95 due on February 10 has not been paid.

At this time I am going to give you until Monday morning, April 10, at 12:00 o'clock noon to have this payment in my office. If this payment is not made in my office as above stated, I can assure you that my feelings will certainly be relieved by having the pleasure of executing on your personal property as quickly as the sheriff can reach your farm.

I cannot understand how a man of your supposed standing in your community can absolutely ignore his obligations.

Expressions like "my feelings will certainly be relieved by having the *pleasure* of executing on your personal property" and "a man of your *supposed* standing" are insulting and dangerous. Regardless of your objective, certain standards of courtesy, decency, and acceptable manners should in all circumstances be observed.

The Cheerful Tone. If credit has been wisely extended, most of the outstanding accounts can be collected not only without punishment but also in a cheerful tone. "Business is friendship, not warfare!" The cannonade of sharp language and insistent threat should be held in reserve, to be called upon only in the ultimate emergency. The cheerful tone can bring astonishing results. Use it as the preferred approach in the early weeks of collection effort.

CHEERFUL REMINDER

We believe a credit reminder should be brief and friendly to be successful. This one is brief. It is friendly. Will you make it successful by forwarding your check? Please.

COURTEOUS REMINDER

When an account runs past the due date, we find that many of our customers appreciate a brief note reminding them so that they may remedy the oversight. Our statement rendered on May 6 showed a balance of $33.75, then due. Your check in an early mail will be an appreciated courtesy.

CHEERFUL STRONG REMINDER

An account is like a train--both are late at times. Here's our reminder: your account with us is overdue. We're asking you, just as you would ask the stationmaster, "What time do you guess she'll roll in?"

How about making out your check for $78.25 and saying, "Here she comes!"

Note the following prize-winning reminder used by the United Autographic Register Company as one of its collection units.

A REMINDER—BRIEF, CHEERFUL, COURTEOUS

It's not going to take much to balance your account because you owe so little.

Only $7.95.

It's for our bill of July 1.

Will you please look it up and take care of it today? Here's an envelope.

Thank you.

A Minnesota undergraduate, completing a course in effective communication, in cheerful tone cleverly personifies an unpaid account.

CHEERFUL STRONG REMINDER TO A "GOOD BUT SLOW" ACCOUNT

Remember me? I'm your unpaid account of $48 waiting for you to come and pick me up.

You know, it's been some time since we last met. In fact
it was six weeks ago when you came in to purchase that new hat.
You charged it to me and then left, and that--as the saying
goes--left me holding the bag!

I'm sure I helped you then, and now I need your help.
Ever since you left me, they have been juggling me around from
book to book until I'm dizzy, and now I'm all alone in the
back of one.

I'm lonely because I haven't heard from you in a long
time. Won't you help me by writing them and arrange to
pay me off?

Please--do it right away!*

The Firm Tone: The Case of the Mistaken Discount. A lithographing company completed an order for a bank. The bank misunderstood the terms of payment because of a fault not clearly traceable to anyone, and expected a cash discount. Note the firm but excellent tone with which the misunderstanding is adjusted.

EXCELLENT TONE—FIRM RESTATEMENT OF CREDIT TERMS

Your check, which you promptly sent us in payment of our
invoice, has already been deposited. No doubt by this time
it has been returned to you through the clearing house.

From your explanation of March 30 we see your position.
Of course, we do not want you to be penalized to even a small
extent for a reason that is traceable to our not expressing
our terms distinctly. So we shall this time gladly waive our
strict policy of no cash discount and run a credit through in
your favor for $4.90. In an instance of this kind even the
strictest rules may be temporarily laid aside without working
an injustice to anyone.

In return for this courtesy we know you will be glad to
abide by our regular terms on future purchases. It will be
a pleasure to serve you soon again.

The Sympathetic Tone: Two Surprising Results. The following note was sent by a manufacturer of school desks and chairs:

STRONG REMINDER—SYMPATHETIC IN TONE

How are you fixed on finances? Is it possible for you
to send us a remittance to cover our invoice of November 30?
There is still a balance of $45 due. Our fiscal year closes
on December 31, and we wish to get in as many of our accounts
as possible before that date. Your check will be appreciated.

HOW THE DEBTOR ANSWERED

I am not flush as to finances, but you people are so
generous and patient with me that I am glad I can respond to
your request. So here is the check for $45. Thanks for your
generous treatment. Happy New Year!

* Reproduced here through the courtesy of Miss Louise I. Martin, Instructor,
Virginia Jr. College, Virginia, Minnesota.

A wholesale house, using a cheerful but insistent tone in the stage of discussion, drew the following earnest reply:

ANSWER BROUGHT FORTH BY A FRIENDLY, BUT FIRM, COLLECTION TONE

It is with considerable regret that I am compelled to write regarding the delay in meeting my obligation to you.

As most of us know, retail conditions have been anything but favorable during the past year. I found it necessary to borrow on certain securities to finance the business. During the market upset these securities went along with the best of them, leaving my bank loan unprotected. The bank insisted that I reduce the loan or put up more collateral. As I could not put up additional collateral, I have had to reduce the loan with the money that has been coming in.

This process has been slow and has left me without funds to pay maturing invoices, although my position is improving. The securities amount to 3,000 shares of Tecla Steel Forge, with a book value of around $35 but a market value of about $20 now. To sell this stock would, of course, mean a tremendous loss, and the return would not cover the loan. I have felt that the best thing to do is to refinance out of current receipts. Within a short period I can commence paying on the invoices again, and I assure you that all receipts are being conserved to that end.

I earnestly hope that you will bear with me until I can work out from under this load.

With this straightforward explanation the wholesaler was able to arrange definite terms and installment payments. The retailer later became one of the wholesaler's best customers.

The Pride Appeal Brings Constructive Results. The pride appeal directs its energizing force to the basic motive of pride-in-oneself or self-esteem—and aims to reinstate the debtor's sense of obligation.

Let us illustrate. A doctor purchased a highly perishable medical item in April of a given year. The bill was $57.50. He paid $35 under collection pressure from the firm and from a collection agency. In October two years later the firm charged off the remainder of the account, $22.50, as a bad debt. In December three years later the credit manager decided to attempt to revive the account through use of the pride appeal:

THE PRIDE APPEAL BRINGS IN THE CHECK

When we ship merchandise to a person of your caliber, either we receive payment or the goods are returned. In spite of lack of response from you to our many reminders, we cannot bring ourselves to believe that it is your habit to accept goods and then ignore the charge.

Had this merchandise been furniture, electrical equipment, or perhaps your surgical instruments, it would have

been returned to our warehouse long ago, and we could have
realized something on the sale.

It is not our desire to cause you any embarrassment
through further collection effort. If you will send us $15
by February 7, we will mark the account "Paid in Full." We
hope you will consider this a fair solution of an honest debt.
We do not want to proceed with other action without giving
you this opportunity to settle. You see, we believed in your
honesty when the merchandise was sent you. We still do.

Here is an envelope (no postage needed) for your reply
and your check.

This letter brought in the check. The debtor could not withstand
the appeal. This is part of his reply:

ONE PARAGRAPH FROM THE REPLY

Your letter is worth the balance of what I owe--$22.50.
Here's my check for the full amount. I don't want to take
advantage of your proposed compromise settlement of $15.
Thanks for your leniency.

How Pride Appeal Brought in Russ Martin's Check. Mr. Russ
Martin, a retailer who has for years enjoyed an "A-1" credit rating,
establishes a dependable, steady-pay record of over eight years of
purchasing from his wholesale hardware supplier. Then, for no
apparent reason and much to the surprise of the wholesale credit
manager, Mr. Martin in a period of six months slips into the delinquent class.

No reply comes to the collection reminders. Yet, in consideration
of his excellent past record, the credit department allows much longer
intervals between collection efforts and in general shows him much
leniency. From past connections and from what the company salesmen report, it is well known that Mr. Martin is normally a careful
buyer and a prudent and foresighted manager.

Armed with these facts, the credit-collection officer drafts the
discussion that appears below. Note the powerful appeals to Mr.
Martin's self-esteem, his pride in himself as a business manager, his
community reputation. This discussion brought in the check.

THE STAGE OF DISCUSSION THAT BROUGHT IN A CHECK

Courteous,
Friendly
Opening;
Appeal to
Self-Esteem

Have you ever waited and wondered why an old
friend, who had always answered you within a few
days in the past, didn't answer your latest note
at all? I'm sure you have. You will realize then
how we have felt while waiting to hear from you--
one of our good friends and valued customers for
the last seven years--in response to our August 1
and September 1 reminders.

<table>
<tr>
<td>Appeal to
Pride as a
Business
Manager</td>
<td>Your business with our firm has been one of our most pleasant connections. You have been the kind of customer that a wholesaler is proud to serve and anxious to serve well. In the past we find you have always taken advantage of the 10-day discount period, a fact that has marked you as a prudent, foresighted businessman. This has proved to us that you are a man who knows the value of an "A-1" credit rating.</td>
</tr>
<tr>
<td>Restates
Facts;
Appeal to
Community
Reputation</td>
<td>Because of your past record with our company, we are unable to give ourselves any satisfactory explanation for your present delinquency of $578. In other springs we extended credit to you to the extent of three times this amount, and you met your obligation promptly. Under the right circumstances, we shall be glad to extend these same amounts again. To do this, however, it will be necessary to get the present situation taken care of before your credit rating is seriously impaired.</td>
</tr>
<tr>
<td>Appeal to
Cooperation</td>
<td>Are you sick? Are you having money troubles? Have you gone to Africa? Or have you just evaporated into thin air? We can't help feeling that some extraordinary condition must have caused this delay. We hope you will let us know at once what the difficulties are. And we urge you to protect your past excellent credit standing!</td>
</tr>
<tr>
<td>Action
Demand</td>
<td>To do this, your check covering the full amount due must be in our hands by noon of November 1. Won't you help us to bring this story to a happy conclusion?</td>
</tr>
</table>

Russ Martin Sends a Check and Explains His Trouble.

To the appeal you have just read, Russ Martin, hardware merchant, made this swift and sudden reply telling about his troubles:

I would certainly like to help you write a happy ending to the story! But I'm afraid the only one I could supply for the present would be of the kind that leaves you only partly satisfied. Maybe, though, not too far in the future, a more agreeable solution can be reached.

This guy, Martin, realizes he has slipped up badly in not having given you the story a long time ago. But I guess I'd better assume my own responsibilities from here on in and tell you just what the trouble is.

I've been hit hard in the present so-called "recession." The hardware business, as you well know, has suffered more than the average. Not only are many of my customers unable to buy, but most of them are neglecting to pay their accounts of several months standing. So I can fully appreciate your position as concerns me, because I'm in the same spot.

You've done me a favor by reminding me that my credit rating was drifting into serious danger. I've been so worried about the ratings of my customers that I pretty much forgot about my own.

Here is what I think we'd better do. I can afford to pay you $50 right now. Then as my customers pay me--and I'm going to try just as skillful tactics on them as you used on me!--I'll pay you promptly. Then you can pay your butcher and baker and together we may help a little toward setting the old business wheels in motion again.

You'll find my $50 check enclosed. Thanks for having been so patient with me.

This forthright reply saved Mr. Martin's credit rating from almost certain disaster and got him and his business affairs back on the right track.

Pride Versus Shame: Use of Contrast. Appeals to pride and self-esteem are powerful in reinforcing the debtor's sense of obligation. Note this contrast: (1) Referring to your customer's *present* good standing, to his *present* business success, to his *present* credit record appeals to his pride; (2) referring instead with emphasis to his delinquency as contrasted with his *former* good standing, his *former* business success, his *former* good credit record appeals to his sense of shame. Shame—a powerful spur to action—is, however, destructive in nature and may undermine the customer's possibly dwindling morale. Yet there are some hard-boiled people who will react to no other spur. The forceful letter on page 461 directs its major appeal to pride, but note the implied appeal to shame in Paragraphs 2 and 4.

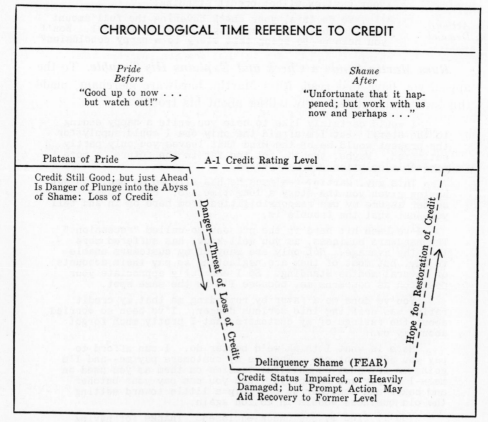

CHRONOLOGICAL TIME REFERENCE TO CREDIT

Pride
Before
"Good up to now . . .
but watch out!"

Shame
After
"Unfortunate that it happened; but work with us now and perhaps . . ."

Plateau of Pride ⟶

A-1 Credit Rating Level

Credit Still Good; but just Ahead
Is Danger of Plunge into the Abyss
of Shame: Loss of Credit

Danger—Threat of Loss of Credit

Hope for Restoration of Credit

Delinquency Shame (FEAR)

Credit Status Impaired, or Heavily
Damaged; but Prompt Action May
Aid Recovery to Former Level

Pride Appeal vs. Shame Appeal

PRIDE VS. SHAME—STAGE OF URGENCY

Courteous
Opening
> We are sorry that we have had no word from you regarding your July 6 invoice, amounting to $575. Our previous two appeals have drawn no response. We feel that it is only fair to you that we make our position clear.

Restates
Facts;
Hidden
Appeal to
Shame
> Having confidence in your ability and willingness to meet your obligations promptly, we extended credit to you--doubting not for a minute that it was your honest intention to pay your account on or near August 1 (as you indicated). Since then, all our correspondence to you has been unanswered.

Appeal to
Cooperation
> In many cases we have been willing to grant extensions of time to customers who have been prevented by circumstances from paying on time. We do feel though that we are justified in expecting your reasons for default, with some evidence of your desire to make the debt good, before we can give this extension privilege.

Appeals to
Shame and
Fear;
Vigorous
Demand
> We cannot believe that you are attempting to evade your obligation. Yet the length of time your account has run, with no word from you, requires that we ask that you mail us a check without delay. A further extension of time we find quite impossible, although we dislike to resort to legal measures.

Appeal to
Pride
> You still have just enough time to preserve the good credit rating that you have held in local exchange reports. Why not act now for your own benefit as well as ours?

The Loyalty Appeal. When an old customer not only fails to pay his bill but also fails to reply to any of the appeals that ask him why, the credit officer is sometimes rightly puzzled. The following discussion appeal written by Russell C. Flom, Credit Manager of the Menasha Products Company, Menasha, Wisconsin, uses the appeal to loyalty in the form of fair play and cooperation. The letter brought in a check by return mail.

A LOW-PRESSURE DISCUSSION USING THE APPEAL TO LOYALTY

Have you ever had to sit down and write to an old friend about a subject that was not very pleasant and wondered just how to start it and what to say? Well, that's the position I'm in right now, Mr. Little.

You have been a customer of ours for a good many years, both in the ice business and through your connection with the fuel company. A connection like that is something we value a great deal, and we certainly want to preserve the friendly relationship that exists between us. Yet we do have a situation that demands attention--right now!

Attached is a statement of items due us--dating back to last May and June. Why these aren't paid is a puzzle to us. It's even more of a puzzle to understand why you haven't at least written us lately in answer to some of our frequent letters about this account. If there is something wrong, surely we should be entitled to that much.

Now then, ordinarily when an account gets this old
there's no question about what to do--it gets placed with
attorneys for collection. However, it isn't our practice to
operate by any rule of that sort; and when we find the account
of some old customer who is loyal to us running delinquent,
we certainly don't treat him the same as some new account
that's running slow on their first bit of business with us.
That's why we've been so very patient on this account, and of
course that's why we feel that now we are entitled to some
action on it.

If you'll just stop to review the facts, I'm sure that
you'll agree we should have your check right away for $398.72.
Or, if circumstances are such that you can't send all of that,
then do send us part of it and let's make some arrangement for
the balance. Any reasonable suggestion you have will meet with
our approval. But let's get it cleaned up promptly. How about
hearing from you by return mail?

The Honesty, Personal Integrity, and Community Reputation Appeals. In the hands of a skillful credit officer the appeals to honesty, personal integrity, and community reputation may be made extremely powerful. The credit manager of Clarence Whitman and Sons, Inc., New York, offers an excellent demonstration of how this may be done in the stage of discussion. So good was his effort considered by a jury of credit experts that it was honored by inclusion in the American Credit Indemnity Company's book, *Fifty Gold Medal Collection Letters.* As you read the paragraphs of the Whitman letter that follow, observe the adroit use of the opening concrete example and its swift application to the problem at hand.

A DISCUSSION APPEALING TO HONESTY, PERSONAL INTEGRITY,
AND COMMUNITY REPUTATION

Suppose a friend of yours proposed your name for membership in a club--a very special club. To be a member of this
club meant that everywhere in the world you would be honored
as a man of reputation and integrity. Wouldn't you be proud
to be elected?

We have proposed your name to be elected to the world-
wide organization of businessmen tied together by a common
belief in honesty and fair play. We did it by extending you
credit--saying to the world, "We believe Mr. Hauser to be a
man of honesty and integrity."

Now, when we receive credit inquiries about you, we must
tell the truth. We do not want to tell the world that a bill
of $279.84 is sixty days past due. That would hurt your credit
standing. It would curtail your purchasing power. It would
injure your bank connections. The total damage to you would
amount to many times $279.84.

Credit standing once lost can never be fully regained.
For your own good we strongly urge that you send us your check
now. Never mind writing. Just enclose the check in the envelope we are providing. We want to get the money quickly so
we can again say, "We believe Mr. Hauser to be a man of honesty
and integrity."

Save Your Customers

Let the Customer Viewpoint Direct Your Appeals. A collection effort is not a complete success unless it gets the money and *keeps the customer*. The ordinary run-of-the-mill collection attempt depends too much on fear and threat. It smashes good will, even if it does frighten the money out of the debtor. One may call it a "Customer-killer."

Good collection procedure unleashes fear and threat only in the closing stages. It relies heavily on the constructive appeals of pride, self-esteem, reputation, fair play, and the Golden-Rule cooperative spirit. So vivid does it make the obligation that the debtor's conscience goads him into paying. In other words, it literally *sells* the delinquent into paying his account. The hammer and tongs of yesterday yield to the collection persuasiveness of today. Tests prove that the selling point of view brings the best collection returns.

The Vast Majority of Customers Are Fair. The majority of customers are honest. They intend to do the right thing. They expect to honor their obligations. They plan to pay their debts. The main trouble, and the trouble that makes credit and collection officers necessary, is that many customers do not feel it quite necessary to honor their obligations and pay their debts until "day after tomorrow," or "week after next," or "in a couple of months."

What Can a Hard-Pressed Customer Do to Protect His Credit Rating? Some customers delay because they are forced to. They simply have no money. And they are sensitive about it. It never occurs to most people that there is anything they can say or do about such a situation. But of course much *can* be done. One intelligent person, deep in debt through no immediate fault of his own, wrote a short note to each of those who had trusted him. He explained that he hoped on an approximate date to make a payment on his bill. And he did not forget to thank his various creditors for the credit and the confidence they had extended.

By return mail he got a fistful of appreciative replies. His biggest creditor wrote:

> If all our customers showed the same consideration, business would be much pleasanter, and we would know far better where we stand. Please do not feel pressed by your little account with us.

Even the credit manager of a department store—a man who certainly must have heard "all the answers"—replied that he appreciated the reply and was ordering a 30-day extension on the bill.

A frank and personal acknowledgment of the debt, stating your good intentions, is the best-known protection for a good credit rating short of an immediate payment in full.

"Save Your Customer." The businessman of today should know the nature of credit, the methods of extending credit, procedures for granting and refusing credit, the resulting difficulties of collecting money, and definite methods for establishing and operating a collection system.

"Save Your Customer" is the modern collection officer's slogan. It is the motto he keeps on the wall. It has been said that, whereas the sales manager of olden times used to direct his sales efforts as if they were collections, the modern collection officer plans his collections as if they were sales efforts. Dominant in his mind is the point of view of his customer.

To Those Who Pay. Credit and collection departments spend so much of their time getting dollars out of the reluctant payers that they are tempted to overlook the opportunity for building good will among those customers who *do* pay their bills promptly. A New York house expresses its appreciation in this message that can be well used, with adaptation, by almost any business offering credit.

APPRECIATION TO THOSE WHO PAY

An Appreciation:

    My Department of Accounts has just called attention to the pleasant regularity with which you meet the monthly statements we send you.

    Because you are the kind of a person who naturally and promptly honors just obligations, I won't embarrass you with my thanks. But I will take the opportunity to point out that such cooperation is helpful in making Starr's an attractive place for you to buy.

    Money is always necessary to the running of a business . . . but rising prices have recently created a sellers' market in which the "slow-pay" store gets scant consideration. Your cooperation helps keep us in fluid condition for cash transactions of worth-while character.

    Sometime when you are congratulating yourself on a particularly fortunate purchase at Starr's, we hope you'll remember that you helped make it possible.

Customers who pay—and do so promptly—are likely to remain your most valuable patrons. They are the ones who are the most worthy of your courteous recognition.

Communication Problems

● **1.** As Credit Manager of the Reliable Builders' Supply Company, you discover that an old and reliable customer, John L. Biggs, building contractor, has not paid his monthly bill by the due date. It is now fifteen days overdue. This is an unusual situation for Mr. Biggs; he has always been a "prompt-pay" account in the past. His account balance is now $790.80 covering purchases of lumber, hardware, and cement products. The home construction industry has held up well and economic conditions indicate that Mr. Biggs should find it easy to meet the obligation.

Directions: Write the reminder. Of course, the assumption must be that Mr. Biggs has simply overlooked the payment and will pay as soon as he reads the reminder. Utilize sales promotion material and personalize your pleasant note.

● **2.** Twenty days have passed since the first reminder was sent to contractor Biggs (Problem 1) and you have not received payment. He has also been permitted to make additional credit purchases during the current month.

Directions: Send him a stronger reminder. Because of his volume of business and past "good-pay" practices, you must still assume that payment has been overlooked. Do not discuss the fact that he has been permitted to make purchases in the meantime, but make the message more stringent than a first reminder by eliminating the sales promotion talk. Make action easy.

● **3.** Ten days after the strong reminder sent to Mr. Biggs (Problems 1 and 2), your accounting department informs you that his new statement for $549.50 has been prepared for mailing. With his 30-day past due account of $790.80, Mr. Biggs now owes you $1,340.30. Write the vigorous discussion to accompany the current month's statement.

Directions: While you still want to retain Mr. Biggs' good will and future business, the situation is becoming extremely serious. You have heard nothing from him. Your obvious appeal is to his sense of cooperation and fair play. You have continued to sell to him despite his large overdue account. Offer to cooperate further by working out some means of payment suitable for both of you. Unless some payment is received within five days, you cannot sell to him. Try to get the $790.80, but keep in mind that the $549.50 is not yet overdue. Would it be a good idea to register the letter?

● **4.** After sending two reminders and a discussion letter to the Central Automotive Parts Company, you (as Credit Manager of Auto-Nite Electric) receive an acknowledgment from Mr. Robert O'Brien,

President of Central Automotive, which includes this closing paragraph.

> We, at Central, appreciate your straightforward collection procedures and your consideration of our problems. With the busy summer season approaching, we assure you that our overdue account will be settled in a few weeks.

Directions: Write, thanking Mr. O'Brien for his reply. In order not to leave the account delinquent ($480), encourage Central Automotive to make the account current by using one of two options: (1) signing a 30-day, 6% note or (2) paying one half of the account now and the remaining half in thirty days. Tabulate the options. Enclose a filled-in promissory note prepared for Mr. O'Brien's signature and send a return envelope. Avoid any suggestion of threat, but appeal to the necessity for keeping accounts out of the delinquent classification—otherwise you must report them to the Retail Credit Association.

● **5.** The Central Automotive Parts Company accepted the second option given in Problem 4 and sent a check for $240 to Auto-Nite Electric. The second payment, however, was not sent within thirty days. It is now ten days past due.

Directions: Write the urgency demand to Mr. O'Brien. Explain the situation once more. Indicate that letter is being sent airmail, registered. Give Central the option of paying within five days or having the account turned over to your legal department for appropriate action. Remind Central of the consequences of court action.

● **6.** To be clear, writing must be simple. On this score Lewis Carroll, author of *Alice in Wonderland*, wrote: "Alice had not the slightest idea what Latitude was, or Longitude either, but she thought they were nice grand words to say."

The following writing illustrates the use of "nice grand words." Do you suppose the average reader of this message would have "the slightest idea" of what the writer is trying to say?

Directions: Rewrite these paragraphs, choosing words that will be understood by the average reader.

> Agreeable to yours of September 25, we have conferred with our credit department to ascertain the status quo of your recent claim pursuant to your request.
>
> Inasmuch as your final payment on said installment is due on October 1, and your credit classification carries a 20-day grace clause, your time of grace does not terminate until October 20.
>
> In accordance with the above, delayed payment may be made up to and including the above-mentioned date.
>
> A 5% carrying charge is added to the balance of all accounts that exceed the stated grace period.

PART VII

Chapter 20

Generating Collection Power
(Concluded)

Modern Credit-Collection Management Calls for Creative Imagination. When an executive deals with the sensitive nerve of personal integrity, he knows that he must maneuver with extraordinary care. He knows that integrity, a priceless character trait, is the foundation cornerstone of both personal and corporate credit. He recognizes the credit phase of finance management, and the resultant collection procedures that go along with it, as presenting challenging complexities that he must approach with insight, expert tact, deep understanding, and creative imagination.

With creative imagination the expert credit officer can adapt his collection procedures with great flexibility to the many highly specialized situations and individual characters that inevitably develop as he faces his daily quota of collection problems. He can, as did one credit bureau executive, draw upon his creative imagination so skillfully, weave his collection appeal so faithfully around the very character of the debtor—in this case the famous leader of a "name band"—that he can bring in money owing on a stubborn indebtedness more than five years old!

Using Creative Imagination to Build the Credit-Collection Portfolio. Each time the collection officer registers a triumphant success, each time he trains his creative imagination into focus on a special situation and evolves a new method of approach and a new application of tested powerful appeals, he files a copy of his successful collection effort in his *Master Credit-Collection Portfolio*. On each copy he makes a notation of the exact results. Year by year the portfolio grows. Year by year it becomes more valuable as a reference—a priceless guide to past successes that may be used over and over again to solve future collection problems. Classified into stages of reminder, discussion, and urgency; classified into special situations such as "new customers," "old customers," "small customers," "large customers," "problem customers," and the like; classified into special characteristics such as "erratic," "stubborn," "tough to budge," "puts it off," "responds to fair play,"—each classification grows, success by success, as the credit executive continues to solve his daily grist of problems. In due course the Master Portfolio becomes a treasure-house of collection experience, reflecting this phase of finance management at its best.

Follow-Up Collection Systems

How Finance Management Uses "Form" Collection Systems. From the Master Portfolio of cumulative collection successes, the collection manager draws exactly the right "master drafts" upon which to base his "form" system. "Forms" are collection messages that are used over and over again, either in identical or in modified versions, and that are sent to debtors whose delinquencies—in terms of amounts owed, periods of time overdue, etc.—are practically identical. Using his creative imagination, the collection manager modifies or adapts highly successful message-appeals of the past, and applies them expertly over and over again (through forms) to collection problems of the present. And he knows that he can do the same thing with collection problems of the future.

Form messages are normally used in about 80 to 90 per cent of all collection work. The other 10 to 20 per cent calls for individual attention. No "standard" collection-form procedure can be designed so that it can be "switched" from company to company. Each must work out the plan that best fits its needs.

The plan should correlate with the work of the accounting department so that duplication is avoided and proper checks and balances are maintained. The collection department as a unit should cooperate closely with other departments in the company, especially with those having direct contact with the customer, so that if there is a difference of opinion about anything other than the collection of the bill, that difference of opinion may be ironed out first.

Consider, for example, the following situation: A customer asks for an adjustment on a faulty order. He corresponds with the adjustment department in an effort to adjust the matter. The collection manager, unaware that an adjustment problem exists and that the adjustment is in process, sets in motion the machinery of the collection system, and the customer gets form requests asking for a remittance because the bill becomes past due during the adjustment negotiations.

Such a situation soon straightens itself out. But common sense tells us that no credit department can make a collection if adjustment trouble is involved, or if the customer doubts the character of the shipment he has received or the correctness of the charge made for it. Hence all departments should work together as a team.

The Form Follow-Up System Provides (1) Cumulative Pressure and (2) Change of Pace. Effective collection follow-up procedure bases its power on the gradual increase of psychological pressure generated through the use of a series of carefully designed messages. To dictate every collection appeal anew each time it is needed would, of course, be a colossal and needless waste.

Theoretically, even a peanut stand, if it extended credit, could profit from a simple collection system. To every organization extending credit, collections are a vital matter. This is equally true, whether the organization is a retail store around the corner of the next block, or a giant concern stretching its financial operations across the continent.

The larger the organization, the greater the need for well-designed master appeals to serve as models from which secretarial assistants may strike off copies when so directed by the collection officer or his staff. Appeals frequently used may be, and in bigger concerns usually are, duplicated by a mechanical process less costly than individual typing. Appeals in advanced stages of collection are, however, always individually prepared. Furthermore, no one identical message should ever go twice to the same customer. The reason for this is obvious. Hence a variety of optional forms are drafted for the collection follow-up series, each of which—through the creative imagination of the expert—can be given the same gripping personal tone that would be found in an individually dictated appeal.

Printed Forms, Stickers, and Statements for the Early Stages. To make as much as possible of the collection system automatic, stickers, forms, and printed statements are used. Gummed slips of paper, measuring perhaps 2 by 3 inches, are printed with individual messages like these:

You have credit standing in your community. Use it. Don't abuse it.
Make a new start by paying this old bill.
Paying an old bill makes you feel like a new man. Won't you take this tonic today?
It's never too late to clear the slate! Please pay today.
That check—get it off your mind and in the mail!
We helped when you needed credit—please help us.
Prompt payment builds credit. Credit builds business.

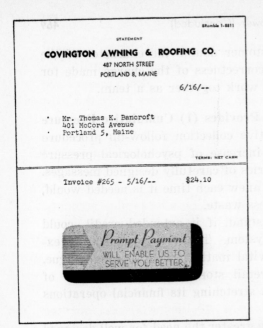

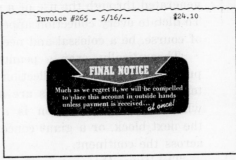

A Series of Three Gummed Reminders That May Be Used on Monthly Statements in the Early Stages of a Collection System

One of these slips is affixed to each statement in a prominent place where it cannot fail to carry its reminder.

A famous metropolitan store uses these forms:

FIRST REMINDER
    We call your attention to the above statement of your account which is now past due. May we have a prompt remittance, please!

*   *   *

SECOND REMINDER
    Your attention is directed to an unpaid balance on our books. Please note the enclosed statement. May we have your check--now?

*   *   *

THIRD REMINDER
    Your account amounting to $----- is past due. If there is any error, please notify us promptly and we will investigate at once. Otherwise, please let us have your check by return mail.

*   *   *

FOURTH REMINDER
    The unpaid balance of $----- on your account is now considerably past due. Observe that our terms provide for payment by the tenth of the month following the date of purchase. Your account should be paid without further delay.

Regularity, Promptness, System, and Clockwork Timing. Additional collection procedure should be timed with clocklike promptness and regularity. The entire program should be systematized so that much of the early work can be automatically handled by an assistant in the collection department. Large organizations standardize the notices, reminders, and strong reminders through form messages and form paragraphs, already made up in large numbers to fit the most common situations. When a prepared form does not cover the situation, the collection officer handles it with a personally dictated appeal. Simple cases can be disposed of with forms from beginning to final ultimatum. Complicated situations and special cases require the creative judgment of the collection officer.

A set collection plan should be followed on all past-due accounts. To allow the thought of the debt to slip from the mind of the debtor or to fade from his memory is fatal to collection success. Prompt notices and regular reminders strengthen the powerful force of habit and take advantage of the fact that a customer normally expects to pay his obligation a certain number of days after the goods are received. Moreover, a customer gains a wholesome respect for the organization that enforces collection exactly on the standard limits with courteous but decisive promptness.

An accurate record of statements and appeals sent should be kept. This is done through card records or notations penciled opposite the entries in the accounts. The control record assures increasing momentum, cumulative pressure, mounting collection force. It also prevents taking steps that would contradict each other. Systematic control is the foundation of effective collection management.

Flexibility and Change of Pace. After regularity, promptness, system, and clockwork timing have been assured, some provision should be made for flexibility and change of pace. It is unwise, for example, to use the identical collection sequence twice in succession on the same debtor. The reason is obvious. The customer who becomes delinquent twice in quick succession should be given drastically different treatment at the first indication of the second delinquency. A different form of strong reminder should be sent immediately. Or the collection officer should give the case individual attention. Thereafter, matters should be brought to quick conclusion, at a much faster pace than normal.

To assure flexibility in collection procedure, it is the usual practice to indicate, with simple code signs on the cards or in the accounts, those customers who are most likely to violate their credit agreements, as proved by their delinquencies in the past. The number of times each customer has been delinquent is also indicated. The collection follow-up is then relentlessly speeded up when applied to those customers with previous bad-pay records. Every collection system should be designed for regularity with allowance for flexibility. After all, it controls a complex problem.

Form Collection Openings. Effective form appeals are expanded from openings like these:

> When we extended you credit, we did so gladly because of the fine reports we received from your references.

> * * *

> How about remembering us the next time you sit down to write checks?

> * * *

> As the vice president of KENCO, INC., you are a man of responsible position. Because of this fact we have been glad to extend credit to you.

> * * *

> You know that we value your business and that you are a welcome customer on our books. But this morning the general manager of our firm said to me that in ten days he was going to ask for a report telling him just who owes us money and why they owe it. Frankly, I don't want to put your name on that list. I want to rate you "A" in that report, and all it takes to enable me to do so is your check.

> * * *

> Perhaps at some time you've written a customer saying that you would appreciate a check in payment of his bill. Of course you know, then, how we feel and can appreciate our present request.

Contrasts and Comparisons. Special attention may be seized by opening with an interesting comparison.

DISCUSSION STAGE—"COMPARISON" OPENING

> I don't know whether you've ever whipped a swirling stream for bass. If you have, you know it's good sport.

> Frankly, I'm fishing this morning, but it isn't such good sport as the other kind. I'm fishing for some money I think you owe this firm. The books show your balance as $200--the exact amount of constructive service rendered you since your last payment on September 15. We've aimed to give you a full dollar's worth for every dollar that is now on the books.

> Now each of us in this firm knows that you are fair and square. Personally, I am convinced, now that you've received this third appeal--the first two went to you on February 15 and March 15--that you will send your check for the balance or drop us a note telling us when it will come. You'll do this, won't you--right now?

Using Questions. Discussion appeals aiming to draw replies are made effective by opening with a series of questions.

Are you ill? Have you been absent from your home? Has some serious trouble overtaken you?

Certainly there must be some unusual situation that has prevented you from answering, with a reasonable explanation, my reminder of May 5 or arranging a settlement of your account.

My offer to help you in clearing up this matter is still open. But I cannot wait much longer for your reply. If you are interested in an amicable settlement, let me hear from you not later than May 25.

Assuming Favorable Action. The following strong reminder is constructed on the assumption of oversight and immediate favorable action. It emphasizes the convenience of sending the check at once.

STRONG REMINDER ASSUMING FAVORABLE ACTION

The check you intended to send us in payment of this month's account of $98.75 has not arrived. No doubt it was simply overlooked. This is not a serious oversight, but for the sake of simplifying the handling of these small accounts, promptness in remitting is greatly appreciated.

Don't go to the bother of writing any explanation. Such oversights occur now and then. We understand how they happen. Just send along your check in the postage-free reply envelope enclosed for your convenience.

Without show of irritation at the delay in payment, this reminder is simple, direct, and friendly.

Materials for Form Follow-Ups. Should the reminder fail to bring the check, material for follow-ups will be found in the reasons why prompt, regular collections must be made. Some of these reasons are:

You need the money for your own business.

If you allow a long extension, he has your money, you lose interest on it, your overhead rises correspondingly and you are forced to charge relatively higher prices. This puts you at a disadvantage with competitors.

The account is justly due for a valuable service rendered.

The customer has willingly assumed this obligation.

To maintain his credit, the customer must pay up.

The finance policies of your firm were made clear when credit was first extended. You want to help him preserve his excellent credit rating. You want to help him to expand his business and enjoy greater profits.

Personal Tone. Forms are written as if each were to go to one person instead of perhaps a thousand. The test is this: When the appeal is read, does it give the impression of a personal message?

Observe that the following urgency appeals (which, by the way, have made impressive records) carry a firm, insistent, personal tone:

STAGE OF URGENCY—BRIEF AND INCISIVE

We have received no response to our September 20 appeal. You will doubtless agree that this leaves us with only one alternative: to instruct our attorney to enforce collection. As this would be extremely disagreeable to you and to us as well, a final opportunity is offered you to effect a settlement before the matter passes out of our hands.

Your account will be turned over to our attorney unless we receive your check for $150 by October 20. We earnestly hope that you will choose to act now!

STAGE OF URGENCY—LAST CHANCE, NOTICE OF LEGAL ACTION

Your failure to reply to our appeal of April 30 can be interpreted in only one way: your past-due account must be settled with Mr. Evans of Harris & Evans, 1694 Shaw Drive, our legal representative in Cleveland.

We hesitated before taking this final step, but we now feel justified in going ahead because of your apparent indifference in this matter. We have exhausted every means of securing your willing cooperation.

We hope, of course, that this balance can be collected without taking court action. But we have instructed Mr. Evans to initiate any proceedings necessary to protect our interests.

STAGE OF URGENCY—STRICT TONE, LAST CHANCE, THREAT OF FORECLOSURE

We are still without settlement covering the long overdue balance under your contract. It seems strange that you have not taken care of this balance or made any response whatever to our several notices and appeals, especially our attorney's demand. Is it possible that after all you are going to compel us to have our attorney proceed further with the collection of this account and, if necessary, to institute foreclosure proceedings under our mechanic's lien to have your property sold to satisfy our claim?

If foreclosure proceedings are instituted, the owner of the mortgage against your property will become a defendant with you. In that event he will, without doubt, feel obliged to take some action to protect his interests. Under the terms of the mortgage you are probably bound to pay all expense that may be incurred in such proceedings by the mortgage owner.

Under the contract terms we hold, you will be required to pay all additional expense that we incur in collecting. The expense of foreclosure probably will amount to several hundred dollars, perhaps as much as $500, all of which you will be required to pay, even though you do not finally lose your property or whatever equity you have in it.

Will you take care of this at once, or shall we communicate with the mortgage owner to notify him of the situation and of the apparent necessity for foreclosure proceedings, in which he will become a defendant with you?

You will have no one but yourself to blame for whatever results may follow if you fail to settle the matter satisfactorily immediately upon receipt of this notice of impending action.

How a Collection Form System Operates. Unless you are a collection officer or a member of his staff, rarely do you see with your own eyes an expertly prepared collection system in operation. For that reason, the following tested and successful set of forms (taken from an insurance company's files) is all the more valuable as an illustration.

The system is made up of twenty-six units in all. The entire sequence is *never* sent to one customer. The method is selective. Out of the six "50-day appeals" (that is, appeals sent after the expiration of a period of 50 days) one is chosen and sent; out of the six "60-day appeals" the one proper unit is chosen; and so on. The appeals in each division are varied in tone and phrasing to fit various classes of customers. Here is a summary of the units:

Insurance Follow-Up System

APPEALS

1 to 6	......Reminders (50-day)
10 to 16	......Stronger reminders (60-day)
20 to 25	......Discussion stage with special appeals (70-day)
30 to 32	......Urgency (80-day): Cancellations for new business, with notice of cancellation enclosed
40	.........Final urgency (90-day): Cancellation put into effect and return of policy called for
41	.........Last-chance appeal (90-day): For reconsideration after cancellation
50	.........Miscellaneous: To follow promise of payment

Observe that the appeals in the series are numbered by groups of tens: 1-6, 10-16, 20-25, 30-32, 40-41, and 50. This is done to make quick reference easy for the dictator in specifying to his assistant what form is to be used. Forms 1-6 are first reminders; 10-16, stronger reminders; 20-25, discussion units; 30-32, urgency units; and 40-41, last chance and reconsideration appeals.

Illustrating Increasing Pressure: Four Insurance Forms. The four appeals that follow are selected to demonstrate increasing pressure.

APPEAL 1: REMINDER (50-DAY)

This is a reminder for the premium payment of $123.45 due on Policy No. 389765A. June 26, 19--, was the effective date of the policy; the premium is now fifty days overdue. If your check is not now in the mail, please enclose one for $123.45 in the attached business reply envelope.

APPEAL 14: STRONG REMINDER (60-DAY)—APPEAL TO PROTECTION

The fire trucks come roaring down Main Street with sirens wide open. They screech to a stop in front of your business! Your first thought is: "I let the insurance company cancel my fire insurance policy yesterday for nonpayment of premium. I personally can't stand the loss of my $40,000 building." But the fire crackles merrily on--and tomorrow you are bankrupt.

Will that be your plight?

We'll still accept your $123.45 check in payment of the premium on your Policy No. 389765A if we receive it by noon of September 25. Don't let the unexpected ruin you. Mail us your check today.

APPEAL 23: DISCUSSION (70-DAY)—SPECIAL APPEAL BY
COMPANY EXECUTIVE

Mr. Loftus of the Credit Department placed your account on my desk this morning with the remark: "Mr. Jens ignores every reminder we have sent him concerning the overdue premium on his fire insurance policy. I suggest that it be canceled for nonpayment of premium."

I do not want to carry out that request, for I feel that you must have some very good reason for not having sent in your remittance or a few words explaining the reason for not having done so. Would you do me the personal favor of writing me a short note of explanation?

The amount you owe on Policy No. 389765A is $123.45. I am confident that you will send either a payment by return mail or an explanation that will be entirely satisfactory.

APPEAL 40: FINAL URGENCY (90-DAY)—CANCELLATION PUT
INTO EFFECT, RETURN OF POLICY ASKED FOR

Your policy is being canceled today for nonpayment of premium, in line with our formal notice of cancellation sent you on October 10, effective October 25.

We now request that you immediately return our policy in the enclosed envelope so that we can complete our cancellation files. Remember this--it is not our decision to cancel. It is yours.

Upon receipt of a cashier's check, we will suggest the reinstatement of your contract to the underwriting department.

This series of form appeals is an instructive demonstration of what may be done in collection procedure. Such a series may be expanded, curtailed, renewed, or revised at will. The series illustrated here is revised every six months. Details of procedure are changed, phraseology is altered and renewed, fresh appeals are inserted to cover new situations.

•

No one policyholder of this company ever receives the same form more than once, for to permit this to occur would be to lose the power of the appeal. When he senses that these forms may not produce the desired results and that special personal appeals may have to be devised, the expert credit executive reinforces the series by taking over in person.

Special Collection Procedures

Among many special collection procedures in common use the following illustrations have proved exceptionally successful.

The "Story" Approach. A "story" opening seizes the debtor's attention. The introductory narrative is compressed into a few opening lines and then at once applied to the collection.

THE "STORY" APPROACH—STAGE OF URGENCY

"Story" Opening
> Two Irishmen were watching steel workers on a large building under construction. After gazing for some time, Pat turned to Mike and said, "I sure would hate to fall from up there." Mike replied, "Sure and I wouldn't mind the fall so much as I would the sudden stop."

Applied to the Subject
> We believe that you are now in the position of Mike. You have not minded the fall, but you are now at the point when the sudden stop that goes with unpleasant collection procedure may really hurt.

Appeal to Pride
> Premier Theaters are old and reliable Herald advertisers. People are accustomed to seeing their advertisement and look for it. The payment of bills has heretofore always been prompt. In fact, the Premier Theaters account has been one we have been eager to serve.

Threat and Final Demand
> Don't force us to adopt stern measures that will endanger your good standing. We must insist that you send a remittance at once to balance your account of $476.35. We shall be disappointed if you force us to take action.

"Turning the Tables" Approach. Letting the debtor decide what he would do if the positions were reversed proves forceful in case after case. "What would you do to collect this account—if you were in *our* place?"

Illustrating this method, the appeal on page 478 (written by the Credit Manager of the Lewisburg Chair & Furniture Co., Lewisburg, Pennsylvania) was the first-prize winner in the American Credit Indemnity Company's group of "Fifty Gold Medal Collection Letters."

"TURNING THE TABLES" APPROACH

What would you do?

If our positions were reversed and we owed you the following?

May 5	$107.00
May 28	71.88

And we failed to mail a check after you made several
requests for payment?

What would you do?

Yes, we could take the same steps, but we believe we know
you better than that. We feel you want to be fair and are willing to do the right thing.

Why not tell your bookkeeper to draw a check payable to
us, for the past-due amount, today?

Thank you.

The "Resale" Approach. Resale material in collections is often
used by those concerns that do an installment business, although
such material is helpful to others as well. The aim of resale material
is to make the order "stick"; that is, to keep the customer satisfied
with his purchase and to make him willing to pay his account. The
first glow of pride in the possession of the article purchased must be
kept fresh and vivid in order that the purchaser's estimate of the
value of the article may not shrink and make him reluctant to pay.
The collection appeal containing resale material "resells" to the
purchaser what he bought, satisfies him that he did the right thing,
and re-establishes for him the value of the article.

In the following example note the resale material, the appeal to
imitation, and the appeal to fair play:

THE "RESALE" APPROACH—WITH FAIR-PLAY APPEAL

Resale	We hope you like those five handkerchiefs, individually monogrammed with your initials, that you ordered a few weeks ago. These handkerchiefs are fashioned of fine linen, stitched and finished to painstaking quality standards. The price, you'll remember, was only $2.95. That was pretty econom-ical, wouldn't you agree?
Appeal to Imitation	Other men answered at once, enclosing their checks for $2.95.
	Prompt payments enable us to offer this remark-able value. Wouldn't it be the fair thing for you, too, to send your check?
Fair-Play Appeal	We have played square. We sent return postage and a shipping label for you to use if you didn't care to keep the handkerchiefs. Now six weeks have gone by. You haven't sent a check or returned the handkerchiefs.
	Yet we know that you are a fair and square man. May we hear from you--by return mail--please?

The following example combines in the first half a strong reminder with collection appeals. The remaining half is devoted to resale.

STRONG IN RESALE MATERIAL AND PERSONAL TONE

Third Reminder

> Won't you <u>please</u> take care of the enclosed statement before you forget it? It's the <u>third</u> we have sent you, by the way--one about two months ago, one about a month ago. Now we come knocking at your door again.

Convincing Appeal; Personal Tone

> The amount is insignificant, I know, and if it were the only small account outstanding, we wouldn't bother you. But your little debt + your neighbor's perhaps + all the rest = many thousands of dollars. And that + bookkeeping + postage + interest = a big debit that may become embarrassing when bills are paid every week as ours are. Please don't think us offensively persistent. Your credit is as good as gold. But we want to know that the WEEKLY is giving you genuine satisfaction, and that you are a <u>pleased</u> member of our family circle--and your payment will tell us so.

Resale

> And while we are on the subject, <u>is</u> the WEEKLY pleasing you? We try to make the WEEKLY act as a secretary to big and busy men and women--a secretary that will read, clip, and translate, when necessary, the best articles in 5,000 periodicals and give you the gist at a glance--a secretary that will save you hours of reading in these breathless days.
>
> I believe we must have succeeded in some measure in our aim; otherwise we wouldn't be able to interest and hold as subscribers year after year 2,500,000 American men and women of the ambitious thinking classes in our American democracy.
>
> It would be a real compliment if we could feel that the WEEKLY had become a permanent part of <u>your</u> equipment.

Action

> Anytime, by the way, that anything goes wrong with our service to you, please let us know. And in the meantime you will attend to the enclosed statement right away, won't you?

The "Sporting" Approach. "Help me win my wager" is the theme of an entire class of effective appeals, illustrated by these paragraphs:

"HELP ME KEEP MY PROMISE" APPEAL

Did you ever make a promise to one of your best friends and then have to rack your brain to figure out how you were going to make good? Well, that is exactly what I am up against.

Our credit manager left for Denver yesterday to attend a convention. And just before he went, I told him we would have a surprise for him in the way of the biggest week's collections the company has made this year. I can do this with your help and am confident that you will let us have a check for $350 to take care of your past-due account.

"We Pay the Freight" Approach. "Enclosed is a self-addressed special-delivery envelope—because for your sake, as well as our own, we are in a hurry to balance up your old account on our books. Pull out your pen now and send that check posthaste!"

The following appeal drew comment from scores of persons who received it from a well-known national magazine. "Did I pay?" remarked a man who got this reminder. "I did indeed!"

NOVELTY APPEAL—MAKES ACTION EASY

"WE PAY THE FREIGHT" proclaims a large mail-order house to its prospective customers.

We know that you want to pay the enclosed bill--that you like to keep small bills off your desk and out of your morning's mail.

So here is the freight--prepaid--in anticipation of your willingness to mail your check today.

Thanks for your promptness and for your interest in TIME.

STAMP

The "Half-and-Half" Approach. An effective device for drawing a reply from a customer who has ignored all reminders is a collection appeal divided into vertical halves in such a way as to make two sides for twin messages. The left side is the space reserved for the typewritten message from the credit officer. The right side is reserved for the customer in the hope that he will use it to explain his delay. Below you see the original appeal and the actual reply it drew.

THIS IS OUR SIDE OF THE STORY	THIS IS YOUR SIDE--USE IT!
You owe us $27.50. Will you	*Gentlemen:*
attach your check to your half of this sheet and rush it back to us,	*This bill as shown is due and should be paid. Business is so quiet—and collections so slow—that I have been unable to do so.*
OR	*You will have this money just as soon as I can get it for you. I have plenty out that I am having to wait on.*
if you cannot attach a check, explain in full why you can't, and tell us when you can.	*I appreciate your kindness. I'll take care of this so soon as possible.*
Please use your half--	*Patrick M. Dennis*
RIGHT NOW!	
Sincerely yours	
J. W. Collins	
J. W. Collins Credit Manager	

"Two-Sided" Appeal and the Reply It Drew

Sharp Language. Sharp language is a dangerous, double-edged weapon. It can cut both ways. In unskillful hands it often does. Needed in later stages of collection, it is a fatal bar to success in early stages. First exhaust friendly methods. Turn to other methods only as the final resort of late stages.

Increasing momentum and cumulative force are thrust into late collection stages through the use of sharper and—if necessary—still sharper language.

From the following list the collection officer selects sharp phrases suitable to the stage in which the debtor falls. Hidden in the middle of a paragraph, sharp phrases are muffled; at the end they fall like bombshells.

Sharp Phrases in the Order of Increasing Force

Reference to past unanswered appeals.

Reference to past unanswered appeals, with dates on which they were sent.

"Immediately."

"Will you not send us your check?"

"Let us have your check NOW!" or "Send us your check AT ONCE!"

Mention of a set time limit: ". . . by May 1" or ". . . within 48 hours."

"We now require that you send us. . . ."
"We must now insist that you send us. . . ."
"We are compelled. . . ."
"We must demand. . . ."
"It is imperative that you send us. . . ."

"Such delinquent conduct makes it impossible for us to go farther in our earnest efforts."

"With regret we are now forced to put your name on the Slow-Pay List. This action means, of course, that you are to lose your preferred credit rating not only with us but also with others."

Generalized threat of other action:
        "We should dislike—and we are sincere in this statement—to be forced to resort to other measures."
        "You force us, with regret, to take steps to protect our interests."

Specific threat of final action:
    "sight draft" (mild)
    "collection agency" (stronger)
    "our attorney" (ultimatum)

"Pin for the Check" Approach. "Enclosed is a *big pin* to serve two big purposes. In the first place, it's a sample of hundreds of similar items we carry in stock. [The collecting company is an office supply house.] In the second place, we're sending a big pin to do a big job. It will do a job that's important to us if you will use it to pin your check to the enclosed bill and rush it back." The record shows that a good many of the delinquent customers used "the big pin."

Telegrams for Urgency Appeals. The effect of a telegram is abrupt. When you receive a "wire," you lay everything aside to read it. So does everyone else. No telegram is discarded unopened. These qualities make telegrams effective in collecting overdue accounts. To urgency expressed in words is added a new kind of urgency—the urgency of time.

An example: one company sent telegrams to twenty of its debtors. These were the results:

> 4 paid within one week after the telegram
> 3 paid within two weeks after the telegram
> 4 paid within three weeks after the telegram
> 2 paid within one week after the second telegram
> 2 paid within two weeks after the second telegram
> 3 paid within three weeks after the second telegram
> 1 claimed additional credit
> 1 did not pay, and his account was placed for collection

Ten Tested Ways to Develop Collection Power

1. Make your appeals exert pressure promptly, regularly, and with ever-increasing force.

2. State in each appeal the exact amount due, or with each appeal send a statement and refer to it.

3. Hold the good will of the debtor as long as you can.

4. Select your appeals to fit him.

5. Reinstate in his mind the value of the goods he ordered. "Resell" him on his purchase.

6. Fix a final date on or before which the check must be received.

7. Be reasonable but never waver. The debtor will respect your firmness.

8. Never resort to anger, pity, or contempt. If you do, you may get the money—but you will lose the customer.

9. Use constructively the powerful leverage of psychological appeals.

10. Be persistent. Keep continually at it.

```
┌─────────────────────────────────────────────────────────┐
│  The Final Aims of a Powerful Collection System:          │
│    1 To hold GOOD WILL                                    │
│    2 To lay the groundwork for FUTURE PATRONAGE           │
│    3 To get the money—and KEEP THE CUSTOMER               │
└─────────────────────────────────────────────────────────┘
```

Systematic Collection Power—Its Final Aims. The winning collection officer is the one who brings in the greatest number of payments with the maximum measure of good will. Like the adjustment manager, he, too, works shoulder to shoulder with the sales manager to save customers and get more business.

Never relaxing his vigilance over delinquent customers, he teams up with other top management officers to earn his company a handsome name for fairness, justice, and efficient management.

Communication Problems

● **1.** Set up a four-stage collection series for a company making small unsecured loans to consumers.

Directions: The first reminder is preceded by a printed notice that says "The _____ payment on your account is now past due." Make each stage an obvious form message with such items as the *amount due* and *date due* filled in in blanks provided immediately beneath the letterhead. The collection series should be relatively short and stringency developed in the language used. Many firms add to stringency by having the reminder signed by a clerk in the credit department, the discussion signed by the collection manager, and the urgency stage signed by the president. In other words, let the delinquent know that the situation becomes progressively more serious until finally the "big brass" is involved. Because such loans usually call for monthly payments (installment loans), your time interval between stages should be short enough to assure that more than one payment does not become due before you have completed the collection cycle.

● **2.** Set up a four-stage collection series for one of these situations:

   A retail department store selling on the installment plan
   A retail department store extending credit on a monthly charge
      account basis
   A public utilities company (telephone, gas, or electrical service)

Directions: Assume that each customer whose account is past due will receive one printed reminder card with a second copy of his statement. Then, prepare a first reminder, a strong reminder, a discussion, and an urgency. Your messages, remember, are going to retail customers whose good will you value and whose knowledge of credit procedure may be inadequate. Use resale material in the reminder and strong reminder. Assume that resale is your original contribution and that the remaining paragraphs are forms.

● 3. As Credit and Collection Manager of the Benson Motor Company—a firm that carries the financing on many of the cars it sells, your job is to make every effort to collect payments on automobile contracts before the distasteful act of repossession becomes necessary. Your full collection procedure uses a printed overdue payment notice, two personal telephone calls to the delinquent, a discussion message, and a final urgency demand.

You are now considering the case of John H. Peters and his wife. They purchased a $3,000 automobile a year ago by paying $1,200 down and financing the remaining $1,800 with the Benson Motor Company on a 24-month, 6% conditional sales contract. Their monthly payments are $84. After making ten payments, they have allowed the eleventh payment to become twenty days past due. The due date of the twelfth payment is only ten days away. In the two telephone conversations, Mr. Peters assured you that payment would be made right away. It is now a week since your last telephone call.

Directions: Write the discussion message.

● 4. Modern collection procedures insist upon good taste—even through the urgency demand. The trend toward using pride, cooperation, and credit-standing appeals is replacing the threat or fear appeal. You are the Collection Manager for the RX Drug Company which wholesales drugs and druggists' supplies to drugstores throughout the country. The account of the Save-Way Drug Company of Midtown, Nebraska, is now over 45 days delinquent. The balance of the account is $634.50. How could you appeal to pride, to cooperation, to credit standing? The first paragraph of your message reads:

> Your frequent orders for RX Drugs indicate that your business must be good. Your current balance with us, however, is $634.50 and still remains unpaid despite our reminders of May 1 and June 1.

Directions: Now write appeal paragraphs for three variations of the massage. First, appeal to pride. Second, write a paragraph appealing to a sense of cooperation. Third, write a paragraph appealing to retention of a good credit rating. The three paragraphs will not, of course, appear in the same message but are to be designed for use in adaptation of form mailings.

● 5. You are Credit-Collection Manager for the Bali-Hi Swimsuit Company of Los Angeles. One account in Miami Beach, The Caribbean Shop, has carried your high-fashion women's swimwear for many years. Occasionally, the manager of The Caribbean, Miss Amy Ward, needs a reminder to clear the balance of her summer account in preparation for the winter vacation business in Florida. It is now October and The Caribbean account has an overdue balance of $89.75.

Directions: Write Miss Ward a personal appeal built around the idea of clearing the overdue balance in preparation for her usual heavy winter business. Because the account purchases about $2,000 from Bali-Hi each year, you usually take this opportunity to subordinate the request for payment by using sales promotion material and your expression of gratitude for her many orders.

PART VIII Management's Guide: The Business Report

Chapter 21   *Creating and Presenting Effective Reports*

The Importance of Reports to Management

Decision-Making at the Top. Top management men are the decision-makers. During the hours of each business day and probably during many other waking hours, they make, or they are in the process of making, crucial decisions that may affect thousands of lives and that may sway the success of a far-flung business enterprise.

"Top Management Decision Simulation." Decision-making is at the very heart of management. And each decision that is made has to be based on facts—clearly organized and intelligently presented facts. To present these facts and to have them instantly available for decision-making purposes, management depends heavily upon the report.

So important has *fact-guided* decision-making become during recent years that the American Management Association now offers a highly advanced training course for top executives and middle executives in the first and second lines of administrative command. This now-famous course is called "Top Management Decision Simulation." The key word, "simulation," means "to assume the appearance of, without the reality." In other words, these experienced management men, taking this advanced executive-training course, play "a sort of war game for business"—a make-believe exercise that turns out to be deadly serious—an exercise in which executives *practice* running a company in competition with their opposing teams and gain priceless wisdom from that experience. The idea of this deadly serious "decision-making game" is to "duplicate" ten years of running a business in two weeks. The American Management Association finds it a far cheaper way to learn *what not to do* than by going bankrupt in real life.

Business Reports Are the Guides. Do the executives playing this serious game use business reports? Indeed yes! As the Red Keystone Corporation executives meet the stern competition of the Blue

Square Company executives (as well as the competition of all the other mythical outfits also in the game), each executive group bases its continuing decisions upon fact-packed reports. These business reports guide them in making up their minds as to what price line they ought to stress, whether to expand their plant capacity, what proportion of their liquid capital funds should go into production, research and development, or sales promotion.

From business reports they learn whether they face a risk of running out of inventory as a result of not planning for an additional plant to meet an expanding market. From reports they learn whether they face a risk of losing part of their market because of too cautious a sales promotion policy. From reports they learn whether they face a risk of being caught in a price war that may drive selling price below their cost of production.

Management Planning, Both Short and Long Range, Is Based on Fact-Packed Reports. These high-powered executive "game-players"—up against the toughest kind of competition—namely, *other* groups of *equally* expert executives—gain practice in using fact-packed reports for long-range planning, for setting manufacturing goals, sales quotas, and general strategy. Using interim periodic reports for equally important short-range planning, they also train in new management flexibility, for each quarter's results (compressed into one day or even a half day or less under the game rules) reveal how their strategy is working out, and they must be quick to adapt to changing competitive conditions.

Through two strenuous weeks of action-packed, fact-based decision-making, they vastly increase their understanding of the decision-making process and sharpen such "analytical report" skills as the collection of data, the analysis and evaluation of statistics, the diagnosis of management problems, and the development of alternative solutions for executive action.

Electronic Computers, Automation, and the Reports of the Future. For A. M. A.'s top management decision-making "training game," the necessary battery of fact-packed reports—the full-length, the interim, and the memorandum—are in part provided by lightning-fast electronic computers linked to "printer-units" alongside for printing the reports. Only in this manner can ten years of actual management experience be condensed into two weeks.

Twenty years from now—much sooner perhaps—electronic computers and similar automation devices with printer attachments may produce most of our reports that are statistical in nature.

But for many years to come, top management executives who "face the real thing" day in and day out will continue to guide their decision-making on the basis of information drawn from carefully prepared business reports submitted in conventional typewritten form. They will use these reports as *valuable and essential tools of management.* For in the final analysis *reports are simply instruments used by management in running a business.*

The Center of Management Communication. In every well-organized business enterprise there is a center of communication, a "report headquarters." As one of the vital tools of management, the function of the communication center is to report and translate *incoming* communications concerning external conditions, the progress of activity, successes, difficulties, and risks, into *outgoing* communications in terms of new activities, preparatory steps, and the like, "all shaped," as C. I. Barnard puts it in *The Functions of the Executive,* "according to the ultimate as well as the immediate purposes to be served." *

Top Management Calls for Better Reports. "The report has become an absolute imperative in the complexity of modern business," assert the editors of *Printers' Ink.* "Unfortunately many of the people to whom the job of preparing reports is entrusted are almost wholly unfitted for the task. The result is confusion, obstruction, muddy thinking, badly conceived plans, and all of the other dangers and disasters that are attendant upon lack of the right ability. We must," conclude these business editors, "have staff people who can develop clear, concise, and logical material."

A Four-Point Check List on Reports

1. Make it readable.
   Keep your sentences relatively short.
   Keep your paragraphs relatively brief.
2. Make it easy to understand.
   Use simple graphs and charts.
   Use nontechnical words.
3. Make it complete.
   Don't "skate over the surface."
   "Get down to brass tacks."
4. Give it handsome form.
   Design an attractive title page.
   Lay out each page to attract the eye.

* Published in Cambridge, The Harvard University Press, p. 178.

The following paragraphs written by a top-rank engineer reflect the crucial importance of the subject:

When a great undertaking is completed, a careful report of it, giving account of every step, is prepared for the proper authorities. . . . Examples are the annual report of a philanthropic institution, such as the Rockefeller Foundation, on its activities throughout the world, or the annual report of a great business organization. . . .

Essentially the same careful record is made on a smaller scale by sub-divisions of business houses and by agencies public and semipublic. In many lines weekly reports are rendered: by traveling salesmen to the home office . . . by managers. . . . Finally, there is the multitude of daily reports. . . .

No prudent executive would dare trust himself in any important action without learning the opinions of his associates, or at least obtaining a comprehensive statement of the important facts in the matter under contemplation. For the information which he needs, the executive of today must rely upon reports. He himself—no less than his subordinates, down to the shipping clerk—is meanwhile engaged in formulating similar reports for the transmission of information to his associates.*

Top Management Also Demands Report Correctness and Accuracy. A top General Electric Company engineer—a senior executive with long years of management behind him—is on the telephone. He's ready to read the riot act, says a delightful article in GE's house magazine. "Right before my eyes," he states, "is a brief report made out by one of our young engineers. I have to guess—yes, guess —what the fellow is driving at. I'm no prose style shark, but I find myself getting a little angry when I see four sentences stupidly tied together into a silly bundle with splice commas!"

"And it gets worse. This clumsy joker uses *principal* when he means *principle*. He misspells *Cincinnati* and *accommodate*. What if some of this chap's stuff escapes us and gets into the hands of our customers?"

Yes—what if it does? The top engineer is really wound up. "At the last meeting of our Association, representatives of practically all the major companies expressed their serious doubts about the way their younger men were putting down their words—*and their futures*—on paper. What's to be done about it?"

General Electric points out that no piece of company business can begin, progress, and achieve its purpose without an accurate command of words. "Writing is an integral part of the electrical manufacturing business. Every day in your future you will be called upon

* Ralph U. Fitting, *Report Writing* (New York: The Ronald Press Co.).

to speak and to write, and when you speak or prepare a report, you will be revealing your potential worth to the company. As you move up the ladder of success, what you write will determine, in part, your rate of climb."

Hammering home this thought with final urgency, General Electric quotes Peter Drucker's famous article in *Fortune*, "How to Be an Employee," concluding that the ability to express ideas in writing and in speaking heads the list of requirements for success. "As soon as you move one step up from the bottom, your effectiveness depends on your ability to reach others through the written and spoken word," concludes Drucker. "And the further away your job is from manual work, the larger the organization of which you are an employee, the more important it will be that you know how to convey your thoughts in writing and speaking. In the very large organizations, whether it is the government, the large business corporation, or the Armed Forces, this ability to express yourself is perhaps the most important of all the skills you can possess."

Concludes GE: "It pleases us at General Electric to go on record as supporters of Mr. Drucker's statement."

One could hardly ask for a more convincing statement of management's demand for correctness, accuracy, and a sound control of report techniques.

A Piece of Paper Goes Along as a Guide. From top to bottom of the modern business enterprise, "pieces of paper," in size all the way from one sentence to a 100 pages or more, help to guide executive decision-making. "No physical activity," states a former president of the General Motors Corporation, testifying before a joint committee of the Congress of the United States, "goes on in our modern age without a piece of paper going along to guide it."

The Report Is a Guiding "Fact Channel." Business reports serve as guides and as "fact channels." As commerce expands, the lines of information, authority, and responsibility become more and more complex. But management executives must have these channels of information in order to make correct decisions. To carry this information is the function of the communication fact channel known as the *business report.**

Note the unusually effective presentation of statistical information from an annual business report on pages 490 and 491.

---

* A list of useful supplementary sources for the study of reports is given on page 521.

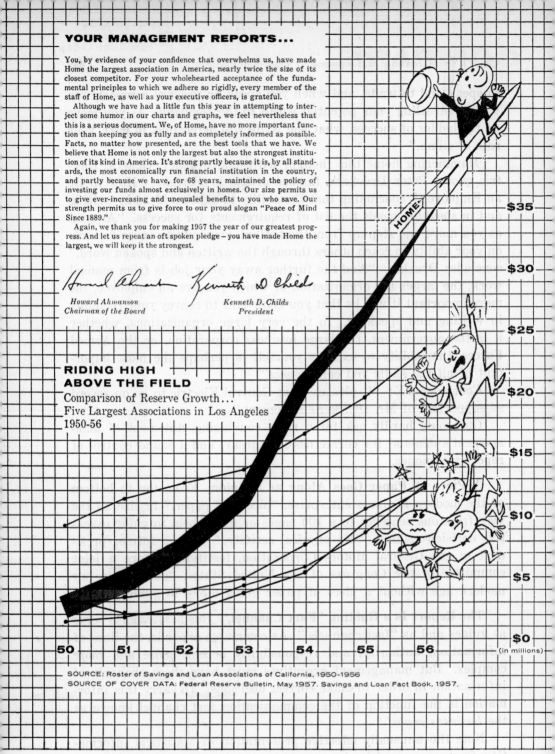

YOUR MANAGEMENT REPORTS...

You, by evidence of your confidence that overwhelms us, have made Home the largest association in America, nearly twice the size of its closest competitor. For your wholehearted acceptance of the fundamental principles to which we adhere so rigidly, every member of the staff of Home, as well as your executive officers, is grateful.

Although we have had a little fun this year in attempting to interject some humor in our charts and graphs, we feel nevertheless that this is a serious document. We, of Home, have no more important function than keeping you as fully and as completely informed as possible. Facts, no matter how presented, are the best tools that we have. We believe that Home is not only the largest but also the strongest institution of its kind in America. It's strong partly because it is, by all standards, the most economically run financial institution in the country, and partly because we have, for 68 years, maintained the policy of investing our funds almost exclusively in homes. Our size permits us to give ever-increasing and unequaled benefits to you who save. Our strength permits us to give force to our proud slogan "Peace of Mind Since 1889."

Again, we thank you for making 1957 the year of our greatest progress. And let us repeat an oft spoken pledge – you have made Home the largest, we will keep it the strongest.

Howard Ahmanson
Howard Ahmanson
Chairman of the Board

Kenneth D. Childs
Kenneth D. Childs
President

RIDING HIGH
ABOVE THE FIELD
Comparison of Reserve Growth...
Five Largest Associations in Los Angeles
1950-56

$35

$30

$25

$20

$15

$10

$5

$0
(in millions)

50   51   52   53   54   55   56

SOURCE: Roster of Savings and Loan Associations of California, 1950-1956
SOURCE OF COVER DATA: Federal Reserve Bulletin, May 1957. Savings and Loan Fact Book, 1957.

Dramatized with Whimsical Humor and Eye-Catching Action—

COMPARE...

Savings Benefits Offered by HOME

Last year, as the graph at right shows, savers continued to show preference for Home. To date, more than 200,000 savers have compared and selected Home as the institution for their savings. Here are their reasons.

Higher Earnings

No higher return is paid by an insured association to its savers . . . a return now paid *quarterly* on all accounts. Savers can plan their financial affairs with complete confidence for Home always declares its rate of return in advance. Accounts opened by the 10th of any month earn from the 1st of that month.

Ready Availability of Funds

Home has always honored every withdrawal request immediately upon demand. Home, like commercial banks and other associations, can require prior written withdrawal notice. This has *never* been done, even during our worst depression. Home's cash balances and unsurpassed reserve strength assure continuation of this time-honored policy.

| HOME 16.8% | SAVINGS & LOAN INDUSTRY 23.9% | BANKS 60.6% |

Overhead...Light as a Feather at Home

Operating Expenses Expressed as a Percentage of Gross Operating Income.

Home is not strapped by overhead. Home's overhead, 30% less than industry average and 72% less than banks, permits higher earnings to be paid to savers without sacrificing the strength of the Association.

68 Years of Experience

Behind our slogan "Peace of Mind Since 1889" stands the experience gained during 68 years of service. During this time, through wars, depressions, and financial crises, Home's doors have never closed . . . your assurance of the safety of your savings. Home stands alone in branch management experience by bringing to savers in 21 Southern California communities the advantages of America's largest and strongest association at the friendly, local level.

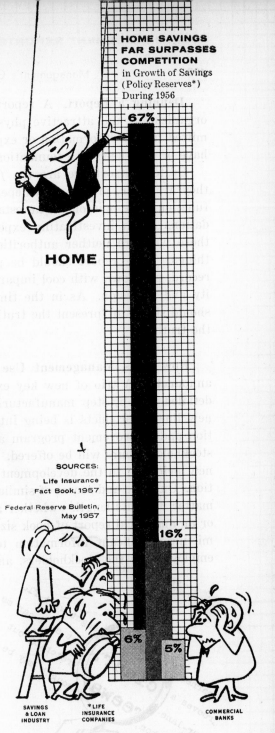

HOME SAVINGS FAR SURPASSES COMPETITION in Growth of Savings (Policy Reserves*) During 1956

67%

HOME

16%

6%

5%

SOURCES:
Life Insurance Fact Book, 1957

Federal Reserve Bulletin, May 1957

SAVINGS & LOAN INDUSTRY

*LIFE INSURANCE COMPANIES

COMMERCIAL BANKS

—Home Savings and Loan Association

—These Full-Page Illustrated Graphs from an Annual Report Present Impressive Statistical Information

Defining a Report. A report is a written document of careful organization and attractive physical form, through which is transmitted factual information or expert opinion that the executive must have or may need as a foundation for his future plans and decisions.

Of top importance are the *facts* that the report transmits. If they are clear, precise, and dependable, they discharge their proper function. The opinions of an established authority or the recommendations of an investigating expert may also be included. But for those who are neither authorities nor experts, facts are the vital things. Your report should be prepared in the form of a concise record, put down with cool impartiality—channeling facts with clarity and precision. As in the time-honored court oath, your report should strive to "present the truth, the whole truth, and nothing but the truth."

How Does Management Use the Report? A merger is being announced. A trio of new key executives have been brought in. A detailed step-by-step manufacturing process is being described. A new line of products is being introduced. As part of a modernization and improvement program a new plant has been erected, and stockholder tours will be offered. Or an engineering group applies a new principle to the development of a revolutionary type of invention. On these and scores of similar subjects the successful report, no matter what its length—whether a one-page progress-announcement, or an analytical report of book size—does an intelligent job of transmitting significant information to the company staff itself, to the employees, to the stockholders, and to other selected audiences.

Are Your Facts Clear, Precise, and Dependable?

Top writing skill becomes "visible" every time a well-organized business report makes a complicated problem crystal clear.

Reports, Too, Win "Oscars" for Excellence. After winning a national award for the most outstanding and informative annual report among savings and loan associations, Standard Federal's President Eason put himself on record thus: "We feel that the annual report is one of the most valuable forms of communication available to us in this industry, and as such, we have done our best to present our members with an interesting, informative, fact-packed review of our Association's record. Members of a mutual organization such as ours are entitled to a complete, factual, and understandable report on the achievements of the year. And they get it."

Demonstrating the degree of competitive interest, more than 5,000 annual reports in 100 industrial classifications were considered in a recent year's international competition. Standard Federal's prize-winning entry in its class called forth wide interest in the savings and loan industry, and thousands of copies were requested by individuals throughout the country. Illustrations from this prize-winning report appear on pages 504 and 505.

New Developments in Report Circulation. In addition to the conventional circulation of its annual report among its many thousands of stockholders, Chas. Pfizer & Company, the famous drug manufacturer, departed sharply from usual corporate procedure and brought its report to the direct attention of some 3,500,000 additional readers. How did it do this? Company management decided to publish the report as a 16-page special supplement in the *New York Times*, in the *Chicago Tribune*, and in the *Los Angeles Times*. Reason for this "new technique in financial journalism," the company announced, was to let readers of three of the largest newspapers in the country "learn first-hand how a typical corporation reports to its shareholders."

Types of Reports

The five chief types of reports are: (1) the periodic report, (2) the progress report, (3) the examination report, (4) the recommendation report, and (5) the statistical report.

The Periodic Report. The periodic report is a record of activities most of which are of "record" character. This type, which summarizes events that have occurred, has come to be called a record report. It is submitted annually, semiannually, quarterly, monthly, or weekly. Daily reports are, for the most part, relatively brief informal memorandums. The periodic (or record) report covers the activities of one of the stated periods mentioned. The frequent brief reports of subordinates supply the material for the less frequent, longer, and more important reports of the junior executives, whose statements, in turn, supply the material for the elaborate record reports of the senior executives and the annual report of the president. The periodic report records essential data in historical form.

SECTION OF A PERIODIC REPORT

Investments in associated companies have been appraised and are carried at a net valuation of $204,810,328.13. This amount includes advances to associated companies as well as securities.

The interest and dividends from associated companies amount to $13,453,654.25. This is 6.9% of the average value at which these investments were carried at the beginning of the year.

Inventory at the year-end was $60,063,418.56. The net billing for the year was $376,167,428.42. The percentage of inventory to net billing was 16%.

Notes and accounts receivable, after deducting reserves, are carried at $41,676,727.47.

The Progress Report. Progress reports show the progress made during the period covered. Annual corporate reports often combine the progress and the record reports issued during the year. The record reports provide the data for the comparisons in the progress report. The usual form of comparison is to establish the status of the business this year as compared with the status of the business at the same time last year. Tabulations of statistics may be included.

SECTION OF A PROGRESS REPORT

The System had a net gain of about 1,000,000 telephones during the first six months of this year as compared with a gain of 970,000 during the first six months of 19--. During the second quarter of this year the gain was about 495,000 as compared with 402,000 for the corresponding period last year. The average number of System telephones in service during the first six months of 19-- was 5.1 per cent greater than for the corresponding period of 19--.

The number of toll and long-distance conversations for the first six months of 19-- was about 6.5 per cent greater than for the corresponding period last year.

An Earnings Report of the Company for the three-month and twelve-month periods ending June 30, 19--, and for corresponding periods ending June 30, 19--, is appended. A System Consolidated Earnings Report for the three-month and twelve-month periods ending May 31, 19--, and May 31, 19--, is shown on page 7.

The Examination Report. The examination report (also called the investigation report) analyzes past and present conditions, often in order to establish a basis for later recommendations. An examination report is founded on a program of study and investigation, which, of course, must precede the organization of the report itself, and any recommendations regarding future action. The actual *process of investigation*, upon which trustworthy conclusions and recommendations may be based, distinguishes the investigation report from the periodic report. The periodic report records known data. The investigation report (1) collects and records essential, but not previously known, data; (2) analyzes these data in order to arrive at definite conclusions; and (3) may include recommendations if they are requested and if the investigator is competent to make them.

The section from an examination report on page 496, written by an expert engineer, illustrates how essential, but not previously known, data are assembled and recorded.

SECTION OF AN EXAMINATION REPORT

Curve #3 on page 8 shows the average moisture as fired and the daily average pounds of fuel per kilowatt hour. The moisture shown is the result of a daily determination of the moisture of fuel taken from the Richardson scales. Previous to April 13 most of the fuel was Westville, having a moisture content of 12% as received, and about 12,300 B.T.U. (British thermal units) dry. The fuel introduced during the latter part of the period was Harrisburg #43 and #47, which has a moisture content of from 6% to 8% with a B.T.U. content of about 13,300.

A tabulation of the effect on the turbine heat consumption, caused by various operating conditions, appears on page 11 of this report.

The Recommendation Report. The recommendation report is an examination report, the results of which lead to specific recommendations. Hence this type of report (1) may be persuasive in manner, (2) may be argumentative in purpose, and (3) may urge a definite program of action. Whereas the examination report restricts itself to facts and to the conclusions that follow in their train, the recommendation report interprets these facts into a series of opinions that recommend a well-defined course of action. If, for example, the examination report, a section of which is reproduced on this page, closed with a set of recommendations suggesting certain actions to improve the efficiency of turbine heat consumption, it would become a recommendation report.

TRENTON, McWHYTE AND GRAVES   PAGE 3

ENGINEERS AND CONSULTANTS   OF 67 PAGES

PROJECT: Production Flow Study, Anaheim, California Plant

CLIENT: American Carton Corporation

The potential for substantially increased production at reasonable capital investment is practical without major structural changes in the plant. Our study substantiates Mr. Winslow's preliminary evaluation that realignment of machines to effect a straight-line production flow can be accomplished within the dimensions of the existing structure.

Basic problem involved is paperboard storage. A productive capacity increase of 40% automatically requires a like amount, at minimum, of board storage area. As illustrated by EXHIBIT 17, page 11, we propose this be provided by the construction of a structure paralleling the present building on the east side. It will enclose the single spur track of the S & F railroad to permit sheltered unloading of raw materials and loading of finished product.

Essential to this plan is the relocation of the present roadway. See EXHIBIT 18, page 12. As 86% of your finished product is delivered by truck, the requirement for bringing the roadway into the proposed new loading dock-storage warehouse is obvious.

Section of a Recommendation Report

The Statistical Report. The top management man, the junior executive, the executive assistant, the engineer, the economist, the physicist, all alike need words, thousands of them, to carry on their daily exchanges. But they also need figures, thousands of them— whole columns of statistics—to take care of another kind of vital communication for which words, in these special cases, would be relatively valueless. For, as you see, only statistical "language" can successfully communicate certain kinds of report essentials. In actual fact, statistics are simply a kind of "shorthand," a stenographic short-cut method of presenting masses of facts of a strictly numerical nature. When the bulk of a report presents statistical material, such as financial data, mathematical charts, tabular columns of figures, and the like, with a relatively brief interpretation of their significance, it is called a statistical report.

A List of Statistical Reports Received by the Top Executive of a Large Retail Enterprise

Balance sheet	General financial
Buyers' trips	Income statement
Cashier's overage and	Insurance
shortage	Merchandise orders placed and
Credit adjustment	amounts outstanding
Credit department	Operating sheet
Comparative sales	Payroll
Delivery equipment	Sales analysis
Department stock	Slow-selling merchandise
Expense	Stock shortage

Direction and Flow of Reports. Business reports are also classified in terms of their direction or flow within the organization as: (1) *horizontal*, (2) *vertical*, and (3) *radial*. The typical information flow (or direction of report movement) in a large industry is pictured in the diagram on page 498.*

Horizontal Information Flow—Direction of Report Movement. The *manufacturing* section of the large industry (inside upper left of the circle diagram) produces occasional periodic reports dealing with materials and processes. Some reports propose new procedures, but others discuss existing manufacturing methods and materials.

---

* The discussion of horizontal, vertical, and radial information flow with the circle diagram on page 498 is based on an interesting analysis by Warren W. Wood, of the Aerophysics Section, Convair, a Division of General Dynamics, Fort Worth, Texas.

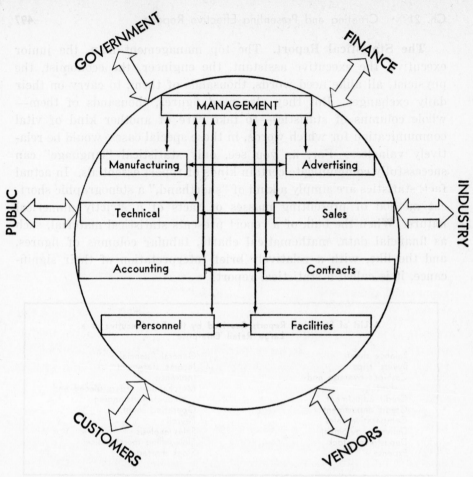

MANAGEMENT

Manufacturing		Advertising
Technical		Sales
Accounting		Contracts
Personnel		Facilities

GOVERNMENT   FINANCE

PUBLIC   INDUSTRY

CUSTOMERS   VENDORS

Typical Information Flow in Large Industry

The manufacturing department also issues periodic reports covering production, manpower, costs, and like subjects.

The *technical* section, usually an engineering department, releases specifications, proposals, and installation and manufacturing drawings. These reports may present design information and data gathered from research and analysis. Since technical reports are closely connected with administrative and financial matters, top management gives them close scrutiny.

The *accounting* department regularly issues statistical analyses of present and proposed work, evaluates its costs and manpower requirements, and carries the responsibility for financial reports, cost studies, and reports on accounting methods and practices.

The *personnel* section produces labor survey reports, recruiting publications, and employee service bulletins.

498

The *facilities* section (inside lower right of the circle diagram) produces reports keeping management and the other sections informed of the status of buildings, equipment, and space. On the basis of these reports the rest of the industrial team can adjust plans and schedules to fit these controlling factors. At this point in the discussion of the diagram, it is interesting to note that the federal government itself also maintains records of the location and condition of large equipment such as presses above a certain size and special milling machines that would be particularly vital during a defense effort.

The *contracts* (legal) section issues reports interpreting or giving opinions on contracts and various other legal matters.

The *sales* department makes periodic reports of sales information. It also conducts market research and customer surveys and makes reports of the results.

The *advertising* section produces similar reports presenting the results of surveys of public opinion, of markets, of advertising media, and the like. It also produces periodic reports summarizing advertising costs and volume for use by the accounting section and by top management.

Vertical Information Flow. Any report information that passes between the functional sections (the eight blocks within the circle) and top management is regarded as having vertical movement. The flow is in both directions, with most of the section reports "ascending" to the management executives, and statements covering administrative, technical, and policy matters "descending" to the sections.

During this vertical movement, there is a marked shift in emphasis in *how a report is read.* For example, on the operating level— on the factory floor, in the tooling sections, in the area of the assembly lines—a report is valued primarily for its *technical* content. But as it "ascends" through the various levels of management, it is valued more and more for its financial and management information. A new production-design proposal, for instance, might be the subject of an enthusiastic report bearing strongly favorable recommendations *at the operating level* but could be thrown out at the top management level because it proves too costly to produce, or because its profit potential is too small.

Radial Information Flow. Distributed around the outside of the circle diagram on page 498 are six important elements: the government, the public, customers, vendors, industry, and finance. These elements overlap. But in a general way they express the need for outside communication.

The government is the outer end of an important two-way communication. Industry has had to devise methods of reporting such things as legislation affecting wages and hours, unionization, strategic materials and equipment, taxation, and the issuance of securities. Reports flow both ways as industry supplies desired information; and government agencies direct, interpret, and otherwise respond to it.

The public is the obvious source of sales revenue, of labor, and of investment capital. Hence, the annual report is as much intended to gain favorable response among the public as among the financial centers. Other reports cover charitable and educational efforts, human-interest situations involving the people and the products of the company, and many other sources of favorable contact.

The customer is the natural target for periodic reports, policy statements, contractual material, production and design data, manuals, parts lists, specifications, and related technical material.

Vendors (manufacturing subcontractors and suppliers of such equipment as business machines and machine tools) receive a huge information and report flow. For example, in a recent annual report General Electric mentions dealing with 42,000 vendors. The number of reports to support such a far-flung effort is enormous. Included are such technical documents as research data, specifications, design proposals, drawings, contracts, policy statements, and a host of periodic reports. Such reports generate questions, modifications and revisions, additions, and comments which add to the flow and exchange of radial information.

Industry, to an increasing extent, shares information concerning technological developments, manufacturing methods, accounting procedure, materials choice, and management techniques. Much of this information appears in service reports and in similar documents designed for circulation within industrial associations. Furthermore, related industries may issue joint policy reports concerning some common problem rather than spend expensive time in individual and duplicated research.

Finally, *finance* appears here primarily in the form of *financial centers* that receive prospectus reports, production reports, and other kinds of financial statements.

A Guide for Analyzing Business Reports

I. **By whom prepared:**

  A. As to organization
    1. Business
    2. Government
    3. Foundations, research committees, engineers, etc.

  B. As to individuals associated with the organization
    1. Executive
    2. Nonexecutive

II. **Direction and purpose—reports which travel:**

  A. Vertically upward, from nonexecutives, junior executives, etc.

  B. Vertically downward, from major executives (policies, orders, etc.)

  C. Horizontally, between departments (as a coordinating device)

  D. Horizontally, from inside out
    1. To stockholders, clients, etc.
    2. To business associates
    3. To regulatory bodies (required by law)

  E. Horizontally, from outside in
    1. Courtesy reports (as from members of a trade association)
    2. Service reports (paid-for reports, prepared by engineers, accountants, etc.)
    3. Reports concerning regulation and procedure (required by law)

  F. Radially, to a region which has been partly, but not wholly, defined

III. **Nature of a report in a given organization:**

  A. Function (Decision to be made as to the result desired)
    1. *Internal*—financial, scientific analysis of product, service, etc.
    2. *External*—market survey, good will, educational, etc.

  B. Form (Decision to be made as to the method of presentation)
    1. Written
    2. Oral
    3. Combination of written and oral

  C. Technique (Decision as to physical presentation)
    1. Formal or informal style
    2. Physical appearance—method of duplicating, graphic devices, etc.

IV. **Appraisal of the qualifications of the report writer:**

  A. Apparent experience and background

  B. Grasp of the subject

  C. Skill in organizing material

  D. Competence in use of sources

  E. Business judgment and natural flair for writing

V. **Extent and quality of illustrative material**

—From a report of Professor Hyla M. Snider,
American Business Writing Association.

A **"Stratosphere" View of Information-and-Report Flow.** Now take a final look at the circle diagram flow-chart. Here you get a "visualization" of the information-and-report flow both inside and outside a major business enterprise. In the lower half of the circle you see representative sections of large industry that are likely to share information among themselves through report exchanges—*the horizontal distribution.* Above these sections is top management, which in turn publishes for, and receives reports from, the subordinate sections—*the vertical distribution.* Immediately outside the circle are representative and highly important areas that both receive and produce reports—*the radial distribution.* The "flow tracks" run both ways and are intricately interwoven throughout the diagram. In addition to the main reports that flow steadily through the indicated channels, *direct reports may also flow between any other pair of elements shown on the chart.*

The "Informalizing" Trend. Today industry tells its story in a manner more effective and more intelligible than ever before. For many companies the annual report is a vital consumer, employee, and public relations effort. Facts are "informalized," figures are illuminated, and interest is heightened by (1) simple, direct, and informal language, (2) illustrations, (3) picture-type charts, and (4) color.

Many companies make the annual report a means to take their employees into their confidence. Enterprises like Monsanto Chemical, Eastern Air Lines, Bethlehem Steel, United States Steel, General Motors, Caterpillar Tractor, Borden Milk, Johns-Manville, Goodyear Tire and Rubber, Stewart Warner, Bridgeport Brass, National Refining, and Revere Copper and Brass send a special report to employees or hand them a copy of the one sent to stockholders. Illustrating the trend toward the "conversational" report to employees is that of the Monsanto Chemical Company, Employees' Edition, Annual Report. A few paragraphs of the report are shown below. But this brief section does reflect an appreciation of the role of clear report writing in maintaining good internal relations in a large enterprise.

SECTION OF AN ANNUAL REPORT TO EMPLOYEES

Let us sit down together and talk for a little while about our business.

You probably know that it is part of my job, as president of our Company, to make a report every year to our Stockholders.

I have just finished making that report for the year 19--. If you would like to see a copy, simply write me for it and I

will send it to you. And now I want to make a similar report
to you who work at Monsanto, just as if I were talking to you.

Probably you have wondered:

"WHO ARE OUR STOCKHOLDERS AND WHY IS IT
NECESSARY TO REPORT TO THEM EVERY YEAR?"

At the close of last year, there were 18,963 Stockholders
in our Company . . . men and women from every state and many
foreign countries . . . life insurance companies, trust estates,
and other investment and savings organizations . . . people and
institutions who have enough confidence in our Company and its
officers to invest their money with us.

It is their money that bought our land, buildings, and
machinery. They supply the money needed to operate a business
as big as ours. Thus, in effect, you and I are working for
them.

Naturally, since the Stockholders are the people who are
employing every one of us, they are entitled to a yearly accounting showing just how their money is being used.

Perhaps you would like to ask:

"WHY DO WE HAVE STOCKHOLDERS?"

It takes money to start and operate any business. The
bigger the business, the more money is needed. Except in very
rare cases, no one man has enough money to provide all the cash
needed for a business the size of Monsanto.

Therefore, we must go to the general public and say: "We
would like to use some of your money. In return for that money
we will sell you stock, which makes you a part owner of Monsanto. If we earn a profit, we will pay you for the use of
your money by issuing dividends."

A report of the United States Steel Corporation indicates modern
progress in simplifying annual statements. Under ten simple headings the report presents the operation of the company for the year,
expressing it in figures, percentages, and on a per-employee basis.
A set of scales presents the balance sheet items, and another table
shows "How the Corporation Earned Its Living in 19—."

Companies like American Telephone and Telegraph, Dictaphone, Goodyear, Masonite, Flintkote, Budd Manufacturing, Borden,
Fansteel Metallurgical, Hobart Manufacturing, Worthington Pump,
Electric Auto-Lite, Pittsburgh Plate Glass, and Owens Illinois Glass
enliven the pages of their reports with numerous pictures of their
products and processes to picture for readers what is under way in
manufacture, sales promotion, and research. Other companies like
General Electric, Pratt & Whitney, Goodrich, National Gypsum,
Freeport Sulphur, and Allis-Chalmers issue supplementary picture-
surveys of operations.

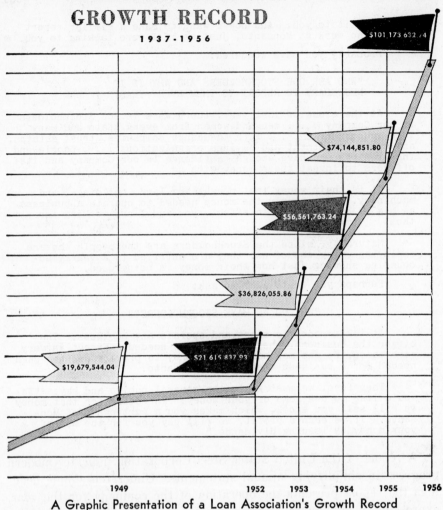

GROWTH RECORD

1937-1956

$101,173,632.74

$74,144,851.80

$56,561,763.24

$36,826,055.86

$19,679,544.04

$21,615,837.93

| 1949 | 1952 | 1953 | 1954 | 1955 | 1956 |

A Graphic Presentation of a Loan Association's Growth Record

This illustration and the one at the top of page 505 appeared in an annual report
that won a prize in a recent year's international competition.

Pictures, graphs, bar charts, maps, tables, blueprints, drawings, rough sketches, diagrams, and other pictorial devices dramatize the contents of many business reports. To highlight its volume of operations in comparison with the general trend of business, the Giddings & Lewis Machine Tool Company projects its sales curve against the monthly index of business activity published by the *Business Week* magazine. Other companies use picture-book techniques to illustrate abstract statistical data such as sales, taxes, and per-employee plant investment. The Atlantic Refining Company pictures a pile of pennies to show how its annual dollar is spent.

How the 19__ Standard Federal income dollar was earned and distributed

	HOW WE EARNED IT	HOW WE DISTRIBUTED IT	
Interest on Loans	64.59¢	9.10¢	Salaries
Escrow, Joint Control and Other Fees	30.98¢	17.39¢	Other Operating Expenses
Dividends and Other Operating Income	4.21¢	.47¢	Interest to Federal Home Loan Bank
Other Non-Operating Income	.22¢	1.25¢	Taxes
		25.76¢	Transfers to Reserves
		45.87¢	Dividends to our Account Holders
		.16¢	Non-Operating Charges
Total	$1.00	$1.00	Total

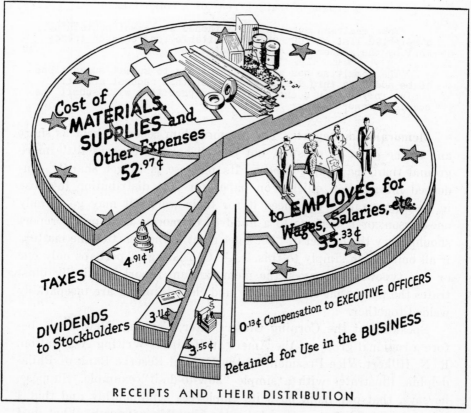

RECEIPTS AND THEIR DISTRIBUTION

Two Types of Pictorial Devices for Business Reports

Preparing the Report

Using Information Sources to Get the Facts. The first essential in preparing reports is to *get the facts*. You will find in Part X, pages 633 to 636, a list of excellent information sources. Use them when you prepare a business report.

The Technique of Report Preparation. The technique of report preparation consists of two basic operations: (1) the arrangement of your thoughts in a clearly organized pattern so that your reader can follow each step in your thinking, and (2) the translation of your thoughts into effective units of words, sentences, and paragraphs—the materials for all communication.

Simple Reports. A simple report may require only a paragraph or two.

A SIMPLE INTERIM REPORT OF A COMMITTEE

Your chairman submits the attached statement containing a selected list of 100 subjects suitable for research treatment by the members of this Association.

The committee has asked all members to submit suggestions to be added to this list. Results of this request are still coming in. Within a short time your committee will submit the complete report.

Memorandum Reports. The memorandum report is kept as short and to the point as possible, but it may have to cover a little more ground than the simple report. Its purpose is to get sharply condensed information quickly on paper for fast distribution to those in the organization who need it for their work. It may go to only one person, or it may go to a hundred or more. Your memo report should carry the impact of "Let's get right to the heart of the matter: it all boils down simply to this. . . ." Consisting of perhaps only one or two typewritten pages, the memorandum report classically illustrates the point that clear writing and clear thinking are inseparably welded together.

Speaking at the Corning Glass Center, Corning, New York, before a regional group of the American Business Writing Association, R. N. Hilkert, Vice President of the Federal Reserve Bank of Philadelphia, illustrates with a simple "how-to-do-it" example. Suppose, he says, that our bank pays its employees semimonthly and that I think we should change the system to biweekly payment. What do I

AMERICAN CYANAMID COMPANY
30 ROCKEFELLER PLAZA
NEW YORK 20, N.Y.

April 22, 19--

To the Shareholders:

At the Annual Meeting of Shareholders, which was held on April 15, 19--, at the Company's statutory office in Portland, Maine, the shareholders gave their approval to the three proposals by the Board of Directors, as follows:

(1) to increase the authorized Common Stock from 12,000,000 shares to 30,000,000 shares

For	8,057,206 shares
Against	55,542 shares
Not voting	33,671 shares

(2) to waive the pre-emptive rights of the Common shareholders with respect to 250,000 Common shares, which shares may be proportionately increased or decreased as a result of any stock dividend, combination or other change

For	7,632,721 shares
Against	217,702 shares
Not voting	302,996 shares

(3) to authorize the Board of Directors to sell such 250,000 Common shares (or the equivalent in convertible preferred stocks) to employees

For	7,678,357 shares
Against	274,456 shares
Not voting	300,606 shares

Of the 10,525,515 shares of Common Stock outstanding and entitled to vote at this meeting, 8,153,449 shares (77.46%) were represented in person or by proxy.

Following this action by the shareholders, Kenneth C. Towe, President, announced that at the quarterly meeting of the Board of Directors scheduled for May 21, he would recommend the distribution, in the nature of a stock dividend, of one share of Common Stock on each share of Common Stock outstanding. Affirmative action by the Directors on this recommendation would increase the Common shares outstanding to approximately 21,134,000, and would raise to 500,000 the number of Common Shares available for sale to employees.

Respectfully,

R. S. Kyle
Secretary

GENERAL ELECTRIC
COMPANY

PUBLIC AND EMPLOYEE RELATIONS SERVICES
INVESTOR RELATIONS SERVICE

570 LEXINGTON AVENUE, NEW YORK 22, NEW YORK • TELEPHONE PLAZA 1-1311

March 31, 19--

Dear Member of the American Economic Association:

A copy of General Electric's 19-- Annual Report is enclosed.

This report should prove to be of considerable interest to you, because General Electric's diversification is such that it in some ways reflects a considerable portion of our national economy.

We have materially changed the format of the report this year, both as a result of formal surveys we have made in recent years and as a result of individual comments and criticisms from economists and others to whom the report has been sent—and any comments you are kind enough to send me will be especially welcome this year.

I am pleased to be able again to offer additional free copies of our Annual Report for use in teaching and similar activities. If you desire additional copies, please let me know, and I shall send them to you promptly.

Very truly yours,

O. Glenn Saxon, Jr.
Consultant—Professional Investor Relations

OGS:rl
Enc.

do? It is not a case of simply issuing an order. What is the procedure? There are several technical sides to the problem that must be examined. Mr. Hilkert continues:

> At the outset I write my general thoughts in a short memorandum to the accounting department, to the machine tabulating department, and to the payroll department. These groups will then unearth every known technical advantage and disadvantage, as they should. They will dig into questions of comparative operating costs. Finally, they will place *their* reports in writing (*their* memorandums this time), and their job is to make *me* understand *them*. There is such a thing as "accounting" language. And as for the machine-tabulating experts, they speak a "language" that is simply out of this world. Now these specialists have to write my language, or we get nowhere fast.
>
> In the course of events there will probably be a conference to iron out the wrinkles, but the time finally comes when I must write my memorandum report for the top management. The statement must be simple and unambiguous. It must set forth the advantages of the change without any attempt to stack the cards. The disadvantages must be stated with equal frankness. The technical difficulties must be listed to show that they have been explored. The methods of surmounting them must be indicated. Then it goes to the boss—for his final decision.

Long Reports: Organization and Arrangement. Long reports are made up of three main divisions, subdivided into nine units as follows:

```
ORGANIZATION OUTLINE FOR THE LONG REPORT

A.  Introductory material
    1.  Title page
    2.  Letter of transmittal
    3.  Table of contents
    4.  Lists of tables, charts, illustrations (if any)
    5.  Summary (or synopsis)

B.  Body material
    6.  Textual content

C.  Supplementary material
    7.  Appendix (or reference section)
    8.  Bibliography
    9.  Index (if one seems desirable)
```

The following paragraphs are numbered to correspond to the foregoing organization outline.

(1) An effective *Title Page* for a report is illustrated on page 509.

(2) The *Letter of Transmittal*, placed just after the Title Page and ahead of the Table of Contents, is an introductory message.

A Title Page for an Examination and Recommendation
Report That Exhibits Attractive Layout

| | | | | | | | | |

REPORT on CANADIAN SALES POTENTIAL and

POSSIBLE CANADIAN AGENCY CONNECTIONS of

ELECTRICAL PRODUCTS CORPORATION

| | | | | | | | | | | | | | | | | | | | | | | | | | | |

Made to
Electrical Products Corporation
Chicago

By
Evan R. Jacobs
Electrical Engineer
November 15, 19--

| | | | | | | |

A Transmittal Letter That Serves as a Personal Introduction
to the Report Accompanying the Title Page at the Left

November 15, 19--

Electrical Products Corporation
Foreign & Export Department
Chicago 10, Illinois
United States of America

Gentlemen:

Following the instructions contained in your letters of July 1, 19--, and July 8, 19--, I am submitting the accompanying report covering investigations and observations, made in your behalf in Canada, relative to the market for your products and to possible agency connections.

The investigations have been made over a period of three and one-half months, during which time numerous authorities have been consulted with a view to obtaining the most reliable information.

The report is concerned first with the present and the future possibilities for the sale of EPC products in Canada, each major field--irrigation, railways, highways, and the like--being considered and analyzed separately, with the sources of information listed and credited, and with prospective sale summarized.

The matter of representation occupies the second part of the report. Recommendations in that respect are made to you only after a searching study was made of all the factors set forth in your letter of July 8 as constituting qualifications for your representatives.

Finally, there are listed certain data relative to current fuel and labor costs, together with an outline of methods for computing Canadian currency in terms of American currency.

My aim has been to investigate and report each matter with the thoroughness that the case demands, both for your present and for your future purposes.

Respectfully submitted,

Evan R. Jacobs
Electrical Engineer

Evan R. Jacobs/mk

Usually less formal and more personal than the body of the report, it states the following:

(a) By whose authority the work has been done
(b) Its purpose
(c) Its scope
(d) Length of time given to the study
(e) Acknowledgments

A Letter of Transmittal is illustrated on page 509. Note that it follows the outline given above. In logical order it introduces the topics that will be covered in the report: irrigation, railways, highways, and the like; representatives; and data on costs. Other examples may be seen in government reports such as the *Annual Report of the Postmaster General.*

(3) The *Table of Contents* is a list of the headings used in the pages of the report, with the number of the page on which each appears. The table provides easy reference to any part. A Table of Contents is illustrated on page 512. Note the use of headings and subheadings to bring the material together into logical groups. Observe how the table guides you through the major divisions and subsections of the material.

(4) *Lists of Tables, Charts, and Illustrations* may be prepared, giving the proper page numbers. These lists are especially helpful to the reader if the tables, charts, and illustrations are numerous.

(5) The *Summary,* or *Synopsis,* follows the Table of Contents. Written *after* the report has been completed, it is NOT an introduction. It is a brief that summarizes the core information, which is expanded in the body of the report. Even in long reports it covers only one or two pages. A paragraph may be enough.

The words *summary* and *synopsis* are close together in dictionary definition. Between them is only a shading of difference. You can get two different shades of useful meanings from the two words, however, so that it may help to combine them in your mind. A summary is an abridgment of a preceding discourse. A synopsis is a condensed statement, often with headings and subheadings.

Summary to most people means a boiling down to smaller scope without particular effort to highlight the high points. *Synopsis* to most people means something with headings or some similar technical treatment that gives emphasis to what the report aims to bring out.

The summary, or synopsis, is given a preferred position at the beginning of the report because the executive who passes upon the content is most interested in the conclusions reached and the action recommended.

(6) The *textual content*, or body, of the report expands the headings listed in the Table of Contents. At the opening of the body material the following statements appear:

(a) Objective of the report
(b) Plan of procedure

In outlining the plan of procedure, you may, for example, present a list of persons interviewed, copies of questionnaires used, methods of selecting the interview list, the scope of the field work, the supplementary value and extent of library work, and the like. Moreover, if a separate exhibit folder accompanies the report, cross reference should be made to its presence and its usefulness.

The rest of the body follows with facts and supporting materials.

Footnotes are used (1) to enable subsequent workers to take up an investigation, (2) to explain and amplify matters referred to in the main text, and (3) to protect the writer against any charge of plagiarism or improper use of materials. Attach them to important statements of fact and to any inferences or interpretations borrowed from other writers. In brief articles number them consecutively. Write the index number above the line and at the end of the passage to which it refers.

Quotations should be brief and pertinent. Make them perfectly accurate. Verify them by direct comparison with their sources. An omission is permissible if the sense of the whole message is not distorted by it. Use omission marks (. . .) to show that part of a quotation has been dropped.

Display your materials, with headings and subheadings, to help your reader find the information he wants. An effective page from the body of a report, showing a suitable use of headings and subheadings, is illustrated on page 512. To help your reader follow your organization, keep these two points in mind: (1) Let your reader *see* just what the divisions of your report are. Remember that he can grasp only one major division at a time. (2) Let your reader also see just how each part of your report is related to the whole; how each subgroup contributes to its division; and how each main group is related to the other main groups and to the whole report.

Table of Contents for an Examination and Progress Report
on a Company's Production and Operation

HOW TO GIVE PROPER DISPLAY TO A REPORT

Importance of Effective Use of Display

Display, which involves the liberal use of white space, is essential in order to make the captions, the section headings, and the main divisions stand out and guide the reader to the information he wants to find.

Specifications to be Followed in Producing Effective Display

Reserve a liberal margin at the left of each sheet of the report. In ordinary work it is well to use standard stationery, white in color, and measuring eight and one-half by eleven inches. Somewhat better display results from the use of the single space because there is a clearer contrast of black and white masses. Some executives, however, prefer the double space. It is advisable to determine in advance which is desired.

Proper Use of Captions and Subcaptions

Captions and subcaptions, which may also be called headlines and subheadlines, may be typewritten in the center of the page or even with the left-hand margin.

Optional Positions of Subheads

Subheads may be inset into the body of a paragraph at the left or may be typewritten in the margins opposite the sections to which they refer. The matter is optional.

General Purpose of Display to Assure Clearness

The general purpose of display is merely to ensure and to increase clearness. For this reason, at least two spaces are allowed above and below display lines, and the most important captions are typewritten in solid capitals.

Illustrations

Illustrating the Contents of a Report

The effect of a business report is often made stronger by the use of pictures, graphs, bar charts, maps, tables, blueprints, drawings, sketches, diagrams, and flat samples. Such items are placed with the sections to which they refer.

A Page from the Body of a Report Showing an Effective
Display of Headings and Subheadings

(7) The *Appendix*, if used, may contain supporting tables, computations, special references and formulae used for algebraic or mathematical procedures, extensive exhibits, and, in general, all other material that may clog the main body of the report.

(8) The *Bibliography* is a list of the sources of information you have used. Books, articles, periodicals, and documents listed should be arranged in alphabetical order by authors, by editors, or by titles (if the authors are anonymous or the sources are periodicals).

(9) An *Index* is necessary only in an elaborate report for which a table of contents is not an adequate key.

Standard Report Form. An effective standard-layout report form—with liberal use of white space—is essential to make the main headings, the section headings, and the subheadings stand out and guide the reader to the information he wants.

Keep a margin of two inches or more at the left of each sheet. Use standard stationery, 8½ by 11 inches. Better display comes from single-spaced material, although some executives prefer double spacing. Determine in advance, if you can, which is desired. Headings and subheadings may be typed in the center of the page, flush with the left margin, or in other ways. A subheading may be inset into the body of a paragraph at the left, may be typewritten in the margin opposite the section to which it refers, or may be arranged in other ways. At least two spaces are reserved above and below each display line. The most important headings are typewritten in capitals, lesser headings in capitals and small letters.

Guide List of Possible Headings for a Long Report. On page 514 is a useful table or guide list of headings, some (but of course *not* necessarily all) of which may appear in a typical annual corporation report. If you will examine the current annual report of a company like DuPont, American Cyanamid, General Dynamics, Westinghouse Electric, AeroJet General, and a dozen others, you will recognize many of these headings.

An excellent discussion of annual corporation reports, and how they are developed under headings similar to those appearing on page 514, is to be found in *Company Annual Reports to Stockholders and Employees,* by K. C. Pratt, editor of Champion Paper and Fibre Company's house magazine, *Stet.* Mr. Pratt skillfully brings the annual report "alive," vividly describes and pictures its many forms and varieties.

Suggested Guide List of Report Headings

Year-to-Year Comparisons

Sales	Dividends	Reserves	Market value
Earnings	Taxes	Financial progress	of stock

The Financial Story

Sales	Changes in officers	Supplies
Earnings	Exports and imports	New policies
Dividends	Research and engineering	Employee relations
Taxes	Inventories	Dealer relations
Reserves	Unfilled orders	Customer relations
Net worth	Capital requirements	Community relations
Industry position	Capital structure,	Anniversary milestones
Expansion of plant	changes	Contract obligations
New equipment	Capital investment	Legal actions
Subsidiaries	Investment per employee	General economic
Branches	Fixed assets	comments
Sales offices	Intangible assets	Market prospects
Changes in directors	Raw material sources	Future outlook

Financial Statistics

Sales	Auditor's certification	Working capital
Earnings	Financial position	Payroll
Dividends	Earned surplus statement	Investments
Taxes	Capital surplus statement	Depreciation, depletion
Balance sheet	Reserves	Value of properties
Operating statement	Income distribution	Nonoperating income
Notes to these	Capital spending	Net worth

The General Story

Brief company history
Company growth
Product history, growth
New product development
Production processes
Sales promotion
Trademarks
Distribution channels
Plant location, size
General offices
Divisions, subsidiaries

Stockholder Statistics

Number, total
Preferred, common, number
Distribution (men, women)
Distribution (geographical)
Average holdings

Management

Organization chart
Biographical briefs of directors and officers

General Information

List of directors and officers
Executive committee
Stock transfer agents
Registrars
Dividend disbursing agents
Attorneys; auditors
Proxy notice
Date of annual meeting
Company publications
Executive, corporate, and
general office addresses

Employee Statistics

Number of employees
Length of service
Age average
Honored veterans

Employee Benefits

Pension plan
Disability protection
Insurance protection
Tenure protection
Productivity bonus
Health provisions
Safety practices
Employee training
Personnel development

"Why do we break our reports up into departments with bold headlines?" comments Owen L. Scott, editor of the *Report for The Business Executive*, issued from Washington, D. C. "To assist you in finding those subjects of greatest interest to you—price trends, tax outlook, business forecasts, and labor-management relations."

Developing the Material

Limiting the Topic. The nature of the problem and the limits of the topic are first to be determined. A frequent error—like that of the college sophomore who chose as the title for his term paper, "The World and All It Contains"—is to try to handle a topic so vast and so unmanageable that any treatment of less than a full-length shelf of volumes will be superficial. The way to avoid such superficiality is to take so *limited* a section of a larger subject that a 1,500- or 2,000-word treatment will be adequate, comprehensive, and complete.

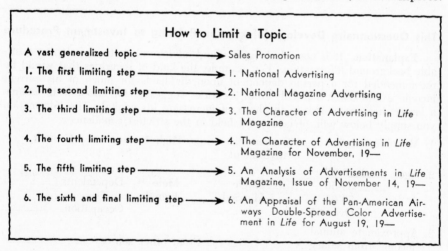

How to Limit a Topic

A vast generalized topic ⟶ Sales Promotion

1. The first limiting step ⟶ 1. National Advertising

2. The second limiting step ⟶ 2. National Magazine Advertising

3. The third limiting step ⟶ 3. The Character of Advertising in *Life* Magazine

4. The fourth limiting step ⟶ 4. The Character of Advertising in *Life* Magazine for November, 19—

5. The fifth limiting step ⟶ 5. An Analysis of Advertisements in *Life* Magazine, Issue of November 14, 19—

6. The sixth and final limiting step ⟶ 6. An Appraisal of the Pan-American Airways Double-Spread Color Advertisement in *Life* for August 19, 19—

Narrowing the Scope. The scope of the topic narrows as the number of words in the title of the topic increases. In deciding when to stop the narrowing process, you must fall back upon your own best judgment. If your judgment proves faulty, you will find, after some progress, that your topic is too broad or too narrow, and that you should cut out parts, or add areas, accordingly. The scope of the topic is controlled by the four factors shown on page 516:

1. The *limits* that have been set for the report or the paper
2. The accessibility of the material
3. The investigator's previous experience
4. The character and the background of those who will read the report or the paper

Assembling the Material. Most of the search for information and raw material proceeds in libraries of classified volumes covering the world's areas of knowledge. For market investigators, of course, the search goes on among consumers through door-to-door research, and through investigation of marketing practices in the actual field of distribution.

The library researcher should know how to find and use books, periodicals, card catalogs, and indexes. Progress in this search is greatly eased by a knowledge of the arrangement of library rooms, desks, shelves, and books. Library sources have been suggested in Section 6 of the Reference Division, pages 633-636.

The field worker should also know how to use questionnaires, an excellent example of which is pictured below. Questionnaires have been discussed on pages 320-323.

This Questionnaire Develops Information Relating to Investment Procedure

Explanation. It is possible to give sound advice only after developing desirable background information. For example, the kind of securities that would be recommended for a person dependent upon dividends for much of his current income would differ markedly from securities suggested for one able to assume a larger measure of risk in the hope of increasing his capital. The information you supply below will, of course, be held in the strictest confidence.

1. My objective is: _____Conservative _____High Income _____Growth
   Investment

2. Age: _____20-35
   _____35-50   _____Single   _____Male   Number of
   _____50-65   _____Married   _____Female   Dependents_____
   _____Over 65
                                                              Occupation_____

3. Approximate annual
   income from salary_____ From other sources_____

4. Funds available for investment_____

5. Securities I now own (*please show quantity and price paid*):

   _____

   _____

   _____

[Attach separate sheet if needed]

An Illustrative Questionnaire for Report Information

The Card Method for Organizing Material

1. With your topic well in mind, jot down on 5" x 3" cards, or on slips of paper, the main headings and the more important subheadings covering the material you have assembled.

2. On other slips or cards, jot down desirable main headings and subheadings for which there appears to be no material yet obtained.

3. Shuffle these cards or slips, testing them with reference to the narrowed limits of your topic. Set aside all cards that do not fit within the limits established, or that do not carry the paper toward its aim.

4. Classify the cards much as you would a hand of bridge, looking for logical interrelationships. Bring together the cards that belong together. See that the entries on coordinate cards are kept coordinate and that the entries on subordinate cards are kept subordinate. Rephrase entries to eliminate overlapping.

5. Now make a fresh single card or slip for each major heading in your emerging outline. Frame each entry in topical form: for example, "Uses of Copper," or "Uses of Copper in Making Electrical Equipment."

6. Clip to each major-heading card all its related subheading cards, so that the original pile of cards is now divided into a series of intrarelated groups.

7. Organize each subordinate group into logical order in relation to the main-heading card for that group.

8. Determine the most logical and effective order in which to present the main units.

9. When the cards have been reshifted into an order regarded as final, number them in sequence to avoid confusion and to preserve the order.

10. With the topical analysis complete, copy the headings and subheadings, from the cards and set them up on a sheet of paper. The result is the first draft of the table of contents.

Organizing the Material. Both the business report and the formal paper profit from careful organization according to a table of contents, the guide outline. An effective method for organizing material is the *card* or *paper-slip* method.

We thus complete the cycle of analyzing data, classifying it, and synthesizing it—bringing it all together. The advantage of the card or loose-slip system is the ease with which various combinations may be discovered and different arrangements may be tried by shifting and reshifting the cards. This method of attacking a problem in writing is confirmed by Professor Barrett Wendell, who adds this testimonial:

On separate bits of paper—cards, if they be at hand—I write down the separate headings that occur to me, in what seems to me the natural order. Then, when my pack of cards is complete—in other words, when I have a card for every heading which I think of—I study them and sort them . . . and it has very rarely been my experience to find that a shift of arrangement will not decidedly improve the original order. Ideas that really stand in the relation of proof to proposition frequently present themselves as coordinate. The same idea will sometimes phrase itself in two or three distinct ways, whose superficial differences for the moment conceal their identity; and more frequently still, the comparative strength and importance, and the mutual relations, of really distinct ideas will in the first act curiously conceal themselves.

A few minutes' shuffling of these little cards has often revealed to me more than I should have learned by hours of unaided pondering. In brief, they enable one, by simple acts of rearrangement, to make any number of fresh plans.

Summaries, Briefs, Digests. To express in a few lines, or at most in a brief paragraph, the sharply condensed gist of a long discussion is an immensely valuable mental discipline, testing your ability to analyze and understand. American civil service examinations use exactly this test—the *summary test.*

A *summary* is the expression (in condensed form) of the gist of a paragraph, a series of paragraphs, several pages, or a whole book. Summaries naturally accompany reports, as we have seen, because it is important that the significant core of a long report be revealed *in brief compass at one point where it may be quickly consulted.*

You will also note the modern fashion of keeping up with the outpouring stream of printed matter by reading it in the form of sharply condensed articles called *briefs* or *digests.* Thus the *Reader's Digest,* through the most skillful summarizing, boils down full-length articles that may have been published previously in other magazines and periodicals, and makes "miniature capsules" out of them. In this manner you can cover, in minutes, an expertly prepared brief or digest of an article that would in its original form occupy perhaps ten times the space and absorb far more of your reading time. When the condensed brief reveals a discussion of great value to you and shows you that you need to know more, you can then go to the original article and read it in its full-length form—exactly the procedure you follow in consulting a business report.

Outlines. An outline is a useful device for representing the framework of a discussion. It helps in preparing long reports, papers, and speeches. An outline should be kept short, simple, and usable. If it becomes intricate, it loses clearness. A good outline seldom uses sentences, seldom carries the subdivisions of the main topics farther than two or three steps, and *is brief enough to be understood and remembered.*

Every writer and every speaker takes certain preparatory steps in drafting his discussion. In other words, he outlines, whether he knows it or not. If his outline is well conceived, his discussion is clear, concise, and complete.

A RECOMMENDED OUTLINE FORM

I. _____
   A. _____
      1. _____
      2. _____
   B. _____
II. _____
   A. _____
   B. _____
      1. _____
      2. _____
   C. _____
III. _____

(*Note:* "a" and "b" subdivisions under "1" and "2" should be introduced only when necessary. The value of an outline is its quick clearness. The simpler it is kept, the better it is. The form here recommended is flexible and easily expanded.)

Three Outline Examples. A reader wants the simplest possible idea of "The Process of Writing a Formal Paper." We reduce the subject to four topics:

SIMPLE, FOUR-TOPIC OUTLINE

I. Selecting and limiting the subject   III. Organizing the material

II. Gathering the material   IV. Writing the discussion

A businessman wants a condensed guide to "Procedure in Writing a Business Report." Here is an expanded outline:

EXPANDED OUTLINE

I. Collecting Facts
   A. Reading
   B. Note taking
   C. Questionnaires
   D. Interviews
   E. Observation

II. Organizing Facts
   A. Loose-slip or card system
   B. Card file
   C. Loose-leaf notebook

III. Interpreting Facts
   A. Definition
   B. Classification
   C. Comparisons
   D. Inferences
   E. Reasoning
   F. Analogies

IV. Summary and
      recommendation

A large enterprise requires frequent reports on factory departments. These reports must be based upon observation and recommendation. Aiding the report writers is the guide shown on page 520.

```
                    EXPANDED OUTLINE
  I. Meeting the foremen and the supervisors
 II. Studying each of the operations.
     A. List of operations
        1. Item 1
        2. Item 2 [etc.]
     B. Purpose of each operation
        1. Item 1
        2. Item 2 [etc.]
     C. Machine and equipment used
        1. Is it difficult to repair?
        2. What amount of power is consumed?
     D. Operators
        1. Number
        2. Qualifications
III. Application of men and equipment to material
     [Similar entries in this division]
 IV. General questions on the department
     A. Questions on main steps in operations
     B. Questions on methods of storing stock in process
     C. Questions on relative use of equipment to capacity
```

A Restatement. The business report is a written vehicle for the transmission of factual information, customarily assembled from tested and classified sources. The report calls for suitable display in order that the captions, the textual divisions, and the illustrations may stand out to guide the reader to the information desired. In some reports, and in many formal papers relating to commercial operations, footnotes, quotations, and bibliography may prove not only helpful but desirable. Such material should be presented in accordance with the standard procedure suggested on pages 628-631.

Let us conclude this chapter with a splendid statement from R. N. Hilkert, Vice President, Federal Reserve Bank of Philadelphia:

Executives must write!

Bear in mind that every large corporation is made up of specialized departments, each run by specialists. Every specialty has its own vocabulary, its own language. But in an organization we must confer with each other and write memoranda and reports to each other. And *we must understand each other.*

We need a common language, a layman's language, for *every man is a layman when he operates beyond the borders of his own specialty.* Too frequently this is forgotten. We find economists writing as though for other economists, lawyers for other lawyers, engineers for other engineers, and so it goes.

Specialists must learn to write for nonspecialists. It is the only way to attain a "meeting of the minds." The executive must make decisions based upon reports and data from the various specialists. His decisions are likely to be no better than his understanding of the reports. This warning is especially applicable to those who are presently immersed in the field of automation. *It is the responsibility of specialists to write for generalists.*

Executives must write—and most of their writing is done under pressure. And their pressure writing must be fitted in between interviews, meetings, and conferences. This fact needs to be understood by students so that they may practice this kind of pressure-writing. Students face assignments calling for a ten-page report to be submitted next week. But they should also face manfully up to assignments calling for a one-page memorandum due twenty minutes from now! For *that is the way top management has to write.*

What of the future? Will more writing be required of us, or less? I believe it will be more. In every aspect of our work we are realizing more than ever before the importance of good communication. This is true in production, sales, finance, engineering, public relations, industrial relations, economic research, in fact every phase of the business.

It is significant that in all the plans for office automation, the point is always made that there will be no reduction in the number of reports. On the contrary, the improved methods make possible the gathering of new data, and old data in new forms and combinations, at a speed that is fantastic. And so the executive writer may look forward in the long future, not to fewer reports, but to far better reports in terms of accuracy, completeness, and fantastically fast, up-to-the-minute currency.

Useful Supplementary Sources for the Study of Reports

Anderson, C. R., A. G. Saunders, and F. W. Weeks. *Business Reports.* New York: McGraw-Hill Book Company, Inc.

Ball, John, and Cecil B. Williams. *Report Writing.* New York: The Ronald Press Company.

Baker, Ray P., and A. C. Howell. *The Preparation of Reports.* New York: The Ronald Press Company.

Brown, Leland. *Effective Business Report Writing.* Englewood Cliffs, New Jersey: Prentice-Hall, Inc.

Crouch, William George, and R. L. Zetler. *A Guide to Technical Writing.* New York: The Ronald Press Company.

Gaum, Carl G., Harold F. Graves, and Lyne S. S. Hoffman. *Report Writing.* New York: Prentice-Hall, Inc.

Hay, Robert D., and Raymond V. Lesikar. *Business Report Writing.* Homewood, Illinois: Richard D. Irwin, Inc.

Selvage, J. P., and M. M. Lee. *Making the Annual Report Speak for Industry.* New York: McGraw-Hill Book Co., Inc.

Tuttle, Robert E., and C. A. Brown. *Writing Useful Reports.* New York: Appleton-Century-Crofts, Inc.

Communication Problems

● 1. Mr. Louis W. Flynn, Marketing Vice President of the Sunray Enterprises, Inc., Los Angeles, has asked you, the firm's market analyst, to prepare a report on the advisability of Pacific City, Parkwood, or Tamarack as *the* location for a new Sunray Paint and Hardware Store. Your problem is to select the most desirable location and substantiate your decision.

Information: The Sunray stores appeal to the home handyman or the do-it-yourself homeowner. You carry the traditional paint and hardware items—all competitively priced. You offer free advisory service to customers. All business is cash and carry. For the new store and building site, Sunray has budgeted $100,000. You have made the following notes about each of the communities:

> *Pacific City:* Beach city with ocean climate; moderate priced homes; considerable new home construction in the shopping area; city located on Highway 101; aggressive Chamber of Commerce; diversified economy, but more families dependent on aircraft and allied industries than on any other activity; stable homeownership.
> Population in 1950—27,000; in 1960—38,000. Population of shopping area served—76,000. Approximate average age of head of household: 41. Average family size: 3.4 members. Average family income before taxes: $6,600. Retail sales in 1958: $65,000,000. Three competitive paint and hardware stores now located in Pacific City.
> Building site cost in downtown Pacific City: $21,400; building cost estimate: $76,000. Building site cost on outskirts (near major shopping area and on a major thoroughfare): $8,000; building cost estimate: $73,000. Parking scarce downtown; space available for customer parking lot on outskirt site.
>
> *Parkwood:* Five miles inland from ocean; little new building with lack of expansion opportunities; older homes, but stable homeownership; citizens are dependent on aircraft industry primarily, but much light manufacturing in area.
> Population in 1950—50,000; in 1960—55,000. Population of shopping area served—91,000. Approximate average age of head of household: 48. Average family size: 2.9 members. Average family income before taxes: $5,800. Retail sales in 1958: $80,000,000. Five competitive paint and hardware stores now located in Parkwood.
> Building site cost in downtown Parkwood: $30,000; building cost estimate: $76,000. Building site on outskirts: $19,000; building cost estimate: $73,000. Parking scarce downtown; space available on outskirt site.
>
> *Tamarack:* Five miles inland from ocean; inexpensive homes; new home construction booming; located near International Airport; about 75% of people dependent on aircraft and airline industries; rather large transient population; frequent changes in homeownership; many rentals; city has room for expansion.
> Population in 1950—21,000; in 1960—33,000. Population of shopping area served—54,000. Approximate average age of head of household: 35. Average family size: 4.1 members. Average family income before taxes: $5,400. Retail sales in 1958: $30,000,000. Two competitive paint and hardware stores now located in Tamarack.

Building site cost in downtown Tamarack: $16,000; building cost estimate: $76,000. Building site cost on outskirts (on major north-south boulevard): $8,000; building cost estimate: $73,000. Parking easily available both downtown and at outskirt site.

Sources of Information and Method of Research: Where can you obtain the type of information given for each community? How can you obtain it?

● **2.** As a member of the staff at Union State College, you have been assigned the task of making a follow-up study of the graduates of the business school. The purpose of the study is to determine graduates' vocational placement, job success, and opinion of the business program at Union. You have mailed out 400 questionnaires and received 320 usable replies. By occupational groupings, you have received returns from: 103 salesmen, 61 accounting workers, 56 employees of financial institutions, 32 graduates engaged in personnel work, 24 industrial management trainees, 16 secretaries, 14 teachers, and 14 women graduates who have married and are not working.

Twenty-seven graduates have held three jobs during the year, 69 have worked for two companies, and the remainder of the employed have worked for the same employer for the entire year.

The following table summarizes salary information gathered from returned questionnaires:

NUMBER OF GRADUATES REPORTING SALARIES AT END OF THE FIRST YEAR							
	$200-$250	$251-$300	$301-$350	$351-$400	$401-$450	$450-$500	Over $500
Sales	—	37	40	9	7	5	5
Accounting	7	9	12	21	7	3	2
Finance	17	9	18	8	4	—	—
Personnel	1	8	14	5	4	—	—
Industrial Management	—	4	6	8	6	—	—
Secretaries	3	6	6	1	—	—	—
Teachers	—	—	7	4	3	—	—

In reporting their job satisfaction, the graduates have replied:

Dissatisfied with present job 37
Satisfied but hope for better 167
Will make this job my career 116

The table on page 524 summarizes graduates' opinions about selected business subjects. These courses were included in the questionnaire, because the Director, who asked you to make the study, was concerned about their places in the curriculum either as required or elective subjects. Note that Columns C and D include the replies of only those graduates listed in Column A. Prepare the report to the Director.

NUMBER OF GRADUATES REPORTING OPINIONS ABOUT SELECTED BUSINESS SUBJECTS				
	A *Number who took the course*	**B** *Number who wish they had taken the course*	**C** *Course very valuable*	**D** *Course of little value*
Market Analysis	77	65	68	9
Communications	320	—	300	20
Salesmanship	211	73	145	66
Industrial Relations	100	7	85	15
Cost Accounting	84	14	75	9
Typewriting	195	120	180	15
Money and Banking	320	—	200	120

● **3.** You are Sales Manager of the Bali-Hi Swimsuit Company. Because of heavy competition in the field, you decide to make a study in cooperation with John Sloan, Advertising Manager, to determine in what magazines to concentrate your advertising for your teen-model swimsuits; the fabric, color, and design to emphasize in your new styles; and the type of store to feature in your sales promotion. After deciding on the survey method, you have had a questionnaire enclosed in the mailings of three prominent teen-age magazines—*Sixteen, After Twelve,* and *Young Moderns.* The same questionnaire has been placed in the teen-shop section of eleven major department stores located throughout the country.

From the keyed symbols on your return envelopes, you find that replies to your questionnaire were received about equally from all sources. Of 70,000 questionnaires distributed, 6,300 were returned. You had assumed that 2,800 (4%) returns would be satisfactory.

Prepare a formal report of your study. Draw conclusions and make recommendations for the consideration of Mr. R. R. Lundborg, President of Bali-Hi. No bibliography is necessary.

Here are the questionnaire entries and the total response to each:

My age is: Under 14 510 ; 15 1,200 ; 16 2,310 ;
17 1,440 ; 18 or over 765 .

When did you last purchase a new swimsuit? Before 1956 1,150 ;
1956 1,420 ; 1957 1,630 ; 1958 1,950 .

Where did you obtain your last suit? Department store 3,225 ;
Women's-Wear store 630 ; Sport shop 1,100 ; It was
a gift 960 ; Can't remember 55 .

How much did your last suit cost? Under $6 405 ; $7-$10
1,227 ; $11-$14 1,450 ; $15-$18 2,008 ; Over $18 650 .

Was it a one-piece suit? Yes 6,017   No 283

Would you buy the same (one- or two-piece suit) again? Yes 5,900 No 400

What size do you wear? 7 832 ; 8 405 ; 9 1,500 ; 10 1,200 ;
11 1,300 (Juniors); 12 400 ; 14 350 (Misses).

What basic color do you prefer? White 795 ; Yellow 1,100 ;
    Blue 1,600 ; Red 612 ; Green 127 ; Black
    1,400 ; Orange 345 ; Brown 27 ; Purple 35 .
Do you prefer: a plain color suit? 3,720 ; a striped suit?
    950 ; a printed multicolored suit? 1,300 .
Please check the fabric you hope to have in your next suit.
    Latex 1,755 ; Wool knit 830 ; Synthetic 1,400 ; Cotton 2,016 .
Where do you shop most for clothing? Small sport shop 1,900 ;
    National chain store 830 ; Department store 3,350 .
Do you get most of your shopping ideas from: Newspapers
    1,700 ; Magazines 4,100 ; Friends 500 .
Which of these magazines do you have at home? Sixteen 1,832 ;
    Metropolitan 2,700 ; After Twelve 1,107 ; Women's
    Companion 4,250 ; Young Moderns 3,200 ; Beauty 1,432 .

● 4. Several employees of the Western Soap Products Company have indicated a desire to have the company adopt some form of group life insurance for employees. As Personnel Administrator, you have been asked by the Board of Directors of the company to make a study to determine the thinking of all the employees regarding such a program. You are to submit the findings of your study in a report that also includes information about the cost of such a program.

You had enclosed with the most recent pay checks to all 550 employees the following questionnaire. All 550 questionnaires were returned. A cross check of the questionnaires revealed that all 75 who said *No* to Question 1 said *Yes* to Question 4.

```
1.  Are you interested in a company group life insurance
    program?  Yes   475      No    75

2.  If the company adopted such a program, would you be willing
    to pay the entire cost of your own insurance?    125
    Or only part of the cost?     350
    Not interested    75

3.  Do you now carry life insurance?  Yes    340      No    210

4.  Do you believe your insurance coverage is adequate?
    Yes   80     No    470
```

Three insurance companies have given you the following information about group life insurance programs. Company A offers either $1,000 or $2,000 policies for each employee, charges 90 cents a month for each $1,000 of coverage, and requires that at least 50 per cent of the employees of a firm be covered for the program to be acceptable. Company B provides $1,000 and $2,000 policies, has a premium rate of $1 a month for each $1,000 of coverage, but requires that only 40 per cent of the employees need enroll.

Company C provides the same policies—$1,000 and $2,000—at a premium rate of only 80 cents a month for each $1,000. Company C makes this plan available, however, only if 75 per cent of the employees are enrolled.

A check of ten companies similar to Western Soap Products indicates that payroll deduction plans for group insurance have received wide acceptance. Of these ten companies, two paid the entire cost of group insurance; two did not contribute to the premiums for group insurance; and in six of the companies, the company and the employees shared the insurance cost equally. The $1,000 and $2,000 policy plan was most popular with about 90 per cent of the employees of these ten companies carrying $2,000 of insurance.

● **5.** You are Office Manager of the Blue Sales Company. You have come to the conclusion that a photocopy machine is needed in your communications and accounting departments. One machine will serve both departments. Generally, the copies you require are used only for a short time, and you seldom make more than one copy of any item. While you strongly believe that the equipment would save many times the cost of having a typist make copies, you must demonstrate this fact to the Controller before he will grant approval for the purchase.

Prepare a report on three different brands of photocopy machines, and make a recommendation for the purchase of the one you consider most desirable. Present information on initial cost, operating cost, cost for each copy, permanence of copies, size, availability of service, and warranties.

● **6.** Prepare a report on the types and quality of paper and printed headings. Sheet sizes, grades of paper, trade names, types of printing, and other areas of information can be studied and reported.

Directions: (a) First, learn all you can about paper from reliable reference books, including the encyclopedia. (Your reading and study background will help you to understand paper when it is discussed with you, and you will be better prepared to ask intelligent questions about the points in which you are most interested.)

(b) Next, visit your local stationery stores or wholesale paper firms. Many firms in either of these categories are able to lend schools or course representatives sample kits of stationery.

(c) Paper dealers may be able to help you with information on printing, too. Or, if you wish, you may visit a printing shop to ask about the various printing methods, the advantages of each method, and the cost. The stationery store, wholesale paper firm, or printing shop may also be able to provide you with samples for your report.

Make Your Report: You may want to use some sort of projection equipment—such as an opaque projector—for your presentation. Another use of visual materials is the bulletin-board display set up a day or two in advance of your report. Still another method of presentation is the use of charts that you display as you present your ideas.

Be sure that you *talk* to the group in your own terms—terms you ordinarily use and that they will understand. Make your presentation interesting. Keep away from too many statistics. Leave some of the material undiscussed so the group will be stimulated to ask questions. Finally, make some recommendations—recommendations of the type that will help your listeners to know how to make intelligent decisions with regard to paper and printing.

PART IX Refresher Division of Communication Skills

Section I Effective Punctuation; Expression of Numbers

Effective Punctuation

Punctuation Controls Thought-Flow. Punctuation is a series of marks or points, convenient mechanical devices, for marking off word groups. The correct grouping of words in sentences is controlled by rules that have been tested until they are known to be right. Any person who masters the simple laws of punctuation guarantees for himself profitable dividends in lucid expression.

Punctuation Control. Punctuation control comes from common sense, training, and practice. The one reason for punctuation is to make sentences clear. It shows how much separation there should be between words and groups of words.

Ideas, Like Traffic, Flow in a Stream. Punctuation shows where one complete idea ends and another begins. It shows also the relation between main ideas and subordinate ideas. Punctuation is used not out of whim but because of the need for clearness. It is not an ornament or a decoration to be peppered in whenever you feel like it. Instead, it is a hard-working essential, controlled by the laws of experience.

The absence of a punctuation mark where it should be present, or its presence where it should be absent, may wholly change your meaning. In business such a change may be costly. Punctuation is therefore a vital business tool. A good writer never puts in too many punctuation marks. He puts in *just enough* to make the meaning clear.

PERIOD

The period is the stop sign in the traffic control of thought. Learn to respect it exactly as you do a stop light in traffic.

1. Most sentences end with a period, which is the mark indicating *full stop* at the end of an assertion. On this page are many examples. All declarative sentences end with a period.

Our office is in Toledo.

2. The period is likewise used at the end of an imperative sentence.

You must have your check in our hands by Friday.

3. The period is used after all initials and after most abbreviations.

R. G. Davis; Mr. L. N. Travis; Acme, Inc.; Kodak, Ltd.; Ph.D.; p.m.; P.M.; f.o.b.; oz.; C.O.D.

Abbreviations composed of several initial letters and written in all capitals are often written solid without periods.

TWA (Trans World Airlines)
FDIC (Federal Deposit Insurance Corporation)

4. The period is used between dollars and cents expressed in figures; as $10.50. Note, however, that a period and ciphers are not required when an amount in even dollars is expressed in figures.

The invoice totals $8.75.
Total fees will be $50 each year.

COMMA

The comma indicates a partial stop. It marks a slight degree of separation, a mild break in thought. It is used with great frequency for many different purposes. To write well, you must learn how to use the comma.

1. Use the comma to point off a subordinate clause preceding its principal clause. Such clauses are often introduced by words like *if, unless, since, because, when, after, although, while, as,* and the like.

> If your report is acccurate, we must call a meeting at once.

2. Use the comma to set off a nonrestrictive clause. A nonrestrictive clause is one that can be dropped without harming the meaning of the sentence.

> Our dean of students, **who formerly was our English teacher,** is very popular.
> This stock, **which has a good dividend record,** is highly recommended.

Note that in the foregoing illustrations the sentences are complete and accurate if the clauses are omitted. The sentences then read:

> Our dean of students is very popular.
> This stock is highly recommended.

A restrictive clause is one that actually restricts the meaning of the main clause and cannot be dropped without harming it.

> The man **who is now chairman of our department** was formerly an economics professor.
> All corporations **that make large profits** can pay satisfactory dividends.

To drop the restrictive clauses would destroy the true meaning of these sentences.

> The man was formerly an economics professor.
> All corporations can pay satisfactory dividends.

Since the sentences without the relative clauses do not convey the meaning intended, the clauses are said to be restrictive. Such clauses are not set off by commas but are left closely joined.

3. Use the comma to set off a nonrestrictive appositive but not a restrictive appositive. Note that the rule for appositives is similar to the one for relative clauses.

> Boise, **the capital,** is the largest city in Idaho.
> Buy the book **Real Estate** at Bell's Bookstore.

The first appositive is properly set off by commas because it is not required to complete the meaning of the sentence. The second appositive is not set off by commas because it is required to complete the meaning of the sentence.

4. Use the comma to separate coordinate clauses joined by one of the pure conjunctions, *and, but, for, or, neither, nor.*

> This book is one of exceptional merit, **and** its sales record has been phenomenal.
> An ample reserve fund had been accumulated, **but** the directors were not forced to use it.
> The office is closed today, **for** it is Founder's Day.
> He will be present, **or** he will send his proxy.

This rule concerns only coordinate *clauses* joined by conjunctions; it does not refer to a clause containing two verbs.

> WRONG: He audited the books, and made his report.
> RIGHT: He audited the books and made his report.

5. Use the comma to point off an introductory phrase containing a verb. One not containing a verb should usually *not* be followed by any mark of punctuation, unless the phrase is parenthetical (such as *For example, In the second place,* and the like).

> After making the survey, the committee will adjourn.
> To complete the contract, they added an extra shift.
> After much debate the motion passed.
> As a gesture of courtesy they agreed.
> For example, consider the modern car.

6. Use the comma to point off a dependent word or word group that breaks the continuity of the sentence.

> There is some doubt, **in view of the huge reserve fund,** about making further collections.
> The committee, **its agenda for the day completed,** adjourned for dinner.

7. Use the comma to point off words, phrases, and clauses that may be omitted without harming the grammatical structure of the sentence. Such words, phrases, and clauses are called *parenthetic.*

Word examples, often transitional helps, are *however, therefore, consequently, perhaps, finally, besides, accordingly, also,* and the like.

> It should be added, **finally,** that no change was authorized.
> We are glad, **however,** to fill your order.
> He was uncertain, **moreover,** of the amount.

Phrase examples are *in fact, as a matter of fact, in point of fact, of course, in short, in brief, in reality, without doubt, in case, by chance,* and the like.

> We believe, **as a matter of fact,** that you will win.
> We, **of course,** will grant the claim.
> There is, **in reality,** no reason why we should.

Clause examples are *I think, I believe, I repeat, he says, as you know, that is,* and the like.

> This is, **as you know,** your last chance.
> This conclusion, **we think,** is wrong.

8. Use the comma to point off words or word groups used in a series when there are at least three units.

> NOUN SERIES: Among the more important commodities are steel, oil, coal, and cotton.
> PHRASE SERIES: There is an upturn in steel mill activity, a hardening of money rates, and a steadily increasing curve in carloadings.
> CLAUSE SERIES: Steel mill activity is increasing, money rates are hardening, and carloadings are up.

9. Use a comma between listed adjectives when the word *and* has

seemingly been omitted—or could be inserted without affecting the emphasis of the descriptive words.

> . . . a strong, progressive firm.
> . . . an honest, reliable man.

Do not use a comma when the adjectives contribute to one complete thought.

> . . . a long blue car.
> . . . a wide bright runway.

10. Use the comma to point off words used in direct address or in explaining other words.

> We are pleased, **Dr. Cain,** that our service to you has been helpful.
> Through television, **the process of seeing along a radio wave,** we shall educate by new methods.
> Mr. Ray Burns, **President of the Kelton Company,** has called for a vote.

11. Use the comma to point off sentence elements that might be wrongly joined in reading if there were no commas.

> MISLEADING: There is no doubt that beneath things are financially sound.
> CLEAR: There is no doubt that, beneath, things are financially sound.
> MISLEADING: Ever since annual figures have been published.
> CLEAR: Ever since, annual figures have been published.

12. Use the comma to indicate the omission of words that are understood by the reader.

> Jay and Bob attended a football game; Ruth and Ann, a movie.
> The desk is listed at $175; the chair, at $50.

SEMICOLON

1. Use the semicolon between the members of a compound sentence when no conjunction is used.

> He is here today; he will not be here tomorrow.

If the conjunction is used in this sentence, place a comma between the clauses.

> He is here today, but he will not be here tomorrow.

2. Use the semicolon between the clauses of a compound sentence that are joined by such words as *also, consequently, for, hence, however, in fact, moreover, nevertheless, therefore,* and *whereas.*

> He arrived early; consequently, he saw the whole program.

3. Use the semicolon before the expressions *as, that is, namely, i.e., e.g., to wit, viz.,* when they introduce an illustration that is a complete clause or an enumeration that consists of several items. A comma is used after each expression.

> John Baczyk is an auditor; that is, he verifies accounting records.
> Three men were nominated; namely, Kent, Marx, and Rank.

4. Use the semicolon to separate the members of a compound sentence when one or both members are punctuated with commas.

> The charts will be finished today; the report, tomorrow.
> If he is nominated, he will run; but since there are three candidates, he does not expect the nomination.

5. Use the semicolon between serial phrases or clauses having a common dependence on something that precedes or follows.

> He demonstrated that the craft will fly; that it will fly faster than the speed of sound; and that it will fly higher than any previous craft.

6. Use the semicolon between the members of a series of clearly defined units, upon each of which special emphasis is to be laid.

> EMPHATIC: The truly creative man in business visualizes a great opportunity; he shapes the materials necessary to take advantage of it; and he creates a going business.
> LESS EMPHATIC BUT CORRECT: The truly creative man in business visualizes a great opportunity, shapes the materials necessary to take advantage of it, and creates a going business.

COLON

The colon indicates greater separation than the semicolon. It suggests that further material is coming. This material may be in explanation, in expansion, or in restatement of the idea.

As a general rule, the colon does not occur with any great frequency in the communications work of the average business day. Yet when it *is* called for, you will very much need to know how to apply it with exactness and precision. Observe the following guides.

1. Use the colon between two independent groups having no connecting word between them, the first group pointing forward to the second.

> Progress lies in one direction: improvement must be made in research and in manufacturing methods.

2. Use the colon after expressions that introduce items of information.

> We must meet these three requirements:
> The members of the board are:
> Please ship the following items:

3. Use the colon before a series of expressions.

> Note these special details: feather touch, velvet carriage, adjustomatic line spacer.

4. Use the colon before a long quotation. Such quotations are often introduced by *thus, the following, as follows,* or *these.*

> The auditor gave the following report: [Two pages of quoted material]
> His statement ran as follows: "You are obligated under the contract to return unsold items."

Before a short, informal quotation, a comma is permissible.

> He said, "Let's go home."

5. Use the colon to separate hours and minutes when expressed in figures.

> 11:30 a.m., 7:30 p.m.

Where all figures refer to time, as on a timetable, the use of the period instead of the colon is permissible.

QUESTION MARK

1. Use the question mark after a direct question.

How many letters has she typed?
He asked, "Where is the report?"

NOTE: The question mark is equivalent to a period. Hence it is normally followed by a capital.

The question mark should not be used after an indirect question, that is, one that does not require an answer.

He asked them if they would vote.

The question mark is not necessary after a courtesy question; that is, a sentence disguised as a question out of courtesy but actually embodying a request or command.

Will you please ship the order not later than tomorrow.
Will you please send me a credit memorandum at once.

2. Use the question mark after the individual members of a series, each one of which might be expanded into a complete sentence.

What is the population of Iowa? of Wisconsin? of California?
Would you guess his age as seven? eight? nine?

EXCLAMATION POINT

The exclamation point is used after a word, a phrase, or a sentence to indicate strong emotion or to carry sharp emphasis.

No! That is not true!
What an amazing climax!
We must get those votes!

APOSTROPHE

Handle the apostrophe with care. Scores of persons and business firms are guilty of letting messages, sometimes mass messages distributed in huge quantity, go before the public eye with the apostrophe *in the wrong place*. Knowing ones, who see the error, smile with amusement—or in contempt.

CARELESS ERROR: The assembly department is operating at **it's** peak.
AS CORRECTED: The assembly department is operating at **its** peak.

The error illustrated above is common. Do not be guilty of it. *It's* means *it is*, the apostrophe indicating the omission of the letter *i* in the contraction. *Its* means *belonging to it*. *Its*, the possessive pronoun, does not need the apostrophe any more than would the possessive pronoun *his*. *His* and *its* follow the same rule.

1. Use the apostrophe to indicate possession. Put the mark in the right place, remembering that the possessor is shown by the part of the word that comes before the mark, no matter whether the word is singular or plural. Master the apostrophe now, and save yourself much future uncertainty.

POSSESSIVE: the firm's patent rights
PHRASE: the patent rights of the firm
POSSESSIVE: the firms' patent rights
PHRASE: the patent rights of the firms
POSSESSIVE: Mr. Hotchkin's office
PHRASE: the office of Mr. Hotchkin
POSSESSIVE: Mr. Hotchkins' office
PHRASE: the office of Mr. Hotchkins
POSSESSIVE: the trainman's wages
PHRASE: the wages of the trainman
POSSESSIVE: the trainmen's wages
PHRASE: the wages of the trainmen

2. Use the apostrophe to indicate the omission of letters in a contraction. Be careful to set the apostrophe properly in a contraction. *The apostrophe stands for the missing letter and takes its place.* Contractions are used (a) in letters to people whom the writer knows in a friendly, informal way, (b) in sales messages to add a personal tone.

I'm	I am	aren't	are not
I'll	I will	couldn't	could not
you're	you are	didn't	did not
you'll	you will	don't	do not
he'll	he will	haven't	have not
we're	we are	isn't	is not
they're	they are	won't	will not

Words like *o'clock* use the same principle of contraction. The apostrophe in this expression stands for *f,* the expression *ten o'clock* expanding into *ten of the clock.*

3. Use the apostrophe to indicate the plural of abbreviations, figures, letters, and words.

> The company hired two Ph.D.'s.
> The 1's, 5's, and 7's are the series he wants.
> Carelessly written **l**'s and **i**'s are often misread.
> Too many **and's, but's,** and **for's** ruin sentences.

4. As a rule it is better not to use the possessive form for inanimate objects. Expressions pertaining to time or measure, or expressions suggesting personification, may, however, be in the possessive case.

> POOR: The door's hinge
> BETTER: The hinge of the door
> CORRECT: A day's trip; two weeks' delay; time's healing effects

QUOTATION MARKS

1. Use quotation marks to enclose every direct quotation. A direct quotation consists of the exact words of the original. An indirect quotation expresses the thought of the original in somewhat different words and does not require quotation marks.

> RIGHT: He said, "Grant Fields can become the best diver in the world."
> RIGHT: He said that Grant Fields can become the best diver in the world.
> WRONG: He said "that Grant Fields can become the best diver in the world."

When the quotation is interrupted by words thrown in by the speaker or the writer, both parts of the quotation must be enclosed.

> "Let us hope," he said, "that the vote is favorable."
> "Only to this degree," the speaker concluded, "can you say you have earned your freedom."

If a continuous quotation consists of two or more complete sentences, quotation marks are used only at the beginning and the end of the quotation.

> The speaker said: "American business is the envy of other nations. To remain a world leader, American business requires strong management."

If a quotation consists of several paragraphs, quotation marks should precede each paragraph and should follow the last paragraph.

Use single quotation marks (' ') to enclose a quotation within a quotation.

> "Then," the speaker continued, "the manager said, 'Excellent,' and approved the report."

2. Use quotation marks to enclose the titles of subdivisions of published works (parts, chapters, sections, etc.) and the titles of magazine articles, reports, lectures, and the like. Titles of books, essays, newspapers, magazines, plays, and other whole publications should be italicized. In typewriting, each word to be italicized is underscored.

> He read the article "Football Fever."
> His lecture, "Automation—A New Age," will be given at two o'clock.
> "How to Ski" is an interesting chapter in **The Book of Sports.**

3. Use quotation marks to enclose unusual or peculiar terms, words used in some special sense, or words to which attention is directed in order to make the meaning clear.

> That is a perfect example of "steam roller" methods.
> This outworn expression is called a "stock phrase."
> The word "furthermore" may be used at this point.

4. When a quotation mark and another mark of punctuation occur together, apply the following rules:

a. Place the period or the comma always inside the quotation mark.

> He wrote an article entitled "The Price of Peace."
> After he quoted the article "Incentive Plans," the motion was passed.

b. Place the colon or the semicolon always outside the quotation mark.

> Klise writes under the head of "Cost of Living": "The index will rise still higher."
>
> He speaks of "improving sales"; but improvement will come only from intelligent effort.

c. Put any other mark inside when it is part of the quotation and outside when it refers to the entire sentence, of which the quotation is only a part.

> The slogan is: "Avoid stock phrasing!"
> May we use "The Trend of Prices"?

DASH

Make the dash of sufficient length to avoid confusion with the hyphen. The typewritten dash is made by striking the hyphen twice.

1. Use the dash to show a sudden break or transition in thought.

> He could learn in an hour—yet why try to convince him?

2. Use the dash to separate the name of an author from an extract from his writings.

> "Motivation is the key to learning."—Lessenberry.

3. Use the dash for desired emphasis before an appositive, especially if the appositive is separated from its substantive by several words.

> He requested one special report—the Bramco report.
>
> One student attended the conference—a young man named Boling.

4. Use the dash instead of a comma where heavy emphasis is desired.

> Those who opposed him—and there was heavy opposition from many—still admired him for his courage.
>
> Courtesy—this is a habit to cultivate in getting along with others.

CAUTION: Do not use the dash indiscriminately for the purpose of concealing ignorance of how to use other punctuation marks. For if you do, you fail to gain the flexible resources of the important points of punctuation over which you should now be gaining mastery.

PARENTHESES

1. Use parentheses when an amount expressed in words is followed by an expression of the same amount in figures.

> The lessee agrees to pay one hundred dollars ($100).

2. Use parentheses to enclose numbers or letters in enumerations which run into the text.

> The report is written in three parts: (1) the introduction, (2) the body, and (3) the conclusion.
>
> The agenda consisted of four items: (a) the minutes of the previous meeting, (b) old business, (c) new business, and (d) adjournment.

3. Use parentheses to set off parenthetic, explanatory, or supplementary material.

> In future announcements (watch for them in your local newspaper) you will get additional facts.
>
> The evidence in this case (see Exhibits 1-5) are conclusive.

CAUTION: The parentheses, like the dash, are dangerous marks for the beginner and sometimes likewise for the veteran writer. Too often, for instance, parentheses are made to serve as a "catch-all" for loose material. Never use either the dash or parentheses as a slipshod substitute for a comma or for the purpose of covering up ignorance of how to use other marks of punctuation.

BRACKETS

1. Use brackets to enclose matter having no connection with the text, that is, something in the way of explanation, comment, or criticism inserted by someone other than the person quoted.

> Twelve states opposed the amendment [the author listed these states in a previous chapter], but it became law.

2. Use brackets to enclose a parenthetic expression within material already in parentheses.

> He confirms your opinion (see, for example, **Seven C's** [3d edition], page 1).

OMISSION MARKS, OR ELLIPSES

Ellipses, frequently termed "omission marks," are printed devices signifying the omission of letters or words in quoted material. Three marks or dots (. . .) are used to signify an omission at the beginning of quoted discourse, or at any other point when the omitted portion or section does not end on a period. Four marks or dots (. . . .) are used when the omitted portion or section does end on a period.

"Twenty delegates . . . voted in favor."
"He explained his position fully. . . ."

HYPHEN

1. Use the hyphen to indicate the division of a word at the end of a line. Rules for the division of words at line endings are given on pages 627 and 628 in the Reference Division of this book.

2. Use the hyphen to join the parts of certain compound words. There is little uniformity in writing compound words. Some are written as two separate words; some, as two words joined by a hyphen; and some, solid as one word.

One cannot set arbitrary rules for hyphening compound words because usage varies greatly. The following guides, however, represent current and accepted practice in the use of hyphens in compound words.

a. A hyphen is frequently used with the prefixes *ex, self,* and *vice.* It is also used to join a prefix to a proper name. It is not used with short prefixes, such as *co, de, pre, pro,* or *re,* except to prevent misinterpretation or mispronunciation.

ex-mayor
self-centered
vice-admiral
un-American
pro-British
co-op (for co-operative)
recover (to regain)
re-cover (to cover again)

b. A hyphen is usually used between two or more words serving as a single adjective *before* a noun.

first-class ticket
eight-room house
ready-to-wear suits
hit-and-run driver
third-class mail
forty-hour week
serious-minded student

When these compound adjectives *follow* the noun, they usually lose their compound characters and are not hyphened.

His up-to-the-minute report was interesting.
His interesting report was up to the minute.
He is a well-known author.
The author is well known.

When an adverb ending in *ly* is used with an adjective or a participle, the compound is usually not hyphened.

highly effective argument
widely praised decision

c. A hyphen is used in compound numbers written as words.

ninety-eight
two hundred twenty-nine
Twenty-four members were present.

d. A hyphen is used between the numerator and the denominator of a fraction written in words, except when one or both of these elements contain a hyphen or when the fraction is used as a noun.

a one-third share
one third of the sum
twenty-one hundredths
twenty one-hundredths
twenty-nine thirty-sevenths

e. When two or more hyphened compounds that have a common basic element are used in a series and the basic element is omitted in all but the last compound, the hyphens are retained in all cases.

one-, two-, and three-year appointments
six-, seven-, and eight-room houses
short- and long-term investments

f. A hyphen is used as necessary to avoid ambiguity or to make reading easier.

> AMBIGUOUS: He is now a junior high school student.
> CLEAR: He is now a junior-high school student.

When you are in doubt as to whether a compound word should be written solid, as two words, or with a hyphen, consult a recent edition of the un-abridged dictionary.

REVIEW OF PUNCTUATION RULES OF ORDER

When two or more punctuation marks occur at the same point in a sentence, they should be placed according to the following rules of order:

1. A period following an abbreviation is used before any other mark of sentence punctuation. When the abbreviation occurs at the end of a declarative sentence, however, the period is not doubled.

> Do you expect them to send it C.O.D.?
> Did he arrive before 10 a.m.?
> "At last," he exclaimed, "I finally did earn that B.A.!"
> J. F. Martin, Ph.D., whom you met last week, is the new research director of Watson and Higgins, Inc.

2. Quotation marks are used with other marks of punctuation as follows:

a. At the end of a quotation, a comma or a period is always placed inside the quotation mark; a colon or a semicolon, outside the quotation mark.

> "I saw them," he said, "as they entered the park."
> I must say this about her "intuition": it is phenomenal.
> John has not read the article "Plastic Wonders"; however, he has read "Modern Living."

b. A question mark, an exclamation point, or a dash is placed inside the quotation mark if it punctuates the quotation only. NOTE: When the quotation including its own mark of punctuation comes first in the sentence, no comma or period is used.

> He inquired, "Where are you going?"
> "Can you be there?" she asked.
> He said, "Well done!"
> "I'm late!" he explained as he hurried down the street.
> "I am so busy that—" is all I heard her say as she rushed past my desk.

c. A question mark, an exclamation point, or a dash is placed outside the quotation mark if it punctuates the entire sentence.

> Why was she "fired"?
> Did he say, "This is good work"?
> How enthusiastically he shouted, "Long live the president"!
> "The activities of the major departments are closely related and must be coordinated if satisfactory results are to be achieved."—Newman.

d. Punctuation for a quotation within a quotation follows the preceding rules for the use of other punctuation marks with quotation marks. When the quotation within a quotation occurs at the end of a sentence, however, note that it precedes the double quotation marks.

> He said, "I read the article 'The Future of the Small Business.'"
> Did he say, "I read the article 'The Future of the Small Business'"?
> He said, "Did you read the article 'The Future of the Small Business'?"
> He said, "I read the article 'What Will Happen to the Small Business?'"

3. Parentheses are used with other marks of punctuation as follows:

a. If the punctuation mark applies to the whole sentence and not to the material in parentheses, the punctuation mark follows the second parenthesis.

> The research has been completed (see Formula 3).
> Pride, in some disguise or other (often a secret to the proud man himself), is the most ordinary spring of action.

b. If the punctuation mark applies to the material in parentheses, the punctuation mark precedes the second parenthesis.

> When I heard him speak (he asked, "Who are you?"), I was startled.
> His article ("Sell the Sizzle!") is most timely.

4. When a parenthetical clause set off by dashes requires a question mark or an exclamation point, the punctuation mark is placed before the second dash.

Kent Smith—is he the vice president or the treasurer of the company?—has an appointment with you at three o'clock.

SPACING AFTER PUNCTUATION MARKS

Within a sentence, space once after a mark of punctuation with the following exceptions:

1. Within a sentence, space *twice* after a colon.

I said: "A male secretary trained under a successful executive is good material for advancement."

2. Within a sentence *do not space* after:

a. A period within an abbreviation—

Dr. Carson, Ph.D., and Dr. Park, LL.D., left at 12:30 p.m. to attend a meeting.

b. A period used as a decimal—

The answer is 3.15 per cent.

c. A dash—

Then we went to--but you are not interested in that.

d. A hyphen—

We want an up-to-date model.

e. An initial quotation mark—

He replied, "My work is finished."

f. An apostrophe within a word—

They couldn't be here.

g. A beginning parenthesis—

(See page 37 of the catalog.)

h. A beginning bracket—

A meeting was held in May [19--].

At the end of a sentence, space *twice* after a punctuation mark.

Type this letter next. How soon can you finish it? There you are! What are you doing?

Expression of Numbers

Handling Numbers. Many an otherwise well-trained writer is puzzled by whether a number should be written in words or in figures. The problem is not found in the writing of business forms such as invoices, sales tickets, or purchase orders, because in them figures are used almost entirely. In letters and in business reports written in paragraph form, numbers are sometimes expressed in figures and sometimes expressed in words. A careful writer observes the rules of expressing numbers, because these rules have been developed for the convenience of the reader. The following guides apply to the use of numbers in letters and other material written in paragraph form.

GENERAL RULES

1. Write a number at the beginning of a sentence in words. If the number is very large, it may be advisable to rewrite the sentence so that the number will not fall at the beginning.

Fourteen dozen pairs of gloves were ordered last month.
Twenty thousand dollars is the goal of the drive.

2. Use figures for numbers greater than 100 except in the case of isolated round numbers.

They registered 375 at the first convention, 1,237 at the second, and 2,119 at the third.
They shipped nine thousand carloads in the first month.

3. Round numbers (numbers in even units, such as tens, hundreds, or thousands) should be spelled in full, except when they are used in the same sentence with other numbers that cannot be expressed in words conveniently.

We saw him ten days ago.
The report contained more than fifty pages.
These machines range in price from $10 to $23,500.

Large round numbers may be written in words or figures or both according to the writer's preference or the nature of the copy. For example, if only one large round number is used, it may be written in words. But in writing of a business nature in which a large number of figures are used in other sentences or paragraphs, a large round number should be written in figures.

fifteen million dollars
$15,000,000
$15 million

4. If several numbers are used in a sentence in a similar construction, write all the numbers in figures, unless all are small or are round numbers that can be written easily in words. If the first word is a number, it may be written out even though the other numbers are written in figures; but it may be possible to improve the sentence by rewriting it so that the first word is not a number.

She ordered 45 typing books, 125 economic books, and 68 law books.
He bought three ties, six shirts, and ten handkerchiefs.
Seventy-seven men, 725 women, and 196 children were called in the poll.
In the poll 77 men, 725 women, and 196 children were called.

When a small number is used in the same sentence with a large number but not in a similar context, it may be written in words.

I asked the two auditors what caused the deficit of $652,890.

5. When one number immediately follows another, it is advisable to spell out the smaller number and to express the larger one in figures.

She purchased 75 four-cent stamps.
He bought four 25-cent notebooks.

6. When one unrelated number immediately follows another, the two numbers should be separated by a comma.

In 1959, 654 new charge customers were granted credit.

ADDRESSES

1. Express house numbers in figures, except for house number *One*.

Roberts lives at One Riverside Drive; Marshall, at 2185 Sutton Avenue; and McKie, at 8 Maple Terrace.

2. Spell out a number naming a street, if it is ten or below. When a street has a number as its name, separate the house number from the street number by a hyphen preceded and followed by a space. The letters *d*, *st*, or *th* may be added to the number that represents a street name.

He moved from 438 West Fifth Street to 867 - 66 Street.
Our office is located at 104 - 131st Street.
Deliver the equipment to 210 West Tenth Street.

DATES

1. After the name of a month, use figures to express the day.

Your letters of June 2, 6, and 9 were answered in full on June 14.

2. When the day of the month stands alone or when it precedes the month, it may be written in figures with *d*, *st*, or *th* added, or it may be spelled out.

In your letter of the 6th you asked for our catalog.
In your letter of the sixth you asked for our catalog.
We sent a check for $200 on the 3d of August.

AMOUNTS OF MONEY

1. Sums of money, whether in dollars or in cents or in foreign denomitions, should be typed in figures except in legal documents.

The total amount of the equipment recently purchased was $769.33.

2. Even sums of money are written without the decimal and ciphers.

She mailed a check for $45 in full payment of her grocery bill.

3. When stating cents, use the figures without the decimal and spell out *cents.*

The little girl purchased a small toy for 89 cents.

4. In legal papers spell out sums of money; write figures in parentheses.

I agree to pay the sum of Five Hundred Sixty Dollars ($560).
I agree to pay a weekly rental of One Hundred Ten (110) Dollars.

FRACTIONS AND DECIMALS

Simple fractions that stand alone are usually written in words. Mixed numbers and decimals are written in figures. When a decimal fraction is not preceded by a whole number, a cipher may be used before it.

She bought one-half dozen erasers.
The average age of stenographers in our department is 24½.
The average age of stenographers in our department is 24.5.
The quotient, 0.758, was obtained swiftly on the calculator.

QUANTITIES AND MEASUREMENTS

Quantities and measurements should usually be written in figures, as in the following examples:

a. Age *(exact)*—

He is 26 years old.

BUT use words in expressing *approximate* age:

Charles is about nineteen years old.

b. Balloting results—

There were 6,756 votes in favor of the amendment and 3,310 votes against it.

c. Dimensions—

They bought bond paper of a standard size, 8½ by 11 inches.

NOTE: Spell *by* in full, except in technical matter where *x* is used for *by.*

d. Distance—

It is 13 miles from my office to my home.
It is 2,098 miles from San Francisco to Honolulu.

e. Financial quotations—

They bought Monarch Utilities at 100 5/8.

NOTE: In financial quotations it is customary to express the plural of figures by adding the *s* without the apostrophe.

f. Mathematical expressions—

We found the total as follows: 125 plus 68 minus 38.

g. Measures—

We produced 200 bushels on every 4 acres.
The chart showed that 231 cubic inches equal 1 standard liquid gallon.

h. Percentages—

Interest on the note was computed at 4 per cent.

NOTE: In business writing the per cent sign (%) is often used to express per cent:

She purchased three 5-year, 4% bonds.

i. Serial numbers—

Policy No. 622147, a new life insurance policy, is discussed in Bulletin No. 3.

j. Temperature—

The highest official temperature record for the city of Dallas is 110°.

k. Time—

The plane leaves at 11:45 p.m.

BUT spell the hour in full when *o'clock* is used in stating time:

The box office of the Shubert Theater closes at ten o'clock.

l. Weights—

It takes 2,240 pounds to make 1 long ton.

MISCELLANEOUS

1. Page numbers are written in figures. Capitalized Roman numerals are often used for major divisions of books, such as chapters, and Arabic numerals for lesser divisions.

> This information is given in Figure 10 of Part 4, Unit IX, page 438.

2. Sessions of Congress and the identifying numbers of political divisions and military bodies are written in words.

> John Hall, of the Eighth District, was elected to the Eighty-fourth Congress. The Forty-fourth Infantry will move into new quarters.

Grammar Review Problems

● **1.** The following message has all the necessary punctuation except commas. Rewrite the message correctly.

Under the statutes the Attorney General is authorized to advise only state departmental heads the seventy-one district attorneys and other individuals specified in the statutes. On that account the Attorney General cannot advise you officially.

The Railroad Commission has jurisdiction over the administration of the common-carrier law as you know and I suggest therefore that you communicate with the Railroad Commission which has available detailed information or which is in a position to obtain if necessary the information you need. If you give it the facts in detail the Commission may already be acquainted with the particular situation. The Commission will I am sure be glad to cooperate.

● **2.** The following message is correct except for lack of punctuation. Punctuate it correctly.

Can you give us an accurate reference for the subject checked on the attached folder Mr. Adams figures which according to our investigation are essentially correct must be given a cross check before they are finally accepted.

These catalogs are in our library Natco No. 152 No 153 No 164A and Smithco No. 63 64 65 67 B Have you any addition which in your opinion should be included in our report.

● **3.** The following sentences contain relative clauses which may or may not restrict (limit) the elements modified. Write these sentences, inserting or omitting punctuation according to whether you think that the relative clause is restrictive (limiting) or merely explanatory. Be prepared to explain your decisions.

1. Enclosed is our descriptive catalog which we have developed for the use of manufacturing chemists.
2. Scientific ventilation which is an important subject in the minds of engineers is of recent origin.
3. The only product that has the unqualified endorsement of heating engineers is the Aero Air Conditioner.
4. The motion that brought such violent debate was on the subject of tax legislation.
5. The advertising copy writer who reads widely is likely to add largely to his resources of knowledge.
6. There is a brilliant future for those graduates who seize this opportunity for special training.

● 4. The following sentences suffer from serious faults in punctuation. Correct them in writing by using any of the available methods you prefer.

1. Please let us have your check before June 30, we cannot wait longer than this, we have made this point clear in our urgent requests of May 18, May 26 and June 10.
2. We should like to serve you, we hope we'll have the privilege soon.
3. Every day we are meeting unusual problems, we have been able to handle them all without difficulty.
4. We want to give you definite information on this laborsaving device, before we can do so however, we must have more detailed information on your production schedule, this should be inserted on the form provided.

● 5. Most of the following sentences contain one or more errors. Rewrite the incorrect sentences; correct all errors.

1. The carton weighed nine pounds and fifteen ounces.
2. The monthly statement showed a delivery charge of 50 cents.
3. The bank charged four per cent on the nine hundred dollar loan.
4. The living room was twelve by twenty feet.
5. The goods were shipped on January third, you should have received them by the sixteenth.
6. A rental fee of nine hundred ($900) dollars shall be paid monthly.
7. On the tour the couple traveled over two thousand miles and drove through eight states.
8. Union Packages 6's were sold at 107 and one half.
9. Our annual catalog lists 216 items at $4.50, eighteen items at $6.50 twenty-two items at $3.00 and one hundred items at $5.00.
10. She had two appointments in the morning one at 8:15 and one at 9:30.
11. A pictorial graph is given on page fifty of volume iii.
12. The temperature in our new freezer was two degrees.
13. In 1788 8 states were admitted to the Union.
14. Fred Kent lives at 914 73d Street his father lives at 1 Elm Road.
15. 70 men, 65 women, and 32 children attended the festival.

● 6. The following sentences include numerous words that require the use of the apostrophe. Rewrite these sentences, preferably on the typewriter, placing the apostrophe at the proper point in each of the words.

1. Theyre determined that theyll win the election.
2. The accountants convention heard the treasurers report.
3. According to the judges decision nobody elses claim can be recognized.
4. Next months meeting of the sales managers group will be held in the Plazas Frontier Room.
5. Several days notice must be given when changing addresses.
6. The advertising managers rules were mimeographed.
7. Was it a mens or a womens petition that was sumitted?
8. After five hours examination of the records at the supervisors desk, the committee defined the three stenographers responsibilities.
9. Both the clerks machines have been repaired.
10. Everybodys interests have been properly defined.
11. The directors committee will adjust the agents commissions.
12. The seasons peak is expected two months from August.
13. The photographers convention meets in Salt Lake City this year.
14. Basketball tickets are obtained at the ticket agents window.
15. The womens section of the convention meets for two successive days.
16. The committees report reviewed the records of the Executives Club.

•
•
•

PART IX

•
•

Section 2   *Using the Dictionary at Top Skill*

Powerhouse of Communication: Your Dictionary. In the chapters of this book you have reviewed the *essential* information regarding the use of words, the tools of business expression. You have noted how to put words together most effectively to solve business problems and to do better business. Every one of these words you will find—in your dictionary.

Words reach certain social levels. Some words are disreputable. Some are rough and colloquial and will pass only in the haste of conversation. Some suit the dignity of formal address.

But note this: the social level of a word seldom remains fixed. Many words have lost both dignity and distinction by overuse, a fate into which certain formerly useful business words have fallen. On the other hand, through the artistry of a powerful writer, a once-common word may be lifted to distinction.

An obvious gap exists between the regularly practiced customs of language on the one hand, and the "rules of usage" so often found in many accepted handbooks on the other hand. The two simply do not harmonize. Yet it is futile to perpetuate an insistence on archaic usage and on unnecessary distinctions when no one observes them. The American language is a great social heritage and a living, changing organism.

No one doubts that the mastery of words is of the highest practical importance for efficiency in living. To the businessman, indeed, few things are more practical—even when appraised in dollars and cents—than the ability to use words as they were meant to be used, to bring them into effective sentences, to mold them into effective paragraphs, to punctuate them so that their collective meaning is emphasized. But even if the mastery of words were not important in a financial sense, it would still be worth the effort. You have heard it said that "the apparel oft proclaims the man." Using words carefully is, in fact, simply a part of good manners, and the part that with relentless truth reveals to others what you are.

The Treasurehouse of the Dictionary. The editor of *The World Almanac*, the annual compendium of world facts, faces each day an inpouring stream of questions. He reports:

The strange thing about my work is that ninety-nine out of a hundred questions that come to my desk could be answered by the questioners themselves if they knew how to use the organized knowledge that is at the command of everybody.

What are the sources?

Now I am going to surprise you. A good unabridged dictionary answers the largest proportion of the questions. If you give a person a good dictionary and cultivate in him the habit of using it every time he encounters an unfamiliar word, you have given him the groundwork of a splendid education.*

This section of the book should be read with a collegiate or an unabridged dictionary near at hand. This discussion is designed to help you take the fullest advantage of the resources of the dictionary, to make available its varied contents, to increase your ability to find the information it contains, and to improve your discriminating selection of words and your precision in the use of words.

* *Vocabulary Building, Word Study, and Bibliography* (Springfield: G. & C. Merriam Company), p. 43.

541

Twelve Tested Ways to Use the Dictionary

1. When you are puzzled by the **meaning** of some word in your news-paper or book (*audion* or *psychopathologist,* for instance)—look it up in the dictionary.

2. When you are uncertain of the **pronunciation** of such a term as *Putsch* or *chargé d'affaires,* or any other difficult one—look it up in the dictionary.

3. When you want to know what the **derivation** of a word is and what its component parts signify—look it up in the dictionary. For example, you will understand *radiotron* better when you know its etymology.

4. When you wish to find the **strongest word for your purpose,** per-haps the only one of a dozen synonyms that just expresses your meaning—look it up in the dictionary. *Hazardous, precarious, un-certain, daring,* and many more words are synonyms, yet each has a distinctly different connotation.

5. When you need to understand the **fine distinction** between two similar words such as *revenge* and *avenge*—look it up in the dic-tionary.

6. When you see or hear a reference to *Mirabeau, Anne Boleyn, Myles Standish,* or some other **historical figure** with whom you are only vaguely familiar—look it up in the dictionary.

7. When you want to know the facts about a **famous character of literature** (*D'Artagnan, Anna Karenina, Uncas,* or thousands more)—look them up in the dictionary.

8. When you want the very **latest official information** about the population of a city, the location of an island, the height of a mountain, the length of a river, or facts about such places as *Manchukuo* and the *Far Eastern Region*—look them up in the dictionary.

9. When you require the **meaning or pronunciation of a foreign word or phrase**—look it up in the dictionary. *Savoir-faire* and *entente cordiale* are typical of many you meet.

10. When you have occasion to use a **table of measurements**—linear, cubic, etc.—look it up in the dictionary. How big is an *acre?* How long is a 400 *meter race?* How many *furlongs* are there in a mile? These are a few of scores of questions answered.

11. When you need information on a **technical point of science or art, industry or civics,** or any other special subject—look it up in the dictionary. You may learn, for example, the nature and use of a *variometer;* the identity of *Paul Cézanne;* the periods and styles of *architecture;* the names, colors, and uses of *dyes;* the duties of the *Vice President.*

12. When you have any question on **words, persons, places, events, or facts**—look it up in the dictionary.

For this is the most reliable and most convenient source of exact knowledge.

From the pamphlet, "Tests for Class Use" (Springfield: G. & C. Merriam Company). Adapted by permission.

Vocabulary Building Through the Dictionary*

General Information. The dictionary covers every field of knowledge and contains much information of an encyclopedic nature. Scriptural, historical, mythological, and general allusions are given in the general vocabulary. In the back of the dictionary are sections which give specialized information of the highest value to business and the professions:

Abbreviations Used in Writing and Printing
Arbitrary Signs and Symbols
Colleges and Universities in the United States and Canada
Common English Christian Names
Foreign Words and Phrases
Pronouncing Biographical Dictionary
Pronouncing Gazetteer
Punctuation, Use of Capitals, etc.

Spelling and Grammatical Information. The dictionary is an indispensable guide in spelling. When two forms are given, the first is preferred by the editors, though both have the support of good usage. When the entry is followed by = or *Var. of*, the form to which you are referred is the preferred spelling. Rules for spelling are given on pages in the front of the dictionary.

Procedure 1: Check the preferred spelling of the following words:

acknowledgment	acknowledgement
advertise	advertize
aesthetic	esthetic
enclose	inclose
gipsy	gypsy
lagune	lagoon
medieval	mediaeval
theatre	theater
today	to-day
traveler	traveller

Plurals of nouns and pronouns, principal parts of verbs, cases of pronouns, and the comparative and superlative forms of adjectives are shown if they are in any way irregular.

Procedure 2: Give the plurals of the following words:

adieu	sheep
bus	stratum
crocus	tomato
delicacy	whimsy
fish	wife

Procedure 3: Give the principal parts of the following verbs:

bite	make
blow	set
drag	sing
go	sit
hang	tell

Procedure 4: Give the comparatives and superlatives of the following adjectives:

bad	lengthy
dim	manly
foggy	red
good	rusty
jolly	weighty

The basis of good diction is grammatical correctness. Often a word is used as more than one part of speech. This use is indicated by the abbreviations *n.* (noun), *v. t.* (verb transitive), *adv.* (adverb), etc., before a definition or before a series of related definitions. Observe, also, that cases of pronouns are shown.

Procedure 5: Give the different parts of speech that each of the following represents.

arm	maroon
as	rough
base	second
best	set
confederate	where
desolate	worthy
fault	wrong
fish	

---

* The discussion that follows is adapted by permission from the pamphlet, "An Outline for Dictionary Study" (Springfield: G. & C. Merriam Company). See also *A Study Plan for The American College Dictionary* (New York: Harper and Brothers), another effective guide to dictionary use.

Pronunciation. Pronunciation is indicated by certain symbols which, for ready reference, are partially explained at the bottom of each page, and fully in the Guide to Pronunciation in the front of the book. Every dictionary user should know this section.

The main vocabulary word is divided into syllables, and the primary accent is marked with a heavy accent mark (′) and the secondary with a lighter one (′). See *floodgate*. This is a great timesaver, for many words can be correctly pronounced without referring to the phonetic respelling, if the accent is known.

Some words have more than one pronunciation indicated. In such cases the first is preferable, although, in the case of many words, good usage (which is the final authority) is about equally divided.

Procedure 6: Determine the pronunciation of these commonly mispronounced words:

appellate	indict
bade	italics
blatant	joust
column	lamentable
condolence	measure
coupon	precedence
exquisite	respite
flaccid	schism
height	senile
impious	suite

Procedure 7: The change of accent from one syllable to another changes the meaning of many words. Determine what change in meaning occurs in the following words when the accent changes.

absent	instinct
collect	minute
contest	precedent
desert	project
increase	object

The Origins of the English Language. The English language is derived from many different sources. Almost every known language has contributed to our vocabulary. A brief statement giving the language or languages from which the vocabulary entry is derived appears in the brackets [ ] which precede the definition, thus: *battalion* [F. (French) *bataillon,* fr. It. (Italian) *battaglione.*].

Procedure 8: Look up the following common words and determine from what languages they are derived:

amen	molasses
arena	potato
bungalow	shawl
chorus	shop
cipher	taboo
grippe	talc
hominy	tea
house	thug
kimono	tungsten
maternal	tulip

A knowledge of a word's component parts and their meanings is most helpful in enlarging one's vocabulary, and in using these words accurately. Once having learned, for example, that words having roots *scribe* and *script* come from some form of the Latin verb *scribo, scribere, scriptum,* meaning "to write," one can determine at a glance the meaning of such words as *transcribe, manuscript, postscript, inscribe,* etc.

Procedure 9: Look up the words *reduce, induce,* and *ductile,* and see from what common Latin root they are derived.

Development of Meanings. In many cases the derivation of a word or sense is most interesting and illuminating.

Procedure 10: Observe the following words in the dictionary and determine the facts as to (1) source and (2) present significance:

almanac	mob
batch	nasturtium
bless	nickname
booby	panic
boycott	pastor
cabbage	pop
calico	puppet
flour	pry
forsythia	satellite
heliotrope	saxophone
lunacy	sherry
martial	shibboleth
meander	vandal

Definition. While the spelling and pronunciation of a given word are important, a word is not mastered until its meaning is clear. Definitions are arranged in a logical order, the meaning which a word had when first used in the language standing first, the meanings which have been acquired later following in regular order. This historical arrangement links older meanings with those more recently acquired and gives a well-rounded picture of a word.

In searching for the meaning of a word in the dictionary, read all of its definitions. One of them will express the precise meaning wanted and the other definitions will help to illustrate it by an analogy or contrast.

Procedure 11: Trace the changes in meaning that have taken place in the following words:

assassin	hospital
bedlam	nice
character	ordeal
dean	piquant
fruition	propaganda
homely	sanction

Illustrative Examples. Many words have acquired secondary or figurative meanings. For such words a sentence illustrating this usage is helpful. A word used idiomatically is more easily understood when the use is shown by a phrase, clause, or sentence.

Procedure 12: Check the illustrative examples used under the following words:

as	give
before	go
but	hard
by	heavy
catch	light
cool	make
cut	set
delicacy	that
fall	the
for	with

Usage. The dictionary records the best usage of words and warns against their incorrect usage. If a word, one of its forms, or one of its meanings,

does not have the sanction of best usage, a label, as *Colloq., Illit., Dial.,* etc., restricts its use or warns against its misuse. Other labels, as *Law, Hort., Mil.,* etc., before a definition show that the definition following applies to the branch of knowledge indicated. After some definitions a note after the index symbol ☞ gives additional information as to the correct use of the word defined or refers to another entry where pertinent information will be found.

Procedure 13: Check the labels or the notes which apply to the following words and serve as a guide to their correct use, or limit their use in certain senses to special fields of knowledge:

auction	phone
awful	post
beside	quit
boss	reckon
ceiling	script
don't	sequence
English	step
hike	straight
hindsight	streak
joint	swell

Synonyms. Accuracy of statement and precision of expression are obtained by the discrimination shown in the selection of synonyms. Words are called *synonyms* and are said to be synonymous when they have nearly the same meaning. Strictly speaking, no two words mean exactly the same thing, and correct usage requires a careful differentiation in their shades of meaning. The treatment of synonyms in the dictionary is of incalculable value to the user of words. Synonyms appear after the definition and are labeled *Syn.* Notice that they are listed logically, the word that has the closest meaning to the vocabulary word coming first. For many of the words the differences in the shades of meaning are explained by illustrations.

Procedure 14: Certain words are often carelessly interchanged in use. Determine the *exact* use of each of the words in the following pairs, and use each of them correctly in a sentence:

ambition and aspiration
apology and excuse
cause and occasion
consist of and consist in
deface and disfigure
discover and invent
eminent and celebrated
error and mistake
explain and interpret
haste and speed
observation and observance
oral and verbal
reparation and amends
restive and restless

Procedure 15: The study of certain groups of business synonyms—especially those used in business administration, marketing, accounting, law, consumer contact, and secretarial procedure—is advisable. The following groups of synonyms come from these special business fields. Those who plan careers in any way related to commerce should be familiar with these terms. Use each of the following words correctly in a business sentence *differing* sharply from the illustrations shown.

GROUP A

Contract, Agreement, Bargain, Stipulation. A *contract* is a legally enforceable agreement. An *agreement* may be made without a contract, but no *contract* can be made without an agreement. A *bargain* is a contract of sale. A *stipulation* is one of the provisions in an agreement.

GROUP B

Discount, Deduction, Allowance, Concession, Refund, Rebate. A *discount* is a reduction usually figured in percentage. A *deduction* is often a lump sum subtracted from the amount to be paid. An *allowance* may be made from the price of goods which prove defective or unsatisfactory. A *concession* is a yielding to a request or a demand. A *refund* is the return of the entire sum paid. A *rebate* is the return of a part of the sum paid.

GROUP C

Invoice, Bill, Statement, Account. A business organization sends an *invoice* for goods which have been shipped. A business sends a *bill* for services that have been rendered. An invoice is itemized. A *statement* is an abstract or summary of an account, showing the balance owed; it is commonly a notice of invoice totals yet unpaid. An *account* is a reckoning of money transactions.

In this group and in the preceding and following groups, note the careful differentiation in the shades of meaning.

GROUP D

Pay, Compensate, Remunerate, Reimburse, Indemnify, Expend, Disburse, Requite. To *pay* is to discharge an obligation due to another, whether for goods delivered or for services rendered. To *compensate* is to make a suitable return for services given, time spent, trouble taken; such compensation may or may not take the form of money. *Remunerate* adds the suggestion of reward. To *reimburse* is to make good an expenditure: He reimbursed his agent for his expenses. To *indemnify* is to insure against loss or to make restitution for a loss. To *expend* is to spend or to use money, time, labor, thought, and the like. To *disburse* is to pay, usually from a treasury or a public fund. To *requite* (in the good sense) is to make a return or to recompense; (in the bad sense) it means to revenge or to retaliate.

Antonyms. Antonyms are words of opposite meanings. Common in legal and business usage, they deserve careful attention and adequate review.

Procedure 16: Of importance in business are the following antonyms. Use each of the words in the following pairs correctly in a business sentence:

assets, liabilities
debit, credit
debtor, creditor
domestic, foreign
extrinsic, intrinsic
inflation, deflation
mortgagor, mortgagee
objective, subjective
predecessor, successor

Prefixes and Suffixes. The English language makes use of prefixes and suffixes so generally to modify and change the meaning of words that a study of a few of the commoner ones is a matter of practical business wisdom.

Procedure 17: (a) Look up the following prefixes and suffixes. Build three words using each and use each word correctly in a business sentence:

PREFIXES

ante-	in-	semi-
anti-	inter-	sub-
arch-	ob-	super-
de-	per-	trans-
ex-	pro-	uni-

SUFFIXES

-able	-hood	-let
-age	-ic, -ical	-ly
-er, -or	-ish	-ment
-ess	-ism	-ness
-fold	-less	-ous

(b) Separate the following words into their component parts, and define the prefixes and suffixes. Then use each word correctly in a business sentence:

antedate	exclude
assignee	grantor
atonement	humanize
behaviorism	misrule
bilingual	novelist
bothersome	object
breakage	precancel
bulbous	reassure
circumvent	threefold
coexist	weakness

Using Prefixes to Form Antonyms.

Prefixes like *in, il, im, ir, un, non,* and *dis* are often used to form antonyms. Since the choice of the right prefix may offer some difficulty, the formation of prefix antonyms deserves study. The base prefix is *in, non,* or *dis.* Note how *in* changes to *il* before words beginning with *l*; to *ir* before words beginning with *r*; to *im* before words beginning with *m* or *p*.

Procedure 18: Use each of the words in the following pairs correctly in a business sentence:

accurate, inaccurate
agree, disagree
assessable, nonassessable
attractive, unattractive
businesslike, unbusinesslike
logical, illogical
movable, immovable
negotiable, nonnegotiable
popular, unpopular
possible, impossible
regular, irregular
resident, nonresident
systematic, unsystematic
usual, unusual

Homonyms. A homonym is a word having the same *sound* as another, but differing from it in meaning. Homonyms (like *there* and *their* or *led* and *lead*) are often confused to such a degree as to cause difficulty in business transactions. Common homonyms should be practiced by repeated use in business sentences.

Procedure 19: Use each of the words in the following pairs or groups correctly in a business sentence:

aloud, allowed	pair, pare
ascent, assent	past, passed
bale, bail	patients, patience
bear, bare	plain, plane
berth, birth	presence, presents
by, buy	principal, principle
canvas, canvass	profit, prophet
capital, capitol	raise, raze
cession, session	sail, sale
coarse, course	scene, seen
complement,	sell, cell
compliment	seam, seem
confidant, confident	serial, cereal
council, counsel	sole, soul
descent, dissent	stationary,
draft, draught	stationery
fair, fare	steal, steel
feat, feet	surge, serge
fore, four	team, teem
hail, hale	tense, tents
heal, heel	there, their
hear, here	to, too, two
hour, our	vain, vane
hoard, horde	ware, wear
incite, insight	wane, wain
indict, indite	weighed, wade
instance, instants	whole, hole
leased, least	who's, whose
new, knew	your, you're
pain, pane	

Capitalization. When a word should be spelled with a capital letter, the vocabulary entry begins with a capital. For illustrations see *American* and *Parthenon*.

Some words ordinarily capitalized have meanings in which the capital is not used. This usage is indicated by [*not cap.*] immediately preceding that particular definition. See, for example, *Atlas, Epicurean, Romanesque*.

The converse is also true, for some words ordinarily not capitalized have meanings which require the capital letter. This usage is indicated by [*cap.*] immediately preceding the definition. See *jovial, grace*.

Syllabication. Syllabication is indicated in each vocabulary entry by separating the syllables with a centered period or with the accent mark, thus: in′de·scrib′a·ble.

Hyphens. Hyphenation of compound words is indicated by a heavy-faced hyphen, thus: a′ble-bod′ied. See also the discussion of hyphenation elsewhere in this book on pages 534 and 535.

Vocabulary Building through the Dictionary. One of the best methods of building vocabulary is to read the works of authors who are recognized masters. Notice unfamiliar words. Look them up in the dictionary. Make sure that you know their meaning. Practice using the words until such use becomes natural.

An extensive vocabulary is an important factor in success, not only in college work, but also in later business and professional life. Years of scientific research have now disclosed a direct relation between vocabulary and success.*

As we have seen in a previous chapter, "an extensive knowledge of the exact meanings of English words accompanies outstanding success in this country more often than any other single characteristic which the Human Engineering Laboratories have been able to isolate and measure."

O'Connor also reports that *vocabulary may always be consciously increased* regardless of the presence or absence of any gift, and that the balance of evidence suggests that "a consciously, even laboriously, achieved vocabulary is an active asset." **

The Dictionary Habit Pays Rich Dividends. The dictionary habit—a habit that pays you rich dividends—has a twin aim: (1) to discover the exact meanings of words already known; (2) to discover the useful meanings of words never before used. A tested program for acquiring the dictionary habit has been presented in this chapter. Use it often.

* Johnson O'Connor, "Vocabulary and Success," The *Atlantic Monthly*, Volume 153.

** *Ibid.*

Grammar Review Problems

NOTE: The seven following projects supplement the nineteen self-training procedures provided in the body of the chapter.

● **1.** Rewrite the following sentences by substituting for the words in parentheses words that seem more exactly to express the thought.

   a. A welcoming committee met the president and (accompanied) him to his headquarters.
   b. The prime minister (abdicated) because of political opposition.
   c. He studied the question by a carefully thought out (mode).
   d. Local businesses cooperated in giving (help) to the depression sufferers.

e. The constitution provided distinctive (names) for the officers.

f. Financial troubles (arrested) his studies for a year.

g. He found his friend's prominence in the community (beneficial) when he set out to get a job.

h. The builders called for a truck to (convey) their equipment.

i. His thrifty, (busy) youth was rewarded with a prosperous old age.

j. He labored to (disengage) himself from his difficulties.

● **2.** Rewrite the following sentences, choosing the correct word from the pair in parentheses. Check your selection with the dictionary. Then write a new sentence using correctly the word that was not correct for use in the sentence given below.

a. He could not answer the inquiry immediately because he had no (stationary, stationery).

b. The (principle, principal) purpose of his trip was to see the sales manager.

c. He was an (excessively, exceedingly) powerful influence in swaying the committee's decisions.

d. His absence did not (effect, affect) the situation.

e. Since he was expert in cases of this sort, they sought his (counsel, council).

f. Being extremely (ingenious, ingenuous), he was able to make a number of improvements in the machine.

g. The uproar outside was (aggravating, irritating).

h. An hour's questioning failed to (illicit, elicit) any information.

i. The city (ordinance, ordnance) forbids parking on University Avenue.

j. He devoted his days to his (avocation, vocation), which was marketing, but in the evenings he often found time for his hobby of philately. (Check your pronunciation of *philately*.)

● **3.** The following sentences reveal cases of repetition. Rewrite each sentence, using the word in parentheses only once in the sentence. To find substitute words, consult the definitions and treatments of synonyms in your dictionary.

a. It (seems) to me that she (seems) more mature.

b. If you (pay) enough to get a good dictionary, you will be well (paid) by the service it will give you.

c. His (clear) explanation of the circumstances won over the committee, and he was (cleared) of blame.

d. He promises to (supply) three loads of gravel, a (supply) which he says should suffice to finish the job.

e. When war was (declared), the ambassador (declared) that it was no longer safe for Americans to remain in the country.

● **4.** For this problem use as large a dictionary as is available. A collegiate dictionary will be satisfactory. (a) Consult the dictionary and bring to class a written explanation of the difference in the meanings of the words of each group. (b) Write a sentence, suitable for use in business, to show your understanding of each word.

GROUP A

active, progressive, up-to-date

certain, unavoidable, inevitable

complicated, involved

comprehensive, far-reaching

educated, skilled

ignore, disregard

marked, prominent, substantial

obstable, impediment

partnership, corporation

permit, license

<table>
<tr><td>**GROUP B**</td><td>**GROUP C**</td></tr>
</table>

GROUP B	GROUP C
advanced, suggested, proposed	adequate, sufficient, suitable
biased, prejudiced	cheap, inexpensive
choice, alternative	enhance, increase, magnify
divested, freed	financial, monetary, pecuniary
expired, terminated, lapsed	insolvent, bankrupt
idle, lazy, unemployed	limit, regulate, restrict
indifferent, neutral	profit, proceeds, return
industrial, commercial	quota, share, proportion
print, publish, promulgate	reduce, minimize
supplemented, augmented	watered, inflated

● **5.** (a) Check the meaning of each of the antonyms given on page 546, making sure that you are familiar with the exact meaning of each. Use a good dictionary. (b) Prepare a written explanation of the difference in meaning between the words in each pair. (c) Use each of these words in a good business sentence.

● **6.** Use each of the homonyms given on page 547 in a business sentence (114 sentences).

● **7.** *A Dictionary Test of Accuracy.*

   a. Write the plurals of the following words:

alumnus	crisis	echo	mother-in-law	parenthesis
basis	cupful	gas	Mr.	ski
bus	datum	lily	oasis	tomato

   b. In the following words indicate orally the syllable to be accented when pronouncing the word:

admirable	condolence	detail	hospitable	precedence
adversary	defects	dirigible	incognito	precedents
comparable	despicable	exquisite	inquiry	romance

   c. Indicate which of the following words are misspelled. Then use each word correctly in a business sentence.

abscence	conceive	encourageing	oblige	seize
adviser	conscience	finally	Phillipines	successful
apparent	desparate	grevious	procede	superintendent
artical	devine	independent	professor	untill
batallion	disappoint	judgement	recommend	welfare
benefitted	embarrass	necessary	relieve	wonderful

   d. Give the principal parts of the following verbs:

awake	choose	flee	get	prove
bid	come	flow	lay	set
burst	dive	fly	lie	wake

   e. Indicate whether the following words are to be written solid, with the hyphen, or as two words:

all right	father in law	in as much	per cent	self educated man
al ready	foot ball	inter collegiate	re write	south west
battle ground	good by	never the less	room mate	to day

Section 3   *Gaining Personal Power Through Words*

Nouns

Nouns, the Namers. A noun is a part of speech that names a thing so that your mind can make a picture of it.

letter   typewriter   desk

As soon as you see the word *letter,* your mind pictures a sheet of stationery on which is typed a message; or your mind may picture the letter *A* or *Z*. When you see the word *typewriter,* your mind may picture the familiar machine with the keyboard on which a letter is typed. When you see the word *desk,* your mind may picture a piece of office furniture on which to place a typewriter or on which to do other office work.

The dictionary broadens the definition a little further: A noun is a word that names a subject of discourse, as a person, place, thing, quality, idea, or action.

Commerce and industry deal largely with facts, and facts are named by nouns. Business could hardly function without nouns. Without them men could not *indicate* things to others; nor could they understand what others were trying to indicate to them.

Common Nouns and Proper Nouns. A name that is common to all the members of a group of persons, places, or things, is called a *common noun.*

man   city   office

The name of a particular person, place, or thing, which distinguishes that person, place, or thing from all others in the group, is called a *proper noun.*

Gary Collins   Detroit   Apex, Inc.

A common noun begins with a small letter. A proper noun is capitalized. You must know the difference between common nouns and proper nouns in order to be certain when to capitalize and when *not* to capitalize.

Let us now translate a list of common nouns into a matching set of proper nouns. Here they are:

COMMON NOUNS

city	man
company	woman
hotel	state

PROPER NOUNS

San Diego	Grant Fields
Acme Corporation	Ann Adams
Hotel Sinton	California

Concrete Nouns and Abstract Nouns. The name of something that can be identified by any one of the five senses is a *concrete noun.* The name of a quality or an idea—something that can only be thought about—is an *abstract noun.*

CONCRETE NOUNS

fragrance	song
paper	rainbow
salt	

ABSTRACT NOUNS

accuracy	initiative
agreeableness	power
courage	

Collective Nouns. The name applied to a group or class as a whole is a *collective noun.*

assembly	crowd
audience	jury
board (of trustees)	multitude
committee	(office) staff
company	regiment

Be able to recognize collective nouns quickly so that you may accurately apply the special rules governing their use in relation to verbs and pronouns. These rules are taken up in later sections discussing verbs and pronouns.

Verbal Nouns. A *verbal noun* names an action rather than a person, place, or thing. Verbal nouns are derived from verbs and end in *ing*.

Typing is a valuable skill.
Dictating and **writing** are two kinds of expression.

You should be able to recognize verbal nouns quickly so that you may accurately apply the special rule governing their use in relation to possessives. This rule is taken up on page 556, which discusses verbal nouns in relation to possessives.

Special Problems Pertaining to Nouns. Common nouns, concrete nouns, and abstract nouns present no difficulties. The special problem in collective nouns is their use in relation to verbs and pronouns. The special problem in verbal nouns relates to the use of the possessive. These uses will be discussed later. The special problem regarding proper nouns is *capitalization*.

CAPITALIZATION

Capitalization of Proper Nouns. How can you tell when to capitalize a word? The answer is logical, definite, and clear. Ask yourself this question: *Is the word, in the place in which it is being used, a proper noun?* If the answer is *yes*, you must capitalize that word.

The general rule that any proper noun must be capitalized does not by itself solve all capitalization problems, because now and then it is hard to tell just what is a proper noun. In deciding what to capitalize, you will find the following rules useful.

1. Capitalize the name of a person exactly as he himself capitalizes it.

Louis E. de La Porte
Robert DeWeese
William R. MacDonough
James F. O'Connor
Charles VanDeRyt
Douglas van Raalte

2. When it is used as a part of a proper name, capitalize a word that is usually an adjective or a common noun.

Carmel River
East Side Restaurant
Lake Tahoe
Pure Products, Inc.
Steamboat Springs
Town House
Western Hills Viaduct
Yosemite National Park

3. Capitalize special names of regions and localities because they are proper names. But do not capitalize nouns or adjectives indicating direction.

CAPITALIZE
the Far East
North Dakota
the South
South America
Upper Peninsula

NO NOT CAPITALIZE
far eastern customs
southern Virginia
the southern part of Texas
upstate New York
western Michigan

4. Capitalize the names of things with specific individuality that are clearly used as proper names.

AIRPLANES: the Executive Flight
CHURCHES: the First Baptist Church
HALLS: Hamilton Hall; the Hall of Mirrors
LIBRARIES: the Richmond Carnegie Library
ROOMS: the Algonquin Room; the Clover Room
TRAINS: the Golden State Limited

5. Capitalize the names of organizations and groups with specific individuality that are clearly used as proper names.

ASSOCIATIONS:	the Society of Automotive Engineers
CLUBS:	the Pacific Club; the University Club
CORPORATIONS:	the Fox River Paper Corporation
DEPARTMENTS:	the Department of Defense
FIRMS:	the National Products Company
INSTITUTIONS:	the Smithsonian Institution
MAGAZINES:	the Atlantic; the Saturday Evening Post
NEWSPAPERS:	the New York Times, the San Francisco Post
ORGANIZATIONS:	the Community Union
SCHOOLS:	Central Technical High School

6. Capitalize the names of the days of the week and the months of the year because they are proper names. But do not capitalize the names of the seasons unless they are personified.

The meeting will be held on Friday, March 5.
The spring and summer prices will be about the same.

7. Capitalize the names of divisions of knowledge when you use them as titles of specific courses. But do not capitalize such names when they are used to denote studies in general or common divisions of knowledge.

He is taking Mathematics of Finance and Report Writing.
The courses they listed were science, mathematics, and engineering.

8. Capitalize words derived from proper nouns unless these words have developed specialized meanings.

CAPITALIZE

American	French
English	Georgian

DO NOT CAPITALIZE

chinaware	pasteurize
italicize	platonic

9. Ordinarily capitalize only the principal words in headings and in the names of books, articles, and subjects.

See Chapter III of the book entitled **The Wonderful Writing Machine.**

10. Capitalize any noun that is personified and that is therefore a proper noun.

If man can destroy his great enemies, War and Pestilence, that villainous pair will fade before the coming of Peace and her healing calm.

11. Capitalize titles in business; professions; rank; honor, and respect, whether civil, religious, or military, (a) when such titles immediately precede or follow a proper name and are directly related to it, and (b) when they refer to specific persons.

Examples of (a):

Dr. R. W. Larkin, Director of Research, and Dr. Mark Freed, Professor of Marketing, will collaborate.
Mr. Albert Bradley is Chairman of the Board, General Motors Corporation.
The Honorable Joseph Burnet, Director-General of Harrod's, Ltd., will address the group.
The Honorable Joseph Burnet is the Director-General.
Dr. Nathan M. Pusey, President of Harvard University, is the speaker.
Dr. Nathan M. Pusey is President of Harvard University.
For information write Mr. Richard A. Michaels, Editor.

Examples of (b):

He is Secretary-Treasurer of Todd, Inc.
She is the President of the National Secretaries Association.

Other Items Requiring Capitalization. Capitals are called for in certain cases other than proper nouns. For example, capitals must be used for the following:

1. The first word of every sentence.

2. The first word and all titles and nouns in the salutation of a letter.

Dear Mr. Daly:
My dear Mr. Daly:

3. The first word in the complimentary close of a letter.

Sincerely yours,
Yours very sincerely,

4. The first word after a colon when the colon introduces a complete passage or sentence having an independent meaning; but not when a colon introduces an element that is explanatory or logically dependent upon the preceding clause.

> He clearly stated: Our studies show. . . .
> He gave two reasons for the decision: the building needs to be enlarged, and the materials are ready.

5. The first word of a long quotation or of one formally introduced.

> Here is what the message said: "Our business messages are valuable pipelines to our customers. Every message is our ambassador and must represent us well."

6. The pronoun *I* and the interjection *O*.

7. Any noun or pronoun used to refer to the Deity.

> "They spoke of God and His legions."

8. A noun or an abbreviation of a noun that refers to a specialized part of a work. Such parts may be followed by a capitalized Roman numeral, or an Arabic numeral, indicating place in a sequence.

Act IV, Scene I	Section 9
Article III	Unit VI
Book II	Volume I
Part 5	Vol. I

BUT: page 1

Verbs

Verbs, the Doers. In the drama of good writing, verbs play the part of action. In the dictating or writing of business messages, sales letters, and special reports, action may rise to high importance, because in this type of writing attention must be held. Nothing engages attention so quickly or holds it so long as colorful and vigorous verbs. The verb is a power-maker and a mover to action. Well-chosen verbs, selected with a trained knowledge of their relationship to other words in the dictated and transcribed thought, make sentences clear, decisive, and forceful.

Command the Simple Verb Essentials. Make your verbs obey your commands. Learn how to channel your action-thoughts with fluent accuracy. To do these things, you must learn a few simple essentials about verbs. You must know them well because you will have to call upon them constantly in the future. Your business sentences will take on the glow of meaning and action when their pivotal power sources—verbs—are deftly slipped into place. But you can express yourself well only when you

know the differences between the various kinds of verbs and can choose each kind intelligently when you need it.

Avoid Typical Verb Difficulties. Failure to understand the differences between the various kinds of verbs gets many people into serious trouble about verbs. When such people have to use verbs like *lie* or *lay*, *let* or *leave*, *sit* or *set*, *rise* or *raise*, they find themselves in a fog of troubled uncertainty, never sure when they are right or when they are wrong. Most of the time they are wrong. Forced to select between the following expressions, they are never certain whether to choose *he don't* or *he doesn't*, *leave it go* or *let it go*, *the letter was laying on the desk* or *the letter was lying on the desk*. Without recognizing their own errors, they blunder into crude mistakes like "It don't matter much," "Leave it go until tomorrow," or "The report you want is laying over there." Such people are often astonished, sometimes mortified, when their work is severely criticized. For their trouble there is only one cure: *they must learn the basic differences between the various kinds of verbs.* Only then can they select the exact verb form that they need in conversation, dictation, transcription. For example, they will have to know the meaning and use of:

Transitive	Infinitives
Intransitive	Participles
Active	
Passive	Shall, Will
	Should, Would
Indicative	
Subjunctive	May, Can
Imperative	Might, Could
Present	Have, Had
Past	
Future	Agreement of
	Subject-Verb

Handling Transitive and Intransitive Verbs. You will need to know that a transitive verb—one that indicates an action passing over from the subject to the object, from the *doer* to the *receiver*—needs an object to complete its meaning.

TRANSITIVE

The president **manages** the company.
The treasurer **collected** the money.
The agent **wrote** the report.

An intransitive verb, however, needs no object to complete its meaning.

INTRANSITIVE

Each month sales **increase**.
A new shipment of goods **arrived**.
Last year business **improved**.

A few intransitive verbs like *be, seem, appear, become, feel, taste, smell, sound,* and *look* call for a pronoun in the nominative case (Examples: *I, he, she, we, they*), an adjective, or a predicate noun (a noun completing the meaning of a connective verb) to complete their meaning.

PRONOUN: It **was he** who won the election.
ADJECTIVE: Report-writing ability **is** [seems, appears] **essential.**
PREDICATE
  NOUN: He **became** the **candidate.**

You will note that an adjective, *not an adverb*, is called for after these intransitive "linking" verbs. The adjective shows some quality or condition of the subject, as: the cloth *feels soft*, the cake *tastes good*, the rose *smells sweet*, the music *sounds harsh*, the future *looks promising*.

Active and Passive Verbs. When you wish to show that the subject is performing the action, use an active verb (a verb in the active voice).

ACTIVE: The **treasurer approved** the statement.

When you wish to show that the subject is being acted upon, use a passive verb (a verb in the passive voice).

PASSIVE: The statement **was approved** by the treasurer.

Only transitive verbs carry an action over from the subject to the object. Hence only transitive verbs may be changed into the passive voice.

Business Prefers the Active Form. Under the direction of the author, a group of students undertook to find out which form of verb, active or passive, modern business appears to favor. In twenty-one advertisements published in seven national magazines, each verb was examined, counted, and checked. Final score: active verbs, 494; passive verbs, 73. *Ratio: about seven to one for active verbs.* Searching further, the students read articles in business magazines and scores of business messages. Again active verbs were most favored by a wide margin. "Business prefers active verbs," the students concluded, "because they picture action surging ahead like an arrow. Active verbs suggest the signal 'Go Ahead!'"

Infinitives. Infinitives are verb forms that assert nothing, but merely indicate in a general way an action or a state of being. They are identified by the word *to*, either expressed or understood. Infinitives are used as nouns, as adjectives, or as adverbs.

NOUN (subject): **To act** requires talent.
NOUN (predicate): Her ambition is **to write.**
NOUN (object): He wants **to write.**
ADJECTIVE: That is a letter **to be treasured.**
ADVERB: She has gone **to order** the gifts.

To, the sign of the infinitive, is omitted after the verbs *bid, let, make, need, help, hear, dare, feel, see,* and a few others.

Will she make us (to) finish now?
Did you hear him (to) go?
Watch him (to) run the machine.

Shall We Split the Infinitive? Good writers ordinarily find it needless to split infinitives. Careless writers often split infinitives for no reason at all, and in the most awkward fashion. The one justification for a split infinitive is the infrequent occasion on which it lends greater clearness and power to certain sentences. Such instances are not numerous. It may be taken for granted that breaking up infinitives often makes writing shoddy. With a little thought nine out of ten split infinitives can be avoided with benefit.

CARELESS:	To promptly fill your order is our hope.
BETTER:	We hope to fill your order promptly.
CARELESS:	They were able to quickly discover the right formula.
BETTER:	They were able to discover the right formula quickly.
CARELESS:	To accurately present the plan is our object.
BETTER:	To present the plan accurately is our object.
CARELESS:	We want you to carefully consider our proposal.
BETTER:	We want to consider our proposal carefully.

Participles (Verbal Adjectives). Business writing calls for participles, which are verb forms used as adjectives and having the double function of verb and adjective. Participles may be present (*writing, dictating, selling*) or perfect (*written, dictated, sold*).

The present participle is the simple form of the verb plus *ing.* It denotes action in progress.

PRESENT PARTICIPLE
The executive **dictating the report** is the chairman of our convention.
[**Dictating** is an adjective modifying the noun **executive**; it is also a verb taking the object **report**.]

In the perfect participle of a regular verb, *d* or *ed* is added to the present tense (*dictate, dictated; order, ordered*).

PERFECT PARTICIPLE
The **report dictated** by the vice president was sent immediately.
[**Dictated** is an adjective modifying **report**.]

The perfect participle of irregular verbs sometimes ends in *t* or *en* (buy, *bought*; think, *thought*; write, *written*; speak, *spoken*; give, *given*; take, *taken*).

Note that participles become absorbed in certain verb forms; for example, *is planning* and *was sent.* These forms are not participles in the foregoing sentences because they are absorbed in the verbs and are not used as adjectives.

Verbal Nouns. Business writing also calls for verbal nouns, which are *verb forms used as nouns and functioning in a sentence as nouns.* They are called verbal nouns because they name actions and because they are derived from their corresponding verbs. The words *writing, dictating, selling, advertising* may often be used as verbal nouns in business. For example:

Writing good reports requires skill.
[**Writing** is a noun and the subject of the sentence; it is also a verb taking the object **reports**.]

When a noun or a pronoun modifies a verbal noun, be sure to put the noun or pronoun in the possessive form. For example:

Does he object to **my** [not **me**] reading the note?
The **manager's** going left a vacancy.

The difference between *naming* an action and *expressing* an action should be observed. *Reading* and *going* in the illustrations just given *name* actions. In the following sentences they are parts of verbs and *express* actions:

He is **reading** the note.
The manager is **going** tomorrow.

Make Verbs Agree with Collective Nouns. Keep the agreement right between a collective noun and its corresponding verb. Group names like *assembly, audience, crowd, office force,* and *company* are collective nouns. They are generally used with a singular verb or a singular pronoun.

> The **assembly votes** to set **its** adjournment ahead.

Sometimes, however, the members of the group are acting as parts or individuals. Such a case calls for a plural verb and a plural pronoun.

> The **crowd were** not agreed among **themselves.**

To put it another way, a collective noun takes a singular verb when the *group* is thought of, but a plural verb when the *individuals* are thought of.

To make the collective use sound natural when *individuals* are thought of, it is sometimes desirable to place the expression *members of* before the collective noun.

> **Members of** the crowd **were** not agreed among **themselves.**

Make Verbs Agree with the Subjects. The verb must agree with the subject in (1) person and (2) number. Look for the exact subject of the verb. Recognize it and fix it carefully in your mind. Do not let elements that fall between the subject and the verb throw you into error.

WRONG: Stenographic service and the salary of the dictator **is** the cause of high letter cost.
RIGHT: Stenograpic service and the salary of the dictator **are** the causes of high letter cost.
RIGHT: High letter cost **is** due to the salaries of dictator and stenographer.
WRONG: You, not he, **is** supposed to have the contract.
RIGHT: You, not he, **are** supposed to have the contract.
WRONG: In the old records **were** found a queer mistake.
RIGHT: In the old records **was** found a queer mistake. [The subject, **mistake,** follows the verb and is singular.]

Subjects Connected by "As Well As" and Like Expressions. When words are joined to a subject by *as well as, in addition to, with, together with, including, no less than,* etc., the verb agrees in number with the subject.

> The summaries, as well as the report, **were** ready.
> The report, together with the two summaries, **was** ready.
> The newest clerk, no less than the president, **is** invited.

Subjects Connected by "Or" or "Nor." Two or more singular subjects connected by *or* or *nor* require a singular verb.

> Neither the professor nor his assistant **is** in the office.

When two or more subjects connected by *or* or *nor* differ in number, the plural subject is placed nearest the verb, and the verb is made to agree with it in the plural.

> Neither the professor nor the students **are** in the room.

When the subjects of the verb *be* differ in person, an awkward sentence is avoided by using a verb with each subject.

> Either **you are** the chairman or **I am.**

Subjects Connected by "And." Two or more singular subjects connected by *and* require a plural verb.

> Mr. Clay and Mr. Johns **are** the new agents.

When the subjects connected by *and* refer to the same person, a singular verb is called for.

> The secretary and treasurer (one man) **is** the next man to be elected.

When the subjects connected by *and* represent one idea or are closely connected in thought, a singular verb is called for.

> Bread and butter **is** the staff of life.

When the subjects connected by *and* are preceded by *each, every, many a,* etc., a singular verb is called for.

> Every nook and cranny **was** searched.

When one of the subjects is affirmative and the other negative, the verb agrees with the affirmative and is understood with the negative.

> The play of the team, and not our hopes about it, determines the score.

Mode in Verbs. Mode is a property of a verb that indicates the manner in which the action or state is expressed. Hence, to express your business thought in exactly the right form and manner, you must know how to handle mode. There are three modes: the indicative, the imperative, and the subjunctive. Each has a useful part to play in business expression.

1. *Indicative mode:* used to express a fact or ask a question.

> The indicative mode is the commonest form in correspondence.

2. *Imperative mode:* used to express a command, a request, or an entreaty; often used in interoffice memoranda and in collection work.

> **Give** this matter close attention.
> **Send** your check without fail by April 31.
> Please **see** that the order is shipped today.

3. *Subjunctive mode:* used to express (a) a statement or a supposition contrary to fact, (b) a wish, or (c) a doubt.

> A FACT (indicative mode): He **is** an excellent writer.
> A WISH, CONTRARY TO FACT (subjunctive mode): He wishes he **were** an excellent writer. [But he is not.]

The subjunctive form of the verb *to be* in the present tense is *were.* This form is used with all persons in both the singular and the plural.

> I wish I **were** able to be there. [I am not.]
> If Dr. Glenn **were** here [but he is not], he would approve the medical report.

The verb *is* should be used in a sentence that refers to the present time and shows an ordinary condition.

> If Dr. Glenn **is** here, he will approve the medical report. [I do not know whether he is or not.]

The verb *was* should be used in a sentence that refers to past time and shows an ordinary condition.

> If Dr. Glenn **was** here yesterday, I am sure he approved the medical report. [I do not know whether he was or not.]

The verb *had been* should be used in a sentence that refers to past time and shows a condition contrary to fact.

> If Dr. Glenn **had been** here yesterday, I am sure he would have approved the medical report. [He was not here yesterday.]

Timing Verbs: the Three Primary Tenses. The accurate timing of verbs is an important business skill. The verb must indicate the exact time of the action. Make sure that you write precisely what you mean by choosing the right tense.

Tense is that form or use of a verb that indicates the time of an action or an event. The three primary tenses are present, past, or future, according to whether they express present, past, or future time.

PRESENT
TENSE: He **dictates** good letters.
PAST
TENSE: He **dictated** good letters.
FUTURE
TENSE: He **will dictate** good letters.
             We **shall dictate** good letters.

The past tense of regular verbs is formed by adding *d* or *ed* to the present tense: *live, lived; like, liked; dictate, dictated.*

Future Tense: Simple Futurity. The future tense indicates what will take place in the future time.

> We **shall be** here Wednesday.
> They **will complete** the report soon.

You must consider two things in choosing between *shall* and *will*: (1) what the person of the subject is and (2) whether the sentence expresses simple futurity, or determination or promise.

To indicate simple futurity, with a subject in the first person (*I* or *we*), use *shall*; with a subject in the second or third person (*you, he, she, it,* or *they*), use *will*. By simple futurity is meant a probable future event, over which the speaker assumes no control.

The plane **will** probably be on time.

Simple futurity also includes the expression of a hope, an intention, an opinion, or a prediction.

We hope we **shall** be able to attend the convention.
They **will** work until they finish their job.
He **will** be glad he made that decision.

Future Tense: Determination or Promise. To express determination or promise, reverse the rule for futurity; that is, with a first-person subject (*I* or *we*) use *will*, and with any other subject, *shall*.

I (or "we") **will** go in spite of opposition.
You (or "he" or "they") **shall** stay, no matter what happens.

When you say, "I *will go*," you express more than a mere intention. You indicate that you are assuming an obligation, or are promising someone, to go; or that you expect to exert your own will power to go, regardless of obstacles or opposition. When someone in authority says, "You *shall* stay," he indicates his intention to use force, if necessary, to see that you stay. The expression reflects unchangeable determination.

Should and Would. *Should* and *would* follow the same rules as *shall* and *will*, *should* corresponding to *shall*, and *would* to *will*. They are used in conditional sentences referring to present time. *Should* is used with *I* or *we*; *would*, with other subjects.

If **I** should go, I shall let you know.
If he **would** come, it **would** assure our success.

To show an attitude of wish, *would* may be used with all pronouns:

I **would** speak if time permitted.
He **would** work faster if he could.
They **would** act at once if approval were given.

Should is also used in the sense of *ought,* in which case it is correctly used with any subject.

I **should** be on my way in an hour.
You **should** report by 10 a.m.
He **should** bring it back with him.
It **should** be called to his attention.
We **should** accept the offer.
They **should** duplicate the order.

Perfect Tenses. Three verb phrases, called perfect tenses, indicate completed action or state of being. The perfect tenses are: the present perfect, the past perfect, and the future perfect.

1. *Present perfect tense:* formed by placing *have* or *has* before the perfect participle.

They **have sent** the order. [Present completion]

This tense is correctly used to indicate an act or an event that began in the past (either a minute or a year ago is past) and that has just now been completed.

2. *Past perfect tense:* denotes an action or an event as completed at or before a stated past time. It is formed by placing *had* before the perfect participle.

They **had sent** the order before the error was discovered. [Action completed at or before an expressed past time]

3. *Future perfect tense:* denotes an action or an event that will be completed at or before a stated future time. It is formed by placing *shall have* or *will have* before the perfect participle.

We **shall have** won the election before they can act.
He **will have** shipped the order by the time our telegram reaches the office. [Action that will be completed at or before an expressed future time]

Indicative Mode—Active Voice

Tense	No.	SIMPLE	PROGRESSIVE	EMPHATIC
Present	*Singular*	1. I pay 2. you pay 3. he (she *or* it) **pays**	1. I am paying 2. you are paying 3. he is paying	1. I do pay 2. you do pay 3. he does pay
	Plural	1. we pay 2. you pay 3. they pay	1. we are paying 2. you are paying 3. they are paying	1. we do pay 2. you do pay 3. they do pay
Past	*Singular*	1. I paid 2. you paid 3. he paid	1. I was paying 2. you were paying 3. he was paying	1. I did pay 2. you did pay 3. he did pay
	Plural	1. we paid 2. you paid 3. they paid	1. we were paying 2. you were paying 3. they were paying	1. we did pay 2. you did pay 3. they did pay
Future	*Singular*	1. I shall pay 2. you will pay 3. he will pay	1. I shall be paying 2. you will be paying 3. he will be paying	*Determination* 1. I will pay 2. you shall pay 3. he shall pay
	Plural	1. we shall pay 2. you will pay 3. they will pay	1. we shall be paying 2. you will be paying 3. they will be paying	1. we will pay 2. you shall pay 3. they shall pay
Present Perfect	*Singular*	1. I have paid 2. you have paid 3. he has paid	1. I have been paying 2. you have been paying 3. he has been paying	
	Plural	1. we have paid 2. you have paid 3. they have paid	1. we have been paying 2. you have been paying 3. they have been paying	
Past Perfect	*Singular*	1. I had paid 2. you had paid 3. he had paid	1. I had been paying 2. you had been paying 3. he had been paying	
	Plural	1. we had paid 2. you had paid 3. they had paid	1. we had been paying 2. you had been paying 3. they had been paying	
Future Perfect	*Singular*	1. I shall have paid 2. you will have paid 3. he will have paid	1. I shall have been paying 2. you will have been paying 3. he will have been paying	
	Plural	1. we shall have paid 2. you will have paid 3. they will have paid	1. we shall have been paying 2. you will have been paying 3. they will have been paying	

Indicative Mode—Passive Voice

Tense	No.	SIMPLE	PROGRESSIVE
Present *Singular*		1. I am paid 2. you are paid 3. he (she *or* it) is paid	1. I am being paid 2. you are being paid 3. he is being paid
Present *Plural*		1. we are paid 2. you are paid 3. they are paid	1. we are being paid 2. you are being paid 3. they are being paid
Past *Singular*		1. I was paid 2. you were paid 3. he was paid	1. I was being paid 2. you were being paid 3. he was being paid
Past *Plural*		1. we were paid 2. you were paid 3. they were paid	1. we were being paid 2. you were being paid 3. they were being paid
Future *Singular*		1. I shall be paid 2. you will be paid 3. he will be paid	
Future *Plural*		1. we shall be paid 2. you will be paid 3. they will be paid	
Present Perfect *Singular*		1. I have been paid 2. you have been paid 3. he has been paid	
Present Perfect *Plural*		1. we have been paid 2. you have been paid 3. they have been paid	
Past Perfect *Singular*		1. I had been paid 2. you had been paid 3. he had been paid	
Past Perfect *Plural*		1. we had been paid 2. you had been paid 3. they had been paid	
Future Perfect *Singular*		1. I shall have been paid 2. you will have been paid 3. he will have been paid	
Future Perfect *Plural*		1. we shall have been paid 2. you will have been paid 3. they will have been paid	

Progressive Form. The progressive form is made by prefixing to the present participle some form of the verb *be.* It denotes that the action of the verb is going on at the time referred to.

SIMPLE
PRESENT: We **write** good letters.
PROGRESSIVE We **are writing** better let-
PRESENT: ters every week.

Both of these examples are in the present tense. The simple present indicates that the action is completed at one time; the progressive present indicates that the action is going on or continuing at the present time.

Emphatic Form. In the present and past tenses (active voice), emphasis may be added by using *do* or *did* and the infinitive without *to.* This form is known as the emphatic form.

SIMPLE
PRESENT: We **write** good reports.
EMPHATIC
PRESENT: We **do write** good reports.
SIMPLE   We **wrote** better reports all
PAST: through the year.
EMPHATIC We **did write** better reports
PAST: after taking the course.

Time Guide for Verbs. A convenient and useful *Time Guide for Verbs* is presented on pages 560 and 561. Use it for quick reference on verb-timing questions.

Using "May, Can, Might, Could." *May* expresses probability or permission. *Might* is the past form of *may.* *Can* expresses power or ability. *Could* is the past form of *can.* A helpful rule is this: *May* equals *please permit* or *it is possible. Can* equals *able.*

May I use your name as a reference?
Can she fill the requirements of this job?
They **may** open the shop tomorrow.
I **can** assure you that those are the facts.

Principal Parts of Verbs. Each verb has three principal parts: the present, the past, and the perfect par-

ticiple. The perfect participle is used with an auxiliary verb, usually *have, has,* or *had.*

Regular verbs form the past tense and the perfect participle by adding *d* or *ed* to the present: *use, used, used; add, added, added.* Most verbs are regular. A few, however, do not follow the normal forms; they are therefore known as irregular verbs.

Irregular Verbs. Irregular verbs are relatively simple. Consider them so, and they will remain so. *Attack them* instead of backing away from them, and you will have no trouble. Become so familiar with the following irregular verbs that their correct use becomes as instinctive to you as to say "Thank you" when you acknowledge a courtesy. To know these irregular verbs is an essential of good manners as well as of good grammar.

Simply memorize the past tense and perfect participle for each present tense in the list on pages 563 and 564. It will not take you long. For good practice attach the three auxiliaries, *have, has,* and *had,* to each past participle as you speak it.*

Control of these irregular verbs is important to dictator and transcriber alike. Without that control neither one can function at his best in business.

Accuracy Is the Watchword. The business writer, in his daily duties, must direct his effort as he would an arrow to a target. He must economize his time, conserve his energy, turn out the maximum amount of work within the available number of office hours. To make a success of these tasks, use verbs with care. See that each verb you use is carefully chosen for its correctness, for its suitability in the sentence, and for its vividness and force. Above all, be accurate!

   * This list may be used as a spelling review, the instructor dictating the present forms, the students writing the past tense and the perfect participle.

Irregular Verbs Important in Business

PRESENT	PAST	PERFECT PARTICIPLE (have, has, had)
am	was	been
arise	arose	arisen
bear	bore	born, borne
beat	beat	beaten
become	became	become
begin	began	begun
bend	bent	bent
bid [command, invite]	bade	bidden
bid [make an offer]	bid	bid
bind	bound	bound
bite	bit	bitten
blow	blew	blown
break	broke	broken
bring	brought	brought
burst	burst	burst
buy	bought	bought
carry	carried	carried
catch	caught	caught
choose	chose	chosen
come	came	come
cost	cost	cost
dig	dug	dug
do	did	done
draw	drew	drawn
drink	drank	drunk
drive	drove	driven
eat	ate	eaten
fall	fell	fallen
fight	fought	fought
find	found	found
flee	fled	fled
fly	flew	flown
forbid	forbade	forbidden
forecast	forecast	forecast
forget	forgot	forgotten
freeze	froze	frozen
get	got	got
give	gave	given
go	went	gone
grow	grew	grown
*hang [suspend]	hung	hung
hide	hid	hidden
know	knew	known
lay [put into place]	laid	laid
lead	led	led
leave	left	left
lend	lent	lent
let	let	let
lie [recline]	lay	lain
lie [falsify]	lied	lied
make	made	made
pay	paid	paid

* The verb *hang*, meaning "to execute," is regular: hang, hanged, hanged.

PRESENT	PAST	PERFECT PARTICIPLE (have, has, had)
put	put	put
ride	rode	ridden
ring	rang	rung
rise	rose	risen
run	ran	run
see	saw	seen
set [put into place]	set	set
shake	shook	shaken
show	showed	shown
shrink	shrank	shrunk
sing	sang	sung
sink	sank	sunk
sit [take a seat]	sat	sat
slay	slew	slain
sleep	slept	slept
speak	spoke	spoken
spring	sprang	sprung
steal	stole	stolen
strike	struck	struck, stricken
strive	strove	striven
swear	swore	sworn
swell	swelled	swelled, swollen
swim	swam	swum
swing	swung	swung
take	took	taken
teach	taught	taught
tear	tore	torn
think	thought	thought
throw	threw	thrown
wake	waked, woke	waked
wear	wore	worn
weave	wove	woven
win	won	won
write	wrote	written

Grammar Review Problems

1. Identify the common, proper, concrete, abstract, collective, and verbal nouns in the following sentences. When optional forms for modifiers of verbal nouns are given, select the correct one.

a. The fleet's arrival is expected hourly, but the mystery of the commercial voyage is deepened because no information has been given out concerning the cargo.

b. Dean Markham's opening statement shows unquestioned courage and foresight.

c. Although his dictating is improving, we are not yet ready to trust his judgment in executive letters.

d. The knowledge and the power he displayed in the last emergency indicate, in the opinion of Secretary Douglas, a new spirit of aggressiveness.

e. America's coming into power as a creditor nation has been relatively sudden.

f. The board wishes to announce to its company that it appreciates the full cooperation of the office staff during the last year.

g. The president has announced [him—his] going.

    h. They seek your approval of [them—their] leaving on the evening train.

    i. His honesty and his integrity led to [him—his] being promoted earlier than he expected.

● **2.** Write these sentences with correct capitalization. Be able to justify each capital letter.

    a. He is a member of the university club, the antlers club, and rotary international. He also holds a staff position in the department of electronics. He will read a paper this Fall at the meeting of the association for the advancement of science.

    b. If he shifts to the department of marketing, he will change his degree to a "general b.a."

    c. The Commercial transport airliner follows a Southern route for two thirds of the distance. It then veers sharply West and continues a Southwestern route to Terminal station.

    d. She lives on the east side. Her mail is sent to her Office on the tenth floor of the union central building, suite 1202. The building is on the North side of commercial square.

    e. The west texas state journal advertises Our Big Sale of Paintings. be sure to read Our Advertisement.

    f. Commercial shipping may now pass from lake michigan into the chicago river. But the slow barges interfere seriously with traffic at the michigan avenue link bridge.

    g. You will never have such a Chance for an Offering like this for a long time. We advise you to act Now, because these mexican green jade rings are almost Priceless.

● **3.** Rewrite the following sentences using *was* or *were* correctly in the blank spaces:

    a. If you _____ asked to speak, would you accept?

    b. If the special bond issue _____ to be floated today, it would greatly depress prices of government securities.

    c. What would you do if you _____ nominated?

    d. If he _____ sending the goods today, there would be no doubt of their acceptance.

    e. He wished it _____ possible for him to be there.

    f. If he _____ really there, as Sherwood reported to me later, someone should have asked him to speak.

● **4.** Rewrite the following sentences using one or more of the following words in the blank spaces: *is—are, was—were, has—have*. Decide which forms are permissible and indicate for each form the difference in meaning in those sentences in which more than one may be used.

    a. Neither the ordinary postal service nor the airmail _____ available for such an article.

    b. The number of unemployed _____ expected to reach not less than three million.

    c. Mr. Richards or Mr. Stagg _____ expected.

    d. Either one or the other of these two _____ right.

    e. One of the orders _____ not sent out.

    f. The comptroller or the accountant _____ responsible.

    g. This subscription with the four premiums _____ a purchase well worth considering.

h. Forty-nine per cent of the shares _____ to be distributed for the account of others.

i. Each of those men _____ loyal to the company.

j. The majority of our stenographers _____ above the standards of accuracy required.

k. Every one of those orders _____ to go out before noon.

l. The majority of the stock _____ in the hands of Kennedy and his group.

m. A quorum _____ lacking because there _____ only fifteen men present.

n. Forty-nine per cent of the stock _____ not enough for control.

● **5.** Rewrite the following sentences using one or more of the following words in the blank spaces: *shall, will, may, can.* Decide which forms are permissible in each sentence, and indicate for each form the difference in meaning in those sentences in which more than one may be used.

a. You _____ have as much time as you need.

b. He is not certain when he _____ pay his bill.

c. They _____ not be able to detect any new trends.

d. Unless you _____ give us assurance that business will improve, we _____ not begin further plant expansion until May.

e. The contract _____ be sent to him today.

f. We _____ suffer a slump in business soon, unless production is held in better control.

● **6.** The following message is typical of the better examples which go through the mails from day to day.

(a) Classify all verb forms in the message under these headings: principal verb, infinitive, participial, or auxiliary; transitive or intransitive; active or passive.

(b) Give the tense of each irregular verb.

(c) Identify any conditional sentences and be able to state why you think they should be so classified.

(d) Determine the number of active verbs and the number of passive verbs. Which form is used more often? In a written paragraph give the conclusion you draw from this comparison.

No longer will you have to begin every business day with a desperate dash for the 8:17. In a short time this curious old custom will have become extinct.

Digestions have improved, tempers have grown tame, all because of Chronos electric time in hundreds of thousands of American homes and offices.

Chronos Master Clocks, in America's powerhouses, have been primarily responsible for this modern promptness and precision. By checking the speed of giant generators, they assure even, regular impulses of alternating current at the electric outlet in the home. Driven directly by these current impulses, every Chronos Clock delivers the same silent, accurate time. Chronos Clocks and Chronos Master Clocks were made for each other.

Mr. C. L. Lawton, one of Denver's leading jewelers, is displaying the newest Chronos. Skillfully designed for mantel, wall, or table, for every room in the house, it is made for long and faithful service. Could you ask for split-second time at a more moderate price than $15.95?

You may choose Chronos, knowing that palatial clubs have chosen it before you. Remember that: No Chronos has ever run down. When you buy Chronos, you buy star time.

See these precision clocks today at Lawton's.

Additional Problems on Irregular Verbs

● 1. Study the list of irregular verbs on pages 563 and 564 until you can spell correctly each part of each verb. Be prepared to write the past tense and the perfect participle when the present form is dictated.

You should not be satisfied with your rating in this exercise *until you make a perfect spelling record.*

● 2. At the end of each of the following sentences one or more verbs appear in italics. Rewrite each sentence, using some form of the verb correctly in the blank space of the sentence to which the verb corresponds.

    a. Price levels last year _rose_ eight points, but they have not _risen_ to any extent this year. (*rise*)

    b. She has _begun_ to plan for next year. (*begin*)

    c. If he had not _seen_ the error in time, the company could not have _broken_ the record. (*see, break*)

    d. Sales have _fallen_ off, but no one seems to have _found_ where they _went_. (*fall, find, go*)

    e. The responsibilities that he _carried_ last month _wore_ him out. (*carry, wear*)

    f. Even if Walker had _arrived_ yesterday, he would not have _won_ the victory for his group. (*arrive, win*)

● 3. Some students have more than normal difficulty with irregular verbs. The following exercise is most helpful. Note the following skeleton sentences:

PRESENT: Today I (*or* it)
PAST: Yesterday I (*or* it)
PRESENT PERFECT: On many occasions I have (*or* it has)

In each of these sentences, write the correct form of each of the verbs listed below. Finish each sentence intelligibly. For example:

Today I *begin* my new job. Yesterday I *began* my new job. On many occasions I have *begun* to doubt it.

bear	come	give	pay	strive
beat	do	go	rise	take
become	draw	know	see	tear
break	eat	lay	show	throw
bring	fly	lead	sink	wear
buy	forbid	leave	speak	win
choose	forget	lie	steal	write

● 4. Write a sentence in which you use correctly the present tense, a sentence in which you use correctly the past tense, and a sentence in which you use correctly the perfect participle, of each of the following irregular verbs.

begin	do	lie (recline)	see
break	fall	pay	sit
choose	give	ride	take
come	go	run	write

Do not be satisfied with your record in this exercise until you avoid all mistakes of form or spelling.

PART IX

Gaining Personal Power Through Words (Concluded)

Pronouns

Pronouns, the Noun Substitutes. A pronoun is a word that is used instead of a noun.

> Dr. Perry agreed to report to **me** as soon as **he** finished **his** research.
> [**He** and **his** are used instead of repetitions of **Dr. Perry**; **me**, instead of the name of the speaker.]

Pronouns Are Useful. Seldom do you realize the usefulness of pronouns in making expression simpler until you try to dictate sentences without them. Suppose you are writing a business report, and that in this task you are not allowed to use pronouns. The first draft below shows how such a report would read; the second, how it should read.

WITHOUT PRONOUNS

When President Murray arose to give President Murray's report to the stockholders, President Murray made the introductory statement that, in President Murray's opinion, President Murray should retire and pass President Murray's responsibilities on to a younger man.

WITH PRONOUNS

When President Murray arose to give his report to the stockholders, he made the introductory statement that, in his opinion, he should retire and pass his responsibilities on to a younger man.

This brief experiment shows that to use the same noun again and again whenever you want to refer to what it represents would be most awkward. Hence, we use a device for *representing* the noun without actually repeating the noun.

Make the Pronoun Agree with Its Antecedent. The form of a pronoun is governed by its antecedent. The antecedent is the word for which the pronoun stands. To make sure of the correct pronoun, think of the noun for which the pronoun stands. Make the pronoun agree with the noun in person (first, second, or third), in number (singular or plural), and in gender (masculine, feminine, or neuter).

> Dr. Kemp promises that **he** will make a report when **he** has finished **his** conference.

The antecedent of *he* and *his* is *Dr. Kemp. Dr. Kemp* is the noun that would have to be repeated if there were no pronouns. *He* and *his* are in the third person, singular number, masculine gender, agreeing with *Dr. Kemp.*

Nominative, Objective, and Possessive Forms. It will pay you to memorize the following forms of pronouns.

NOMINATIVE	OBJECTIVE	POSSESSIVE
I	me	my, mine
we	us	our, ours
you	you	your, yours
he	him	his
she	her	her, hers
it	it	its
they	them	their, theirs
who	whom	whose

When the pronoun is the subject of the sentence, use the nominative form.

(The one exception: a pronoun following the infinitive *to be* or *to have been* agrees in case with the noun or pronoun preceding the infinitive. "I know *you* to be *him* who presented the gift." Of course, a far more natural way to say it would be, "I know you're the one who presented the gift.")

When the pronoun is the object of a transitive verb or of a preposition, use the objective form. When the pronoun indicates possession, use the possessive form. When the pronoun completes the meaning of a connective verb (some form of the verb *to be*), use the nominative form.

> SUBJECT: **We** shall arrive Saturday. **They** will come too.
> OBJECT OF A TRANSITIVE VERB: We invited **them.**
> OBJECT OF A PREPOSITION: The sales report came from **them.**
> POSSESSIVE: She got **her** bonus Tuesday.
> POSSESSIVE: The two divisions merged **their** offices.
> SUBJECT: **He** was the one **who** headed the committee.
> OBJECT: The man **whom** he introduced was Mr. Phillips.
> POSSESSIVE: The man **whose** name you heard was Mr. Phillips.
> AFTER THE VERB "TO BE": It was **he.** Who are **they?**

Antecedents Connected by "And." When the pronoun represents two or more antecedents in the singular connected by *and,* the pronoun must be plural.

> The secretary and the treasurer made **their** statements.
> [Note that the article **the** is repeated.]

When, however, the antecedents are different names for the same person or thing, the pronoun is singular.

> The famous author and lecturer made **his** visit today.
> [The article **the** is not repeated.]

When two or more antecedents connected by *and* are preceded by *each, every,* or *no,* the pronoun must be singular.

> Every minute and every second has **its** duties.

Antecedents Connected by "Or" or "Nor." A pronoun with two or more antecedents in the singular connected by *or* or *nor,* must be singular.

> Neither Paul nor Jack read **his** report.

When one of the antecedents is plural, it should be placed last, and the pronoun should be plural.

> Neither the guide nor his followers reached **their** goal.

Antecedents in Common Gender. When the antecedent requires a common gender pronoun, the masculine *he, his,* or *him* is used.

> Every man and woman in this community is urged to give **his** loyal support to this project.
> [**His** indicates common gender. Use some form of the pronoun **he** when referring to both sexes. Avoid the somewhat awkward **he** or **she, his** or **hers, him** or **her,** except in legal documents, in which this use may be necessary to indicate the proper distinction.]

Collective Nouns as Antecedents. What has been said earlier about a collective noun and a verb applies also to a pronoun of which the collective noun is the antecedent. The pronoun in such a case must agree with the antecedent in number, which is indicated by the sense of the sentence.

If the antecedent of a pronoun is a collective noun conveying the idea of unity, the pronoun should be singular.

> The firm enters **its** fifth year this month.
> The committee is ready to make **its** report.
> The air force has announced **its** training program.
> The company published **its** annual catalog this week.

If the antecedent is a collective noun conveying the idea of the plural, the pronoun should be plural.

> The office staff and **their** families have been invited.

Whether the antecedent expresses the singular or the plural is determined from the evidently intended meaning of the entire sentence.

In expressions like *one of the people who, one of the things that, one of the men who*, the relative pronoun refers, not to *one*, but to the plural object of *of*.

> He is one of those men **who keep** rigidly at the task.
> [Not **who keeps** . . .]

The words *kind, sort, type, class*, etc., are singular and should be modified by a singular demonstrative pronoun. Demonstrative pronouns are *this, that* (singular), *these, those* (plural).

> WRONG: He likes **these** kind of pencils better than **those** kind.
> RIGHT: He likes **this** kind of pencil better than **that** kind.
> RIGHT: He likes **these** kinds of pencils better than **those** kinds.

Verbal Nouns Call for the Possessive Case. The word governing a verbal noun should be in the possessive case. Distinguish carefully between a verbal noun and a participle (see page 556). The noun or pronoun preceding the participle is not possessive.

> Do you object to **my** [not **me**] dictating the instructions?
> They will approve **his** [not **him**] going to the convention.
> We recommend **their** [not **them**] attending the conference.

Indefinite Pronouns. Pronouns that do not name any particular individual or thing are known as *indefinite pronouns*. Some of the more common ones are *anybody, someone, somebody, one, none, nobody, everybody, everyone, either, neither, each, any, anyone, another*. These indefinite pronouns (except *none* and *any*) are singular, and any pronouns that refer to them must also be singular. *None* and *any*, by approval of both the dictionary and modern usage, may be used as pronouns in either the singular or the plural. *None* more commonly takes the plural verb.

> **Neither** of the men had prepared **his** report.
> **Anyone** can do this job if **he** tries.
> **Everybody** should work for **his** own success.

Do Not Use "You" for "One." Avoid the error of using *you* instead of *one* for general indefinite reference.

> One [not **you**] should make definite progress each day.

The "indefinite *you*" is sometimes called upon at the easy, colloquial "slang" level; but it is not desirable in formal writing.

Using the Word "One" as Antecedent. The word *one* is obviously singular, and any pronoun of which *one* is the antecedent must also be singular.

> **One** should make some progress in **his** [not **their**] work each day.

Using "Its" and "It's." Personal pronouns in the possessive case do *not* require the apostrophe. *Its* is the correct possessive form of the personal pronoun. *It's* is the contraction for *it is*. Master this difference *now* and you will save yourself much painful embarrassment later.

> The company has moved into **its** [not **it's**] new building.

Using the Indefinite "It." The "indefinite *it*" is a type of expression that has won its way into our language through sheer usefulness.

> **It** appears that business is good.
> **It** is a cold day.
> **It** is easy to believe that.

In most such expressions *it* is the grammatical subject of a verb of which the logical subject is the following noun, infinitive phrase, or clause. The pronoun *it* merely anticipates the real or logical subject of the verb. The real subjects appear thus:

> **That business is good** appears to be true.
> **The day** is cold.
> **To believe that** is easy.

Constructions like the latter are permissible, but if used too often they sound stilted and superformal. The "indefinite *it*" construction is more natural.

Pronoun Control, An Index to Language Accuracy. Certain "corners" of our language are treacherous to careless people. In one of these corners are pronouns. No one in business can afford to juggle pronouns and let errors slip through. If he does, he creates an impression of slipshod carelessness that no amount of painful perfection elsewhere can offset. Train yourself in pronoun control.

Adjectives

Control of Adjectives Adds Business Force. The experience of thousands of business people who have gone through their basic training and progressed in due course to executive levels proves that we need to gain control over certain elements of grammar, which in this book we have called the tools of business expression. Among these tools are nouns, verbs, and adjectives, without a knowledge of which we are virtually helpless in the business office.

Adjectives create pictures. Anyone who has recently passed a newsstand will be aware of the huge popularity now enjoyed by the picture magazines, a development supporting the accepted belief that the eye is one of the quicker channels to the brain. This truth gained recognition thousands of years ago. Down the dim corridors of time has come the oft-quoted saying of a Chinese philosopher, "A picture is worth ten thousand words." Adjectives are picture-makers.

Adjectives Spur Interest and Yield Picture Power. Choice of adjectives has often been found to add power and interest to the written word and to add force and entertainment to the spoken word. Adjectives make definite the meanings of nouns in such a way as to make the picture carried to the mind of the reader or the hearer match, point for point, the picture in the mind of the writer or the speaker.

Special Problems in Regard to Adjectives. The few special problems connected with adjectives can be mastered quickly. Adjectives are words used to modify nouns or pronouns and to describe the persons, places, or things named by them.

A *compound adjective* is a modifying word made by joining two or more words that are ordinarily used by themselves. The two or more words that make up a compound adjective used before the noun modified are joined by a hyphen. If the compound adjective is used after the noun, the hyphen is not used.

> That vase is made of **hand-blown** glass.
> The glass in that vase is **hand blown**.
> The **well-known** author sent him that book.
> The author of that book is **well known**.

In some compound adjectives the hyphen may be omitted, and the adjectives may be written as one word.

> **lifelike** puppet
> **everlasting** peace

The singular form of the noun is used when the compound is a number written before a noun indicating distance, quantity, or the like.

> five-**year** course
> fourteen-**foot** pole vault
> ten-**story** building

A hyphen is used in numbers like those in the following examples.

> fifty-seven stories
> thirty-nine steps

A hyphen is used in fractions written in words only when the fractions are used as adjectives. A hyphen is not used when a fraction is used as a noun or when a fraction, used as an adjective, contains a hyphen in either of its parts.

ADJECTIVE

a one-fifth share
the two-thirds rule

NOUN

one half
three fourths

ADJECTIVE WITH HYPHEN
IN A PART

a one twenty-fifth portion
a five thirty-sixths share

A hyphen is not used when a compound adjective consists of an adverb ending in *ly* and an adjective or a participle.

widely known lecturer
fairly good reproduction

Comparison: Fitting Adjectives to Your Meaning. An adjective suggests a quality of the object modified. To make the adjective fit the meaning closely, it is possible to change its form to express a greater degree and a greatest degree of this quality.

The Rolls-Royce is a **fast** car.
The Rolls-Royce is **faster** than the Renault.
The Rolls-Royce is the **fastest** car in England.

Comparative degree: used to compare two objects. Form it by adding *r* or *er* to simple adjectives of one syllable and to a few of two syllables.

strong, strong**er**
angry, angri**er**
handsome, handsom**er**

To form the comparative of most adjectives of more than one syllable, prefix the word *more* (or *less*) to the simple (positive) adjective.

trustworthy, **more** trustworthy
expensive, **less** expensive

Superlative degree: used to compare three or more objects. Form it by adding *est* to adjectives of one syllable and to a few of two syllables.

fast, fast**est**
angry, angri**est**

To form the superlative of most adjectives of more than one syllable,

prefix the word *most* (or *least*) to the simple adjective.

effective, **most** effective
variable, **least** variable

Irregular Comparisons. Note the irregularity in the comparison of the following common adjectives.

POSITIVE	COMPARATIVE	SUPERLATIVE
bad [ill, evil]	worse	worst
far	farther	farthest
good	better	best
little	less	least
many	more	most
much	more	most

Special Adjective Groups. There are six groups of adjectives that deserve special attention.

1. "This, That, These, Those." *This* and *that* are the only adjectives that have a plural form. The plural forms *these* and *those* must be used with plural nouns. *Those* kind is incorrect; *that kind* or *those kinds* should be used. *Them* is not an adjective and should not be used to modify a noun.

2. "Either, Neither." *Either* or *neither* refers to one of two. *Either* should be used correlatively with *or*; *neither*, with *nor*.

The words *either* and *neither*, like the words *this, that, these,* and *those,* are adjectives when they are used with nouns. But they are pronouns when they stand alone.

3. "First, Last." The words *first* and *last* when used with adjectives that express numbers are placed before the adjectives.

the **first three** sections
the **last ten** chapters

4. Each Other, One Another. *Each other* refers to two objects only; *one another*, to more than two.

The two salesmen help **each other**.
The three salesmen help **one another**.

5. Anyone, None. *Anyone* refers to one of several. *None* means literally *not one* and, when used in that specific sense, takes a singular verb.

> Anyone who can write well is invited to apply.
> None of the reports is satisfactory.

If the reference is obviously to a group of individuals, the verb should be plural. In fact, when used as a subject, *none* with a plural verb is now the commoner construction.

> None of us have completed our work.

6. Above, Below. *Above* is normally an adverb or a preposition; but modern dictionaries have also admitted it to usage as an adjective, and so it may be mentioned at this point. Examples:

> The track ran above. (Adverb)
> Place it above the chair. (Preposition)
> The above comments are clear. (Adjective)

Below is used as an adverb or a preposition but is not recognized as an adjective and should not be so used.

> The track ran below. (Adverb)
> Place it below the clock. (Preposition)
> WRONG: The below list is inaccurate.

The word *above* is sometimes used in combinations as in *above-listed*, *above-mentioned*, *above-named*, and *above-cited*.

Careful writers reduce to a minimum their use of *above*, and always avoid the use of *below*, in the form of adjectives.

Numbers as Adjectives. Numbers used as adjectives are written in words when they can be expressed in one or, at most, two words.

> The president serves a term of **four** years, or **forty-eight** months.

Higher numbers carried out to exact units should be written in figures.

> The counters recorded **4,823** subscribers.

In a series of numbers follow one plan consistently.*

* For a comprehensive guide to the correct expression of numbers in business letters, reports, and related forms of communication, see pages 536 to 539.

Using the Articles "A, An, The." *A* and *an* are indefinite articles used to limit a noun to any one thing of a particular class.

> a letter; an address

The is the definite article, so named because it selects a definite individual or object from a particular class.

> The man who issues the order.

Use *a* before nouns beginning with a consonant sound.

> a dividend; a corporation

Use *an* before words beginning with a vowel sound.

> an issue; an order

Using "A, An, The" in Titles of Books, Periodicals, Etc. When you use the titles of books, newspapers, periodicals, pamphlets, documents, reports, proceedings, or the like, consult the following rules:

1. If the title of a book or other single literary, musical, or artistic work begins with one of the articles, *A, An,* or *The,* write this word as part of the title, which is underlined when typewritten and italicized when printed.

> WRONG: Be sure to read Harry Scherman's **Promises Men Live By** and Walter Lippman's **Preface to Morals.**
> RIGHT: Be sure to read Harry Scherman's **The Promises Men Live By** and Walter Lippmann's **A Preface to Morals.**

2. Do not include *A, An,* or *The* in the name of a newspaper or other periodical, or pamphlet, document, report, proceeding, leaflet, or the like. Thus, in writing the name of a newspaper or other periodical, do not capitalize and italicize *a the* limiting the noun of the title, even if it is part of the title.

> Our library has a complete file of the **Century Magazine** and the **Post-Gazette.** The **Reader's Digest** for April and the **Atlantic** for May contain helpful references.

Adverbs

Control Adverbs. Adverbs make up one group of words that, with other groups, add descriptive force and contribute accurate shades of meaning.

Special Problems in Regard to Adverbs. Adverbs modify and make definite the meaning of verbs, just as adjectives modify and make definite the meaning of nouns. Adverbs may also modify and make definite the meaning of adjectives and other adverbs.

ADVERB MODIFYING A VERB: He **easily** obtained that order. [Tells how.]
He was **fully** prepared. [Tells how much.]
He cabled us **immediately** after the contract was signed. [Tells when.]
ADVERB MODIFYING AN ADJECTIVE: It is **almost** impossible to see him.
Quotations reached **exceptionally** high levels.
ADVERB MODIFYING ANOTHER ADVERB: The matter was **quite** thoroughly discussed. But when the motion was put to a vote, it was **very** promptly defeated.

Note that adverbs answer the questions "When?" "Where?" "How?" "How Much?" Note, again, that *adverbs may be used to modify verbs, adjectives, or other adverbs.*

Using "-ly." Manner adverbs, telling how actions take place, usually end in *-ly*: *constantly, completely, thoroughly, effectively.* Such adverbs modify only verbs of action. Note that sense verbs—*look, sound, smell, taste, feel*—and connective verbs—*be, seem, appear, become*—are followed by adjectives and may *not* be modified by *-ly* (manner) adverbs.

He **clearly** explained the problem.
He finished the job **satisfactorily**.
The agreement sounded **satisfactory**.

All too common is the error of using an adjective where an adverb should be used. Learn the difference in form and use the correct word.

Special Adverb Groups. Five groups of adverbs deserving special attention are:

1. "As—As and So—As." If equality is stated, use *as—as*; if negative comparison is made, use *so—as*.

Sales are **as** great this year **as** they were last year.
Sales are not **so** great this year **as** they were last year.

2. "Farther, Further." *Farther* and *further* (each of which may be used as both adjective and adverb) are not always differentiated, but (1) *farther* is often preferred for reference to spatial distance, and (2) *further* for reference to time, quantity, or degree.

He built his home at a **farther** point.
His home is **farther** away than yours.
He made no **further** effort to succeed.
His success goes much **further**.

3. "Good, Well." *Good* is usually an adjective; *well* is usually an adverb.

The report is very **good**. (Adjective)
Mr. Hart dictates **well**. (Adverb)

In speaking of health, *well* is used as an adjective.

She has been ill, but she is now **well**.

After *look, sound, taste, smell,* and *feel* (sense verbs), use the predicate adjective, NOT the adverb.

The reports look **good** (not **well**) today.

4. "Real, Very." *Real* is an adjective of quality. *Very* is an adverb of degree. *Real* may be used to modify a noun; *very* to modify an adjective or an adverb.

He is a writer of **real** ability.
The report is **very** (not **real**) clear.
He spoke **very** (not **real**) slowly.

5. "Sometime, Some Time." *Sometime* (one word) is an adverb meaning at one time or other in the future, or at some not definitely known time.

Some time (two words) is a phrase combination in which the noun, *time*, is modified by the adjective *some*.

They will go **sometime** next week.
It took **some time** to get ready.
We plan to go there **sometime**.

Comparison: Fitting Adverbs to Your Meaning. Most adverbs are compared by prefixing the word *more* (or *less*) or the word *most* (or *least*) to them.

more effectively; **least** thoroughly

A few add *er* or *est* to the simple form.

often, oftener, oftenest

But the preference is to use *more* and *most*.

more often, **most** often

A few adverbs are compared irregularly.

well, better, best
far, farther, farthest

Where to Put Adverbs. Place the adverb where it will most clearly show the meaning you intend. Modifiers should be put close to the words they modify. Hence an adverb should ordinarily be placed near the adjective, the adverb, or the verb it modifies. Use care in handling the adverbs *only, too, also, merely*. See page 588 for illustrative sentences showing how the meaning changes with the shift of the modifier *only*.

Connectives: Prepositions and Conjunctions

Special Problems in Regard to Connectives. Business would find it just as awkward to get along without prepositions and conjunctions as without pronouns. How prepositions and conjunctions make expression easier is seldom realized until we try to compose a few sentences without them. Suppose we take a sentence from an informal business memorandum and strike out every preposition and conjunction, leaving as substitutes nothing but empty parentheses. The first draft below shows how the memorandum would look; the second, how it should look.

WITHOUT CONNECTIVES

He presented this proposal ( ) me ( ) the last meeting ( ) the board, ( ) that time was not, ( ) my opinion, a favorable moment ( ) its consideration.

WITH CONNECTIVES

He presented this proposal to me at the last meeting of the board, but that time was not, in my opinion, a favorable moment for its consideration.

When ideas are closely related, it is often desirable to combine them. For this purpose connecting words are needed. The awkwardness of trying to get along without connectives is evident.

Prepositions Are Words That Connect. A preposition is a word used to connect a following noun or pronoun to some other word or element in the sentence. In making the connection, the preposition also indicates the relation.

. . . **to** me **at** the last meeting **of** the board.

The preposition is followed by its object, which is a noun or a pronoun or an expression so used.

. . . to **me** at the last **meeting** of the **board**.

To identify the object of a preposition, put the question "What?" or "Whom?" after the preposition.

To whom? To **me**.
At what? At the **meeting**.
Of what? Of the **board**.

A prepositional phrase is a group of words formed by a preposition and its object. Example: *to me*. When a pronoun follows a preposition, it must be put in the objective case.

Prepositions Most Commonly Used. The following prepositions are the principal ones in business:

aboard	except
about	for
above	from
across	in
after	into
against	of
along	on
amid	over
among	past
around	round
at	through
before	throughout
behind	till
below	to
beneath	toward
beside	under
between	underneath
beyond	until
but [except]	up
by	upon
concerning	with
down	within
during	without

Phrase Prepositions. Certain prepositions are made up of two or more words; hence they are called phrase prepositions.

apart from	in place of
as for	in reference to
as regards	in regard to
as to	instead of
by way of	on account of
contrary to	to the extent of
devoid of	with respect to
from beyond	

Special Problems in Regard to Conjunctions. Conjunctions are words used to connect words, phrases, or clauses.

The letter **and** the enclosure [Connects words.]
The broadcast will come from New York **or** California. [Connects phrases.]
Business is improving, **but** the process is slow. [Connects clauses.]

Coordinate Conjunctions. A coordinate conjunction joins elements of the same rank or grammatical relation.

Stocks **and** bonds are widely used for investment. [Compound subject.]
Businessmen buy **and** sell them often. [Compound verb.]

Clauses holding the same rank in the sentence are joined by a coordinate conjunction.

Business improves, **but** the progress is slow.

The word *but* connects two independent clauses. Neither clause is dependent upon the other for its meaning.

The principal coordinate conjunctions are:

and	likewise
but	moreover
for	neither—nor
neither	nevertheless
nor	not only—but also
or	notwithstanding
———	now
accordingly	otherwise
as well as	so
besides	so that
both—and	still
consequently	then
either—or	therefore
furthermore	thus
hence	whether—or
however	yet

Use a comma to separate independent clauses in pairs or in a series joined by one of the pure conjunctions listed above (*and, but, for, neither, nor, or*). Use a semicolon, however, between independent clauses joined by a conjunction that indicates a greater change of thought than is indicated by the pure conjunctions. Typical of such conjunctions are *accordingly, consequently, hence, however, moreover, nevertheless, notwithstanding.*

Sales volume is increasing; **nevertheless** costs are rising.

Subordinate Conjunctions. A subordinate conjunction joins a subordinate clause to some word in the principal clause.

You work **in order that** you may earn.

In order that joins the subordinate clause, *you may earn,* with *work* in the principal clause. *Work* leads to the use of the subordinate clause. The subordinate clause is dependent upon *work* for its meaning and clearness.

The principal subordinate conjunctions are:

after	so that
although	supposing (colloquial)
as	than
as soon as	that
because	though
before	till
if	unless
in case that	until
in order that	when
inasmuch as	where
lest	whereas
on condition that	whether—or
provided	while
since	

Guard against These Errors. Errors may arise from the choice of conjunctions not used in the correct idiomatic manner, or by the introduction of needless or redundant conjunctions.

No one can doubt **that** [not **but that** or **but what**] he is influential.
No one can deny **that** [not **but**] she has tried hard to succeed.
Seldom, **if** [not **or**] ever, should that rule be waived.
He will try **to** [not **and**] use every chance to study.
She had scarcely entered the door **when** [not **but**] the storm broke.
The book was sent to 530 Glenway Avenue, **which** [not **and which**] was the correct address.

How Connectives Control Phrases and Clauses. A *phrase* is a group of closely related words *not* containing a subject and a predicate. Phrases are introduced by prepositions, participles, or infinitives.

A *clause* is a part of a sentence that contains a subject and a predicate. Clauses are connected with other parts of the sentence by conjunctions or relative pronouns.

A clause contains a verb; a phrase does not. A clause (that is, an independent clause) makes sense in itself; a phrase in itself asserts nothing.

INDEPENDENT CLAUSE: **The letter has been written.**
SUBORDINATE CLAUSE: **When the letter has been written,** please let me see it.
PHRASE: **To write the letter,** I shall need a machine.

Correlative Conjunctions. Correlative conjunctions are conjunctions used in pairs, the first of the pair introducing and the second connecting the elements. The principal correlatives are:

both—and	not only—but also
either—or	whether—or
neither—nor	

Place correlatives *just before* the words or the phrases connected.

This lesson requires **both** copy **and** layout.
Let me have **either** the pen **or** the pencil.
She has **neither** telephoned **nor** telegraphed.
He is **not only** secretary **but also** treasurer.
We are not sure **whether** we will earn the dividend **or** fall short.

"Like" and "As." *Like* and *as* are often confused. *Like* is a preposition and introduces a phrase. *As* is a conjunction and joins clauses. In careful writing *like* is not approved as a substitute for *as*. *As* is often used as a conjunction, and in such constructions *like* as a substitute is undesirable, even though today it is colloquially so used.

UNDESIRABLE: It looks **like** they will come.
RIGHT: It looks **as if** they will come.
RIGHT: Her sister looks just **like** her.
UNDESIRABLE: He writes just **like** you write.
RIGHT: He writes **as** you write.

"Provided" and "Providing." *Provided* may be used as a conjunction. *Providing* is normally a present participle. Dictionaries in their latest editions have, however, begun to reflect the widespread and commonplace usage of *providing* as a rough alternative of the more accurate *provided*.

LESS DESIRABLE: **Providing** he **can** arrive in time, he will speak.
RIGHT: **Provided** he can arrive in time, he will be glad to speak.
LESS DESIRABLE: He will study **the** lesson **providing** he can find his book.
RIGHT: He will study the lesson **provided** he can find his book.

"Except, Without, Unless," and "But." *Except* and *without* are prepositions and introduce phrases. They are followed by the objective case. *Unless* is a conjunction and joins clauses. *But* may be either a preposition or a conjunction, depending upon its use in a sentence. As a preposition it is followed by the objective case.

They are all going **except her.**
No decision can be made **without him.**
They cannot leave **unless they** get a pass.
Everyone has left the building **but him.**

Grammar Review Problems

●1. Rewrite the following sentences, correcting where necessary the faulty use of pronouns:

    a. We have in stock all different grades of printing paper, which assures you prompt filling of all our orders.
    b. One must be careful lest they overestimate.
    c. The man is a real leader who heads that organization.
    d. To each person who makes a request on their business stationery, we will send them one of our illustrated maps.
    e. Enclosed are full details showing latest improvements at lowest cost which gives you the information requested.
    f. That habit is a little one, but unless you take firm steps you will have to fight them all the rest of your life.
    g. Our huge volume and our direct methods of selling have made it possible for us to cut down a large amount of our expense. This we gladly pass on to you.
    h. The enclosed booklet will tell you all you need to know about Chronos. It shows you how it will fit on your mantel and how it operates. Give it a thorough study.
    i. It is clear that any added delay will undermine your credit standing, which neither of us desires.
    j. A person should watch their sales talk carefully and use the best arguments in all their future interviews.
    k. Any one of our men will take care of you if you will ask them to do so.

●2. Give the grammatical reason why each of the following pronouns is correctly used.

    a. The promotion is to go to *whoever* can win that order.
    b. The president will call *you* and *me* into conference.
    c. He wants to talk immediately with *you* and *me.*
    d. It was *he* who ordered the investigation.
    e. The winners of the sales contest are Robinson and *I.*
    f. *Whom* did they nominate for the office of secretary?
    g. If you were *I,* would you take that course?

●3. Write six business sentences illustrating the proper use of six different manner (*ly*) adverbs.

●4. Write six business sentences illustrating the proper use of the six different adjectives from which the adverbs in Problem 3 were derived. Example: He *rapidly* explained the plan. [Adverb.] The next year was marked by a *rapid* increase in output. [Adjective.]

●5. Illustrate, by writing a business sentence for each, the correct use of the following words (ten sentences in all):

    fine—finely   satisfactory—satisfactorily
    good—well   slow—slowly
    real—very

● **6.** Study the following block of copy from an advertisement of the Republic Steel Corporation, Youngstown, Ohio. Then give the solutions to the problems that appear below it.

Eighty-Five Stories up . . . Go the Silvery Lines of ENDURO, The New Perfected Stainless Steel.

On the historic site of the famous old Waldorf Astoria, the tallest structure in the world pierces the changing sky line of New York . . . a majestic study in gray and shimmering silver. It is the Empire State Building.

Stretching up two sides of the building for more than 1,200 feet, glittering ribbons of Enduro catch and reflect the light, producing the same impressive effect that this new perfected stainless steel gives to the silvery summit of the Chrysler Building.

Enduro fits into the modern trend in industry. Because it does not tarnish or rust, automobile manufacturers have adopted it for radiator shells, head lamps, and other lustrous parts.

Because it resists acids and is so easily cleaned, it is widely used in the manufacture of dairy machinery, soda fountains, hospital and restaurant equipment. In the oil and chemical fields, where for years corrosion has been a constant spectre, Enduro has brought new economies . . . and greater efficiency.

The uses of this revolutionary metal seem almost limitless, for, in spite of its amazing properties, Enduro is easy to work. It can be welded, stamped, cast, deep drawn, or wire drawn . . . and is stronger than carbon steel. Its glittering finish cannot chip or wear thin because it is the same all the way through.

Republic's tremendous facilities are backed by a special metallurgical department, which will work with any manufacturer in applying this new metal to his product.

A request will bring you an instructive series of booklets dealing with Enduro and its uses.

CENTRAL ALLOY DIVISION
REPUBLIC STEEL CORPORATION

(a) Classify the adjectives in this piece of copy as positive, comparative, or superlative in degree of comparison.

(b) After you have identified the degree of comparison for each adjective, write the other two comparative forms which it may take.

(c) Be able to justify the use of each of the three articles (*a, an,* and *the*) by citing six examples of each from this copy and showing how the use accords with rules already studied.

● **7.** Use correctly in sentences, in written or oral form as directed: (a) the prepositions listed on page 576; (b) any ten prepositional phrases; (c) the coordinate conjunctions listed on page 577; (d) the subordinate conjunctions listed on page 577; (e) each of the correlatives, *both . . . and, not only . . . but also, neither . . . nor, either or, whether . . . or.*

● 8. Study the following sales message from the Aluminum Company of America. Then give the solutions to the problems that appear below it. The sentences are numbered for convenient reference.

(1) Those swiftly rolling vehicles that make up modern transportation—the sleek motor car, the interurban coach, the burly truck, the electric coach—have been lifted out of the web of deadweight, thanks to the strong alloys of Aluminum.

(2) Shattering old traditions, structural shapes in sizes up to ten inches in depth and ninety feet in length are now available. (3) These shapes are made of the strong alloys of Alcoa Aluminum, which, strength for strength, are the equivalents of structural steel but weigh only one third as much. (4) This fact is more than news, for it shows a new epoch in the making.

(5) Apply this new type of construction to railroads and this is what happens. (6) Relieved of tons of deadweight, trains sweep forward to faster time and lower cost schedules. (7) Power is saved. (8) Starting and stopping are quicker and smoother. (9) Riding is more comfortable.

(10) Electric coaches, scientifically lightened, compete more easily with heavily jammed traffic conditions, because these strong alloys are steadily clipping off ton after ton of deadweight drag.

(11) In buses, nearly fifteen hundred pounds can be stripped from body weights, a reduction which saves money on gas, oil, and tires. (12) Aluminum bodies for trucks reduce deadweight from one thousand to sixty-six hundred pounds.

(13) Airliners become safer because of Alcoa Aluminum, "the metal that flies best." (14) Besides being light for flight, the strong alloy of Alcoa Aluminum is noninflammable, shatter-proof, splinter-proof.

(15) After it has been forged, cast, and smoothly rolled into sheets, it is transformed into standard shapes and tubes, most carefully inspected. (16) As you can easily see, it is then in shape for working with the same machines used for other metals. (17) It can be instantly welded, or it can be most firmly put together with aluminum alloy rivets, bolts, or screws.

(18) As a progressive engineer, you will want our engineering handbook, *Structural Aluminum*, which will be sent to you with our compliments upon request.

(19) The enclosed business reply card already carries your name and address. (20) Merely drop it in the outgoing mail.

(a) The message contains sentences illustrating the uses of nouns, verbs, adjectives, adverbs, pronouns, prepositions, and conjunctions. The message, as a whole, provides ample material for drill in quick recognition and classification. In the sentences, numbered for convenience, be able to classify, orally or in writing, the parts of speech you have studied in Sections 3 and 4.

(b) Mark off seven vertical columns on a sheet of typewriting paper. Head them as follows: Noun, Verb, Adjective, Adverb, Pronoun, Preposition, Conjunction. Classify all these parts of speech found in the first four sentences of the sales message.

● 9. (a) From the pages of a leading daily or weekly news periodical make a written list of ten expressions that you believe to be idiomatic, including enough of the context to give the full meaning of the idiom in its prose setting. (b) In an original sentence differing entirely from that quoted as one of the examples under (a), make correct written use of each of the idioms in the list you have gathered.

Section 5 Effective Business Sentences: How to Write Them

Sentence Control. The forceful sentence ranks at the top of all the business tools. Business, in some ways a stern taskmaster, demands that its sentences have clearness, power, and flexibility. When a sentence swings into action, it becomes the shortest distance between two minds—if it is properly built.

Through tested methods discussed and illustrated in this book, the good business sentence closes agreements, negotiates contracts, presents technical data, and may even sway public opinion. Forceful in its structure, the good business sentence carries a swift-running message with crystal clarity. You, yourself, may create this kind of forceful expression if you master the several techniques of sentence power now to be reviewed.

Sentence Power Techniques. Important as it is to know words and how to mold them into strong sentences, it is perhaps even more vital to know the different types of sentences and how to build them into forceful letters, memorandums, summaries, and reports. After you know the several types by their technical names, you are then in a position to master the techniques of their use. *How to build and use sentences* is the matter of real and final importance.

Sentences Classified as to Function. In terms of function—of what it does—a sentence may be:

Declarative: makes a statement or an assertion.

The price trend is up.
Your report needs revision.

Interrogative: asks a question.

Is the price trend up?
Does the report need revising?

Imperative: expresses a command or an entreaty.

See that the check is in our office by noon tomorrow.
By all means try to be there!

Sentences Classified as to Form and Internal Structure. By far the quickest and most practical way to learn to use sentences for business purposes is to be able instantly to *recognize their form and internal structure.*

Recognizing Simple Sentences. A simple sentence contains one principal clause. This one principal clause may be a statement, a question, a command, or a request.

STATEMENT: Commerce and industry move the world.
QUESTION: How soon can you ship the order?
COMMAND: See that we have your check by noon Monday.
REQUEST: Please wire your decision as soon as you can.

Recognizing Compound Sentences. A compound sentence contains two or more principal clauses joined by one of the pure conjunctions *and, but, for, or, neither, nor.*

The market is strong, **and** prices are steady.
Business continues its long-term expansion, **but** this expansion is now under wiser guidance.
Conditions have improved, **and** they may improve still further.

The main (also called principal or independent) clauses of a compound sentence are joined by coordinate conjunctions. In the foregoing examples the coordinate conjunctions are set in boldface.

Recognizing Complex Sentences. A complex sentence contains one principal clause and one or more subordinate clauses. Such subordinate clauses are often introduced by words such as *if, unless, since, because, when, after, although, while,* and *as.*

> **Although** the market is strong, prices are steady.
> **Although** American business continues its long-term expansion, this expansion is now under wiser guidance.
> **Although** conditions are already satisfactory, they may improve still further.
> Even **though** they have been slow to accept the truth, industrial leaders have agreed **that** it is wise to gear production more closely to demand **because** this type of manufacturing program tends to prevent oversupply.

Note that these complex sentences are composed of two or more simple sentences, brought together in such a way that one is the main member and the other or others are dependent upon it for their meaning. The main members and the dependent members are all called clauses.

Recognizing Clauses. A clause is a subdivision of a sentence containing a subject and a predicate. A *main* clause is one the meaning of which is complete or clear without reference to any other clause.

> MAIN CLAUSE: Industrial leaders have agreed.

A *subordinate* clause is one that makes a statement the meaning of which is not clear without reference to the main clause.

Subordinate conjunctions, boldface in the following example (and also in those illustrating complex sentences on the preceding page), are used to introduce subordinate clauses.

> Even **though** they have been slow to accept the truth, industrial leaders have agreed **that** it is wise to gear producton more closely to demand **because** this type of manufacturing program tends to prevent oversupply.

Recognizing Phrases. Phrases are naturally coupled with clauses in this type of language review. Hence this is a logical point at which to define and illustrate phrases. A phrase is a group of related words, without a predicate, used as a part of speech.

It is well to become familiar with the several kinds of phrases so useful in business. They are:

Prepositional phrase: a group of words formed by a preposition, its object, and often modifiers.

> She wrote **with great care** each letter **in the series.**
> Here is report **of international affairs.**

Infinitive phrase: an infinitive with or without modifiers and an object.

> **To dictate good letters** is not easy.
> Our object is **to dictate better letters.**
> Here are prices **to fit every purse.**
> We want **to make this order satisfactory.**

Participial phrase: a participle and its modifiers, or a participle and its object.

> The person **writing the best application** will get the job.
> A prize will be given to the salesman **having the best sales record.**

Verbal-noun phrase: a verbal noun and its modifiers or object.

> We regret **asking you to wait.**
> **Dictating good letters** is a valuable skill.
> The advantage of **shipping the order** by freight is economy.

Use Clauses and Phrases with "Change of Pace." To stimulate interest and hold attention, use clauses and phrases with change of pace. Get variety and freshness by putting expression into different molds.

First Version—With Simple Sentences

Perhaps you have noticed the development of an unfortunate situation in this country. Very serious charges of dishonesty have been made concerning aircraft production.

This branch of the military service is important. Therefore I feel these charges should be investigated. This should be done as soon as possible. There may be some guilty parties. We should prosecute them vigorously. Then, there may be some innocent parties. The investigation should be just as prompt for them. By prompt action we may clear their reputations.

I requested the Department of Justice to investigate these charges. I instructed it to use every instrumentality available. I have another idea, too. The Attorney General approves of it. I want you to investigate these charges with him. This is a matter of great importance in my opinion. Your services would be valuable in connection with it. We need you to study and pass upon the questions. I hope you will do so.

SUBORDINATE CLAUSE: Because we wanted the package to reach Chicago as soon as possible, we sent it by air express.

PARTICIPIAL PHRASE: Desiring the package to reach Chicago as soon as possible, we sent it by air express.

INFINITIVE PHRASE: To get the package to Chicago as soon as possible, we sent it by air express.

Use Simple, Compound, and Complex Sentences in Combination in Dictating or Writing. Note that a complex sentence has only one principal clause; a compound sentence, always two or more. You may put two complex sentences together, or a complex and a simple sentence together, just as you may join two simple sentences together. Any one of the three types of joining results in a compound sentence.

SIMPLE SENTENCES JOINED: He has dictated the letter, and it is ready to be transcribed.

COMPLEX JOINED WITH SIMPLE: Since the first draft has been finished, copies have been prepared in triplicate; and the manuscript should now be edited.

COMPLEX JOINED WITH COMPLEX: It is clear that a revolution in metals is just starting, and it is further believed that the remaining years of the century will see startling advances in steel, aluminum, copper, and other basic metals.

Variety in Sentences. The human mind welcomes variety and a change of pace. It craves the freshness of different kinds of sentences. It does not want them to come marching out all the same, like so many cartridge boxes off the end of an assembly line.

Let us select an important situation that calls for the writing of an urgent request. The first version of the request (shown above) is written with simple sentences. No one could read this communication without a sense of growing monotony. The childish choppiness begs for correction.

Now we enter the second stage of sentence structure. This time, using the same message, we draft a fresh edition with compound sentences (shown on page 584). Even the amateur business writer will sense the monotonous tetter-tottering of these lines. Because it loosely couples all ideas, important or trivial, with *and, but,* or *for,* this message once again echoes the speech of children and reflects immaturity. Technically the fault is too much coordination. The choppiness of the first stage is now the see-saw of the second.

As an individual matures with experience, he learns to adjust his ideas to their relative importance. With

Second Version—The Same Request with Compound Sentences

An unfortunate situation has developed in this country, for very serious charges of dishonesty have been made about aircraft production.

This branch of the military service is important, and I therefore feel much alarmed. These charges should be investigated, and this should be done as soon as possible. There may be some guilty parties, and we should prosecute these vigorously. Then, there may be some innocent parties, and the investigation should be just as prompt for them. By prompt action we may clear their reputations, and we may also thereby disprove the charges.

I have not been idle in this matter, for I have requested the Department of Justice to investigate all charges. I instructed it to use every instrumentality available; but I have another idea, too, and the Attorney General approves of it. My idea is to have you investigate these charges with him, for this is a matter of great importance, and your services would be very valuable in connection with it. We need you to study and pass upon the questions, and for this reason I hope you will agree to do it.

sentences of varied structure, some simple, some compound, some complex, he expresses his thought with flexible change of pace.

The message used for illustration in the preceding discussion was written in its correct and original version by Woodrow Wilson, World War I President of the United States, to Judge Charles Evans Hughes. The original letter is reproduced on page 585. Note how, through the use of sentence variety, the letter masterfully expresses the ideas that were so badly mauled in the previous versions.

What President Wilson did in his original version was simple in its essentials. He proceeded to (1) place minor ideas in subordinate clauses, (2) reduce still less important ideas to phrases (participial or prepositional), and (3) omit trivial details altogether. You can learn to do the same.

Sentence Unity

What "Top Management" Thinks about the Subject You are Studying. "Ability to handle your language effectively," writes the president of a leading American air transport company, "and to express thought and action clearly is, beyond the slightest doubt, of great value to anyone in the business world. Clear thinking, accurate writing and speaking, and good appearance are all attributes eagerly sought by all executives. It would be impossible," concludes this executive, "to give too much emphasis to these high qualities."

Whether you find your life work inside or outside air transport, you will find the twentieth-century pace swift indeed. To meet its challenge, you must turn in part to clearer expression, because you will find that it has a market value, that it enlarges your business output, and that it increases your personal power. Leading to the attainment of these aims is the control of sentence unity.

Sentence Unity. The principle of unity requires that a sentence contain *only one main idea. Modifying* ideas

THE WHITE HOUSE
WASHINGTON

May 13, 1918

My dear Judge Hughes:

You have doubtless noticed that very serious charges of dishonesty have been made in connection with the production of aircraft.

Because of the capital importance of this branch of the military service, I feel that these charges should be thoroughly investigated and with as little delay as possible, in order that the guilty, if there be any such, may be promptly and vigorously prosecuted and that the reputations of those whose actions have been attacked may be protected, in case the charges are groundless.

I requested the Department of Justice to use every instrumentality at its disposal to investigate these charges, and, with the approval of the Attorney General, I am writing to beg that you will act with him in making this investigation. I feel that this is a matter of the very greatest importance, and I sincerely hope that you will feel that it is possible to contribute your very valuable services in studying and passing upon the questions involved.

Cordially and sincerely yours,

Woodrow Wilson

Hon. Charles E. Hughes
9 Broadway
New York City

The Letter of President Wilson to Judge Hughes

may be attached, but the main idea must be left in supreme command. In order that unity may be assured, two rules must be observed:

1. Do not omit anything necessary to an understanding of the main idea.

2. Do not include anything that is not needed.

Fragment Fault. A sentence is more than "just a group of words." A group of words, to be a sentence, must have at least one independent subject and predicate. If it has not, it falls into the fragment fault. This is the fault of pointing off part of a thought as if it were an independent unit. Usually the error takes the form of separating a subordinate clause from the independent clause and punctuating it as a separate sentence.

> FRAGMENT FAULT: Each day we are coming into contact with pressing problems. Which require immediate solution for the good of business.
> CORRECTED: Each day we are coming into contact with pressing problems which require immediate solution for the good of business.
> FRAGMENT FAULT: This is the usual procedure. Although there is no reason why we cannot modify it.
> CORRECTED: This is the usual procedure, although there is no reason why we cannot modify it.
> MORE EMPHATIC: Although this is the usual procedure, there is no reason why we cannot modify it.

Loose Hook-up Fault. A good writer includes in a sentence nothing that is not needed. One idea should not be hooked to another unless it is needed to round out the thought or unless it is so related that it helps to clarify the thought. A careless string of *and's* and *but's* between equal and loosely related ideas flattens writing into a weak hodgepodge. The effect of joining two loosely related thoughts between a capital and a period is stringy and unpleasant.

> LOOSE HOOK-UP: Our company maintains a research division, and the home office is in Chicago.
> BETTER: Our company maintains a research division. The home office is in Chicago.

> CONFUSING: The report shows many ways in which our Standard machine can be used, and your business should profit from increased efficiency and decreased costs, but a trial of the machine will cost you nothing, and we suggest that you send in the enclosed card at once without delay.
> CLEAR: Your business should profit from increased efficiency and decreased costs through the multiple use of our Standard machine. A trial costs you nothing. Why not put the card in the mail today?

Even when the ideas are well connected, a sentence is sometimes allowed to become so long that it is difficult to follow the thought. In such cases it is a sensible precaution to divide the material into units easier to grasp.

Omission of Words. Clearness is the object for which every writer strives. It is a great mistake to think that a hasty and telegraphic kind of dictation, in which words are omitted at random, adds anything to business brevity or to clearness. Exactly the opposite is true. It is not good form to put the reader to the labor of supplying missing words.

> CRUDE: Your letter of Jan'y 12th rec'd. Glad to see that order suited. Was sure it would meet with satisfaction. Wish to state you can depend on us at all times. Credit terms mentioned satisfactory. Hoping for further business. Y'rs.
> RIGHT: It is pleasing to know from your letter of January 12 that our shipment exactly suited you. You can depend on our filling all your orders promptly. The credit terms you suggest are satisfactory.

Follow safe usage: Do not omit any word necessary to a quick understanding of the sentence. Such omission not only fogs clearness but also mars courtesy.

Comma Fault. The comma fault—the placing of a comma between two complete ideas when a period is called for—is a serious violation of unity.

> WRONG: Here are six copies of our report, this summarizes our annual operations.

Correct the comma fault by (1) substituting a period for the comma and beginning the following word with a capital, or (2) supplying connecting words that show the proper relation between the two clauses.

RIGHT: Here are six copies of our report. It summarizes our annual operations.

RIGHT: Here are six copies of our report, **which** summarizes our annual operations.

JUNGLE TALE

A jungle of lushest verbiage crept over him. He panted, and hewed and slashed his way into language no white man had ever dared penetrate.

A forward step, and the heavy foliage of "inasmuch as" snapped back in his face. He slashed at the underbrush of redundancy, and a coiled double negative sprang at him swiftly. A split infinitive flew up from the teeming path and stung him.

A top-heavy adverbial clause lay in wait for him around the bend of the next semicolon; and the tom-toms of an unwieldy paragraph sounded sinisterly near.

But on he fought, yet on—brave, stubborn, single-handed—till the foliage grew thinner, parted, and "with the kindest of personal regards," gave way to the blessed sunlight and safety of "very truly yours"; and he brilliantly covered his tracks by saying casually, "Just change that around, Miss Whiffleberry, any way you see fit."

—Courtesy of Edith Pellow and
The *Saturday Evening Post.*

Sentence Coherence

To put straight thinking on paper is something every business person would like to be able to do. You can develop this ability through learning to control sentence coherence.

Sentence Coherence. Coherence, the quality of *hanging together*, is essential in the writing of business sentences. To hang words and ideas together *in such a way that their intended meaning cannot be misunderstood* is to assure coherence. Good coherence prevents double meanings and fogginess, two costly errors. The misreading of business messages because of misplaced words, inexact connections, and poorly arranged ideas costs American business huge sums each year. To send a clear message through the mail, you must arrange words so that the sentences carry the meanings intended.

Put Words in the Right Order. Put modifiers next to the words they modify. Grammatically related words should be joined as snugly as possible within the sentence.

NOT CLEAR: The critic points out that the book discusses the principles that guide in writing effective credit letters in a preceding chapter with clearness.

BETTER: The critic points out that in a preceding chapter the book discusses with clearness the principles that guide in writing effective credit letters.

FAULTY MEANING: He saw the Empire State Building towering high into the sky from the middle of the Hudson.

CORRECTED: From the middle of the Hudson, he saw the Empire State Building towering high into the sky.

Placement of "Only, Alone, At Least," and Other Modifiers. See that *only, alone, at least,* and other such modifying words and phrases are placed close to the elements they modify. Usually the best position is right before the element modified.

In the following sentences note how the meaning changes with the shift of the modifier *only*:

1. **Only** they could get the speaker to deliver one address to the business conference. [Meaning: They alone, no other group, could persuade the speaker to do it.]
2. They could get **only** the speaker to deliver one address to the business conference. [Meaning: They could persuade this speaker alone to deliver an address; **or** They could persuade this speaker alone to limit himself to one speech.]
3. They could get the speaker to deliver **only** one address to the business conference. [Meaning: one address and no more.]
4. They could get the speaker to deliver one address **only** to the business conference. [Meaning: one address and no more; **or** the business conference alone and to no other group.]
5. The speaker delivered one address to the **only** business conference in the eastern area. [Meaning: no other conference held in that locality.]

Connect Action to the Right Agent.

Always *connect an action to the right agent.* To set up a false connection is to clog clearness and befog the meaning. In business this costs money; in writing it is bad form.

WRONG (Dangling Participle): **Speeding** rapidly down Wall Street, **the Stock Exchange** came into sight.
RIGHT: **Speeding** rapidly down Wall Street, **we** came into sight of the Stock Exchange.
WRONG: When **classified** and **indexed, you** may have the manuscript for a first reading.
RIGHT: When **classified** and **indexed,** the **manuscript** may be submitted for your first reading.
RIGHT (An Equally Good Method): When the manuscript has been **classified** and **indexed,** you may have it for your first reading.

WRONG: The cable from European headquarters came in at the very moment **the board** had **adjourned** and **canceled** the proposed sales plan. [Fault: The cable, not the board, canceled the plan; but the meaning is falsely reversed.]
RIGHT: At the very moment the board had adjourned, a **cable** from European headquarters **came** in and **canceled** the proposed sales plan.
RIGHT (An Equally Good Method): A **cable canceling** the proposed sales plan **came** in from European headquarters at the very moment the board had adjourned.

Give Parallel Ideas Parallel Form.

When ideas are parallel in character and alike in importance, use a similar structure to bring out the parallelism. When two or more parts of a sentence have the same relation to the main thought, give them parallel form in order to help the reader recognize their similarity. Hence *avoid shifts in construction.*

INEFFECTIVE: Please recommend a man who can take charge of the office and to supervise correspondence. [Noun and infinitive phrase]
PARALLEL: Please recommend a man who can take charge of office routine and correspondence supervision. [Noun and noun]
INEFFECTIVE: We make a point of having our representative follow up all orders promptly, and that he should be careful as to details. [Phrase and clause]
PARALLEL: We make it a point that our representative should follow up all orders promptly and that he should be careful as to details. [Clause and clause]
INEFFECTIVE: Selling, adjusting, and to collect bills are not always easy tasks. [Noun, noun, and infinitive phrase]
PARALLEL: Selling, adjusting, and collecting are not always easy tasks. [Noun, noun, and noun]
INEFFECTIVE: The end of the year is considered the best time for reinvesting dividends and to check up inventories. [**For** and **to**]
PARALLEL: The end of the year is considered the best time for reinvesting dividends and for checking up inventories. [**For** and **for;** or **to reinvest** and **to check**]

Use Joining Words Accurately to Get Parallel Structure. Apply the rule of parallel construction to words, phrases, and clauses joined by correlatives. Familiar correlatives, or joining words, are *either . . . or, both . . . and, neither . . . nor, not only . . . but also.* See that the same structure follows each member and that the ideas are logically related.

WRONG: Send **either** the order at once, **or cancel** it.
RIGHT: **Either send** the order at once, **or cancel** it.
WRONG: Such a system forecasts **not only trends, but also suggests** the extent of the cycle.
RIGHT: Such a system **not only forecasts** trends **but also suggests** the extent of the cycle.
WRONG: We ask you to delay **neither the shipment nor must you** be late with the confirmation.
RIGHT: We ask you to delay **neither the shipment nor the confirmation.**

Be Sure to Complete Comparisons. Comparisons are often left incomplete. The result is confusing. Parallel structure will avoid the fault or will correct it if it occurs.

WRONG: The production curve of this company is rising faster than any other company.
RIGHT: The production curve of this company is rising faster than **that** of any other company.
WRONG: He likes this model better than any in the list.
RIGHT: He likes this model better than any **other** in the list.

Hold the Same Point of View. To avoid shifts in construction, avoid illogical shifts in point of view. Keep person, number, and voice parallel.

WRONG: For the patronage **you** have given us, we wish to thank all **our customers.**
RIGHT: For the patronage **they** have given us, we wish to thank all **our customers.**
WRONG: **A person** working for this organization has to watch **their** sales record constantly. [False agreement]
RIGHT: **A person** working for this organization has to watch **his** sales record constantly. [True agreement]

Keep the Reference of the Pronoun Clear. A sentence is ambiguous when either of two words may be interpreted as the antecedent of a pronoun.

AMBIGUOUS: When the manager talked with Mr. Brieske, he felt certain that the report would be done by noon.

Which of the men, our manager or Mr. Brieske, expected the report to be finished by noon? A small change in the wording makes the meaning clear:

The manager felt sure, when he talked with Mr. Brieske, that the report would be done by noon.
or
Mr. Brieske felt sure, when the manager talked with him, that the report would be done by noon.

When using relative clauses, avoid the ambiguity by placing the clause near the noun it modifies—the antecedent of the relative pronoun.

AMBIGUOUS: Consumers are sure to be aware of modern improvements in retail stores that are in touch with new business methods.
CLEAR: Consumers who are in touch with new business methods are sure to be aware of modern improvements in retail stores.

A noun or pronoun used as the antecedent of a relative pronoun should be in the nominative or objective case—not in the possessive.

INFERIOR: He inspected a club's headquarters that has occupied the same premises for a half century.
BETTER: He inspected the headquarters of a club that has occupied the same premises for a half century.

The use of a pronoun to refer to a clause should be avoided.

FAULTY: He has delivered the wrong machine, which means that we must wait until tomorrow.
IMPROVED: He has delivered the wrong machine and has thus caused us to have to wait until tomorrow.
IMPROVED: Since he has delivered the wrong machine, we must wait until tomorrow.

Sentence Emphasis

Put the Most Important Thoughts in the Most Emphatic Places. One of the great language improvements is putting the most important ideas in the most emphatic places. Known as emphasis, this quality is essential in the writing of practical and effective business sentences.

Sentence Emphasis. Emphasis gives force and adds thrust to a sentence that is already clear. In the business message each sentence should deal with one main idea (UNITY). The material in the sentence should fall into place in a way to make the meaning clear (COHERENCE). When appropriate, added force should thrust the meaning into even the most reluctant mind (EMPHASIS). In all your writing try to make those shifts in sentence structure that put the important ideas in the important places. In short, apply the "headline" principle.

Important Ideas Deserve Important Placement. A person's hat and shoes are conspicuous. Similarly the beginning and the ending of a sentence gather special attention and are therefore logical spots for ideas of prominence that you wish to emphasize.

LESS EFFECTIVE: One way of improving ability to write well is to use a good handbook whenever you feel puzzled.
MORE EMPHATIC: To improve your skill in writing and to settle questions that puzzle, use a good handbook.
ALSO STRONGER: A good handbook helps to settle puzzling questions and to improve writing skill.

Reading keeps the human brain busy. Help the reader to seize the important points. When a speaker stresses certain words or larger elements, you know that he regards these as important. You *hear* him emphasize. But in writing, emphasis must be *seen*. Words that you emphasize by vocal stress in speaking, you must emphasize *by position* in writing.

Choose the Right Place for Important Words. The beginning and the ending of a sentence, a paragraph, a letter, or a book are the parts that most forcibly impress the reader. Force is increased if the sentence is so arranged as to bring the important words at the beginning and the end, and the others, such as connectives and modifying phrases, in the middle.

In the opening sentence of a letter, for example, reference to the date, and sometimes to the subject of the message to which it is a reply, is necessary. But this date and subject reference is *not* the part that should be emphasized. Usually words to express this reference can easily be placed in the middle of the sentence.

INFERIOR: In reply to your inquiry of May 3 asking about the building agreement, we are glad to say that the contract has been signed.
IMPROVED: We are glad to say, in reply to your inquiry of May 3, that the contract has been signed.

To violate this principle of emphasis by placement may cost you the attention of your reader. You may make him search so long for the meaning that he may become weary and quit. Make the reader's task as light as possible by stressing prominent ideas. Put them in places of force.

How to Handle the Words "However, Therefore, Nevertheless, Moreover, Also," and the Like—to Preserve Emphasis. For the sake of beginning or ending the sentence with words that deserve distinction, it is often an advantage to place *however, therefore, nevertheless, moreover, also,* and the like within the sentence. Such words should be placed early in the sentence so that their qualifying effect is seen at first glance.

LESS EMPHATIC: The dean is strict in enforcing the rules. However, the record shows that he is just.

IMPROVED: The dean is strict in enforcing the rules. The record shows, however, that he is just.

NOTE: This caution includes such expressions as *I think* and *it seems to me*. Do not place these particles and expressions at the end of clauses.

INFERIOR: His method is one we ought to use, I think.

IMPROVED: His method is, I think, the one we ought to use.

Climax for Emphasis.

Useful and sometimes highly effective is the arranging of words, phrases, and clauses in a series of rising force. The sentence gains momentum and ends with great power. This device, known as climax, strengthens all writing.

EMPHASIS BY CLIMAX: ". . . and that government of the people, by the people, for the people, shall not perish from the earth."

A boy who is taught to save his money will rarely be a failure; will rise to success in his profession; will forge ahead in the estimate of his fellowmen.

The planned budget is so sure, so strong, and so necessary that no great empire can long exist without it.

Balance or Contrast for Emphasis.

Balancing one idea against another in the same sentence lends added power to both. In this type of sentence the words and the phrases of one part correspond in form and position with those of the other part. The effect is artificial; yet if it is not used too often, it adds strength.

EMPHASIS BY BALANCE: The one is a man of action; the other a man of thought.

In emphasis by contrast, or antithesis, the balance of word against word need not be observed, but ideas are contrasted in such a way as to lend force to each other.

EMPHASIS BY CONTRAST: In business as in life, "Character is what we are; reputation, what people think we are." "Read not to contradict and confute, but to weigh and consider."

True selling is the art of introducing to a man something he needs; not the art of tricking a man into buying something that he does not want.

Position, climax, balance, and contrast are forceful tools with which to give a sentence energy and momentum.

Periodic Sentences Lend Emphasis.

A periodic sentence is one in which both the main clause and the meaning are incomplete until the end is reached. Such a sentence keeps the reader in suspense. It spurs his curiosity. It holds back the important point until the close. Not until the whole sentence has been completed does the reader know the full meaning. The loose sentence, on the other hand, may blurt out the most important point in the opening clause. Then may come phrase after phrase, clause after clause, strung together as long as the sentence will stand the strain. Yet a sentence may be seriously weakened if it is allowed to trail off into an unimportant element. Amateurs often make this blunder.

PERIODIC: After the students had reviewed the assignments for the semester and the instructor had illustrated each of the main points, the class adjourned for the long Christmas vacation.

LOOSE, LESS EFFECTIVE: The class adjourned for the long Christmas vacation after the students had reviewed the assignments for the semester and the instructor had illustrated each of the main points.

PERIODIC: To help solve many of its daily problems, our company has set up, at the home office in Cleveland, a well-staffed research department.

LOOSE, LESS EFFECTIVE: Our company has set up a well-staffed research department to help solve many of its daily problems, this department being located at the home office in Cleveland.

Of course, it would not be wise to make all your sentences periodic. If you did, your manner of writing would be stiff and unnatural. But there is little danger of your overdoing the periodic style. The author has yet to see an example of a student whose writing has become "too periodic." Hence, write in the periodic form when it best fits your thought.

Subordination, a Powerful Device for Emphasis. The only way the mind can detect the importance of an idea in writing is to watch the flow of the word groups. This quality is to writing what modulation and pitch and loudness of tone are to speaking.

The principle of subordination requires that one statement be made independent and that the others in the sentence be made subordinate to it. In brief, you subordinate one idea to another by using a suitable connecting element to show the subordinate relation of one clause to another.

The most important statement, of course, deserves the command. The less important thoughts should yield to its leadership. Yet, in hastily dictated business paragraphs, the best ideas are often overlooked because they have been hidden away in subordinate clauses. Meanwhile a trivial idea creeps into a main clause and parades under false colors. Do not make the first statement, whatever it happens to be, always the main clause. If the first statement is unimportant, subordinate it to a position of lesser importance. This subordination is one secret of effective writing. You will find it characterizing the pages of all first-rate writers. In a sense, it is the "hallmark" of the skilled professional.

> EMPHASIS INVERTED: I think that Mr. Roberts did wrong in accepting the presidency of a corporation, the operating principles of which he could not conscientiously approve.

> EMPHASIS CORRECTLY PLACED: In accepting the presidency of a corporation, the operating principles of which he could not conscientiously approve, Mr. Roberts, I think, did wrong.

In the first example, the least important statement, *I think*, is made the main clause and awarded an important position. On the other hand, *Mr. Roberts did wrong*, the main statement, is put in a subordinate relation and hidden away in the middle of the sentence, the least emphatic place. In the rearrangement of the second, proper emphasis is provided.

Finally: Let Conciseness Yield Emphasis. The fewer the words used to express an idea, the clearer the thought stands forth—*if* it has been made complete. Modern times demand brevity. Completeness and courtesy must be assured; but to accomplish these aims, just enough words should be used.

Strike Out Needless Words. A sentence that is already clear and correct can often be made more forceful through the use of the principle of conciseness. Let your sentence contain only enough words to express the idea to be conveyed.

> WORDY: Within a short time after the receipt of the report from your company, we set ourselves almost immediately to the task of putting its principles into effect in connection with our own operations. (33 words.)
> IMPROVED: Shortly after receiving your company report, we began applying its principles to our own operations. (15 words.)

Grammar Review Problems

● 1. Apply the principle of parallel structure in correcting all the weaknesses in the following sentences.

    a. The sales record of that corporation is outstripping all other companies combined.

    b. The head of the publicity division must be a man of wide experience, original, and have unusual ability.

c. We call your notice to the fact that you still owe a hundred dollars on account and all future payments should be made to the new address.

d. He was responsible for placing that order, and the charges were paid for in full by him.

e. The specifications for both the front axle and for the front springs are to be changed.

f. He urged me to give my business to those firms from which you get the quickest service.

g. A person makes rapid progress only through courtesy, and you should therefore cultivate tact.

h. The ability to give good service as well as effective adjusting of complaints and being skillful at closing sales is both necessary and we must develop more of it.

i. From the result of the vote, it was clear that the convention refused to approve not only the move but wanted to reconsider the previous action also.

j. The factory was large, new, and it was well equipped.

k. The applicant states that he has had experience in report writing and that collection procedure has also been handled by him in his previous position.

l. Hurrying through these tasks, and to skimp duties here and there are faults that warrant criticism and making a careful inspection.

m. The wind resistance of the Bonar Special Racer is less than other cars.

n. The hardest job this year has been traveling and to collect accounts.

● 2. In the following sentences shift the order of the words and, if necessary, change the construction so that there can be no misunderstanding as to the meaning.

a. The adding machine in the auditor's office which had been cleaned and adjusted was in good condition.

b. The new gasoline-electric railway cars can save much money for the railroads by putting them on the short runs when they want to accommodate light traffic.

c. The re-order should be sent without delay to the Uranium Mining Company which was approved yesterday by the Credit Department for three dozen grade-one bars.

d. Wisconsin as a state is famous for producing dairy products the world over.

e. A request sent to a person with a notice of an account due inside is called a collection request.

f. On the first page of a four-page folder, the secretary can lay out a handsome message before the mailing piece is put in the mail with a typewriter.

g. The report should not be released without further investigation to the Chesna Corporation.

h. The sheet was mailed on January 3 which contains the necessary items in plenty of time for your revision.

● 3. At the end of each of the following sentences is a word or a phrase in parentheses. Place each word or phrase in the sentence in the position which gives the exact meaning you intend. Note that in some of the examples several different positions may be possible. The particular answer you give will depend on the meaning you wish to convey.

Only

a. The board of directors could authorize the president to sign his contract. (*only*)
b. Five special offers are given to subscribers. (*only*) *Only*
c. After the meeting the secretary said he would send for a special *immediately* messenger. (*immediately*)
d. You have ten days in which to take advantage of this offer. (*only*)
e. You should finish by noon. (*at least*)
f. The salesmen of this company did it. (*alone*)
for a long g. They have intended to inspect the factories. (*for a long time*)
h. Every salesman can hope to equal this record. (*not*)
i. This contract expires in thirty days. (*only*)
j. The supervisor intends to check one fourth of the items every two *at least* weeks. (*at least*)
k. Every soap is good for washing sheer silks. (*not*)

● 4. Examine these sentences and correct any false connections you find.

a. As pointed out in our previous communication, we shall not be able to execute this contract until next year.
though argument b. When argued, you will find the decision good.
c. After determining whether the figures total correctly, the ledger is ready for the next step.
d. Although not entirely satisfactory, we plan to keep the order this time.
e. When examined carefully, you will see some interesting new points on the chart. *through close examination*
f. Coming to the point at once, this action may not be allowed without danger to all.

● 5. Make each of the following sentences so clear that its meaning cannot be misunderstood. You may shift the order of words and, if necessary, change the construction.

a. I saw your advertisement *for a society* in last night's *Times-Star* newspaper and want to be considered as an applicant for it. *for the position*
b. Please ask George Stevens as soon as he comes to see me. *he came*
c. It is our aim to give you, as one of our good customers, all the practical information that we have obtained through years of experience in the retail hardware field without cost.
d. Thank you for your order for the ten electric ranges which came *received* today.
e. A cross-section blueprint is enclosed with this note which gives complete and accurate details.
f. In our request of August 19 we asked for payment for the shipment of cookware sent you on June 3 which was due on July 1.
g. Edward Simpson told Kevin Arnold the other day that he would be *Kevin* promoted to assistant sales-promotion manager.

● 6. The following paragraphs are ineffective because of errors or deficiencies discussed in detail in this section. Rewrite them as you would approve them for the mail. Introduce (a) variety, (b) sentence correctness, and (c) emphasis.

(a)

I have your notice in regard to Note of 500.00 due at your Bank. I have been laid up at home sick for past two weeks. I am better but not able to be out yet. I expect to be at my office first of next week. I will then attend to it.

(b)

Replying to your letter of Jan. 8th. The price to you such as you got is the correct price. We cannot in no condition give better price and if you cannot use them return them as we are obligated under the patent right on this article, we couldn't reduce it in no respect.

We are very sorry but if you can't use them please return them, everyone gets this price so you are not handicapped.

(c)

Meant to answer yours of the 10th before this but I did want to get in touch with Mr. Sorenson before doing so. Failing to find him in his office the first week following receipt of your inquiry and then the fact that I went to Chicago and Philadelphia interfered and so I did not see Mr. Sorenson until today, when he told me he had the matter before the Program Committee and you would soon hear definitely from them.

(d)

Having made an estimate on painting the exterior of your House, the following proposal is submitted.

Propose to furnish labor and materials to paint all exterior wood trim, metal decks and gutters also blinds, two coats of pure lead and oil paint. All loose paint to be scraped off before is done. Interior of sleeping porch to be painted one coat.

All above complete for sum of Six hundred dollars. All so agree to paint Iron Fence one coat of black for sum of Eighteen dollars.

● 7. The following message is relatively effective. Construct an analysis by writing a list of the reasons and qualities that make it direct and workmanlike. A major requirement of this problem is to organize your critical appraisal in such a manner as to assure that you cover all the points discussed and illustrated in this section.

It is with regret that I must decline to grant your request of March 25, asking for leaves of absence for Cadets Harrison and Carter from Friday, April 4, until Sunday, April 6.

Saturday with us is a school day, Monday being our weekly holiday. The best I could do for you would be to permit them to leave here Saturday afternoon after their duties are over, about 3 p.m., to return Sunday afternoon in time for parade at 4 p.m. Moreover, this privilege is dependent upon certain other factors: They must have approval from their parents for the absence and must be free from any special duties.

Will such an arrangement be agreeable to you?

● 8. Rewrite the following paragraphs, using subordination as much as possible and introducing periodic sentences where you think it necessary to improve sentence variety and emphasis.

Situation: A customer has ordered an imported ring. There is delay in filling the order. The customer inquires. This is the reply.

We have received your inquiry of October 1 and we have read its contents carefully. We find that you are inquiring about the ring you ordered some weeks ago, and we wish to inform you that we have already ordered this ring. It is imported, and we had to order it from abroad. It will take a little longer than usual to get it, but as soon as it arrives we will send it.

We had hoped to fill your order at once, but the salesman did not have the right sample on hand, and we had to order direct from abroad. We get our rings direct, and they are imported from southern Europe. They are hand-engraved by peasants, noted for their fine workmanship.

We thank you for your order, and we are sure it will please you.

Letter 1

ROBINSON AND ASSOCIATES, INC.   MANAGEMENT CONSULTANTS

3658 Hamilton Avenue • Cincinnati 24, Ohio • Linwood 1-7365

March 5, 19--

Mr. John C. Worthington
Cincinnati Lithographing Co.
38 West McMicken Avenue
Cincinnati 10, Ohio

Dear Mr. Worthington

One of the basic decisions every writer of business letters
must make has to do with the "style" or layout of the letter
on the page. Any one of several styles may be used, but
generally only <u>one</u> is used by a single business.

The style in which this letter is typed, for example, is known
as the <u>block style</u>. It is so called because each line begins
at the left margin--or as communication experts say, "It is
'blocked' at the left." Its chief advantage is its simplicity.
It requires <u>no</u> special machine adjustments! Consequently, the
typist can "make tracks" when typing it because she doesn't
have to remember to tabulate for indentions. Furthermore, no
time is lost in using the tabulator mechanism (even if the
typist <u>remembered</u> to do so when she should!).

Notice also that there is no end-of-line punctuation in the
opening and closing lines except for the period to punctuate
"Co." in the address. This punctuation style is known as <u>open
punctuation</u>. It saves small amounts of time for the typist.

Remember that this letter style's chief advantage lies in the
speed and efficiency with which it can be typed. Its chief
disadvantage is that, to some people at least, it "looks" off
balance to the left.

Sincerely yours

Joy E. Condorodis

Consultant, Communication Division

JECondorodis/m

(1)

Letter 2

ROBINSON AND ASSOCIATES, INC.   MANAGEMENT CONSULTANTS

3658 Hamilton Avenue • Cincinnati 24, Ohio • Linwood 1-7365

March 5, 19--

Westerman Print Company
2116 Colerain Avenue
Chicago 10, Illinois

Attention Miss Jeanne Etienne

Gentlemen

You will like the style in which this letter is typed.
It is called the <u>modified block style without paragraph
indentions</u>.

Notice, as you compare it with the block style, that the
date line has been moved to end at the right margin and
that the closing lines have been blocked at the horizontal
center of the letterhead. In other words, we
have "modified" the block style. All other lines begin
at the left margin.

Open punctuation has been used in this letter to harmonize
with the limited modification of the block style.
Some other punctuation style might have been used, but
open punctuation is appropriate.

The modified block style without paragraph indentions is
more popular than the block style because it gives better
balance on the letterhead. It retains much of the
efficiency of the block style in that only two modifications
are made in the arrangement of letter parts.

You will like this style if you will give it a try.

Sincerely yours

Joy E. Condorodis

(Miss) Joy E. Condorodis
Communication Division

lm

(2)

Letter 3

ROBINSON AND ASSOCIATES, INC.   MANAGEMENT CONSULTANTS

3658 Hamilton Avenue • Cincinnati 24, Ohio • Linwood 1-7365

March 5, 19--

J. L. Osberger and Company
Textile Building, Room 340
Gay and Broad Streets
Columbus 1, Ohio

Gentlemen:

Here are some facts, gentlemen--facts about the most
popular style of business letter. <u>Modified block style with
indented paragraphs</u> is its name, and its features are observed
in the layout of the letter you are now reading.

You have studied the block style letter with all lines
typed flush left. You have seen it modified to type the date
at the right margin and the closing lines blocked at the horizontal
center. Now you are studying still another modification
of it--the indenting of paragraphs and the centering of
the date.

Notice, too, that a colon is used to punctuate the salutation;
a comma, to punctuate the complimentary close. This
style of punctuation is called <u>mixed punctuation</u>. A majority
of businessmen favor this style because it is slightly less
informal than the open style.

Even though this letter style cannot be typed so rapidly
as the other styles you have studied, businessmen prefer it
because of its balanced layout and the eye-catching quality
of its indented paragraphs. If these factors are more important
to you than the slight saving that comes from improving
typing efficiency, then here is a letter style you can use
with comfortable assurance that it will be accepted by your
business friends.

Very truly yours,

Jerry W. Robinson

Jerry W. Robinson, Director

ck

(3)

Letter 4

ROBINSON AND ASSOCIATES, INC.   MANAGEMENT CONSULTANTS

3658 Hamilton Avenue • Cincinnati 24, Ohio • Linwood 1-7365

March 5, 19--.

Miss Mary Burnet,
    Marsh & Kelton, Inc.,
        485 Hamilton Avenue,
            Evansville, Indiana.

Dear Miss Burnet:

This letter is typed in the <u>indented style</u>. It is so called
because of the following features:

1. The first line of the address begins at the left
    margin, but each line after the first is indented
    five spaces from the beginning of the preceding line.

2. The first of the closing lines begins about five
    spaces to the left of the horizontal center of the
    letter, but each subsequent line is indented five
    spaces from the beginning of the preceding line.

3. The first line of each paragraph is indented five
    or ten spaces.

The punctuation style used in this letter is called <u>close
punctuation</u>. It requires punctuation at the end of each line in
the date, the address, the salutation, and the complimentary close
as indicated in this letter.

Both the indented style letter and close punctuation are being
used less and less in business. This is true because they
suggest extreme formality and are much less efficient to type than
the other letter styles.

Sincerely yours,

ROBINSON AND ASSOCIATES, INC.

Joy E. Condorodis

Communication Division

JECondorodis:lm

(4)

Four Styles of Layout: (1) Block Style—Open Punctuation, (2) Modified Block Style with Block
Paragraphs—Open Punctuation, (3) Modified Block Style with Indented Paragraphs—
Mixed Punctuation, (4) Indented Style—Close Punctuation

PART X Reference Division

Section I   ***Letter Layout: Variations in Arrangement of Introductory Parts, Body Material, and Concluding Parts***

Layout Styles

Letters may be arranged in a variety of styles, the most common of which are the block, the modified block, the NOMA, and the indented. The modified block style was discussed in detail on page 44 of Chapter 2; other styles are discussed and illustrated below.

In the **block style** each line begins at the left margin. This style interferes with picture-frame symmetry, but it enjoys some favor because it saves small amounts of time for the typist. The amount of time saved on each letter may become a significant factor when the number of letters handled in a day, week, month, or year are considered.

The date line is ordinarily considered to be a part of the heading and not a part of the letter itself. Therefore, if the date line balances the letterhead more satisfactorily when it is centered under the heading or when it is typed to end at the right margin, it may be typed in one of these positions even though the rest of the letter is in the block style.

Simplified Styles. An interesting example of the movement toward simplifying letter form is the *NOMA simplified*, supported by the National Office Management Association. An illustration of the NOMA simplified letter is presented on page 598. This form follows the block style. It differs from the usual block style in the following details:

1. The salutation is omitted.
2. The subject heading is typed in capital letters at least three spaces below the address.
3. Questions, listings, or like items in the body of the letter are indented five spaces from the left margin except when they are preceded by a number or a letter.
4. The complimentary close is omitted.
5. The name of the dictator is typed in capital letters at the left margin at least five spaces below the end of the letter.
6. The names of individuals to receive carbon copies are typed on a line three spaces below the signature.

Another simplified style is shown in the illustration on page 598. This form is a less radical change from the conventional than is the NOMA simplified form. It does drop the *Dear* in the salutation, making *Dear Mr. Crawford* simply *Mr. Crawford*. It also drops the complimentary close. Otherwise, it follows a standard modified block style.

Indented Style. In this style each line after the first in the heading, the address, and the closing is indented five spaces to the right of the preceding line. The first line of the heading is started at a point so that the longest line in the heading will not extend into the right margin. The

597

ROBINSON AND ASSOCIATES, INC.   MANAGEMENT CONSULTANTS

3658 Hamilton Avenue • Cincinnati 24, Ohio • Linwood 1-7365

March 5, 19--

Miss Antoinette Peters
W. C. Tyirin & Company
Ingalls Building, Suite 5
Erie, Pennsylvania

NOMA'S SIMPLIFIED LETTER

Here, Miss Peters, is a letter typed in the style known as the
NOMA Simplified. It is simplified, or more appropriately streamlined by the elimination of the salutation, the complimentary
close, and the company name. This is something quite different
in letter layout, and I thought you might be interested in trying it.

NOMA has made additional innovations in letter style that characterize the simplified letter. Here they are:

1. The block-left format is used
2. A subject heading, typed in ALL CAPS, is used three line
   spaces below the address
3. Paragraphs are blocked at the left
4. The writer's name and title, typed in ALL CAPS, appear at
   the left margin at least three line spaces below the last
   line of the body of the message
5. The initials of the typist (when used) are typed at the
   left under the writer's name

The adoption of this letter style will help to reduce your letter-
writing costs. Although it is considered too extreme by some
firms, the NOMA letter is gradually "catching on" in others.

Jerry W. Robinson

JERRY W. ROBINSON - DIRECTOR

ck

(1)

ROBINSON AND ASSOCIATES, INC.   MANAGEMENT CONSULTANTS

3658 Hamilton Avenue • Cincinnati 24, Ohio • Linwood 1-7365

March 5, 19--

Mr. Walter H. Evans
Evans Advertising Agency
298 West Berry Street
Fort Wayne, Indiana

Mr. Evans:

Many thanks for your letter of February 26, asking about the
proper visualization of business letters.

Visualizing is the process of seeing in your mind's eye how
a letter should look when you lay it on paper in its final
form. If you develop an eye for symmetry, proportion, and
balance, if you learn how a picture ought to look in its
frame on the wall, you can give a letter great advantages.

The "picture-frame" rule is a safe one to apply to letter
form. A letter should be made to assume the same proportions as those of the sheet upon which it is placed. The
resulting display is attractive and high in attention; it
makes the message stand out; and it thrusts the meaning upon
the mind in a form easy to read.

Most business firms approve a standard letter form that all
typists are asked to follow. The larger the company, the
more likely you are to find a standard form in use.

Accept my best wishes, Mr. Evans, for all your business
correspondence in the coming year.

Jerry W. Robinson

Jerry W. Robinson, Director

cx

(2)

ROBINSON AND ASSOCIATES, INC.   Jerry W. Robinson Director

3658 Hamilton Avenue • Cincinnati 24, Ohio • Linwood 1-7365

March 5, 19--

My dear Mr. Whitmore:

    The official style of letter, of which this is
an example, differs from the modified block style primarily in the position of the address.

    Note that the letter address is blocked at the
left margin four to six line spaces below the complimentary close. The precise placement of the address, as of
the salutation, depends upon the length of the letter.

    Letters typed in this style usually do not,
although they may, include a department name or title in
the closing lines. Since the paper on which such a letter is typed generally includes the name of the writer
as part of the heading, the initials of the writer are
not included in the signature identification and stenographic reference line. Instead, the initials of the
typist alone may be shown.

    As its name implies, the official style is used
in letters of official character. It may also be used in
personal letters of a formal and dignified nature.

          Yours very sincerely,

          Jerry W. Robinson

Mr. Frank E. Whitmore
4738 Duck Creek Road
Cincinnati 27, Ohio

ck

(3)

1201 Edgecliff Road
Cincinnati 6, Ohio
March 5, 19--

Dear Jim,

    It was most thoughtful of you to send me a
copy of the series of sales letters you developed
as a case study in your communications course. The
series is exceptionally well prepared, and you certainly deserve the "A" you received as a grade.

    In answer to your question regarding styles
of layout for personal letters, let me suggest that
you follow the one I am using for this letter.

    Note that it includes my return address and
the date blocked so that no line extends into the
right-hand margin; it uses a personal salutation
followed by a comma; its paragraphs are indented to
the comma following the salutation; and it ends with
an informal close.

    While there are many acceptable variations
in personal letter styles, you will be safely in
good taste if you follow the plan of this one.

          Cordially yours,

          Jerry

(4)

**Four Additional Layout Styles: (1) NOMA Simplified, (2) Simplified,
(3) Official, (4) Personal**

first line of the address begins at the left margin, and the first of the closing lines begins about five spaces to the left of the center of the letter. The first line of each paragraph is indented five or ten spaces.

Personal and Official Letter Styles. The personal letter style (see the illustration on page 598) is used for informal messages to personal friends and acquaintances. In this type of letter the address is usually omitted.

The official letter style, illustrated on page 598, is used in (a) messages of an official character, (b) formal messages to persons of prominence, and (c) nonbusiness messages to individuals not personally known. This style differs from the ordinary only in the position of the inside address, which is placed flush with the left margin from two to five spaces below the final signature line. The reference initials are placed on the second line below the final line of the inside address.

Punctuation Styles. *Mixed punctuation*, the punctuation style most used in business, is illustrated in selected letters on pages 596 and 598. Note that mixed punctuation requires a colon after the salutation and a comma after the complimentary close. No other end-of-line punctuation is used in the opening and closing lines; however, any abbreviation that ends a line must be followed by a period.

Open punctuation permits the omission of the colon after the salutation and of commas and periods at the *ends* of lines, unless a line ends in an abbreviation. An abbreviation must always be followed by a period. Modern usage shows a trend toward open punctuation.

Close punctuation, also known as end-of-line punctuation, requires commas or periods at the ends of lines of the date, the heading, the address, the salutation, and the complimentary close. It is being used less and less in business.

Single Spacing. Business prefers single spacing for the body of a message. Single spacing brings economy and better display. Many more words can be put on a page typed with single spacing. Hence less stationery may be required. Because the eye is accustomed to reading the printed book and magazine, it finds the single-spaced letter familiar. Paragraphs have greater visual unity when typed in single-spaced blocks with double spacing between paragraphs. Their darker mass is better displayed against the light background of the letterhead. Penwritten messages may adopt the same principle.

Double spacing is sometimes used for the body of a message of under fifty words. Even when double spacing is used, however, the lines of the address are single-spaced.

The Introductory Parts of the Letter

Heading. The heading shows where the message comes from and when it was written. The mail address should be arranged in logical order, the most definite point (for example, *25 Standish Hall*) being placed first. The longest line of the heading should not run into the right margin of the letter. Normally the heading should not extend to the left of the center of the sheet. The preferred order of the information in the heading is: room and building (if they are included) on the first line, otherwise street and number on that line; city, with zone number, and state, on the next line; date, on the last line.

BLOCK HEADING

```
25 Standish Hall
201 College Place
Des Moines 8, Iowa
May 1, 19—
```

INDENTED HEADING

```
25 Standish Hall
    201 College Place
        Des Moines 8, Iowa
            May 1, 19—
```

Date Line. Write the date in full: *August 23, 19—*. Upon the accuracy of the date may rest a legal decision. Figures alone, like *8/23/63, 8-23-63, 8:23:63,* invite misunderstanding. Avoid their use except in office memorandums. Avoid also the needless additions of *st, d, nd, rd,* and *th* after the day of the month.

Letters are usually dated the day they are dictated, not the day they are transcribed. This is the more common practice because it is then unnecessary to alter statements referring to time when the message cannot be transcribed on the same day that it is dictated.

Armed Forces Date Line. The Armed Forces favor writing the date thus: *23 August 19—,* with the number of the day in Arabic numerals first, the name of the month second, and the figures for the year third. This procedure is logical, and it has come into civilian use as an approved form.

Unusual Arrangements of the Date Line. With certain kinds of letterheads unusual arrangements of date lines are sometimes pleasing, but they are time consuming to type. Although few offices adopt them, it is well to know about them.

August 23,
   19—
	August
	   23
	   19—

August
Twenty-third
   19—
	Twenty-third
	August
	   19—

August Twenty-third Nineteen Sixty-three	Twenty-third August Nineteen Sixty-three

Preferred Positions for the Date Line. The date of a message is a part of the reference material, much of which is supplied by the printed letterhead. The date gives information in terms of *time;* while the city, postal zone, and state name printed on the letterhead give information in terms of *place.* As time and place information are related, it is a good practice to place the date on the second line below the city and state names printed on the letterhead. In the block style the date line may be started at the left margin, and in all three styles—block, modified, and indented—it is acceptable practice to center the date line under the letterhead or type it so that it ends at the right margin. If the letterhead is unusual in arrangement, the date line may be placed in relation to the body of the letter so as to achieve an impression of balance.

Address. The address states (1) the name of the person or the business to which the message is to be sent, (2) the street address, (3) the city, postal zone, and the state. In the block style each line of the address is typed even with the left margin. In the indented style the first line is typed even with the left margin; the second line is indented five spaces from the left margin; the third line, ten spaces; and so on. Three lines are normally used. When a title or a descriptive phrase is used with the name of the person or the business, four or more lines may be necessary to prevent the use of a long line that would mar the layout.

```
Mr. Edward Andrews
1521 Bond Avenue
Flint 6, Michigan
```

```
Mr. Ralph Johnson
Executive Secretary
Automatic Processes, Inc.
204 Woodlawn Avenue
Flushing 11, New York
```

```
Mr. J. R. Newcombe, Vice President
Evan K. Menninger Company
312 Crescentville Road
New Orleans 8, Louisiana
```

The address is typed four to twelve single spaces below the date, depending on the length of the letter. Double spacing is used between the last line of the address and the salutation.

In messages to persons of prominence and to others for whom a formal style may be desired, the address is often typed below the signature in the manner illustrated on page 598. This style is also frequently used when a letter is addressed to a friend of the writer. The complete address may be desired so that it will show on the carbon copy and thus be available for filing purposes, but the letter seems a bit more personal if the address is given at the bottom rather than in its usual position at the beginning of the letter.

If window envelopes are used, the address must be arbitrarily positioned so that it will show in full through the envelope window when the sheet is folded and inserted.

Handling Numbers in the Address.
1. Express house numbers in figures, except for house number *One.*

> Harold lives at One Cedar Drive; Mark, at 2015 Bedford Street; and Charles, at 8 Francis Lane.

2. Spell out a number naming a street, if it is ten or below. When a street has a number as its name, separate the house number from the street number by a hyphen preceded and followed by a space. The letters *d, st,* or *th* may be added to the number that represents a street name.

> He moved from 721 Fifth Street to 864 - 37 Street.
> Our plant is located at 381 - 123d Street.

Selecting the Correct Title. Use the correct title before the name of the person addressed, both in the address on the letter and in the address on the envelope. Do not address a letter to an individual without using *Mr.* or whatever *other* personal title is correct. The correct general titles for the first line of the address are:

Individual: *Mr., Miss, Mrs.* *

Firm: *Messrs.* (the abbreviated form of the French *Messieurs*) is used in addressing men, or men and women; *Mmes.* (the abbreviated form of the French *Mesdames*) is used in addressing women. Modern usage tends to omit these two titles and to use instead the name of the firm as it appears on the letterhead.

Corporation: *Name of the Corporation.* To determine (a) whether to use or to omit the word *The* before a company name, and (b) whether to use the sign "&" (called an *ampersand*) or the word *and* in the corporate name, and (c) to settle any other possible points of doubt, follow the exact style used on the letterhead of the company to which the letter is addressed.

Punctuating Titles. The period must be used with the following titles because they are abbreviated forms:

Mr.	man
Messrs.	two or more men
Mrs.	married woman

The period is not used with the following titles, which are not abbreviated forms:

Miss	unmarried woman
Misses	two or more unmarried women
Mesdames	two or more married women

Special Titles. Certain titles, in addition to those already mentioned, often occur in correspondence. They are:

Dr. is the title of one who holds a doctor's degree, whether of philosophy, law, literature, theology, education, or medicine. As a title it is abbreviated.

---

*It is proper to assume that women are to be addressed as *Miss* unless they themselves indicate that they are married (see page 610). A few organizations have experimented with *Ms.* as a "universal" form covering both *Miss* and *Mrs.*, but the practice has not been generally adopted.

Professor (Prof.) is the proper title of one holding a professorship in a college or a university. It should be written in full, although abbreviation is common.

The Reverend (Rev.) is a title properly carried by a minister, a priest, or a rector. The following guides are important:

1. *The,* as an article preceding the title *Reverend* or the title *Honorable,* is the conservative and preferable usage, although the growing practice in America (as distinguished from that in England) is to use the title *Reverend* or *Honorable* alone.

Preferable:

The Reverend Dr. C. E. Frederick
The Reverend Mr. Bradshaw
The Reverend J. J. Bowen
The Honorable George Sherwood
The Honorable Mr. Sherwood

In the case of direct *oral* address *The* is dropped.

2. Although abbreviation is common, it is better usage to write such titles in full.

3. When preceded by *The,* such titles should *not* be abbreviated.

4. Correct usage does not approve the use of *Reverend* or *Honorable* with the last name alone. Avoid: *The Reverend Crane; The Honorable Towne.*

5. When *the* is not the only word used before Reverend or Honorable, it should not be capitalized.

We sent this suggestion to the Reverend Nicholas Towne and to the Honorable N. W. Johns.

The Honorable (Hon.) is a title given to an individual who holds, or has held, a prominent governmental position. It is used with the names of cabinet officers, ambassadors, members of both houses of Congress, governors, mayors, and judges. Courtesy often extends it to others. As in the case of *Professor* and *Reverend,* it is better to write *Honorable* in full, although abbreviation is common. When preceded by *The,* the title *Honorable* should not be abbreviated. Do not use *Honorable* with the last name alone. Avoid: *The Honorable Wiley.*

Difficult Titles for Special Classes. For certain public officials, educators, and church dignitaries, other special titles and salutations are reserved. For these titles and the matching salutations, see pages 621 to 626.

Using Double Titles. Common sense dictates when it is correct or incorrect to use a double title. The multiplication of titles and degrees with a given name is not objectionable *if each one represents a different kind of status or achievement from the other.* Hence, double titles are justifiable when the second title adds new information or distinction and does not merely duplicate that which appears in the first title.

Compare and analyze these examples:

RIGHT

Mr. Richard E. Crawford, Manager
Dr. W. L. McGregor, Director
The Honorable K. L. Cameron,
     President
The Reverend H. H. Davenport,
     Moderator
Mrs. M. J. Anders, Superintendent

WRONG

Dr. Stewart R. Jones, M.D.
Dr. R. N. Barnes, D.D.
Mrs. Dr. J. G. Watts

Typing the Official Title. The official title in an address should be placed at the beginning of the second line and followed by a comma and a space. This title indicates the official position in relation to the company named in the second line. If the second line is long, however, the official title may be typed on the first line, with the personal name, to equalize line lengths.

Mr. James Harrison
Manager, Ross Company
2078 Kellerman Avenue
Camden 10, New Jersey

Mr. C. F. Wells, Vice President
Petroleum Refining Corporation
2099 South Fordham Place
San Francisco 9, California

If the title itself is rather long, it may be typed on the second line by itself.

```
Mr. C. D. Nelson
Chairman of the Board
The Donovan Corporation
315 Randolph Street
Chicago 10, Illinois
```

Handling Proper Names. An error of the worst kind is to misspell the name of the person addressed or to take undue liberty with that name in the way of abbreviation or the omission of an initial. Men with the names *Robert* and *Albert* may detest seeing them slashed to *Robt.* or *Alb.* Men with the initials *R. R.* and *A. C.* may have a deep personal distaste for initials cut to *R.* and *A.* Nothing is more individual than our names as we spell them and present them to others. Do not alter names without authority. In the address of a letter and elsewhere, write a name exactly as it is written by the bearer. This rule applies likewise to the word *Company,* which should be shortened to *Co.* only when the business itself does so in its own letterhead.

To misspell a proper name is bad enough; but even worse is to mispronounce it. In a sales presentation it is a cardinal sin to mispronounce the name of the man whom you are addressing. Such mispronunciation may offend him. In using the name of another, be sure to pronounce it as it is pronounced by the bearer himself or by one who knows him. Always take pains to determine the correct pronunciation before you speak. You will find that such care will reward you in a great many ways.

Attention Line. Two acceptable ways may be used to reach by letter an individual in a business concern. One is to address him personally at the address of the business. The other is to address the concern and to follow that address with an attention line, which directs the letter to his notice,

and which becomes a related part of the address. The attention line is typed on the second line below the last line of the address. In the block style of letter the attention line is customarily typed even with the left margin between the address and the salutation. In the indented style the line is either centered after the salutation or begun at the paragraph point two lines above the salutation.

BLOCK STYLE

```
Michaels and Cox, Inc.
General Contractors
6300 Decatur Place
Dallas 6, Texas

Attention Mr. Cox *

Gentlemen **
```

INDENTED STYLE

```
Michaels and Cox, Inc.
     General Contractors
        6300 Decatur Place
           Dallas 6, Texas

Gentlemen **      Attention Mr. Cox
```

On the envelope, type the attention line in the lower left corner or immediately below the name of the company in the address itself. (See illustrations on page 612.)

A letter carrying an attention line will be opened at once, along with general correspondence. If the person specified is absent, and a prompt answer is required, the letter will be referred without delay to another member of the staff. A letter bearing a personal address may await the attention of the addressee and, as a result, may for some time lie unanswered on his desk. In larger companies, however, *all* letters—except those marked *Personal*—are opened, irrespective of the character of the addresses.

Mr. Cox, Please is sometimes used as a variant of *Attention Mr. Cox.*
** Usage, logic, and practical considerations now justify the use of *Dear Mr. ....* after an attention line. See the *Bulletin* of the American Business Writing Association, Volume XX, Number 6, Page 6.

Subject Line. The subject of a message is sometimes emphasized with a subject line, thus: *Subject: Unions* or *Subject: Order No. 3572.* If the printed letterhead does not indicate the place for the subject line, the subject (if one is used) may be (a) centered in the space after the salutation and on a line with it or (b) placed on the second line below the salutation. In the latter case the body of the letter begins on the second line below the subject line. The word *Subject* should be followed by a colon. The subject heading is not necessary if the position of the subject line makes its nature clear.

```
Watson Corporation
2913 Drexel Road
Austin 3, Texas

Gentlemen:          Subject: Unions

Watson Corporation
2913 Drexel Road
Austin 3, Texas
Gentlemen:
                    Order No. 3572
```

In the full block letter style the subject line may optionally be typed flush with the left margin on the second line below the salutation.

```
Watson Corporation
2913 Drexel Road
Austin 3, Texas

Gentlemen:

Subject: Unions
```

Attention and Subject Lines Used Together. If the same message should call for the use of both subject and attention lines, follow this procedure: (a) Type the attention line on the second line below the last line of the address; (b) type the salutation on the second line below the attention line; (c) center the subject line to the right of the salutation and on a line with it.

```
Watson Corporation
2913 Drexel Road
Austin 3, Texas

Attention Office Manager

Gentlemen:          Subject: Unions
```

Reference Line. Occasionally a correspondent will place, somewhere at the top of his letter, the following request: "In your reply please refer to File 586." Your reply will then carry the following reference line, typed at the same point as the subject line:

```
Reference:  Your File 586
```
or
```
Your File 586
```

Salutation. The salutation of a letter is a form of courtesy to the reader, an interpretation of good manners exemplified both in letter form and in business usage.

When you meet another, perhaps you say, "How do you do?" Just so you may write: *Dear Sir* or *Gentlemen.* For the business letter these are two common salutations. They are "correct" (in the purely formal sense). *Dear Sir* is always singular. *Gentlemen* as a term is always plural. Do not use *Dear Sirs.*

Whatever the salutation, type it on the second line space below the address and flush with the left margin. If there is an attention line, type the salutation on the second line below the attention line unless that line is centered after the salutation. Double-space between the salutation and the first line of the body of the message.

Approved Salutations. Certain salutations are approved by the preference of authorities and by the weight of usage of famous organizations. In the order of decreasing formality, these salutations are:

```
                FOR MEN
Sir
My dear Sir
Dear Sir
My dear Mr. Brock
Dear Mr. Brock
My dear Brock
Dear Brock
My dear Paul
Dear Paul
```

FOR WOMEN

Madam
My dear Madam
Dear Madam
My dear Mrs. Adams
Dear Mrs. Adams

My dear Ruth
Dear Ruth

In the plural the approved salutations are:

Gentlemen—This salutation is standard for addressing a company, a committee, a numbered post-office box, a collective organization made up entirely of men (or of men and women) and other group units of similar type. It is optional to use (1) *Dear Sir and Madam* in writing to a firm consisting of a man and a woman; and (2) *Ladies and Gentlemen* in writing to a club or social organization consisting of both men and women.

Mesdames—This salutation is standard for addressing a company, a committee, or a collective group made up exclusively of women. *Ladies* is an alternate salutation that is gaining favor.

The Test: How Well Do You Know Your Correspondent? Naturally you seek a standard by which you can choose the correct salutation from these lists, no matter what the situation. The test is found in the answer to the question, How well do you know your correspondent?

Choose the salutation that represents the degree of acquaintance you enjoy, that properly reflects the relation existing between you and the person addressed, and that matches the tone of your message. For those whom you have never met, the formal *Sir* or *Madam* may be used, although in such instances the less formal *Dear Mr. Brock* (or whatever the name may be) is approved. When *Printers' Ink* some time ago made a survey of the letter production of five hundred companies, it found that the salutation *Dear Mr. Brock* was used a hundred times to each use of *Dear Sir.*

When you are on a level of personal acquaintance, the less formal and the informal salutations may be used. Modern communication prefers personal directness. For this reason the *Sir* and *Madam* groups are falling into disfavor.

How to Capitalize a Salutation. Capitalize the first word of a salutation. The word *dear* is not capitalized unless it is the first word. The following words are always capitalized:

Sir
Mr.
Every surname (Williams, for example)
Every first name (John, for example)
Madam
Mrs.
Miss
All titles (President, Professor, Superintendent, Director, Dr., and the like)

How to Punctuate a Salutation. The only correct punctuation for the salutation of a *business letter* is the colon (:). It should be placed at the end of the salutation line. Example:

Dear Mr. Morris:

Do not use a comma as the punctuation after a business salutation. (The comma, in this usage, is acceptable in personal correspondence.) Use only the colon (:). Do not use a colon and a hyphen (:-).

The use of the colon after the salutation is optional. When mixed punctuation is used, the colon is retained after the salutation. If open punctuation is used, the colon is omitted.

Special Salutations Involving Familiar Titles. Certain familiar titles are used almost every day. Many of these find their places in salutations. The most important follow.

Dr.—It is permissible to abbreviate this title in the salutation, although many leading concerns write it in full.

Dear Dr. Sterling
Dear Doctor Sterling:

Professor (Prof.)—Although the abbreviation is common in salutations, it is better practice to write this title in full.

Dear Professor Bell:

The Reverend (Rev.)—Although the abbreviation is common in salutations, it is better to write this title in full.

My dear Reverend Cowley:
Dear Reverend Father:

Difficult Salutations to Special Groups. Some business messages must go to persons not directly, and in some instances not even remotely, connected with business. To address these people correctly, you must be familiar with the special titles and salutations or you must know where to go to find them.

Two special groups of persons considered difficult to address are: (1) governmental and other officials prominent in public life; (2) church dignitaries.

The difficulty is that the suitable titles and salutations are unfamiliar because they are not often used. Furthermore, in messages to these special classes formal address must be observed. Beginning on page 621 of this book is a list of special address forms and matching salutations for these special groups. This list has been painstakingly edited and will prove a useful guide. The list is based upon the prevailing practice of the leading organizations of America.

Dropping Salutations. The simplified letter style of the National Office

Management Association drops the salutation (see the illustration on page 598) and puts a subject-heading in its place.

A few firms have also experimented by dropping the salutation and substituting such forms as:

Mr. Rand, Please
Greetings, Mr. Rand
Good Morning, Mr. Rand
How Do You Do, Mr. Rand

A variation lifts the opening words of the first paragraph into the salutation position:

Here, Mr. Rand,

is our idea of how you should proceed. Lay your plans for the first month, (etc.)
                    or
So You May
Get Acquainted

For one month I am going to send you the weekly United Forecasts of Business, (etc.)

Still another variant launches the message abruptly without lifting the introductory words:

Mr. Robert Rand
987 Waverly Drive
Louisville 9, Kentucky

Here, Mr. Rand, is our idea of how you should proceed in the matter about which you wrote on July 7. Lay your plans, etc.

The sheer weight of long-honored tradition is likely to extend the use of the salutation for many years to come.

The Body and The Concluding Parts

Body of the Letter. The paragraphs in the body of the letter are indented or are in block form according to the layout style used. Indented paragraphs may be used in letters written in indented or modified block style. Paragraphs in block form may be used

in letters written in full or modified block style. When the indented paragraph style is used, the first line of each paragraph is most commonly indented five or ten spaces.

Paragraphs are usually typed single-spaced with double spacing between paragraphs. In very short letters with indented first lines of paragraphs, however, the entire body of the letter may be double-spaced.

Paragraphing in the Body. As a rule, paragraphs in business letters are shorter than those in other forms of writing. The rapid pace of the modern office has made them so. The business paragraph is on its way to get something done. It aims straight at the bull's-eye of a target, and the path of its thought should be as straight as an arrow.

Consider your reader's convenience. Make it easy for him to understand what you have written. Keep the first paragraph short. An opening block of two to five lines is easy to see and to grasp. Remember that it is easier to read four paragraphs of six lines each than one solid paragraph of twenty-four lines. You will also find it easier to read four paragraphs of six lines each than twelve paragraphs of two lines each. Do not overparagraph. Strike a happy medium. In general, vary the later paragraphs within four to ten lines or so.

Abbreviations. Use abbreviations sparingly. To write names and titles and expressions in full is a courtesy that many well-known firms thoughtfully extend. Certain abbreviations should be avoided at all times.

USE	AVOID
account	acc't, acct., a/c
amount	am't, amt.
received	rec'd
Philadelphia	Phila.

USE	AVOID
San Francisco	S. F.
Dear Sir	D'r S'r
Gentlemen	Gents
Secretary	Sec'y
and Company	& Co.
Yours	Y'rs
March 6, 19—	3/6/—

In routine correspondence, in which the addressees are familiar with the terms used, shortened forms are permissible. In such cases the correspondents should standardize their abbreviations according to a list like that in the *Style Manual of the United States Government Printing Office.*

Second Sheets. Most business messages can be put on one sheet. Only when necessary should second pages be used.

The use of the smaller elite type permits the inclusion of more copy on a single page and makes possible more one-page messages. Yet this warning is important: *Do not crowd one page merely to avoid the use of a second.*

Top and side margins on the second page should match those on the first. The heading of the addressee is preferably written in one of the styles illustrated above approximately one inch below the top edge of the sheet.

Leave three to six lines between this second-page heading and the continuation of the message from the first page.

Stationery used for second pages, in messages of more than one page, should *exactly match* the first sheet in quality, weight, color, and size.

Faithfully yours, Yours faithfully, Faithfully,	Close personal friendship with or without business Close confidential relations involving business
Cordially yours, Yours cordially, Cordially,	Daily business contacts Close business friendship Informal business relations Personal friendship
Very sincerely yours, Yours very sincerely, Sincerely yours, Yours sincerely, Sincerely,	Semiformal Ordinary business matters Business acquaintance Ordinary business friendship
Very truly yours, Yours very truly,	Formal, but widely used
Respectfully yours, Yours respectfully, Respectfully submitted,	Severely formal or for use in official messages, reports, or communications to superior authority, or to indicate special respect.

An Approved List of Complimentary Closes

Complimentary Close. The complimentary close is the fifth structural part of the letter. Like the salutation, its choice is controlled (1) by good taste, (2) by the practice of leading business organizations, and (3) by the degree of acquaintance you have with the reader.

Match the Complimentary Close to the Salutation. Note the direct link between the salutation and the complimentary close. The most commonly used closes in business letters are:

Very truly yours
Yours very truly
Sincerely yours

The close *Yours truly* is less often used in modern correspondence because it sounds abrupt.

Choose the complimentary close to match the salutation. Let it also match the tone and spirit of the message. Keep them in step. If the salutation is familiar because of a long-standing acquaintance, the complimentary close may be so. If the salutation is reserved because the message is directed to a person of high position with whom correspondence has never before been carried on, the complimentary close should be likewise. In brief, the two parts should match at beginning and end, should keep in step, grade by grade, from the most severely formal at one extreme to the most familiar and friendly at the other. An approved list of closes is given above.

"Good-Will Closes." Closes that pivot on the good-will words *sincerely,* *cordially,* and *faithfully* gain in use. Their choice should be governed by good taste and by the spirit of the message. In cases of doubt choose the more conservative closes: *Very truly yours, Yours very truly.*

Form of the Complimentary Close. (1) Type the complimentary close on the second line below the last line of the body. (2) Begin it (a) flush with the left margin in the block style; (b) at a point even with the date line; or (c) if the date line has been centered, begin the close slightly to the left of the center of the paper. (3) Capitalize only the first word of the close. (4) When close punctuation is used, follow the complimentary close with a comma. When strict open punctuation is used and the colon is not used after the salutation, omit the comma after the complimentary close. If the colon is used after the salutation, with open punctuation in the heading and the address, the comma should be used after the complimentary close (mixed punctuation).

Signature. In its usual form the signature of a business letter has three parts:

1. Dictator's signature (penwritten)
2. Dictator's name (typed)
3. Dictator's title in the organization (typed)

A number of firms still follow the practice of typing the company name in all capital letters a double space below the complimentary close. This practice is unnecessary if the company name appears in the letterhead.

In the block style each part of the signature is begun even with the complimentary close. In the indented style the first signature line is indented five spaces from the beginning of the close and each of the other signature lines is indented five spaces from the beginning of the line preceding it.

Company Name. The company name, if used, is typed in solid capital letters on the second line below the complimentary close. If the company name is long, it must begin far enough to the left so that it will not extend noticeably into the right margin.

Penwritten Signature. A penwritten signature should, if possible, be readable. Make your signature legible, if it is not already so, before your writing habits become too set. Standardize your personal signature in a simple form and do not deviate from that form in business matters. This plan reduces the chance of questions arising when signatures of the same individual vary. In legal disputes signatures are scrutinized to the minutest detail. Adopt the form of your name you like best and use that form.

Dictator's Name and Title. As a courtesy, type the name of the dictator (not just the initials). The spelling of the dictator's name may thus be positively identified even if the handwriting is beyond the power of the eye to decipher.

The dictator's name is typed directly under the penwritten signature on the fourth line below the company name or on the fourth line below the complimentary close when a company signature line is not used. An optional arrangement is to type the dictator's official title directly under the penwritten signature and to combine the full name of the dictator with the stenographic reference initials.

If the name of the signer appears on the letterhead in such a line as *Office of A. B. Horton, Executive Director,* it is unnecessary to type an identification. Here initials are sufficient.

If the dictator's name is typed below the penwritten signature, the official title is usually placed on the line below the dictator's name. Only when both the name and title are short is it possible to combine these two itmes on the same line.

BLOCK STYLE

GOODNER-ARMS, INC.

Henry J. Erickson

Henry J. Erickson
Vice President

INDENTED STYLE

ILLINOIS GLASS COMPANY

L. V. Simms

L. V. Simms, Manager

Optional Personal Signature Style. It is permissible to place the penwritten signature on the second line below the complimentary close. This penwritten signature may be followed by (a) the typed signature or the official title (typed), or both, on the fourth line below the complimentary close and (b) the name of the company typed in solid capitals on the line following one or both of these elements.

Very truly yours

Keith J. Andrews

Keith J. Andrews, President
NATIONAL COPPER CORPORATION

* * *

Sincerely yours,

D. M. Kensington

D. M. Kensington
Secretary and Treasurer
JUDD CHEMICAL COMPANY

Indicating the Status of Women.
Married women should identify their
status by one of the following
methods:

Sincerely yours

Kathryn D. Lynn

Kathryn D. Lynn
(Mrs. J. L. Lynn)

* * *

Sincerely yours

Kathryn D. Lynn

(Mrs.) Kathryn D. Lynn

An unmarried woman may type the
title (Miss) preceding her typewritten
signature as a courtesy to the person
who may later need to write her and
who does not know her marital status.

**Signature Identification and Steno-
graphic Reference.** When there is
more than one dictator and more than
one stenographer in the office, it must
be possible to know who has dictated
a letter and who has transcribed it.
Initials or figures are used to indicate
the stenographer.

If the name of the dictator is typed
below his penwritten signature, the
stenographic identification is typed
after his initials, which appear at the
left margin, thus: *SFL:JC.* Otherwise
the name of the dictator is typed flush
with the left margin, followed by the

stenographer's initials. The preferred
form is:

SFLowell/jc

or

Stephen F. Lowell
JC

The reference line is typed even
with the lowest line of the signature
or on the second line space below that
line, flush with the left margin. The
former method keeps the base line of
the letter *even* and hence greatly en-
hances the attractiveness of the picture-frame margins, thus:

Sincerely yours

TRI-STATE, INC.

P. A. Leeds

PALeeds/ld   Vice President

Special guide lines for mailing and
carbon copy instructions are placed
below the reference line, flush with the
left margin.

Enclosures. Call attention, in the
body of the letter, to enclosures if any
are included. Add a notation (usually
the word *Enclosure,* or the abbreviation *Enc.* or *Encl.*) at the left margin,
on the second line below the stenographic reference.

WFKeeling/jao

Enclosures 2

or

WFK:JAO

Encs. 2

The use of the double space after
the identification line causes the word
Enclosure or the abbreviation *Enc.* to
stand out clearly for the attention of
the mail clerk. When the letters have
been signed by the dictator and are
being folded and prepared for the
mail, the enclosure reference provides
a check against failure to include the
enclosure called for.

Separate-Cover Notations. When the letter refers to items sent in a separate envelope or package, an appropriate notation should appear at the left margin below the last enclosure line or below the reference line if there is no enclosure line. The notation should indicate the method of transportation used in sending the separate-cover material and the number of envelopes or packages.

```
Separate Cover - Express
Separate Cover - Mail 2
```

Mailing Instructions. When a special postal service is to be used (airmail, special delivery, or registered mail), a notation to that effect should be typed in all capital letters even with the left margin (a) below the reference, enclosure, or separate-cover notation line (whichever is last) or (b) midway between the date line and the first line of the address.

```
AIRMAIL

SPECIAL DELIVERY
```

Carbon Copies. A carbon copy of each typewritten letter is usually filed for reference. Additional copies are sometimes made for special purposes, such as conveying information to others interested in the correspondence. In such instances it is correct to sign the carbon copy. If the carbon copy is used under circumstances that make a personal tone desirable (for example, an identical message to several committee members), the signature should be placed on each as if it were an original.

If you wish to indicate, on the original letter, those to whom copies are being sent, you may write *Copy to* or *Copies to* (optionally *cc*) on the second line below the reference, enclosure, separate-cover notation, or mailing-instruction line (whichever is last) flush with the left margin, with the names of the copy recipients on the spaces immediately following, thus:

```
MVH/ac

Copy to Dr. John C. Halterman
```
or

```
MVH/ac

cc: Mrs. Mary Robertson
    Dr. W. G. Sprague *
```

If the information regarding carbon copies is not for the benefit of the addressee, this notation may be placed on the carbon copies only. In that case it may be placed at the top of the sheet rather than at the bottom.

Multiple Guide Lines. It is at times necessary to use more than one guide line. In such cases place the first at a point two lines below the stenographic reference line. Single-space or double-space the additional ones according to the length of the letter.

```
KDA

Enclosures 2

cc:  Mr. R. D. Wood
     Mr. W. R. Steele
```

Postscripts. A postscript consists of one or more paragraphs added to the letter after it has been typed in the usual form. It may be used (1) to cover a point thought of after the message has been typed, or (2) to give special emphasis to some particular point. The postscript is not often used. Logical construction of the message makes most postscripts unnecessary, except for those few cases in which deliberate special emphasis is wanted.

A postscript may be started on the second line below the reference initials and may be typed in the same

---

* When carbon copies are sent to a number of persons in an organization, the names may be arranged (a) alphabetically, (b) according to rank (highest on down), or (c) according to the relative degree of interest in the particular subject. The alphabetical arrangement is the simplest and most "foolproof" of the three.

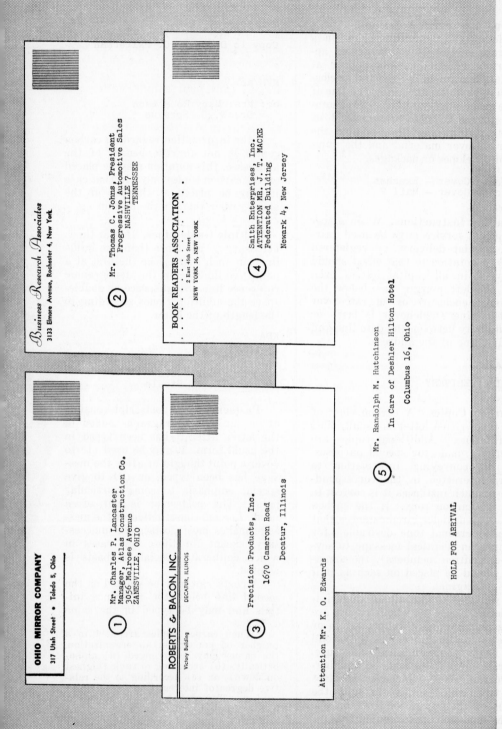

Styles of Envelope Addresses

form as any other paragraph of the letter. If special guide lines are used, the postscript may be started on the second line below the last one. The postscript may also be preceded by the letters P.S., the abbreviation for postscript; or the letters N.B., the abbreviation for the Latin *nota bene*, "Note well."

Addressing the Envelope. The illustration on page 612 shows five popular styles of envelope addresses. They are:

1. Single-spaced, block-form, four-line address. Note the method of emphasizing the city and the state.
2. Single-spaced, indented, four-line address. This form is used with indented letters when the address is written in four lines. Note the method of emphasizing the city and the state.
3. Double-spaced, indented, three-line address, showing one placement of the attention line.
4. Single-spaced, block-form, four-line address, showing one placement of the attention line. Note the extra space before the last line. This extra space makes mail sorting easier.
5. Double-spaced, indented, three-line address. This form is used with indented letters when the address is written in three lines. Note the *Hold for Arrival* notation.

Special Lines on the Envelope. When an attention line is a part of the address, it may be typed either on the line immediately following the company name or on a separate line in the lower left corner of the envelope.

An *In Care of* line may be typed in either of the positions indicated for the attention line on the envelope. If space permits, it is better to spell out *In Care of* instead of using the symbol *c/o.* Do not use the percentage sign % for this purpose.

Other special lines, such as *Hold for Arrival* and *Please Forward*, are usually typed in the lower left corner.

Why Some Mailings Never Arrive. An official of the Chicago post office, explaining why millions of pieces of mail each year are undeliverable, de-

layed in delivery, or returned to the sender, points out that eight to ten per cent of the staff in the main Chicago office alone spends full time correcting common preventable errors. The six biggest causes of mailing wastes, he asserts, are these:

1. Failure to give street and number in the envelope address.
2. Failure to put the complete return address in the upper left corner of the envelope.
3. Careless errors in typewriting or handwriting addresses.
4. Omission of North, South, East, or West (N., S., E., W.) street directions.
5. Failure to place the necessary postage on the envelope (millions of pieces of unstamped mail are received yearly by the Chicago post office).
6. Failure to wrap parcel-post packages securely.

Window Envelopes. The window envelope—a special type—has a transparent "window" (of cellophane or similar material) at or near the center of its face, permitting the address typed on the letter itself to show through. The chief advantage of the window is that it cuts out the cost of addressing the envelope by letting the address on the letter serve the purpose. The window envelope is popular for sending out checks, invoices, bills, and similar items. Its chief disadvantage for use with letters is that it requires special framing, spacing, and folding which, in turn, may force the letter layout far out of balance.

Folding the Sheet. The size of the envelope largely controls how the letter must be folded. The folding method should economize time and energy and should make the unfolding easy for the receiver. An unfolded letter must be neat and attractive as it comes forth from the envelope and first strikes the eye. The folding directions on page 613 are recommended.

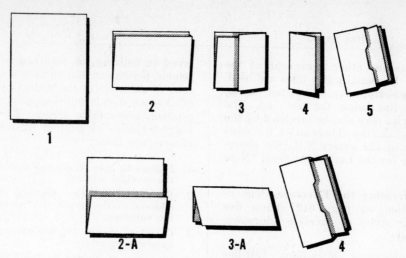

Folding the Sheet for Small and Large Envelopes

FOLDING FOR A SMALL ENVELOPE

(Size: Approximately 6½ by 3⅝ inches)

1. Place the sheet face up on the desk.
2. Fold the sheet up from the bottom to a point a half inch from the top edge. With the edges even at the sides, crease the fold.
3. Fold from right to left not quite a third of the width of the sheet.
4. Fold from left to right, leaving a margin of about a half inch at the right.
5. Hold the envelope in your left hand, face downward, flap open toward the right; take the letter in your right hand last crease at left, last fold up; insert it into the envelope.

FOLDING FOR A LARGE ENVELOPE

(Size: Approximately 9½ by 4⅛ inches)

1. Place the sheet face up on the desk.
2-A. Fold the bottom third of the sheet toward the top. With the edges even at the sides, crease the fold.
3-A. Fold the top downward not quite a third of the sheet. With the edges even at the sides, crease the fold.
4. Hold the envelope in your left hand, face downward, flap open toward the right; take the letter in your right hand, last crease at left, last fold up; insert it into the envelope.

The folding methods illustrated above assure the natural reading position of the letter, top edge up, as the sheet unfolds.

Special Folds for Window Envelopes. Fold an 8½- by 11-inch sheet of stationery for a window envelope measuring 9½ by 4⅛ inches as follows:

1. A fold is made from the bottom, one third the length of the sheet.
2. The top third of the sheet is folded backwards from the first fold so that the address will be on the outside.

To place the same sheet in a window envelope 7½ by 3⅞ inches, about one and a half inches of the right end of the folded letter is folded back in order that the inside address will appear in the proper position in the window of the envelope. The following illustration shows how a properly folded sheet is inserted in a window envelope.

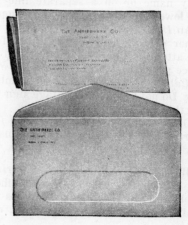

Communication Problems

● **1.** From the information given in each of the following items, type or write in the style specified an appropriate inside address, salutation, subject (when supplied), and complimentary close. Refer to pages 621-626 for correct addresses and salutations for special groups. Use the appropriate city of your own state in the address.

BLOCK STYLE; OPEN

a. Dr. Sherman W. Layman, President of City College, 333 University Drive, 101 Administration Building.

b. J. Kirk Fielding. Fielding is Commanding General of the Third Army Air Base with offices in the Federal Building.

MODIFIED BLOCK STYLE; MIXED

c. Thomas C. Pine, M. D. Doctor Pine's office is in the Medical Arts Building, 3205 First Street.

d. Professor Mary O'Connell. Miss O'Connell is Director of the School of Social Service at City College. Her office is located at 34 Campus Terrace.

e. W. B. Henry, a prominent Protestant minister, who resides at 2101 Mark Twain Boulevard.

OFFICIAL STYLE; MIXED

f. Henry C. Coon, a justice of the Supreme Court, who resides at 123 Lake Street. Use his home address.

g. Joseph Callan. Callan is the mayor of the city. He receives his official mail at 400 City Hall.

INDENTED STYLE; CLOSE

h. Peter L. James. He holds the ecclesiastical title of Monsignor and resides at the rectory of St. James Church in St. James Square.

i. Stephen O. Feldman, Ph.D. Feldman is a rabbi at Congregation B'Nai Israel, 22 Field Street.

j. Sister Mary Paul, O. F. M. She is Superintendent of Mt. Mercy Hospital for the Poor.

● **2.** Copy the following courtesy introduction in each of the following styles:

   a. Block; open punctuation.
   b. Modified block with blocked paragraphs; open punctuation.
   c. Modified block with indented paragraphs; mixed punctuation.
   d. Indented; close punctuation.

   (Current Date)   Mr. Robert J. Goodwin   The Acme Electric Company   126 North Devers Avenue   Chicago 8, Illinois   Dear Mr. Goodwin

   Mr. Paul W. White, a personal friend and business acquaintance of mine, is moving next week to Chicago to assume his new duties as the office manager of the Pencol Oil Company. For the past four years Paul has been the assistant to the office manager of the Grew Tool Company in this city.

   Paul is a fellow member of the National Office Management Association and has been most active with this group.

Paul plans to telephone you when he gets to Chicago. At that time I would appreciate it if you would make the necessary arrangements for him to accompany you to the next monthly meeting of NOMA and introduce him to the group.

I shall appreciate whatever courtesies you extend him. Sincerely yours   William G. Cramer, President   NOMA Chapter of Detroit

Suggestions: In setting up this problem solution, use blank sheets of 8½- by 11-inch typewriting paper. Preferably type your work, observing the picture-frame rule for pleasing appearance. Be sure that the keys of your typewriter are clean so that nothing will detract from the neatness and readability of your letters. Use as your guide the layout styles illustrated on pages 596 and 598.

● 3. Copy the introduction given in Problem 2 in the NOMA Simplified style. In setting up your solution, keep in mind the suggestions in Problem 2. From your reading of the book you will remember that this particular style has no salutation or complimentary close. Let the subject line read: INTRODUCING MR. PAUL R. WHITE. Do not use a period after the subject line. Before starting this problem, review what the book has to say about this particular style (page 597). Note the punctuation used in the example on page 598.

● 4. Assume that you have accepted the appointment to be the local chairman of the Red Feather Drive in your community. One of your first responsibilities is to extend a written invitation to a group of prominent civic leaders in business, government, and church circles to serve with you in this worth-while community activity. Here is the invitation you plan to use in requesting their cooperation:

Because of your long experience in community work and because of your keen interest in the progress of our community, will you attend a meeting to be held at the Civic Center on Monday, October 6, for the purpose of discussing initial plans for this year's Red Feather Drive?

This gathering will be attended by various civic leaders like yourself and by others who are interested in community pride and welfare.

Your presence and wise counsel will do much to make the meeting a success. The place is the Civic Center, and the time is one o'clock, Monday, October 6.

Directions: It is your desire to have this invitation a formal and dignified impression upon your readers. You decide, therefore, to have the message set up in the official style illustrated on page 598 of this book. You have decided on this particular form because you plan to use the letterhead of your company for prestige purposes. To lessen the "business" look, you plan to shift the traditional placement of the inside address to the official style.

Suggestions: Keep in mind that this is an invitation going to a number of different individuals. Decide upon a standard salutation, complimentary close, and signature. Note, too, that you are writing on your company letterhead in a civic capacity. Follow the form of punctuation illustrated for this style on page 598 of the book. Use your instructor's name and address for the inside address. Date the letter *September 25.*

Section 2

Condensed Letter-and-Transcription Guide
(A General Reference)

The business executive and his secretary are concerned with a common aim: to produce effective communication. A business message produced by an expert dictator and an expert secretary always possesses two notable qualities:

1. Attractive external form.
2. Effective internal content.

The guides to good usage and accurate punctuation provided on the following pages are definite and should be consistently followed. These guides are based on authoritative practice and on a consensus of leading business organizations.

Note that the letter on page 618 has been prepared in modified block style with indented paragraphs and that the rules on this and the following pages are keyed to that letter.

Guides for the Illustrated Letter on Page 618

1. Make the layout look like a picture in a frame. Let it assume the same proportions as those of the sheet upon which it is typed.
2. Some cities are now divided into postal zones. If your message is addressed to such a city, include the postal zone number in both letter address and envelope address. (Do *not* place a comma before the zone number.) Examples of the correct form:

   New York 7, New York
   Chicago 17, Illinois

3. Center the date line immediately under the letterhead or place it so that it ends even with the right margin. In either case type it on the second line (a double space) below the city and the state line of the letterhead.
4. Spell names of months in full, both in the date line and in the body of the letter.
5. Use *st, d, nd, rd,* and *th* after the number of the day only when the month is not mentioned. Omit at other times.

6. Separate with a comma the day of the month from the year.
7. Omit punctuation after the year at the end of the date line if the letter is written with open or mixed punctuation. Insert a comma after the year within a sentence.
8. Type the address in block form even with the left margin and three to eight single spaces below the date line, depending on the length of the message.
9. Make the several lines of the address as nearly equal as possible. To this end you may place the addressee's title
   (a) on the same line as his name,
   (b) on the following line preceding the name of the firm, or
   (c) on a line by itself.
   Your decision will depend on the length of the title, the length of the addressee's name, and the length of the name of the firm.
10. Separate with a comma the addressee's title from his name or the firm name as the case may be.

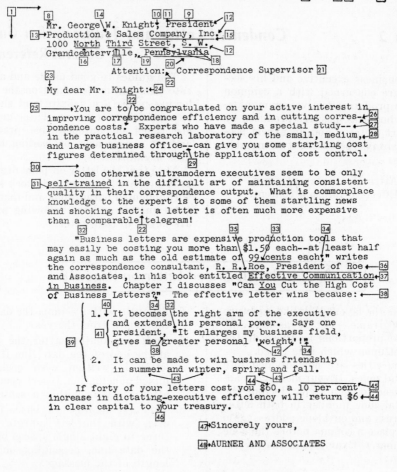

Illustrated Letter

The numbered items shown on this letter are discussed on pages 617, 619, and 620.

11. Capitalize the principal words of titles and the names of departments, as:

    Credit Department
    Sales Promotion Department

12. Use no punctuation after the lines in the address except after permissible abbreviations.

13. It is good practice to write the firm name as it appears on the firm's own letterhead.

14. The sign & (and) is permissible only when the firm itself uses it.

15. It is permissible to abbreviate *Incorporated* (*Inc.*) and *Limited* (*Ltd.*), preceding them with a comma. Only when they occur within a sentence are they followed by a comma. Write in full the words *Company* and *Corporation*.

16. Write in full the words *North, South, East,* and *West* in street directions.

17. Spell out the number naming a street, if it is ten or below; for eleven or above, use figures. Example:

    345 South 47th Street

18. For postal sections of a city, use initials followed by periods, but do not abbreviate *Avenue, Boulevard,* or *Street.*

19. Type the state on the same line as the city in the address. Separate with a comma the state (or country) from the city. It is wise to use a three-line address on the envelope; if there is no street address, put the state on a separate line.

20. Write in full the names of states. Exception: the District of Columbia may be abbreviated *D. C.*

21. If an attention line is necessary, center it on the second line (a double space) below the address. In the block style of layout the attention line is typed even with the left margin. Capitalize only the principal words. Choose the proper salutation without regard to the attention line.

22. Leave two spaces after a colon, exclamation point, question mark, or period (except a period following an initial or abbreviation). Leave one space after a comma or semicolon. Leave two spaces between sentences.

23. The first word of a salutation is always capitalized. Note that the word *dear* is not capitalized unless it is the first word.

24. Type the salutation even with the left margin on the second line (a double space) below the last line of the address, or a double space below the attention line if one is used. The salutation is followed by a colon in mixed and close punctuation. *Do not* use a hyphen.

25. Begin the body of the message on the second line (a double space) below the salutation. Indent the paragraphs five to (not more than) ten spaces for the indented style of letter. For the block style begin the body even with the left margin.

26. To maintain a reasonably even right margin requires occasional hyphenation. Avoid too many hyphens. Divide a word only when it is necessary.

27. A hyphen or dash is placed not at the beginning of a line but at the end of the preceding line.

28. Use the comma to point off words or word groups used in a series when there are at least three units. Always place a comma before *and, or,* or *nor* in a series of three or more.

29. The dash is made by typing the hyphen twice, without spacing before or after.

30. Double-space between paragraphs.

31. The hyphen is used to link together compound words.

32. Capitalize the first word of a direct quotation.

33. Use figures and write in full the word *cents.* (In tabulating work the characters *99¢* or *$.99* are acceptable.)

34. At the end of a quotation a comma or a period should precede the quotation mark. A semicolon or a colon should follow the quotation mark. In a quotation, a question mark or an exclamation point is placed inside the quotation marks when a part of the quoted matter; outside when not a part.

35. Set off with commas a word or words in apposition.

36. Within a sentence a title following the name is both preceded and followed by a comma.

37. When referring to articles and books, it is customary to place in quotations the titles of articles, short monographs, and chapters; and to underline or type entirely in capitals the titles of books. Such titles are preceded and followed by commas only when they are in apposition.

38. Use a colon after the words that introduce an enumeration or a long quotation. Use a comma before a short quotation.

39. Block in and center enumerations and long quotations. Double-space between paragraphs.

40. Place a period after a point number of an enumeration, and space either once or twice after the period.

41. Begin the second and following lines of centered material directly under the first letter of the first word of the first line.

42. A quotation within a quotation is enclosed in single quotation marks (' '). Double quotation marks are placed with relation to other punctuation marks according to Guide No. 34. Examples:

    I said, "He 'met his Waterloo.'"
    He asked, "Who shouted, 'Help'?"

43. Seasons of the year are capitalized only when they are personified. Example:

    "Harsh Winter and his minions fade
    . . . and gentle Spring takes o'er
    her reign."

44. Express even sums of money without the decimal and ciphers.

45. Express percentages in figures; spell out *per cent*.

46. Use a hyphen to connect two or more words compounded to express a single idea.

47. Type the complimentary close on the second line (a double space) below the last line of the body of the message. Begin it at the horizontal center or, if the closing lines are long, five spaces to the left of center.

48. Type the company name in all capital letters a double space below the complimentary close, beginning it even with the beginning of the complimentary close. The modern practice is to omit the company name in the closing lines, especially when letterhead paper is used.

49. Type the official title on the fourth line below the company name, beginning it even with the beginning of the company name.

50. Type the signature identification and the stenographer's reference initials flush with the left margin and on a line even with the dictator's official title, or a double space below.

51. Type the word *Enclosure*, or the abbreviation *Enc.* or *Encl.* (if this notation is necessary), flush with the left margin a double space below the signature identification. More than one enclosure is indicated by adding the correct figure:

    Enclosure 2
    Enc. 4
    Encl. 6

52. The phrase *Copy to* or *Copies to* (*cc* or *CC*) may appear preceding the name or names of individuals or firms to whom carbon copies are being sent. Type the phrase flush with the left margin a single space, or a double space (if the message is short), below the item above it.

Section 3

Correct Addresses and Salutations* for Special Groups**

THE PRESIDENT OF THE UNITED STATES

ADDRESS | SALUTATION

The President
The White House
Washington 25, D. C.

The Honorable Dwight D. Eisenhower
The White House
Washington 25, D. C.

Sir:
To the President:
Mr. President:
Dear Mr. President:
My dear President Eisenhower:

VICE PRESIDENT OF THE UNITED STATES

The Vice President
United States Senate
Washington 25, D. C.

The Honorable the Vice President of the
United States
Washington 25, D. C.

The Honorable Richard M. Nixon
Vice President of the United States
Washington 25, D. C.

Sir:
My dear Sir:
Dear Sir:
Mr. Vice President:
My dear Mr. Vice President:
Dear Mr. Vice President:

THE CABINET

The Honorable the Secretary of State
Washington 25, D. C.

The Honorable John Foster Dulles
Secretary of State
Washington 25, D. C.

Sir:
My dear Sir:
Dear Sir:
My dear Mr. Secretary:

The Deputy Secretary of the
Department of Defense
Washington 25, D. C.

The Honorable Donald A. Quarles
Assistant Secretary of the
Department of Defense
Washington 25, D. C.

Sir:
My dear Sir:
Dear Sir:
My dear Mr. Quarles:
Dear Mr. Quarles (but *never* Mr.
Secretary) :

THE SUPREME COURT

The Chief Justice of the United States
Washington 13, D. C.

The Honorable Earl Warren
Chief Justice of the Supreme Court of the
United States.
Washington 13, D. C.

Sir:
Mr. Chief Justice:

The Honorable Hugo L. Black
Associate Justice of the Supreme Court
Washington 13, D. C.

The Honorable Hugo L. Black
Justice, Supreme Court of the United States
Washington 13, D. C.

Sir:
Mr. Justice:
Your Honor:
My dear Mr. Justice:
My dear Justice Black:

* All salutations are listed in the order of decreasing formality.
** Useful Supplementary References: (1) C. O. Sylvester Mawson, *The Secretary's Guide to Current Modern Usage*; (2) H. L. Mencken, *The American Language*; (3) Webster's *New International Dictionary* (Second edition, Unabridged).

SPEAKER OF THE HOUSE

ADDRESS	SALUTATION
The Honorable the Speaker of the House of Representatives Washington 25, D. C.	Sir: My dear Sir: Dear Sir:
The Speaker of the House of Representatives Washington 25, D. C.	Mr. Speaker: My dear Mr. Speaker: Dear Mr. Speaker:
The Honorable Sam Rayburn Speaker of the House of Representatives Washington 25, D. C.	My dear Mr. Rayburn: Dear Mr. Rayburn: (informal)

OTHER WASHINGTON OFFICIALS

The Honorable Frank J. Lausche The United States Senate Washington 25, D. C.	Sir: My dear Sir: Dear Sir:
Senator Frank J. Lausche The United States Senate Washington 25, D. C.	My dear Mr. Senator: My dear Senator: Dear Senator:
The Honorable Frank J. Lausche United States Senator Cleveland, Ohio (When at headquarters away from Washington)	My dear Senator Lausche: Dear Senator Lausche:
The Honorable Joseph W. Martin, Jr. The House of Representatives Washington 25, D. C.	Sir: My dear Sir: Dear Sir:
Representative Joseph W. Martin, Jr. The House of Representatives Washington 25, D. C.	My dear Congressman: My dear Representative Martin: Dear Representative Martin: My dear Mr. Martin:
The Honorable Joseph W. Martin, Jr. Representative in Congress North Attleboro, Massachusetts (When at headquarters away from Washington)	Dear Mr. Martin: (informal)
The Honorable Lawrence G. Derthick Commissioner of Education Department of Health, Education, and Welfare Washington 25, D. C.	Sir: My dear Sir: Dear Sir: My dear Mr. Commissioner: My dear Mr. Derthick: Dear Mr. Derthick: (informal)

STATE OFFICIALS

ADDRESS	SALUTATION
His Excellency The Governor of Montana Helena, Montana	Sir: My dear Sir: Dear Sir:
The Honorable J. Hugo Aronson Governor of Montana Helena, Montana	My dear Governor Aronson: Dear Governor Aronson: Dear Governor: (informal)
The Honorable the Governor of Montana Helena, Montana	

ADDRESS	SALUTATION
The Honorable John W. Chapman Lieutenant Governor of Illinois Springfield, Illinois	Sir: My dear Sir: Dear Sir:
The Lieutenant Governor of the State of Illinois Springfield, Illinois	
The Honorable Adrian Burke Associate Judge of the Court of Appeals New York, New York	Sir: My dear Sir: Dear Sir: My dear Judge Burke: Dear Judge Burke:
The Honorable Mark French The State Senate Madison 1, Wisconsin	Sir: My dear Sir: Dear Sir:
Senator Mark French Senate Chamber The State Capitol Madison 1, Wisconsin	My dear Mr. Senator: Dear Senator: My dear Senator French: Dear Senator French:
The Honorable George Reed Member of the Assembly Harrisburg, Pennsylvania	Sir: My dear Sir: Dear Sir:
Representative George Reed *or* Assemblyman George Reed Assembly Chamber The State Capitol Harrisburg, Pennsylvania	My dear Representative Reed: Dear Representative Reed: My dear Mr. Reed: Dear Mr. Reed: (informal)

CITY OFFICIALS

The Honorable Donald Clancy Mayor of the City of Cincinnati City Hall Cincinnati 2, Ohio	Sir: My dear Sir: Dear Sir: My dear Mr. Mayor: Dear Mr. Mayor:
The Mayor of the City of Cincinnati City Hall Cincinnati 2, Ohio	My dear Mayor Clancy: Dear Mayor Clancy: (informal)

EDUCATORS

ADDRESS	SALUTATION
President (*of a College or University*) Dr. Fred D. Fagg, Jr. President of University of Southern California Los Angeles 7, California	My dear Sir: Dear Sir: My dear President Fagg: Dear President Fagg:
M. E. Sadler, LL.D. (*or if not an LL.D., use the initials of his highest degree*) President, Texas Christian University Fort Worth 9, Texas	

Doctor of Philosophy (*or Laws, or Medicine*)
Samuel J. Warren, Ph.D. (*or* LL.D., *or*
    M.D.) *or* Dr. Samuel J. Warren *or* (to
    man and wife)
Dr. and Mrs. Samuel J. Warren
1416 Beckwith Avenue
Los Angeles 49, California
	My dear Sir:
	Dear Sir:
	My dear Dr. Warren
	Dear Dr. Warren: *and*
	Dear Dr. and Mrs. Warren:

ADDRESS   SALUTATION

Doctor of Divinity
W. R. Robinson, D.D. *or*   My dear Sir:
Dr. W. R. Robinson *or*   Dear Sir:
The Reverend Dr. W. R. Robinson   My dear Dr. Robinson:
(Specific address here)   Dear Dr. Robinson:

Professor (*in a College or University*)
Professor Herman Underwood   My dear Sir:
School of Business   Dear Sir:
Indiana University   My dear Professor Underwood:
Bloomington, Indiana   Dear Professor Underwood:

W. E. McKendrick, Ph.D. (*or* LL.D.,
    M.D., etc., using only the initials of
    his highest degree)
Professor of Accounting
University of California
Los Angeles 24, California

CHURCHMEN

Bishop (*Protestant Episcopal*)
To the Right Reverend Horace W. B.   Right Reverend and dear Sir:
    Donegan   My dear Bishop Donegan:
Bishop of New York   Dear Bishop Donegan: (informal)

Bishop (*Methodist*)
Reverend Bishop Hazen G. Werner   Dear Sir:
Bishop of the Ohio Annual Conference   My dear Bishop Werner:
438 Rowlands Building   Dear Bishop Werner:
12 North Third Street
Columbus 15, Ohio

Bishop (*Anglican*)
The Right Reverend the Lord Bishop of   My Lord Bishop:
    (name of bishopric here)   My Lord:
(Specific postal address here)

Bishop (*Scottish*)
The Right Reverend Bishop (name of   Right Reverend Sir:
    church official here)
(Specific postal address here)

Clergyman (*Protestant*)
The Reverend W. B. Waltham   Reverend Sir: (formal)
2001 Park Avenue   My dear Sir:
Cleveland 10, Ohio   Dear Sir:
    or (if a doctor of divinity)   My dear Mr. (*or* Dr.) Waltham:
The Reverend Dr. W. B. Waltham, etc.   Dear Mr. (*or* Dr.) Waltham:

(*Note:* Most authorities disapprove the use of Reverend with the last name
alone. There is also a well-defined preference for spelling the word Reverend
in full.)

Rabbi   Reverend Sir: (formal)
Rabbi S. W. Stern   My dear Sir:
The Reverend S. W. Stern   Dear Sir:
(Place specific address here)   My dear Rabbi Stern:
                                                   Dear Rabbi Stern:

(*Note:* If a doctor's degree is held, *Dr.* may be substituted for *Rabbi.*)

ROMAN CATHOLIC HIERARCHY *

ADDRESS   SALUTATION

Pope
His Holiness Pope Pius XII   Most Holy Father:
Vatican City   Your Holiness:
Rome, Italy

Cardinal
His Eminence Francis Cardinal Spellman   Your Eminence:
St. Patrick's Cathedral   My Lord Cardinal: (to cardinals
481 Fifth Avenue   of foreign countries)
New York 22, New York

(*Note:* Such salutations as My Lord, Your Lordship, My Lord Cardinal, etc., are not ordinarily used in the United States of America, but should be used by an American writing to dignitaries of foreign countries entitled to such a title.)

Archbishop
Most Reverend Albert G. Meyer   Your Excellency:
2000 West Wisconsin Avenue
Milwaukee 3, Wisconsin

Bishop
Most Reverend Matthew Francis Brady,   Your Excellency:
    D.D.
St. Joseph Cathedral
Manchester, New Hampshire

Monsignor
The Right Reverend Monsignor   Right Reverend and dear
    Carl J. Ryan, Ph.D.   Monsignor:
5418 Moeller Avenue
Norwood 12, Ohio

Priest
Very Reverend Valentine Scherrer *or*   Dear Reverend Father:
Reverend Valentine Scherrer   Dear Father Scherrer:
St. Peter's Church in the Loop   Dear Father:
110 West Madison Avenue
Chicago 2, Illinois

Superior of Sister Order
Mother M. Angela, Mother General *or*   Dear Mother General:
Mother M. Anne, Superior General *or*   Dear Mother Superior:
Sister M. Gertrude, Superior   Dear Sister Superior:
1863 Maple Avenue
Philadelphia 37, Pennsylvania

Sister
Sister Mary Priscilla   Dear Sister:
St. John's School
459 Cass Street, North
Trenton 5, New Jersey

* The list of proper titles and salutations for churchmen of the Roman Catholic Hierarchy has been checked for acceptability by competent and eminent authorities. The list is believed to be a safe and reliable guide. It has, according to the confirmation of the *Catholic School Journal*, the consent of the Hierarchy and the Clergy.

THE ARMED FORCES

ADDRESS	SALUTATION
General Nathan F. Twining Chairman of the Joint Chiefs of Staff United States Armed Forces Washington 25, D. C.	Sir: My dear Sir: Dear Sir: My dear General Twining:
General Maxwell D. Taylor Chief of Staff United States Army Washington 25, D. C.	
Admiral Arleigh A. Burke Chief of Naval Operations Navy Department Washington 25, D. C.	Sir: My dear Sir: Dear Sir: My dear Admiral Burke:
General Thomas D. White Chief of Staff United States Air Force Washington 25, D. C.	

Special Note I: In the case of Lieutenant General, Major General, Brigadier General, Vice Admiral, Rear Admiral, follow the same form as in addressing a full General or Admiral, using one of the salutations shown above. Use the salutation *My dear General* (or *Admiral*) *Blank,* if you wish to use the surname in the salutation; NOT *My dear Major General Blank;* NOT *Dear Rear Admiral Blank.* The same rule applies in forming the salutation for Lieutenant Colonel (Army) and Lieutenant Commander (Navy).

Special Note II: In the case of Colonel, Major, Captain, Lieutenant (Army); and Captain, Commander, Lieutenant, Lieutenant (J. G.), and Ensign (Navy):

For army, air force, marine, navy, or coastguard officers of these ranks, liberal current practice approves a salutation using the appropriate designation of rank or title. Examples:

Dear Colonel Royce: Dear Commander Lowe:
Dear Captain Fields: Dear Lieutenant Grant:

Enlisted Man: Army

Private Frank M. Baker (Army Serial Number) Company G, 169th Infantry APO 711, Care of Postmaster New York, New York	Dear Sir: My dear Mr. Baker: Dear Mr. Baker: Dear Frank: (Personal)

Enlisted Man: Marine Corps

Private Richard D. Anderson, USMC U. S. Marine Corps Unit No. (Insert Number) Care of Postmaster San Francisco, California	Dear Sir: My dear Mr. Anderson: Dr. Mr. Anderson: Dear Dick: (Personal)

Enlisted Man: Navy or Air Force

Gary M. Collins, Seaman First Class
    [or appropriate Air Force designation]
(Naval Unit or Ship)
    [or appropriate Air Force unit]
Care of Postmaster
New York, New York
	Dear Sir:
	
	My dear Mr. Collins:
	
	Dear Mr. Collins:
	Dear Gary: (Personal)

Word Division: How to Divide Words at Line Endings

One cannot serve long in a business office without discovering why a knowledge of correct word division is necessary. To make the right margin of a letter, a report, or any other type of manuscript relatively even, it is often necessary to divide words. When a word is divided at the end of a line, the division is indicated by a hyphen following the syllable or syllables at the end of the line.

Word Division Is Called Syllabication. We really have syllabication of three kinds: (1) Dictionaries show *all* the syllables into which a word may be divided. For readability, however, it may not be desirable to divide at a point permitted by the dictionary. (2) In *printed* material the left margin and the right margin must be exactly even. To keep these margins even, it is now and then necessary to divide a word at a point that does interfere somewhat with the readability of the material. (3) In *type-*

written material, unlike books, the right margin does not have to be exactly even. Hence it becomes possible for the typist to make a choice. As a result a set of principles has been developed for the syllabication of typewritten material. The purpose of these principles is to make the right margin as attractive as possible without interfering with the readability of the copy.

In word division there are certain rules that must always be observed, and there are certain other rules that it is desirable to follow but that may be broken if following them would make the right margin too uneven. A person typing a letter or a manuscript (or writing it in longhand) is not forced to have an exactly even right margin; therefore he can usually follow the second group of "desirable" rules as well as the first group of "must" rules.

The dictionary is the final authority on the syllabication of words.

"Must" Rules for Dividing Words

1. Divide only between syllables.
2. Never separate a single-letter syllable at the beginning or the end of a word from the remainder of the word.

RIGHT	WRONG
above	a-bove
steady	stead-y

3. Never separate a two-letter syllable at the end of a word from the remainder of the word.

RIGHT	WRONG
really	real-ly
teacher	teach-er

Since a single-letter syllable at the beginning or end of a word and a two-letter syllable at the end of a word are never separated, it follows that a four-letter word is never divided and that a five-letter word is seldom divided.

4. Do not separate a syllable that does not contain a vowel from the remainder of the word. Do not divide contractions.

RIGHT	WRONG
doesn't	does-n't
wouldn't	would-n't

Desirable Rules for Dividing Words

5. Put enough of the word to be divided on the first line to suggest what the completed word will be.

THIS DIVISION	RATHER THAN
clearing-house	clear-inghouse
diffi-cult	dif-ficult
gentle-men	gen-tlemen
recom-mend	rec-ommend
stenog-rapher	ste-nographer

6. Avoid dividing words at the end of more than two successive lines, or the final word on a page.

7. Avoid separating a two-letter syllable at the beginning of a word from the remainder of the word.

8. Avoid dividing hyphened words and compounds, such as: *eight-sixteenths, brother-in-law, record-breaking*, and *self-explanatory*, except at the hyphen.

9. Avoid dividing a surname and separating titles, initials, or degrees from a surname.

•

•

•

Section 5   *Formal Papers and Reports: Guide for Quotations, Footnotes, and Reference Lists*

Quotations

Quotations should be brief and pertinent. They must be perfectly accurate and should be verified by direct comparison with the sources. An omission is permissible if the sense of the whole passage is not distorted by it. It is customary to use omission marks (. . .) to show that part of a quotation has been dropped.

Omission marks, also called ellipses, are devices signifying the omission of letters or of words in quoted material. Three marks or dots (. . .) are used to signify an omission at the beginning of the quoted discourse or at any other point, when the omitted portion or section does not end on a period. Four marks or dots (. . . .) are used when the omitted portion or section does end on a period. An editorial explanation within a quotation is enclosed in square brackets [ ]:

"President [Arthur W.] Sherwood pioneered the new wage scale."

If parentheses are used, the reader understands that the material enclosed, as well as the parentheses, was taken verbatim from the original source:

"President Sherwood (always a bold executive) pioneered the new wage scale."

Footnotes

Footnotes are used (1) to enable subsequent students to take up an investigation, (2) to explain and amplify matters referred to in the main text, and (3) to protect the writer against any possible charge of plagiarism or improper use of his materials.

They should be attached to important statements of fact and to any inferences or interpretations borrowed from other writers. In brief articles they should be numbered consecutively. The index number should be written above the line and at the end of the passage to which it refers. In books and theses the numbering usually begins anew at the beginning of each chapter.

If only one or two references are made to footnotes, it is permissible to use the asterisk (*) and the double asterisk (**). It is also permissible to use the dagger (†) and the double dagger (‡) to identify footnote references.

Placement of Footnote References. Footnotes should not be allowed to fall below a one-inch margin at the bottom of the page. Separate the footnotes from the regular manuscript page by a line made through the use of the underscore key. This line should extend from the left margin at least to the center of the page and preferably to the right margin.

Spacing. Single-space footnotes. They may be written flush with the left margin, the footnote numeral and the beginning of the first line being indented five spaces; or the entire footnote may be indented five spaces.

Footnotes Illustrated. The first time any source of information is referred to in a footnote, the complete reference should be given. The approved forms are described below and illustrated on page 630.

Books. When the footnote refers to a book, write the source of information in this order: the author's name, the name of the book, the place and name of the publisher, the copyright date, the volume (if any), and the page number.

Observe these points in the footnote: (1) the author's name is not transposed (as it is in the alphabetical bibliography), (2) the name of the place of publication is followed by a colon, although commas are used elsewhere, (3) the place, the name of the publisher, and the date of publication are given in parentheses.

If a book has gone through more than one edition, the number of the edition is indicated immediately after the title by the words: *3d ed.* or *10th ed.*

Magazine Articles and Periodicals. When the footnote refers to a magazine article, write the source of information in this order: the author's name, the name of the article, the name of the magazine, the volume number, the month and year of issue (in parentheses), and the page number.

When the footnote refers to a periodical, write the information in this order: the name of the periodical; the city in which it is published (unless this is already evident in the name of the periodical); the month, day, and year of publication; and the page number.

Repetition of Footnotes. Subsequent footnotes to the same authority should be abbreviated as much as is consistent with clearness.

Ibid. When two or more citations from the same authority immediately follow one another, it is permissible to use the Latin abbreviation *ibid.* (*ibidem*, meaning *in the same place*) for the second and later citations.

Note that *ibid.* is used only when the footnote refers to a book cited immediately above it.

op. cit. When two (or more) citations from the same authority are separated by a different citation falling between, it is customary to use the Latin abbreviation *op. cit.* (*opere citato*, meaning *in the work cited*) in the second of the two citations from the same authority.

loc. cit. The abbreviation *loc. cit.* (*loco citato*, meaning *in the place cited*) following an author's name, denotes a reference to the same work previously referred to and to the identical passage of the work.

References to Volume and Page. It is permissible to omit *Vol.* and *p.* when both items are given in one reference.

In a footnote referring to more than one authority, the items should be separated by semicolons.

Additional Use of Footnotes. It is customary also to use footnotes to discuss or amplify points in the text when such discussions or digressions, if incorporated in the body of the text, would complicate the presentation of the subject.

Model Footnotes

Ibid. refers to the source immediately preceding it. *Op. cit.* refers to a reference previously cited when other references intervene. *Loc. cit.* refers to the same passage in a reference previously cited.

BIBLIOGRAPHY

Three-Author Book →	Anderson, Chester Reed, Alta Gwinn Saunders, and Francis William Weeks. Business Reports, Third Edition. New York: McGraw-Hill Book Company, Inc., 1957.
One-Author Book →	Aurner, Robert R. Effective Communication in Business, Fourth Edition. Cincinnati: South-Western Publishing Company, 1958.
Newspaper Article →	Cincinnati Enquirer, December 10, 1958, pp. 38-39.
Articles in Periodicals →	Murphy, Herta A. "How to Help Cut Your Company's Letter Costs," University of Washington Business Review, Vol. 17, No. 5 (February, 1958), pp. 40-58.
	Riebel, John P. "Writing Star Reports," The ABWA Bulletin, Vol. XX, No. 2 (December, 1955), pp. 4-10.
Unpublished Material →	Silverthorn, James E. "The Basic Vocabulary of Written Business Communications." Ed.D. Thesis, Indiana University, 1955.

Model Reference List (Bibliography)

Reference Lists

A reference list (or bibliography), in which are listed the sources of information used in the preparation of the report or formal paper, should (if possible) accompany every piece of written work of any importance in which source material is employed.

The books, articles, periodicals, or documents listed should be arranged in alphabetical order by authors, editors, or titles (if the authors are anonymous or the sources are periodicals), unless the nature of the material requires a classified treatment. The items may be accompanied by a few words of description or criticism.

Exact information as to author, title, place, publisher, and year of publication should be given in order to identify each reference cited. In special cases (government documents, periodicals, etc.) even more information may be required in order to complete the positive identification of the works. The titles of books and periodicals are ordinarily underlined in manuscript or typewritten material and *printed in italics*; the titles of magazine articles are enclosed in quotation marks.

The correct form for listing books, magazine articles, and periodicals in the bibliography, with all necessary punctuation, is given in the illustration on page 630. Note that in the bibliography (1) the author's name is written last name first and (2) the punctuation differs from that in footnotes.

Section 6

Reading for Business Background

The Power of Books. You will be wise to recognize the power of books and to give yourself some background regarding the main trends of business thought as reflected in the literature of business. Make an effort to understand, just as far as possible, the significance of business in human life.

The reader who dips into Harry Scherman's *The Promises Men Live By*, Calkins' *Business the Civilizer*, Filene's *Successful Living in This Machine Age*, Selfridge's *Romance of Commerce*, Meeker's *Work of the Stock Exchange*, or Professor Ripley's *Main Street and Wall Street*, opens for himself a few of the thousand vistas down which he is privileged to look. The purpose of studying such literature is to unveil the meaning of business and to present its ideas in the proper setting.

Chief Aims in Reading the Literature of Business. The chief aims in acquainting oneself with the literature of business are these:

1. To strengthen the power to read with understanding and appreciation.
2. To familiarize oneself, through books and periodicals, with the body of business literature and with the progress of thought in the business world.
3. To improve the power of self-expression by stimulating thought and by discovering new information on which to base one's own writing and speaking. Clear thinking in the field of general ideas is stimulated by following the worthy and well-expressed thoughts of others. Clear thinking is as essential for effective self-expression as is a knowledge of facts and of models of form.
4. To familiarize oneself with rising ideals of life and conduct by becoming acquainted with rich personalities and admirable characters both inside and outside the world of business.

Hints on Rapid Reading. The more rapidly a person reads, the more he reads in a given time. Most of our knowledge is secured through reading. Much of our thinking is stimulated by what we read. Obviously, fast reading is important. Slow reading is no guaranty of careful reading. In fact the opposite is true. Rapid reading is in itself one of the best guaranties of good reading.

For the person who reads too slowly, dangers lurk. The mind is not absorbed, and the attention wanders away woolgathering. The mind gets from slow reading only a mental hodgepodge instead of a clear-cut impression.

Most people can with surprising ease increase their rate of reading. Experiments indicate that by a moderate amount of definite practice, with conscious effort to improve, a person can increase his speed of reading from 50 per cent to 100 per cent without losing the sense of the ideas he has read.

A good reader should be able to read ordinary textbook material at the rate of about 200 to 225 words a minute. He should also understand the meaning of what he is reading. Note the difference between talking and reading: businessmen seldom average better than 80 to 100 words a minute in their talk. But if they are properly drilled, they can easily read between 200 and 300 words of serious material a minute.

If you are a slow reader, your eyes probably stop too often in a line of print. To increase your reading speed, try making only three, or at most four, stops in a line. Practice on something easy. At first simply shift the eyes correctly without trying to pick up the meaning. Then begin to pick up some of the sense. If this process slows you down too much, go back to the simple three shifts of the eye in a line until you have established a firm new habit. Presently you will find yourself picking up the sense without conscious effort, and soon you will be reading much faster without losing any of the meaning. Do not expect instantaneous improvement. Be patient with yourself and your practice. You can check your progress by the mirror test.*

Avoid lip reading and movements of the throat. You can test at once whether you are a lip reader by placing a finger on your lips as you read. If you are silently pronouncing or whispering your words, you are slowing yourself to a reading crawl, whereas you should be racing fleetly along. To read fast, read with your eyes only.

* If you are curious to discover what kind of reader you are, try the following experiment:

The materials needed are one book and one mirror for each two people, who work in pairs, each successively testing the other's reading rate.

Sit at the desk, with the book open. Place the mirror on one page of the book. Hold the mirror and book at the proper reading angle. Read from the other page. Have the other person stand back of you and count, by looking into the mirror, how many times your eyes stop in reading a line of type. If your eyes stop *more* than four times, your reading rate is below the average. After a moment's practice the checker, who is standing behind, can easily follow your eyes as they cover a line and sweep back to the next. A few lines will show about how many pauses you average. When a person reads a simple novel, the eyes should not stop more than three times in each line. There should be one stop near the beginning, one in the middle, one near the end.

After your reading rate has been carefully checked and given to you, exchange places with the other person and repeat the test. The accuracy of the test can be checked at any time by requiring the person being tested to repeat orally the gist of the passage he has read. He must understand the meaning of what he is reading.

Do you have a report to prepare? Do you have an article to write? Do you have a speech to make? Not all the information needed can be kept in a private office. So the library is the logical starting place.

The modern library is not the simple one of yesterday. Wide new ranges of information now available make necessary a means of access. Your access to the fact-storehouse is furnished by guides and indexes, the tools of the swift worker. These tools tell him where to turn quickly for information. They help him to avoid the futility of hunting for hours for a fact that should be found in a few minutes.

But even the system of guides and indexes has become so elaborate that it is often confusing to the casual worker. The purpose of this article is to suggest the most basic general sources. This short selected general list constitutes a starting point for any investigation. It will suffice for the ordinary speech or paper, or it will point the way for a more detailed search into specific divisions of business. The businessman is often concerned with the latest information; this list accordingly emphasizes periodicals because magazines, newspapers, and bulletins contain much information that never appears in books or that is still too recent to have been published in book form.

Sources of Information and What They Contain

In using an index, if you do not find material under one head, try another. There is probably another logical key word. For instance, many references on "management" will not be found under that head but may, instead, be found under "business management," "administration," "business administration" "executive action," "executive decision making," and other variants.

A glance at the prefatory pages of each source will tell whether the entries are listed under author, title, or subject—or under all three—what magazines are indexed, whether books, pamphlets, etc., are included, and what the abbreviations mean. For further information, ask the librarian. That is her business, and she will be

glad to help. Before starting to work, ask the librarian if she has a special bibliography on your subject.

Every field has its own basic source —Moody's Investor Service in securities, *Labor Relations Reporter* for labor information, and *Standard Federal Tax Reports* for tax information. Such detailed titles are beyond the scope of this discussion, but the general guides listed will lead the way into any specialized fields desired.

Accountants' Index: Bibliography of all accounting literature printed in English. Increasing attention given to Canadian, British, and Australian articles. (Also use supplements in the *Journal of Accountancy*.) Most important source for accounting references.

* This material is adapted, by permission, from an article by Professor C. R. Anderson, for many years Secretary of the American Business Writing Association, in *Opinion and Comment*, Bureau of Economic and Business Research, University of Illinois.

Agricultural Index: With business so closely joined with agriculture, this index opens the door to source material not only in farm periodicals but also in some books, bulletins of experiment stations, Department of Agriculture, and universities, both foreign and domestic.

Ayer's Directory of American Newspapers and Periodicals: Detailed information about publications, including trade, class, technical, religious, fraternal. Gives circulation figures, date of publication, size of page. Descriptive and statistical matter about each state, county, and city, such as size, population, products, etc. Has some good maps.

Business Literature: An outstanding monthly business bibliographic aid prepared by the Newark, New Jersey, Business Library. Books, periodicals, and government publications on a specific topical business subject are listed and evaluated in each issue.

Business Bookshelf: A weekly column in the financial section of the *New York Times.* The best single source of book reviews of new business titles.

Cumulative Book Index: Standard list of books in print in the United States. Before 1928, it was called the *United States Catalog.* This index lists each book under author, title, and subject or subjects that describe the contents of the book. Published monthly and cumulated each year. Broadened to include books published in English throughout the world. Should be used to find the newest books on any subject.

Dictionary for Accounts: Author, Erich L. Kohler. A dictionary with alphabetized accounting terms and definitions.

Encyclopedia Americana: Excellent general encyclopedia, especially strong in business, science, and government.

Kept up-to-date by its supplement, *Americana Annual.*

If the *Americana* is not available, use the *Britannica,* which gives an exhaustive treatment of almost every topic of general interest.

An encyclopedia is always a good starting point in the search for information, not only because of the thorough and excellent material found there, but because at the end of many articles there are bibliographies which speed further research.

Encyclopedia of the Social Sciences: Contains articles written by specialists covering the whole field of the social sciences. Especially useful to the businessman in the fields of political science, economics, and possibly in law, geography, and social work. Good bibliographies.

Engineering Index: Especially useful to industrial management men in business. Articles on such subjects as production, management, report writing, etc., will be found in some excellent magazines. Indexes the best technical and engineering publications, including foreign.

Industrial Arts Index: A technical and industrial subject index to a selected list of engineering, trade, and business periodicals, books, and pamphlets. More specialized in the industrial field than the *Public Affairs Information Service (PAIS)* described below, but not so technical as the *Engineering Index* and does not contain so many foreign titles. The first source for general industrial subjects, although if time permits it should be used with *PAIS.*

The Management Almanac: Printed annually by the National Industrial Conference Board, is a handbook of facts for executives and labor officials.

A Manual of Style: University of Chicago Press. A widely used authority for manuscript and printing preparation.

Market Data Book: Primary information on industrial and trade markets, and the business publications serving them.

New York Times Index: An index to the thorough *New York Times.* Applies indirectly to all newspapers since they all handle current news on the same dates.

Public Affairs Information Service (PAIS): Probably the most useful and practical general index for the businessman. Indexes over 900 periodicals, as well as many books, pamphlets, government documents, etc., in the field of political science, economics, sociology, commerce, and finance.

Readers' Guide to Periodical Literature: Indexes general, nontechnical periodicals. Touches business primarily in the field of economics. Not a prolific source of information for specialized business topics, but oftentimes helpful for general business subjects.

Thomas' Register of American Manufacturers: The place to find who manufactures what, and where.

Statesman's Year Book: Descriptive and statistical information about the governments of the world, including size, political aspects, financial and industrial data. Good bibliography for further study.

Statistical Abstract of the United States: A digest of the most important statistical data gathered in the U. S.—population, education, finance, utilities, commerce, transportation, etc. Similar publications are issued by many foreign governments. For more detailed data, see Census reports.

United States Government Publications: Sources of Information for Libraries: Author, Ann M. Boyd. Comprehensive guide to the use of the myriad of government publications. Intended for students of library service, but affords considerable information for business and public administration persons.

Government Publications and Their Use: Author, Lawrence F. Schmeckebier; 2d rev. ed. Another good guide to government publications.

United States Government Publications; Monthly Catalog: A current, up-to-date listing of all government publications. Supplements the *Document Catalog,* which is the permanent and complete catalogue of all government publications but does not appear regularly.

World Almanac: A yearbook giving up-to-date facts and figures over an enormous range of subjects. Usually reliable. Available in any library. A useful, inexpensive book to own.

Additional Sources of Information for Business Reports

Library Work

1. Unabridged dictionary for concise information.
2. Encyclopedia as a treasure house of human knowledge (with valuable references and a bibliography).
3. Public-library catalog.
4. Private business libraries.
5. City, telephone, and trade directories.
6. Organization files. (Associations such as National Association of Credit Men, etc.)
7. Check list of United States Public Documents.
8. Federal, state, and municipal reports.
9. Bureau of Foreign and Domestic Commerce. (Consult Bureau's nearest district office or write Washington, D. C. for further information.)

Library Work (Continued)

10. Current periodicals and trade papers not yet indexed.
11. Printed and tabulated results of previous investigators in the field (to save needless duplication of effort).

Reference Books for Travel

1. Timetables (for schedules and maps showing lines operated and principal cities served).
2. *The Official Guide of the Railways*, containing (a) tables for railroads in other North American countries and in Cuba, (b) tables for airlines, with information about fares and connections with other types of carriers, (c) tables for steamship lines with dates of sailing and arrival.
3. Maps.
4. *Hotel Red Book* (current geographical classification of principal hotels, divided according to states of the United States and the provinces of Canada, and then according to cities).

Reference Books for Mail and Transportation

1. *United States Official Postal Guide.* Published by the United States Government Printing Office, Washington 25, D. C. Contains complete information on postal department services (including all classes of domestic and international service).

2. *Official Directory of the Railway Express Agency.* Lists all express offices in the United States alphabetically under the names of states, and contains carefully classified rate information.
3. *Express and Parcel Post Comparative Rate Guide.* Contains general information about express service, parcel-post service, air express service, and foreign mail, and facilitates the comparison of express and parcel-post rates from one shipping point to various points in the United States and Canada.
4. *Bullinger's Postal and Shipper's Guide.* Used in determining routes for freight shipments, since it is a compendium showing the railroads serving each city, town, or village, or (for a town or village not on a railroad) the nearest railroad station and the roads serving it.

Business Directories

1. City directories.
2. Directory of manufacturers.
3. Telephone directories.
4. Financial directories (such as credit rating books published by Dun and Bradstreet, Inc., and investment manuals published by Moody's Investors Service and the firm of Standard and Poor's).

Field Work

1. Personal interviews in the field of investigation.
2. Mailed questionnaires.

Index

How to Use PUNCTUATION MADE EASY!

On the next two pages is a highly condensed quick-reference table for the use of those who wish a source of punctuation information in easily accessible space. This table is of special value to executives, secretaries, and stenographers who use this book continuously as a reference.

PUNCTUATION

USE THE PERIOD: (Page 527)*

1. At the end of a declarative sentence.
2. At the end of an imperative sentence.
3. After all initials and after most abbreviations (*C.O.D., Inc., R. R. Ames* but *SEC*).
4. Between dollars and cents expressed in figures (*$8.75*).

USE THE COMMA: (Pages 528-529)

1. To point off a subordinate clause preceding its principal clause (clauses often introduced by words like *if, unless, since, because,* etc.).
2. To set off a nonrestrictive clause.
3. To set off a nonrestrictive appositive but not a restrictive appositive.
4. To separate coordinate clauses joined by one of the pure conjunctions (*and, but, for, or, neither, nor*).
5. To point off an introductory phrase containing a verb.
6. To point off a dependent word or word group that breaks the direct continuity of the sentence.
7. To point off parenthetic words, phrases, and clauses.
8. To point off words or word groups used in a series when there are at least three units.
9. To point off words used in direct address or in explaining other words.
10. To point off sentence elements that might be wrongly joined in reading if there were no commas.
11. To indicate the omission of words that are understood by the reader.
12. To separate numbers (*7,891,000*).
13. Before a short quotation.

USE THE SEMICOLON: (Pages 529-530)

1. Between the members of a compound sentence when no conjunction is used.
2. Between the clauses of a compound sentence that are joined by such words as *also, consequently, for, hence, however, in fact, therefore, whereas,* etc.
3. Before the expressions *as, that is, namely, i. e., e. g., to wit, viz.,* when they introduce an illustration that is a complete clause or an enumeration that consists of several items.
4. To separate the members of a compound sentence when one or both members are punctuated with commas.
5. Between serial phrases or clauses having a common dependence on something that precedes or follows.
6. Between the members of a series of clearly defined units, upon each of which special emphasis is to be laid.

USE THE COLON: (Page 530)

1. Between two independent groups having no connecting word between them, the first group pointing forward to the second.
2. After forward-looking expressions.
3. Before a series of expressions.
4. Before a long quotation.
5. To separate hours and minutes when expressed in figures (*10:15 a. m.*)
6. After the salutation of a business message.

USE THE QUESTION MARK: (Page 531)

1. After a direct question.
2. After a question in abbreviated form (*What is your opinion of the Baltimore & Ohio? the Santa Fe? the Union Pacific?*)
3. In parentheses (?) to denote doubt or uncertainty.

---

* Page references are to pages in this book.